Faith and Faction

Faith and Faction

W. R. Ward

EPWORTH PRESS

Copyright © Epworth Press 1993

0 7162 0490 8

First published 1993
by Epworth Press
1 Central Buildings
Westminster, London SW1H 9NR

Phototypeset by Intype, London
and printed in Finland by
Werner Söderström Oy

Contents

Preface

My best thanks are due to the committee of the Epworth Press for agreeing to undertake the publication of the present volume and to the holders of the copyright of those chapters which have been previously published for permission to reprint. These include: the committee of the Ecclesiastical History Society (for chaps. 2, 3, 8, 10, 14, 19, and 21); the editors of *Victorian Faith in Crisis* (for chap. 4); the editor of the *Bulletin of the John Rylands University Library of Manchester* (for chap. 5 & 7); the editors and publishers of *Kerkhistorische Opstellen aangeboden aan Prof. Dr. J. van den Berg* (for chap. 6); the editors of the *Journal of Ecclesiastical History* (for chap. 9); the editor of the *Baptist Quarterly* (for chap. 11); the Oxford University Press (for chap. 12); the editor of *Erweckung am Beginn des 19. Jahrhunderts* (for chap. 15); the editor of *Kirchliche Zeitgeschichte* (for chap. 16); the German Historical Institute, London (for chap. 17); and the editor of *Durham University Journal* (for chap. 20). As on previous occasions gratitude is due to my wife for coping with a series of enterprises which are not at all her cup of tea.

Petersfield, November 1992

Introduction

Like preachers of special sermons in the eighteenth century, modern scholars are from time to time subject to kindly pressure from their colleagues to reprint papers which have appeared in inaccessible places or in volumes which have disappeared from libraries; and, like preachers of any age, they tend to accumulate pieces prepared for particular occasions which have never gone to press. The present selection from the normal output of a life largely devoted to sustaining academic institutions placed under increasing strain, and to meeting the demands of students of various levels to be taught things of quite other sorts, partakes of both these kinds; but it is hoped that the pleasure given by the work which has gone into them, and by the assistance of other busy scholars, may in some measure be communicated to other readers with too much to do, and that the choice of studies made over a period of twenty years may not lack the coherence required of a book. For despite a continuous shift of interest, there has been a continuous thread running through my own research over the last forty-five years, the interplay between politics and other forms of human existence. It began with politics and fiscal administration, and continued with a series of studies of the political setting of academic life, which have gained in actuality since they were written. But it was impossible to write about nineteenth-century Oxford without paying heed to the religious stance of the parties involved; and in the later stages of that work another group of questions of religious belief and practice came rather closer home. The proposals for Anglican-Methodist union inevitably raised sharp differences of opinion on both sides, and on the Methodist side were marked by appeals to Methodist history which amply compensated in stridency what they lacked in illumination. But there was no mistaking the fact that what Methodism *had been* was part of the question of what Methodism was and ought to be. A situation characterized by so much heat and so little light almost required of a working Methodist historian that he examine some of the questions for himself; and in my own case this impulse came at a juncture when work I had been doing upon the religious history of Manchester had reached a point where the history of the town was requiring explanations which the town itself could not provide. Here was an invitation to explore some of those wider aspects of Methodism which were then in contention among Methodists, including some of those forms of popular belief and practice which found a home among them and were sometimes valuable, which resisted connexional manipulation, and seemed to have little to do with that Methodist image offered for acceptance by the church. These studies, here represented by the essays on 'Revival and Class Conflict' and 'The Religion of the People' were balanced by an attempt to re-examine the old Wesleyan doctrine of the ministry in 'The Legacy of John Wesley', and to cast light on the central administration of the old Wesleyanism by reassembling and editing the correspondence of Jabez Bunting, the Methodist Pope. With him I must confess never to have sustained wholly charitable relations, and in the sixties and seventies it was difficult to avoid seeing him through the prism of contemporary problems. Issues of the ecclesiological status of new church machinery were also faced by the Baptists (among others), and are discussed here in the essay on 'The Baptists and the Transformation of the Church'. The viewpoint which emerged from these studies was described by one learned and generous Nonconformist critic as Arnoldian, related, that is, to the stance not of Matthew, but of Gottfried, Arnold; readers will form their own views about this, assisted or impeded by the fact that a recent conference of the Ecclesiastical History Society on martyrs and martyrologies afforded an opportunity to examine Arnold himself in the essay 'Is Martyrdom Mandatory?'.

The Arnold essay exemplifies another aspiration of my more recent work, namely to make available to British students a personal view of some of the remarkable work of German scholars in the field of modern religious belief and practice, and to escape from the insularity which characterizes much British work in this area, without being shipwrecked upon the artificialities of the comparative approach or on the institutional presuppositions of what is offered as 'ecumenical' church history. Two practical considerations played their part. In 1972 the church history section of the Deutscher Historikertag devoted its session to the theme of social Christianity, and invited me to read a paper on British Protestant social Christianity, later reflection on which appears here as 'The Way of the World'. The effort of making the British enterprise comprehensible to a German audience finally convinced me that the German counterpart to the story was a good deal more interesting than our own. This conviction led me to attempt a book-length critique of the German story, published in Switzerland as *Theology, Sociology and Politics*, fragments of which, appearing on the way, reappear here as 'Max Weber and the Ritschlians' (the more precise title of a German version of the English original) and 'The Socialist Commitment in Karl Barth'. These studies are here complemented by an attempt, produced by invitation at the time of the *Rerum Novarum* celebrations, to elicit the salient features of the vast and tangled story of German Social Catholicism in 'Faith and Fate'. Whoever gives his mind to the interaction of religion and politics is unlikely to complain of serious attempts to produce a theological politics, but I must confess to a good deal of disappointment with the outcome of such attempts. Whether the sorry record of unreality in social Christianity is the result of attempting something impossible, or whether its failures were any worse than those of policy prescriptions upon a secular basis, are interesting questions awaiting further inquiry.

The second practical reason for a change of field was provided by the opportunity to produce a new edition of Wesley's *Journal*, a work now complete and well advanced in publication. Wesley's early adventures on one frontier of the Protestant world in Georgia and on another in Herrnhut, prompted the question why the fringes of the Protestant world were acting upon the centre in this way, and what, in terms of *mentalité*, the Protestant world then was. The final outcome of this work was embodied in an attempt to portray the religious revival of the eighteenth century in its European setting in *The Protestant Evangelical Awakening* (1992), but among the papers generated on the way were the Conference lecture on 'Power and Piety', the essays on 'Orthodoxy, Enlightenment and Religious Revival', the paper on the Austrian Protestants, and the Moravian studies which appear here. These studies will be supplemented by another series of papers on Pietism, Hallesian and radical, at present in the press. To lay the groundwork for these papers in the archives of Central Europe required at the time a spell of work behind the Iron Curtain, and created an interest in what the historians of the Eastern Bloc made of the topics with which I was concerned. Two of the following essays, on 'Spener and the Unitarians' and on 'Bach as an Expositor of the Bible', were, among other things, an attempt to create modest memorials to what they achieved before they were swept into oblivion, and were, as essays for the press, themselves left behind by the pace of events which they anticipated. The subjects themselves, however, are of sufficient interest to warrant inclusion here.

In the eighteenth century, religious revival was often a form of resistance to assimilation, an American theory about which had concerned me long before in the person of Will Herberg, an essay on whom appears here. Members of the Church of England have not often been exposed to assimilation, but in the eighteenth-century form of ethnic cleansing Scottish Episcopalians were, with the curious results discussed in the last paper in the volume. Three final contributions complete the harvest. The paper on the 'Pastoral Office and the General Priesthood' discusses the fortunes of the doctrine of the priesthood of all believers before and during the revival of the eighteenth century, and may or may not be Arnoldian; 'Faith and Fallacy' is a contribution to the history of Anglo-German theological diplomacy, and received its special shape from the requirements of a co-operative volume on the Victorian crisis of faith; 'John Wesley, Traveller' was written for a staff seminar devoted not to religion but to the history of travel. It lacks any reference to the light cast by Wesley's travel narratives upon his aesthetic sensibilities, since that topic had been dealt with in the introduction to Wesley's *Journal*. But it may justify its inclusion in a collection of religious studies if only as an antidote to the romantic delusion, still present among us, that Wesley rode into the sunset solo, to address throngs assembled by the unaided agency of the Holy Spirit. To this extent it is like the other studies in this volume, a small attempt to put the historiography of religious belief and practice upon a more realistic basis. In this respect at least, the spiritual and the scholarly support each other.

Part One

Orthodox, Evangelical and Rational Religion

Spener and the Unitarians

There has been little to be said for the government of Poland over the last few years, but its dire necessities have had one useful result: in its desperate efforts to deny the Roman Catholic Church the exclusive possession of the national tradition, it has encouraged some good work on Polish religious dissidence, and not least Unitarianism. Now that that church has returned to bask in fitful sunshine, it has replied in kind with the doctrine that the proper place for Polish Protestants is in Germany and for Polish Orthodox in the Ukraine; and it may well be that the historiography of Protestantism will again come to be regarded as an anti-national if not actually an unnatural activity. All the more reason therefore for English students in the field to take note of what has been done.[1] And if in the case of my small offering this involves the tedious business of observing a movement through the eyes of one of its critics in whom I am interested for other reasons, I take heart from the fact that no religious body can be more inured to this process than the Unitarian.

The enormous German *Pietismusindustrie* which generates a bibliography of some two hundred items a year has seen to it that the career of Philipp Jakob Spener (1635–1705) is explored from every conceivable angle, and his controversy with Lutheran Orthodoxy has been subject to the same variety of scholarly technique and of scholarly fantasy as the history of early Methodism. What is barely mentioned at all is that his last great literary work, the *Verteidigung des Zeugnüsses von der Ewigen Gottheit Unsers Herrn JESU CHRISTI . . .* , was directed against the Unitarians. At this stage in his career Spener had taken refuge under the confessionally benign rule of Prussia, was Provost of the Nicolaikirche in Berlin, and a Brandenburg consistorial councillor. But the work was thought to be of sufficient public importance for the king to excuse him from attendance at the consistory to give him more time to labour at it,[2] and Spener indeed devoted all the strength of the last five years of his life

Historical lecture delivered to the annual conference of Unitarian and Free Christian Churches, 1990.

to the task. He is reckoned to have introduced over 179 authors into the discussion and endeavoured to make an orthodox reply to a series of significant anti-Trinitarian theologians. When Spener thought his strength was running out he arranged for the theological faculty at Halle to complete it for him, but, recovering somewhat, he forced the work through to the end. He did not live to see his blockbuster of nearly 1000 pages through the press, and it was produced for him posthumously in 1706 by Paul Anton. Nor was this last will and testimony neglected in the great German compendia of polemical theology of the next half-century, Walch[3] and Baumgarten.[4] It is modern scholarship, substantially derived from the great struggle against confessional orthodoxy, and never threatened by Unitarianism, which has forgotten the curious fact that Spener allowed Unitarianism, not Orthodoxy, to kill him.

There clearly are two quite different questions here. One belongs at least ostensibly to the history of Unitarianism, and is the question why Spener, who never lived to see the Pietist movement safe from the onslaughts of its Orthodox enemies, should exhaust himself in the end in a defence against rational Christianity. The other is a question in the slipperiest of all subjects, the definition of Pietism, the question whether there are characteristic differences between Spener's appraisal of anti-Trinitarian religion and that of its Orthodox critics. I would like to say a little on each of these subjects.

At a superficial level there is no problem in answering the first question. Gottfried Arnold in his famous *Unpartheyische Kirchen- und Ketzer-Historie* makes the snide remark that:

> especially in recent years Socinianism has spread unperceived very widely through Germany, and that in some great courts even the greatest ministers are inclined to it. In Holland and England, the Socinians enjoy no great freedom, but spread surreptitiously ever further, so that many of the clergy themselves confess outwardly, but cherish these doctrines in their hearts.[5]

Arnold took the view that the more clergy were attracted by the new doctrines, the more the Orthodox party raised Cain against them. In a letter of 1694 Spener made remarks to much the same effect.[6] The bugbear here was the very court of Berlin which had taken the Pietists under its protection. For the great grievance of the Lutheran Orthodox against the Great Elector and his immediate successors was not just that they were Reformed in their church allegiance, and packed their court with adherents of the Reformed churches in the West, but that these so-called Calvinists on the make were men commonly of very shallow religious conviction. The Lutheran loss was not a Reformed gain. Here the word Socinianism was being used not to define a theological position, but to abuse torpid convictions with a rationalistic label. But with John Toland visiting the court in Berlin in 1701, and gushing his way round Europe as to how marvellous it was,[7] the label easily stuck.

At any rate Spener who had not scrupled to jeopardise his previous appointment as court chaplain in Dresden at an early stage by saying unpopular things, took the risk again and preached twice in 1691 on the eternal Godhead of Christ, and again in 1693 on the eternal procession of the Son from the being of the Father.[8] These sermons were indeed of a piece with earlier remarks of Spener to the effect that Socinians were no more Christians than were the Turks,[9] and that Socinianism and Quakerism were opposed theological extremes to be avoided at all costs.[10] It was not, however, a Quaker who took up the cudgels against him, but a Socinian who replied to his sermons in a short series of anonymous *Betrachtungen* published in Amsterdam in 1700. This was Samuel Crell (1660–1747), the grandson of the famous Socinian theologian Johann Crell (1590–1631) who had been taken out of Poland by his father after the edict of banishment in 1658, had been educated at the Arminian gymnasium in the Netherlands, and had served as a Socinian preacher at various places in Germany including Berlin and Silesia, the theatre of the first great Pietist rescue operation.[11] Crell,

> the last significant representative of Socinianism . . . was everywhere distinguished and valued by the most significant men of that time, La Croze, Pierre Bayle, the famous bookseller, Reynier Leers, the Earl of Shaftesbury, Isaac Newton, the famous English theologian Grabe [i.e. a Prussian who settled in England on Spener's recommendation] and others on account of his delightful personality and brilliant scholarship. In a letter to Mosheim, La Croze says, that, heresy apart, he was the best and most delightful man in the world.[12]

At one level, therefore, Spener was goaded into devoting his final years to Trinitarian controversy by the spur of an opponent who was in every way worthy of his steel. It is hard to believe, however, that this was the whole story, for anti-Trinitarian doctrines were not making progress in Prussia, and while every Pietist was bound to have his doubts about the court of Frederick I, the fact was that that court had given Spener sabbatical leave from part of his duties in order to promote what it was hoped would be the ultimate hatchet job on Samuel Crell.

It was, of course, the case that Prussia, and especially East Prussia which lay outside the bounds of the Empire and was therefore not covered by the religious provisions of the Westphalia settlement, could not be immune to the destruction of Polish Unitarianism. The alliance of the great Polish magnates and the Jesuits in the struggle against Russia and Sweden which made Poland the country of the Counter-Reformation *par excellence* was sealed by the peace of Oliva in 1660, and led to the betrothal of the kingdom, like that of Hungary, to the Virgin. The fact that Poland is still a Marian state and Hungary is not, is due chiefly to the fact that the religious dissidents in Hungary, and the ethnic groups with which many of them were associated, had substantial aristocratic backing. Aristocratic rebellion was to be a feature of Hungarian politics right into the eighteenth century. It took Hungarian Protestants up some appalling blind alleys and led too many of them to flee from reality into a crazy apocalyptic; but it provided the necessary minimum of protection, and allowed forces of self-help to work in the eighteenth century with such effect, that despite Habsburg brutality, Protestantism of various kinds retained the allegiance of one third of the population.[13] In Poland, which in the early seventeenth century, like America at the end of the following century, was ostensibly the land of liberty achieved, and had harboured the chief numerical and intellectual centres of anti-Trinitarian strength, aristocratic backing was never enough, and was perhaps weakened further by Unitarian tendencies to social radicalism. At any rate the Unitarians backed the Swedes, lost their gamble, and were expelled, the aristocracy often going first. Their catastrophe was simply a preface to a series of acts of violence against other Protestant communities whose very existence was held to constitute blasphemy against the Virgin.[14]

Some of the refugees made for the principality of Siebenbürgen, south-east of Hungary and independent until 1699 when it was absorbed into that kingdom, the surviving Protestants of which have in late years had a bad time under the Ceausescu regime. But the bulk went north into the New March of Brandenburg or into what we call East Prussia. In Mark Brandenburg there were one or two spectacular episodes which kept the local estates on their toes against a supposed Unitarian menace. In 1626 the Potsdam pastor Joachim Stegmann confessed a Unitarian position, was removed from office and went off to be Rektor of the famous Unitarian gymnasium at Rakow in Poland.[15] The Mark was also subject to the influence, as long as it lasted, of the Unitarian congregation just across the Polish border at Meseritz. In 1655 a Unitarian conclave there appointed the minister, Preuss, to be a missionary to spread the faith in Silesia, Lusatia (which was already filling up with Protestant refugees from Silesia and Bohemia) and in the Mark itself. His most notable convert was a pastor who was of course dismissed from office and expelled from the country. For although the Hohenzollerns were pertinacious upholders of religious toleration, they preferred in the Empire to stick to the three religions which were tolerated in the Empire. On the Selchow and Schmettau estates Unitarians found aristocratic protection, and on the latter there were in

1718 seventy-two of them of whom twenty lived in Koenigswalde; of this group only four were adult males, three of them unkindly described as 'idiots' who could not write their name. In that year Frederick William I authorised their continued residence on condition that they abstained from all propaganda, but already they had, to avoid additional fees on marriages, broken up their congregation into small private house groups. No further disturbance was to be expected from them.[16]

In East Prussia Unitarians enjoyed much greater prosperity but the end product was much the same. Unitarian propaganda came across the frontier, and early in the seventeenth century secret meetings and services began to take place. A trickle of clergy adopted the new views, and the three Polentz brothers despised Luther's catechism, claimed to have found 600 mistakes in his translation of the Bible, but insisted they were not forming a sect. Then in the middle of the century one of the teachers at the university in Königsberg, Valentin Baumgart (1611–1673), picked up Unitarian doctrines in the Netherlands, and, after being required to recant, pushed off to join the Socinians, first in Poland and then in Siebenbürgen. The Elector of Brandenburg then required the theological faculty at Königsberg to oppose a book by Melchior Schäfer, and they entrusted the work to the subsequently famous Abraham Calov, whom we shall meet again. At the same time (1640) the Landtag adopted a sharp edict against Socinian literature and meetings.

Fortunately for the Polish Unitarians in their hour of need, by the time they were expelled from their native country, the governor of East Prussia was a Lithuanian of Reformed convictions, Prince Boguslaus Radziwill. He was aware that other Lithuanian-Polish nobility were of Socinian opinions, and he brought them in, promoted a number of them in state service and got them landed property in Masuria, one of the underdeveloped parts of the state. They in turn brought in their brethren in the faith, and before long not only were congregations being formed but even a synod was held at Kessel in 1665. Needless to say none of this was palatable to the estates of East Prussia, and they had the Great Elector hooked on an ambiguity of policy. His constitution of 1661 forbade the dissemination of 'Arian, Jewish and Mennonite' doctrines, but also required that no conscience should be constrained. The short history of what was a long and alarming story to the Unitarians, was that the Elector was pushed by the estates into promises of maintaining religious uniformity, which, so far as the Unitarians were concerned, he did not fulfil. And although the estates did not succeed in securing the expulsion of the Unitarians, they effectively stopped them recruiting. This was the moral of the case of the Elector's Chief Secretary in Königsberg, Christoph Sand. He had become acquainted with Unitarian doctrines in the course of an education in the Netherlands, and on his return to Königsberg abstained from Lutheran worship. This was sufficient for him to be brought to book in 1668. He first of all confessed to Unitarian doctrine, and then, when required within two weeks to confess that Jesus was the Son of God, contested the right of the prince to compel conscience in this way. The Elector's sympathy with toleration did not extend to the free market in religion implied by conversions of this kind. Sand lost his job.

Unable to recruit, the Unitarians could do little but decline, and in fifty years the pressure to which this subjected them showed that they too were capable of constraining conscience. Increasing numbers of Unitarians began to go over to the Lutheran establishment (or in Königsberg, to the Reformed church), and in 1725 one of them, a tailor called Isbedsky from Kosinsken received instruction, was admitted to baptism, and was badly beaten up in the street by a bunch of his former co-religionists. There was now very little advantage to the kings of Prussia in fighting the corner of the Unitarian community. One edict of 1721 forbade them to hold public services or circulate their literature, another anti-Unitarian edict followed in 1730. Limited toleration on the basis of private meetings continued, and about 1750 what had been their big settlement at Andreaswalde was reckoned to number about seventy Polish-speaking Unitarians, with twenty more in Rudowken, and about a hundred in Prussia. The sad end to the tale was that in 1776 the remnant petitioned Frederick the Great to grant them respectability by allowing them a proper church; this he did, but it took till 1788 to get a small stone meeting-house with a thatched roof erected in Andreaswalde; the Religionsedikt for the Prussian states of the very same year did not include the Unitarians among the sects who enjoyed public protection, and in 1803 the congregation at Andreaswalde dissolved.[17]

This sad story far exceeds our chronological limits, but is germane to the theme; if the unbridled commitment of the Polish government to its Marian allegiance meant sudden death to the Unitarians, the grudging toleration conceded by the kings of Prussia, however generous compared with the demands of their estates, simply meant slow death. It is this obvious fact that creates the chief mystery behind our present subject; it was not new for Lutheran theologians to write against anti-Trinitarians, but they chose to do so on a scale and with a bitterness without precedent at the very moment when the Protestant world as a whole had lost some 60 per cent of its numerical strength to the Catholics, and when Unitarianism, always a small movement, was facing, after expulsion from Poland, extinction in eastern Europe. Abraham Calov's classic 2000-page anti-Socinian epic of 1684[18] seems an entirely disproportionate sledgehammer to take to this particular nut, and so, in its way, was Spener's *Verteidigung*. Why did they do it?

In a small measure this was no doubt due to the political situation. As I hope to explain in my forthcoming book, the Lutheran Orthodox, having pinned their own hopes of survival on the terms of the Westphalia settlements, and abandoned enormous numbers of Protestants in the great triangle bounded by Salzburg, Transylvania, and Poland to their fate, were now finding insuperable difficulties in getting the terms of those settlements implemented in their own favour; any public deviation from those terms, and the admission of Polish Unitarians to the Empire was a deviation, would undercut the international guarantees on which they had staked everything and play into the hands of a still rampant Counter-Reformation. This explanation, however, does not help much with the case of the Pietists who were not only embarked on a programme of spiritual renewal designed to supplant delusive reliance upon the diplomatic arm of flesh, but had also achieved a world perspective entirely beyond purview of the Westphalia treaties or the Empire.

The explanation seems to lie in circumstances internal to Protestant apologetic.[19] Socinianism had grown up with the Reformation, shared many of its characteristic features, and in Poland had created an *ecclesia minor* connected with the *ecclesia major* of the Reformed church. It shared a humanistic basis with at least part of the magisterial Reformation movement and the more that movement got into the hands of the self-described Orthodox parties the more important it was for them to distinguish themselves from deviationists, and, in some respects, the more difficult it was to distinguish themselves from Socinians. For the long-term movement in Protestant Orthodoxy was away from treating justification by faith as the article by which the church stood or fell, to that of the Scripture principle; so that by the mid-eighteenth century polemicists of both Catholic and Enlightenment provenance correctly understood that it was the Scripture principle they must destroy. Moreover Protestant Orthodoxy came increasingly to be presented in a metaphysical setting, which did not become unpalatable till the eighteenth century. In particular, I am told by those who work on these things that the Lutherans found it impossible to expound the doctrine of the Trinity without the scholastic logic in which it had been expounded long before the Reformation; and in any case the long reign of Aristotelianism in Protestant universities would have produced a result of this kind. Certainly by the early eighteenth century Socinian scholars had shown that the Scripture principle was no direct and immediate help to the doctrine of the Trinity which is not a New Testament doctrine. They had also hooked the Orthodox on the horns of a dilemma, the latter having on the one hand to show why their rationalism

produced results so different from that of their critics, and, on the other,
how the very unrationalistic study of history could disprove the Socinian
allegation that the doctrine of the Trinity was an invention of the Papacy.
It did gradually become clear that the basic differences between two sides
which had much in common were on the understanding of the relations of
faith and reason, and on the understanding of personality. For the Socinian,
faith was historic assent to the doctrine of the Lord Jesus; for the old
Orthodoxy faith was also the assent to sound doctrine, but it had to be
assent to an integrated doctrinal system a good deal more elaborate than
could be historically imputed to the Lord Jesus. Similarly the Orthodox
notion of person had a Trinitarian standpoint behind it; to the Socinian
God was a morally active person, and man, created in his image, must be
understood in the same way. He had the actual freedom to do good or evil.
The Formula of Concord had been prepared to allege that whoever did
not believe in the Trinity was not a Christian, but it was not until the
Hochschule at Rakow produced a catechism and the fruits of what
amounted to a humanist university that the depth of the challenge
which the anti-Trinitarians produced from very similar premises became
apparent. Indeed as late as 1659, Jancovius, a pastor near Züllichau,
summoned to appear before the consistory on charges of holding Socinian
doctrine, took himself off instead to Wittenberg, and got himself a
certificate of orthodoxy from the theological faculty of that fortress of
theological purity. He still preached Socinianism on his return, and was
finally expelled from Brandenburg by the government.[20] It is therefore not
surprising that Calov's vast treatise incorporated the results of disputations
he had held in various parts of eastern Europe, Rostock, Königsberg,
Danzig and Wittenberg, nor that, as the Lutherans began to realise the
extent of the Socinian challenge to the Nicene tradition, they characterized
it not only as profligate and ruinous to salvation, but in an heretical
succession to Ebionites, Cerinthians, Arians and Samosatenians.

This was the controversial context which Spener entered. Like the
Orthodox, the Pietists had some striking resemblances to the Socinian
position. They too wished to get round the spirit of confessional Orthodoxy
and to cultivate a common Protestant consciousness against Rome. They
too were deeply interested in Bible texts, languages and exegesis, and
prized the New Testament higher than the Old. They too wished to move
the emphasis from doctrine to life, to esteem ethics above dogmatics. Halle,
it might be said, was a second and greater Rakow. And if Rakow produced
a celebrated catechism, Spener made his name as a catechist.[21] Spener was
indeed himself accused in 1690 by the Orthodox Daniel Hartnack of
Socinian tendencies.[22]

There was, of course, one fundamental difference which separated the

Socinians from Spener even more sharply than from the Orthodox. This was his rejection of religious rationalism, the combination of the Scripture principle with the principle of reason. If the Socinians looked to reason as the norm of Scripture exegesis, Spener taught the corruption of reason by the Fall, and the impossibility of understanding the revelation of God except by the illumination of the Holy Spirit.[23] Spener indeed reduced the issue to a formula declaring that Socinianism made reason the mistress of faith and denied our dependence upon divine illumination.[24] Whether this difference is to be distilled into a clash between religious rationalism and religious fideism we need not now inquire; but it is notable that the pulling apart of faith and reason which was to characterize the whole process of religious revival, and usually occurred on the initiative of the evangelicals, here took place on the initiative of the rationalists.

Was Spener's anti-Socinian polemic in any way distinctive from that of the Lutheran Orthodox?

There were differences both of style and substance from the Orthodox polemic, of which Calov may stand as the type, which are worth noting as they contribute to the profile of the Pietist party. In the first place while Calov attempted to dispose of the whole body of Socinian literature, listing some seventy Socinian authors in his index, Spener undertook to controvert only three, Georg Enyedi, Johann Ludwig von Wolzogen, and Jeremias Felbinger, later adding Johann Preuss, and, when he discovered his identity, Samuel Crell. It is clear from Spener's earlier works that he had read the classic Socinian writers from Sozzini onwards; but he was now engaged, not in an academic exercise, but in an effort to controvert writers whom he knew were in circulation in Berlin. Wolzogen and Felbinger were indeed the only Socinian writers to have several titles printed in German in the Netherlands in the seventeenth century.[25] (Enyedi, who died in 1597, and had been superintendent of the Socinian churches in Siebenbürgen, got in because Spener thought he was the subtlest of his opponents, and the one on whom they most depended).[26] His literary purpose also came out in the fact that he wrote in German rather than Latin. This had not been usual in the Lutheran anti-Socinian polemic.[27]

Then, secondly, whereas Calov, in the Orthodox manner, had dragged the Socinians relentlessly through every department of the Orthodox theological system, Spener was content to concentrate on a single point, on which he thought the whole issue rested, the eternal Godhead of Christ. If, as he believed, this could be established on the basis of a Scripture principle which both sides acknowledged, then controversy was at an end. This was moreover the basic article of true Christianity, and the one on which salvation rested. Here already was proclaimed the Christocentric character of modern theology from the Revival to Schleiermacher and to the twentieth century.

In the third place Spener clearly believed himself confronted by a different problem of theological strategy. To Calov the issue was the preservation of a system of pure doctrine not only against Socinian errors, but against compromising Lutherans like the syncretist Calixtus. Spener by contrast was prepared to quote endlessly from Calvinist theologians like Jacques Abbadie,[28] or Anglicans ike Peter Allix,[29] or even Hugo Grotius, with a view to getting up the same kind of pan-Protestant front against the Unitarians as he wished to see against the Catholics. Spener's argument was also purely exegetical, and to this extent has dated worse than the systematics of Calov. The direct biblical evidence for the participation of Christ in the work of creation, still less that of the distinction between created and uncreated angels and the interpretation of the latter as appearances of Christ, is not likely to carry much contemporary exegetical support. On the other hand Calov's argument has a curiously modish ring. The effect of the Unitarian view, he claimed, was that the image of God in man was that of the creator of the world and therefore implied lordship over the creation. Calov maintained that this lordship could not be the image of God in man because it was not the highest gift man received in creation, and was more obviously characteristic of tyrants and the children of this world than the saints, for they did most of the lording over creation. Seen from the standpoint of the Trinity, the image of God in man consists in his participation in the divine wisdom, righteousness and immortality, without which lordship over creation is a dangerous business.[30] One can imagine some trendy Cambridge dean discovering any day now that Calov was a Green theologian three centuries before his time.

On the other hand Spener saw more clearly than Calov that Unitarianism was much more than a recurrence of an ancient heresy written off long ago. It represented a first attempt to reshape Christianity into a humanist ethic, radically secularizing in the sense that it denied the Godhead of Christ. Spener's instinct that Unitarianism presented mankind with a choice altogether more important than was suggested by Calov's defence of Orthodox system, was surely the true one.

Notes

1 The two papers to which this essay owes more than to anything else are: Paul Wrzecionko, 'Die Sozinianer und der Sozinianismus im Widerstreit der Beurteilungen' in *Reformation und Frühaufklärung in Polen. Studien über den Sozianianismus und seinen Einfluss auf das westeuropaische Denken im 17.*

Jahrhundert ed. Paul Wrzecionko, Göttingen 1977, pp. 244–72; Johannes Wallmann, 'Pietismus und Sozianismus. Zu Philip Jakob Speners antisoziniani-schen Schriften', in *Socinianism and its role in the culture of the 16th to the 18th centuries*, ed. L. Szczucki, Z. Oganowski & J. Tazbir, Warsaw, 1983, pp. 145–156. East Germany has also made its contribution, not least in E. Winter, *Frühaufklärung. Der Kampf gegen den Konfessionalismus in Mittel- und Osteuropa und die deutsch-slavische Begegnung*, East Berlin 1966, esp. pp. 255–66.

2 Paul Grünberg, *Philipp Jakob Spener*, Göttingen 1893–1906, I. 346.

3 Johann Georg Walch, *Historische und theologische Einleitung in die Religions-Streitigkeiten ausser der Evangelisch-Lutherischen Kirche*, Jena, 1733–36: repr. Stuttgart/Bad Canstatt, 1952 I. 579.

4 Siegmund Jacob Baumgarten, *Geschichte der Religionsparteien* ed. J.S. Semler, Halle, 1766: repr. Hildesheim, 1966, p. 942.

5 Gottfried Arnold, *Unpartheyische Kirchen und Ketzer-Historie* . . . Frankfurt/M., 1699–1700, 2. 557–8. A similar view was put forward by H.L. Benthem, a superintendent in Brunswick in the 1690s: 'It occurs to me that England is regarded by some with suspicion on account of Socinianism, and it is held inadvisable to send young people there . . . [But] whoever wishes to stay at home on account of Socinians, must now be continually imprisoned between the narrow frontiers of his dwelling, for this offensive sect are to be found among all the others, not only in foreign places, but also in our Germany'. *Neueröffneter Engelandischer Kirch- und Schulen-staat*, 2nd ed. Leipzig, 1732, Preface 9. An obituary of Benthem is to be found in *Unschuldige Nachrichten* 1723, pp. 838–9.

6 Wallmann, 'Pietismus und Sozianismus', p. 151 n. 21.

7 J. Toland, *An account of the Courts of Prussia and Hanover*, 2nd ed. London, 1706.

8 *Drei christliche Predigten von des wahren Christentums Art, Pflichten und Vorteil samt der ewigen Gottheit Jesus Christi*, Berlin/Frankfurt, 1692, and reprinted both in the *Verteidigung des Zeugnüsses* and in Spener, *Kleine Geistliche Schriften* ed. Johann Adam Steinmetz [in his youth the revivalist of Silesia], Magdeburg/Leipzig, 1742 2. 1183–1266. The third sermon was *Die ewige Geburt des Sohnes Gottes aus dem Wesen des Vaters*, Berlin, 1694, and was also reprinted in the *Verteigung des Zeugnüsses*. At Christmas 1701 he preached a fourth sermon on *Des Sohnes Gottes vor seiner aus Maria geschehener leiblicher Geburt bereits gehabter wesentliche Gottheit*, Frankfurt/M., 1702 as a foretaste of the major work on which he was now engaged. The full reference to the *Verteidigung* is: Philipp Jakob Spener, *Verteidigung des Zeugnüsses von der Ewigen Gottheit Unsers Herrn JESU CHRISTI, also des Eingebohrnen Sohns vom Vater* . . . , Frankfurt/M., 1706. The successive numbers of these works in Grünberg's Spener bibliography (*Spener* vol. 3) are 44, 26, 27, 306. I have so far failed to trace copies of any of them in this country.

9 P.J. Spener, *Erste Geistliche Schriften*, Frankfurt, 1699, p. 37.

10 P.J. Spener, *Letzte Theologische Bedencken*, Halle, 1711 3. 129, 240, 742 (Repr. in Spener, *Schriften* 15 pt. 2). Cf. Spener's *Einfältige Erklärung des christlicher Lehr* under the first commandment: 'Q. 46. Who is this that speaks in this commandment? [A.] The Triune God, Father, Son & Holy Spirit, to whom alone is honour due'. Spener, *Schriften* 2 pt. 1.

11 On this see W.R. Ward, 'Power and Piety: the origins of religious revival in the early eighteenth century', *Bulletin of John Rylands University Library of Manchester* 63, 1980, pp. 231–52.

12 Otto Fock, *Der Sozianianismus nach seiner Stellung in der Gesamtentwicklung des christlichen Geistes, nach seinem historischem Verlauf und nach seinem Lehrbegriff dargestellt*, Kiel, 1847; repr. Aalen, 1970, 1. 240. The eighteenth-century bibliography puts Crell's *Betrachtungen* against Spener at the head of his writings (F.S. Bock, *Historia Antitrinitariorum Maxime Socianismi et Socinianorum*, Regiomonti/Lipsiae, 1774; repr. Leipzig, 1978, 1. i. 172). His *Cogitationes novae de primo & secundo Adamo examini eruditorum compendiosi propositae*, Amsterdam, 1700, provoked a long-running controversy.

13 On all this see Béla Obál, *Die Religionspolitik in Ungarn nach dem Westfalischen Frieden*, Halle, 1910; Mihály Bucsay, *Der Protestantismus in Ungarn, 1521–1978*, Vienna/Cologne/Graz, 1977–79, vol. 1; Béla Köpeczi, *Staatsräson und christliche Solidarität. Die ungarischen Aufstände und Europa in der zweiten Hälfte des 17. Jahrhunderts*, Vienna/Cologne/Graz, 1983.

14 On this see the account of the crisis at Thorn in my book on *The Protestant Evangelical Awakening*.

15 Cf. Joachim Stegmann, *Prob der einfältigen Warnung für die New [sic] Photinianischen oder Arianischen Lehr von Johanne Botsacco, Th. D. des Gyymnasii zu Dantzig Rektore und Predigern in der Kirchen zur h. Dreyfaltigkeit in Druck gegeben*, Rakow, 1633.

16 F.S. Bock, *Historia Socinianismi Prussici*, Regiomonti, 1753; Georges Pariset, *L'État et les Églises en Prusse sous Frédéric-Guillaume Ier (1713–1740)*, Paris, 1897, pp. 716–17; Martin Lackner, *Die Kirchenpolitik des Grossen Kurfürsten*, Witten, 1973, pp. 283–4; Arthur Rhode, *Geschichte der evangelischen Kirche im Posener Lande*, Würzburg, 1956, pp. 69–71.

17 Walther Hubatsch, *Geschichte der evangelischen Kirche Ostpreussens*, Göttingen, 1968, 1. pp. 162–8.

18 A. Calov, *Scripta Anti-Sociniana*, 3 vols. Ulm, 1684.

19 On the following see Wrzecionko, 'Die Sozinianer und der Sozinianismus'.

20 Lackner, *Kirchenpolitik des Grossen Kurfürsten*, p. 284.

21 Spener's *Einfältige Erklärung der christlichen Lehr nach Ordnung dess Kleinen Catechismi des theuren Mannes Gottes Luther*, Frankfurt/M., 1677: repr. in Spener, *Schriften* 2 pt. 1 went through over twenty editions and was his most widely circulated work. Cf. J. Wallmann, *Philipp Jakob Spener und die Anfänge des Pietismus*, Tübingen, 1970, p. 211.

22 Grünberg, *Spener* 1. p. 149. Spener's defences against this suspicion are to be

found in *Theologische Bedencken* (Halle, 1702) 4. 600–601; *Letzte theologische Bedencken* 3. pp. 129, 240, 742, Repr. in *Schriften* 15 pt. 2.

23 In his early controversy with Dilfeld, Spener did not deny that natural knowledge may contribute to theological understanding, but held that a saving knowledge of God required not only a natural literal knowledge of Scripture, but also divine illumination. P.J. Spener, *Die allgemeine Gottesgelehrtheit aller gläubigen Christen und rechtschaffenen Theologen* . . . , Frankfurt/M., 1680. On the Dilfeld controversy, see J. Wallmann, 'Spener und Dilfeld. Der Hintergrund des ersten pietistischen Streites' in *Theologie in Geschichte und Kunst*. Festschrift Walter Elliger, ed. Siegfried Hermann & Oskar Söhngen, Witten, 1968, pp. 214–35.

24 'Quod rationem nostram fidei etiam facit magistram, nec divina illuminatione nos egere perhibet'. P.J. Spener, *Consilia et judicia theologica latina*, Frankfurt/M., 1709, 3. p. 747 (Quoted in Wallmann, 'Pietismus und Sozinianismus' 149).

25 See J. Bruckner, *Bibliographical Catalogue of Seventeenth-century German Books published in Holland*, Hague/Paris, 1971. For Felbinger see nos. 203, 239, 283, 340, 363; for Wolzogen, nos. 124, 150, 535.

26 A posthumous edition of his chief work *Explicationes Locorum Veteris & Novi Testamenti. Ex quibus Trinitatis dogma stabiliri solet* . . . appeared in Transylvania in 1598; but there was a reprint in Spener's lifetime at Groningen, 1670.

27 Cf., however, Johann Botsack, *Eine Warnung für denen neuen Photinianern oder Arminianischen Lehre*, Danzig, 1632: Konigsberg, 1646.

28 Jacques Abbadie, *Traité de la divinité de Nôtre Seigneur Jesus Christ*, Rotterdam, 1690. Among the passages quoted by Spener was pp. 337–343, which argues that if Christ were not God, religion must be regarded as superstition, comedy and magic. Abbadie appeared in English dress as *A Sovereign Antidote against Arian Poyson: or the Divinity of our Blessed Saviour asserted and plainly proved* . . . *in full answer to Dr. Clarke, Mr. Whiston, Mr. Emlyn and the rest of their adherents*, London, 1719.

29 Peter Allix, *Judgment of the ancient Jewish Church against the Unitarians, in the controversy upon the Holy Trinity* . . . , London, 1690. To what purpose, asked Allix (p. iv), should Christ exhort the Jews to search the Scriptures of the OT because they testified of him, if the Scriptures could only give a false notion of him by intimating that the promised Messiah was the God of Israel. Spener used this text in a translation by an unnamed friend. This was Christoph Matth. Seidel whose translation appeared at Berlin in 1707 with a foreword by Gottfried Arnold.

30 Calov, *Scripta Anti-Sociniana* 3. 128.

2

Orthodoxy, Enlightenment and Religious Revival

Everyone has his favourite squibs to illuminate the animosity of the devotees of the Christian application of modern knowledge towards the partisans of religious revival. R.B. Aspland, the Unitarian, summed them all up succinctly in the early nineteenth century in his case against Wesleyanism. 'Wine', he declared, 'is the beverage of the gentleman, spirits of the herd. So with religion'.[1] Something of this edge had been there from the beginning, long before attitudes had been struck and the French Revolution had become a divider of spirits everywhere. Much of the fascination of the Turretini correspondence is provided by the conscious sense of intellectual superiority of the Swiss fathers of rational orthodoxy. 'We are here much occupied with the scandalous affairs of Toggenburg', writes Jean Gaspard Escher with an almost audible turn of the nose. 'These are mountain people rather like Vaudois, Miquelets or Camisards', and their murderous politics were of the Ulster variety.[2] Neither the Toggenburgers, nor the Vaudois or Camisards were part of the history of religious revival, but they were very like Protestant minorities from Central Europe who were; the Salzburgers, for example. 'The majority of these men', writes Escher of the latter, 'can neither read nor write; their fundamental doctrine is that worship is due to God alone and that salvation is by Jesus Christ. This doctrine fills them with a horror of popery: . . . they are ill-instructed in the other articles of religion. They know by heart some fine passages of Scripture and some Lutheran hymns to which they hold'.[3] Pastorally, if not confessionally, the mountain men were a different cup of tea from the practitioners of polite learning; but as late as 1800 it was possible to turn American Methodists and Baptists out in droves to vote for the deist Jefferson, and it is the purpose of this paper to suggest that the fate of the revivalist and that of the men of enlightenment was more

First published in *Studies in Church History* 28 (1982), pp. 275–96.

closely linked at an early stage than the text-book categories usually suggest.

It is notable, indeed, that Turretini's friends did not confine their snobbery to the mountain men – practically everything German fell under the ban. To them, Lutheran theologians were unspeakably rebarbative,[4] but even in reformed Hesse 'the profession of the ministry is regarded as a degradation, and such is the state of the academies that the majority leave them without cultivation, without knowledge of life, without manners and almost without knowledge'.[5] 'I would not dare to trust to paper all my fears for Protestantism in Germany', wrote another; 'humanly speaking only the King of Sweden can prevent its ruin; but what am I to say of the religion? The majority of the great lords have none at all, self-interest guides their consciences and this threatens great evils to Europe. I imagine they lived in no other way before the flood; with most of them chastity, good faith, justice, charity are only empty words. Yet there are some devoted to a mystical religion which I do not understand'.[6] Of course the original reformers had been very nearly as bad. Even in 1726 Dr Prittius of Frankfurt was reported to have 'a very false idea of the Reformed and . . . imputed to the greater part of their theologians the harshest sentiments of the first reformers on the matters disputed between the Reformed and the Lutherans; he was quite surprised when I told him that the greater part, especially at Geneva were of much more moderate sentiments'.[7]

This correspondence bears out, what has long been recognised, that there was a kinship between the early Enlightenment, Pietism, and that different but related phenomenon, religious revival, by virtue of their loudly trumpeted opposition to confessional orthodoxy. Among the most moving documents in John Wesley's *Journal* are the testimonies of the Moravians he met at Herrnhut; they made it clear that, having been through the fires of persecution in Bohemia, and of revival after their escape, they were not much enamoured of what they found in orthodox Saxony.[8] The prescription of the two parties for what they found lacking – piety based on knowledge – was also the same, and if there were differences in the kind of knowledge they had in mind, the practical upshot was similar. One of the marks of Pietism and religious revival everywhere was the supplementing of the regular round of parish devotions by other, often clubable, religious practices; the men of rational orthodoxy and enlightenment, while admitting sadly that 'in England the people are no more instructed nor more devout than elsewhere, although, since their liturgy requires them to respond to the minister they must, it seems suffer less distraction and be more attentive',[9] sought tirelessly, and especially in Germany, to wake up their own flocks by liturgical reform, to establish liturgical studies as an academic discipline within the field of pastoral theology, and to get the subject into the professional handbooks published for the clergy.[10]

The Turretini correspondence also illustrates another factor common to the men of reason and the man of piety, namely that their case against confessional orthodoxy was in some respects not a very good one, that, indeed, they shared two of the principal concerns of late orthodoxy, their fears for Protestantism in the empire, and their alarm about atheism; and that the Swiss at least, made a serious misjudgment about the social structure within which any progress in Germany would have to be made. Some comment on each of these points is in order. The standard case of both the *Aufklärers* and the pietists against confessional orthodoxy was that it had become 'hard' and 'dry', and certainly the pertinacious way in which Lutheran theologians refused to have dealings with the reformed on the basis of common acceptance of the Augsburg confession, the latter being unwilling to accept every jot and tittle of the *Invariata*, invited this description.[11] There was, however, nothing hard or dry about the significance of the issue between general and special grace to the orthodox; it was a 'basic article through which faith must be kindled and maintained',[12] and the late orthodoxy had done a great deal to redress the balance created by the reformation in the sixteenth century. The reformers had felt no option but to expose popular piety to a powerful theological critique, of which liturgical reform had been only a part. One of the questions which the orthodoxies of the seventeenth century had faced was the equally important fact that theology must expect a critique from the standpoint of piety, that it must yield depth and inwardness of life.[13] The seventeenth century had been the great age in Germany for church building, church art, the writing of hymns, psalms and prayers in verse; it developed a tradition of church music which culminated in Bach; its hymns moved markedly in an existential direction[14] – in Paul Gerhardt the sense of personal communion with God and release from guilt were what attracted John Wesley;[15] it produced not merely rogue spiritual writers like Jakob Boehme, but men like Johann Arndt whose texts were absolutely crucial to the age of religious revival, or like Joseph Schaitberger (1658–1733), one of the first great working-men revivalists amongst the Austrian Protestants, who actually contrasted the 'old Lutheran' tone of his own devotional writings with that of the 'new Pietists'.[16]

Necessarily common to all religious parties were fears for the future of Protestantism in that baffling organisation about which English writers almost all prefer to remain uninformed, the Holy Roman Empire. The Peace of Westphalia was not merely a fundamental law of the empire, it was fundamental to the future history of Protestantism. Outside the protective ring fence which it created, in the great triangle bounded by Transylvania, western Poland and Salzburg, a Protestantism, numerically strong, and commonly of much more recent vintage than in the old lands of the Reformation, a Protestantism inextricably connected with the defence not only of older social customs against intensified serfdom, but often oppressed nationality as well, must generate new resources quickly or go under, and must frequently do so without the ordinary mechanisms of church life. The urgency of the situation was what distinguished revivalism from Pietism, and the setting in which revival had to be accomplished left a permanent mark, a propensity to offer not so much an alternative church as an alternative to the church. Within the protective ring fence, the Westphalia settlement created a Protestant frame of mind which lasted over a hundred years, one of timorous conservatism; after generations of propaganda by liberals, Marxists and theorists of modernisation who flatter Protestantism by setting it in a context of progress, this frame of mind is now hard to recover, but it is central to the story.[17] Johann Jacob Moser, a Württemberger who himself embodied the complex of religious attitudes we are discussing, favouring enlightenment to the point where it threatened to encroach on revelation,[18] makes this abundantly clear in the marvellous work, *Teutsches Staats-Recht* (1 ed., 21 vols, Nuremberg etc., 1737–54) in which he established the public law of the empire as a subject of ordinary university study, combining history, law and politics in a way that has usually eluded the English lawyers. 'The religious peace [he writes] is an arrangement effected for ever, between the Empire and the Catholic estates of the empire on the one side, and the imperial estates adhering to the Augsburg Confession on the other, as to the way religious and ecclesiastical affairs shall be maintained in the Holy Roman Empire'.[19] 'On such a rock was the peace of Germany founded,' he concludes, 'Take heed, ye thoughtless hell-raisers'.[20] For hell-raisers had plenty to work on, almost all to the Protestant disadvantage. It was not just that a long trail of Protestant rulers, of which Saxony and Württemberg were only the most important, had converted to Rome, nor that the reformed house in the Palatinate had died out and been succeeded by a Catholic branch, nor even that it had taken some devious diplomacy to secure the last Protestant vote in the electoral college for the house of Hanover in 1692, though all these were bad enough. It takes some application to the lawbooks like Moser,[21] Struve's history of religious grievances,[22] or to the endless volumes of the proceedings of the *Corpus Evangelicorum* at Regensburg, edited in the middle of the eighteenth century from the notes of the Württemberg embassy, with the heart-felt prayer 'that the God of peace will fill all Christian hearts in such a way that Germany may know *for the first time* what conduces to its peace',[23] to drive home what an immense proportion of the time and effort of public authorities in Germany since Westphalia had been directed to salvaging the fundamental law of the empire. Much of the business concerned the rights of religious refugees, of whom there were many; again the change of religion in the ruling house in the Palatinate exposed the overwhelmingly Protestant subjects of that unhappy state to some very shabby treatment, and still worse, revealed a structural defect in the whole Westphalia system. The baseline that treaty established for settling confessional boundary disputes was the year 1624, but in the 1690s before these had all been painfully settled, the French fell furiously upon the Palatinate and occupied part of it till the peace settlement in 1697. Behind the French troops the building of Catholic churches recommenced, and in many places Catholics were permitted to use Protestant church buildings. By the fourth clause of the Peace of Ryswick the French also secured the concession that, in the places they now gave up, Catholicism should retain its present status. To the Protestant interest in the empire this was a clear breach of the Westphalia principle, accomplished under duress and not binding in conscience, and they set up a bray which was not silenced for fifty years. To this the Catholics replied that Westphalia itself was an act of force in which they had been pillaged by the Protestants with foreign assistance from France and Sweden, and the way the whole house of cards might be threatened by Moser's 'hell-raisers' was only too clear. It is also clear why Moser was pushed towards the law of nature and of nations in trying desperately to prove to Catholics as well as to Protestants that the Westphalia settlement was eternally binding and was not to be overthrown by the authority of the Pope or the Council of Trent, that it was based either on the principles of the Catholic religion itself, or upon religion as such.[24] In all this enlightenment and the anti-French sentiments which were a staple of Württemberger Pietism, could feed each other. Clause IV was, alas! anything but an academic matter. It filled the politics of the empire and occupied the international conferences. It encouraged the Elector Palatine and the spiritual princes of the Rhineland to behave worse to their reformed subjects, and led the king of Prussia to threaten reprisals against his Catholics. Finally, a major crisis was brought on in 1719. The church of the Holy Spirit, regarded as the cathedral of Heidelberg, exemplified only too fully the anomalous condition of the Palatinate. The choir, owned by the electors who were buried there, had been used by the Catholics for forty years, and separated from the rest of the building by a wall from top to bottom. The wall was now pulled down and the reformed turned out, with, indeed, specious promises designed to induce them to forgo their internationally guaranteed status, and, prospectively, that large part of the ecclesiastical revenues of the Palatinate attached to the church.[25] Moreover, concluding that the glosses to the eightieth question of the Heidelberg catechism to the effect that the Mass was 'abominable idolatry' were not part of the original catechism that he was bound to tolerate, the Elector set about the seizure of all the copies he could find, notwithstanding that the new edition of 1719 bore his arms and permission to print, and, as the Palatine reformed ruefully reflected, notwithstanding that even Louis XIV had taken no special exception to his Protestants' addressing the Pope as anti-Christ. The final upshot was a tremendous diplomatic crisis, maintained to the brink of war, in which the Palatine Protestants regained their rights, but much more importantly, a serious check was given to the counter-reformation pressures which had been gathering force in the empire for seventy years.[26] The whole episode gave an impulse on the one side to schemes of Protestant church union, alarming to the orthodox, and, on the other, to those schemes for the forcible extirpation of Protestantism in Germany under the auspices of assorted dignitaries from prince Eugene to the Vienna allies of 1725[27] or the College of Cardinals,[28] the documents of which did yeoman service to the Second Reich as propaganda for the *Kulturkampf*.

The history and prehistory of this crisis help to illuminate many features of the intellectual situation which are otherwise hard to understand. The decisive force in securing the settlement was George I acting as elector of Hanover, and forging one more link in the chain which was binding England to the religious situation in Germany as she had never been bound before; he strengthened that complex of influences which was increasing the sensitivity of the perceptive to what was going on in the Protestant heartlands, preparing the politicians for new Protestant crusades in the sordid Polish affair of the bloodbath of Thorn in 1724, and softening up the ordinary carnal Englishman to dedicate a host of public houses to the Protestant chivalry of the sceptical Frederick the Great on the occasion of his Silesian adventure in 1740, and revel in Protestant pornography on the theme of 'The Queen of Hungary Script'.[29]

English involvement was symptomatic of the fact that no interested party could escape stating an attitude to the Protestant crisis within and without the empire, nor circumvent its constitutional complexities. What made the Lutheran theologians so repellent to the Swiss was that they could see no hope of salvation except in the letter of the Westphalia settlement and the dogmatic documents which lay behind it. The sheer vituperativeness of Saxon orthodoxy sprang from no arrogant sense of being in possession both of Luther and secure religious establishment; it was a confession of weakness. The heart had gone out of the Saxon establishment when the ruling house exemplified all the orthodox abhorred as 'indifferentism' by becoming Catholic to gain the Polish crown; the orthodox (much like Queen Anne's Tory clergy) knew that the number of their communicants was dropping sharply. Dabbling in revival offerred them even less hope than it offered the clergy of George II: in domestic terms revival was inextricably intermeshed with the separatist politics of the nobility of Upper Lusatia,[30] the most recently acquired territory of the Electorate; in foreign policy terms revival was part of the politics used by Prussia to build up its interest in the Oder valley, to prepare remotely for Frederick the Great's onslaught on Silesia, and to secure more immediately that Saxony was kept separated from the lands of the Polish Crown.[31] And, not least, to dabble in revival meant incurring the hostility of the House of Habsburg, the only power at present capable of keeping Prussia in her place. What else could the Saxon clergy do, but stand relentlessly upon an orthodox platform, and hope that in the long run the legal guarantees they had inherited from the past would save the day? Meanwhile their great spokesman Valentin Ernst Löscher[32] was using his famous journal, the *Unschuldige Nachrichten*,[33] to moan year in and year out that the truth fell victim to everything, indifferentism and popery, Pietism, revival, and atheism; and indeed Saxony, like ex-Protestant parts of Austria was already being steadily prepared for the ultimate reception of the next live popular religion on offer, Social Democracy. From a Lutheran standpoint things were no better in Prussia. Adopting the reformed faith with a view to territorial acquisition in the Rhineland, the Hohenzollerns bestowed their favour in the two generations following 1660 mostly upon men born and educated in the west and of reformed profession. The orthodox position was undermined by relativising it, or as they said, God was betrayed for Mammon in the shape of profitable colonisation by immigrants. The court chaplaincies were used to form a privileged reformed body from which prestigious places were filled. Yet the Lutheran loss was hardly a reformed gain, for the court society which counted, though of Calvinist origin, remained confessionally indifferent. The way to preferment for the ordinary clergy, too, was through the army chaplaincies, managed from 1717 by a special *Kriegskonsistorium*, separate from the other spiritual authorities, and dedicated to ironing out the differences amongst the Prussian church provinces.[34] No wonder that the Lutheran clergy, seeing their *ständisch* redoubts steadily undermined, scented indifferentism, even atheism.

All parties to this story made it their business to settle accounts with the atheists. It is characteristic of the use of language in this period that in Baumgarten's treatment of religious parties,[35] atheists were the first religious party to be discussed.[36] For on orthodox principles there could not be a real atheist, since it was impossible to root out the inborn witness of conscience to God. Orthodoxy had no doubts, however, that theoretical atheism was a plague imported from abroad, and consisted largely of Herbert of Cherbury, Hobbes[37] and Spinoza. Atheist was an acceptable description of all who questioned the personality of God, providence, immortality and the authority of the Bible, and all these religious deviationists, enthusiasts, Pietists and Catholics who were solemnly resurrected in the 1920s by Fritz Mauthner in his monumental history of atheism.[38] The orthodox also discovered the existence of practical atheism, and even during the Thirty Years' War the consistorial records of Württemberg were filled with complaints of moral brutalisation succinctly characterised as atheism.[39] How neatly the pioneers of Pietism and of enlightenment could combine to make this orthodox theme their own is illustrated in the case of Leibniz and Gottlieb Spizel. Spizel was a Protestant clergyman who died in 1691 as Senior of Augsburg, having made the campaign against atheism his life's work. Educated in the shade of Leipzig orthodoxy, Spizel became in due course a follower of Spener, an enthusiastic admirer of the *Pia Desideria*, the founder of a Pietist collegium in Augsburg and so forth. Long before this, however, Spener had recommended to Spizel a treatise he knew Leibniz had written, the *Confessio naturae contra atheistas*, and in 1668 he obtained it from Boineburg and sent it to Spizel with a covering letter. In the following year Spizel published it along with the concluding volume of his first atheism trilogy, *De Atheismo eradicando*.[40] In the atheist controversy solutions might be sought similar to those canvassed for the more general problem of Protestant survival. Some might concentrate on the development of a watertight doctrine of Scripture which jeopardised continued contact between faith and the progress of knowledge,[41] others might try what could be done by natural theology, or by tackling the problem of practical atheism at a pastoral or evangelistic level. Along these routes orthodoxy, enlightenment and Pietism or revival came to distinguish themselves. But the king of the German enlightenment, Christian Wolff himself, acknowledged how far his own work rested on the development of natural theology in late Lutheran orthodoxy and stressed the importance of natural theology for the struggle against atheism.[42]

The German crusade against atheism will contain few surprises for English students raised upon recent comment, insular as it is, upon English controversy in the later seventeenth century.[43] It is worth noting that the English controversies left their mark in Germany, and fuelled the xenophobia which entered into both orthodoxy and Pietism, not only at the points where foreign literature entered, like Hamburg,[44] but also in the learned journals of the Saxon orthodox. In 1721 the *Unschuldige Nachrichten* gave extensive coverage to George I's championship of orthodoxy against Socinianism, Arianism and unbelief, and to the lurid stories of the Hellfire Clubs;[45] six years later it turned a review of a German translation of a catechism written by Archbishop Wake when Bishop of Lincoln, into a slashing attack on his schemes of church union. Union with a church as riddled with Arianism and Socinianism as that of England was impossible. The author had never had any confidence in what the Church of England offered in the way of confessional orthodoxy; thirty-two years before he had been a student in England and had met many distinguished orientalists, mathematicians and philosophers, but the theology had been bad. As one of its more distinguished practitioners had jested, 'it was created like the English language which was put together out of many others, such as Lower Saxon, Danish, Latin French and old British; so also is English theology created from religions of many kinds'.[46] The status of the Church of England in Lutheran eyes was now of importance, for since the 1690s a very large number of German ordinands had come here for part of their education, so large that H.L. Benthem, a consistorial councillor in Brunswick, produced a vast tome of almost 1300 pages, conveying all the information about the English church, universities and scholars required by even the most discriminating German student. Lower Saxony now came to the rescue of the Church of England, for the work was brought up to date and reissued by one of the general superintendents of Hanover,[47] and Benthem's sturdy defence of *ecclesia Anglicana* restored to public notice. Was there anxiety about Socinianism in England? 'Whoever wishes to stay at home on account of Socinians', declared Benthem, 'must now be continually imprisoned between the narrow frontiers of his dwelling, for this offensive sect are to be found . . . not only in foreign places, but also in our Germany; and meanwhile many of the so-called Pietists and enthusiasts are willing to be bound to no certain *formula confessionis*, and others are almost solely concerned how they can pursue enthusiasm and chiliasm. One does the English injustice if one thinks that Socinians have greater privileges among them than elsewhere'. Anxiety that theologians might be corrupted among English students was rebuffed with equal vigour. 'The student is either dissolute beforehand or not. If he is of that sort he should be made to stay at home and begin another course of life; for God wants not only scholarly but also pious servants. But if he is not reckless and voluptuous, in God's name let him go, for at English universities he will not be seduced'.

The English church had other robust defenders in reformed Switzerland and these portended an important change in the intellectual atmosphere. If in 1700 the system of confessional orthodoxy was working anywhere in the Protestant world, it seemed to be here. Under pressure of a mounting crescendo of Catholic conversions, and under the leadership of the canton of Bern, the chief towns had adopted the *Formula Consensus* in 1675, and Bern, at least, was prepared to uphold it in no kidglove manner. The reality, however, was more complicated. The *Formula* was not printed till 1710, partly because there was powerful resistance to it abroad. The Great Elector tried to get it dropped in 1686 when taking on board Huguenot refugees who inclined to Amyraldism and the school of Saumur, and Werenfels managed to free the church of Basel from it. In Neuenburg the clergy generally managed to avoid subscription, and when that territory passed to Prussia in 1707, there was no question of maintaining strict orthodoxy. The great crisis in Germany in 1719 brought renewed and repeated pressure on reformed Switzerland from the king of Prussia, the king of England and the *Corpus Evangelicorum* not to divide the Protestant front. And there was always internal opposition not only in Zürich, and in Geneva which felt the immediate hostility of the French reformed and finally dropped subscription in 1725, but also in the French-speaking Vaud, chafing under Bernese domination.[48] Even in Bern, orthodoxy came under pressure from the mixture of forces we have been discussing, those which led to rational orthodoxy and enlightenment, and those which led to Pietism and revival, both of them drawing encouragement from England. One of the earliest portents of enlightenment in Bern, Ludwig von Muralt (1668–1749), claimed in his *Lettres sur les Anglais et les Français* (circulated in manuscript and published only in 1725) that English liberty of thought was no misfortune, 'for all those who in England are unbelievers, are in other lands hypocrites, and which of these is worse everyone knows'. Curiously enough, exiled from Bern, his alienation took another form and he ended his life a solitary mystic.[49] Albrecht von Haller also noted in his diary that the English clergy had more success in putting down denials of God than others, and wrote the best Protestant mystical books. It was in this vein that his philosophical poems owed much to English example, that Tscharner translated Young's *Night Thoughts* into German hexameters, that Sigmund Gruner put *Paradise Lost* into German verse, that the English moralists, and, most of all, the expository paraphrases of the new testament of that Englishman who more than anyone stood with one foot in the camp of the Enlightenment and the other in that of revival, Philip Doddridge, were highly prized. But the standard English pabulum at the end of the seventeenth century which nourished a piety never contained within the *Formula Consensus* was the works of Baxter and Bunyan; these encouraged, in the blessed English puritan phrase which underlay so much continental Pietism, the *praxis pietatis*, and opened the door to German devotional writers.[50] How close together common discomfort might bring the rational orthodox and the Pietist is revealed in Ostervald's account of a conversation he had in 1702 with the son of a big bourgeois of Bern who had refused to have his son baptised. 'After an hour's conversation [he relates] he appeared to me amenable, and he told me that if they used that language at Berne there would be no talk of Pietism'.[51] The tone of this comment is eloquent. Werenfels, Ostervald and Turretini, the Helvetic triumvirate, wanted to do their work for the church through religious establishments, if possible through unions of religious establishments. Neither church union nor contact with healthy culture were to be frustrated by high Protestant orthodoxy. Confessional isolation and the cultural isolation which later produced the *gemeinnützige Pfarrer* (public-spirited parsons), known for all manner of economic, agricultural and even historiographical good works, but unknown for any religious position, were equally dangerous.[52] Orthodoxy had linked church with church on a confessional basis; the rational orthodox wished to find common ground between the confessions, and between religion and a culture dominated by French names, though it also included Tillotson and Locke, Leibniz and Pufendorf, from the Protestant world. But in Swiss, as in Württemberger, Pietism there was a strong, anti-French vein, and in the long run, Bernese Pietists, less 'amenable' than Ostervald's friend, became heavily tarred with the brush of opposition to the Bernese oligarchy.[53] One of the factors which seems to have undermined the comfortable relations the rational orthodox established with England through the SPCK and SPG seems to have been their final fear that religious societies would end in just such a way.[54] Nor were the results more positive on the German side. It was not difficult for the triumvirate to see that confessional orthodoxy offered no solution to their problems, to Switzerland's lack of a political champion since the death of Cromwell, to the long-term survival of the reformed diaspora in the Rhine valley which they had financed for so long, to the perennial agony of the reformed churches in Hungary, or even to the handling of the flood of French refugees in their own midst, some of them worldly and skittish, others crazy and prophetic. Their disappointments with the Lutherans, however, show that they did not grasp what the cultural situation in Germany was, nor why the Lutheran theologians were so rebarbative. Though the number of journals in Germany was increasing all the time, it was not until the end of the eighteenth century that an independent lay culture could come into being on the back of the publishing boom which Germany shared with much of Europe. In the linguistic sense Zürich was one of the main centres of the German enlightenment; in 1747, Sulzer, recently called from Zürich to Berlin, wrote home that 'the sort of men who live comfortably on their incomes and are masters of their time, is entirely lacking here. For every ten in Zürich who read and think there is only one in this part of the world'.[55] The sole market for learning in Germany was provided by the state through the church and universities, and the state had enough ecclesiastical problems on its hands without a repetition of the fracas between the orthodox and the Pietists. Swiss rational orthodoxy was in all conscience conservative enough, but in Germany even in the 1770s when Lessing edited the *Fragments* Reimarus had not published for himself, passionate protests against the *status quo* were still very exceptional. And as we have seen the prospective destructiveness of 'hellraisers' in Germany made the *status quo* precious to all German states, even to Prussia.

Moreover, the Pietist tools of Prussian policy at Halle had assessed the potentialities of a religious appeal at a popular level better than the rational-orthodox. Of course even in the age of orthodoxy the effective religious appeal had varied much from one social stratum to the next. If orthodoxy had been inextricably linked with *ständisch* politics in Saxony and Prussia, and with the patrician order in Bern, rational orthodoxy in one sense continued its work; certainly in an age which attached a good deal of importance to lucidity and clarity, simplification, classification and co-ordination were required in the elaborate doctrinal tangle of the old orthodoxies. Then there had always been a prevalent conventional church-manship which the orthodox, the Enlightenment and the Pietist had all tried to animate in their own way, its connection with establishment and a sacramental system always tempting the latter to separation and dissent. There was also much of what Wernle called 'natural religion'[56] to be found at various social levels from the peasantry to the educated classes; this was a simple belief in providence and rewards, little supported by doctrine but much nourished by scripture, a conviction that men were involved in a moral order, and would come off best if they were men of virtue and religion. On the one side this arose from a familiarity with common-place worldliness which could hardly regard religion as the supreme temptation it had appeared to Luther, a professional religious (in both senses), and on the other it could issue in enlightenment once the harmony of the earth and the richness of its potentialities had made an impression. At the lowest social level Christianity was accompanied or displaced by all manner of the primitive superstition ridiculed in the later popular literature of the Enlightenment.[57] What Halle showed was that the literature of a bygone age, reinforced by Pietist pamphleteering, could unite portions of these social segments in a way that historians have been reluctant to admit.

The rise of Halle and its connection with the beginnings of religious revival in the Habsburg empire is too large a story to relate in the present paper, but illuminates the way literature was received by the movements which concern us and shows that one of the forces which kept enlightenment, Pietism and religious revival in touch, and turned them against the orthodoxy to which they were related, was Prussian state policy. Having acquired the duchy of Magdeburg in 1680, a run-down post-Thirty-Years'-War province, Brandenburg proceeded to develop it economically at a great rate, and to exploit its potentialities at the crossroads of the great German trade routes from south to north (Leipzig to Hamburg) and west to east (the Rhine to Frankfurt-on-Oder, the junction of the Polish and Silesian trade, the latter of which led to Breslau and Russia). The Prussian drive up the Oder valley had important political as well as economic objectives. The foundation of the university at Halle (1690–94) was designed not only to train civil servants and keep Brandenburger ordinands out of the orthodox universities of Saxony, but to compete directly with the celebrated neighbouring Saxon university of Leipzig, and it was staffed with Pietists and champions of enlightenment, many of whom were Saxon-born or Leipzig-trained. To Francke, Halle and the Prussian state were not merely the eleventh-hour saviours of Pietism; they were a base for a mission of universal regeneration.[58] Halle took in students from all the Slavonic peoples that counted, planted out its agents right across Europe, financed its huge institutions by a hair-raising mixture of commerce, politics and begging, and began to cultivate a sphere of interest extending from western Siberia, India and Constantinople,[59] eventually to the American colonies in the other direction.[60] Peter the Great saw in Halle an agency of modernisation; Francke propped up the Ests, Letts and Lithuanians against the ravages of Swedish orthodoxy; most especially an enormous work was done in the provision of literature in the tongues of the west and south Slavs.[61] Some of this was for the benefit of enserfed Slavonic populations in Germany, like the upper and lower Wends of Lusatia, whom the Pietist nobility were as determined as any to keep down. But the bulk of what they did was for the Protestants of Silesia, German and slav,[62] and of Bohemia, Moravia, and other parts of the Habsburg empire, and was subversive in intent. Prussia had an immediate interest in raising the Protestant minorities of the Habsburg empire on the basis partly of religion and partly of resistance to the intensified serfdom; this would weaken the emperor, and foster the recruiting of new settlers for the kingdoms of Prussia. In the long run it would prepare for major adventures like those which began with the Silesian wars in 1740. Religious revival was the joint product of Protestant self-help, peasant resistance, and Prussian propaganda. Halle provided dictionaries and other scholarly apparatus which ultimately did much for the literary development of these languages, but the enormous volume of material they disseminated through the Grace church at Teschen, the Protestant embassy chaplains at Vienna[63] and other sources was of a different kind. This tremendous bombardment which makes the assault which the SPCK is now known to have made upon Wales in the generation before the revival[64] look like a battery from peashooters, consisted mostly of a relatively limited range of texts, the Bible, which as a forbidden book was the most subversive text of all, and a number of

Protestant classics – Luther's *Shorter Catechism*, his *Romans*, the works of Arndt and so forth. These works proved admirably calculated both for the job in hand and for linking populations of low literacy with élites far removed in place and educational level.

In the middle of the eighteenth century the object of the *Aufklärers* who produced an enormous literature for peasant consumption was summed up by von Rochow in thoroughly anti-emancipationist terms as 'to form good Christians, obedient subjects and capable farmers'. Halle, in the Habsburg domains at least, was batting on a better wicket in seeking to form good Christians, disobedient subjects, and peasants who resisted their dues or left the country. Peasants would not touch the literature provided for them by the *Aufklärers*, partly from a not unfounded suspicion that economic efficiency only benefited the landlord, partly from the ingrained hatred of Slavonic peoples against German lordship, partly from their level of reading readiness. Peasants would buy the almanacs, ghost stories and crime which were distributed all the way from France to Russia through fairs and colporteurs, but, for the rest, reading for them was an intensive affair, a matter as much of ear as of eye, a process of deciphering a text often heard before, the continuation of a tradition of family reading. For this purpose the vernacular Bible and the Reformation classics were ideal, their very lack of *aktualität* adding to their authority.[65] It was for this reason that central European Protestants had always feared total inability to read as the gateway to coarse worldliness or to popery, well known to be the religion of illiterates; what astounded the Saxon orthodox in the eighteenth century was the discovery that literature used in this way was capable of reproducing the faith from generation to generation among oppressed populations deprived of the church, a thing impossible on orthodox principles. When twenty thousand Protestants were dislodged from the archbishopric of Salzburg in 1731, they were marched across Europe and catechised in every town. To Löscher's astonishment the catechising proved that they were Lutherans with rights under the Westphalia settlement, and the charity sermons which went out on their behalf were accompanied by harrowing line drawings showing these mountain men turning their back on their homeland for the sake of the gospel, a baby under one arm, Luther's Bible or the shorter catechism under the other.[66] Even if Wesley had not met these men with their Halle pastors in Georgia, he and the other proto-evangelicals would have had their eyes opened to the forgotten sustenance contained in this kind of literature. As everyone knows Wesley's heart was strangely warmed at Aldersgate Street 'while one was reading Luther's Preface to Romans'.[67] But Francke too had been converted thus; and Luther's preface played a central role in the literature of Pietism, revival and the early overseas missions.[68] Reformation literature read apart from dogmatic presuppositions of orthodoxy forged a link among men of the most varied national origin, social status and level of literacy, in a political context which separated them from orthodoxy, rational orthodoxy, and also from enlightenment. Nowhere was this problem more serious than in orthodox Saxony whose theologians had been equally ferocious against Pietists and against the schemes of church union sponsored by the rational orthodox. While the population of Saxony more than doubled between 1550 and 1750, the proportion of that increased number who were peasants diminished by half, and the proportion who were merely gardeners and cottagers increased six and a half times; and both these trends were maintained into the next century when the whole population inceased by another 85 per cent.[69] Orthodox censorship[70] ensured that there was nothing for this swelling rural proletariat, and when orthodoxy collapsed before enlightenment in the middle of the eighteenth century, enlightenment had nothing to offer. Saxon religion was then in a poor way. A sad example of this was afforded unwittingly by J.G. Carpzov in one of his anti-Moravian polemics. In an interesting personal reminiscence he describes how in his youth the Bohemian persecuted 'came every year unto Upper Lusatia, Dresden, Freyburg and other Chur-Saxon places where Bohemian services were held, in order to enjoy Holy Communion there. A form which I myself well recall to have often heard . . . when the preacher M. Rühr at Dresden, conducted the Lutheran service in the Bohemian church and tongue, so that in summer-time he had many travelling communicants out of Bohemia', 'many' meaning thousands.[71] The mass communion, particularly of the oppressed, the classic formula for revival, whether at Kirk o' Shotts or in Antrim in the 1630s, in Cambuslang and Kilsyth in 1742–3, or Cane Ridge, Kentucky, in 1800, had presented itself to the orthodox, but they had feared for the church order and made nothing of it.[72] The Pietist nobility of Upper Lusatia, exploiting the fact that they were not subject to the central censorship of Saxony, had by contrast provided the setting for the celebrated Moravian revival of 1727 at Herrnhut.

This tangle of events and attitudes does something to clarify the intellectual and practical options available to John Wesley in his formative years. The concurrent crises of Protestantism within and without the Westphalia ring fence were only too well known, and, in their effect, like the creeping canker of political corruption at home. If Wesley was sufficiently like the continental orthodox to rant against 'those . . . *first born of Satan*, the Deists, Arians or Socinians', he could tilt in the same breath against Tillotson;[73] the confessional state was as impracticable in England as it was hopeless in Saxony, and church union, the solution strenuously pressed by Wake and the rational-orthodox admirers of

Tillotson, had run into the sands in the mid-twenties.[74] Private enterprise and older doctrinal inspiration seemed the only hope, first the non-jurors, then, indeed, the key texts of the reformers. How strangely English Methodism could add its weight to the literary and spiritual impulses of central Europe was illustrated in the 1760s when the first Methodist society was created in America by two Irish immigrants, Barbara Heck and Philip Embury. Little is known of Barbara Heck, but there is a surviving portrait of her, devoutly clasping her Bible. The Bible, like that of the Salzburgers in the cartoons, is Luther's Bible. Embury and Mrs Heck were not Irish by descent, but the offspring of a previous European persecution, the poor Palatines rescued from the French in 1709 and settled on plantations in the west of Ireland.[75] But if such pillars of progress as Frederick the Great and Karl Friedrich, Margrave of Baden-Durlach, were unwilling to let Pietism lose touch with enlightenment, and kept issuing Pietistic school ordinances,[76] circumstances would not let Wesley evolve into a neo-Protestant shellback; the empiricism required to create and sustain a religious community kept him within reach of enlightenment, and it is no surprise in the eighties to find him in touch with the latitudinarian American Episcopalians.[77] And in America, though revival seemed, even to the former establishments of New England, to be a way to the recovery of Calvinist orthodoxy, the sheer purposiveness of the American churches, their need to construct not merely the kingdom of God but the kingdom of this world from the foundations upwards, ensured a great levelling of denominational differences and a triumph of pragmatic churchmanship which was nearer enlightenment than most things on offer in Europe. Of course, this fresh blurring of the lines in Britain and the British Empire, had already been foreshadowed in Hanover. The university of Göttingen, a model of enlightenment, devoted from the beginning to natural sciences and conceding no special privilege to theology, was created by Baron von Münchausen, an alumnus of Halle who stood close to the Pietists and wished to steer a middle course in church contests; the early theologians he appointed sought to unite inherited orthodoxy with 'enlightened Pietism'. And if, on the academic side, this bore fruit in mid-century in the efforts of the church historian Mosheim to mediate between orthodoxy, Pietism and enlightenment, on the practical side it led H.M. Mühlenberg, to found an Orphan House in the town, to organise the Pietistic and revivalist Germans of America into a Lutheran church, and to create those close relations which still subsist between the Lutheran church of the USA and the theological faculty in Göttingen.[78]

Notes

1 R.B. Aspland, *The rise and present influence of Wesleyan Methodism*, London 1831, p. 20.

2 *Lettres [inédites addressées à J.A.] Turretini*, ed. E. de Budé, 4 vols, Paris/ Geneva 1887, 2. p. 23.

3 *Ibid.* 1 pp. 376–7.

4 *Ibid.* 1 p. 157: 2 pp. 92–3, 120.

5 *Ibid.* 1 p. 302.

6 *Ibid.* 1 p. 340.

7 *Ibid.* 2 p. 50.

8 *Journal [of the Rev. John Wesley]*, ed. Nehemiah Curnock, 8 vols, 2 ed. London 1938, 2 pp. 20–57.

9 *Lettres Turretini* 2 p. 111. It is entertaining to see the Catholic enlightenment coming back to this point after Catholics had wrought havoc for generations in the name of a strict confessionalism. A report made to Joseph II in 1771 after a tour of the old protestant territories of Bohemia, Moravia and Silesia, declared that 'there is a great lack of education in all your majesty's hereditary lands and in the real Christian and moral virtues; the mob lives in the greatest ignorance, the townsmen and many who regard themselves as pious souls are held in a really tasteless and superstitious piety, which brings religion to breakup and scorn, through the ignorant clergy, overstocked in these towns, who give occasion to petty devotions partly from self-interest, partly from their own stupidity.' *Aus der Zeit Maria Theresias. Tagebuch des Fürsten Johann Josef Khevenhüller-Metsch, 1742–1776*, ed. Rudolf Graf Khevenhüller-Metsch and Hans Schlitter, 7 vols, Vienna 1907–25, 7 p. 381. Cited below as *Khevenhüller Tagebuch*.

10 Detlef Reichert, 'Der Weg protestantischer Liturgik zwischen Orthodoxie und Aufklärung', D. Theol. thesis, University of Münster (1975) pp. 295–6, 347–8. Pietism itself could be active in liturgical reform, taking up into itself themes both of orthodoxy and enlightenment. In Thuringia, for example, the Pietists got rid of public confession, introduced public confirmation, and greatly developed the musical side of public worship, *Geschichte Thuringens*, ed. Hans Patze and Walter Schlesinger, 4 vols, Cologne/Vienna 1968–73 in progress, 4 pp. 30–1. The Pietist court in Denmark abolished exorcism as a normal part of the baptismal liturgy in 1737, *Acta Historico-Ecclesiastica*, Weimar 1737–56, 4, p. 93.

11 [J.G.] Walch, [*Historische und theologische Einleitung in der*] *Religionsstreitigkeiten [welche sonderlich] [ausser der Evangelisch-Lutherischen Kirche [entstanden]*, 5 vols, 3 ed. Jena 1733–6: reprint Stuttgart/Bad Canstatt 1972, 1 p. 508. The *Invariata* was a text of the original Augsburg Confession drawn up for the Book of Concord in 1580, and, despite its name, is said to differ in more than 450 places from the text of 1530. The Reformed were willing to accept the *Variata*, Melancthon's revision of 1540.

12 Walch, *Religionstreitigkeiten ausser der Evangelisch-Lutherischen Kirche* 1 p. 54.

13 Winfried Zeller, *Theologie und Frömmigkeit*, Marburg 1971, esp. pp. 85–116. Compare Susi Hausamman, ' "Leben aus Glauben" in Reformation, Reformorthodoxie und Pietismus', *T[heologische] Z[eitschrift]* 27, Basel 1971, pp. 263–89; also [Paul] Wernle, [Der] *schweizerische Protestantismus* [*im XVIII. Jahrhundert*], 5 vols, Tübingen 1923–42, 1 pp. 92–103.

14 Cornelis Pieter van Andel, 'Paul Gerhardt, ein Mystiker zur Zeit des Barocks', *Traditio-Krisis-Renovatio aus theologischer Sicht*, ed. Bernd Jaspert and Rudolf Mohr, Marburg 1976, p. 183.

15 John Wesley, *Journal* 5, p. 117; John Wesley, *Letters*, ed. J. Telford, 8 vols, London 1931, 4 p. 299. Amongst the 33 German hymns translated by Wesley were several by Gerhardt, four of which are in current use.

16 Zeller, *Theologie und Frömmigkeit*, pp. 109–10.

17 The reality of these fears is in no way diminished by the fact that the Catholics in the empire continually harrowed themselves (and kept their party together) by fears that the Protestant party was about to capture the Imperial dignity itself. On this see Heinz Duchardt, *Protestantisches Kaisertum und altes Reich*, Wiesbaden 1977. For Habsburg use of an alleged plot to subvert the Catholic estates of the empire, see *Khevenhüller Tagebuch* 2 pp. 382–3.

18 Reinhard Rürup, *Johann Jakob Moser, Pietismus und Reform*, Wiesbaden 1965, pp. 29–31.

19 *Teutsches Staats-Recht* 1, pp. 123–4.

20 *Ibid.* 1 pp. 167–8.

21 Modern introductions like Aloys Schulte, *Der deutsche Staat. Verfassung, Macht und Grenzen, 919–1914*, Stuttgart 1933, repr. Aalen 1968, while useful are no substitute.

22 Burcard Gotthelf Struve, *Ausführliche Historie des Religions-Beschwerden zwischen denen Römisch-Catholischen und Evangelischen im Teutschen Reich*, Leipzig 1722.

23 E.C.W. von Schauroth, *Vollständige Sammlung aller Conclusorum, Schreiben, und anderer übrigen Verhandlungen des hochpreisslichen Corporis Evangelicorum . . . bis auf die gegenwärtigen Zeiten*, 3 vols., Regensburg 1751–2, preface to vol. 1, n.p. (Italics mine).

24 Moser, *Teutsches Staats-Recht* 1, p. 171.

25 An interesting report on all this was subsequently prepared for Turretini, *Lettres Turretini* 3 pp. 375–82.

26 On the whole question see Karl Borgmann, *Der deutsche Religionsstreit der Jahre 1719–20. Abhandlungen der mittleren und neuren Geschichte. Heft 80*, Berlin 1937. Andreas Biederbick, 'Der deutsche Reichstag zu Regensburg im Jahrzehnt nach dem Spanischen Erbfolgkrieg, 1714–24. Der Verlauf der Religionsstreitigkeiten und ihre Bedeutung für den Reichstag', Diss, University of Bonn (1937).

27 Wolfgang Michael, *Englische Geschichte im achtzehnten Jahrhundert*, 5 vols., Hamburg, Leipzig and Basel 1896–1955, 3 pp. 410 seq.

28 J.G. Droysen, *Geschichte der preussischen Politik*, 4 vols., Leipzig 1874–86, 4er Theil, 4e Abtheilung, pp. 416–33. Compare *Acta Historico-Ecclesiastica* 3 p. 563: 6 pp. 529–34.

29 Manfred Schlenke, *England und das friderizianische Preussen, 1740–63*, Freiburg/Munich 1963.

30 J.B. Neveux, *Vie spirituelle et vie sociale entre Rhin et Baltique au XVIIᵉ siècle*, Paris 1967, pp. xxxiii–xxxiv.

31 On the general situation see G. Jaeckel, 'Die Bedeutung der konfessionellen Frage für die Besitzergreifung Schlesiens durch Friedrich den Grossen', *Jahrbuch für schlesische Kirche und Kirchengeschichte*, NF 34, Düsseldorf 1955, pp. 78–121.

32 On whom see Martin Greschat, *Zwischen Tradition und neuem Anfang. Valentin Ernst Löscher und der Ausgang der lutherischen Orthodoxie*, Witten 1971.

33 First published at Wittenberg 1701, and at Leipzig 1704–61.

34 G. Heinrich, 'Amsträgerschaft und Geistlichkeit. Zur Problematik der sekundaren Führungsschichten in Brandenburg-Preussen, 1450–1786', *Beamtentum und Pfarrerstand, 1400–1800*, ed. Günther Franz, Limburg/Lahn 1972, pp. 179–238.

35 S.J. Baumgarten's *Geschichte der Religionspartheyen* was edited by Semler, Halle 1766, repr. Hildesheim 1966, from lectures given in 1754 and 1755.

36 *Ibid.* pp. 25–60.

37 In Baumgarten's rational orthodoxy Hobbes was promoted to the rank of 'indifferentist', since he permitted the sovereign to require not merely conformity, but conscientious adherence, by his subjects, to the religion he prescribed, *Ibid.* p. 107.

38 Fritz Mauthner, *Der Atheismus und seine Geschichte im Abendland*, 4 vols., Stuttgart/Berlin 1920–23.

39 Dietrich Blaufuss, *Reichstadt und Pietismus – Philipp Jacob Spener und Gottlieb Spizel aus Augsburg*, Neustadt a.d. Aisch 1977, p. 268.

40 Dietrich Blaufuss, 'Korrespondenten von G.W. Leibniz. 3. Gottlieb Spizel aus Augsburg (1639–91). Ein Anhänger Phil. Jac. Speners, des Führers des lutherischen Pietismus', *Studia Leibnitiana* 5, Wiesbaden 1973, pp. 116–44; Gottfried Wilhelm Leibniz, *Sämtliche Schriften und Briefe*, Erste Reihe 9, Berlin 1975, p. 595.

41 Hans Leube, 'Ideen und Taten im deutschen Protestantismus nach dem Dreissigjährigen Kriege', *Zeitschrift für deutsche Geisteswissenschaft* 5, 1943, pp. 97–120, reprinted in Hans Leube, *Orthodoxie und Pietismus, Gesammelte Studien*, Bielefeld 1975, p. 111.

42 On this whole question see Hans Leube, 'Die Bekampfung des Atheismus in der deutschen lutherischen Kirchen des 17. Jahrhunderts', *ZKG* 42 (1924) pp. 227–44, reprinted in Leube, *Orthodoxie und Pietismus* pp. 75–88.

43 John Redwood, *Reason, Ridicule and Religion. The age of Enlightenment in England, 1660–1750*, London 1976; Margaret C. Jacob, *The Newtonians and*

the English Revolution, 1689–1720, Hassocks 1976, p. 15; Roland N. Stromberg, *Religious Liberalism in eighteenth-century England*, London 1954.

44 Leube, *Orthodoxie und Pietismus* p. 77.

45 *Unschuldige Nachrichten* 1721 pp. 493–7.

46 *Ibid.* 1727 pp. 432–9. Wake's catechism was published at Frankfurt and Leipzig in 1725; a Basel edition contained a foreword by the ferocious Cyprian opposing union with the reformed and others among whom Socinianism was gaining ground as rapidly as in the Church of England.

47 Henrich Ludolff Benthem, *Neu-eroffneter Engländischer Kirch- und Schulenstaat . . . nebst einer Vor-Rede Hern. Consistorial-Rat und General-Superint. Mentzers in Hannover*, Leipzig 1732, preface paras 9–10. An obituary of Benthem who died 9 July 1723 is given in *Unschuldige Nachrichten* 1723 pp. 838–9.

48 Rudolf Pfister, *Kirchengeschichte der Schweiz*, 2 vols., Zürich 1964–74, 2 pp. 486–96; [Max]Geiger, 'Die Unionsbestrebungen [der schweizerischen reformierten Theologie unter der Führung des helvetischen Triumvirates]', *TZ* 9 (1953) p. 128. Compare Martin Schmidt, 'Ecumenical activity on the Continent of Europe in the 17th and 18th centuries', *A history of the ecumenical movement, 1517–1948*, ed. R. Rouse and S.C. Neill, 2 ed. London 1967, p. 109.

49 [E.] Bloesch, [*Geschichte der schweizerischen-reformierten Kirchen*], 2 vols., Bern 1899, 2 p. 46.

50 [Kurt] Guggisberg, [*Bernische Kirchengeschichte*], Bern 1958, pp. 370, 401, 471–2; Geiger, 'Die Unionsbestrebungen' p. 125.

51 *Lettres Turretini* 2 p. 398.

52 Bloesch, 2 pp. 136–7.

53 Guggisberg p. 378; Bloesch 2 p. 104.

54 This matter and the whole question of Anglo-Swiss participation in the much-canvassed Protestant front in the war of the Spanish Succession is discussed by Dr Eamonn Duffy in a paper contributed to Professor C.W. Dugmore's Festschrift and kindly made available before publication, ' "Correspondence Fraternelle": the SPCK, the SPG and the churches of Swizterland in the War of the Spanish Succession'.

55 Herbert Schöffler, *Das literarische Zürich, 1700–1750*, Frauenfeld/Leipzig 1925, p. 108.

56 Wernle, *Schweizerische Protestantismus* 1, p. 107.

57 Hans Otto Lichtenberg, *Unterhaltsame Bauernaufklärung. Ein Kapitel Volksbildungsgeschichte*, Tübingen 1970, *passim* esp. pp. 112–17.

58 Carl Hinrichs, *Preussentum und Pietismus*, Göttingen 1971, pp. 1–125.

59 Eduard Winter, *Halle als Ausgangspunkt der deutschen Russlandkunde im 18. Jahrhundert*, [East] Berlin 1953.

60 Karl Zehrer, 'Die Beziehungen zwischen dem hallesischen Pietismus und dem frühen Methodismus', *Pietismus und Neuzeit* 2, Witten 1975, pp. 43–56.

61 Eduard Winter, *Die Pflage der West- und Süd-slavischen Sprachen im 18.*

Jahrhundert, [East] Berlin 1954: Eduard Winter, *Die tschechische und slavische Emigration in Deutschland im. 17. und 18. Jahrhundert*, [East] Berlin 1955.

62 Jaeckel (see n. 31 above) has lately argued that the Silesian wars (to which this propaganda led) were indeed of religion; certainly Prussia spared no pains to make them appear so. Polish commentators, much less enamoured than those of the DDR in presenting the intercourse between Halle and Peter the Great as a progressive foreshadowing of the present eastern bloc, prefer to talk about class conflict and see the Poles (many of whom in Silesia were indeed Protestant) as the vanguard of peasant resistance to the exploitation of a (largely German) nobility (Stanislaw Michalkiewicz, 'Einige Episoden aus der Geschichte der schlesischen Bauernkämpfe im 17. und 18. Jahrhundert', *Beitrage zur Geschichte Schlesiens*, ed. Eva Maleczynska, [East] Berlin 1953, pp. 356–400. Some recent West German scholarly work is of pre-war intellectual vintage: *Geschichte Schlesiens*, band 2, *Die Habsburgerzeit, 1526–1740*, ed. Ludwig Petry and J. Joachim Menzel, Darmstadt 1973, pp. 1–135.

63 The role of Protestant embassy-chaplains as smugglers of forbidden literature may explain the curious fact that though prospective clergy were as a class debarred from the scholarships endowed to support the new Regius Professors of Modern History of Oxford and Cambridge in 1724, three scholarships were reserved for ordinands willing to serve as embassy-chaplains. N. Sykes, *Edmund Gibson, Bishop of London 1669–1748*, London 1926, p. 96.

64 Geraint H. Jenkins, *Literature, Religion and Society in Wales, 1660–1730*, Cardiff 1978.

65 On this whole subject see the seminal paper by Reinhard Wittram, 'Der lesende Landmann. Zur Rezeption aufklärerischer Bermühungen durch die bäuerliche Bevölkerung im 18. Jahrhundert', *Der Bauer Mittel- und Osteuropas im sozioökonomischen Wandel des 18. and 19. Jahrhunderts*, ed. Heinz Ischreyt, Cologne/Vienna 1973, pp. 142–96. Compare the situation among the French peasantry, Robert Mandrou, *De la culture populaire aux XVIIe et XVIIIe siècles. La Bibliothèque bleue de Troyes*, Paris 1964.

66 The British Library has a collection of these sermons and cartoons at 1012 d. 30; see especially V.E. Löscher, *Drey Predigten von Erkänntnis und der Ehre des Sohnes Gottes*, Dresden 1733, p. 26. Compare J.G. Hillinger, *Beytrag zur Kirchen-Historie des Erzbischoftums Salzburg*, Saalfeld 1732.

67 John Wesley, *Journal*, 1 pp. 475–6.

68 Martin Schmidt, 'Luthers Vorrede zum Römerbrief im Pietismus', enlarged version in his *Wiedergeburt und neuer Mensch. Gesammelte Studien zur Geschichte des Pietismus*, Witten 1969, pp. 299–330.

69 *Aufklärung, Absolutismus und Bürgertum in Deutschland*, ed. F. Kopitsch, Munich 1976, p. 21.

70 This matter is explored in the unpublished doctoral dissertation of Agatha Kobuch, 'Die Zensor in Kursachsen zur Zeit der Personalunion mit Polen (1692–1763). Beiträge zur Geschichte der Aufklärung', Humboldt University, East Berlin, 1965.

71 J. Gottlob Carpzov, *Religions-untersuchung der Böhmisch- und Mährischen*

Bruder von Anbeginn ihrer Gemeiner bis auf gegenwärtigen Zeiten, Leipzig 1742, p. 406.

72 Arend Bucholtz, *Die Geschichte der Familie Lessing*, 2 vols., Berlin 1909, 1 pp. 98, 109–10.

73 Sermon CXXXIV (1741). *Works of John Wesley*, 14 vols., London, 1872: repr. Grand Rapids n.d., 7 p. 454.

74 N. Sykes, *William Wake, Archbishop of Canterbury, 1657–1737*, 2 vols., Cambridge 1957, 2 pp. 1–88.

75 *The history of American Methodism*, ed. E.S. Bucke, 3 vols., New York/ Nashville 1964, 1 pp. 13–14.

76 Gerhard Schmalenberg, *Pietismus-Schule-Religionsunterricht. Die christliche Unterweisung im Spiegel der von Pietismus bestimmten Schulordnung des 18. Jahrhunderts*, Bern/Frankfurt 1974.

77 W.R. Ward, 'The legacy of John Wesley', *Statesmen, Scholars and Merchants*, ed. A. Whiteman, J.S. Bromley and P.G.M. Dickson, Oxford 1973, pp. 331–3 (below, ch. 12). On Wesley's relations with the Anglican equivalent of Orthodoxy, see Eamon Duffy, 'Primitive Christianity Revived: Religious renewal in Augustan England', *SCH* 14 (1977) p. 299.

78 Eric Beyreuther, 'Halle und die Herrnhuter in den Rezensionen der Göttingi-schen Zeitungen von gelehrten Sachen auf dem Hintergrund niedersächsischer Religionspolitik zwischen 1739 und 1760' *Jahrbuch der Gesellschaft für niedersächsische Kirchengeschichte* 39, Göttingen 1975, pp. 109–34; Günther Meinhardt, *Die Universität Göttingen. Ihr Entwicklung und Geschichte von 1734–1974*, Göttingen 1977 esp. pp. 34–5.

3

Art and Science: or Bach as an Expositor of the Bible

For a long time before dramatic recent events it has been clear that the German Democratic Republic has been in the position, embarrassing to a Marxist system, of having nothing generally marketable left except (to use the jargon) 'superstructure'. The Luther celebrations conveniently bolstered the implicit claim of the GDR to embody Saxony's long-delayed revenge upon Prussia; still more conveniently, they paid handsomely. Even the Francke celebrations probably paid their way, ruinous though his Orphan House has been allowed to become. When I was in Halle, a hard-pressed government had removed the statue of Handel (originally paid for in part by English subscriptions) for head-to-foot embellishment in gold leaf, and a Handel Festival office in the town was manned throughout the year. Bach is still more crucial, both to the republic's need to pay its way and to the competition with the Federal Republic for the possession of the national tradition. There is no counterpart in Britain to the strength of the Passion-music tradition in East Germany. The celebrations which reach their peak in Easter Week at St Thomas's, Leipzig, are like a cross between Wembley and Wimbledon here, the difference being that the black market in tickets is organized by the State for its own benefit. If Bach research in East Germany, based either on musicology or the Church, has remained an industry of overwhelming amplitude and technical complexity, the State has had its own Bach-research collective located in Leipzig, dedicated among other things to establishing the relation between Bach and the Enlightenment, that first chapter in the Marxist history of human liber-ation. Now that a good proportion of the population of the GDR seems bent on liberation by leaving the republic or sinking it, the moment seems ripe to take note for non-specialist readers of some of what has been achieved there in recent years.

Paper delivered to the Ecclesiastical History Society, 1990. Published in *Studies in Church History* 28 (1992), pp. 343–53.

The old image of Bach as the Fifth Evangelist has been effectively undermined by the musicologists and is not, I think, to be restored by the enormous effort put in over the years by the bibliographers (one notable one being English)[1] on what are called Bach's 'Spiritual Books' or 'theological library'. A word is in order on each of these points. Bach's career is only to be understood in the light of his descent from an old musical family in the technical sense of that word. His forbears were town-pipers, professional fiddlers, musicians to councils and courts, who pursued their trade as artisans and were appropriately unionized in guilds. The organists, too, emerged from these trades, and were distinct from the academically trained *Kantors* (or precentors) who studied music as a science in a liberal arts course at the university, obtained the qualification to teach in Latin schools, and could unite school and church service. This distinction was beginning to disappear as organists rose in status with the increased significance of instrumental music, and the rise of spiritual recitals from which the cantata developed. Eventually the distinction between *Kantor* and organist disappeared, but although it was bridged by Bach, it remained in full force in his lifetime.

Bach himself followed the family pattern in detail, becoming by a process of apprenticeship a practical violinist and organist, developing as an autodidact into the leading virtuoso of his day, and then maturing into a composer. Not only was a theoretical education at a university beyond his means, even the few months' study he enjoyed at Lübeck under Buxtehude would now be thought very informal, a matter of listening, discussing, making music of his own. The kind of musician Bach was and conceived himself to be was brought out by the fact that right through his earlier appointments he was in demand not only as a virtuoso performer, but as an adviser on the mechanical construction of organs. Moreover, his first major appointment as *Kammermusicus* and court organist to Duke Wilhelm Ernst in Weimar (1709–18), illustrated his merit as a musical jack of all trades. As *Kammermusicus* he had to pick up the latest fashions in Italian orchestral music, and did so largely from the works of Vivaldi. Bach indeed undertook to transcribe Vivaldi for the organ, a work which was characteristic of the lifelong interest of the honest journeyman in musical forms and techniques for their own sake. As *Kammermusicus* he performed with the ducal orchestra on the violin and harpsichord, often directing the orchestra in the place of the ageing kapellmeister. Given his double-barrelled appointment, the organ could not be neglected, but it may be significant that his youthful intention of creating 'a regulated church-music to the honour of God'[2] – that is, a year's plan for liturgical music, attained only 45 of the planned 164 pieces, and the title had a ring of the artisan rather than the liturgical mystic: *Little Organ-book, in which the aspiring organist is introduced to the execution of a chorale of any kind, and also to qualifying himself in pedal study, for in the chorales to be found in it the pedal is treated quite compulsorily. To the sole honour of God in the highest and for the instruction of one's neighbour.* Bach became adept in this period at the cantata form, but here again there might be no clear distinction between liturgical and non-liturgical music. Cantata no. 61, we are told, is in the instrumental form of a French overture, and secular orchestral work is included.[3]

The Weimar experience, however, bears on the story in another way. Bach did not receive the recognition which was his due, for Drese, the kapellmeister, was succeeded on his death by his son. Bach got himself another appointment as court kapellmeister at Anhalt-Köthen in 1717, and such was the ill odour in Weimar that he had to do a month in gaol before he could leave to take up the new job. In the age of the baroque to be the director of a court orchestra, even of a small court like that at Anhalt-Köthen, was the summit of the ambition of a working musician such as we have seen Bach to be. This no doubt is why he took it, notwithstanding that it included no responsibilities towards the Lutheran liturgy, since the prince and his territory adhered to the Reformed faith. Equally he displayed unparalleled creativity in orchestral and chamber music; and in the family way, too. He married his second wife, and embarked on a family of thirteen, of whom many died, though two became composers of note. He seems, however, to have been upset by the remarriage of his prince to a woman of narrow musical interests, and began to look for another appointment. This he found in 1723, as *Kantor* of St Thomas's, Leipzig.

Quite apart from the fact that in the original competition Bach was placed third to Telemann and Graupner, the kapellmeister to the Landgrave of Hesse, and finally received the appointment on very humiliating terms, the appointment itself was a professional step backwards, and was felt by Bach to be so.[4] What made it tolerable was that the Prince of Anhalt-Köthen allowed him to keep his title on a non-resident basis, and he continued to use it in signatures ahead of his Leipzig titles.[5] Again for four years he displayed immense creativity, writing new cantatas Sunday by Sunday, and both the St John and the St Matthew Passions. Then the creativity slackened, he went in for secular concerts in the Zimmermann coffee house, and eventually more court compositions for the king of Poland. He did in this final period gather together a great deal of what he had done for music in general from the *Goldberg Variations* to the second part of the *Well-tempered Klavier* and the *Art of Fugue*; but here Bach spoke as an autonomous though not emancipated artist addressing the possibilities and limits of his art. In these years he hardly appears as a figure in church history, and when he died in 1750 he was already old-fashioned and about to go out of fashion altogether. Given the disappointments with which he began at St Thomas's and the way he wound up there, Bach might have derived a wry satisfaction from the stained-glass window introduced on the south front by a nineteenth-century superintendent who helped to found the Gustav-Adolf Verein, that fog-horn of the Protestant interest; in three panels this depicts him in a rake's progress between Luther and Gustavus Adolphus.[6] An honest workman, after all, should be able to turn his hand to anything.

It has frequently been thought that a view of this kind, not to mention any Marxist attempt to claim Bach for the Enlightenment, might be nullified by appeal to what is called Bach's theological library. This was, in fact, not a library at all, still less a library catalogue, but chapter 12 of a posthumous assessment of Bach's property, which was discovered in legal archives in Leipzig in 1870. It is headed 'To Spiritual Books' and puts a rather low valuation on fifty-two short titles running to eighty-one volumes.[7] With enormous labour the great bulk of these short titles have been identified with a high degree of certainty. They include two sets of Luther and are mostly of an old Lutheran character, but include Francke, Spener, and Rambach, from the Pietist side, and, in Josephus, a non-theological text much used by church historians. The material thus identified is not without significance for assessing Bach's religious position, but is virtually useless for instant application. For it is quite clear that a list of books which contains none of the Latin works which would be in a scholar's library, and none of the devotional works, especially English devotional works, which a Protestant German bourgeois family would have, and, above all, the list of a professional musician which contains not a single title in that field, is not a library at all, but the sorry remnant that was left when Bach's sons had rifled all they wanted. And the valuer was right to put a low assessment on this rump, because he knew no one else wanted them. For in the middle of the century the same change in taste which carried Bach's music into oblivion, dealt dramatic execution to the demand for the literature of Lutheran Orthodoxy.[8]

All, however, is not lost. There remain the questions of whether anything can be inferred from Bach's musical use of biblical texts, what a correspondent of Goethe referred to as his 'absolutely barmy German church-texts',[9] or from his own informal exegesis in the shape of his marginal notes to his Calov Bible, a treasure, preserved, appropriately or otherwise, in the library of that Middle Western fortress of pure Lutheranism, the Concordia Seminary, St Louis, USA. The first question requires a lengthy working-out on paper which is neither appropriate nor possible in a conference communication, and the interested inquirer is best referred for it to the researches of Elke Axmacher.[10] One or two of his examples, however, cast light on our point. A particularly 'barmy text' appears in Cantata BWV 161:

> Komm, du süsse Todesstunde,
> Da Mein Geist,
> Honig speist
> Aus des Löwen Munde.

Messrs Tate and Lyle have ensured that at least no English listeners will fail to grasp the reference to Samson's riddle in Judges 14.8, 14. But what has this to do with death? Eighteenth-century hearers were presumed to be familiar with a sermon on this passage in Heinrich Müller's *Evangelischer Hertzens-Spiegel* (1st edn, 1679):

> When Samson found honey in the lion, he propounded this riddle . . . Sweetness proceeded from the terrible. What is more terrible than death when it breaks bones like a lion? How Isaiah complains of this (Isa. 38:13). Yet a Christian finds honey in the lion and comfort in death.

The cantatas stand in a tradition, well-established since the early Church and especially since the Reformation, of poetry based on the lectionary and especially upon the Sunday Gospels, the object of which is to produce not a metrical version of the Scripture, but an exegesis with a contemporary application. Thus, for example, in the cantata BWV 23 the poet appropriates to himself the cry of the blind man in Luke 18.38, 'Jesus, thou Son of David, have mercy on me.'

> Du wahrer Gott und Davids Sohn,
> Der du von Ewigkeit in der Entfernung schon
> Mein Herzeleid und mein Leibespein
> Umständlich angesehn, erbarm dich mein.

And blindness is interpreted as spiritual darkness, much as, in many passages, tears of suffering are interpreted as the water at the wedding in Cana transformed by the act of Jesus into the wine of joy.[11] These exegetical procedures had, of course, an ancient lineage in the fourfold sense of Scripture in which alongside the *sensus litteralis* (or *historicus*) there were various applications of the *sensus spiritualis* (or *mysticus*) to the Church and its dogmatic history, to the conditions of individual believers, and to metaphysical and eschatological secrets.[12] And as the same exegetical procedures were widely employed in the lectionary sermons, those sermons were the great reservoir of motifs employed by the cantata poets. By the same token, Bach's works, and especially the cantatas, are full of passages from the Old Testament, and especially from the Psalms and the Song of Solomon, which are taken not as prophesying what was realized in the New Testament, but as representing the New Testament itself, exactly as in Handel's *Messiah* the bulk of the saving events of the birth, death, and Resurrection of Christ are proclaimed with Old Testament passages.[13] This Christianized Old Testament was one of the presuppositions of the exegesis which Bach inherited and his text-writers used.

Of course, in the same way as the cantata texts were not just metrical versions of the Scriptures, they were not just metrical versions of lectionary sermons. They enjoyed a life of their own, and in Bach's time underwent a development which ended in their breaking away not only from the text of the biblical passages, but also from the old spiritual, allegorical, tropological, and anagogical exegesis. This may be illustrated by the parable of the unjust steward (Luke 16.1–9), the Gospel lesson for the Ninth Sunday after Trinity. This story, in which the steward, threatened with dismissal for poor performance, secured his retreat by writing down the obligations of his master's debtors, had, of course always posed problems for the exegetes, not least in the Lord's commendation of the steward's cunning and his injunction, 'Make to yourselves friends of the mammon of unrighteousness.' Most of the sermons dealt with this by saying that what was commended was not the dishonesty of the unjust steward, but the speed and skill with which he dealt with his plight; it was the part of the Christian to repent in good time before the judgement, and to give the same attention to his eternal salvation as the children of this world give to their temporal interests. Müller, however, applies the plans of the unjust steward tropologically to the Christian. If the unjust steward would not dig or beg, but live on the property of others, Müller's advice to his congregation is: 'O my heart, begin to dig, beg and provide for yourself with the substance of others.' Here digging signifies searching the depths of conscience till tears of penitence arise, begging is seeking forgiveness for sin or debt, and the Christian provides for himself with the substance of others when he lays hold of the work of Christ, of his blood as the redemption for sin.

When Solomon Franck came to use this passage for Bach (in BWV 168) he followed the main lines of this exegesis. Great emphasis is laid on the idea of judgement, but whereas the traditional preaching had acquired a Christological motif by allegorizing the intentions of the steward, Franck presents the death of Jesus as the judgement suffered representatively which frees men from the death sentence. A part is also played by the idea of the blood of Jesus as a ransom for sin. And being skilled in the use of an exegetical tradition as a source of verbal images he can get away from the preaching tradition of expounding the passage sentence by sentence or even word by word. He also uses the Passion theme to give the cantata a more powerful eschatological twist than did the sermons:

> Stärk mich mit deinem Freudengeist,
> Heil mir mit deinem Wunden,
> Wasch mich mit deinem Todesschweiss,
> In meiner letzten Stunden;
> Und nimm mich einst, wenn dir's gefällt,
> In wahrem Glauben von der Welt
> Zu deinen Auserwählten.

Yet when Picander, by this time Bach's 'house poet',[14] came to work over the same passage in 1728–9, comparison shows how close to Orthodoxy Franck still was. He does not take over the Christological interpretation of the passage, and so the problem of sin loses the weight which it had in Müller and Franck. The closing chorale is on a different level altogether:

> Lass mich mit jedermann
> In Fried und Freundschaft leben,
> So weit es christlich ist.
> Willt du mir etwas geben,
> An Reichtum, Gut und Geld,
> So gib auch diess dabey,
> Dass von unrechtem Gut
> Nichts untermenget sey.

Here Picander's cantata reveals already the thought of the early Enlightenment.[15]

Bach was, of course, a good Lutheran, who not merely communicated regularly, but also coupled this with regular confession at a time when this was going out of fashion; though the hot sacramentarians of the late twentieth century might not be impressed with a regularity which consisted of twice a year. But he seems to have consulted his confessors on the choice of Scripture passages for his liturgical music, and they were of the Orthodox party.[16] Moreover, as a matter of musical theory Bach was prepared to affirm the good old ecclesiastical doctrine of the thorough-bass.

> The thorough-bass is the most perfect foundation of music, which is played with both hands in such a way that the left hand plays the prescribed notes, the right adds the consonants and dissonants, so that it is a pleasing harmony to the honour of God and the permissible delight of the spirit, and should, like all music – and this is the be-all and end-all of the thorough-bass – be solely to the honour of God and the recreation of the spirit; where this is not observed, it is not actually

music, but a diabolical bawling and lack of expression [Geplärr und Geleier].[17]

This is not the utterance of an autonomous or emancipated musician; but emancipation of a sort was creeping in by another door.

The author of the libretto of the *St John Passion* is not known, but has often been thought to be Bach himself. Be this as it may, the piece makes substantial use of six pieces of the Passion by B.H. Brockes (1712–13), but is more Orthodox than Brockes to the extent that it does not use Brockes's dramatic methods to make the Passion a contemporary event. What is contemporary about the Passion is comprised in its eternally valid results of reconciliation, redemption, and discipleship. Bach brings this out by separating the Passion narrative from reflection upon it. In the *St Matthew Passion*, Bach's text was provided by Picander on the basis of the sermons by Heinrich Müller, who, as we have seen, was much drawn on in the cantatas. The conclusion of Axmacher's careful comparison of the texts of the three Passions is that they reveal the steady dissolution of the Anselmian doctrine of reconciliation as it had been held in early Protestantism. The reasons for this were both intellectual and existential. Difficulty in accepting the paradox that God punished the innocent Christ led gradually to the elimination of the idea of punishment from the understanding of the Passion. As God disappeared from the story in this sense, the sufferings of Christ and human consciousness of sin were both more intensely represented. If the action of God was to be replaced by Jesus' sacrificial love for man, there was inevitably a concern that that love must be capable of being experienced or, in other words, made accessible to feeling.[18] A generation after Bach's death, in the age of sensibility, feeling could take a leading role, and one of the objects of liturgical music might be to balance or even offset the effects of rationalist preaching. This is not a situation which Bach himself contemplated; but the solvents applied to Orthodoxy by Pietism and revival were not absent even from the *St Matthew Passion*.

This, of course, is not enough for the Marxist critics who, objecting quite reasonably to the blanket application of the term 'baroque',[19] and exaggerating the progress of the bourgeoisie in music patronage,[20] claim 'to set free the core of the new in Bach's creativity'.[21] But at the bottom the crude appeal to politics has to do duty for the refining of concepts or the weighing of evidence. As E.H. Meyer put it in a discussion,

If the word baroque is used for Bach and Handel, there is the danger they will be heard out of the great central area of the music today to be performed for the masses of men. For us, Bach and Handel are also the greatest masters immediately before the *classics* . . . [22]

A socialist state competing for the national tradition cannot say otherwise; but the appeal to politics will do nothing to define how deeply Bach was rooted in Lutheran Orthodoxy nor the ways in which he reveals the disintegration of that system of doctrine, still less will it explain why there was no contact between Bach and Gottsched, the *aufklärerisch* professor of poetry in Leipzig, and himself an energetic composer of texts for music.

Bach's own annotations to his Calov Bible assume the pre-critical realism common to his age and embody a mixture of genuine personal piety, of pride in the religious and liturgical function of music, with doubtless an edge against the Reformed who did not see things in the same way, and in his office to provide it. Thus, for example, on Genesis 26.33[23] Calov, like many versions of the Authorized Version, has a note saying that the word Beersheba means 'well of the oath', and adds that a well had been given the same name in Erfurt. Bach's comment is 'N.B. There is a village of that name about an hour from Erfurt.' The Bible, even Beersheba, was very much Bach's native land.[24] On I Chronicles 25, in which David and the captains of the host separated, many to 'prophesy with harps, with psalteries, and with cymbals', he notes, 'This chapter is the true foundation of all church music pleasing to God'; more convincingly perhaps, on the great chorus of choral and instrumental music which accompanied the dedication of Solomon's temple, 'In devotional music God is always present with his grace.' I Chronicles 28.21, in which David instructs Solomon how to set up the temple, refers in the Authorized Version to the 'courses of the priests and Levites' and 'to all manner of workmanship', but in the Luther version refers to the offices of the priests and to all the other officers. This to Bach is evidence that his office as organist or *Kantor* is equivalent in its sphere to that of the pastoral office in its sphere: 'N.B. A glorious proof that alongside the other institutions of the liturgy music was also specially ordained by the spirit of God through David.' On Exodus 15.20, in which 'Miriam the prophetess . . . took a timbrel in her hand; and all the women went out after her with timbrels and with dances', Calov commented that this was not a new song, but a response or echo to the song which Moses and the men of Israel had sung before. To Bach this signified the element of dialogue in the liturgy: 'N.B. The first anticipation of two choirs making music to the honour of God.' And there are two entries of a more personal nature. On the sacramental level, Leviticus 17.11, 'The life of the flesh is in the blood,' is silently underlined. And the elaborate marginal transcription of Mark 10.29–30, 'There is no man that hath left house, or brethren, or sisters, or father, or mother, or wife, or children, or lands for my sake and the gospel's but he shall receive an hundredfold now in this time', speaks volumes for the piety of a man who lost four brothers and sisters in infancy or childhood, and two more later, a mother when he was nine, and a father at ten; and who was himself widowed at the age of 35, having lost four of the seven children of his first marriage, and was in due course to lose seven of the thirteen of his second marriage at a very early age. The reward he notes for losses for the Gospel's sake is not that of eternal life in the world to come, but that of recompense 'an hundredfold now'. This was the response of a man of faith.

Notes

1 Robin A. Leaver, *Bachs theologische Bibliothek. Eine kritische Bibliographie*, Neuhausen and Stuttgart, 1983.

2 *Bach-Dokumente*, 4 vols., Leipzig and Kassel, 1963–79, 1, p. 19.

3 For this biographical material see the brief study by the doyen of Bach research, Walter Blankenburg, 'Johann Sebastian Bach', in M. Greschat, ed., *Orthodoxie und Pietismus = Gestalten der Kirchengeschichte*, 7, Stuttgart 1982, pp. 301, 304–5.

4 *Bach-Dokumente*, 1, p. 67.

5 Ibid., 1, p. 53.

6 There is a colour reproduction of this window in Martin Petzoldt and Joachim Petri, *Johann Sebastian Bach. Ehre sei dir Gott gesungen*, [East] Berlin and Göttingen, 1988, pp. 168–70.

7 This list has been most recently reprinted in *Pietismus und Neuzeit*, 12 (1986), pp. 180–1.

8 On all this see Johannes Wallmann, 'Johann Sebastian Bach und die "Geistlichen Bücher" seiner Bibliothek', *Pietismus und Neuzeit*, 12 (1986), pp. 162–81.

9 *Briefwechsel zwischen Goethe und Zelter*, ed. L. Geiger, Leipzig, n.d. [1902], 2, p. 468.

10 Elke Axmacher, *'Aus Liebe will mein Heyland sterben'. Untersuchungen zum Wandel des Passionsverständnisses im frühen 18. Jahrhundert*, Neuhausen und Stuttgart, 1984, 'Die Deutung der Passion Jesu im Text der Matthaus-Passion von J.S. Bach', *Luther*, 56, (1985), pp. 49–69, 'Ein Quellenfund zum Text der Matthäus-Passion', *Bach-Jahrbuch*, 64 (1978), pp. 49–69, 'Bachs Kantaten in auslegungsgeschichtlicher Sicht', Martin Petzoldt, ed., *Bach als Ausleger der Bibel. Theologische und musikwissenschaftliche Studien zum Werk Johann Sebastian Bachs*, [East] Berlin and Göttingen, 1985, pp. 15–32.

11 On the above see Axmacher, 'Bachs Kantaten', pp. 15–16.

12 See G. Ebeling's article 'Hermeneutik', in *RGG*, 3, cols. 249–50.

13 Helene Werthemann, *Die Bedeutung der alttestamentlichen Historien in Johann Sebastian Bachs Kantaten*, Basle, 1959, pp. 1–5.

14 Friedrich Blume, *Syntagma Musicologicum II*, ed. A.A. Abert and M. Rulinke, Kassel, Basle, Tours, and London, 1973, p. 192.

15 Axmacher, 'Bachs Kantaten', pp. 17–23. Cf. Winfried Zeller, 'Tradition und

Exegese. Johann Sebastian Bach und Martin Schallings Lied, "Herzlich lieb hab ich dir, o Herr"', in Petzoldt, *Bach als Ausleger*, pp. 151–76.

16 M. Petzoldt, 'Christian Wiese d. A. und Christoph Wolle – zwei Leipziger Beichtvater Bachs, Vertreter zweier auslegungsgeschichtlicher Abschritte der ausgehenden lutherischen Orthodoxie', in Petzoldt, ed., *Bach als Ausleger*, pp. 109–29.

17 Quoted in Walter Blankenburg, 'Johann Sebastian Bach und die Aufklärung' in Walter Blankenburg, ed., *Johann Sebastian Bach = Wege der Forschung*, 170, Darmstadt, 1970, pp. 100–10, at p. 103 [repr. from *Bach Gedenkschaft*, Freiburg im Breisgau and Zurich, 1950, pp. 25–34]. For a brief introduction to the thorough-bass see the article 'Figured bass', in Percy A. Scholes, *The Oxford Companion to Music*, 8th edn, London, 1950, pp. 317–18.

18 Axmacher, *'Aus liebe will mein Heyland sterben'*, pp. 149, 152–61, 204–8.

19 For a non-Marxist argument to the same effect see Ulrich Siegele, 'Bachs Ort im Orthodoxie und Aufklärung', *Musik und Kirche*, 51 (1981), pp. 3–14.

20 As Werner Neumann harshly put it in a public discussion, the innumerable dedications and addresses of homage to princes and nobility by Bach and his contemporaries would be odd garb for an anti-feudal, anti-absolutist emancipation movement. *Johann Sebastian Bach und die Aufklärung* ed. for the Forschungskollektiv 'Johann Sebastian Bach' by Reinhard Szeskus, Leipzig, 1982, p. 131.

21 Ibid., 4, pp. 8–9.

22 Walter Blankenburg, 'Die Bach-forschung seit etwa 1965', *Acta Musicologica*, 55 (1983), pp. 39–40. Cf. his 'Aufklärungsauslegung der Bibel in Leipzig zur Zeit Bachs. Zu Johann Christoph Gottscheds Homiletik', in Petzoldt, ed., *Bach als Ausleger*, pp. 97–108.

23 'And he called [the well] Sheba: therefore the name of the city is Beer-sheba unto this day.'

24 The texts are usefully assembled and commented on in Petzold and Petri, *Johann Sebastian Bach*, pp. 18–21, 44–7, 8–11, 86–8, 104–7, 120–3, 136–8.

4

Faith and Fallacy: English and German Perspectives in the Nineteenth century

1   The Victorian Crisis of Faith: Myth or Reality?

The agony of faith that failed is one of the familiar echoes of Victorian England, as familiar as the conservative rant against the corrosive scepticism of 'Garman' professors who would have been better at the bottom of the 'Garman Ocean'. A crisis of faith, however, is less easy to detect, define, and date, and the hunt for it is much obfuscated by characteristic perceptions of both the mid-nineteenth and the late-twentieth centuries. The *Religious Census* of 1851 seemed more shocking to contemporaries than it does to us because of two assumptions which they shared neither with previous nor with later generations, that there should be a parson in every parish and that everyone free and able to darken the doors of a place of worship should do so weekly. And our own day has blinkers of its own. Is the present religious situation in western Europe an adequate hermeneutic for the whole story? Or is the problem of believing as encountered in Victorian England a chapter in a complicated web of many plots, in which belief finds new social roles as well as losing old ones, not least because of a radical redistribution of Christian belief and practice in the world as a whole. Is there one story, that of secularisation, or are there several?

How uncertain even the best of the current literature is on this question of perspective comes out in the work of that eminent scholar, Owen Chadwick. His history of the Victorian church[1] contains chapters entitled 'Unsettlement of Faith', 'Science and Religion', 'History and the Bible, and 'Doubt', but the general effect is flattening, and secularisation is treated as a vague word for a non-subject. Certainly no church suffered very much from secessions or disciplinary actions based on intellectual appraisals of

First published in 'Victorian Faith in Crisis', ed. R.J. Helmstadter and B. Lightman, London, 1990.

the content of its teaching, any more than in the golden age of secession and expulsion between 1790 and 1850. But the second volume of this great work was scarcely off the press when he took the opposite line in his Gifford Lectures.[2] Secularisation was now not merely the truth, but the peculiarly stark truth. Insisting that 'if it were proved by historians, for example, that whole societies spent unfold centuries believing in a god or gods and then within a hundred years suffered such an intellectual *bouleversement* that they no longer believed in any such person or things, it would have momentous consequences for those whose business is not history but a study of the nature of religious experience,'[3] Chadwick asked the reader to believe that some such change took place in the twenty or thirty years after 1860. The only balm to the wounded spirits of the believer was the silent (and absolutely implausible) implication that secularisation was a transformation of the context within which the Christian faith was held or proclaimed, and did not involve failures in the proclamation itself.

Some light may be cast on this dark matter by both lengthening and broadening the historical perspective in which it is discussed. Neither the pessimistic sociologists who try to persuade us by statistics that hardly anyone has been to church in England since the Reformation,[4] nor those modest Anglicans who are prepared to settle for religious practice in the Establishment at no more than 10 per cent of the population even in 1660, have left any room for the supposition that there could be a popular crisis of faith after 1860. The religious census, moreover, confirmed other evidence that the churches were now of limited use either as vehicles of social policy or as devices of social control, and in the next generation this discovery doubtless cost them the loyalty of members of the political classes who had valued them chiefly in this respect; but this loss of confidence could not be described as a crisis of faith. Moreover, in the early years of the present century, there was sufficient evidence of recent and present good performance by the churches to convince many churchmen as well as later historians[5] that all was well. Certainly the English churches as a whole made a much bigger splash in the world than they had ever done before, and had created the situation in which, in the next half century, it was natural for English to become the sacred language of the ecumenical movement. All the churches had contributed to a great effort to take religion to the people, and Roman Catholics and dissenters might (perhaps with justice) persuade themselves that England was becoming non-Anglican much faster than she was becoming non-Christian.

Moreover, after 1850, once the older social tensions had been dissipated, the churches were spared one potent source of religious disenchantment. The 1830s and early forties had been the great age of the religious (as well as the political) doctrinaire. The great spur to total commitment against the bogy of the moment, be it establishment or disestablishment, revolution or new poor law, ungodliness or liquor, had been the conviction that nothing could be worse than the present state of affairs, a facade behind which one evil interest or another manipulated the nation's affairs; Newman at Littlemore, trying to promote galloping sanctification by chewing rhubarb,[6] may stand for the army of revivalists, teetotallers, ecclesiastical disciplinarians like Bunting, who could screw up courage and induce exaltation to levels absolutely impossible to sustain. Froude's title, the *Nemesis of Faith* was but too apt. Balleine, implausibly, suggested that the millenarian issue was wound up for Anglican evangelicals by Bishop Waldegrave's Bamptons in 1853,[7] but the end of the world as an issue in polite society unquestionably came to an end, when the strains which had involved even Arnold's obsession with it,[8] themselves eased. The two political heroes of the fifties embodied the religious ideals of the age before the doctrinaires took over. There was the ghost of Peel whose religious rationalism had elicited shakings of head even from Bishop Charles Lloyd; and there was the very unghostly Palmerston who had actually been a pupil of Dugald Stewart. Things looked up for Enlightenment, and, certainly, none of the political and religious issues of the next two decades was fought to a finish. Even Dwight L. Moody's fatal heart attack owed more to his twenty stone of modish corpulence, than to the stress of attempting the conversion of the world in his generation.

Social and economic developments often dealt more harshly with the churches' competitors than with the churches themselves. The great age of the Man of Letters was that of early Victorian years. From Carlyle to Macaulay they were great synthesisers, presenting and interpreting the world of knowledge to their contemporaries and assisting a compact and opulent middle-class public to understand itself in the light of that knowledge; they produced their own body of scriptures in the heavyweight reviews, and set the tone for all those novelists who believed in the necessity (and compatibility) of realism and moral elevation. The menace of Carlyle to organised religion was not his low estimate of the Churches, still less his affectation of greater familiarity with German idealism than he had, but the fact that he was a commercially successful Ranter, usurping one of the churches' functions with such effect, that long after his death he could be regarded by certain Nonconformists as a true prophet against humbug. Yet the men of letters could not long keep up with either the *Natur-* or the *Geisteswissenschaften* the development of which came to turn on specialised publications and institutions. And they were outflanked on the opposite side by publishers who learned how to tap a mass market of a lower level of literacy.[9] The developments which took the wind out of the sails of the men of letters were not so inimical to the churches. They could obtain a theology school in Oxford and develop journals to match; and they (especially the dissenters and Roman Catholics) had always drawn at least some preachers, who retained the ear of their fellows, from the milieu now catered for by the popular press.

In a more fundamental sense, not all was well. As the men of letters transformed themselves into dons, they paid the price of ceasing to interest a public of commercial proportions, and laid hands on university endowments which had long been used to give budding lawyers and parsons a start in life. The clergy found the transition from the crass amateurism of their past to the professional amateurism of their new status particularly difficult. Nothing has ever produced a theologically minded ministry in England; but clergy put a fair amount of work into the Bible, only to find, as the Germans had found before, that the Scriptures were becoming harder to preach from. This might not have mattered had the Social Gospel ever really materialised. When, during the Great Depression, the dominant economic ethic was partially repudiated by sections of the hitherto economically influential classes, it was partially repudiated also by sections of the clergy, particularly of the Establishment, and particularly by liberal Catholics whose fortunes had been closely linked with Gladstone.[10] The Social Gospel, however, which in Germany, despite massive intellectual input, was neither an intellectual nor a practical success,[11] was in England little more than a fraudulent sleight of hand;[12] English working men knew what they were about in putting their trust in uncontrived improvements in the terms of trade, in Lib-Labism, and in a State of limited ambiance. Moreover, although the disappearance of revolutionary tension after 1850 had in the short run made life easier for the churches as for other social institutions, other social developments were much to their disadvantage. Between the middle of the eighteenth-century and the middle of the nineteenth, the commercialisation of all sectors of the economy had weakened old forms of deference and given entirely new scope for fresh religious appeals, Protestant and Catholic. Social strains had broken through old habits and broken up the ground for the revivalists in a way they conspicuously failed to do in the second half of the century. The geographical redistribution of resources which underlay the revolt of the fringes of the country against the centre had turned the evangelical awakening into something like a mass movement. The second half of the century, however, sprang the unpleasant surprise, that the rise of the provinces had in no way impeded the relentless growth of London, a Great Wen beyond the power of any organisation, religious or political, to organise; a metropolis situated (like Paris) in the old heartland of the establishment, a heartland itself of low religious practice; a metropolis which increasingly attracted the provincial elites who had done so much for the religious as well as the public life of provincial towns,[13] and took control of the economic assets which had supported them. One of the unmentionable calamities of modern British history was to allow London to continue as both a commercial capital and a centre of government spending; and this was calamitous for religion, even before the twentieth-century development of the media thrust the ethos of London into every home. None of these developments, however, could be described as a crisis, still less a crisis of faith; and the erosion, though ceaseless, was slow.

Cox's famous quip, that the obsessive speculation of young men in Oxford about the marks of the one true church was transformed in the forties into speculation in railway shares,[14] does not however, disguise the agony sometimes occasioned by loss of faith, nor discount the damage suffered by tender mortals like Clough and J.A. Froude.

Amongst those most seriously at risk from the new developments were men of evangelical upbringing within the Church of England. Their immediate forbears had been clear that an inherited *Kulturprotestantismus* would never pull the established institutions of England (not to say Ireland) through the strains of the Revolutionary and Napoleonic Wars. International threats then meshed perilously with domestic discords, and social discontent was sharpened by a popular political programme given actuality by sympathy with the struggles of the Convention in France. In a society in which (to use the modern jargon) the private sector overwhelmingly outweighed the public, survival depended on inculcating an interior discipline. This, it seemed, could spring only from a much more intense religious commitment than had sufficed in the recent past. Indeed one of the reasons for the perplexing resemblances and continuities between the new evangelicalism and the Puritanism of the seventeenth century, was that the latter had aimed (amongst other things) to plant out Protestantism as a popular faith in the dark corners of the country for the first time, a work resumed by evangelicals on a great scale. Evangelicalism had prospered (as had quite different forms of religious appeal, native Roman Catholicism, for example) on the widening freedom of choice in English society, but it had always sought to set voluntary bounds to the freedom of choice on which it throve; and for many it had been made into a social policy by the stresses of the Revolutionary era, however broad the gap between the details of their faith and the concrete reality of social questions. Before the middle of the nineteenth century the two great connexionally-organised communions, the English Wesleyans and the Church of Scotland, had, nevertheless, been brought to spectacular schisms by the need to reappraise inherited policies. The English Church, almost as much an independent denomination as the Baptists, had only the ructions in the annual meeting of the National Society to set beside the upheavals in Conference and

Assembly, but the evangelical party could not escape the pressure created
by the doctrinaires; indeed that pressure was compounded by the family.
The great discovery of Protestant religious revival in the later years of the
seventeenth century and the early years of the eighteenth had been that in
the Habsburg lands where the Protestants had lost their church structure
the family could, on its own, be an effective means of transmitting
and reviving the faith; and that the devotions prescribed by Spener to
supplement the parish round were capable of bearing the whole weight of
Christianising successive generations. Anglican evangelicalism was by no
means a copy of the revivalism of central Europe, but the family was one
of the forms of unecclesiastical action it had sought most energetically to
use; and at the very moment when churches were most perplexed by
unavoidable changes of course, family pressure produced the paradox that
religious 'deviance' or changes of denominational allegiance became more
painful to individuals than they had been a century before. Whether what
hurt was the inadequacy of the church to fill the role assigned to it by
Wilberforce and his friends, or whether the problem was to cope with
doctrinal difficulties created by science and history, some evangelicals were
in trouble.

Now (as always in the past) there were moral difficulties in believing,
some of them sharpened by the unpleasant clerical ramp on the eternity of
infernal punishment; but laymen were notably nimble in evading them.
When they concluded that their offspring were innocents needing neither
baptismal grace nor converting power, they soon found professionals to
tailor doctrines of baptism accordingly.[15] Between 1860 and the end of
the century, however, there emerged scientific or historical reasons for
believing that some things which the churches had taught with confidence
or even authority, were not true, even that some things which the Bible
had taught or had been thought to teach, were not true. But because the
issue fundamentally was one about church teaching, those affected were
primarily clergy and prospective ordinands, very scrupulous laymen of
intellectual bent, and less scrupulous laymen whose confidence in the
church (though not perhaps in God or Jesus)[16] had suffered, and who were
not averse to finding the church in difficulties of its own. Science was no
great problem except in so far as it impinged on the Bible.[17] In any case
science was English enough; laymen had partly ignored, partly absorbed
Newtonian cosmology; they had done the same with geology; in the
Bridgwater treaties they had recently found traditional arguments from
natural theology acceptable; even evolution might be harnessed to the
argument from design. For those with inadequate flexibility there was
some choice of shelter to hand. Liddon was arguing that one must accept
the entire Catholic system or watch Christianity crumble piece by piece;

and the Plymouth Brethren offered millenialism and an inerrant Bible in an evangelical framework, all in a withdrawn society devoted to avoiding embarrassment.

History was more difficult because it involved a shift of attitude towards the Scriptures, and perhaps towards Jesus himself. Moreover, it was known that more advanced and shocking things were being said about Scripture and Christology in Germany than in England; and this knowledge inflamed durable prejudices going right back to the beginning of the eighteenth century, prejudices which distinguished those who thought England should go it alone in religion and diplomacy, and those who held that this was neither desirable nor possible. If this line of argument reduces the Victorian 'crisis of faith' almost to the dimensions of books like *Robert Elsmere* (1888), it also raises the excruciating question of the intellectual traffic between two nations, whose fates and religious circumstances moved apart in the nineteenth century as the whole Protestant world fragmented into mutually incomprehending regional enterprises.

2 Politics and the Origins of Modern German Theology

The wars of Queen Anne's reign and the alarums of the following decade had occasioned bitter disagreements. Those of Whiggish and latitudinarian mind held that the United Kingdom could not be indifferent to the tottering Protestant interest in the Holy Roman Empire; and those of Tory and High Church bent not merely wished their country well out of such entanglements, but were hot for those peculiarities of the English church which distinguished it both from English dissenting communities, and from the non-episcopal Protestant churches of the continent.[18] To their chagrin the United Kingdom fetched up with a German dynasty, and drew closer not merely to the internal disputes of the Holy Roman Empire, but to the terrors and the consolations of the German religious mind, than it had ever been before. For the first time Luther, in the guise of the archetype of evangelical conversion, became an English religious hero.

Differences of English attitudes towards continental Protestants were fully matched by differences among German Protestants towards England. At the official church level the Orthodox Lutheranism of the Saxon Church and its friends (especially in the Imperial cities) was sharply separated from virtually all the movements for religious change and adaptation. These movements, which had an anti-Saxon slant, might well enjoy the patronage of the Hohenzollern dynasty, who, as the reformed rulers of an overwhelmingly Lutheran state had domestic as well as anti-Saxon reasons for wishing to get round the entrenched religious divisions of the past. So also, in a complicated way, had the Hanoverians after they had succeeded to the

English throne. They eased the domestic problem in Hanover by agreeing to accept only local ordinands into the ministry of their church,[19] thus conceding a permanent monopoly to a party of peculiarly dead Orthodoxy. But they would not let Prussia seize the leadership of the Protestant interest in the Empire without a contest. When they founded the University of Gottingen in 1734 they adopted the Prussian recipe of an alliance of enlightenment and Pietism exempt from church control, and, in Hanoverian England, the Pietist interest was publicly kept up by a succession of distinguished German court chaplains and the open patronage of the thinner of George I's two mistresses, the Duchess of Kendal.[20]

The Lutheran Orthodox, the pro-Saxon party, shared the same sense of confessional isolationism as English High Churchmen, and, from the time the Saxon dynasty turned Catholic, shared also their embarrassment in dealing with a monarch of alien faith. All the more reason, it seemed, to insist that Luther was, in effect, the normative doctor of the church, and was a Saxon possession. The Orthodox were prepared to entertain almost unlimited fantasies as to the unsoundness of English religion. The Protestant states of the Empire had been much troubled in the late seventeenth century by anti-institutional movements of a Quakerish kind, as well as actual Quaker missions; 'Quakerism' became the shorthand abuse for radical Pietist movements of any sort, the natural product of 'overheated English blood'.[21] England had foisted several varieties of Fifth Monarchy men upon the Lutheran world,[22] spawned the comic doctrines of Eva von Buttlar and her gang,[23] and was well known to be the source of damaging literature.[24] The Orthodox press retailed politically inspired reports of scandalous hellfire clubs in England,[25] and could believe that the American colonies were the 'outer darkness' of Matt. 8:12 where the lost were cast with weeping and gnashing of teeth.[26] A steady stream of German ordinands seeking education in England set in late in the seventeenth century, but they could only be defended by the superintendent of the church in Brunswick by the backhanded argument that Socinianism was no more rampant in England than in Germany, and that England was not especially morally corrupting except to those who were already susceptible to corruption.[27] And although some of the enthusiasts thought that 'English' or 'psychic spirits' were good angels,[28] many of them reproduced the prejudices of the Orthodox. Even the inspired were inclined to describe their physical symptoms as 'English movements' and suspect them of satanic origin;[29] and to critics of Moravians an appropriate title for anti-Christ was 'Englischer Lichtes-Schein'.[30]

No one, however, doubted, that England mattered. English theology of all kinds was reviewed in quantities in the journals, much was translated, and large stocks, both in translation and in the original tongue, were bought in for libraries like that of the Stift at Tübingen.[31] Indeed the very breadth of German exposure to English theological output makes English influence hard to profile with precision. There is no question, however, as to who the Anglophiles were; they were Pietists with a respect for English Puritanism,[32] and an English Bible exegesis unencumbered by Lutheran Orthodoxy or Moravian fantasy;[33] and the *Aufklärer* who, in the field of secular letters, were also devotees of the English moral weeklies.[34] J.R. Schlegel, rector of the gymnasium at Heilbronn, whose *Kirchengeschichte* is a model of enlightened scholarship, beat the drum about the English inspiration to research abroad, and its especial importance in the fields of the philosophy of religion and Old Testament studies.[35] In other words, exactly as the English latitudinarians had political as well as intellectual and theological reasons for wishing to outflank the isolationist High Church party, the Anglophile groups in Germany consisted of precisely those anti-Saxon parties rallied by Prussia and used by Hanover, which had political as well as intellectual, theological and religious reasons for wishing to outflank Lutheran Orthodoxy. Like spoke to like. And a bridge was built between the two from the German side.

Sigmund Jacob Baumgarten, the most significant of the transitional theologians, in his final, historical, phase, produced a series of works on foreign religious movements, translating English authors by the dozen, especially the historians, and rhapsodising about the *Biographia Britannica*: 'England and the lands connected with it are more fruitful in noteworthy people of all conditions who attract and hold the attention of their rational fellow creatures, or can yield more notable examples of the most glorious virtues or most shameful vices, of the exceptional use and misuse of unusual capabilities and advantageous opportunities, as well as the most audacious and unsuccessful enterprises, and of the most rapid and unexpected changes of good and ill fortune, than other nations [who lack the exaggerated political liberties of England] . . . For this reason they have not attained the levels which corporately developed scholarship, wit, shrewdness, industriousness, bravery, arts, science, business, riches, extravagance, boldness, folly, enthusiasm and evil have reached there.'[36] Baumgarten might well respect English liberty, for he would have been ejected from Halle with Spangenberg (with whom he shared a single appointment) but for the personal protection of the Queen of Prussia. Baumgarten, in the current manner, had combined orthodox theology with practical ideals of piety; his offence was to have subjected his propositions to Wolffian logic, as the most rigorous test available. His turning from Wolff to history marked his conviction that what was now required was the rigour of history (regarded by Wolff as factual knowledge and prescientific), especially in apologetics and exegesis.[37] It was liberty which made England so rich a field of historical study, and an historical character was firmly impressed on the theological side of the German Enlightenment after 1750 by Baumgarten's greatest and most affectionate pupil, Johannes Salomo Semler.

With Semler the history of modern Protestant theology begins. In a vast series of works, written in what Hirsch described as 'the worst [German] ever written by a German of intellectual standing'.[38] Semler contributed to every part of the theological field. In one sense he limited that field by stressing the human element in the reception of revelation; in another sense he broadened it by his very emphasis on the historical and variable element in it. Private and public (or theologically organized) religion were indeed two different things, and the latter bore all the marks of time, place and circumstance. The same was true of Scripture, and Semler plunged boldly into the historical criticism of the New Testament, even of the canon itself. Semler's impact on German thought was not, however, as great as that of Lessing, who bridged two important gaps. For Lessing was a successful man of letters before he became a theologian,[39] and his struggle against the dead hand of a biblical literalism was so much part of a struggle for literary freedom and creativity, that it could not be simply repudiated when the German Romantics turned against the Enlightenment. Lessing beat the drum about Providence and the *Education of the Human Race*: he re-established Leibniz's metaphysical determinism and did not despise the 'positive' religions (including Christianity) which he certainly did not hold, because he viewed them as part of the development of mankind, a growth towards a more perfect moral and religious rationality. And he used his right as librarian of the famous ducal library at Wolfenbuttel, to publish posthumous *Fragments* of Hermann Samuel Reimarus (1694–1768). Reimarus was a Hamburg Wolffian and an adherent of English deism. He had made his assault on Orthodoxy on general rational grounds, designed to demonstrate the impossibility of the Christian reading of either Testament, and the frailty of the proofs from miracle and the fulfilment of prophecy. Nor did Reimarus spare the New Testament testimony to Jesus. The scriptural writers, he held, embodied the apostolic system of Christianity which deviated from that of Jesus, who intended neither to set up new articles of faith (like the mystery of the Trinity) nor to free his followers from Jewish religious practice.[40] By showing that the New Testament could be made to yield a portrait of Christ quite different from that favoured by Orthodoxy, Reimarus opened the door to that long series of Lives of Christ, some of which so alarmed the Victorians.

From Lessing, German thought could proceed in either of two directions. Kant who was bred in mathematics and Wolffian logic, pressed beyond it to a universal human *Bildung* which included studies in human and natural sciences. He sought also to lay the foundations of a rational knowledge which should be proof against the confusion of opinions. This object and the synthetic work which was to crown his critical studies proved to be beyond him; but in the last dozen years of his life he produced a series of important works to which German theologians and philosophers would return when the need to get rid of metaphysics became urgent, and which ended in *Religion within the limits of mere Reason* (1793). The other line was to take up the theme of history, and especially of the history of cultural creativity, and find in it a revelation or a substitute for one. If Lessing had been a man of letters turned theologian, Herder was one of the few theologians to have earned an important place in the general intellectual and literary history of his people, fetching up appropriately in 1776 as General Superintendent in Weimar. Behind the events of everyday, Herder saw a divine force, and sought to awaken his fellows to a sense of beauty and harmony, a poetic perception of humanity. For Herder, indeed, there was no difference of nature and spirit which was not embraced by the deeper unity of a creative original force. Creation was the self expression of a living and active God. The documents of religious history could be made to yield a message in terms of religious psychology. Psychology and history went together, for revelation was constituted not by the ideas and concepts it contained, but by the movement of the heart towards a humanity devoted to God.

Herder's most powerful impact was upon the young Goethe. After being raised in a cool and reasonable Christianity, Goethe had come under Moravian influence, but never quite to the point of conversion. Goethe's obstacle was not rational objection to points of doctrine which concerned him little, but the power of his poetic imagination, the feeling (as one of his biographers later put it)[41] that he must choose between being an author and a Christian. At the crucial point in 1770/1 he met Herder who opened his eyes to Shakespeare, Ossian, Homer, and folk-poetry, and led him to his first great poetic achievements.[42] Goethe's poetic liberation involved a separation from Christianity of a sort that seemed to require no decision, and he left it to his readers to make up their mind how much Christian piety they would combine with the inward awakening brought about by his poetry. He found it impossible to make any person the centre of his thought and life as his friend Lavater made Jesus. Lavater, he maintained, plucked feathers from all the world's birds to adorn the bird of paradise. In the same way it was untrue that God spoke to men only through the Bible; this was a denial of the whole world of literature of which Goethe had come to drink so deeply. The biblical miracles, the Virgin Birth and Resurrection, also left Goethe cold; if there was a revelation it was in the unity which underlay the manifold forms of creative activity. The Bible, indeed, included images of the three different kinds of religion which Goethe thought inculcated the proper respect for man as the highest of the works of God. Ethnic religion (as in the Old Testament) taught a proper respect for the power above embodied in the pages of world history. Philosophic religion taught the relations of man to mankind, and respect for his equals. The Christian religion taught men to recognize the divine in poverty, suffering, and death; it inculcated respect for what is below us, and was only indispensable to those in adversity. But ultimately religion, the true awakening, was respect for man in his full humanity.

By the end of the Napoleonic Wars the cultural relations of theology in England and Germany were the reverse of what they had been three quarters of a century before. Then radical English criticism in the field of the philosophy of religion had given a lead to German theologians, a lead enhanced by an English reputation for being libertarian and larger than life, a reputation justified to the extent that deist literature could actually appear in print. After the Seven Years' War German literary creativity, assisted by the fact that no major state was now prepared to put its weight behind Lutheran Orthodoxy, and that even in the Imperial cities brittle Orthodoxy was crumbling to decay, had 'taken off' on a scale which defies simple analysis. In part at least this rise was due to the fact that German nationalism had no political focus and gathered round a set of cultural traditions defined with new historical precision, and freshly developed. If this process enabled Pietists, for example, to mistake the ploys of patriotism for their inherited soteriology,[43] it enabled Goethe to slip out of Christianity altogether. But on the Protestant side, the legacy of Lutheran Orthodoxy, a highly articulated system of doctrine, guaranteed true upon the basis of an infallible Bible, was simply too tough to be ignored by intelligent men who had been bruised by it. For this reason the German enlightenment, bolstered by the confidence and sense of moral outrage of the English deists, tackled the problem of applying reason to religion with much greater thoroughness than was ever attempted in England, and found, in particular, that history was a better way of overturning the Orthodox exegesis of Scripture than 'reason' in the deist sense of the word. History which did so much to uncover traditions round which national sentiment was gathering, might deal a knock-out blow to one divisive tradition, that of Lutheran Orthodoxy.

When the war was over, and Weimar classicism was spent, when there were religious revivals on both the Catholic and Protestant side, when the Orthodox and Pietists made an unholy alliance with each other and the conservative forces in political possession, when the political atmosphere again became bitterly intolerant, even Prussia, hitherto the most unconfessional of entities, proclaimed itself a Christian state in the narrowest of senses. There being no political activity to hand, and the life of the nation being focused upon a culture rather than a state, the work of ideological demolition must begin all over again.[44] And the aggressiveness on the radical side was justified by the fact that the conservative forces in possession were not merely as isolationist as their Orthodox predecessors, but have proved of even less intellectual interest.

It was this situation which gave such explosive power to the *Life of Jesus* first published by David Friedrich Strauss in 1835, notwithstanding that criticism since Reimarus had approached no consensus of a *Life* without presuppositions to replace the image of Orthodoxy, and notwithstanding that Strauss could only deploy the old weapons with more ruthlessness than his predecessors. What made Strauss a man commemorated by a plaque in the Stift at Tübingen as a bitter offence to the church, was that his renewed assault on Christology had political implications. Old English deism had found little room for an incarnation, but the German criticism of the previous generation had grappled with the question in its own way. Kant had seen the moral perfection of humanity in the harmonious community of free individuals, of which the archetype might be the perfect person willing to die for others. Schleiermacher, understanding religion as the feeling of absolute dependence on God, could conceive Kant's archetype as actualised in Jesus, the religious genius, unique in his consciousness of God. Hegel, holding that the content of his philosophy was that of Christianity in another form, and that its built-in understanding of contradiction fitted it to embrace the contradictions in the idea of the God-man, concluded that the real was the rational and vice versa, and that the incarnation was both real and rational. Strauss was not a stable politician. As recently as 1830 he had been telling his congregation that it was 'better to perish from a lack of earthly bread than suffer a lack of heavenly manna'. The *Life of Jesus*, by contrast was 'democratic' in the sense that the properties which the church (contradictorily) ascribed to Christ were united in humanity; *pace* Hegel, Absolute Spirit was actualised not in a man, but in the human species. Bad news for the Christ, this was also bad news for kings. Strauss could not keep up this radicalism for long. The third edition (1838) of the *Life* was 'aristocratic' in the sense that Strauss admitted the historicity of the Fourth Gospel, took up the category of genius, and saw in Jesus a genius who gave shape to the inner life. He was the genius who of all the geniuses on offer in the late thirties was the least likely to realise the outer ideals of the liberal, the rationalist, or the social critic. Strauss had sold the pass[45] (there were reversions later). And though this may have helped him to a chair at Zürich, it did not save him from dismissal as the result of a revolution. It was entirely in order that his fourth edition should be put into English by George Eliot in 1846. Heine could sum up the matter in the phrase that in Germany philosophy had fought the same victorious fight against Christianity as in ancient Greece it had fought against mythology.[46]

3 The Victorian Encounter with German Scholarship

It is convenient to resume the English side of the story with the translation of Strauss's *Life of Jesus*, more than fifty years after the outbreak of the Revolutionary Wars. During that time Britain and Prussia had been political allies, there had been a good deal of economic interaction between the two sides,[47] the evangelical world had had its own go-betweens in men like K.F.A. Steinkopf,[48] but the English world of intellect, and especially of theology, had lost contact with the great developments in German theology, and encouraged by the celebrated revulsions against Germany of A.J. Rose and E.B. Pusey, did not want to know what had been going on. The 'pro-German' and the isolationist parties were as they had always been, but the balance between them had changed completely (as in America it notably had not).[49] The universities and the clergy of the Church had, under the pressures of the late eighteenth century, been much more fully incorporated into the new establishment created in those years than their predecessors had ever been, and, in their revulsion against enlightenment, were more completely isolationist in their defence of English ways and institutions than were their predecessors. This did not harm the German establishments; even without the sympathies of the English church, they did better out of the Vienna settlement of 1815 than they had done from any settlement under the Empire. Nor did isolationism solve the domestic problems of the English church. The Whig triumph of 1830 was far more menacing than that of 1715; it was met, especially at Oxford, by a passionate resistance which parodied that of the early Hanoverian era. Then there had been heads who were latitudinarian and Whig; now they were solidly protestant High Churchmen, and the only way the Oxford juniors could twist their arms to last-ditch resistance, was themselves to advance from Protestant High Churchmanship to a Catholicism intense equally against Protestant dissenters and Romanists. This artificial construct represented an extreme of isolationism.[50] It was only too clear what a church of low achievement, intellectual and otherwise, the Church of England was,[51] and so, when English divines lost touch with the German developments in an obsession with their own traditions and peculiarities, the Germans, even liberal Germans, avid consumers of the English output in the first half of the eighteenth century, stopped reading English work on the irreproachable ground that it was not worth reading, and, certainly, no longer bore on the progress of German idealism.

Emanuel Hirsch, old, blind, and dismissed from his chair by the victorious Allies, atoned after the Second World War for a lifetime of nationalism by writing his immense *Geschichte der neueren evangelischen Theologie* against the whole history of the West. He cannot, I think, be faulted in the proportion of his space allocated to English theology; more than two-fifths of the first of his five volumes (devoted to the late-seventeenth and early-eighteenth century), but of the three volumes extending from the mid-eighteenth to the mid-nineteenth century (and totalling 1536 pages) a mere 82 pages. There were, of course perils in the isolation of superiority as well as in the very second-rate *Sonderweg* favoured in England. By the 1940s Thomas Mann was writing savagely that it was 'nothing but German provincial conceitedness' to deny depth to the world; and castigating his native land 'where the word "international" has long been a reproach, and a smug provincialism has made the air spoilt and stuffy'.[52] And Rudolf von Thadden has lately spoken of the 'catalogue of ghosts which alienated the [Wilhelmine] intellectual world from the realities of modern life'.[53] Still, if it took exile in America to open the eyes of Thomas Mann to latter-day German isolation, it took exile in Natal to save Colenso from English isolation and make a scholar of him. It happened that the curator of the museum and library in Cape Town, was the son of the notable German Old Testament scholar, Friedrich Bleek, and he kept Colenso supplied with good German work in the field that he would probably not have obtained in England.[54]

As has often happened in England, nonconformists took their cue from the Church. When the Congregationalists created the *British Quarterly Review* in the 1840s, it contained valuable bibliographies of the current German output; but when Samuel Davidson, professor of Biblical literature and ecclesiastical history at Lancashire Independent College, 1843–57, a friend of various German theologians of relatively conservative views, contributed to the second volume of the tenth edition of Horne's *Introduction to the Sacred Scriptures* (1856), the college committee made him resign his chair. The very last extant letter of Jabez Bunting, the so-called 'last Wesleyan', was to forbid the teaching of German to voluntary classes in the Didsbury College seminary;[55] the 'first Wesleyan', John Wesley, himself, it is noteworthy, had been a principal channel of the influence in England of Bengel, Buddeus, and the Pietists, and translated no fewer than thirtyfour German hymns, much to the advantage of his flock. Most conservative of all were the atheists who organised themselves publicly in the Secular Society in 1851, still firmly wedded to the doctrines of Tom Paine, and the deists of the eighteenth century.[56] Nor were the men of letters more open than the theologians. The German contacts made by letter or by visit, of

Wordsworth, Coleridge, Crabbe, Robinson and the rest, do not amount to much, nor were they greatly enhanced by reading in the literature.[57]

It was outsiders who responded positively to the German achievement, Unitarians, by this time so much outsiders as to be of small general influence, liberal Anglicans interested in German historiography,[58] a learned recluse like Connop Thirlwall (Melbourne had his translation of Schleiermacher's *Critical Essay on the Gospel of St. Luke* vetted by two bishops and the Primate before he felt able to raise him to the least desirable of all episcopal sees)[59] literary men like Carlyle who found in Goethe a painless exit from Christian profession, and one literary in-man, in the shape of Coleridge who had indeed been a Unitarian for a time. Carlyle's understanding of Goethe is not now regarded as profound, but he corresponded with him, regarded him in 'the hero as Man of Letters' as 'by far the notablest of all Literary Men', and helped Sterling out of the Church of England with him. It was a fitting memorial to this succession that George Eliot, despite her association with Positivists, had much of the Goethean about her, and that her association with G.H. Lewes began when she joined him in Germany where he was completing his *Life of Goethe* (1856). And with that association George Eliot discovered herself as a novelist. Curiously enough, there was something in this for Germany. Carlyle translated one of Goethe's poems in *Past and Present*.[60] He filled up the metre at the end with an admonition of his own: 'Work and despair not'. This somewhat Calvinist exhortation summed up what Carlyle thought he had learned from Goethe, and, translated into German, it became in the present century one of the mottoes of the Weimar system.[61] Coleridge, a layman with a message for the Church, who evoked a succession of his own to preach it, was a curious case. Neither he nor his disciples made any bones that his Platonism took the form it did as a result of his application to Kant, Fichte and Schelling, even if 'the matured theory of the clerisy which one finds in the *Church and State* arose from the accommodation of his development of German idealist philosophy to English cultural traditions [and] as such . . . is specifically English, and Coleridgean'.[62] What Coleridge valued in the Germans, in other words, was not the critical achievement, but the possibilities of metaphysical construction he perceived in them; and given that this perception was open and legitimate, it is extraordinary that he should have proceeded to the extent he did by way of unacknowledged plagiarism.[63] The one 'in-man' who found a conservative message in Germany took great care not to reveal the sources of all he had poached.

The other group of outsiders seeking to be insiders who took up the German cause were the university reformers, and they were quite as selective as Coleridge. After the murder of Kotzebue in 1819, the German liberal students were praised because they had 'adopted the universal wish of the nation, and the professors, so unlike the generality of their brethren in other places, [were] almost without exception the strenuous supporters of national liberty and inalienable rights of mankind.' The excellence of their scholarship matched the excellence of their politics.[64] Thomas Hodgskin was more cautious, but thought that, even at the lowest, 'without placing much confidence in [German] sovereigns, it may at least be supposed that . . . they are as capable of organising a university as the same class of men were three or four centuries ago'.[65] This view of the matter was implicitly conceded by conservative opinion, which professed no surprise at the subversiveness of German institutions in which professors offered novelties for fees, instead of expounding approved books in the manner of the English tutors.[66] And for most of the century the issue between men of conservative bent, and liberal (often Unitarian) reformers, over the planting out of new German universities in London and the provinces was discussed largely in these terms; the real fact was, of course, that German state patronage secured professors who on major issues regarded themselves as lions under the throne, and who, where technological studies were concerned, were as opposed to novelties as the *Quarterly Review*. It was religious and scholarly orthodoxy which was corroded by the critical power of professorial liberalism. Appropriately enough, the broadest critique of the English university system came from the man most seriously engaged with the German philosophical challenge, Sir William Hamilton. He maintained that the universities' defence of chartered liberties was misplaced since the colleges had illegally swallowed up the universities, and that religious tests to enter the arts faculties could hardly be warranted, when they were unknown in universities outside England.[67] Certainly the absence of tests would not explain German scepticism. When Hamilton visited Germany for the first time in 1817 to buy books for the Advocates' Library in Edinburgh, he knew no German, but he speedily put this right, and employed his new knowledge to combine the common-sense philosophy on which he had been raised with the transcendental philosophy of Kant. In Hamilton there was a genuine reception of Kant, hitherto barely known in Scotland, together with an attempt to take the argument further. From Kant Hamilton derived the view that the existence of a God conceived as a being absolute in himself was as undemonstrable as the ground of our freedom. The evidence of our consciousness for God's moral government of the world and for our responsibility did not extend to a speculative proof of how God exists and how our freedom is possible. A recent German inquiry maintained that he was the only one of the Victorian agnostics to have made a genuine encounter with German philosophy.[68]

We come finally to what is conventionally treated as the main part of the subject, the topics treated by Professor Chadwick under the headings of 'History and the Bible' and 'Doubt'. Once university teachers found German texts in classical, historical and theological studies indispensable, they could not avoid some kind of encounter with German scholarship. The furore over *Essays and Reviews* was sufficient to put Jowett and Stanley off their projected reconstruction of New Testament criticism; and, though a somewhat dated Hegelianism became modish amongst philosophers,[69] there were deep-rooted habits of mind among theologians which discouraged genuine engagement. Locke had regarded knowledge as something external to man, perceived by sense impressions. Revelation was in the nature of the case external to man, though it was recognizable by supporting evidences. Among these were miracles and the fulfilment of prophesies, that is, principally biblical evidences, and all was well as long as the Bible was secure. The boldness of German historical criticism owed, as we have seen, much to the need to dislodge a peculiarly tough doctrinal system; but it was also encouraged by the turn taken by German philosophy. This philosophy had gone inward rather than outward, and encouraged a view of religion as the experience of a liberating God, to be perceived in history as well as within, and confirmed and sustained in Scripture. The evidences that mattered were those within. De Wette, the great Old Testament critic of the early nineteenth century, wrote that the supernaturalists 'believe in miracles, and conceive them in a natural and material manner. They consider that the laws of nature are temporarily suspended, that Nature's machine is differently set. With all their exaltation of Faith they are unable to believe without seeing. And if they had lived in the days of Christ, they would indeed have beheld no marvellous works, for, like the Pharisees, they would have asked for a sign from heaven'. On this view, the English theologians were pharisees. The philosophical stress on 'inner truth' eased the critic's way to recognizing the importance in antiquity of myth, and encouraged him, perhaps too readily, to think that the truth could be restated in contemporary terms through speculative philosophy. At the beginning of the nineteenth century there was no English counterpart to the body of the Old Testament criticism already available in Germany, and the later practice of T. & T. Clark and others in publishing translations of predominantly conservative German authors encouraged the view that there was no critical case to answer.[70] Eventually the German Old Testament work was summed up and presented in English dress by S.R. Driver, whose *Introduction to the Literature of the Old Testament* (1883) still earns high marks from Old Testament specialists.[71] But Driver's frame of mind had not changed much from that of his Lockean predecessors of the eighteenth century. He accepted a double theory of the truth of the Bible, according to which its inner or spiritual truths could be distinguished from its outward expression. Thus if, on scientific grounds, it became impossible to hold with Genesis 1 that the world was created within seven days, it was permissible to regard this statement as the disposable outer husk of some spiritual truth conveyed by the narrative. That is to say that the Bible was still, in the old manner, to be regarded as conveying external truths. Driver, moreover, did actually believe that the narrative of the Fall was a picturesque description of an event, of man's failure when he had developed to the point of being conscious of the moral law, and breaking it; indeed he thought that if the human race had arisen in several independent quarters of the world, each group would have gone through this event. Real (and otherwise unknown) history lay behind the image. Compare this with Schleiermacher. He maintained that even if the Mosaic narrative were acceptable as 'an historical account communicated in an extraordinary way, the particular pieces of information would never be articles of faith in our sense of the phrase, for our feeling of absolute dependence does not gain thereby either a new content, a new form, or clearer definition'.[72] No comment is needed as to which of these views was more likely to lead to a 'crisis of faith' in an age when historical studies were in the full flood of progress.

It was a similar story with the key issue of Christology. Though Strauss's *Life* was followed up by best-selling successors in England, France and Germany, what was made available in English was not the German critical work on the New Testament which had Christological implications, but church history and the like. Anglicans in particular took comfort from the fact that Lightfoot was now addressing himself to the whole question of Gospel criticism; Lightfoot said (or at any rate implied, for he was economical of words, in both speech and writing) that accepted views of the Incarnation were all right, and wrote that the critical views of the Tübingen school were too extravagant to last. It is not now thought that Lightfoot engaged with the Tübingen school in any fundamental degree,[73] and where the shoe pinched was made clear in his anxiety to defend the historicity of the Fourth Gospel. The Fourth Gospel presented a clearly Christian view of Jesus, and if the historical accuracy of the Gospel were basically reliable, then Christian claims about the Incarnation could be held to be rooted in historical reality. The information would have been conveyed in the Lockean manner. Yet in the main Lightfoot stuck closely to his exegetical last, creating the impression that all would come out all right if historical criticism were honestly pursued, and avoided wider issues. The degree of reassurance his fellows required may be measured by the abundant veneration he received.

This need for reassurance is in itself evidence for the sense of unease that marked so many during the long Victorian crisis of faith. With that unease no longer with us, it is interesting to observe that in our own time a much fuller exposure to nineteenth-century German scholarship is taking place. A great deal of important German work on Gospel criticism nearly a century old has recently been translated into English, some of it for the first time. In 1973, after almost 140 years, the English version of Strauss's *Life of Jesus* reappeared, and was well received;[74] in comparison with other weapons, this particular hand grenade now seemed benign.

Notes

1 Owen Chadwick, *The Victorian Church*, London, 1966–70.

2 Owen Chadwick, *The secularization of the European mind in the nineteenth century. The Gifford Lectures in the University of Edinburgh for 1973–4*, Cambridge, 1975.

3 *Ibid.*, p. 2.

4 Clive Field in an unpublished paper on 'Religious Practice in England: 17th and 18th centuries'.

5 On the 'golden age of the Church of England' see Desmond Bowen. *The Idea of the Victorian Church. A Study of the Church of England, 1833–1889*, Montreal, 1968.

6 Owen Chadwick, *The Mind of the Oxford Movement*, London, 1960, p. 50.

7 G.R. Balleine, *A history of the evangelical party in the Church of England*, London, 1957, pp. 164–5.

8 W.R. Ward, *Religion and Society in England, 1790–1850*, London, 1972, p. 287.

9 On all this see T.W. Heyck, *The Transformation of the Intellectual Life in Victorian England*, London, 1982, pp. 24–49.

10 W.R. Ward, 'Oxford and the origins of Liberal Catholicism in the Church of England' *Studies in Church History* I (1962) 233–52.

11 W.R. Ward, *Theology, Sociology and Politics. The German Protestant Social Conscience 1890–1930*, Bern, 1979.

12 W.R. Ward, 'The Protestant Churches, especially in Britain, and the social problems of the Industrial Revolution', *Religion und Kirchen im industriellen Zeitalter*, Schriftenreihe des Georg-Eckert-Instituts für internationale Schulbuchforschung Bd. 23, Braunschweig, 1977, pp. 63–72.

13 For the case of Reading see S. Yeo, *Religion and voluntary Organisations in crisis*, London, 1976. Cf. G.E. Milburn, 'Piety, profit and paternalism: Methodists in business in the North-East of England, c.1760–1920', in *Proceedings of the Wesley Historical Society* 44 (1983) 45–92.

14 G.V. Cox, *Recollections of Oxford*, 2nd ed., London, 1870, p. 355.

15 For a Canadian study of this which could be paralleled in contemporary England see Neil Semple, ' "The Nurture and admonition of the Lord" ':

Nineteenth-century Canadian Methodism's response to "Childhood", *Histoire Sociale – Social History* 14 (1981) 157–75.

16 In a famous book *Dreimonate als Fabrikarbeiter und Handwerksbursche*, Leipzig, 1981, Eng. tr. *Three months in a workshop*, London, 1895) Paul Göhre reported that Jesus had not gone down the hill in the esteem of the Chemnitz textile workers, among whom he had spent three months incognito, as had the Church. He proposed therefore to take them the historical Jesus. A similar situation obtained in England.

17 The best study of this subject is by James R. Moore, *The Post-Darwinian controversies. A study of the Protestant struggle to come to terms with Darwin in Great Britain and America 1870–1900*, Cambridge, 1979. For an earlier period there is a suggestive American study which makes use of German material: H. Hoverkamp, *Science and Religion in America 1800–1860*, University of Pennsylvania Press, 1978. See also T.D. Bozeman, *Protestants in an age of science*, Chapel Hill, 1977.

18 On all this and on continuing alarm for the Protestant interest on the continent see my paper, 'Orthodoxy, Enlightenment and religious revival', in *Studies in Church History* 17 (1980) 275–96. Above, Ch. 2.

19 *Unschuldige Nachrichten* 1735 pp. 235–7, 52: 1741 p. 57. Cf. the ordinances of 1744 forbidding foreigners to preach in Hanover. *Acta Historico-Ecclesiastica* 9, 264–5.

20 *Zeitschrift der Gesellschaft für nieder-sächsische Kirchengeschichte* 39 (1934) 185 and n 54. The Duchess of Kendal was also a contact of Zinzendorf. Another Pietist at the Hanoverian court in London, 1714–28, was the Countess Johanna Sophie of Schaumburg-Lippe. *Ibid.* 63 (1965) 187.

21 J.G. Walch, *Historische und theologische Einleitung in die Religions-Streitigkeiten ausser der Evangelisch-Lutherischen Kirche*, Jena, 1733–6: repr. Stuttgart, 1972 I. 606.

22 Johannes Reiskius, *Commentatio de Monarchia Quinta*, Wolfenbüttel, 1692.

23 F.W. Barthold, *Die Erweckten im protestantischen Deutschland während des Ausgangs des 17. und der ersten Halfte des 18. Jahrhunderts besonders die frommen Grafenhöfe*, reprinted from *Historisches Taschenbuch 1852–3* at Darmstadt, 1968 I.166. Eva von Buttlar gave it out that her lover, a theologian called Winter, and a medical student from Jena were God the father and God the Son, while she was no less than the Holy Spirit.

24 *Acta Historico-Ecclesiastica* 9. 298.

25 *Unschuldige Nachrichten* 1721 p. 493. Cf. *Ibid.* 1726 pp. 841–3, 1727 p. 437.

26 For Löscher's assault upon the alleged unorthodoxy of the English Church see M. Greschat, *Zwischen Traditionund neuem Anfang*, Witten, 1971, p. 236.

27 H.L. Benthem, *Neu-eroffneter Engländischer Kirch- und Schulenstaat*, 2nd ed. Leipzig, 1732, preface paras. 9–10.

28 Dr. Kayser, 'Hannoversche Enthusiasten des siebzehnten Jahrhunderts', *Zeitschrift der Gesellschaft für niedersächsische Kirchengeschichte* 15 (1905) 59.

29 Max Goebel, 'Geschichte der wahren Inspirations-Gemeinden von 1688 bis 1859'. Part III. *Zeitschrift fur die historische Theologie* N.F. 19 (1855) 98.

30 Andreas Gross, *Vernunftiger und unpartheyische Bericht über die neuaufkom-*
    mende Herrnhutische Gemeinde, 3rd ed. Frankfurt/Leipzig, 1740, p. 21.

31 M. Brecht, 'Die Entwicklung der alten Bibliothek des Tübinger Stift in ihren
    theologie- und geistesgeschichtlichen Zusammenhang', *Blätter für Wurttem-*
    bergische Kirchengeschichte 63 (1963) 59, 63. The holdings of the library at
    the Stift are a marvellous continuous record of what was thought worth buying.
    Whitefield and Watts, for example, were thought more important than Wesley.

32 There was strong English representation in J.H. Reitz, *Historie der Wiederge-*
    bohrnen, 5th ed. Berleburg, 1724.

33 Carl Heinrich von Bogatsky, *Aufrichtige und an aller Kinder Gottes gerichtete*
    Declaration über eine gegen ihn herausgekommene Herrnhutische Schrift,
    Halle, 1751, p. 10.

34 Wolfgang Martens, *Die Botschaft der Tugend. Die Aufklärung im Spiegel der*
    deutschen Moralischen Wochenschriften, Stuttgart, 1971.

35 Johann Rudolf Schlegel, *Kirchengeschichte des achtzehten Jahrhunderts*, Heil-
    bronn, 1784–96, esp. 2.814.

36 Siegmund Jacob Baumgarten, *Samlung von merkwürdigen Lebensbeschreibun-*
    gen grossten Teils aus der britannischen Biographen ubersetzt . . . Halle,
    1754–7, unpaginated preface. As late as 1798 it could be reported that
    'the English imperial constitution . . . without doubt one of the best in the
    world . . . opens to all foreigners without distinction access to this blessed
    island . . . English freedom causes the land . . . to blossom', but it was already
    noticeable that 'the Briton is not himself inventive, but . . . follows the track
    pointed out to him by the foreigner'. J.G. Burckhardt, *Kirchengeschichte der*
    deutschen Gemeinden in London, Tübingen, 1798, pp. 9–13.

37 Martin Schloemann, *Siegmund Jacob Baumgarten. System und Geschichte in*
    der Theologie des Überganges zum Neuprotestantismus, Göttingen, 1974.
    Among the English authors whom Baumgarten had gone out of his way to
    introduce to German readers were the deists and their critics.

38 Emanuel Hirsch, *Geschichte der neuern evangelischen Theologie*, 5th ed.
    Gütersloh, 1975 4.50.

39 A substantial East German Lessing reader (*Lessing für unsere Zeit. Ein*
    Lesebuch, 25th ed. Berlin/Weimar, 1984, almost excludes Lessing the theo-
    logian. This imbalance may be rectified by *Lessing's Theological Writings* ed.
    H. Chadwick, London, 1956.

40 *Reimarus: Fragments* ed. C.H. Talbert, London, 1971.

41 H. von Schubert, quoted in Hirsch, *op. cit.* 4.248.

42 *The Autobiography of Johann Wolfgang von Goethe* ed. K.J. Weintraub,
    Chicago, 1974, 2.8–23.

43 Gerhard Kaiser, *Pietismus und Patriotismus in literarischen Deutschland*,
    Wiesbaden, 1961.

44 The political parallel was explicitly drawn by Heine in his *Zur Geschichte*
    der Religion und Philosophie in Deutschland (1834) in *Sämmtliche Werke*,
    Bibliothek Ausgabe, Hamburg, n.d. 7. 126.

45 For a fuller development of this argument, see Marilyn Chapin Massey, *Christ*

Unmasked. The meaning of The Life of Jesus in German Politics, Chapel Hill, 1983.

46 Heine, *Sämmtliche Werke* 7. 147.

47 Hans-Joachim Braun, *Technologische Beziehungen zwischen Deutschland und England von der Mitte des 17. bis zum Ausgang des 18. Jahrhunderts*, Dusseldorf, 1974.

48 Ward, *Religion and Society in England*, p. 45.

49 Carl Diehl, *Americans and German scholarship, 1770–1870* (New Haven, 1978) esp. p. 1.

50 W.R. Ward, *Victorian Oxford*, London, 1965, chs. 5 and 6. Walter Harley Conser Jnr., shows indeed that the confessional frame of mind was an international phenomenon, but does not admit that confessionalism could only become international by following migrations of population. 'Church and Confession: conservative theologians in Germany, England and America, 1815–66'. Unpublished Ph.D. thesis, Brown University, 1981. Published under the same title, Macon, Ga., 1984.

51 Writing in 1890 Otto Pfleiderer ascribed the difficulty to the fact that no English counterpart of German idealism was to hand when popular Lockeanism, 'that barren view of things which binds man to the world of the senses', ceased to satisfy. But he did not mince the 'fact that the church life of England . . . , has remained almost completely untouched by the vast progress of . . . scientific thought . . . and that whenever the two come into contact, such a violent collision is the consequence that popular feeling is shocked'. *The development of theology in Germany since Kant, and its progress in Britain since 1828*, London, 1890, p. 307.

52 Thomas Mann, *Doctor Faustus*, Penguin ed. London, 1978, pp. 175, 174.

53 *Troeltsch Studien* Bd.3, ed. Horst Renz and Friedrich Wilhelm Graf, Gütersloh, 1984, p. 119.

54 John Rogerson, *Old Testament Criticism in the nineteenth century. England and Germany*, London, 1984, p. 221.

55 W.R. Ward, *Early Victorian Methodism*, Oxford, 1976, pp. 420–421. More information of this kind, mostly of a later date, is to be found in Willis B. Glover Jnr., *Evangelical Nonconformists and Higher Criticism in the 19th century*, London, 1954.

56 S. Budd, *Varieties of Unbelief. Atheists and Agnostics in English Society*, London, 1977, p. 10.

57 On this point see R. Wellek, *Confrontations. Studies in the intellectual and literary relations between Germany, England and the United States during the Nineteenth Century*, Princeton N.J., 1965, pp. 6–11.

58 Duncan Forbes, *The liberal anglican idea of History* Cambridge, 1952.

59 *Letters literary and theological of Connop Thirwall*, ed. J.J.S. Perowne and L. Stokes, London, 1881, pp. 159–61.

60. 'Mason Lodge'. Thomas Carlyle, *Past and Present. Works*, London, 1897: repr. 1969, 1974 10. 237–8.

61 On the 'Goethe Gemeinde' see W.H. Bruford, 'Goethe and Some Victorian

Humanists' in *Publications of the English Goethe Society* N.S. 18 (1949)
34–67. On Carlyle see R. Wellek, 'Carlyle and German Romanticism', and
'Carlyle and the Philosophy of history' in *op. cit.* pp. 34–113; C.F. Harrold,
Carlyle and German Thought 1819–34, New Haven, 1934.

62 Ben Knights, *The idea of the clerisy in the nineteenth century*, Cambridge,
   1978, p. 65.

63 On the plagiarism see N. Fruman, *Coleridge, the damaged Archangel*, London,
   1972, e.g. pp. 31–4, 80–83. On Coleridge as a philosopher, see J.H. Muirhead,
   Coleridge as a philosopher, London, 1930; René Wellek, *Immanuel Kant in
   England, 1793–1838*, London, 1931; T.B. McFarland, *Coleridge and the
   Pantheist tradition*, Oxford, 1969: Donald MacKinnon, 'Coleridge and Kant'
   in *Coleridge's Variety* ed. John B. Beer, London, 1975, pp. 183–203.

64 *A memoir of Charles Louis Sand: including a narrative of the circumstances
   attending the death of Augustus von Kotzebue; also a defence of the German
   universities*, London, 1819.

65 T. Hodgskin, *Travels in the North of Germany*, Edinburgh, 1820, 2. 265–9.

66 *Quarterly Review* 23. 446–8.

67 Ward, *Victorian Oxford*, pp. 82–3, 92.

68 Karl-Dieter Ulke, *Agnostisches Denken im Victorianischen England*, Freiburg/
   München, 1980.

69 The study being commended in a book which delighted Emerson and Carlyle,
   J.H. Sterling, *The Secret of Hegel*, Edinburgh, 1865.

70 On this whole subject see John Rogerson, *Old Testament Criticism in the
   nineteenth century . . .*

71 J.W. Rogerson, 'Philosophy and the rise of Biblical criticism; England and
   Germany in *England and Germany. Studies in Theological Diplomacy* ed. S.W.
   Sykes, Frankfurt, 1982, pp. 22–3. Cf. *The Cambridge History of the Bible* 3.
   274–95.

72 Quoted in Rogerson, *op. cit.* p. 73, Strauss likewise pleaded that he had cut
   across old divisions in the interests of truth. 'Orthodox and rationalists alike
   proceed from the false assumption that we have always in the gospels testimony,
   sometimes even that of eyewitnesses, to fact. They are, therefore, reduced to
   asking themselves what can have been the real and natural fact which is here
   witnessed to in such extraordinary ways. We have to realize that the narrators
   testify sometimes not to outward facts but to ideas, often most practical and
   beautiful ideas . . . [This] results in narrative, legendary, mythical in nature,
   illustrative often of spiritual truth in a manner more perfect than any hard
   prosaic statement could achieve.' *Life of Jesus* Preface.

73 R. Morgan 'Historical Criticism and Christology: England and Germany' in
   S.W. Sykes *op. cit.*, p. 87.

74 e.g. *Theology* 76 (1973) pp. 602–3. Even Reimarus appeared in English
   translation in 1971.

Part Two

Revival

5

Power and Piety: the Origins of Religious Revival in the Early Eighteenth Century[1]

John Wesley may have claimed that the world was his parish, but Methodist historians have been strongly tempted to make his parish their world, or, on the ecumenical rebound, pretend that Methodism has no firm connection with time and place but is a sort of *philosophia perennis* providentially welling up in the church universal from time to time.[2] I suspect that God is as little glorified as I know the historian is little enlightened by either of these attitudes. For Methodism illustrates the complex of early eighteenth-century forces which were uniting England to Germany closer than ever before, to its politics and piety, to its theology, and to the private comforts and overt terrors of the German religious mind. Wesley's own development was crucially influenced by events not only on the fringes of the Protestant world, but on opposite fringes – by Salzburgers and Moravians in Georgia and on the Atlantic passage, and by those other Moravians at Herrnhut on the frontiers of Saxony and what is now Czechoslovakia, whither amongst hundreds of others, Wesley made a pilgrimage in 1738, to see if sinless perfection really existed in this world, and to write some of the most moving pages in the whole of his *Journal*.[3] Why were the fringes operating upon the centre in this way? The question is the more urgent because of what one hears scholars describing as the 'tunnel' period of English history, the twenty years or so before the beginning of Wesley's evangelistic ministry in 1739. Something at least is known of the grandiose panorama of the religious struggles under Queen Anne, of the alliance of theology and eastern studies, of England, Prussia and the Russia of Peter the Great to frustrate a putative take-over of Greek Orthodoxy in the interests of Popery and French power; and the international negotiations of Archbishop Wake afer Anne's death were explored by Dean Sykes. But then the darkness falls, and there seems no

Methodist Conference historical lecture. First published in *Bulletin of the John Rylands University Library of Manchester* 63 (1980), pp. 231–52.

accounting for religious revival when it comes. In this paper, ignoring what was happening in the Reformed world for reasons of space, I would like to approach these questions by examining some developments in Central Europe, and assuming that there were shared anxieties in the Protestant world which gave rise to shared expectations. In these shared expectations, rather than in the sociology of parish or denomination lies the explanation of the random outbreak of religious revival all the way from Carinthia to New England.

Among the most powerful unifying factors in the whole Protestant world were the ambitions and problems of the new kingdom of Prussia. Long before she acquired Stettin in the Oder estuary in 1714, Prussia had ambitions in the Oder valley, and the construction of a canal between the Spree and the Oder in 1669 had given Berlin direct access to Breslau, one of the most important of German cities and the starting point of the Russia trade. The importance of this connection was enhanced by the aquisition of the duchy of Magdeburg in 1680. At that time a thoroughly run-down post-Thirty-Years-War province, Magdeburg mattered to Prussia as a junction to its possessions in the West, as a bridgehead against Saxony, and as an asset capable of rapid improvement. Under Prussian management the mines of salt, copper and hard coal began to boom, the Saale was made navigable, the population doubled in two generations, and manufactures were exported via the Silesian route to Hungary and Moravia. It was a bold move to do all this on the doorstep of Leipzig, the seat of an ancient and famous university, the home of an international trade fair, one of the two leading German book markets, and the chief place of a Saxony which was itself the chief mining and manufacturing state in Germany, and whose Elector acquired the Polish crown in 1697. But the Berlin government meant business and, as was their wont, they made it plain by founding a university at Halle. A Lutheran university to turn out clergy and officials for the state was indeed required. Duisberg and Frankfurt-on-Oder were both reformed universities, while the Saxon universities of Leipzig and Wittenberg were strongholds of Lutheran Orthodoxy, perilous to the affections of Brandenburger ordinands for their Reformed monarchy.[4]

There was also an anti-Saxon slant to the religious policy of the Berlin government. They had somehow to gain acceptance of the Reformed religion of the court and their Rhineland provinces against the ingrained prejudices of the established Lutheran churches of their main territories. Politics as well as religion drove the Berlin court to play with all kinds of movements which sought to circumvent the entrenched theological positions of the past. The patronage rights which Orthodoxy acknowledged in the gentry constituted it not only a theological party, but a politics of gentry, a politics nowhere more deeply rooted than in the outlying territories of Magdeburg and East Prussia. Moreover, Lutheran Orthodoxy was the confessional platform for Prussia's immediate rivals in the great international game, Sweden and Saxony. In this conflict the Berlin government found one ally in the early champions of Enlightenment, another in the leaders of Lutheran Pietism. Rather like English Methodism, Pietism combined a reliance on one set of past traditions with a sharp criticism of others. Building on a movement of generalized and unconfessional puritanism which had been widespread in the early seventeenth century and in which the literature of English puritans and of German writers like Arndt of a markedly anti-Saxon bent was still highly prized, the Pietists also followed their predecessors in calling for a second Reformation of the ecclesiastical forces in possession; in Germany this meant the Orthodoxy sustained in the old Lutheran heartland of Saxony, and institutionalized in the teachings of the universities of Wittenberg and Leipzig. Unjust as the Pietist criticisms of Orthodoxy as 'hard' and 'dry' often were, they gave vent to a disquiet common in Catholic as well as Protestant Europe at the policy of Christianizing the people by the device of privileged religious establishment operating at one level by a closely articulated doctrinal system guaranteed against defeat in polemical warfare, and, at another, by parish oversight. If Christianity was for ordinary people, it must be something other than the complicated orthodoxies of the seventeenth century; if it was to be transmitted from generation to generation, it looked as if some other mechanism must at least supplement the round of parish devotions; if it was to exert an effective leverage upon conscience, it must find some substitute for the increasingly ridiculous Orthodox insistence upon repentance before the imminent end of all things. But if the end was not at hand, time was limited. The prospects for Protestantism in Germany looked bleak. The decline of France and the rise of the Habsburg house encouraged the formation of a powerful Catholic party in the empire.[5] There was a sorry trail of conversions of Protestant princes to Rome, of which Saxony was only the chief. Still worse, the legal constitution of Protestantism in Germany gave increasing trouble, bringing the Empire to the brink of confessional war in 1719, generating a series of hair-raising plans for the forcible extirpation of protestantism under the aegis of Prince Eugene or the Vienna allies of 1725 or the college of Cardinals, which harrowed opinion throughout the twenties and thirties, and kept the machinery of the Empire at full stretch resisting, with only partial success, constant Catholic encroachments on Protestant church property and other rights.[6] And, as we shall see, where the provisions of the Westphalia settlement did not apply at all, or applied still less effectively than they did in Germany, the situation was even more urgent.

One solution to this set of problems was offered by mystical and enthusiastic movements of a Quakerish type which had little use for the formalities of church life and were as common in Germany as they were in England. Spener, the founder of Lutheran Pietism, took another line. Beating the drum about the New Birth, the conditions of vitality in the faith, Spener treated the doctrine of justification less as the personal consciousness of the forgiveness of sins than as the real transformation of the newly-born; he repudiated the things of this world and yet demanded their improvement on the basis of the real improvement worked by faith upon mankind. In his *collegia pietatis* or class meetings he found a form of religious practice which seemed to provide something missing in the preaching and sacraments of the church. And in his 'hope of better times', his insistence that the end of all things would not come till all the scriptural promises to the church had been fulfilled, he afforded another motive to strive for the kingdom of God on earth.[7] Like Wesley, Spener claimed in no way to differ from the doctrines received in his church, but the Orthodox did not at all take to his effort to make faith dependent on an active piety and regarded his devotional groups as an invitation to schism. In the Orthodox view there were enough schismatic enthusiasts in Germany already, and it was known that Spener's right-hand man, August Hermann Francke, stood near them. The upshot was that a big drive against the Pietists was put on between 1689 and 1692. Spener and Francke were spectacularly drummed out of Saxony, their friends elsewhere were expelled, and it became clear that Pietism was bound for the underworld of visionary enthusiasm if some new protector could not be found. That protector turned up in Brandenburg–Prussia. Senior appointments were found for Spener and his friends, and above all the theological faculty at the new university at Halle was staffed with Pietists. This alliance between the Pietists and the Prussian court, which occasioned the most ferocious disputes with the Orthodox clergy of Halle and the estates of Magdeburg, lasted till Francke's death in 1727, and in a less intimate form till the accession of Frederick the Great in 1740.[8]

This reversal of fortune was not more singular than the uses to which Francke put it. He was one of the most extraordinary organizers in the whole history of Christianity. He began by systematizing what the stages of the Christian life were, beginning with a conviction of sin under the law, working through fear of the wrath to come to a total breach with the old Adam, a faith and sanctification continuously tested by rigorous self-examination. Francke indeed laid the basis for that pattern of Christian existence against which Methodist class-members and leaders were eventually experimentally to test their progress, a pattern the total absence of which is one of the distinguishing features of Christianity today. He also established characteristic forms of charitable and educational activity which marked the whole subsequent history of evangelical religion. Everybody knows, and everybody knew from Francke's calculated propaganda at the time, of the Orphan House he created at Halle, of the dispensary, the schools, the teacher-training institutions, and the Bible Institute attached to it. But Francke's Orphan House bore no resemblance to the minuscule reproductions of it set up by Wesley in Newcastle and Whitefield in Georgia, nor was the dispensary primarily a device for pumping pills into orphans. The Orphan House was one of the biggest buildings in Europe, if not the biggest – 3,000 people were soon living and working there[9] – while the dispensary was the first producer of standardized branded medicaments on a commercial scale, able and anxious to sell a complete public health kit for a city or province and marketing its wares by brochures in Latin, French, English, Dutch and Greek. How else indeed was Francke's vast enterprise to be paid for? His institutions received royal privileges which had a cash value; there were charitable collections all over Europe; but the whole organization turned on commercial ventures on an enormous scale, Francke's spiritual agents tapping the markets for a wide range of products all the way from Venice to the Far East. But the great business of Halle lay in the supply of medicaments and Bibles and other religious literature. The press speedily became one of the chief in Germany, publishing not only in German and Greek and Russian Cyrillic type, but in a whole range of Slavonic languages where nothing of the kind had been available before. These works were partly for the benefit of Wends and other enserfed populations on the estates of the Pietist nobility in Germany, but still more for the restless Protestant populations of the Habsburg lands.[10] To these peoples the Bible was a forbidden and revolutionary book, and the strategy underlying Francke's hope of creating a second Halle at Teschen, the point at which Silesia made a junction with Hungary on the one side and Bohemia on the other needs no comment. Francke indeed began with Utopian aims of setting the whole world to rights, and supported them by a gigantic correspondence, by establishing his agents in all the key points of central and eastern Europe, and by alliances with a number of important imperial counts outside Prussia, especially in Silesia and in Lusatia, the most recently acquired and dissident portion of Saxony. These connections explain why Francke was useful to Prussia, and also explain the link between a Pietism which was not itself revivalist and the origins of Protestant religious revival.

The Peace of Westphalia of 1648 is commonly spoken of as having secured the establishment of Protestantism, and certainly it put a ring-fence around the principal Protestant church-establishments. But this ring-fence excluded enormous numbers of Protestants in Salzburg, Bohemia, Moravia, Austria, Hungary, Silesia and Poland, populations often locally in a numerically dominant position. No rights of toleration were secured for those in Bohemia, Moravia and Austria; in Hungary there were constant persecutions, even while Transylvania was preserved as a sort of Botany Bay for Protestants deported from all parts of the Habsburg lands. In all these areas the Reformation had been as much a plea for social justice as a theological or liturgical programme,[11] and a steady intensification of serfdom had led to a long succession of peasant revolts in which the defence of Protestantism, the defence of older social customs, and in places, the defence of oppressed nationality were inextricably mingled together. In all these areas the problem of securing the survival of the faith was far more acute than in Germany or England; slow decline seemed hardly a practical possibility; the Protestants must generate new power from their own resources quickly or go under; and they must do so in the more or less complete absence of the ordinary mechanisms of church life.

Silesia was a fascinating half-way case. Under the Westphalia settlement the free exercise of the Protestant religion was preserved only in Breslau and a few indirectly ruled territories. The rest of Silesia had to make do with three churches newly built before the walls of Glogau, Jauer and Schweidnitz; all the other churches were withdrawn and the pastors, soon followed by the schoolmasters, were driven out. For formal worship Protestants resorted by hundreds to the frontier churches of the neighbouring areas of Saxony, Brandenburg, Poland and Liegnitz, but in 1675 Liegnitz itself fell to the Habsburgs and was Catholicized. The Jesuits worked hard in Breslau, created a university in a splendid baroque building by the Oder, and clearly aimed to cream off the educated strata of Protestant society. Help eventually came from Charles XII of Sweden, who marched victoriously into Silesia in 1707, and secured very extensive concessions to the Protestants by the Convention of Altranstädt. One hundred and twenty churches were to be returned to them in the indirectly governed principalities, six new 'grace' churches were to be built in the Habsburg family lands, and to these and some other churches schools were to be attached. The city of Breslau got back four churches in the neighbouring countryside. There was no religious equality, but the worst pressure was off.[12]

What is interesting is what happened to the religion of the Silesian Protestants who were in the toils, but not afflicted by the demoralizing oppression which came upon the Protestants of France or Hungary. What could not be accomplished by the ordinary mechanisms of church life must be accomplished in some other way. Domestic piety, informal class-meetings, must replace public worship. Clergy, dispossessed of their livings, lived perilously, keeping in touch with their flocks on an itinerant basis, known already as *Busch-prediger*, the local equivalent of the later Methodist field-preachers. Deprived of public standing, the Silesian Protestants turned to inwardness of faith, a patient steadfast trust in God, a certain tenderness of piety[13] which became one of the hallmarks of Protestant revival. If Silesian Protestantism at the beginning of the eighteenth century was more sober in tone than later revivalism, this owed much to the empirical scholarship of its inherited leadership. Caspar Neumann, then chief pastor in Breslau, professor at the gymnasium and theological adviser to the town council, was in touch with Leibniz and other leading scholars abroad, a member of the Royal Society of Sciences in Berlin and a correspondent of the Royal Society in England. Of course the Breslau Protestants could not afford to let the Jesuit educational ladder draw off the upper ranks of society. Their gymnasium must be as good as their competitors', and, while sending off their prospective professional men to Jena and Leiden, they must find a substitute for a local university. Already in 1652, before any of the big scientific societies in the West, an Academia Naturae Curiosum had been founded in Schweinfurt, and the Breslau doctors soon formed a branch of their own. They launched the world's first scientific medical journal, and developed academy sections to pursue physics and chemistry, mineralogy and meteorology, zoology and palaeontology, to the same standard as medicine. The Breslau clergy, concluding, unlike most clergy at most times, that if they were going to hold forth on the great facts of life and death, they had better know what they were, cooperated with the doctors to produce better tables of vital statistics than those which could be obtained from the Bills of Mortality in England. Caspar Neumann and one of the doctors, Gottfried Schultz, sent the data on to Halley in 1692, who used them as the basis for the first satisfactory calculations of annuity tables. This was the same Caspar Neumann whose hymns were prized all over Germany, and whose book of prayers, *Kern alle Gebete*, went through twenty-two editions in his lifetime, and was translated into almost all European tongues, including English (in 1705).[14]

Yet there had been not only Swedes at the Altranstädt negotiations; Francke had been there too and it was Halle that exploited the opportunities there created. And there were other things besides sober piety in Silesia, and these put Neumann in 1707 much in the position of John Wesley dealing with the Ranters. When the Swedish army entered Silesia there were no Protestant churches for their use, so their church parades were held in the open air, introducing another familiar Methodist word, camp-meetings (Feldgottesdienste). When the troops moved on, the children of Lower Silesia took over where they had left off, meeting several times a day in the open air, without adult cooperation, standing in circles around their elected leaders in prayer and singing. Despite the winter, this 'uprising of the children' as it was called, spread across the country, and reached Breslau in 1708.

The objects of the camp-meetings – the re-establishment of Protestant churches and schools – were politically sensitive in the highest degree, and behind them came a new wave of Pietist camp-meetings, a new race of itinerant preachers backed by Halle, and, we are told, 'enormous balderdash leading to fanaticism was heard'. Neumann turned this corner by baptizing the movement, setting aside newly returned churches for children's use, and established clerical leadership.

It was quite impossible for Silesia's embarrassments to be locally confined. There were, first of all, substantial population movements in a part of Europe still very short of labour. Eighteen hundred Protestant weavers went off to Lusatia; in 1724 the Jesuits got the Schwenkfelders out of Liegnitz and they went (via Herrnhut) to America. The Governor of Schweidnitz expelled a group of the 'awakened' ('Erweckten' – the German word for revival is 'Erweckungsbewegung'); there were also substantial immigrations of Poles and of German Lutherans escaping persecution in Hungary. Above all, Halle with the Prussian government behind it was determined to exploit the key situation of the grace church at Teschen, the natural meeting-ground for Poles, Czechs, Slovaks and Hungarians. Voigt, the original preacher there, was a former tutor to Francke's own children; he was succeeded by other able agents from Halle, and when the Jesus Church was finally dedicated, there was a congregation of 40,000, three-quarters of whom were Poles.[15] The Polish work continued on so large a scale as to tempt the historians of communist Poland to see the whole affair in terms of Polish hatred of German lordship and their leadership of the oppressed.[16] But the openings which most interested Halle were in Bohemia and Moravia. A great peasant revolt in 1680 against increasing Catholicization and intensified serfdom, had led to a steady emigration centred on Zittau and Upper Lusatia. After the Convention of Altranstädt 7,000 peasants appealed to Sweden for religious freedom, and the repression, war and taxation which followed, led to another rising in 1713–14. Religion blended with politics on both sides.[17] Among the Czechs, resistance to forced labour combined with secret Protestantism and revolutionary elements in the Hussite tradition; the Bohemian government accompanied a Forced Labour Patent in 1717 with an edict against secret Protestant emissaries.

This legislation was directed in the first instance against the activity of the Jesus Church in Teschen. The Jesuits were too clever to allow the creation of a second Halle in that place, but they could not stop religious literature produced at Halle going through it to the tune of scores of thousands of volumes, nor could they stop illegal journeys by the Teschen preachers into Bohemia to inflame the troubles there. Things became particularly difficult after the Pietist John Steinmetz was appointed to Teschen in 1719. His assistants, Liberda, Sargánek and Macher, trained at Halle in the Polish and Czech languages, were powerful characters, and Liberda in particular, in whom the preacher and political agitator were almost indistinguishable, must have been one of the most effective revivalists of all time. The success of the preachers in Bohemia may be measured by the determination of the Jesuits to get them out of Teschen; after a seven-year trial they succeeded in 1730, and the preachers were expelled.

The Jesuit counter-attack was only the overt sign of an inward competition for the religious roots of Czech nationalism which passes unmentioned in the books. For it was now that the Habsburgs took up the veneration of a fourteenth-century Bohemian, John of Nepomuk, and pressed it on a great scale. Charles VI and his consort Elizabeth Christine effectively urged Pope Clement XI in 1720–1 to speed his canonization, and obtained it in 1729. At the crisis of Habsburg survival in 1742, with Silesia lost and French and Bavarian troops in Prague itself, a great veneration of the Bohemian saint began at the court of Maria Theresia. In Vienna itself two churches, six chapels, statues by the score at every bridge and river bank, and religious fraternities with their altars, testified to the new standing of the only Bohemian saint of international significance.[18] Czech Protestants could now hardly avoid a rival effort to appropriate their country's religious past, and if their efforts to do so never seemed to the Lutheran Orthodox anything but arbitrary,[19] they generated a religious revival which not only beat the canonization of John of Nepomuk by a short head, but considerably outdid him in international impact.

By 1730 a considerable wave of Czech emigration had been got going, most of it into Saxony, and especially into a few parishes in Upper Lusatia. The first name here was one of John Wesley's heroes, Christian David from North Moravia. He had been converted and later strengthened in the faith by the preaching of Steinmetz at Teschen, and had been put in touch with a young Pietist nobleman, educated at Halle, Count Zinzendorf, who had bought an estate at Berthelsdorf, on the borders of Bohemia, with a view to creating a religious community. It was here at Herrnhut, 'The Lord's Watch', that David felled the first tree in 1722, and peopled the settlement with illegal emigrants brought out on his repeated perilous sorties across the frontier; it was here that the famous revival broke out in 1727 and the renewed Unity of the Moravian Brethren was created; it was here that the famous troubles with the Saxon church and government took place, and that one of the most famous missionary forces of the revival was born of the necessity to secure alternative bases, the Moravians of John Wesley's youth, of Fulneck and Droylsden, of Gracehill in Ireland and Bethlehem,

Pennsylvania, of mission stations as distant as Greenland and the West Indies. But these Herrnhuters were Germans, and Wesley's *Journal* had no reason to note that the movement which Christian David let loose in North Moravia spread far into East Bohemia and produced a large Czech emigration as well. This emigration poured into Gross Hennersdorf, a parish adjacent to Berthelsdorf, owned by Zinzendorf's aunt, Henriette von Gersdorf, one of the lay supporters of Francke. Milde, who translated Francke's works into Czech, and got them into Bohemia at the rate of 10,000 a year, had long spells in Hennersdorf organizing the inflow, clearly preparing the parish to be a staging-post for a migration. And when it became necessary to appoint a Czech preacher there in 1726, who should be installed but the inflammatory Liberda from Teschen. This was important for the future. The Pietist nobility of Upper Lusatia might hope to populate their estates with Protestant refugees, but they wanted to have them in the same bondage as they had the Wends. But of all the nationalities in this part of the world, the Czechs were the most determined to preserve their nationality, and, having fought *Leibeigenschaft* in Bohemia, were adamant against submitting to any such thing in Germany. And Liberda was the last man to persuade them to do otherwise.

A generation of policy had now rewarded the Prussian government and its henchmen at Halle with the leadership of the Protestant interest inside Germany and out. Rousing the Protestant minorities weakened the Habsburgs and was producing a flow of immigration so profitable as to be denounced by the Lutheran Orthodox as selling gospel truth for Mammon. For quite apart from the vast empty spaces in Prussia, there were in 1721 three thousand two hundred and fifty seven deserted peasant lots in Brandenburg alone, and multitudes more further east. From 1718 the King advertised throughout Europe annually, offering favourable conditions for colonists, and it was a measure of the Emperor's concern that he did his best to divert the King of Prussia's acquisitiveness to the Rhineland territories of Jülich and Berg and made privately encouraging noises when in 1732 Prussia's immigration policy accomplished its most signal triumph in the neighbouring territories of the Archbishop of Salzburg.[20] Of course, the great difference between the Salzburg crisis and the great Catholic assault in the Reich in 1719 was that Charles VI was now buying approval of the Pragmatic Sanction by any means to hand.

The Archbishopric was a sovereign state, allied to the Habsburgs, with, it was supposed, a modest Protestant minority of five or six thousand, miners of gold, salt and other minerals, hill and valley peasants. In 1685 at the time of the Revocation of the Edict of Nantes, there had been a clash between the government and the Protestants in the Defereggertal which led to a small emigration to Prussia and Baden. But the real crisis did not come till the election of Baron Leopold von Firmian to the see in 1727.[21] Firmian was a mechanically-minded man, zealous according to his lights who had tried to raise the moral tone of the diocese of Lavent by minutely regulating the moral conduct of the clergy; as Bishop of Seckau (1724–7) he had turned to the Jesuits, and he now resorted to Jesuit missions again.[22] These produced evidence of a peasant Protestantism in the mountains, kept going through the generations by Luther's Bible and Protestant hymnbooks, and began to take ever more severe measures against suspects, against the weak and against children. Gastein was full of heretics, with a long tradition of private devotions and itinerant peasant preachers, and in the early thirties heretical gatherings were taking place at night and during mass in many places. The Protestant estates of the Empire defended their co-religionists and kept up the smuggling of forbidden books; and preparations for Protestant resistance began in Salzburg amid scenes of religious excitement which became part of the regular expectation in religious revivals. Over the winter of 1730–1 the peasants of the Lungau and Pongau began to associate and petitioned the Corpus Evangelicorum at Regensburg on behalf of their 19,000 brethren in the Protestant faith that they might have the rights assured by the Peace of Westphalia of the free exercise of their religion or of emigration. This petition showed for the first time what the statistical proportions of the problem were. Finally, the Salzburg government called in Austrian troops, and in November 1731, in midwinter, expelled all Protestants over twelve at eight days' notice, with no opportunity to clear up their affairs. There were rumours that a Prussian army was to be sent in; instead a rescue operation was mounted which was one of the most remarkable achievements of eighteenth-century government. Thousands of Salzburgers made their way through neighbouring territories which did not want to give rights of passage, were picked up by Prussian commissaries in various parts of Swabia, marched in columns by different routes to ease the billeting problem, to Berlin, and then on to Pomerania, East Prussia and Lithuania, paid a daily subsistence allowance on the way, and rapidly settled in domestic service or on peasants lots. The poor Salzburgers had to face a second winter without proper housing, but they did get themselves provided for, and soon the Prussian government supplied them with churches, clergy and schools, and set about getting some return on the property they had had to abandon in Salzburg. After an initial contumacy, in which some even threatened to turn Papist, the Salzburgers settled down, and those who read contemporary novelists like Bobrowski and Siegfried Lenz, who write about East Prussia and Lithuania as they were just before the last war, will have come across them, still a distinct population marked out by its own customs and methods of making sauerkraut. The whole operation cost the Prussian government half a million thalers, but they got about 20,000 settlers, the largest group to be displaced in Germany since the Reformation. The Dutch subscribed 400,000 thalers and got 788 Dürrenberger miners and settled them partly at Flushing and partly on an island in the Mass estuary, where they mostly sickened and died.[23] The English subscribed 228,000 thalers and got a first instalment of 200 who were settled near Savannah by the Georgia Trustees with two ministers sent from Halle, and put under the general spiritual oversight of the Wesley brothers. The Archbishop of Salzburg got the enthusiastic congratulations of the Pope, but, unable to fill the spiritual vacuum he had created, also got what is supposed to be the oldest centre of hard-core working-class atheism among the salt miners at Hallein, and a diocese in which female dress was regulated with exemplary minuteness but in which money was not safe in the bank and collapse was imminent.

The propaganda generated by the episode is as interesting as the episode itself. As the Salzburgers marched across Europe they were catechized in every town and treated to endless sermons which were sold to raise funds on their behalf.[24] The catechizing proved that, notwithstanding the allegations of the Salzburg government, after centuries without a church, they were still Lutherans with rights under the Westphalia settlement, not an unrecognized sect. The Salzburgers, even more than the Silesians before them, had found not so much an alternative church as an alternative to the church, and in doing so had left an indelible mark on the history of Protestant revival. As Valentin Ernst Löscher, the great spokesman of Saxon Orthodoxy,[25] put it in amazement:

> it is astonishing that so many thousands should become Protestants without teachers, in the midst of the Kingdom of anti-Christ under the power of the Pope of Rome, without special human leadership . . . We knew almost nothing of them, and those who did know something of them reckoned the secret brethren of the faith at scarcely some hundreds and behold there are many thousands of them . . .

The charity sermons went out with emotional line-drawings of the Salzburgers turning their back on their mountain homeland for the sake of the faith, and depicted them carrying a fat baby under one arm and the Luther Bible under the other, or with a fat baby under each and Luther's shorter catechism. The evidence was that in the absence of all the routines of church life, the Bible and a quite small number of Reformation classics were capable of keeping faith alive. Is there any wonder that the English proto-evangelicals, sick at the feebleness of the church and their own personal failings, should have their eyes opened to the forgotten sustenance still contained in this kind of literature?[26] Their agonies, indeed, were perfectly well-known in Germany, the spies of Halle reporting back on the respective merits of Mr Wesley and Mr Whitefield (whom they preferred),[27] and the great Weimar Orthodox journal, the *Acta Historico-Ecclesiastica*, giving a highly circumstantial account of the toils Wesley got into in Savannah, which reads very oddly beside his own account.[28]

But there was another kind of propaganda for which the Prussian government made itself responsible with the minimum of disguise. One huge work of seven enormous volumes, published at Halle, gave the crop yields for every settler in Georgia; another monster, written in the house of one of the members of the Prussian government, described in similar detail the settlements around the Baltic.[29] The case was clearly being made in the most circumstantial way possible that to leave the realms of Anti-Christ and Habsburg was a way to serve not merely God but Mammon, and was speedily to be put to the test. There were, as we have seen, Czechs at Gross Hennersdorf bitterly opposed to the living conditions, religious restrictions and the attempts of Henriette von Gersdorf to put them in bondage. Led by Liberda, and supported by the other exiles from Teschen, Sarganek and Steinmetz, and by the younger Francke, a deputation obtained an audience with the King of Prussia in 1732, and proposed to make the Hennersdorf Czechs the advance guard of a new train of 30,000 Czechs from Bohemia who should be settled with the Salzburgers in East Prussia. Frederick William, as usual, temporized, but patience was not in the nature of any of the parties he was dealing with. Liberda dashed off into Bohemia armed with supplies of his spiritual works, the *Key of David* and the *New Harp*, which had a proved revolutionary effect. No sooner had he left Hennersdorf than the bulk of the Czechs there uprooted, and marched off to Berlin in mid-winter, where they were set to work in a textile factory and became one of the basic units of the Berlin proletariat. When Liberda got into Bohemia, he found a peasant revolt already under way, with agitators claiming to bring great promises from the King of Prussia, and he drafted the rebels' petition, Salzburg style, claiming freedom of conscience or an unimpeded passage to Prussia. Alas! the Habsburg government hit hard and crushed the rebels. But the basic situation remained unchanged, the Protestant emissaries still came in, a steady trickle of secret emigrants went out, and there was another peasant revolt in 1738. When Liberda got back to Hennersdorf he was dragged off in chains to Dresden, convicted of high treason, and imprisoned in one of the most notorious gaols in Saxony. The Czech congregation in Berlin, however, begged the King to get them Liberda as their minister. Frederick William actually laid on a gaol-break attempt and at the third try Liberda escaped, taking his gaoler with him, and both took refuge in Berlin. The next stage of the story, Frederick the Great's direct assault upon Silesia, and his cynical efforts, with Liberda's assistance, to get up another Czech revolt in 1741, all of which made the young sceptic the Protestant hero of innumerable public-house signs in England,[30] falls outside the limits of this paper. It is worth, however, seeing what was happening in Inner Austria.

In Styria and Carinthia features familiar from Salzburg and Bohemia were combined.[31] As in Bohemia, the persecutions of the previous two centuries had dislodged the Protestant nobility, leaving only peasants behind; but, as in Salzburg, the Protestant peasantry were a minority, conforming on occasion to Catholic worship, though in the long mountain valleys of Upper Styria and Carinthia many of them lived miles from a parish church and were not much disturbed. In these equivocal circumstances the only prophylactic against absorption into a dead Catholicism lay in basing a live family-worship upon the Bible and a few other approved books.[32] There had been a lively sympathy in Austria for the victims of persecution in Salzburg in the 1680s, and one of those expelled, Joseph Schaitberger, became the first of the working-men revivalists in Austria, leaving a permanent memorial in his spiritual writings and songs. The crisis in Salzburg in 1731 produced great excitement in Austria. The Government closed the passes into Salzburg on pretext of cattle-plague to keep out the Salzburgers, only to be embarrassed by the efforts of their own Catholic peasants to break into Salzburg on a massive scale to take advantage of the collapse of land prices after the Protestant emigration. In Graz and Klagenfurt religious commissions were established to keep the situation under control and to keep a lookout for Prussian agents. The Austrian government produced the names to the Corpus Evangelicorum of Salzburgers and Carinthians sent in with religious literature and assistance to those who wished to emigrate; Prussian agents were well known to be there too, but were not taken red-handed.[33] There is no mistaking, however, the level of religious excitement. The Habsburgs resorted to their heavy weapons, drafting Protestants into the army and transporting others to its own frontier area in Transylvania. Yet the troubles went on; there was more unrest in Carinthia between 1738 and 1741, and when the whole Habsburg system was imperilled by Frederick the Great's incursion into Silesia, Vienna feared a Protestant uprising in Carinthia.

The later stages of the Protestant movements in Inner Austria and Bohemia fall outside the scope of this paper. It could hardly have been accidental that there were serious troubles as events led up to the Seven years' War, and that disturbances in Inner Austria immediately preceded the great Czech peasant uprising of 1775. Each of these troubles produced fresh emigration to Prussia, though nothing more on the Salzburg scale. For this there were several reasons. Frederick was too cynical by half in manipulating religious grievances and the Czechs, bent on preserving nationality and liberty at all costs, became too clever for him. So, too, in their way did the Habsburgs. If they had to cede Silesia, they would not give up the key-point of Teschen; they confronted heresy not only with force, but with improved church organization and a missionary appeal of a new character.[34] Above all, the thoroughly anti-Protestant government of Joseph II began by ending the worst forms of personal servitude in 1780 and introducing religious toleration in 1781. This was trebly profitable. It produced immediate relaxation of political tension; it tempted some of Prussia's ill-used Czechs back home; and it ensured that the next round of peasant discontent went not into the now tolerated Protestant churches, but into weird sects with often fantastic views. The days when religious revival sprang from the conjunction of Protestant self-help and Prussian conspiracy were over. The sign of Habsburg victory at home was that nineteenth- and twentieth-century statues of St. John of Nepomuk could bear the face of Hus; the proto-Protestant could be pressed into Catholic service.

The impulse given by these events was now, however, beyond the reach of any of the Central European governments. Revival began to break out in America, first among those German communities most closely in touch with Halle, and then amongst New Englanders also in touch with Halle. When Halle finally became the prisoner of a Prussian state which cared nothing for its universal ends, Zinzendorf's Moravians developed a world-wide mission, and both directly and on the rebound from America left their mark in England. Above all, the evidence, at a time when the Protestant world outside the Westphalia ring-fence reached its crisis, that with a bit of assistance, with the scriptures and the pure milk of the Reformation word, popular Protestantism could pull itself up by the boot-straps in a remarkable and unecclesiastical way, created self-fulfilling expectations which lasted on a large scale till the end of the nineteenth century and are not yet dead.

Moreover, the political and social ambiguities which are usually dis-cussed on an absurdly narrow basis in relation to Halévy and Methodism were there from the beginning. The religion which was a tool of state policy at Halle was that of a country opposition to a baroque court in Württemberg much as the earliest Methodism seems to have been related to the opposition to Walpole. The same Lusatian Pietist gentry who incited the Czechs to rise against serfdom proposed to enserf them as soon as they got over the border. Germans and Czechs from adjacent Bohemian villages went opposite ways; the one into universal evangelism and a forswearing of politics, the other into the defence of a national tradition by a mixture of intense trade unionism and political intrigue. The so-called 'tunnel', decades before Wesley's conversion, had seen many of the themes of

Methodist history rehearsed in advance by a strange mixture of forces of revival, renewal and resistance operating in the most varied contexts between the Russian and the American frontiers of the European world.

Notes

1 Lecture delivered in the John Rylands University Library of Manchester on Wednesday, 7 May 1980.

2 Rupert Davies, *Methodism*, London, 1963, pp. 11–23. The affirmation in the first sentence of this chapter clearly counts much more than the qualification in the last.

3 *Journal of the Rev. John Wesley*, ed. Nehemiah Curnock, 2nd ed., London, 1938, ii. 20–57.

4 On this see E. Winter, *Halle als Ausgangpunkt der deutschen Russlandkunde im 18. Jahrhundert*, [East] Berlin, 1953, and E. Winter, *Die Pflege der West- und Süd-slavischen Sprachen in Halle im 18. Jahrhundert*, [East] Berlin, 1954.

5 On this see e.g. Hugo Hantsch, *Reichsviezekanzler Friedrich Karl Graf von Schönborn*, Augsburg, 1929; Alfred Schröcker, *Ein Schönborn im Reich*, Wiesbaden, 1978; and cf. Norbert Huber, *Österreich und der Heilige Stuhl (1714–21)*, *Archiv für österreichische Geschichte*, Bd. 126, Vienna, 1967.

6 On the crisis of 1719 see Karl Borgmann, *Der deutsche Religionstreit der Jahre 1719/20* (Berlin, 1937); Andreas Biederbick, *Der deutsche Reichstag zu Regensburg im Jahrzehnt nach dem Spanischen Erbfolgekrieg, 1714–24*, Unpub. diss., Bonn, 1937). Only the contemporary discussions (e.g. J.J. Moser, *Teutsches Staatsrecht*, 21 vols. Nuremberg & c., 1737–54, i 119–78; Burcard Gotthelf Struve, *Ausführliche Historie des Religionsbeschwerden zwischen denen Römisch-Catholischen und Evangelischen im Teutschen Reich*, Leipzig, 1722; and the resolutions of the Corpus Evangelicorum, (E.C.W. von Schauroth, *Vollständige Sammlung aller Conclusorum, Schreiben, und anderer übrigen Verhandlungen des hochpreisslichen Corporis Evangelicorum . . . bis auf die gegenwärtigen Zeiten*, Regensburg, 1751–2), give any impression of the labour involved in getting the provisions of the religious peace agreed at Westphalia, to work. A brief introduction to all this is given in my paper, 'Orthodoxy, Enlightenment and Religious Revival', in *Studies in Church History*, xvii above pp. 16–37.

7 The voluminous literature on Pietism is briefly introduced by Martin Schmidt, *Pietismus*, Stuttgart/Berlin/Cologne/Mainz, 1972; for an example of the recent work, Johannes Wallmann, *Philipp Jakob Spener und die Anfänge des Pietismus*, Tübingen, 1970.

8 Klaus Deppermann, *Der Hallesische Pietismus und der preussische Staat unter Friedrich III (I)*, (Göttingen, 1961); Carl Hinrichs, *Preussentum und Pietismus*, Göttingen, 1971.

9 Gerhard Oestreich, *Friedrich Wilhelm I*, (Göttingen, 1977), p. 82.

10 See reference in note 4 above.

11 *Sozial Revolution und Reformation. Aufsätze zur Vorreformation, Reformation und zu den Bauernkriegen in Sudmitteleuropa*, ed. Peter F. Barton, (Vienna/Cologne/Graz), 1975; *Rebellion oder Religion?*, ed. Peter F. Barton and László Makkai, Budapest, 1977.

12 G. Biermann, *Geschichte des Protestantismus in Oesterreichische-Schlesien*, Prague, 1897, pp. 65–92; *Geschichte Schlesiens*, ed. L. Petry and J. Joachim Menzel, Darmstadt, 1973, ii 95–135. On the diplomacy of Altranstädt see Norbert Conrads, *Die Durchführung der Altranstädter Konvention in Schlesien*, Cologne/Vienna, 1971.

13 On the past history of this see Gustav Hoffmane, *Die religiöse Bewegungen in der evangelischen Kirche Schlesiens während des siebzehnten Jahrhunderts*, Breslau, 1880. For Silesian religious verse, see Julius Mützell, *Geistliche Lieder der evangelischen Kirche . . . von Dichtern aus Schlesien . . .*, Brunswick, 1858; repr. Hildesheim, 1975.

14 Hildegard Zimmermann, *Caspar Neumann und die Entstehung der Frühaufklärung. Ein Beitrag zur schlesischen Theologie- und Geitesgeschichte im Zeitalter des Pietismus*, Witten, 1969.

15 On this subject in general see E. Winter, *Die tschechische und slavische Emigration im 17. und 18. Jahrhundert*, [East] Berlin, 1955; on the Jesus Church at Teschen, Oskar Wagner, *Mutterkirche viele Länder. Geschichte der evangelische Kirche im Herzogtum Teschen, 1545–1918/20*, Vienna/Cologne/Graz, 1978.

16 E.g. Stanislaw Michalkiewicz, 'Einige Episoden aus der Geschichte der schlesischen Bauernkämpfe im 17. und 18. Jahrhundert', in *Beiträge zur Geschichte Schlesiens* ed. Eva Maleczynska [East] Berlin, 1953, pp. 356–400. Compare Czech views in papers by Polišenský and others in *Probleme der Ökonomie und Politik in den Beziehungen zwischen Ost- und Westeuropa von 17. Jahrhundert bis zur Gegenwart* ed. Karl Obermann, [East] Berlin, 1960; also Wladyslaw Czoplinski, 'Die Polnische-deutschen Beziehungen in den Jahren von 1525–1795', in *Polen und Deutschland*, ed. H. Ludart and G. Rhode, Cologne/Graz, 1963, pp. 73–7.

17 For independent revivals in Bohemia, D. Cranz, *The Ancient and Modern History of the Brethren*, London, 1780, pp. 91–2.

18 Elisabeth Kovács, 'Die Verehrung des hl. Johannes von Nepomuk am habsburgischen Hof und in der Reich- und Residenz- hauptstadt Wien im 18. Jahrhundert', in *250 Jahre Hl. Johannes von Nepomuk. Katalog der IV Sonderschau des Dommuseums zu Salzburg*, Salzburg, 1979, pp. 69–85. Characteristically, one of the favourite atrocities of the Protestant hordes let loose on Silesia in 1740 by Frederick the Great was to bowl over the statues of St. John of Nepomuk (A. Theiner, *Zustande der katholischen Kirche in Schlesien, 1740–58*, Regensburg, 1852, i. 4).

19 J.G. Carpzov, *Religionsuntersuchung der Böhmisch- und Mährischen Brüder von Anbeginn ihrer Gemeinen bis auf gegenwärtigen Zeiten*, Leipzig, 1742, pp. 405–7.

20 L. Ranke, *Memoirs of the House of Brandenburg and the history of Prussia*

during the seventeenth and eighteenth centuries, repr. New York, 1969, i 231, 336–7. For the diplomatic setting of the Salzburg crisis see Loesche (n. 21 below,) and J. K. Mayr, 'Zur Geschichte der Emigration der Salzburger Protestanten von 1731/2', in *Jahrbuch der Gesellschaft für die Geschichte des Protestantismus im ehemaligen und im neuen Österreich*, lii (1931), 136–47.

21 On the following, generally, see Gerhard Florey,*Geschichte der Salzburger Protestanten und ihrer Emigration, 1731–2*, Vienna, 1977. Cf. H. Widmann, *Geschichte Salzburgs*, Gotha, 1907–14, iii 315–449; Georg Loesche, 'Neues über die Ausrottung des Protestantismus in Salzburg, 1731/2', in *JGGPÖ*, I (1929), 4–201.

22 Karl Klamminger, 'Leopold II Anton Eleutherius Freiherr von Firmian', in *Die Bischöfe von Graz-Seckau, 1218–1968*, ed. Karl Amon, Graz/Vienna/Cologne, 1969, pp. 336–9.

23 Since 1972 the descendants of the Dürrenbergers have had their own historical journal published at Groede (Netherlands). The East Prussian Salzburger Verein, founded in 1911, was dissolved by the Russians in 1945, but was reconstituted at Bielefeld in 1952/3, and since 1962 has also had a journal. Bernard H. Zimmerman, 'Salzburger Glaubensfluchtlinge in dem Nederlanden und in Ostpreussen', *JGGPÖ*, lxxxix (1973), 183–7.

24 The British Library has a collection of these sermons and cartoons at 1012 d. 30; see especially V.E. Löscher, *Drey Predigten von der Erkanntnis und der Ehre des Sohnes Gottes* (Dresden, 1733), p. 26. Cf. J.G. Hillinger, *Beytrag zur Kirchen-Historie des Erzbischoftums Salzburg* (Saalfeld, 1732).

25 For Löscher see Martin Greschat, *Zwischen Tradition und Neuen Anfang. Valentin Ernst Löscher und der Ausgang der lutherischen Orthodoxie* (Witten, 1971).

26 The Protestant crisis inside and outside the Westphalia ring-fence was being circumstantially reported in England at the time of Wesley's conversion (see e.g. *The Present State of Germany*, London, 1738, vol. 1, pp. vii, 36) but was in any case perfectly well-known. English historians neglect the Hanoverian role of George I and even George II as Protestant crusaders; on this see Martin Naumann, *Österreich, England und das Reich 1719–1732*, Berlin, 1936.

27 Karl Zehrer, 'Die Beziehungen zwischen dem hallesischen Pietismus und dem frühen Methodismus', in *Pietismus und Neuzeit*, ii (1975), 43–56.

28 *Acta Historico-Ecclesiastica*, ii. 405–24; iii. 1087; iv. 885–95.

29 S. Urlsperger, *Ausführliche Nachricht von dem Saltzburgischen Emigranten die sich in America niedergelassen haben*, Halle, 1744–52; Gerhard Gottlieb Guenther, *Vollkommene Emigrationis Geschichte von deren aus den Ertz-Biss-thum Saltzburg vertrieben und grössentheils nach Preussen gegangen Lutheranern*, Frankfurt/Leipzig, 1734–7.

30 Manfred Schlenke, *England und das friderizianische Preussen, 1740–1763*, Freiburg/Munich, 1963. On the later history of the religious question in Silesia, see G. Jaeckel, 'Die Bedeutung der konfessionellen Frage für die Besitzergreifung Schlesiens durch Friedrich den Grossen', in *Jahrbuch für schlesische Kirche und Kirchengeschichte*, N.F. xxxiv, Düsseldorf, 1955, 78–121.

31 For the following: Hans von Zwiedenek-Südenhorst, 'Geschichte der religiösen Bewegung in Inner-Österreich im 18. Jahrhundert', in *Archiv für österreichische Geschichte*, liii, Vienna, 1875, 457–546; Bernhard Raupach, *Evangelisches Oesterreich das ist historische Nachricht von dem vornehmsten Shicksalen der evangelisch-Lutherischen Kirchen in dem Ertz-Herzogthum Oesterreich*, Hamburg, 1732; *Acta Historico-Ecclesiastica*, i. 769–808, 293–307, 403–4; ii. no. 7, 6–10, 734–42; iii. 1162–6.

32 Assimilation could be a spiritual peril even in Protestant Upper Lusatia. On how it might be offset by revival see Cranz, *Ancient and Modern History*, p. 86n.

33 August Leidl, 'Die religiöse und seelsorgliche Situation zur Zeit Maria Theresias (1740–1780) im Gebiet des heutigen Österreichs', in *Ostbairische Grenzmarken*, xvi, Passau, 1974, 176.

34 On this see Rudolf Reinhardt, 'Zur Kirchenreform in Österreich unter Maria Theresia', in *Zeitschrift für Kirchengeschichte*, lxxvii (1966), 105–19; Adam Wandruszka, 'Geheimprotestantismus, Josephinismus und Volksliturgie in Oesterreich', in *Zeitschrift für Kirchengeschichte*, lxxviii (1967), 94–101; Heinrich Ferihumer, *Die Kirchliche Gliederung des Landes ob der Enns im Zeitalter Josefs II*, Linz, 1952; Elisabeth Kovács, *Ultramontanismus und Staatskirchentum im Theresianisch-Josephenischen Staat*, Vienna, 1975, pp. 13–55; August Leidl, 'Die religiöse und seelsorgliche Situation zur Zeit Maria Theresias'; Ferdinand Maas, *Der Frühjosephinismus*, Vienna/Munich, 1969, pp. 36–40.

6

Enlightenment in early Moravianism[1]

Sustained by Marxists and by non-Marxists the historiography of the Enlightenment has become a major intellectual industry. Yet the relation of the pioneers of religious renewal and revival, Francke, Zinzendorf, Wesley, even Jonathan Edwards, to the new currents of thought and feeling remains as obscure as it ever was. The first three seem to be middlemen between so many pairs of opposites as to form a standing trap for unwary inventors of ecumenical pedigrees,[2] while even Edwards could not say what he wanted to say without adapting the psychology of Locke. It seems inappropriate to grant to Zinzendorf and Wesley, who were intelligent, practical men, the status of colossi bestriding their age, gathering up and harmonizing all its currents;[3] and whether the historian pins his faith to the structure of thought or reports the changing nuances of sentiment and opinion, he is hard put to explain why Wesley could borrow heavily from the Moravians and from Bengel, when the latter and Zinzendorf were not on speaking terms, or how Zinzendorf could pursue lifelong a philadelphian ideal and yet quarrel with everyone of independent mind whom he encountered, driving even the faithful Spangenberg to complain that 'to me his addresses often appeared paradoxical and his methods of business extraordinary'.[4] Again, one of Scholder's tests for the religion of enlightenment, that of 'religion as the means and way to a better life',[5] is too catholic a category to be useful, and would exclude hardly anyone in the milieu of Herrnhut or Halle.

In a brief article it would be foolhardy to attempt to restructure eighteenth-century intellectual history as a whole; but the difficulties in the Zinzendorf literature are worthy of note. Too much of the literature about Zinzendorf, from Spangenberg's official *Life* onwards, has been written by professional theologians, treating Zinzendorf as if he were a professional theologian, which, for both good and ill, he was not; and too much of this theological literature has been directed to the question whether

First published in Kerkhistorische Opstellen aangeboden aan Prof. dr. van den Berg (Kampen, 1988), pp. 114–127.

or not he was a Lutheran. Given what Cranz called the ancient and modern history of the Brethren, this is not a negligible question; but, however it is resolved, it will not cast much light on the relations of Zinzendorf, an eminently international man,[6] and the head of a cosmopolitan missionary community, to wider currents of thought and feeling. As many difficulties arise if the student commences from the revivalists' fresh approach to the age-old problem of Christianising the people, and their new stance towards inherited confessional divisions. Granted the periodisation long current in German theological scholarship, in which the age of Orthodoxy is followed by those of Pietism and Enlightenment, and allowing for the necessary overlaps, Zinzendorf must be located near the common frontiers of the ages of Pietism and Enlightenment. This placing runs counter to the commonest explanation of the 'time of sifting', that Zinzendorf was reacting hard and early to the spiritual pressure of the Enlightenment, and, more importantly, to the brilliant and sympathetic portrait of Zinzendorf written from within his community and from an Enlightenment standpoint by Baron von Schrautenbach. He held that 'in the times in which we now live such a community institution would develop with difficulty, and entail much joyless toil upon its creators and promoters. How astonishingly different from today were those times which have scarcely passed from us. Education, light, generally diffused knowledge, were much less than they are now. There was less international fellowship among men across the globe . . . Habits were rough, always a step nearer nature, fierceness, too, irritability, energy . . . a general longing among all men for fellowship, with a whole caboodle of opinions and very uncertain foundations.'[7]

Even had Zinzendorf not thus been summarily consigned to a period which, twenty years after his death, seemed already like ancient history, two difficulties would still remain. Even within the field of religion and theology, the alleged transition from Orthodoxy to Pietism to Enlightenment excludes too much that matters. Religious revival was not the same as Pietism, and neither had any necessary connexion with the Spanish mystics and with the French writers like Mme Guyon and Antoinette Bourignon who were often at loggerheads with their own church authorities; yet the leaders of revival, and especially Zinzendorf, were in fact greatly taken up with them, and with a range of other intellectual concerns secular and sacred. And what of Enlightenment? A notion that once had a precise and particular reference[8] has been extended to cover two continents and over a century in time,[9] and now resembles the hazy global concept used for blanket condemnation by the propagandists of the romantic era. In this respect the boom in Enlightenment studies has perpetuated an obstacle to understanding from which it promised release. It is not helpful to be told of so vast and undifferentiated a phenomenon, that a change of mood set in after 1786, or that the 'true Enlightenment' began then to be perceived.[10] Notwithstanding all the local variations, so cosmopolitan a concept as the Enlightenment[11] must itself be given some kind of structure and periodisation if it is to be usable. The one serious attempt to do this has been made in America with American conditions in mind. Henry May divides the history of the Enlightenment into four periods.[12] The first period, which he calls the moderate or rational enlightenment, 'preached balance, order and religious compromise, and was dominant in England from the time of Newton and Locke until about the middle of the eighteenth century'. This was followed by the sceptical enlightenment in which the lead was taken in France. 'Its method was wit, its grand master Voltaire . . . if it was pursued systematically it issued either in the systematic epistemological scepticism of Hume or the systematic materialism of Holbach'. The third category, 'the Revolutionary Enlightenment', beginning with Rousseau and culminating in Paine and Godwin is too late to concern a Zinzendorf who died in 1760, but the fourth category, in which May has most trouble with dates, 'the Didactic Enlightenment, a variety of thought which was opposed both to scepticism and revolution but which tried to save from what it saw as the débâcle of the Enlightenment the intelligible universe, clear and certain moral judgments, and progress', is of some interest for comparative purposes. Its chief triumphs in Scotland came in the years following the Seven Years War; its American heyday in the first quarter of the nineteenth century.

The biggest differences between the history of the Enlightenment in Protestant Germany and the Protestant West came in the later eighteenth century when the men of *Aufklärung* got to work on the scriptural and theological bases of a tougher Orthodoxy than any which existed in the West. Despite all the political differences, there was a good deal in common between them in the first half of the eighteenth century. It proved impossible anywhere fully to implement the ideals of the confessional state, and, on the back of failure, ideas of toleration flourished. These ideas might be given a distinctively religious content, or might embody the Enlightenment principle that the state must deal with its subjects as it found them, and not as confessional organisation promised ineffectively to make them. There was a coherence in the Protestant world which enabled the foundation ideas of Leibniz, Newton, and Locke to be discussed everywhere, and this coherence was sustained by large and durable compromises. Leibnitz wanted to bridge over the confessional divide in Europe,[13] and with rather more success, justified the ways of God to men.[14] To Locke the lighthouse-beam of reason was powerful but narrow; to the delight of more conservative rationalists it proved the existence of God, but it left so much in darkness as to create little embarrassment for spokesmen of red-

blooded revelation like Wesley.[15] Newton testified impressively to the
regularities of the stellar universe, without surrendering the idea that he
was investigating the ways of an active and benevolent God, and helped
to push the radicals who saw the new principles issuing in republicanism,
materialism and pantheism into an underworld of conspiracy and freemasonry.[16] Christian Wolff, the uncrowned king of German philosophy
in the period, saw no reason to abandon the old metaphysics where
its useful life could be prolonged.[17] The old warring Orthodoxies had
somehow to accommodate that new knowledge of God which modern
science had made available to mankind in general without respect to
confessional distinction,[18] and in the first half of the eighteenth century the
leading prophets of Enlightenment offered eclectic compromises calculated
to minimize the drawbacks of the old metaphysics and the most painful
excesses of the confessional state, and to contain religious and political
radicalism. The epistemological scepticism that was to confront their
fudges in Hume was not yet to be foreseen. If they compromised, so did
the pioneers of religious revival who achieved prominence right across the
Protestant world between the late twenties and early forties. This is why
it is not difficult to represent Zinzendorf as an eccentric pioneer of early
enlightenment or as an inveterate opponent of it.

On the latter front, the Christocentrism of Zinzendorf put him decisively
against the creeping, or as he believed in later life, the galloping, Socinianism
of the Enlightenment, an opposition which involved far-reaching matters
of intellectual vocabulary and style. A Moravian conference in 1747 raised
'the distinction between Arianism & Socinianism; the first is a downright
poysonous enmity against our Son; & a scandalous speculation about
what place & ranke he has with his father. But Socinianism declares our
Sav.ʳ to be a meer man, but ye most sweet & lovely man that ever liv'd,
who has for *himself* merited to be God, & for *us* has obtained happiness
by his satisfaction. The Arians also used to make very little of Baptism &
ye Lord's Supper; but ye Socinians are not so, but are only too nice &
critical about them & will subtilize much.'[19] More brusquely, Zinzendorf
'once said to a Unitarian, "Your opinion is damnable because no converted
person ever held it."'[20] These opinions were reinforced by the fact that in
the Netherlands, where Zinzendorf chiefly encountered Socinianism and
where he professed to believe that a couple of hundred churches were
surreptitiously[21] being taken over by it,[22] he recruited successfully among,
and received invaluable financial support from,[23] those Mennonites who
were resisting the inroads of the new views.[24] But the same forces were
at work in the established church (where Zinzendorf championed the
resistance of Domine Bruinings),[25] and seemed to him to be related to the
general feebleness of the old establishments. 'The teachers in ye religions

saw yt. there was no more any coming thro' with their medley of Law & Gospel, sin & vanity prevailing so very much, & therefore they have kept Synods, Conferences, Chapters &c. in order to put a stop to ye disorder, & to give a lift to decaying Christianity. Hence they have come upon this: the fault must be in ye doctrine concerning our Sav.ʳ Faith there is no want of, ye people know enough, if they did but practise it, & hereupon [they] have preached up morality with all earnestness, & ye Philosophers, Deists, Socinians & Arians, have directly joined them & strengthen'd those stupid persons in their idle conceit' to get round the law.[26] This emphasis so coincided with Spangenberg's own as to be prominently represented in his *Life* of the Count.[27]

For all his Trinitarianism, Zinzendorf sharply rejected the school theology which he had inherited with it, and the metaphysical setting of that theology, and ranted against 'system' with all the vehemence of a *fin-de-siècle* English evangelical.[28] Opposition to system carried over into denunciation of the Franckean scheme of the Christian life, the Hallesian method of conversion. All such schemes Zinzendorf castigated quaintly as 'Methodisms', as 'pedantic, scholastic, fanatical or even nonsensical'[29] believing that the *Busskampf* was a 'self-induced sickness', an affront to the cheerful Christianity for which he stood.[30] On his own reckoning Zinzendorf had 'no systematic head',[31] and this encouraged a fair amount of writing and preaching against 'philosophy'. Philosophy encouraged slavery to system, the belief that reason established the limits of religious questions,[32] and it worked with bloodless abstractions ('transcendent ideas of God's incomprehensibleness & philosophical perfection . . . by which [the philosophers'] high-mind and self-conceit can always be maintained').[33] Zinzendorf always had a preference for concrete and sensual images,[34] for blood and wounds; he did not care for 'precision' in the use of language,[35] but as befitted a writer who was a poet rather than a professional theologian, was adept at using words in new ways to convey what was to him the intimate reality of the Saviour in the heart.[36]

Having discovered two generations before the English evangelicals and nearly three before Newman, that the Bible was not a text book of systematic theology, Zinzendorf created as well as solved difficulties on the points both of language and of 'heart religion'. Zinzendorf was a practitioner of what became known in the English evangelical tradition as the 'language of Canaan'. The problem was that the Brethren must speak the word of grace in a Babel of not merely secular but also theological languages. If they entered into 'the language of the Saviour and his apostles' they could put the 'simple meaning of Scripture which is as clear as day and moves the heart' to 'Mennonite, Socinian, Arian, Gichtelian, Behmenist, Anglican, Nonconformist, Remonstrant, Quaker, Separatist and whatever else is non-Lutheran, (all of which lack insight rather than commitment of the heart)', as well as to Lutherans if what they spoke (and here Zinzendorf was paradoxical but lucid) was '*Apostolisch Teutsch (nicht aber Theologisch und Lateinisch Teutsch)*.'[37] This process of sympathetic identification, of 'entering in', was the key not merely to appropriating the benefits of the cross, but of appropriating the Bible, and grasping the real meaning of church history. The essence of the Bible was its testimony to the reconciliation of men with God through the blood of Christ,[38] and to grasp this required not scholarship but the prayer and industry to interpret one part of the Bible by another.[39] It ought indeed to be possible to get a church history which should be not theological polemic teaching by examples but the real history of the true philadelphia, the heart-believers of whatever confession, down the ages, and for this the Count applied to both Jena and Tübingen.[40]

Zinzendorf admitted that 'heart religion' 'makes the great difficulty between us and the rationalists and men of reason . . . We do not argue that the cause of the Saviour would not be solidly reasonable and deep wisdom . . . But the thing which is controverted between us and occasions their ridicule, is that they think, if they are to speak of things with understanding and wisdom, then they must be found absolutely appropriate to the standards of their reason . . . What is not illuminated to them by their indescribably limited reason, this the dear God has not willed.'[41] The doctrine of the Trinity, in short, was not to be put out of court by the rules of arithmetic. Nevertheless the depreciation of 'reason' as compared with the 'heart' appeared consistent with Zinzendorf's use of the lot as a solution to disagreements and a brake on feelings.[42] Zinzendorf believed himself warranted in the use of the lot both by biblical example and the sanction of Luther, but he developed its use on a scale altogether beyond what current opinion approved as a means of concluding evenly-balanced decisions;[43] and he took it into the realm of personal choices, marriages, travel and business arrangements. The use of the lot received merited obloquy in that monument of the *Aufklärung*, Schlegel's *Kirchengeschichte*,[44] while the 'heart-religion' encouraged Emanuel Hirsch to conclude that Zinzendorf rooted religion in the feelings, a view decisively rejected by the main line of German theological development in the eighteenth century[45].

In fact the 'heart religion' shows how close Zinzendorf, the international man, was to Enlightenment of another kind, that of Locke and the English. Locke had held that 'all ideas come from sensation or reflection . . . from EXPERIENCE',[46] and Hume too reckoned that 'belief is more properly an act of the sensitive than of the cogitative part of our natures.'[47] Wesley and Jonathan Edwards had believed that the Holy Spirit created a spiritual sense; if it was in the end impossible to explain this experiential basis, this Anglo-Saxon 'heart-religion', to those who did not have it, it provided a bond of unity amongst those who did, much as Zinzendorf said. At the height of the 'time of sifting' Zinzendorf could declare that 'we cannot sing, "Litle Side Hole, thou art mine", the Holy Spirit our dear church-mother, must intervene with us, at least with the imperceptible ideas which one cannot bring into words and developed ideas, but which are certainly present, accompanied by the tenderest feeling and the exhalation of the most inward tenderness and love, which belong to the words which no one can utter but the Holy Spirit understands . . . Before [our ideas] reach the level of apprehension by the brain, He understands what they mean for He produces [*fabriziert*] them'. This passage is said to illustrate the dependence of Zinzendorf on the psychology of Leibniz,[48] but it closely resembles the use the Anglo-Saxon evangelicals had to make of Locke as they sought to escape the thraldom of seventeenth-century theology to system and metaphysics. As Zinzendorf put it elsewhere, 'Religion cannot be rationally apprehended while it is repugnant to experience' (*Empfindung*).[49] This was not a turning from reason to emotion, but a use of Enlightenment for the purpose in hand.

The portrait of an anti-Enlightenment Zinzendorf may be balanced by a portrait of an Enlightenment Zinzendorf. The German Enlightenment, it has been noted, began and ended with attempts to popularize things French. In 1687 Christian Thomasius gave a university lecture for the first time in German on the theme, 'How best to imitate the French in everyday life?' In 1792 the Mainz Jacobin club championed the same cause on a popular political level. Thomasius had to take refuge in Prussia, the Mainz Jacobins in France.[50] Zinzendorf (who fetched up in England) also began with Thomasius and French culture. Thomasius seems to have seen in Zinzendorf a representative of the sort of modern lay culture and religion for which he stood; he encouraged the publication of his journal, *Der Teutsche Sokrates*, and told him that though his enemies were legion he might 'see a peasant who could combine philosophy and faith. [Zinzendorf] answered, "I might have the pleasure of presenting to him a great number of such peasants".'[51] Unable to follow up these enlightened pleasantries by a visit to the great man as he lay dying, Zinzendorf sent him a poem.[52] His aristocratic appropriation of French literature was exemplified in the *Lecteur royale* (1733 and 1736) which he produced for the Crown Prince of Denmark, which presupposed a knowledge of Montaigne, La Rochefoucauld, La Bruyère, Montesquieu, and Fénélon's *Télémaque*. He liked reading Molière and La Fontaine before going to sleep, and concerned himself with Saint-Évremond, Ninon de Lonclos, and Manon Lescaut von Provost.[53] Even at the height of the 'time of sifting' Zinzendorf could say that fanaticism was much worse than philosophy, was indeed a sort of pseudo-philosophy (*Afterphilosophie*) making pretentions to ultimate truth on behalf of men 'who could say as little certain about the origin, coherence and harmony of the universe as could a couple of mice in the cellar of the Escorial about building plans of the palace'.[54]

This last passage illustrates both the fact that Zinzendorf had more options than Orthodoxy and Enlightenment to choose among, and also his curious relationship with the two early pillars of enlightenment, German and French, Leibnitz and Bayle. Towards Leibnitz whose global plans had attracted the great Halle generation of Pietists,[55] Zinzendorf was at first well disposed. He was impressed by his historical sense and his development of the use of source materials;[56] he kept a personal copy of Leibniz's plan for the reunion of the churches;[57] he was permanently marked by Leibniz's treatment of God's omnipotence and was as touched by his *Theodicy* as by Racine's *Alexandre* or Corneille's *Cinna*.[58] In later life the Count was markedly cooler. It was partly a question of his difficulties with philosophy in general and system in particular,[59] partly that he feared that forcing religion into a fine-spun rational harmony was no substitute for faith, and made faith harder by giving the impression that belief was a mathematical problem.[60] Still worse, the world was not only irrational, it was also evil. Philosophy transformed human need into ignorance, and Christian perfection into knowledge; an age of research somehow remained shallow.[61]

This cooling towards rationalism owed much to a precursor of enlightenment as paradoxical as Zinzendorf himself, Pierre Bayle, the stormy petrel of the Huguenots.[62] Zinzendorf once shocked Dippel by declaring that Bayle's *Dictionnaire historique et critique* was his favourite reading after the Bible.[63] He studied him hard in 1727[64] and referred to him in print as 'in his ill-starred way, the incomparable Bayle.'[65] The abiding impression made on Zinzendof by Bayle was the divorce both in style and substance between philosophy and theology. 'I believe and teach: philosophy has nothing to do with theology: our metaphysical, physical, mathematical ideas ought not to be, and must not be, mixed in theology, whether we want to help or hinder theology . . . Let people clarify their minds with philosophy as long as they like, but tell them as soon as they wish to become theologians, they must become children and idiots . . . let us bid philosophy good-night for ever and lay the foundations of our wisdom'.[66] This view of the matter opened some rather dangerous doors during the 'time of sifting'; it barred the way to a simple *aufklärerisch* aspiration to revivify Christianity by the pure streams of modern knowledge, and it undercut the metaphysical proofs of the existence of God. On the other hand it aided the progress of Enlightenment by encouraging a relaxed attitude to rational corrosion of the props of Orthodoxy, and in particular its notion of the verbal inspiration of Scripture. As the Count noted, this doctrine could hardly have been known to the apostles who habitually quoted Old Testament Scriptures from the Septuagint.[67] And if Zinzendorf did not believe that the essence of Christianity consisted in an opinion or resided in the brain,[68] he held firmly to the liberal notion that there was an essence of Christianity, and that that essence was faith in the Lord Jesus Christ.[69] Pure reason, even basing itself on Christ produced 'a pure skeleton or *corpus inanimatum*'. Pure imagination, even starting from the same point, built a house of straw. The two in balance (that classic characteristic of the first period of the Enlightenment) generated 'skilful preaching of the Word and pastoral guidance. *Physica experimentalis* is the model of theology'.[70] Zinzendorf is back to practical ends and the desire for a 'useful reason.'[71]

Zinzendorf's aristocratic contempt for 'academic moles'[72] and his eclectic approach to the intellectual resources of his generation were reinforced by the fact that he had more interests to provide for than the champions of Orthodoxy. He had to free himself from mysticism, while recognising that in the mystical literature, and perhaps especially in the great wave of Spanish literature which had impressed the Pietists before him,[73] there was nourishment for spiritual vitality. He was a man of letters whose *Teutsche Sokrates* took its cue from Addison's *Spectator*,[74] and whose defensive autobiography was also in the style of the moral weeklies which took the German literary market by storm.[75] He praised the English moderns, Tillotson and Stillingfleet,[76] though his friend and biographer Schrautenbach thought he did not achieve Tillotson's fine finish.[77] He was a major hymn writer and minor poet whose verse expresses the spirit of Enlightenment,[78] and was approved by his inveterate theological enemy Sigmund Baumgarten, the modernising and historicising spokesman of Halle.[79] The other side of the coin was formed by the curious paradoxes in Zinzendorf's doctrine of toleration. He was from his youth up hostile to the confessional Orthodoxies, even those deriving from the 'idea of a Reformation where one himself thought & acted, & did not let ye Sav[iou]r think & act' which led 'on one side [to] heat and vehemence, & on ye other side [to] tyranny, & at last open wars'.[80] Small wonder that, notwithstanding his affection for the Augsburg Confession, his advice to the Cardinaal de Noailles was that 'Je ne vous conseille pas vous faire enrôler chez Les dits Réformés ou Lutheriens, dont je ne suis pas moins, qui suis Chrétien simple et adhérant à la Confession d'Augsbourg, parce que je n'en sais pas de meilleure qui soit publisé et parce qu'elle et le Commencement du rétablissment de l'Evangile'[81] A Zinzendorf who as a young man in the Netherlands learned how many confessions there were,[82] had at one and the same time to deny that any of the warring parties possessed a monopoly of grace and truth, and to affirm that all possessed some portion, that each was a realisation of Christian belief and practice in different conditions of climate and national character,[83] and that for that reason, syncretism and watering down were anathema.[84] The same Zinzendorf who counselled (though did not always practise) gentleness to those whose doctrine or practice was repugnant to him,[85] was unwilling to allow liberty of reading to himself or anybody else.[86]

Spangenberg declared that Zinzendorf loved both the natural and political peculiarities of Upper Lusatia,[87] and in many ways he is to be looked on as a naturalised and acclimatised Upper Lusatian. In Jakob Boehme's lifetime it had been clear that the independence of Upper Lusatia would fall victim to one or other of the warring Orthodoxies, Lutheran (embodied in Saxony), Reformed (embodied in the Winter King of Bohemia), Counter-Reformation (championed by the Habsburgs). Boehme's life is most easily understood as an attempt to provide an alternative to all three, and so, in the changed conditions of the eighteenth century, was Zinzendorf's. As a young man he read all the opposition writers, everything except dogmatic literature; and he embodied much of the mystical tradition of Silesia and Lusatia. Zinzendorf pioneered his own middle way, which had to take account of modern rationalism, and, in the spirit of the early Augustan age, hold in balance what was valuable in the religion and the culture of the day. The effort to do so was very characteristic of the first period of the Enlightenment; when substantial changes in political organisation became unavoidable after the Seven Years War, Enlightenment itself became more doctrinaire.

Of course once, at the peak of his career, in the 'time of sifting', Zinzendorf himself failed to preserve the balance, and toppled into a *Schwärmerei* from which he himself had to order the retreat.[88] It is instructive both of Moravianism and of the age generally, that, after his death in 1760, the balance could not be maintained at all. Spangenberg pushed the flock steadily back towards Lutheran Orthodoxy in language theology and devotion. By this device Spangenberg obtained the recognition of *Landeskirchen* but lost even the relative independence of a school or style of Lutheranism. From Kant to Harnack the Brethren followed whatever was the dominant current in Lutheran theology, distinguished only by their avoidance of radical extremes – no 'German Christians', no *Bekennende Kirche*, no truck with Karl Barth till he was an established figure after the Second World War, and, of course, very little Zinzendorf.[89] Indeed in 1880 the Brethren sold Zinzendorf's books in order to invest in factories.[90] In Denmark the settlement at Christiansfeld, promoted by the dynasty in the name of Enlightenment, turned against that standpoint only when radical rationalism began to establish itself in the state church.[91]

On the other hand the reconciliation with Orthodoxy did not inhibit a notable development of scientific studies among the Brethren,[92] nor the Count's cousin Lutz taking up Enlightenment with enthusiasm.[93] Those who wished to look back sympathetically on their early history from an Enlightenment standpoint found no difficulty in doing so. Most memorably the Baron von Schrautenbach wrote a brilliant biography of Zinzendorf under a text taken from the Enlightenment in the world of letters – 'Hence we find our happiness in religion alone, in virtue and the witness of a good conscience, in the hope of a better life which cheers our outlook and leaves no room for anxious misgivings about missing the true and the blessed' (Laurence Sterne)[94] – not least comparing him with David Hume's portrait of Cromwell. Lessing, quite in the spirit of Sterne could praise Zinzendorf for pointing men 'to the only thing which can create us a happy life, to virtue', though he complained that he did not set up as a theological reformer.[95] Herder too could rejoice that Zinzendorf had directed men to the 'end of religion which consists in active love in fraternal and sociable harmony',[96] and others could note that the Count's view that 'religions are matters of nationhood, modified according to the ordinary sociable disposition of the people'[97] anticipated much that Herder had to say about national character. In a famous passage Goethe admitted the fascination of the Brethren's model of peace, harmony and active employment, no less than the example of his cousin Katherina von Klettenberg, though he was not in the end able to accept the doctrine of total depravity.[98] And sometimes the sympathetic retrospect was coloured by nostalgia for a great eccentric who, right or wrong, could address his contemporaries with distinction. Here Lavater may stand for the rest: 'In Spangenberg's *Idea fidei fratrum* I find the most reasonable compromise between Lutheranism and Herrnhutism, but no beam of higher light . . . I find very little in the more modern literature of the Brethren to strike out (*auszustreichen*) as unscriptural, but also much less to strike up (*unterstreichen*) as great, original or deeply felt, than in Count Zinzendorf's unworldly writings.'[99] Not until Schleiermacher who could claim to 'have become after everything a Hernhuter again, only of a higher order'[100] was there a fresh synthesis; and he was a German romantic counterpart of Scottish Moderatism.

Notes

1 *Abbreviations*: The Olms reprint of the works of Zinzendorf (Hildesheim, 1962–) is referred to by the following abbreviations:

ZW *Zinzendorf Werke*
HS *Hauptschriften*
EB *Ergänzungsbände zu dem Hauptschriften*
Other volumes referred to by series and volume numbers.

2 E.g. A.J. Lewis, *Zinzendorf the ecumenical pioneer. A Study in the Moravian contribution to Christian mission and unity*, London, 1962: ZW EB 10 p. cxxx.

3 Even if the idea of 'representative personality' were acceptable. M.R. Breitwieser, *Cotton Mather and Benjamin Franklin. The price of representative personality*, Cambridge, 1984, pp. 1–4.

4 A.G. Spangenberg, *Declaration über die Zeither gegen uns ausgegangen Beschuldigungen*, Leipzig/Görlitz, 1751, p. 18 (Repr. in ZW EB 5).

5 Klaus Scholder, 'Grundzüge der theologischen Aufklärung in Deutschland', in *Geist und Geschichte der Reformation. Festgabe Hanns Rückert zum 65. Geburtstag*, Berlin, 1966, pp. 460–486 (Repr. in *Aufklärung, Absolutismus und Bürgertum in Deutschland* ed. Franklin Kopitsch, Munich, 1976, p. 297).

6 Zinzendorf gave more practical substance to the claim that the world was his parish than did Wesley. Hans-Walter Erbe, *Zinzendorf und der fromme hohe Adel seiner Zeit*, Leipzig, 1928, p. 120 (Repr. in ZW Reihe 2 Bd. 12 p. 492).

7 Ludwig Carl Freiherr von Schrautenbach, *Der Graf von Zinzendorf und die Brüdergemeine seiner Zeit*, Gnadau/Leipzig, 1851), pp. 16–17 (Repr. in ZW Reihe 2 Bd. 9). Schrautenbach handed over the original MS. to the Brethren in 1782.

8 John Lough, 'Reflections on *Enlightenment* and Lumières', *British Journal for Eighteenthy-Century Studies* 8 (1985) 1–15.

9 '. . . den Zeitraum vom ausgehenden siebzehnten Jahrhundert bis zur Mitte des neunzehnten Jahrhunderts'. Franklin Kopitsch in *Aufklärung, Absolutismus und Bürgertum in Deutschland* p. 47.

10 Werner Schneiders, *Die wahre Aufklärung. Zum Selbstverständnis der deutschen Aufklärung*, Freiburg/Munich, 1974, pp. 82–6.

11 Thomas J. Schlereth, *The cosmopolitan ideal in Enlightenment thought*, Notre Dame, Indiana, 1977.

12 Henry F. May, *The Enlightenment in America*, New York, 1976, p. xvi.

13 F.X. Kiefl, *Der Friedensplan des Leibniz zur Wiedervereinigung der getrennten Christlichen Kirchen*, Paderborn, 1903: repr. Hildesheim, 1975.

14 When John Witherspoon arrived from Scotland to be President of Princeton in 1766, and proved unexpectedly to be a champion of Scottish Moderatism, he placed 'Leibnitz's Theodisays and Letters' at the head of his student reading-list. May, *op. cit.* p. 63.

15 Frederick Dreyer, 'Faith and Experience in the Thought of John Wesley', *American Historical Review* 88 (1983) 21–24.

16 Margaret C. Jacob, *The Radical Enlightenment: Pantheists, Freemasons and Republicans*, London, 1981.

17 Christian Wolff, *Logic or Rational Thoughts on the powers of the human understanding*, London, 1770, p. lxvi.

18 Thomas P. Saine, 'Was ist Aufklärung? Kulturgeschichtliche Überlegungen zu neuer Beschaftigung mit der deutschen Aufklärung', *Zeitschrift für deutsche Philologie* 93 (1974) 522–545 (Repr. in Kopitsch, *op. cit.* (n. 5 above) pp. 319–44 esp. p. 327).

19 Moravian Church House, London MSS. Gemeinhaus Diarium. (Eng. tr.), Nov. 19, 1747.

20 Schrautenbach, *Graf Zinzendorf* p. 52 (Repr. in *ZW* Reihe 2 Bd. 9).

21 Surreptitiously, because the open profession of Socinian views was still illegal. A.G. Spangenberg, *Leben Zinzendorfs*, Barby, 1773–5, 4, 949 (Repr. in *ZW* Reihe 2 Bd. 4).

22 Nikolaus Ludwig von Zinzendorf, ΠΕΡΙ ΕΑΥΤΟΥ. *Das ist Naturelle Reflexiones* . . . (n. pl. or d. [1746]) p. 236 (Repr. in *ZW EB* 4).

23 See my paper on 'Zinzendorf and Money' in *Studies in Church History* vol. 25, pp. 283–305.

24 Moravian Church House MSS. Gemeinhaus Diarium May 30, 1747: May 29, 1747.

25 David Cranz, *Alte und Neue Brüder-Historie*, 2nd ed. Barby, 1772, p. 433 (Repr. in *ZW* Reihe 2 Bd. 11).

26 Moravian Church House MSS. Gemeinhaus Diarium Feb. 19, 1748.

27 Spangenberg, *Leben Zinzendorfs* p. 1562 (Repr. in *ZW* Reihe 2 Bd. 6). Zinzendorf had the prudence to avoid the familiar trap awaiting Trinitarians of explaining the doctrine of the Trinity. 'When our Count had to do with Socinians, he witnesses with a warm heart and much emphasis on the Godhead of our Lord Jesus Christ. Among brethren and sisters, however, who had been saved from their sins by him, and had experienced him as Lord and God in their hearts, he was not in the habit of going into lengthy proofs of his divinity.' *Ibid.* pp. 1342–3 (Repr. in *ZW* Reihe 2 Bd. 5). However his language in relation to the Trinity (Father, mother and bridegroom) was singular to himself, and created a good deal of offence, as late in life Zinzendorf candidly acknowledged. Otto Uttendörfer, *Zinzendorf und die Mystik*, Berlin, [1950], p. 333.

28 N.L. von Zinzendorf, *Der Predigten die der Ordinarius Fratrum von 1751 bis 1755 zu London gehalten hat* Zweyter Band, London/Barby, 1757, p. 37 (Repr. in *ZW, HS* BD. 5). He greatly admired Benjamin Whichcote, the Cambridge theologian of the Commonwealth period for his defence of toleration and opposition to systematic theology N.L. von Zinzendorf, *Der Teutsche Sokrates*, Leipzig, 1732 p. 98 (Repr. in *ZW HS* Bd. 1).

29 N.L. von Zinzendorf, *Die gegenwärtige Gestalt des Kreuz-Reichs Jesu in seiner Unschuld* (n. pl., 1745) p. 27 (Repr. in *ZW EB* 5): *ZW HS* 6 p. IX: N.L. von Zinzendorf, *Theologische und dahin einschlagende Bedenken* (Büdingen, 1742) p. 63 (Repr. in *ZW EB* 4): Zinzendorf, *Naturelle Relfexiones* pp. 38, 65. (Repr. in *ZW EB* 4): Schrautenbach, *Graf Zinzendorf* p. 76 (Repr. in *ZW* Reihe 2 Bd. 9). The Count had, however, a 'method of converting savages' in 25 steps: *Büdingische Sammlung*, Büdingen, 1742–1745, 3.90–91 (Repr. in *ZW EB* 9).

30 N.L. von Zinzendorf, *Einiger seit 1751 . . . zu London gehalten Predigten*
    Bd. 1. London/Barby 1756, p. 205 (Repr. in *ZW HS* Bd. 5): Moravian Church
    House MSS. Gemeinhaus Diarium May 12, 15, 1747: Herrnhut MSS. R2
    A23a: R20 A2, 22, 33.

31 Zinzendorf, *Der Teutsche Sokrates* p. 231 (Repr. in *ZW HS* 1).

32 *Ibid.* p. 133.

33 Moravian Church House MSS. Gemeinhaus Diarium March 5, March 19,
    1747.

34 Gerhard Reichel, *Zinzendorfs Frömmigkeit im Licht der Psychoanalyse*,
    Tübingen, 1911, p. 125 (Repr. in *ZW* Reihe 2 Bd. 13 p. 125).

35 *ZW HS* 1 p. IX. This is clearly a reference to Wolff's attempt to apply
    mathematical logic in every sphere of intellectual life.

36 *ZW HS* 3 pp. xvi–xvii.

37 *Büdingische Sammlung* 1. 226–8 (Repr. in *ZW EB* 7): A.G. Spangenberg,
    Apologetische Schlussschrift, Leipzig/Görlitz, 1752, p. 69 (Repr. in *ZW EB*
    3).

38 *Ibid.* p. 204.

39 N.L. von Zinzendorf, *Sonderbare Gespräche zwischen einem Reisenden und
    allerhand andern Personen* . . . , Altona, 1739, p. 5 (Repr. *ZW HS* 1).

40 Moravian Church House MSS. Gemeinhaus Diarium March 2, 1748.

41 Quoted in Sigurd Nielsen, *Intoleranz und Toleranz bei Zinzendorf*, 3 vols.
    Hamburg, 1952–60 2. 170.

42 Cf. Spangenberg, *Apologetische Schlussschrift* pp. 212–3, 314–5 (Repr. in
    ZW EB 3).

43 Cf. *Journal of John Wesley* ed. N. Curnock, 2nd ed. London, 1938, 2. 56.

44 Johann Randolph Schlegel, *Kirchengeschichte des achtzehnten Jahrhunderts*,
    3 vols. Heilbronn, 1784–96, 2. 874.

45 Emanuel Hirsch, *Geschichte der neuren evangelischen Theologie*, 5th ed.
    Gütersloh, 1975, 12. 406–7.

46 John Locke, *An essay concerning human understanding* Bk 2 Ch. 1 § 2.

47 David Hume, *The Philosophical Works* ed. T.H. Green and T.H. Grose,
    London, 1886: repr. Aalen, 1964, 1. 475.

48 Otto Uttendörfer, *Zinzendorf und die Mystik*, Berlin, [1950], p. 249.

49 Zinzendorf, *Der Teutsche Sokrates* p. 290 (Repr. in *ZW HS* 1). On the
    equivalence of *Empfindung* and 'sensation' see *Historisches Wörterbuch der
    Philosophie* ed. Joachim Ritter, Darmstadt, 1972 2. 457, 462: Rudolf Eisler,
    Wörterbuch der philosophischen Begriffe, Berlin, 1927, 1. 325.

50 Thomas P. Saine, 'Was ist Aufklärung?' (see n. 16 above), Kopitsch, p. 323.

51 Zinzendorf, *Der Teutsche Sokrates* Vorrede (Repr. in *ZW HS* 1): Spangen-
    berg, *Leben Zinzendorfs* 2. 337–9 (Repr. in *ZW* Reihe 2 Bd. 2).

52 *Ibid.* 3. 505 (Repr. in *ZW* Reihe 2 Bd. 3).

53 *ZW EB* 2 pp. x–xi.

54 *Zeitschrift für Brüdergeschichte* 13 (1919) 12–13 (Repr. in *ZW* Reihe 3 Bd.
    4).

55 Peter Baumgart, 'Leibnitz und der Pietismus. Universale Reformbestrebungen um 1700'. *Archiv für Kulturgeschichte* 48 (1966) 364–386.

56 *ZW HS* 3 p. XIII.

57 *ZW EB* 10 p. L.

58 *ZW EB* 2 p. XXVIII: Zinzendorf, *Teutsche Sokrates* Vorrede n. (Repr. in *ZW HS* 1).

59 N.L. von Zinzendorf, *Die an den Synodum der Brüder in Zeyst . . . gehaltene Reden* (n. pl. 1746–7) p. 179 (Repr. in *ZW HS* 3).

60 *Ibid.* pp. 246–7 (Repr. in *ZW HS* 3).

61 Zinzendorf, *Londoner Predigten* 1. 341–2: 2. 337 (Repr. in *ZW HS* 5).

62 On this subject generally see Erich Beyreuther, 'Die Paradoxie des Glaubens. Zinzendorfs Verhältnis zu Pierre Bayle und zur Aufklärung', in his *Studien zur Theologie Zinzendorfs. Gesammelte Aufsätze*, Neukirchen, 1962 pp. 201–234.

63 Uttendörfer, *Zinzendorf und die Mystik* p. 85.

64 Spangenberg, *Leben Zinzendorfs* 3. 467 (Repr. in *ZW* Reihe 2 Bd. 3): Schrautenbach, *Graf Zinzendorf* p. 86 (Repr. in *ZW* Reihe 2 Bd. 9).

65 Zinzendorf, *Teutsche Sokrates* p. 252 n. (Repr. in *ZW HS* 1).

66 N.L. von Zinzendorf, *Jeremias, ein Prediger der Gerechtigkeit*, 2nd ed. Frankfurt/Büdingen, 1741, p. 100 (Repr. in *ZW EB* 6).

67 On Zinzendorf's exegesis generally see Erich Beyreuther, 'Bibelkritik und Schriftverstandnis' in *Studien zur Theologie Zinzendorfs* pp. 74–108.

68 Zinzendorf, *Teutsche Sokrates* pp. 212–3 (Repr. in *ZW HS* 1).

69 Zinzendorf, *Londoner Predigten* p. 146 (Repr. in *ZW HS* 5). The phrase 'das Wesen der Religion' occurs in the *Teutsche Sokrates* p. 267 (Rep. in *ZW HS* 1).

70 *Zeitschrift für Brüdergeschichte* 6 (1912) p. 201 (Repr. in *ZW* Reihe 3 Bd. 2).

71 Zinzendorf, *Teutsche Sokrates* p. 38 (Repr. in *ZW HS* 1).

72 'Academische Maulwürfe'. *Zeitschrift für Brüdergeschichte* 4 (1910) 96 (Repr. in *ZW* Reihe 3 Bd. 2).

73 E.g. Herbert Stahl, *August Herrmann Francke. Der Einfluss Luthers und Molinos auf ihn*, Stuttgart, 1939.

74 P. 24 (Repr. in *ZW HS* 1).

75 Zinzendorf, ΠΕΡΙ ΕΑΥΤΟΥ *Das ist Naturelle Reflexiones*. Cf. Wolfgang Martens, *Die Botschaft von Tugend. Die Aufklärung im Spiegel der deutschen Moralischen Wochenschriften*, Stuttgart, 1968.

76 *Teutsche Sokrates*, pp. 102–3 (Repr. in *ZW HS* 1).

77 Schrautenbach, *Graf Zinzendorf* p. 73 (Repr. in *ZW* Reihe 2 Bd. 9).

78 *ZW EB* 10 p. xxvii.

79 *Geistliche Gedichte [von Zinzendorf]. Erster Samlung mit einer Vorrede Sigm. Jacob Baumgartens*, Halle, 1748 pp. 7–8.

80 Moravian Church House MSS. Gemeinhaus Diarium, May 28, 1747.

81 *ZW EB* 10 p. xxvii–xxviii.

82 Peter Baumgart, *Zinzendorf als Wegbereiter historischen Denkens*, Lübeck/

Hamburg, 1960 pp. 20–21. Zinzendorf tried to account for this by an elaborate argument based on the two natures of Christ. Pierre Deghaye, 'Die Religionen und die eine wahre Religion bei Zinzendorf', *Unitas Fratrum* 14 (1983) 58–94. But cf. the attack on Deghaye in Leiv Aalen, 'Die esoterische' Theologie des Grafen von Zinzendorf. Zur Auseinandersetzung mit der Abhandlung von Pierre Deghaye: *La doctrine ésoterique de Zinzendorf*, in *Pietismus – Herrnhutertum – Erweckungsbewegung. Festschrift für Erich Beyreuther* ed. Dietrich Mayer, Köln, 1982, pp. 207–263.

83 Nielsen, *Intoleranz und Toleranz bei Zinzendorf* 2. 136.

84 Zinzendorf, *Die gegenwärtige Gestalt des Kreuzreiches Jesu* p. 29 (Repr. in *ZW EB* 5).

85 Spangenberg, *Leben Zinzendorfs* pp. 639, 678 (Repr. in *ZW* Reihe 2 Bd. 3): Zinzendorf, *Sonderbare Gespräche* . . . pp. 150–2 Repr. in *ZW HS* 1).

86 Spangenberg, *Apologetische Schlussschrift* p. 459 (Repr. in *ZW EB* 3): Theodor E. Schmidt, *Zinzendorfs soziale Stellung und ihr Einfluss auf seinen Charackter und sein Lebenswerk*, Basel, 1900, p. 51.

87 Spangenberg, *Leben Zinzendorfs* p. 178 *(Repr. in ZW* Reihe 2 Bd. 2).

88 Oskar Pfister, *Die Frömmigkeit des Grafen Ludwig von Zinzendorf. Eine psychoanalytische Studie*, 2nd ed. Leipzig/Wien, 1925, p. 95 (Repr. in *ZW* Reihe 2 Bd. 13 p. 727): *ZW HS* 3 p. xxiv.

89 Werner Reichel, 'Samuel Christlieb Reichel in seiner Entwicklung zum Vertreter des 'Ideal herrnhutianismus', '*Zeitschrift für Brüdergeschichte* 6 (1915) 1–44 (Repr. in *ZW* Reihe 3 Bd. 2): *ZW EB* 10 pp. xii–xiii.

90 *ZW EB* 7 p. xii.

91 A. Pontoppidan Thyssen, 'Die Bedeutung der Herrnhuter im Kampf gegen die Aufklärung am Beispiel Christiansfeld' *Unitas Fratrum* 16 (1984) pp. 38–44.

92 J.W. Stolz, 'Bibliographie der naturwissenschaftlichen Arbeiten aus dem Kreise der Brüdergemeine' *Zeitschrift für Brüdergeschichte* 10 (1916) 89–127 (Repr. in *ZW* Reihe 3 Bd. 4.)

93 Horst Weigelt, *Die Beziehungen zwischen Ludwig Friedrich zu Castell-Remlingen und Zinzendorf sowie ihr Briefwechsel*, Neustadt a.d. Aisch, 1984, p. 46.

94 Schrautenbach, *Graf Zinzendorf* p. 1 (Repr. in *ZW* Reihe 2 Bd. 9). A less successful defence of Zinzendorf in the same vein was made by another propertied adherent of the community, von Schachmann. Horst Orphal, 'Karl Adolph von Schachmanns Leben und Apologie für Zinzendorf', *Unitas Fratrum* 9 (1981) 71–101.

95 G.E. Lessing, *Sämtliche Schriften* ed. K. Lachmann, Stuttgart/Leipzig, 1886–1924, 14. 154–63 esp. p. 160.

96 J.G. Herder, *Sämtliche Werke* ed. B. Suphon, Berlin 1877–1913, 24. 36–7. Cf. Gerhard Meyer, 'Zinzendorf als Vertreter des Ost-deutsch-schlesischen Frömmigkeitstypus', *ZW* Reihe 2 Bd. 12. 758.

97 Quoted in Baumgart, *Zinzendorf als Wegbereiter historische Denkens* pp. 41 n. 246, 55.

98 J.W. von Goethe, *Autobiography* ed. K.J. Weintraub, Chicago, 1970 2. 269–73 (Bk. 15). Fraulein von Klettenberg was of course the original of the 'schöne Seele' of *Wilhelm Meister* Bk. 6.

99 Gerhard Reichel, *August Gottlieb Spangenberg. Bischof der Brüderkirche* (Tübingen, 1906) pp. 203–31 (Repr. in ZW Reihe 12, 13. 246–7).

100 *Aus Schleiermachers Leben. In Briefen* ed. L. Jonas and W. Dilthey, 2nd ed. Berlin 1860–63, 1. 295.

7

The Renewed Unity of the Brethren: Ancient Church, New Sect or Interconfessional Movement?

The origins of the Renewed Unity of the Brethren – 'Moravianism' in common English parlance – are of more than normal complexity. Regarded by some, though not all, of its original adherents as a rebirth of the old Unity of the Brethren, a body which had succumbed to the violent pressure of the Counter Reformation in its old heartlands of Bohemia and Moravia, it was attacked by its Orthodox opponents either as a new sect with no right to toleration in the Holy Roman Empire, or as 'indifferentist', i.e. as denying the ultimate importance of confessional loyalty on the way to salvation. By its principal champion, Zinzendorf, it was usually prized as an interconfessional movement, but even he had no scruple in accepting an Act of the British Parliament on behalf of his followers in America in 1749 based on the claim that the Unity was 'an antient apostolical and episcopal church'.[1] For each of these views there was some solid evidence, since the Renewed Unity arose from the conjunction of three distinct elements. There were German-speaking Protestant emigrants from Bohemia and Moravia; there was a much larger number of religious refugees of other sorts attracted by the toleration which became available at Herrnhut; and there was Zinzendorf himself who bought the Berthelsdorf estate on which they settled, and who came to pursue his own religious objectives through the heterogeneous flock he found he had gathered. Amid so many shifting sands it is well to begin by sketching the complex progress of the Count himself.

Nikolaus Ludwig von Zinzendorf (1700–1760) was the grandson of an Austrian Protestant nobleman, who in 1661 had joined the great emigration

First published in *Bulletin of the John Rylands University Library of Manchester* 70 (1988), pp. 77–92.

of the Protestant aristocracy, and the son of a privy councillor in the service of Saxony. Dying less than two months after Nikolaus was born, his father's principal legacies to the boy were a connexion through his mother, Charlotte Justine, Baroness of Gersdorf, with the restless aristocracy of Upper Lusatia,[2] and the tradition of a family which had grown great in the struggle against the Turks,[3] but had finally put confessional solidarity with the Protestants ahead of service with the Habsburgs or the defence of Christendom against the heathen. From the beginning, the young Zinzendorf was marked by traditions of piety which had grown up in East and South-East Europe,[4] and to the end he was concerned with the settlement of most of the frontiers of the Protestant world, with Silesia, the Baltic, Georgia and Pennsylvania alike. In 1704 his mother married the Prussian Field Marshal Dubislav Gneomar von Natzmer, and left the boy to be brought up at Gross Hennersdorf in Upper Lusatia by another widow, his grandmother, Henriette Catherina von Gersdorf, née Friesen. As a business-like blue-stocking possessed of all manner of languages she, like her new son-in-law, was intimately associated with the Pietist clans pushing the new university and charitable institutions at Halle. As a Friesen she was in the thick of the aristocratic resistance to the centralizing policies pursued by the Electors of Saxony, now kings of Poland. She shared the family view that new methods, administrative, educational and religious, were needed to put the enserfed Slavonic populations of Lusatia, the Sorbs and Wends, to rights. Material for this was supplied from Halle.[5] Devout but shrewd, she was a model of the aristocratic political commitment on which, much against her will,[6] Zinzendorf was eventually to turn his back; but Upper Lusatia and his grandmother were to leave an indelible mark upon him, an independence of mind and spirit. A supporter of Halle, Henriette was not a slavish adherent of Halle Pietism.[7] Spangenberg declared that Zinzendorf, who but for the untimely deaths of his father and grandfather would have been brought up in court society at Dresden, loved both the natural and political peculiarities of Upper Lusatia.[8] And as late as 1753 a German tourist in London was surprised to hear him preaching at the Fetter Lane chapel in 'a quite simple and common Upper Lusatian dialect'.[9]

In his official biography of Zinzendorf,[10] Spangenberg felt committed to producing a portrait of a boy of quite unusual religious virtuosity and to support it by legends and by the other other material available to him, viz. Zinzendorf's own recollections of his youth, preserved long afterwards in publications and addresses. There seems no doubt that Zinzendorf early conceived a lively personal devotion to his Saviour,[11] sustained by an affection for the old Lutheran hymnody. He claimed that at the age of five he was persecuted for laying claim to a dependence on the Saviour it was supposed he could not have, and that an unflattering portrait of him was transmitted to Halle which he could never live down.[12] But later testimony about Halle is all coloured by the world-wide contest between Halle and Herrnhut which began in the 1730s. Cranz, the official historian of the Brethren, did his best to obliterate altogether the Hallesian background to their history and thus achieved a smoother transition from what he called the ancient to the modern history of the Brethren than the facts warranted. Zinzendorf was impressed by the preaching he heard at Halle and still more by the sense of being at the hub of a world-wide movement of grace.[13] He learned a healthy distrust of children's revivals (prominent as these were to be in the awakening at Herrnhut), but out of a revival movement he gathered a circle of friends who were to form his Order of the Grain of Mustard Seed, his international and interconfessional mission to the whole church.[14] His poems suggest that he combined a sort of Bernardine Christ-mysticism and the contemplation of the sufferings of the Saviour with an impulse to conversion.[15] From Halle he proceeded to Wittenberg where he was certainly an odd fish. With much exaggeration he later claimed that he left 'with Wittenberg theory and Halle practice'.[16] In fact a good deal of his time there was spent in experimenting with 'things indifferent', dancing, billiards, balloons, and, worst of all, one of his fundamental aristocratic traits, gambling.[17] Finally, however, he did form an Order of the Slaves of Virtue on the model of the English SPG which rejected 'things indifferent' entirely,[18] and made serious contact with Luther himself at least once.[19] The Grand Tour was more educational. Holland opened his mind to the possibilities of religious toleration, one of the great themes of his life thereafter.[20] A stay in Paris improved his acquaintance with the religious struggles of the Jansenists, Mme Guyon and Fénelon, and brought him the friendship of Cardinal de Noailles, who was later a member of the Order of the Grain of Mustard Seed[21] and godfather to two of his children.[22] It brought also an exaggerated impression of the money to be made out of Law's Bubble.[23] He returned from his journey convinced that God had his true followers in every confession and that he would on no account adopt a party standpoint.[24] He had come round to the mystical outlook of the radical Pietist, Gottfried Arnold.

Between 1721 and 1727 Zinzendorf obtained an independent position and, most importantly, in 1722 married Erdmuthe Dorothea, Countess Reuss of Ebersdorf. Erdmuthe Dorothea was very much Zinzendorf's second choice as a wife.[25] But she proved an admirable helpmate in his labours and travels, possessed a much better head for business than he had, and brought him invaluable financial assistance in his early years. The marriage, moreover, connected Zinzendorf with a family which was central to that network of intermarried imperial courts which did so much to sustain the Pietist enterprise.[26] His wife's grandmother had been a highly prized friend of Spener; and the Ebersdorf court was in the inner circle of the Halle policy-makers with its connexions across the Empire from Silesia to the Wetterau. More immediately, Ebersdorf offered a pattern of Christian existence of the sort for which Zinzendorf was now looking. It was not a parish in its own right. The castle congregation easily separated from the parish church, inviting preachers of their own like the revivalist Hochmann von Hochenau.[27] The important positions at the Ebersdorf court were filled by Christians without respect to sect or party, and they cohered harmoniously in the castle congregation on the basis of a common love of the Saviour. This model deeply impressed Zinzendorf and was what he wanted to reproduce when he built a house for himself and his wife at Herrnhut.[28] As it transpired, the Ebersdorf *ecclesiola* eventually joined the Renewed Unity of the Brethren.

Zinzendorf's personal development towards a philadelphian reconciliation of mysticism, pietism and orthodoxy was not at all interrupted by events on the estate at Berthelsdorf which he purchased from his grandmother; but it encountered strains of its own. There is no question that he suffered severe intellectual doubts.[29] These, combined with his personal devotion to the Saviour, though allowing him to take communion peacefully, would often cause him to shake for twenty-four hours before or afterwards.[30] Like many of the original Halle generation, he was at first strongly attracted by Leibniz.[31] But he had difficulties with philosophy in general and system in particular.[32] He came to feel that forcing religion into a fine-spun rational harmony was no substitute for faith; it made faith harder by creating the impression that belief was a mathematical problem.[33] Moreover, the world was evil as well as irrational; Christian perfection was not, in the mathematical sense, knowledge.[34] Some relief in this quandary was provided by that stormy petrel of the early Enlightenment, Pierre Bayle, whom Zinzendorf studied assiduously in 1727 and came to admire.[35] The moral drawn by the Count from Bayle was the divorce both in style and substance between philosophy and theology:

> I believe and teach: philosophy has nothing to do with theology: our metaphysical, physical, mathematical ideas ought not to be, and must not be, mixed in theology whether we want to help or hinder theology . . . Let people clarify their minds with philosophy as long as they like, but tell them as soon as they wish to become theologians they must become children and idiots . . . [36]

This view had its perils during the 'time of sifting' in the 1740s. But for the moment it protected faith and the Living God[37] on two fronts, against a mechanistic view of the universe and against the Orthodox insistence on the literal inspiration of the Bible. Zinzendorf developed, but never abandoned, the religious objectives which he pursued in the 1720s. Originally they had nothing to do with those of the Moravian refugees brought on to his estates from 1722 onwards by Christian David.

David was a characteristic product of the Habsburg attempt forcibly to recatholicize Bohemia and Moravia. He was the son of a Czech father and a German mother, both poor and both strict Catholics. He had, however, a speculative mind and pronounced independence of character. At the age of twenty, having been in touch with secret Protestants, he underwent a severe spiritual struggle in which he almost became a Jew,[38] but ended with firm Protestant convictions. Conversion was followed by emigration to a Protestant land, an experience which taught David that there were innumerable German Protestants who could see no hope of survival except in the guarantees of the Treaty of Westphalia and who did not want to know about the problems of Protestant minorities in the Habsburg family lands where they had no internationally guaranteed rights. He was directed to Görlitz, one of the six towns of Upper Lusatia, where there had been a town fire and where there was plenty of work for carpenters. There he met a sympathetic soul in the parson Melchior Scheffer, who was involved in planning and financing Zinzendorf's philadelphia on the Berthelsdorf estate. He also met Johann Schwedler, another connection of the Count, whose church at Niederwiesa had been built on the northern, Saxon, bank of the Queis to provide a refuge for the churchless Protestants in Silesia. He was a man of unrivalled repute for his pastoral and political care of the Silesians, not to mention his nine-hour sermons.[39] Christian David could not be restrained from making the perilous journey home, where he found that the secret Protestants with whom he was in touch were responding to the revivalist preaching and inflammatory politics of Steinmetz and his coadjutors at the grace church in Teschen, not far away in Upper Silesia.[40] Revivals were breaking out amongst those who could no longer bear with the equivocations involved in the secret practice of the faith,[41] and thoughts were turning to the possibility of emigration to lands where there was liberty for Protestants, thoughts which in the 1730s culminated in a vain attempt to get out a train of 30,000. David's contacts were limited to three villages, Sehlen, Zauchtental and Kunwald, which were peculiar in that before the Thirty Years War they had been strong centres of the generally weak German branch of the mainly Czech church of the Brethren.[42] It was from these obscure villages that the first handful of refugees who were to leave an indelible mark on the history of Protestanism were brought by David, via Schwedler in Niederwiesa and Scheffer in Görlitz, to Berthelsdorf in 1722.[43] Zinzendorf was away, but Heitz, his Swiss estate manager, saw the possibilities of creating a craft village for the refugees, so he settled them at the far end of the estate, around the main road from Zittau to Löbau. On 17 June 1722, Christian David felled the first tree for the first house in what became the village of Herrnhut.

Herrnhut grew rapidly, its population reaching 300 in 1727 and 600 by 1734, despite the fact that, two years earlier, the Saxon government had stopped the inflow of Moravian emigrants.[44] But, from the first, the new settlement grew up in an atmosphere of crisis, both external and internal. The external threat came from the Emperor's determination to stop the leakage of labour by migration under the banner of religious liberty. The agent of the Emperor's threats was the generally client government of Saxony which in this matter had the willing assistance of the Saxon church. For now that the dynasty had turned Catholic, the Lutheran church in Saxony clung more than ever desperately to its rights as an establishment and had no love for the religious toleration now obtaining on the Berthelsdorf estate. Moreover, the pastors throughout Upper Lusatia felt the ground quaking beneath their feet. Apart from their old suppressed Slavonic minorities, the Sorbs and Wends, the area was now full of footloose immigrants from Silesia, Bohemia, Moravia and Hungary, some German, many Slav, and when Schwedler and other revivalist preachers were abroad, they would assemble in their thousands from every quarter.[45] Public order and every notion of a parochially-based church were at stake.

Moreover, the Herrnhuters suffered divisions of their own, in addition to the grinding poverty of a new start. Though well-known figures among them, including Christian David, were tradesmen, the bulk were peasants who had had to forsake everything in order to escape. Of the first 300 settlers at Herrnhut, only half were Moravians, and most of the rest were artisans of every kind – weavers, shoe-makers, potters, tailors, turners and the rest. The disparity of origin, social character and religious belief could only be increased by Zinzendorf's own recruiting campaigns in Silesia.[46] And religion itself proved a divisive factor even among the Moravians. As the Lutheran Orthodox polemicists were not slow to point out, the old Unity of the Brethren had stood nearer to the Reformed than to the Lutheran churches. And the key figure among the Moravians who had no roots in the old Unity, Christian David, became enamoured of the predestinarian doctrines of the Count's Zürich-Reformed manager, Johann Georg Heitz.[47] Disputes which followed led not merely to Heitz's return to Switzerland, but to David's building a new house well out of the village. The Moravians divided into a Lutheran party, which supported the Count and Richard Rothe, the pastor he presented to the living at Berthelsdorf, and an anti-church group, led by Christian David[48], wishing to separate itself from the parish.

Given the external threats to Herrnhut, nothing could have been more

embarrassing to the Count than the emergence of separatism. He came
back to reside on the estate, imposed a village constitution, and a religious
constitution which should be co-ordinated into the church-structure of the
province. One of its first features was the bands in which the settlers could
share their religious experience.[49] The lay office of elder was revived, and
David was chosen as one of the twelve. Soon afterwards, he was elected
by lot one of the four Senior Elders (*Oberältesten*). But it was no longer
possible to save the day in Herrnhut by seigneurial action alone. For
religious revival was in the air, originating in Silesia, spreading in Upper
Lusatia, concentrated in the Moravians' own parish by the increasing
resonance of the preaching of Richard Rothe. Christian David was
harrowing opinion by asking what use it had been for him to risk his life
bringing souls out of Popery if they were to be entangled in Lutheranism
and thus made doubly children of hell.

The emotional temperature was being raised by the visits of inflammatory
preachers like Johannes Liberda, the old Czech preacher at Teschen, and
Schwedler. Overspill at the parish church at Berthelsdorf reached the point
where services had to be duplicated at Herrnhut. News came of great
awakenings in Silesia, and signs and wonders began to appear in Herrnhut
— 'great grace was among them and in the whole district'. Christian David
began to hold men's Bible classes; there were all-night prayer-meetings on
the Hutberg. It needed only one more sign of the recent revivalist past, an
intense spirit of prayer among the children (as in Silesia a generation
before), to precipitate one of the most remarkable of all religious revivals.

Within the limits of an essay it is not possible to relate the extraordinary
chain of events which began with the conversion of the eleven-year old
Susanne Kühnel and generated an amazing spirit of prayer among the
whole community, the Herrnhut diary[50] carrying self-conscious echoes of
the great events in Silesia twenty years before. In this high-pressure
awakening the community at Herrnhut, which had been on the verge of
disintegration, pulled itself up by its bootstraps, discovered a usable past
and created a remarkable future. Separatism was not yet over in Herrnhut;
but there was now no difficulty in getting acceptance for the elaborate
arrangements which Zinzendorf made for mutual edification and pastoral
oversight. David Cranz, the Brethren's historian, artlessly records:

> When soon afterwards they received Johann Amos Comenius's history
> and church order of their forbears in Buddeus's[51] edition from the Town
> Council library at Zittau, they found to their joy that their organization,
> in its inmost being, conformed closely to the church discipline and order
> of their fathers. So they resolved to stand by it now and in the future.
> Several times afterwards, and especially in 1728 and 1731, the question

arose amongst them whether for the sake of peace and to avoid defamation and persecution, they should not abandon their peculiar institutions. But the Moravian Brethren always rejected this and pressed forward the more zealously completely to reestablish the old constitution of the Brethren.[52]

As the kings of Prussia met their match with the Czech emigrants, Zinzendorf met his match with the Germans. He would have to realize his philadelphian ideals through their objectives, and it was his particular genius to divert them into a mission to the universal church. Despite the confusion in Zinzendorf's mind, confusion between him and the Moravians, confusion between the Moravian and non-Moravian Herrnhuters, confusion among the Moravians themselves, and confusion between them and their parish minister, there had so far been very little interference with Herrnhut from the outside. This was partly because Upper Lusatia possessed no consistory of its own and partly because the Dresden theologians, who might have regarded its statutes as deviating from Lutheran symbols, were a long way off and lacked the machinery to intervene.

Events far beyond Herrnhut had precipitated the original emigration, however, and others were now to put a stop to the movement and bring in not only the Saxon church but also the Saxon government. On 15 August 1731 the Imperial ambassador in Dresden lodged a written complaint from the Emperor against Zinzendorf's practice of tempting away his subjects, claiming that Herrnhut sheltered twice as many as in fact it did.[53] This was altogether more serious than the Emperor's previous interventions. For Charles VI was now alarmed at the turn of events in Salzburg which led to the emigration of 30,000 Protestants from that province the following winter, while in September 1732 chronic peasant discontent in Bohemia issued in open rebellion. This outbreak, in which religious and economic grievances were blended, was exploited by Liberda, the former Czech preacher at Teschen, now the minister of a Czech congregation in Berlin, who had a house at Herrnhut. He had been conspiring with the king of Prussia to get up a train of 30,000 Czech Protestants, using the Hennersdorf estate, the property of Zinzendorf's neighbour and aunt, as a staging post. The Czech rebellion was a disaster, and Henriette von Gersdorf had Liberda imprisoned as soon as he returned to Hennersdorf.[54] But the Emperor had reason to be more than ever importunate on the always sensitive subject of the loss of labour.[55] The Saxon Privy Council therefore forbade Zinzendorf to receive any more Moravian emigrants. Although a commission which they sent down to the village reported in relatively favourable terms, Augustus the Strong banished Zinzendorf and, on account of his 'shocking and grave behaviour', required him to sell his estates.

The crisis, however, fizzled out. On 1 February 1733, Augustus the Strong died, and, in a display of clemency, his successor temporarily suspended the sentence of exile. The Count sold his estates to his wife, and only the Silesian Schwenkfelders, who had sought refuge at Herrnhut, were expelled.[56] But at once negotiations began for bases abroad, first in Denmark, then in Georgia in case Herrnhut should become untenable. The Moravians had no option but to become a missionary body. The Count took two other defensive measures. He obtained from the theology faculty at Tübingen the opinion that, presupposing an agreement in evangelical doctrine, the Moravians might keep the institutions and discipline they had possessed for 300 years and might also 'maintain their connexion with the evangelical church', a position of institutional pluralism which he believed Luther had provided for in the *Deutsche Messe*. Zinzendorf also divided the colony at Herrnhut into two parts. The first was to consist of exiles from Moravia only. They were to adhere strictly to their peculiar institutions and hold themselves ready for migration at any time. The others could adhere to the Moravian constitution if they wished, but could expect to stay in Herrnhut. All these events were calculated to strengthen the Moravian sense of separateness. When in 1735 David Nitschmann was consecrated bishop by Jablonsky to lead the second group of Moravian setters to Georgia, a step had been taken which was calculated to convince others as well as Moravians that the Brethren were now an independent church. Nor did the Lutheran orders acquired by Zinzendorf himself do anything to strengthen impressions to the contrary.

The next crisis was a Saxon affair; but it had international consequences. One of the effects of the great revival of 1727 upon a province stuffed with refugees was the beginning of a large-scale diaspora work based on Herrnhut. This aroused a good deal of complaint from the clergy.[57] The final spur to government action, however, was applied by Baron von Huldenberg, the British envoy extraordinary to the Imperial court at Vienna. In 1733 he inherited property in Upper Lusatia and made a scene about Moravian activities in the Bautzen parliament. This time the Dresden government acted decisively. They reactivated the banishment order against Zinzendorf while he was in Amsterdam, so that he could not give evidence before a second commission sent down to Herrnhut in 1736 – a commission on which the Count had no friends and which was part of a general move against conventicles.[58] The final outcome was a royal decree of 1737 which tolerated the Brüder-gemeine at Herrnhut provided they adhered to the Augsburg Confession, avoided conventicles and did not intrude into strange parishes. But the Saxon government would have no further truck with the Count.[59] All he could do was to move the Moravians proper, under the name of the Pilgrim Congregation, off to Marienborn in the Wetterau, leaving Herrnhut peopled by Lutherans, and abandoning its diaspora work to half a century's decay. Moreover, the settlements in the Wetterau were never anything but independent of the local established (Reformed) churches. Against Zinzendorf's will, the general concession granted soon afterwards by the Prussian government for new settlements to be established on its territories, subjected the Moravians to no consistory, i.e. regarded them as a dissenting body. The negotiations successfully carried through the British Parliament by Zinzendorf's agents in 1748–1749 for the grant of special privileges in America, began from the premise 'that the church known as the Unitas Fratrum is an ancient, apostolical and episcopal church', deriving its doctrine from the Greeks, and recognized by the Synod of Constantinople as recently as 1740. What they sought was the toleration and privilege not of a spiritual movement within Anglicanism or Lutheranism, but of an independent church.[60] This was, of course, a worse rub in Germany than in England. Baumgarten, the transitional theologian, did not mince the matter: 'the Moravian Brethren did not belong to the evangelical church, but must be reckoned a fourth religion of their own in the German Empire', and hence were not entitled to toleration under the Westphalia settlement.[61] Zinzendorf could only reiterate '*my* basic principle, according to which the societies of the Brethren must in perpetuity never become a separate religious body or, at least, if they do, forsake all connection with me and mine'.[62]

The problem clearly was that the Moravians were not prepared to forego what they believed to be their traditions, imperfectly understood and remembered as they were, while Zinzendorf was not prepared to surrender his original philadelphia ideal. Both needed toleration, and toleration was easier to appeal for in German conditions on the basis of the Count's principle. Even so, he had the vexation to find that neither the Orthodox nor the Hallesian defenders of Lutheran traditions were prepared to accept the view which he shared with Spener, that Luther himself had provided for the existence of community institutions of the sort he had created at Herrnhut within the Lutheran church. His one way out of the dilemma was to establish what he called 'Tropuses' or institutionalized movements within the Lutheran, Reformed or English churches. However, it would be flattery to describe even Zinzendorf's views of the Tropuses as ambivalent. He could say: 'we have the lovely Tropus-business as a poison from which the Saviour has prepared a medicine',[63] or again:

as to that ill conclusion: So then you are a church by your own choice? We answer as a weighty doctor concerning church matters in Germany has put into our mouths, No, we are only one of ye societies in ye church . . . By means of Tropuses in ye hands of understanding divines, there will be more obtained than by all apologies whatever . . . ye Moravian church nevertheless abides by itself having her own form & without any other's direction. The Ord[inary] declared that this was none of our own inventing, but within these 26 years, he only follows ye thread & now sees afterwards ye reason & views of our Sav[iou]r.[64]

The result of constant pressure from his enemies was that, with every year, the Moravian church seemed to become a more distinct body and, in the first instance, to put down secure roots, not within the bosom of the historic Reformation confessions, but in those lands where the state was prepared to tolerate dissenters, namely in the Wetterau, in Holland, in Prussia and Sweden, in Britain and the American colonies. The Renewed Unity of the Brethren was neither the 'antient apostolical and episcopal church' of the application to the British parliament, nor the new eclectic sect envisaged by Bengel, nor the rump, either Lutheran or Calvinist, of the Orthodox propagandists, nor Zinzendorf's philadelphian ideal. But it contained something of each, and it still contains a large dual membership with the Evangelische Kirche Deutschlands of the sort which no longer subsists between English Methodism and the Church of England. Moreover, a crucial part in its revival had been played by the preaching and propaganda of Halle, a fact which neither side now wished to recognize.

The Moravians' critics on both right and left scored a good many points and missed the mark mainly in trying to prove too much. J.G. Carpzov, Superintendent at Lübeck, held that in the first period of their history the Brethren

> were *Wycliffites*, in which at the beginning they still cherished many popish errors . . . in the second [from Luther to the end of the seventeenth century] they were complete Calvinists as they united openly with them in the assembly at Sandomir;[65] in the third [period of the early eighteenth century they were] *Innovators* whose religious pretexts were created outwardly according to the condition of each country and people where they stayed, but were inwardly filled with many fanatical, enthusiastic, Weigelian, Behmenish and Quakerish opinions.[66]

In the nature of the case, 'with the long discontinuance of public worship, Protestant schools and preachers . . . their children's children became less informed in evangelical doctrine, cooler in their Christianity, more neglectful in devotional exercises'.[67] Nor did the long history of emigration justify what Zinzendorf had made of it. In an interesting personal reminiscence, Carpzov admitted that may be some of them came every year to enjoy holy communion into Upper Lusatia, especially to Pirna, Dresden and other Chur-Saxon places where Bohemian services were held. I myself well recollect having heard this form often in my youth, when the preacher M. Rühr at Dresden conducted the Lutheran service in the Bohemian church and tongue. In the summer-time he had many travelling communicants out of Bohemia. Yet it cannot be said whether they were Lutheran or Brethren or co-religionists of both kinds, who found edification and strength in the pure religion wherever it could be found nearest.[68]

Many of them may have been descendants of the old Moravian Lutherans, but, whether they were or not, 'their service, doctrine and confession in Saxony were never other than according to the Confession of Augsburg'. Certainly the old Moravians knew nothing of the indifferentism or syncretism of the new.[69] Many of these charges reappeared from the left. Andreas Gross, the spokesman for the radical Pietists of the Wetterau, maintained that the Moravians had brought to Herrnhut, 'a jumble of doctrine, a total ignorance of the constitution and discipline of the Bohemian church, and were, in addition, unconverted persons'.[70] The last point might be thought sufficiently met by the revival after they had arrived. But Zinzendorf's story about the miraculous discovery in Zittau public library made it hard to controvert the second, while the private narratives of the exiles themselves gave only too much force to the first. In 1742 Martin Liebisch and David Schneider wrote a narrative of their heritage in which they claimed descent from the old Moravian and Bohemian Brethren and 'as such' recognition by the Reformed in Holland.[71] What neither of these critical accounts admitted was that, to all those like Zinzendorf who now were concerned to get behind the entrenched lines of division in European religion, there might be positive value in the confused traditions of a religious body which had worked under very unfavourable circumstances in a pluralistic milieu. Though even Zinzendorf was known to say 'that the Moravian and Bohemian religion [i.e. confessional tradition] is much worse than the Lutheran and Reformed; the Bohemian Confession does not hold a candle to the Augustana', and its adherents were always making unholy compromises with more powerful neighbours.[72]

The singularities in the history of a sect whose patron insisted was not a sect, and whose original adherents insisted was not a new sect, enhance rather than diminish the interest of the Moravians to the student of sects in general. What they illustrate is the difference between those sects which originate in schism, and are in fact conflict-groups, and those which have their origin in religious revival. To the conflict-group, the enemy is clearly delineated, and the lines are drawn. To the revival-group, the world which has to be overcome is too protean to admit of simple prohibition, and if the past (even the Catholic past) contains well-springs of spiritual vitality, it is folly not to draw upon them. Indeed, the whole revival movement aspired to be orthodox without Orthodoxy, to be puritan without precisionism, to be alert to what Catholic spiritual writers had to say (often against the managers of Catholic establishments), to be eclectic towards both past and present. The weight of discussion devoted to religious affections and to the marks of the New Birth showed clearly enough that religious vitality was not readily to be reduced to a formula; that, on the one hand, the devil did mimic the work of God, and that, on the other, God's true children were to be found in the most unlikely confessions. Empirical tests might properly determine the outward forms of church life, the inner forms of church discipline and fellowship, even, what a Wesley might refer to, in no proprietary sense, as 'our' doctrines. The revival-groups were thus in a real sense not 'dissenting' sects, even where the public law of the societies in which they were born required them to be classified as such. The characteristic expression of their belief was not the confession of faith, in the Reformation tradition, but the accumulation of archives, the evidence of the way God operated in history. Their leaders, though they were usually theologically aware, were not professional theologians defending a line, but pastors and evangelists writing letters and journals, preaching daily. And if their 'openness' offered many advantages over the compact citadels of the other type of sect, it was a question in the long run whether a mind open on so many fronts could retain even the eclectic connection with the past which had been so important at the beginning.

Notes

1 Report of Committee to House of Commons, 14 March 1748. In Archiv der Brüder-Unität DDR-8709 Herrnhut, Oberlausitz (cited below as Herrnhut MSS), R 13 A 24 no. 22.

2 Valuable family trees of the Zinzendorf family are to be found in *Zeitschrift für Brüdergeschichte*, i, 204ff; reprinted in the Olms reprint of the works and other materials of Zinzendorf, published in Hildesheim, 1962–77, and cited below as *Zinzendorf Werke*. Here 3 *Zinzendorf Werke*, i.

3 *Zinzendorf Werke, Hauptschriften*, i. viii–ix.

4 E. Beyreuther, 'Zinzendorf und der deutschen Osten', *Jahrbuch der Schlesischen Friedrich-Wilhelms-Universität Breslau*, 7 (1962), 132 (Repr. in 2 *Zinzendorf Werke*, xii. 764). Silesian Pietist noblemen were known to pray in the field in broad daylight. H.W. Erbe, *Zinzendorf und der fromme hohe Adel seiner Zeit*, Leipzig, 1928, 27 (Repr. in 2 *Zinzendorf Werke*, xii. 399).

5 On the von Gersdorf family and their part in religious reform see Walther von Boetticher, *Geschichte des Oberlausitzischen Adels und seiner Güter, 1635–1815*, Görlitz, 1912–23, i. 424–608; Christian Knauthe, *Derer Oberlausitzer Sorbwenden umständliche Kirchengeschichte*, ed. R. Olesch, Cologne/ Vienna, 1980: A. Mietzschke, 'Lusatica aus dem Anfang des 18. Jahrhundert', *Zeitschrift für Slavische Philologie*, xvii: 2 (1941), 123–42.

6 A strongly drawn portrait of Henriette Katherine von Gersdorf is given in Gerhard Reichel, *Die Anfänge Herrnhuts. Ein Buch vom Werden der Brüdergemeine*, Herrnhut, 1922, 10–29.

7 At one time she knew Hochmann, the revivalist; she supported the chiliast Petersen with money. Zinzendorf said of her, as he might have said of himself, 'she new no distinction between the Catholic, Lutheran and Reformed religions'. Otto Uttendörfer, *Zinzendorf und die Mystik* [East] Berlin, 1950, 22–3. On the theological peculiarities of the Upper Lusatian aristocracy generally see *Ausführliche historiche und theologische Nachricht von der Herrnhutschen Brüderschaft*, Frankfurt, 1743, 17–18, 187 (Repr. in 2 *Zinzendorf Werke*, xiv.)

8 A.G. Spangenberg, *Leben des Herrn Nicolaus Ludwig Grafen von Zinzendorf und Pottendorf* (cited below as *Leben Zinzendorfs*), Barby, 1773–75; repr. in 2 *Zinzendorf Werke*, i. 178.

9 E. Vehse, *Geschichte der Höfe des hauses Sachsen*, pt. 7 (being vol. 34 of his *Geschichte der deutschen Höfe seit der Reformation*, Hamburg, 1854, 71.

10 See no. 8 above.

11 Ibid., i. 33n.

12 A.G. Spangenberg, *Apologetische Schlussschrift*, Leipzig/Görlitz, 1752, 654 (repr. in *Zinzendorf Werke, Ergänzungsband*, iii).

13 Spangenberg, *Leben Zinzendorfs*, i. 42.

14 Gerhard Reichel, *Der 'Senfkornorden' Zinzendorfs: Ein Beitrag zur Kenntnis seiner Jugendentwicklung und seines Charakters*, Gnadenfeld. n.d.), 30, 207, (repr. in 2 *Zinzendorf Werke*, xii. 174, 351).

15 Uttendörfer, *Zinzendorf und die Mystik*, 27.

16 N.L. von Zinzendorf, *ΠΕΡΙ ΕΑΥΤΟΥ Das ist: Naturelle Reflexiones*, n. pl., 1746, 11 (repr. in *Zinzendorf Werke, Ergänzungsband*, iv).

17 Spangenberg, *Leben Zinzendorfs*, i. 62–3, 78–9. See further in my paper on 'Zinzendorf and Money', *Studies in Church History*, xxiv (1987), 283–305.

18 Uttendörfer, *Zinzendorf und die Mystik*, 29–30.

19 Ibid., 32.

20 On this see Sigurd Nielsen, *Intoleranz und Toleranz bei Zinzendorf*, 3 vols., Hamburg, 1952–60.

21 Uttendörfer, *Zinzendorf und die Mystik*, 33–6.

22 *Zinzendorf Werke, Ergänzungsband*, x. cxxiv.

23 Otto Uttendörfer, *Alt-Herrnhut: Wirtschaftgeschichte und Religionssoziologie Herrnhuts während seiner ersten zwanzig Jahre, 1722–42*, Herrnhut, 1925, 144.

24 Herrnhut MSS, R 20 A 17.

25 Erich Beyreuther, *Der junge Zinzendorf* Marburg a. d. Lahn, 1957, 212–22.

26 On this group see Friedrich Wilhelm Barthold, *Die Erweckten im protestantischen Deutschland während des Ausgangs des 17. und der ersten Hälfte des 18. Jahrhunderts, besonders die frommen Graftenhöfe*, repr. from *Historische Taschenbuch*, 1852–53, ed. F. von Raumer, Darmstadt, 1968: also Erbe, *Zinzendorf und der fromme hohe Adel.*

27 For whom see Heinz Renkewitz, *Hochmann von Hochenau (1670–1721): Quellenstudien zur Geschichte des Pietismus*, repr. Witten, 1969.

28 Beyreuther, *Der junge Zinzendorf*, 226–8; Uttendörfer, *Zinzendorf und die Mystik*, 43.

29 N.L. von Zinzendorf, *Büdingische Sammlung*, Büdingen, 1742–45, footnote to Preface, n.p.(repr. in *Zinzendorf Werke, Ergänzungsband*, vii). Zinzendorf referred to the same experience in the *Teutsche Sokrates* (1732 ed.), 209–10 (repr. in *Zinzendorf Werke, Hauptschriften*, i) and in a letter to Liborious Zimmermann in 1728. *Zeitschrift für Brüdergeschichte*, v. 202 (repr. in 3 *Zinzendorf Werke*, ii). See also ibid., i. 151 and the later entries quoted in Uttendörfer, *Zinzendorf und die Mystik*, 74–5.

30 Spangenberg, *Apologetische Schluss-Schrift*, 452; Spangenberg, *Leben Zinzendorfs*, i. 52n.

31 Peter Baumgart, 'Leibnitz und der Pietismus: Universale Reformbestrebungen um 1700', *Archiv für Kulturgeschichte*, xlviii (1966), 364–86; *Zinzendorf Werke, Hauptschriften*, iii, xiii; Zinzendorf, *Der Teutsche Sokrates*, Preface, first footnote (n.p.).

32 N.L. von Zinzendorf, *Die an den Synodum der Brüder in Zeyst . . . gehalten Reden* (n. pl., 1746–47), 179–80 (repr. in *Zinzendorf Werke, Hauptschriften*, iii).

33 Ibid., 246–7.

34 N.L. von Zinzendorf, *Londoner Predigten* (London/Barby, 1756–57), i. 341–2: ii. 337 (repr. in *Zinzendorf Werke, Hauptschriften*, v).

35 Spangenberg, *Leben Zinzendorfs*, iii. 467; Ludwig Carl Freiherr von Schrautenbach, *Der Graf Zinzendorf und die Brüdergemeine seiner Zeit* (Gnadau/Leipzig, 1851), 86 (repr. in 2 *Zinzendorf Werke*, ix); Erich Beyreuther, 'Die Paradoxie des Glaubens: Zinzendorfs Verhältnis zu Pierre Bayle und zur Aufklärung', *Studien zur Theologie Zinzendorfs: Gesammelte Aufsätze*, Neukirchen, 1962, 201–34; Uttendörfer, *Zinzendorf und die Mystik*, 86; *Teutsche Sokrates*, 252 n. 6.

36 N.L. von Zinzendorf, *Jeremias, ein Prediger der Gerechtigkeit* (2nd. ed., Frankfurt/Büdingen, 1741), 100 (repr. in *Zinzendorf Werke, Ergänzungsband*, i).

37 Zinzendorf's concerns here were very similar to those of Johann Christian Edelmann, who after a brief flirtation with Moravianism went over wholesale to Enlightenment. See my paper 'Johann Christian Edelmann: A Rebel's Progress', *Modern Religious Rebels*, ed. S.P. Mews; Walter Grossmann, *Johann Christian Edelmann: From Orthodoxy to Enlightenment*, The Hague/Paris, 1976.

38 As Czech Protestantism came under the hammer and lost touch with institutionalized Protestantism it fell apart and followed strange courses. A sect of Israelites arose who came close to Judaism, near Neu Bydžov after 1720; apocalyptic had its devotees, and, especially in East Bohemia, deism. Rudolf Ričan, *Das Reich Gottes in dem Böhmischen Ländern: Geschichte des tschechischen Protestantismus*, Stuttgart, 1957, 148.

39 For a biography of Scheffer see *Acta Historico-Ecclesiastica*, iii. 389–413. On Silesia, Gerhard Meyer, *Gnadenfrei: Eine Herrnhuter Siedlung des schlesischen Pietismus im 18. Jahrhundert*, Hamburg, 1950, 12–14.

40 For this story see my paper, 'Power and Piety: The Origins of Religious Revival in the early Eighteenth Century', *Bulletin of the John Rylands University Library of Manchester*, lxiii (1981), 231–52. Above, Ch. 5.

41 David Cranz, Alte und Neue Brüder-Historie, Barby, 1772, 107–10 (repr. in 2 *Zinzendorf Werke*, xi).

42 Joseph Theodor Müller, *Zinzendorf als Erneuerer der alten Brüderkirche*, Leipzig, 1900, 1–2 (repr. in 2 *Zinzendorf Werke*, xii. 7–8).

43 Cf. the way later Moravian refugees were passed from hand to hand by the Pietist nobility of Silesia before arriving, sometimes after a decade, in Herrnhut. *Zeitschrift für Brüdergeschichte*, vi (1912), 187 (repr. in 3 *Zinzendorf Werke*, ii).

44 Uttendörfer, *Alt-Herrnhut; Zinzendorf und die Herrnhuter Brüder. Quellen zur Geschichte der Brüder-Unität von 1722 bis 1760*, ed. H.C. Hahn and Hellmut Reichel, Hamburg, 1977, 61–110.

45 Erich Beyreuther, *Zinzendorf und die sich allhier beisammen finden*, Marburg a.d. Lahn, 1959, 155; Cranz, *Brüdergeschichte*, 143; Arend Buchholtz, *Die Geschichte der Familie Lessing*, Berlin 1909, i. 91, 98, 109–14.

46 Meyer, *Gnadenfrei*, 46–70.

47 Heitz was the unnamed Calvinist mentioned in the reminiscences of Christian David collected by John Wesley. *The Journal of John Wesley*, ed. Nehemiah Curnock, 2nd. ed., London, 1938, ii. 31. See also Beyreuther, *Zinzendorf und die sich allhier beisammen finden*, 116.

48 Ibid., 166–8.

49 On the history of these see Gottfried Schmidt, 'Die Banden oder Gesellschaften in alten Herrnhut', *Zeitschrift für Brüdergeschichte*, iii (1909), 146–207 (repr. in 3 *Zinzendorf Werke*, i).

50 The Herrnhut diary between May and August 1727 is printed in *Zinzendorf und die Herrnhuter Brüder*, 95–108; Beyreuther, *Zinzendorf und die sich allhier beisammen finden*, 206–7.

51 Buddeus left a philosophy chair at Halle to enter on a distinguished period as professor of theology at Jena, in 1705. His influence was at least not hostile to the revivals which developed there, revivals in which both Zinzendorf and Spangenberg had a hand.

52 Cranz, *Brüder-Historie*, 142, 147.

53 This letter is printed in Gudrun Meyer, 'Herrnhuts Stellung innerhalb der sächsischen Landeskirche bis 1737', *Unitas Fratrum*, ii (1977), 42–3 n. 50A.

Propaganda against Herrnhut had also been forthcoming from the Emperor's
Jesuit missionary among the Schwenkfelders, Fr. Carl Regent, *Unpartheyische
Nachricht von der in Lausnitz überhandnehmenden . . . neuen Sect der so-
gennanten Schefferianer und Zinzendorfianer . . .* Breslau, 1729; (repr. in 2
Zinzendorf Werke, xiv).

54 On Liberda and these events see Eduard Winter, *Die tschechische und slovakische Emigration in Deutschland im 17. und 18. Jahrhundert: Beiträge zur
Geschichte der hussitischen Tradition*, [East] Berlin, 1955, 104–13. After three
gaol-break attempts, the king of Prussia 'sprung' Liberda and his gaoler, and
they returned to Berlin in 1737.

55 Zinzendorf believed that he had been a victim of a local eddy of the larger
whirlpool. A crowd of Bohemian (i.e. Czech) refugees in a very poor state of
health turned up against his will at Herrnhut, and after being given medical
assistance were sent on their way. This he thought had been magnified by his
enemies into a breach of the requirement to accept no more refugees. *Naturelle
Reflexiones*, 132; *Büdingische Sammlung*, iii. 653–67.

56 On these events see Mayer, 'Herrnhuts Stellung', 32–5; Müller, *Zinzendorf als
Erneuerer*, 44–5 (repr. in 2 *Zinzendorf Werke*, xii. 50–1); Herrnhut MSS,
Johannes Plitt MS, Neue Brüdergeschichte 159; Ferdinand Körner, *Die kursäs-
chsische Staatsregierung dem Grafen Zinzendorf und Herrnhut bis 1760
gegenüber* (Leipzig, 1878), 14–24.

57 Even in 1742 the Orthodox press reported that the clergy of Upper Lusatia
had much to suffer from the Herrnhuters, who came swarming in with the
complaint that 'Luther was indeed a good man, but the Lutherans of today
were damned wretches [*Luderaner*] and stank like beasts [*Luder*]'. *Acta
Historico-Ecclesiastica*, viii, 936: *Unschuldige Nachrichten* (1735), 241–2.

58 On all this see F.S. Hark, 'Der Konflikt der kursächsische Regierung mit
Herrnhut und dem Grafen von Zinzendorf, 1733–38', *Neues Archiv für
sächsische Geschichte und Alterthumskunde*, iii (1882), 12–25: Zinzendorf,
Naturelle Reflexiones, 135; Körner, *Die kursächsische Staatsregierung*, 27–31;
Acta Historico-Ecclesiastica, iii. 381.

59 Körner, *Die Kursächsische Staatsregierung*, 35–56: Hark, 'Der Konflikt der
kursächsischen Regierung', 26–64; Martin Greschat, *Zwischen Tradition und
neuem Anfang: Valentin Ernst Löscher und der Ausgang der Lutherischen
Orthodoxie*, Witten, 1971, 322–4.

60 Meyer, 'Herrnhuts Stellung', 38: Spangenberg, *Leben Zinzendorfs*, iv. 958,
969–70, 1104; Herrnhut MSS, R 13 A 24 no. 22. Even in 1737 during the
Georgia negotiations Archbishop Potter had agreed that the Brethren were 'a
true apostolic and episcopal church which held nothing contrary to the Thirty-
nine Articles of the Church of England'. *Acta Historico-Ecclesiastica*, iii. 450.

61 Müller, *Zinzendorf als Erneuerer*, 83 (repr. in 2 *Zinzendorf Werke*, xii. 89).

62 Zinzendorf, *Naturelle Reflexiones*, 127.

63 Müller, *Zinzendorf als Erneuerer*, 101 (repr. in 2 *Zinzendorf Werke*, xii. 107).

64 This rather awkward translation was made for the English Moravian com-

munity and is to be found in MS in the archives in Moravian Church House, Muswell Hill, London. MS Gemeinhaus Diary, 11 Nov. 1748.

65 By the Consensus of Sandomir (in Poland), 1570.

66 J.G. Carpzov, *Religious-untersuchung der Böhmisch- und Mährischen Brüder von Anbeginn ihrer Gemeinen, bis auf gegenwärtigen Zeiten*, Leipzig, 1742, Preface n.p.

67 Ibid., 407–8.

68 Ibid., 406.

69 Ibid., 405, 413, 416.

70 Andreas Gross, *Erste und letzte Antwort auf die so-genannte Erklärung des Herrn Grafen N.L. von Zinzendorf*, Frankfurt, 1742, Appendix, 97–119, 306–56.

71 *Zeitschrift für Brüdergeschichte*, vi (1912), 186–95.

72 Müller, *Zinzendorf als Erneuerer*, 100–1 (repr. in 2 *Zinzendorf Werke*, xii. 106–7).

8

Zinzendorf and Money

There are problems with this topic. Zinzendorf himself would certainly have considered it a non-subject, as he would certainly have regarded the counsel of his contemporary Wesley to 'gain all you can, save all you can, and give all you can'[1] as unspeakably bourgeois, an adjective I have no recollection of Wesley's applying to himself. The severer kind of economic historian might also regard what I have to say as a non-treatment of a non-subject, for I cannot present you with a profit-and-loss account of Zinzendorf's transactions; I know no more about his income than he did, which was not very much; and although I shall refer later to the successive valuations of Zinzendorf's property which that remarkable scholar Otto Uttendörfer dredged up from the Herrnhut archives sixty years ago, I attach no great importance to them. They seem to me the same kind of artificial enterprise as the annual revaluations for borrowing purposes which were made of the empty Centre Point building in its earlier years. Moreover, the straightforward introduction to the theme which I enjoyed not long ago is not readily available to historians in the West. It is to work first in the archive of Francke's Orphan House at Halle, and then move on to that of the Renewed Church of the United Brethren at Herrnhut. Francke's Orphan House, one of the biggest buildings of eighteenth-century Europe, has the Thatcherite principle of cost-effectiveness written all over it, and is clearly based on the Prussian barracks. The whole community at Herrnhut combines baroque lavishness with simplicity in a way not easily put into words, but most movingly experienced in the Grosse Saal in which the Brethren now hold their services. A visit to the Moravian settlement at Zeyst in the Netherlands, however, may sufficiently illustrate the point.

A treatment, even in general terms, of Zinzendorf's attitude to money and its consequences is nevertheless worth attempting. The Moravian historians, both ancient and modern, have been less coy about this matter than those of any other religious community I have studied, but have not

First published in *Studies in Church History* 24 (1987), pp. 283–305.

taken it up systematically. Then again, allegations of financial malpractice were a constant if subordinate theme in the anti-Moravian polemic which was a major international intellectual industry in the 1740s. 'Where does the money come from?' asked an anonymous freemason,[2] and Orthodox and conservative Pietist scribblers were not reticent in their views. Zinzendorf's Moravians were not stout Protestants who forsook all rather than bow the knee to the Popish Baal – declared one Orthodox pamphleteer: 'They run like dumb cattle to the crib'; and what they came for was Saxon liberty and a table prepared for them by Zinzendorf with money collected from the Mennonites and the Inspired in Holland and England.[3] Another critic maintained that at Marienborn, where Zinzendorf created his second settlement, he had furnished all ninety rooms in the castle, that Popery peeped out in every corner, and the idlers he had assembled there employed the leisure provided by 'amazingly rich' English and Dutch supporters endlessly wittering on about 'wounds, wounds, wounds'.[4] The Herrnhuters' Saviour, it was noted, built his kingdom in bricks and mortar, and when Zinzendorf required 12,000 florins from a rich Frankfurter, he told him that his lifestyle was like an over-loaded boat, and that it was time to cast the excess burden into the sea; if, however, creditors pressed the Moravians to pay, they said that the capital had all been consumed for the Saviour and that he would repay in due course.[5] Whitefield, a kindly man, accused Zinzendorf in 1753 of ruining families and accumulating debts in excess of £60,000 in England alone.[6] They were also accused of losing their first love, and recklessly injuring the trade of all the towns round about Herrnhut by the pursuit of trade and manufacturing to sustain political ends.[7] Then there was the *Heilandscasse*, the Saviour's fund at Zinzendorf's disposal, to which all brethren and sisters were supposed to pay over their worldly wealth. It was thought clearly to be a device for getting money out of the country, and to be one of the reasons for which the King of Denmark had hunted the Moravians out of his Pietist realm.[8] Shadier transactions were hinted at in the allegation that a well-known merchant had contributed 100,000 *Taler* to the *Heilandscasse* on condition that Zinzendorf changed his name for a time, a thing which, oddly enough, he did at intervals.[9] Spangenberg, Zinzendorf's right-hand man and successor at the head of the *Unitas Fratrum*, denied that there ever was a *Heilandscasse*, arguing that if there had been, the financial crisis encountered by the community in the 1750s would never have come about.[10] These charges, which show to a demonstration that what the eighteenth-century Orthodox lacked in charity they more than made up in incisiveness, compel one to ask what was the reality to which they referred.

More importantly, Zinzendorf, at the peak of his career in the later forties underwent a dizzy series of changes of fortune, which gain cohesion and meaning if approached from the standpoint of his resources. Why, for example, was the Zinzendorf who had been compelled by the Dresden government in 1732 to sell his estates, and in 1736 had been banished from the Electorate, warmly welcomed back in 1747? Why was the Zinzendorf who seemed to have come to terms with the major powers of this world, and to have received important concessions from the monarchies of Prussia and Saxony and from the British Parliament, with his whole community expelled from the tiny principality of Ysenburg-Büdingen in the Wetterau, hitherto one of the shining lights of toleration in the Empire? Why, thirdly, did that strange outburst of religious emotionalism and calculated *naïveté* known in the history of the Brethren as 'the time of sifting' (*Sichtungszeit*)[11] occur when it did in the later forties, and drive them ultimately to remedies which were not just theological and spiritual, but economic and institutional? Any light on these questions is welcome, if only because the most brilliant of the recent interpretations of Zinzendorf, that by his editor, Gerhard Meyer,[12] is so completely cast in terms of *Geistesgeschichte* as to be not quite credible. Moreover, answers will help to show how much in the eighteenth century could be accomplished on a shoe-string, even on other people's shoe-strings, and may help to define, if hardly to resolve, some of those moral questions to which the President has dedicated this conference.

Zinzendorf was an imperial count and remained an aristocrat first and foremost.[13] In 1728 he confessed in a poem written on the second marriage of his brother:[14]

> I was a Zinzendorf, and for Zinzendorfs life is not worth living
> If it cannot be devoted to proper causes.

These proper causes, of course, included those of oppressed Protestantism in the Habsburg lands, his grandfather having left his property in Lower Austria during the wave of aristocratic Protestant emigration in the seventeenth century. Zinzendorf was raised by his grandmother Henriette von Gersdorf, a Friesen by birth, and so could hardly fail to be touched by the peculiar double-edged politics pursued by the nobility of Upper Lusatia,[15] Saxony's most recently acquired province. One the one hand there was resistance, led by the Friesens, to the centralizing policy of the Electors of Saxony, now Kings of Poland; and on the other there was the conviction that the enserfed populations of Sorbs and Wends had emerged from the Thirty Years War living the life of Riley and must be got to rights by a mixture of new measures, administrative, educational, and religious.[16] For these latter Halle came to supply the material;[17] Henriette von Gersdorf and her daughter were stout supporters of Halle, whither the young Zinzendorf was despatched for part of his education. But the real business of aristocracy was not actually to do anything, but to be a display,[18] and this Zinzendorf understood to perfection: 'His aspect was tall, powerful, and distinguished in a crowd', and though he dressed simply he made a minor sensation even in the streets of London and Amsterdam.[19] The legends he attracted were all of the same kind. In 1742 when Zinzendorf was in the American backwoods, and wished on the Lord's Day to observe the Litany, devotions were made impossible by a noisy performance put on by the Indians, complete with drumming and singing; at a word from Zinzendorf, even delivered at second hand, all was still.[20] It was the same with entertainments. Zinzendorf, a youth of abnormal religious virtuosity, reports: 'I was taught gambling by my tutor, and I liked it.'[21] As a student at Wittenberg, Zinzendorf could justify chess because it sharpened the mind, and billiards because it exercised the body, or even balloons which occupied the tired mind; gambling was now more problematic because his grandmother disapproved. The solution was not to give it up, but to devote the winnings to the poor, or to buying Halle Bibles for them.[22] On a broader front, Zinzendorf's propensities to gambling were a menace less to himself than to his friends. One of his friends, whose sister he eventually married, was Henry XXIX of Reuss-Ebersdorf. The house of Ebersdorf, a Thuringian principality reputed to be the smallest in the Empire, but equipped in the best Pietist manner with an orphan-house which still stands, was central to that network of intermarried imperial counts which did so much to sustain the Pietist enterprise,[23] and like almost all the rest it was financially on the rocks.[24] Zinzendorf was in Paris during Law's speculative bubble, and kept clear of it himself. But he had no more sense than to write to Henry XXIX: 'Dear brother, why have you not staked your salvation in Mississippi, since the biggest profit is assured. An Irishman put in 100,000 francs and cleared 25 million on it.'[25] Still worse was the case of Friedrich von Watteville, Zinzendorf's Swiss student friend, whom he had wanted to take to Wittenberg with a view to securing him employment at the Polish court. Von Watteville, however, went into his father's bank at Bern, receiving from Zinzendorf the somewhat back-handed encouragement that 'the Bank needs people who give their yea and nay as in the sight of the most high Judge . . . [though] a pious banker enjoying the peace of God is alas! almost as rare a bird as a Christian courtier'.[26] Apparently with Zinzendorf's encouragement von Watteville did plunge into the Mississippi bubble – 'won tons of gold and then lost them again'. Still worse he blew his father's bank, and lost all his father's capital. Zinzendorf's letter of comfort could hardly have expressed more clearly his contempt for money: 'The time of our abiding here is but brief, you will easily come through it.'[27] This was the Zinzendorf who could not travel alone without confusion because he did not understand the kinds of money in circulation even in Germany;[28] in 1737 he arrived penniless in Halle, and, not surprisingly failing to borrow from the now hostile theologians there, cadged the necessary from a peasant.[29] It is pleasant to record that Friedrich von Watteville did much to help Zinzendorf through the difficulties he encountered later in life.

Thus in Zinzendorf an aristocratic commitment to display based on contempt of money, reinforced a genuine Christian intention to seek first the kingdom of God without counting the cost. It is characteristic that Zinzendorf in a German work could use the French word *entrepreneur* (which meant then much what it means now) as the equivalent of *Schleicher* – pussyfooter or intriguer.[30] He was launched into public life as a *Hofrat*. in Dresden, an unpaid office which might eventually lead to the profits of politics, but which did nothing for the moment to offset the financial embarrassments created by his charitable giving. Then in 1722, having lost his intended bride, Theodora of Castell-Remlingen, to his friend Henry XXIX, Zinzendorf in a rather casual way married Henry's sister Erdmuthe Dorothea,[31] whose grandmother had been a highly prized friend of Spener. In the long run Erdmuthe Dorothea proved one of the best assets Zinzendorf ever had; in the short run his marriage involved creating a second household on the estate he had brought from his grandmother at Berthelsdorf in Upper Lusatia; and as, inevitably, no house seemed fit to live in, fresh building was undertaken much in excess of what could be accomplished by the labour dues on the estate. What Zinzendorf intended to create was a *Schloss-ecclesiola* on the lines of that at Ebersdorf, in which he could put into practice his interconfessional philadelphian views. What actually happened in his absence was that German-speaking refugees from Bohemia turned up on his estates, like the Czech refugees who were foregathering on his grandmother's adjacent property at Hennersdorf, and that his Swiss estate manager, Heitz, hoping to find employment in the craft trades for them, settled them away from Berthelsdorf on the main road between Zittau and Löbau. Once it became known that in this new settlement, Herrnhut, 'the Lord's watch', religious toleration was to be had without *Leibeigenschaft*, other religious refugees came in of a quite different religious cast and economic background. A village founded in 1722 had reached a population of 600 by 1734. One hundred and fifty of the first 300 were Moravians, mostly peasants who had forsaken everything to come; but the inflow of Moravians was prohibited by the Saxon government in 1732, and the place was increasingly colonized by tradesmen, weavers, shoemakers, potters, tailors, turners, and the like. Thus Zinzendorf had greatly increased the supply of one of the factors of production, namely labour, at the expense of having to assist with the housing of the new labour force and the provision of all such amenities as were to be had;

and at the further price of compounding the acute religious difficulties of the new community by political menaces from the Emperor (who had no desire to see his labour force denuded by the seductions of Protestant agitators), from the Saxon government (which could not face the wrath of the Emperor), from the Saxon Church (which had enough trouble on its plate since the dynasty turned Catholic, without having the Slavonic minorities of Lusatia convulsed by immigrants and revivalists). This price had its cash aspect, for when religious separatism broke out in Herrnhut, Zinzendorf decided he must come back to live there to sort the place out, and that in turn meant forgoing the prospect of an income from Saxon politics. There was a great financial crisis in 1726, and in retrospect one can be sure that, if the frictions in Herrnhut had not been sublimated in religious revival, the whole enterprise would have fallen disastrously apart. In fact, in 1727 the revival took place; it brought Zinzendorf to pursue his philadelphian ideal through the creation of the Renewed Unity of the Brethren, a renewal of that fellowship of the forbears of the Moravian exiles which in the Kingdom of Bohemia had gone down before the onslaughts of the Counter-Reformation. It also produced one of the first great missionary forces of the Protestant world, one at least of the impulses of which was the necessity to provide alternative bases if Herrnhut should become untenable.

How meanwhile had things gone in terms of institutional structure and economic viability? In 1727 and 1728 Zinzendorf, as lord of the manor, issued two documents giving a constitution to the village; no one was required to join the Unity of the Brethren, but everyone must accept the village constitution or leave. Like contemporary improving German authorities in general, Zinzendorf grossly over-regulated his flock, but embodied clearly enough in his sketch of a little Christian commonwealth three kinds of obligations in return for his protection and freedom from *Leibeigenschaft*. Heads of families must each pay him one *Taler* protection money, one *Taler* ground-rent for his house, or the lease of house, garden and field, and must bear their proportionate share of the dues payable to the parish of Berthelsdorf. Tradesmen must pay an annual handling charge. Every inhabitant was required to earn his own bread, though the old, sick, and impoverished were to be supported by the community. Then there were obligations to each other, administrative, moral, and economic; to repair the roads, and put down sand not ash when there was ice; to have no dances, drinking-bouts, pub-crawling, or wakes at burials, baptisms, or weddings; craftsmen were to stick to their delivery dates or indicate to the purchaser why they could not.[32] Of course, as Herrnhut became organized as an artisan colony there were protests from guilds and other monopolies in the towns round about. To one of these, the printers,

Zinzendorf bowed, moving the press he intended to establish at Herrnhut to Ebersdorf.[33] That minuscule Pietist Zion[34] became the Count's Wapping, and that is why the version of the Scriptures which brought so much Orthodox wrath upon him was known as the Ebersdorf Bible.

The central institutions and most of the trade of Herrnhut were in the hands of the manor and their management showed no such rigour of intent as the village constitution. There was an orphan-house, dispensary, and guest-house. The orphan-house began, Zinzendorf style, as a school for nobility, but when this did not succeed, Zinzendorf changed its function, and it grew steadily, educating an increasing number of children of the village at the Count's expense. Zinzendorf's failing was that he would not collect for the school in any systematic way, and could always attribute his negligence to reluctance to compete in the organized charity market with the Francke foundation at Halle. The result was that debt on the orphan-house increased steadily, and it had finally to be transferred to the Wetterau. Henceforth the village must organize their own school and pay for it. The dispensary was begun by one of Zinzendorf's staff, Dr Gutbier, who prepared and supplied medicaments. In 1731 Zinzendorf bought it from Gutbier, added a laboratory, and found that he was putting in 100 *Taler* a year and drawing no profit. The dispensary was therefore privatized, and von Dürr, who took it on, anticipated the American drugstore by supplying a wide range of grocery and stationery products, introducing retail trade to the village. This development must have been a success, for the capital involved increased thirteen-fold in a decade; but it is not known where the profits went. Herrnhut needed a guest-house, as it still does, for it attracted swarms of visitors, like John Wesley who made the journey in 1738 to see if sinless perfection really existed in this world. The guest-house offered one answer to that question which he failed to discover, for the weights and measures proved to be all fraudulent and had to be replaced. Small wonder that when in 1733 Zinzendorf attempted to require the village to buy their salt at the guest-house, the Brethren rebelled. But how did the Count, who had sunk more than all the capital he possessed in real estate, manage to create even these institutions?

The answer is that the Francke foundation at Halle offered a completely new pattern of enterprise. It was an institution of neither Church nor State, though its objectives were spiritual, and State privileges were among its minor financial assets. The Francke foundation depended partly upon internationally organized charity, but mainly upon hard commerce pursued for the Kingdom of God. Halle was modern in the sense that the contractual principle displaced inherited symbols, and so too was Herrnhut. The Herrnhut *Diarium* for 31 December 1734 proclaimed:

All institutions exist for a purpose. When that purpose is no longer attainable, or ceases, the institution itself must be abandoned. That is how it must be in a community of God, or its salt loses its savour, and things go on only *ex opere operato*.[35]

When a penurious Zinzendorf was founding his institutions Melchior Schäfer, a preacher with whom he had dealings in Görlitz, pressed the Halle principle upon him. Schäfer proposed a sort of joint-stock arrangement in which the Count should provide a site, wood, and land for a kitchen-garden to the value of 300 *Taler*; Schäfer and Richard Rothe, the famous hymn-writer and minister of Berthelsdorf, should give as much in money, and the three together should borrow 1,000 *Taler* from Frau Nichtin in Görlitz, and the institutions thus created should pay 6 per cent on the capital. When this scheme was got going an orphan-house and poor school should be founded in Görlitz, supported by shops and workshops. The Count should be director and his two partners managers (*Inspecktor*). In fact, in 1724 the three with Watteville and others put together 1,500 *Taler* for a large institution-house and borrowed a further 700 at 6 per cent. But the toughness of purpose which characterized Halle was foreign to Zinzendorf's nature, and he had no taste for spiritual business of this sort. He changed his mind as to the purpose of the building, bought out his partners, and survived the ensuing crisis by traditional methods; the Countess pawned her jewels to the parson Schäfer, and the Count begged from his grandmother.

The most surprising element in this situation was probably not yet known to Zinzendorf: it was that his circumstances were actually improving. His original patrimony had been about 40,000 *Taler*, but he had settled a dispute with his stepbrother by giving him a little over half. He had then bought Middle and Lower Berthelsdorf from his grandmother for 26,500 *Taler* leaving him with no money and a debt of 6,000 *Taler*. This was before any of the improvements, and before the purchase of Upper Berthelsdorf in 1727 for 6,000 *Taler*. Cutting out the intermediate stages, we find Zinzendorf valuing his estate in 1732 at 126,160 *Taler*, against debts of 25,000 and an income of 4,388 — not a marvellous return upon the capital, but an income nevertheless. Zinzendorf wrote off to his cousin Lutz at Castell-Remlingen in high glee: 'Do you know how, we began with 80,000 *ecus*, spent more than 60,000, and at the end of a thorough reckoning, after allowing for debts, have 100,000 *écus* . . . I present you with this story to fortify your faith.'[36] Edifying the story undoubtedly was, but success flowed from two sources only. The first was the self-sacrifice and business acumen of Erdmuthe Dorothea, to whose bookkeeping is due the fact that it is possible to give a better account of Zinzendorf's affairs at this stage than at any later point in his career, and whose resources sustained the Count till the death of his grandmother in 1726. He had also profited comfortably from those assets which swilled unpredictably around the aristocracy. He had received by inheritance 8,000 *Taler*, by gifts and presents 11,800, from his mother 6,300, from his grandmother 4,000, from his great-aunt Meusebach 2,300, from Denmark 1,000; the invaluable Erdmuthe Dorothea had come into 20,000 *Taler* and incorporated it in the estate; a total of 53,400 or more than two and a half times the capital with which he had begun. And a formerly undeveloped estate now included not only white elephants, but a substantial village well equipped with craft trades.[37]

Zinzendorf's good fortune was now to be severely tested. He claimed the world as his parish[38] and treated it as such more realistically than Wesley. So on top of his normal living expenses were now added the costs of his journeys to all parts of northern and western Europe and to America as well.[39] The Moravians quickly established missions from Greenland to the West Indies, inevitably at some expense to the Count. The Countess could not be expected to go on increasing the value of the Berthelsdorf property, especially as there were sharp political restraints on the intake of new immigrants, and most of the new recruits simply replaced bankrupts or Brethren who had gone elsewhere on the work of the Unity. Above all, the political situation changed for the worse. The impending blow of expulsion incurred by the Schwenckfelders at Herrnhut never fell on the community as a whole, but there were powerful commissions of inquiry into its affairs in 1732 and 1736. After the first of these Zinzendorf was required to sell his estates, and before the second he was banished from Saxony. The first of these penalties Zinzendorf minimized after the manner of a bankrupt councillor of Clay Cross, by conveying his estates to the Countess. The second brought on another financial crisis, and indirectly ensured that the estate was deprived of the firm managerial hand of the Countess for long periods as she accompanied her husband abroad. The contract of sale permitted Zinzendorf to take both capital and an income out of the Berthelsdorf estate; the public contract priced the deal at 70,000 *Taler*, the private contract at 100,000. Of this the Countess paid her husband 24,000 *Taler*, took on 26,000 *Taler* of debts and agreed to pay 5 per cent (more than the estate was earning on its capital as a whole) on the remaining 50,000. This was not an economically prudent arrangement, but long-term considerations became suddenly irrelevant when the Count was banished in 1736 and many of his old 6 per cent creditors called in their loans. Spangenberg, Zinzendorf's biographer, taking his cue from the Count himself, saw a special providence in the fact that at the end of March, at the very time when the banishment order reached the

Oberamtshauptmann in Upper Lusatia, a pious friend from the Netherlands arrived with relief.[40] The fact was that Zinzendorf was in the Netherlands from 4 March till 16 April, most of the time in Amsterdam; he had discovered through pious circles there that the Dutch rate of interest (at 3 or 4 per cent) was a good deal lower than that in Saxony, and recomended the fact to his cousin Lutz as a way out of the financial difficulties of Castell-Remlingen.[41] Those who came to the rescue were Johann Deknatel, a Mennonite minister,[42] Isaac Lelong,[43] an Amsterdam merchant, and Matthäus Beuning, a wealthy Holland Labadist and sympathizer with Zinzendorf.[44] Two years later the first two were among Wesley's contacts in the Netherlands on his way to Herrnhut,[45] but it was the third who now saved the day with a loan of 120,000 florins which enabled the Count to pay off the most urgent of his Saxon debts and make a permanent saving of almost half the service-charge.[46] The subterranean Labadist connection with Western Pietism, which had surfaced at intervals since Spener's salad days in Frankfurt, had again made its mark, this time not to Zinzendorf's benefit in the long term.

Characteristically it was Erdmuthe who signed the contract with the Dutch; after this she seems to have been substantially excluded from the business, and the whole story becomes harder to trace. But she managed to establish some order in the administration under the name of the General Diaconate, and ran it with the aid of a devout Nuremberg merchant, Jonas Paulus Weiss, who in 1738 entered the community and devoted his wealth to its work.[47] One of the Count's connections may have been valuable for cash, or may principally have illustrated Zinzendorf's extraordinary capacity for picking up threads of the revivalist past. In 1734 Zinzendorf, seeking ordination and impeccable Lutheran credentials, took a job under an assumed name with a merchant of Stralsund, Abraham Ehrenfried Richter, obtained a certificate of doctrinal rectitude from the rigidly Orthodox faculty at Greifswald in Swedish Pomerania, and ordination. The Orthodox press maintained that Zinzendorf had squeezed 100,000 *Taler* from Richter, and sent him to his death in Algeria.[48] Zinzendorf said that Richter was financially in low water when they met, and, having begged to join the Moravian community, came to Herrnhut with only 1,000 *Taler*, as *Inspektor* of the Count's manufacturers. Here he bought and extended the Vogtshof, which became the administrative headquarters of the Unity, and after preaching to gypsies in the Wetterau, felt a call to preach to Christian slaves in Algiers, and died in the plague of 1740.[49] Whatever the truth about the money, it is curious that Richter had been one of the backers of Charles XII's crusade in Silesia, behind which revival had begun.[50]

It was the Dutch consul who obtained permission for Richter's entry from the Dey of Algiers,[51] and it was Dutch money which played the leading role in the rapid development of the Unity in the next few years. Zinzendorf must provide a retreat should Herrnhut become untenable, and he turned first to those curious reformed principalities in the Wetterau where, for a generation, religious toleration had been made an economic asset,[52] and where for some years he had been fruitlessly negotiating with the Inspired and other enthusiasts.[53] After securing the castle at Marienborn on a temporary basis, Zinzendorf obtained a new lease and began negotiations for a ruined castle on the Ronneburg. The accommodation at the Ronneburg was too restricted for a settlement, but Zinzendorf acquired it on lease, put in a congregation and a children's institution, and, remarkably, often returned there himself for solitude. Marienborn was in the territory of the Count of Ysenburg-Meerholz, and Zinzendorf at first thought to build a colony there, but the Count of Ysenburg-Büdingen offered a site by the Haag churchyard, and it was there, Zinzendorf now being under sentence of perpetual banishment from Saxony, that Herrnhaag was built. Thither Zinzendorf transferred some of the central institutions and the original Moravian exiles under the name of the Pilgrim Congregation, and soon Herrnhaag surpassed the growth Herrnhut had attained in twenty years. Meanwhile after various developments an important settlement was begun in the Netherlands at Zeyst: Zeyst was an estate belonging to Count Nassau, a son of William III, who had built a fine house upon it occupied in 1672 by Louis XIV, and an elegant settlement was developed in the grounds. The Marienborn estate was obtained by means of a loan of 150,000 *Taler* to the heavily indebted Count of Ysenburg-Meerholz, the money being provided by Mathäus Beuning, and Zinzendorf taking no part in the negotiation.[54] The Büdingen negotiation was conducted by a Salzburger member of the community, Hofer, and was clinched by a loan from Beuning of 150,000 florins. Another 16,000 was paid for two other plots.[55] Zeyst cost 200,000 florins, the money being provided by Cornelius and Jakob Schellinger, two Mennonite financiers who had come over to the Brethren, Mathäus Beuning, Cornelius van Laer, and Jan Verbeek.[56] These great sums were of course independent of what was required for lavish building-projects and missions world-wide, but there seemed nothing which cheap Dutch credit could not accomplish. The strength and the weakness of the almighty florin were, however, speedily to be revealed.

Zinzendorf, ten years an exile, had never given up hope of getting back to Saxony, and in 1747 began to use language understood in an electorate now much bruised by Frederick the Great, by offering a loan of 100,000 *Taler* at a moderate rate of interest. His correspondence makes it clear that he hoped the Saxon government would send another commission down to Herrnhut in order to establish that that community adhered to the

Augsburg Confession. At the same time a negotiation was staged with the faculties at Leipzig and Wittenberg, by Arvid Gradin, a Swedish Brother who turns up in John Wesley's *Journal*,[57] to show why Orthodox Lutheran Sweden had accepted the Moravians. At this moment Lutheran Orthodoxy in Germany was in full cry against Zinzendorf and his followers. The theologians were not to be bought, but in 1747 the government permitted the Count to return, the following year a commission of inquiry accepted the orthodoxy of Herrnhut, and the castle of Barby which had come to hand through the death of the Duke of Weissenfels was made over to the Brethren, and the press was shifted there. The Saxon government coolly followed up its complacency by asking Zinzendorf to raise it £100,000 sterling at 4 per cent in London, while the Count pressed the community to keep the favour of the government by industrial progress.[58] The whole episode was a preface to the reorganization of Saxony after the Seven Years War by Pietists.[59] Orthodox Saxony, humiliated once by the conversion of the electoral house to Catholicism, endured the second humiliation of being saved by Pietism.

Money, however, did not always talk, and in Ysenburg-Büdingen things were changing. The Moravians' principal friend, Regierungsrat Meyerhof, died in 1745, and the Count himself died in 1749. He was succeeded by his second son, Gustav Friedrich, who was entirely in the pocket of his Regierungsrat Christoph Friedrich Brauer, a ferocious exponent of territorial sovereignty. At the beginning of 1750 he issued a decree requiring the inhabitants of Herrnhaag to take a new oath of homage and to separate themselves from Zinzendorf, or leave the country within three years. The response was that they would accept the oath, but would on no account separate from Zinzendorf; an expulsion order was issued on 18 February, and before the end of the summer the entire community, a thousand souls, had abandoned the Wetterau, leaving only a diaspora congregation at Marienborn, and a graffito on the wall of the prayer-room at Herrnhaag: *Maledicta sit memoria Braueri.* The early Moravian historians looked for an explanation of this calamity to the extraordinary personal animosity which developed between Brauer and Zinzendorf, but it is clear that there were irreconcilable issues of subsistence between them. The years prior to the expulsion were the peak of the 'time of sifting', and the violent animosity which that evoked among the Orthodox made the Moravians less welcome guests. Zinzendorf's incautious language about the theocracy of the Saviour, and the feasting and fireworks at Herrnhaag, which were the normal accompaniment of sovereignty, created a bad impression. But worst of all were the financial relations. In 1747 Zinzendorf had acquired the Wetterau mortgages from Beuning for 300,000 Guilders and became much the largest creditor of both branches of the house of Ysenburg. Then in the course of the complicated transaction he had carried through in Saxony at the time of his loan, the mortgages had passed into the hands of the Saxon *Rent-Cammer*. Scarcely had the Büdingen administration heard of this than an emissary of the Saxon government arrived on their doorstep. Clearly, whatever happened to the Moravians, Zinzendorf must be got rid of, and Brauer stated his case anonymously in a huge tome of nearly 650 pages which, in translation, made a considerable impression in England.[60] The heavy building investment in the Wetterau had always been, in a worldly point, a folly, for the concessions received by the Brethren had all been on short-term contracts. Now the whole house of cards had collapsed, and besides the loss of fixed assets and expensive concessions in the Wetterau, the Brethren must face the expense of resettling those who lived there, the bulk in Pennsylvania, many in Barby and Zeyst, others again in an expensive new French-speaking settlement at Neuwied on the Rhine.[61]

The mood of reappraisal evoked by this calamity extended to the most recent phase of Moravian spirituality, that phase of *Schwärmerei* led by Zinzendorf himself, known as 'the time of sifting', which one historian of the Brethren felt able to date very precisely from 19 September 1745 when the Count wrote his poem on the 'little cross-air bird' (*Kreuzluftvögelein*).[62] The Moravian method for inducing conversion quicker than the Francke scheme had always been that of imaginative identification with the Crucified Lord; now in Moravian parlance there were rivers of blood; it was discovered that the wound in the side made by the spear, and endlessly adored as 'the little side-hole', was the straight and narrow way the Christian must tread,[63] the place where the 'little cross-air bird' devotedly circling the cross must nest. Zinzendorf always had a streak of childishness in him,[64] and he now launched a wave of circulated *naïveté* which had the Moravians singing exuberantly of a whole menagerie of twee diminutives, the little cross-air dove, the little cross-air sponge, the little cross-air hen, the little cross-air lamb, the little cross-air bee, the little cross-air lark, the little cross-air swallow, and untold others. Almost every kind of explanation from depth psychology to folk-lore, has been called in to interpret what was actually Zinzendorf's most fertile and creative period. It seems to me that two different questions require an answer. As regards the substance of the *Schwärmerei* we need to know the origins of the imagery, some of it clearly very ancient, and how it got into Zinzendorf's mind to be conjured up in the later forties. This is a vast subject in its own right. The second question is why the outburst came when it did. With remarkable unanimity contemporary and modern historians of the Brethren say that Zinzendorf felt the pressure of the Enlightenment and was trying to seal his followers against its dread influence.[65] This explanation seems to me entirely unacceptable. So far as Enlightenment went, the one new factor in Germany was the accession of the Count's hero Frederick the Great[66] in 1740, and this showed every sign of being one of the best things that ever happened to the community. Their inveterate enemies at Halle lost the ear of the Prussian government after almost fifty years. The shoemakers of Herrnhut were swamped with orders for army boots for the Silesian campaigns, and Silesia itself was opened to the Brethren. Whereas Charles XII's Protestant crusade in Silesia was followed by preachers from Halle, Frederick the Great was followed by the Moravians, picking up the survivors of the revival of 1707–8, and using them to help establish new Moravian settlements which basked in royal favour.[67] Of course, for long enough Zinzendorf's agents had been getting up pro-Prussian sentiment in Silesia.[68] The new and oppressive things in the forties were internal to the community; Zinzendorf's followers had tried to organize themselves as a sect, and had been restrained only by the assertion of dictatorial authority by the Count, and that dictatorship had been confronted by immediate financial strain. Zinzendorf in effect gambled wildly, and from 1747 was unable to meet all the interest on the debts he had contracted. In 1727 the social strains in the community had been sublimated in revival; perhaps now a great outpouring of childlike innocence might be the best way out of the sophisticated tangle in which the community's affairs were involved. Certainly in Spangenberg's account of the motives which led to the summoning of the Synod of Barby in 1750 the need to get rid of the excesses of the 'time of sifting' and to face dire financial emergency stand side by side.[69] And in the most personal of his apologetic works he coupled the two again.

> I cannot deny that to me his [Zinzendorf's] addresses often appeared paradoxical and his methods of business extraordinary. I must also admit, that I was often reluctant towards them, and on this account not seldom let myself out in my free way. But in all this his basis remained in my view rock-firm, and his pure intention, his heart burning for his Saviour, commended itself to my heart, no less than his orthodox, old-theological, and caring attitude to the Lutheran church.[70]

For a double-edged problem a double system of control was prepared. Spangenberg was not loathe to have Zinzendorf in London for the rest of his life, and on the spiritual and intellectual side pushed the community steadily back towards Lutheran Orthodoxy. By origin a professional theologian who had once shared a post at Halle with Sigmund Jacob Baumgarten,[71] Spangenberg had never really cared for the autodidact in Zinzendorf, and thought that his unprofessional use of theological language had caused avoidable trouble with the Orthodox. If Zinzendorf had aimed to realize the unity of Christians divided by confessional systems, and had been blessedly free from the quirks of the schools, Spangenberg's well-schooled language was taken up into a systematic theology, which did not go beyond the utterances of Scripture[72] and which, in the words of a modern Moravian commentator, was

> ... intended to place before ministers and members of the Moravian Church a scheme of Christian doctrine expressed in biblical language and to present to friends of the Unity a vindication of its orthodox and catholic character ... It ... answered any question regarding the soundness of their doctrinal position.[73]

How burdensome the purging of Zinzendorf's eccentric language might become may be illustrated by the following prayers. The Count's Litany of the Wounds in 1743 contained the following simple petition: 'May the dear sweat of thy toil lighten all our labour; may thy faithful craftsmanship make us faithful in our turn'. Fourteen years later this had been expanded to half a page of modern type and commenced:

> Dear lord God, bless us with your industry in toil . . . Grant . . . that our prince and all his ministers may guide and protect us so that we under them may lead a peaceful and quiet life in all godliness and integrity. May we be subject to all human ordinance for thy sake. Teach us to seek the best for the place thou hast for us . . . Take on thyself the pressing needs of the congregation . . . Grant us managers, so that things may go honestly among us not only before the Lord, but also before man. Sanctify our commerce. Bless the sweat of our brow and our faithful craftsmanship that noone in trouble may discern the aftertaste of sin.[74]

And so on for petition after petition.

If on the one side the Brethren were subjected to a new rigour of language, thought, and devotion, they were subjected on the other to the discipline of the market. In Herrnhut itself this meant official encouragement for Abraham Dürninger, a successful linen-merchant, who undertook to develop the business for the benefit of the community, speedily got into the export markets, opened the first cotton and chintz factory in Saxony, and made a fat profit from the Prussian effort in the Seven Years War.[75] The spectacular efforts of Dürninger were matched in Yorkshire and encouraged elsewhere,[76] with the result that in the long run the Unity was deeply marked by the relative economic dynamism of the larger host-communities. The firm of Abraham Dürninger still survives in the Socialist DDR, supported by West German capital, and the subject of some rather anxious casuistry by Moravian apologists.[77] The economic functions of the Yorkshire settlement at Fulneck were detroyed by the superior power of Yorkshire capitalism; while Bethlehem, Pennsylvania, became the headquarters of the mighty Bethelehem Steel Corporation.[78]

That these disciplines were badly needed was to be revealed by events in England, the Moravian field least affected by the 'time of sifting',[79] and from 1749 the headquarters of their enterprise.[80] The Moravian fields furthest from the centre, namely Pennsylvania and Livonia, were independently financed, and England would have been much better off in like case. But in 1749 Zinzendorf negotiated successfully to obtain an act pronouncing the Brethren to be an ancient episcopal church and granting them privileges in the colonies; and British finances could not help being confused with expenses incurred for the benefit of the Unity as a whole. Nor did Zinzendorf's ambitions in the way of bricks and mortar diminish. He rented Northampton House in Bloomsbury Square; then rented Ingatestone Hall, twenty miles out, as well, to provide peace and quiet; and then, to set up the Brethren in a style befitting the English aristocracy, he acquired Lindsey House, the residence of the Dukes of Ancaster, complete with park, on the Thames at Chelsea, and the Beaufort grounds next door. The cost of converting and extending these premises of course also greatly exceeded the estimate.[81] The long-impending financial crisis broke in January 1753 when the Brethren's correspondent, a Portuguese Jew called Jacob Gomez Serra, failed, owing them over £76,000. The Dutch credit network collapsed in a most un-philadelphian confusion of lawsuits and theological bickering. An English statement of the indebtedness here (to the tune of £132,000) was not made more palatable by the attacks of Whitefield. Zinzendorf prepared to go to prison, but, assured by the lot that he would not have to do so, 'enjoyed a quiet siesta'.[82] In the nick of time a favourable wind brought the Dutch packet in early, bearing just sufficient money to turn the corner again. But Lindsey House did not long remain in the hands of the Brethren, and Zinzendorf was suspended from his office.[83] It took fifty years to pay off his debts, and in the effort to do so, the Brethren hit on a device which has escaped the mainstream episcopacies. Zinzendorf's suspension enabled the management of the Church to be put under administrators, whose successors still have their shoulder to the wheel. Pastoral care, which bulks so large in the theory of episcopacy and plays so small a part in its usual practice, is actually the business of the bishops of the Brethren.

This curious story is uncommonly difficult to sum up. Zinzendorf had little success with his philadelphian ideals, and even in Lusatia where many Brethren retain a dual membership with the *Landeskirche* of a sort that Methodism mostly lost with the Church of England, they suffer, arguably, an unreasonable brake on their liberty. On the other hand a valuable addition was made to the ranks of the Protestant denominations with, at its best, an unusual capacity for supporting missionary zeal by an ability to realize a Christian ideal within the terms of unfamiliar cultures. From the historian's point of view it is clear that the kind of networks of pious businessmen which were the making of Moody and Sankey and their twentieth-century successors, already existed in the eighteenth century, and were not only one of the subordinate factors moving the axis of revival westwards, but, finding that the revivalist of the day, against every reasonable expectation, was a count of the Holy Roman Empire, were actually prepared to pay the rate for the job. From the standpoint of our conference theme, it is plain that those who aspire to be as innocent as doves, let alone as innocent as the little cross-air bird nesting in the little side-hole, had better be as wise as serpents; Zinzendorf was a good deal less wise than even bourgeois old Wesley. And the successes of Dürninger, among so many failures, do not weaken the force of Adam Smith's sly thrust that 'I have never known much good done by those who affected to trade for the public good'.[84] But what of Spangenberg? By an heroic effort of enforcing the scholarly disciplines in various areas of the community's life he built a long-term future for the Brethren out of parlous circumstances, and an assembly of scholars will not underestimate that achievement. But whereas Zinzendorf was blessedly free of academic nostrums, had perhaps an excess of liturgical fertility, and restored Christianity as a cheerful religion after the churches had devoted a century to putting the flock through the mangle of Orthodoxy, the price of survival and acknowledgement by the Lutheran churches was the transformation of the Brethren into *die Stillen im Lande* which they have been ever since. The scholarship of mainstream Christianity has a great deal to answer for.

Notes

1 This theme is most fully worked out in Wesley's Sermon no. 50 on Luke 16.9, 'Make to yourselves friends of the mammon of unrighteousness', but he was sufficiently confident of it to return to it on several occasions, for example, *The letters of John Wesley*, ed. J. Telford, London, 1931 5.8–6.207. Compare also Sermon no. 116§8.

2 *Das neueste Gespräch im dem Reiche der Lebendigen zwischen dem Herrnhutischen . . . Grafen von Zinzendorf und einem Freymaürer . . .* Frankfurt/Leipzig, 1741, p. 27.

3 *Ausführliche historische und Theologische Nachricht von der Herrenhuthischen Brüderschaft . . . mit einer Fortsetzung,* Franckfurth, 1743, p. 50. reprinted in the Olms reprint of the works of Zinzendorf (referred to below as *Zinzendorf Werke*) Reihe 2, Bd. 14, Hildesheim, 1976). It was also maintained that the attraction of Herrnhut was freedom from *Leibeigenschaft* [C.F.

Demelius], *Vollständige sowohl historisch- als theologische Nachricht von der Herrnhutische Brüderschaft . . .* Frankfurt/Leipzig, 1735, pp. 10–11.

4 'I.C.T.' [otherwise anonymous], *Sammlung einige Briefe beruhmter und gottseliger theologorum zur Erläuterung des Zinzendorfischen Unwesens*, Hamburg, 1748, pp. 25–31.

5 *Ausführliche Nachricht . . . Fortsetzung* [see above n. 3], pp. 47, 108.

6 G. Whitefield, *An Expostulatory letter addressed to Nicholas Lewis, Count Zinzendorf*, in *Works*, London, 1771, 4, pp. 251–61 (German tr. *Ein Bestraffungsschreiben an hrn . . . Grafen von Zinzendorf*, Halle, 1753. This edn included a letter from Zinzendorf denying the charges of his indebtedness).

7 Ludwig Carl Freiherr von Schrautenbach, *Der Graf Zinzendorf und die Brüdergemeine seiner Zeit*, ed. J.W. Kölbing, Gnadau, 1851, p. 452 repr. in *Zinzendorf Werke*, Reihe 2, Bd. 9, Hildesheim, 1972.

8 Otto Andreas Woldershausen, *Gegründete Nachrichten von dem Ursprung, Fortgang und Mitteln zur Ausbreitung der Herrnhutische Secte*, Wittenberg/Zerbst, 1749, pp. 49, 55: Johann Philip Fresenius, *Bewährte Nachrichten von Herrnhutischen Sachen*, 4 vols, Frankfurt, 1746–51, 2.318, 330.

9 Otto Andreas Woldershausen, *Das Leben des Herrn Grafen Nicolaus Ludwig von Zinzendorf*, Wittenberg/Zerbst, 1749, p. 9.

10 August Gottlieb Spangenberg, *Apologetische Schlussschrift*, Leipzig/Görlitz, 1751, p. 379 repr. in *Zinzendorf Werke, Ergänzungsband 3*, Hildesheim, 1964: August Gottlieb Spangenberg, *Leben des Herrn Nicolaus Ludwig Grafen und Herrn von Zinzendorf und Pottendorf*, 8 vols, n.pl. [Barby], 1771–5, p. 1586, repr. in *Zinzendorf Werke*, Reihe 2, Bde. 1–8, Hildesheim, 1971. Zinzendorf did not always weigh his words carefully, and some of what he published invited charges of this kind. *Büdingische Sammlung*, 3 vols, Büdingen, 1742–3, 3.228 [Rept. *Zinzendorf Werke, Ergänzungsband 9*, Hildesheim, 1966].

11 The reference is to Luke 22.31.

12 See especially his introduction to the reprints of the *Teutsche Gedichte* (1766) (*Zinzendorf Werke, Ergänzungsband 2*, Hildesheim, 1964 and the Catholic writings (*Zinzendorf Werke, Ergänzungsband 10*, Hildesheim, 1970). Compare Archive of the Renewed Unity of the Brethren [hereafter Herrnhut MSS] R. 20 A1. Darstellungen Zinzendorfs aus seiner früheren Zeit.

13 He spoke even of 'the nobility' of Christ's decision to become man. Schrautenbach, *Graf Zinzendorf*, p. 83, repr. in *Zinzendorf Werke*, Reihe 2, Bd. 9.

14 *Teutsche Gedichte*, p. 178, repr. in *Zinzendorf Werke, Ergänzungsband 2*.

15 On whom see Walther von Boetticher, *Geschichte des Oberlausitzischen Adels und seiner Güter, 1635–1815*, 4 vols, Görlitz, 1912–23. The von Gersdorf family is treated at 1.424–608. Spangenberg declared that Zinzendorf loved both the natural and the political peculiarities of Upper Lusatia. *Leben Zinzendorfs*, p. 178, repr. in *Zinzendorf Werke*, Reihe 2, Bd. 2. As late as 1753 a German tourist in London was surprised to hear Zinzendorf preaching in the Fetter Lane Chapel in 'a quite simple and common Upper Lusatian dialect'. E.

Vehse, *Geschichte des Höfe des hauses Sachsen*, pt 7 – *Geschichte der deutschen Höfe seit der Reformation*, 34, Hamburg, 1854, p. 71.

16 On this see C. Knauthe, *Derer Oberlausitzer Sorbwenden umständliche Kirchengeschichte*, ed. R. Olesch, Cologne/Vienna, 1980: A. Mietzschke, 'Lusatica aus dem Anfang des 18. Jahrhundert', *Zeitschrift für slavische Philologie*, 17, pt 2 (1941), 123–42. Compare R. Lehmann, *Geschichte des Markgraftums Niederlausitz. Der Schicksalsweg einer ostdeutschen Landschaft und ihrer Menschen*, Dresden, 1937, pp. 326–45: H. Petri, 'Der Pietismum in Sorau N-L', *Jahrbuch für Brandenburgische Kirchengeschichte*, 9–10 (1913), pp. 126–203.

17 E. Winter, *Die Pflege der West- und Süd- slavischen Sprachen in Halle im 18. Jahrhundert* [East] Berlin, 1954, pp. 31–42.

18 O. Brunner, *Adeliges Landleben und Europäischer Geist*, Salzburg, 1949.

19 Schrautenbach, *Der Graf Zinzendorf* 66, repr. in *Zinzendorf Werke*, Reihe 2, Bd. 9. Zinzendorf also shared the eating habits of the German aristocracy and became corpulent in old age.

20 Spangenberg, *Leben Zinzendorfs*, p. 1442, repr. in *Zinzendorf Werke*, Reihe 2, Bd. 5).

21 *Büdingische Sammlung* I, Vorrede [n.p.] Footnote. repr. in *Zinzendorf Werke*, *Ergänzungsband* 7.)

22 Spangenberg, *Leben Zinzendorfs*, p. 79, repr. in *Zinzendorf Werke*, Reihe 2, Bd. 1.

23 On this group see F.W. Barthold, *Die Erweckten im protestantischen Deutschland während des Ausgangs des 17. und der ersten Hälfte des 18. Jahrhunderts, besonders die frommen Grafenhöfe*, repr. from *Historische Taschenbuch 1852–3*, ed. F. von Raumer, Darmstadt, 1968: also H.-W. Erbe, *Zinzendorf und der fromme hohe Adel seiner Zeit*, Leipzig, 1928 repr. in *Zinzendorf Werke*, Reihe 2, Bd. 12.

24 *Zeitschrift für Brüdergeschichte* 8 (1914), 13, repr. in *Zinzendorf Werke*, Reihe 3, Bd. 3, Hildesheim 1973.

25 O. Uttendörfer, *Alt-Herrnhut. Wirtschaftsgeschichte und Religionssoziologie Herrnhuts während seiner ersten zwanzig Jahre, 1722–42*, Herrnhut, 1925, p. 144.

26 J. Grosse, *Studien über Friedrich von Watteville. Ein Beitrag zur Geschichte des Herrnhutertums*, Halle, 1914, p.25.

27 T.E. Schmidt, *Zinzendorfs soziale Stellung und ihr Einfluss auf seinen Charakter und sein Lebenswerk*, Basel, 1900, p. 43.

28 Uttendörfer, *Alt-Herrnhut*, p. 145.

29 Spangenberg, *Leben Zinzendorfs*, p. 1080, repr. in *Zinzendorf Werke*, Reihe 2, Bd. 4. Compare E. Beyreuther, *Zinzendorf und die sich allhier beisammen finden*, Marburg an der Lahn, 1959, pp. 254–5.

30 Zinzendorf's defenders followed suit: '*Entrepreneurs* of all classes with large and extensive views, misunderstanding the Count, took him at first for a man whom they could use to accomplish their own chimerical projects; but when he spoke against them or showed in practice that he wanted nothing to do with

them, took offence, and threatened controversy or attacked him without warning'. [Imprimatur – Polycarp Müller] *Siegfrieds Bescheidene Beleuchtung*, n.pl., 1744, p. 97, repr. in *Zinzendorf Werke*, Reihe 2, Bd. 16, Hildesheim, 1982, p. 317. On the French usage compare R. Cantillon, *Essai sur la nature du commerce en general*, ed. H. Higgs, London, 1931, p. 54; J.A. Schumpeter, *History of Economic Analysis*, Oxford, 1954, p. 555.

31 On all this see H. Weigelt, *Die Beziehungen zwischen Ludwig Friedrick zu Castell-Remlingen und Zinzendorf so wie ihr Briefwechsel. Ein Beitrag zur Geschichte des Herrnhuter Pietismus in Franken*, Neustadt an der Aisch, 1984, pp. 9–10: E. Beyreuther, *Der junge Zinzendorf*, 2nd edn Marburg an der Lahn, 1957, pp. 215–21.

32 Uttendörfer, *Alt-Herrnhut*, pp. 18–45.

33 Christian Knauthe, *Annales Typographici Lusatiae Superioris oder Oberlausitzchen Buchdruckereien*, Lauban, 1740: repr. Cologne/Vienna, 1980, p. XI*. The printers were also championed by Zinzendorf's uncle, Privy Councillor von Gersdorf, Oberamthauptmann of Gorlitz, who forbade the establishment of the press, and was attacked by his nephew for hostility to 'the appearance of the Kingdom of God in Upper Lusatia'. Beyreuther, *Zinzendorf und die sich allhier beisammen finden*, p. 96.

34 Ebersdorf also had the advantage of being free of the Saxon censorship. A. Kobuch, 'Die Zensur in Kursachsen zur Zeit der Personalunion mit Polen (1697–1763). Beiträge zur Geschichte der Aufklärung', Dr. Diss. Humboldt Universität zu Berlin, 1965, 1.160.

35 Quoted in Uttendörfer, *Alt-Herrnhut*, p. 25.

36 Weigelt, *Beziehungen zwischen Castell-Remlingen und Zinzendorf*, p. 95.

37 This account is based mainly on material gathered by Uttendörfer, *Alt-Herrnhut*, pp. 125–34, 146–60. See also W. Jannasch, 'Erdmuthe Dorothea, Gräfin von Zinzendorf geborene Gräfin Reuss zu Plauen', *Zeitschrift für Brüdergeschichte*, 8 (1914), pp. 1–507, esp. pp. 87, 94–8, repr. in *Zinzendorf Werke*, Reihe 3, Bd. 3: N.L. von Zinzendorf, *Die gegenwärtige Gestalt des Kreuz-Reichs Jesu in seiner Unschuld* (1745), pp. 112–14, repr. in *Zinzendorf Werke, Ergänzungsband* 5, Hildesheim, 1965.

38 Erbe, *Zinzendorf und der fromme Adel*, p. 120, repr. in *Zinzendorf Werke*, Reihe 2, Bd. 12, p. 492.

39 Jannasch, 'Erdmuthe Dorothea', *Zeitschrift für Brüdergeschichte*, 8 (1914), p. 127, repr. in *Zinzendorf Werke*, Reihe 3, Bd. 3. The Count's itineraries are appended to the second and third volumes of Erich Beyreuther's biography, *Zinzendorf und die sich allheir beisammen finden*, pp. 289–90: *Zinzendorf und die Christenheit*, Marburg an der Lahn, 1961, pp. 291–4.

40 Spangenberg, *Leben Zinzendorfs*, p. 963, repr. in *Zinzendorf Werke*, Reihe 2, Bd. 4: N.L. von Zinzendorf, *ΠΕΡΙ ΕΑΥΤΟΥ. Das ist naturelle Reflexiones . . . n.pl. or d.* [1746], p. 237, repr. in *Zinzendorf Werke, Ergänzungsband* 4, Hildesheim, 1964.

41 Weigelt, *Beziehungen zwischen Castell-Remlingen und Zinzendorf*, p. 145.

42 Johann Deknatel (1698–1759), a leading Mennonite minister in Amsterdam,

who brought about an evangelical revival among a religious community tending to unitarianism, and strove actively for a union among the scattered Baptists of Hungary. He was listed as one of the Amsterdam Brethren in 1744 (A. Reincke, *Members of the Moravian church and of persons attached to the said church . . . between 1727 and 1754*, Bethlehem, Pa., 1873, p. 45), but his financial assistance ended in his instituting lawsuits against them. His portrait is preserved in the archive at Herrnhut.

43 Isaac Lelong (1683–1762) seems not to have been a member of the Moravian community.

44 J. Taylor Hamilton, *A history of the church known as the Moravian Church or Unitas Fratrum*, Bethlehem, Pa., 1900: repr. New York, 1970, p. 147. Catharine Beuning, probably his wife, became a member of the Moravian congregation in Amsterdam. Reincke, *Members of the Moravian church*, p. 45.

45 John Wesley, *Journal*, ed. N. Curnock, 2nd edn, London, 1938, 2.6: *The Works of John Wesley*, 25, *Letters* I, ed. F. Baker, Oxford, 1980, p. 584–5.

46 David Cranz, *Alte und Neue Brüder-Historie* (Barby, 1772), p. 561, repr. in *Zinzendorf Werke*, Reihe 2, Bd. 11, Hildesheim, 1973: Eng. tr. *The ancient and modern history of the Brethren* by Benjamin La Trobe, London, 1780, p. 409. Taylor Hamilton, *History*, p. 147 says the loan was 20,000 fl.; Jannasch 'Erdmuthe Dorothea', p. 193 says 30,000; the figure quoted is given in Herrnhut MSS R 20 A. 2. 33.

47 Jonas Paulus Weiss (1695–1775) was given charge of the small congregation of the Brethren at Nuremberg, Weigelt, *Beziehungen zwischen Castell-Remlingen und Zinzendorf*, p. 135, n. 22, and later distinguished himself by advocating the formation of a college of businessmen to finance the unity by promoting commerce and manufactures. (O. Uttendörfer, *Wirtschaftsgeist und Wirtschaftsorganization der Brüdergemeine von 1742 bis zur Ende des Jahrhunderts*, Herrnhut, 1926, p. 37.) On the Diaconate, Schrautenbach, *Graf von Zinzendorf*, p. 487, repr. in *Zinzendorf Werke*, Reihe 2, Bd. 9. Compare Woldershausen, *Gegründete Nachrichten*, p. 17.

48 Woldershausen, *Leben des Grafen*, pp. 9, 46–52: Woldershausen, *Gegründete Nachrichten*, p. 17.

49 Beyreuther, *Zinzendorf und die Christenheit*, pp. 76, 82: Zinzendorf, *Naturelle Reflexiones*, pp. 121, 186, repr. in *Zinzendorf Werke, Ergänzungsband* 4.

50 This seems to be the implication of Spangenberg, *Leben Zinzendorfs*, p. 829 n., repr. in *Zinzendorf Werke*, Reihe 2, Bd. 4. Compare Schrautenbach, *Graf Zinzendorf*, p. 215, repr. in *Zinzendorf Werke*, Reihe 2, Bd. 9.

51 Taylor Hamilton, *History*, p. 65.

52 On the origins of this see M. Benad, *Toleranz als Gebot christlicher Obrigkeit. Das Büdinger Patent von 1712*. Studia Irenica, 27, Hildesheim, 1983.

53 M. Goebel, 'Geschichte der wahren Inspirations-Gemeinden von 1688 bis 1850. Als ein Beitrag zur Geschichte des christlichen Lebens aus bisher unbenutzten Quellen', *Zeitschrift für historische Theologie*, N.F. 19 (1855), pp. 137–60, 327–42; M. Goebel, *Geschichte des christlichen Lebens in der*

rheinisch-westphalischen evangelischen Kirche, 2 vols in 3, Coblenz, 1849–52 3, pp. 150–4.

54 Beyreuther, *Zinzendorf und die Christenheit*, p. 120: Spangenberg, *Leben Zinzendorf*, pp. 1490–2, repr. in *Zinzendorf Werke*, Reihe 2, Bd. 5.

55 Beyreuther, p. 163: A.G. Spangenberg, *Darlegung richtiger Antworten auf mehr als dreyhundert Beschuldigungen gegen den Ordinarium Fratrum*, Leipzig/Görlitz, 1751, pp. 27–8, 224–32, repr. in *Zinzendorf Werke, Ergänzungsband* 5.

56 Taylor, *History*, p. 122; Schrautenbach, *Graf von Zinzendorf*, p. 414, repr. in *Zinzendorf Werke*, Reihe 2, Bd. 9.

57 Wesley, *Journal* 2.47–9. Arvid Gradin (1704–54) was born at Wiks, Sweden, the son of a clergyman. He came under Pietist influence in 1724, and made contact with Dippelianism in the 'thirties. He was won to Moravianism by reading a book and by a personal visit. In 1740 he was despatched to Constantinople to negotiate with the Greek Church through personal interviews with the Patriarch. The negotiations were fruitless but he served as a chaplain to the Swedish embassy. In 1741 he was sent on an evangelistic mission in Sweden and Norway which finally obtained the approval of the Archbishop of Stockholm. He was imprisoned in Russia on a diplomatic mission to the Holy Synod in 1743. He wrote a short history of the *Unitas Fratrum* which was translated into English in 1743 and sold by James Hutton (*Svenska Män och Kvinner*, 3.80). For Gradin's theological views see G. Hök, *Zinzendorf's Begriff der Religion*, Uppsala Universitets Arsskrift, 6 (1948), pp. 147–52. He is said to have declined the offer of a chair at Uppsala soon after arriving at Herrnhut.

58 F. Körner, *Die kursächsische Staatsregierung den Grafen Zinzendorf und Herrnhut bis 1760 gegenüber*, Leipzig, 1878, pp. 59–71; Cranz, *Alt-und Neue Brüder-Historie*, pp. 459–63, 465–9, repr. in *Zinzendorf Werke*, Reihe 2, Bd. 11: Eng. tr. pp. 336–9, 341–3.

59 H. Schlechte, 'Pietismus und Staatsreform 1762/63 in Kursachsen' in *Archivar und Historiker. Festschrift für H.O. Meisner*, Berlin, 1965, pp. 364–82.

60 *Historische Nachricht von den Mährischen Brüdern zu Herrnhaag* . . . Frankfurt/Leipzig, 1751, repr. and splendidly introduced by Hans Schneider in *Zinzendorf Werke*, Reihe 2, Bd. 18, Hildesheim, 1978 (Eng. tr. by Henry Rimius, *The history of the Moravians, from their first settlement at Herrnhaag* . . . *down to the present time* . . . London, 1754).

61 On this see T. Wotschke, 'Herrnhuter Briefe aus Neuwied', *Monastsheft für Rheinische Kirchengeschichte*, 26 (1932), pp. 108–28: T. Wotschke, 'Neuwieder Gemeinde Nachrichten von Juli 1753 bis Juli 1754', *Ibid.*, pp. 136–51.

62 Herrnhut MSS. Johannes Plitt's MS. Neue Brüdergeschichte [1829] 4, fol. 303.

63 Moravian Archive, Muswell Hill: MS Gemeinhausdiarium 1747, March 26.

64 Spangenberg, *Leben Zinzendorfs*, p. 2012, repr. in *Zinzendorf Werke*, Reihe 2, Bd. 7.

65 Cranz, *Alte-und Neue Brüder-Historie*, p. 510, repr. in *Zinzendorf Werke*,

Reihe 2, Bd. 11: Eng. tr. p. 373: O. Uttendörfer, *Zinzendorf und die Mystik*, Berlin, n.d. [1950], p. 286: Beyreuther, *Zinzendorf und die Christenheit*, p. 238.

66 Zinzendorf had almost become confessor to Frederick's father. G. Meyer, 'Zinzendorf als Vetreter des Ostdeutsch-schlesischen Frömmigkeitstypus', *Jahrbuch der Schlesischen Friedrich-Wilhelms-Universität zu Breslau*, 5 (1960), p. 93, repr. in *Zinzendorf Werke*, Reihe 2, Bd. 12, p. 757: J. Klepper, *Der Soldatenkönig und die Stillen im Lande*, Berlin, 1938, pp. 135–59.

67 Taylor Hamilton, *History*, pp. 114–15: Cranz, *Alte und Neue Brüder-Historie*, p. 378, repr. in *Zinzendorf Werke*, Reihe 2, Bd. 11: Eng. tr., p. 279): *Zinzendorf Werke*, Reihe 2, Bd. 16, Hildesheim, 1982, pp. 22*–3*.

68 See *Zinzendorf Werke*, Reihe 2, Bd. 14, Hildesheim, 1976, pp. XXV, XXIX, LXXII, n. 32: Carl Regent, *Unpartheyische Nachricht von der . . . neuen Sect . . .* Breslau, 1729, repr. in *ibid.*

69 Spangenberg, *Leben Zinzendorfs*, p. 1839, repr. in *Zinzendorf Werke*, Reihe 2, Bd. 6.

70 A.G. Spangenberg, *Declaration über die zeither gegen uns ausgegangen Beschuldigungen* (Leipzig/Görlitz, 1751), p. 18, repr. in *Zinzendorf Werke*, *Ergänzungsband* 5.

71 M. Schloemann, *Siegmund Jacob Baumgarten. System und Geschlichte in der Theologie des Überganges zum Neuprotestantismus*, Göttingen, 1974, p. 37.

72 The Eng. tr. was entitled *An exposition of Christian Doctrine*, London, 1784 (French version, Barby, 1782).

73 D.A. Schattschneider, 'The Missionary Theologies of Zinzendorf and Spangenberg', *Transactions of the Moravian Historical Society*, 22 (1975), p. 225: G. Reichel, *August Gottlieb Spangenberg, Bischof der Brüderkirche*, Tübingen, 1906, p. 229 (repr. in *Zinzendorf Werke*, Reihe 2, Bd. 13, Hildesheim, 1975, p. 245.)

74 O. Uttendörfer, *Wirtschaftsgeist und Wirtschaftsorganisation der Brüdergemeine von 1743 bis zur Ende des Jahrhunderts*, Herrnhut, 1926, p. 34.

75 *Ibid., passim*: Hamilton Taylor, *History*, pp. 155, 159.

76 In 1760 another Dürninger was sought for Ireland: Uttendörfer, *Wirtschaftsgeist*, pp. 53–4.

77 T. Kootz, 'Kapitalismus und Christentum im Blick auf die Wirtschaftsordnung Alt-Herrnhuts', *Unitas Fratrum*, 4 (1978), pp. 94–109.

78 G. Lindt Gollin, *Moravians in Two Worlds. A Study of Changing Communities*, New York, 1967.

79 *Zinzendorf Werke, Hauptschriften* 5, p. XIV, Hildesheim, 1963.

80 Herrnhut MSS. Johannes Plitt, MS. Neue Brüdergeschichte 5, fol. 5.

81 Spangenberg, *Leben Zinzendorfs*, pp. 1764, 1820–3 (repr. *Zinzendorf Werke*, Reihe 2, Bd. 6): D. Benham, *Memoirs of James Hutton*, London, 1856, p. 257.

82 *Ibid.*, pp. 275–7.

83 Spangenberg, *Leben Zinzendorfs*, p. 1933, repr. in *Zinzendorf Werke*, Reihe 2, Bd. 7.

84 E. Roll, *A History of Economic Thought*, London, 1938, p. 48.

9

'An Awakened Christianity'.†
The Austrian Protestants and Their
Neighbours in the Eighteenth Century

The Austrian Protestants of the eighteenth century are not without their memorials; the noble series of *Jahrbücher* produced by the Society for the History of Austrian Protestantism and the bicentennial celebrations of Joseph II's Toleration Patent in 1981 have seen to that. But whereas the Hungarian Protestants are perceived as central to the history of their kingdom, the great Protestant emigration from Salzburg in 1731–2 receives a mention in general histories produced outside England, the Moravian propaganda machine has ensured that the religious fate of Bohemia and Moravia figures in the general myth of Protestant revival, and even the development of Silesian Protestantism has attracted new attention,[1] the Austrian Protestants seem never to be centre stage, though their irritating presence in the wings is admitted to goad the Habsburgs in their search for new methods of government. Contemporaries allowed them a greater significance: the archbishop of Salzburg was warning the bishop of Seckau against the 'incorrigible and contumacious' Protestant members of his Styrian flock as early as 1710;[2] in 1731 the Emperor Charles VI feared that confessional conflicts might endanger negotiations for the Pragmatic Sanction;[3] at the time of the Habsburgs' greatest peril in 1741, Maria Theresia feared an uprising among the Carinthian Protestants;[4] in 1744 an experienced parish priest reckoned that, in the Schladming and Ramsauer district, not more than a third of the adult parishioners could be reckoned

First published in *Journal of Ecclesiastical History* 40 (1989), pp. 53–73.

†'Man könnte ... sagen, dass die Geschichte unserer evangelischen Kirche in Österreich, wenn auch zeitweise auf kleine Wurzelgebiete reduziert, die Geschichte eines sehr intensiven, entschiedenen und erweckten Christentums ist', Oskar Sakrausky, 'Der österreichische Protestantismus', *Carinthia I* clxxi (1981), 11–28 at p. 27.

to be genuine Catholics;[5] and the Jesuits were in full cry there in the 1750s.[6] More importantly the affairs of the Austrian Protestants, though never achieving the astonishing newsworthiness of those of Salzburg at the time of the great emigration, were very widely reported in the context of the fate of Protestantism within the area of Habsburg power and influence[7] and generated a number of serious studies,[8] not to mention attempts to interpret their history in the light of the observations of Bishop Burnet.[9] Some of the modern neglect originates in the very act of memorial building. For the attempts of Austrian Protestants to demonstrate their pedigree in a once-great movement encourage the view that their eighteenth-century period was an uninteresting relic of something formerly much more significant; while the efforts of Protestant polemicists in the Reich at the time to seize on the 'hidden seed' of the secret Protestantism of the Habsburg lands as at least a partial answer to the Catholic question, 'Where were the Protestants before the Reformation?',[10] were equally uninteresting to their successors, who were less interested in the continuity and invariability of religious belief than with its congruity to reason. Moreover, the framework of modern German church historiography, a succession of (doubtless overlapping) periods – Reformation, Counter-Reformation, Orthodoxy, Pietism, Enlightenment – is particularly unhelpful to the history of Austrian Protestantism.[11] In important ways this was always different from that of the Northern Reich. It arrived much later; it was never imposed from above; and it was always in latent or vigorous conflict with a Counter-Reformation which, in one sense, outlasted even Enlightenment and survived into the nineteenth century. And although the Austrian Protestants, having no local Confession, clung in their way to the *Confessio Augustana Invariata*,[12] they never had an age of Orthodoxy. The Orthodox solution to the problem of Christianising successive generations was to concentrate temporal authority behind a religious establishment and a parish system and to reinforce both with a highly articulated doctrinal system guaranteed against polemical assaults by critics of all kinds. The Austrian Protestants never enjoyed the political presuppositions of the former and – having, before the eighteenth century, lost virtually all their leadership, clerical, intellectual and noble – had neither the need for, nor the capacity to produce, the latter. Whatever the failings of the Austrian Protestants in this period, they were not ideological shellbacks. They were a peasant remnant whose confessional grievances were compounded by the fact that their landlords were often religious orders (including the Jesuits) more interested in drawing an income from their properties than in providing pastoral assistance;[13] the peasants of the Reich were adept at securing redress for their grievances through the Reich courts, but this complaint was not actionable.[14] And their confessional stance was

Map of principal places mentioned in the text

reinforced by political judgements, especially the view that the trials of the Turkish wars were occasioned by the policies of the Counter-Reformation in Hungary.[15]

Right or wrong, this view attested the capacity the Austrian Protestants shared with quite ordinary co-religionists elsewhere in the Protestant world to interpret their fate upon a very broad canvas. They were particularly sensitive to what went on in other areas of Habsburg power or influence and in Salzburg, all of which shared the fate of being more or less completely excluded from the international guarantees given to Protestants in the Westphalia settlement, betrayed, so a choice of legends went, either by the self-seeking of the Protestant estates of the empire or by the susceptibility of the Swedish delegation at the peace conference to bribery by Trauttmansdorf, the emperor's chief ambassador.[16] Carinthians were indeed supposed to have introduced Protestanism into the Defereggental,[17] a remote portion of the principality of Salzburg and the first from which Protestants were to be expelled in 1685, at the time of the Revocation of the Edict of Nantes. At the same time the archbishop also clashed with Protestant salt-miners in Hallein, one of whom, exiled for the rest of his days to Nuremberg, turned into the most notable Protestant propandist and evangelist over the whole area of Salzburg, Styria and Carinthia. This was Joseph Schaitberger (1658–1733), the fame of whose exile songs and *Trost-Schreiben* earned him a place immediately after his death in the collected annals of Protestantism since the Reformation, along with such celebrities as Spener and Francke, James II and John Locke.[18] Schaitberger illustrates much of the personal and public history of the religious persecutions of these years and the equivocations to which it gave rise.

His father was a peasant and miner in the Archbishop of Salzburg's
Dürrenberger salt mines, a concern so crucial to the finances of the
principality that covert Protestantism had long enjoyed official connivance;
his mother came from the mining community on the other side of the hill
at Berchtesgaden. Both were Protestants, but Joseph was sent to the
Catholic school. The schoolmaster, however, was his brother, who taught
him reading and writing and read Protestant books with him. At thirteen
Joseph went into the salt mines and at eighteen, on his father's death,
inherited property worth about 1,100 thaler. By twenty-five he was married
and had accumulated a theological library of some 300 volumes. In a
paradoxical way the burdens upon conscience involved in the secret
profession of Protestantism seemed most intolerable when there was
persecution, and equivocation seemed not even to pay; and Schaitberger
and a close circle of friends who 'frequently met, prayed, sang, read the
Scriptures, the catechism and other good books together', anticipated
countless numbers of their fellow Protestants over the next hundred years
in feeling called to make a public profession of their faith at the very time
that the axe was falling in the Defereggental and they themselves were
under pressure. The upshot was that Schaitberger was expelled and left
with a party of fifty, intending to seek employment in the mines in Saxony.
Offers of assistance in Nuremberg, however, induced them to settle there.
Emigration was financially costly. Schaitberger could bring little money
with him and eked out a living by unskilled manual labour; the reward of
fame at the end of a long life was to be specially admitted to a poorhouse,
a former Carthusian monastery, normally reserved for citizens of Nurem-
burg. But the personal cost was even higher. Like the others, the Schaitbergers had been forcibly separated from their daughters, and soon after their
arrival in Nuremberg his wife died of consumption and a broken heart, on
her death-bed constantly begging him to get their children out. It was while
considering how he might do this that Schaitberger began to write the
letters to his countrymen which made him famous, spread right through
Inner Austria and were carried by the exiles of conscience from those
provinces to Pressburg and even to Siebenbürgen at the remotest end of
Hungary;[19] letters of comfort, but also letters to revive and stiffen faith;
letters which remained forbidden literature in Austria even after the Patent
of Toleration in 1781.[20] A legendary reputation right through the area of
secret Protestantism and emotional receptions on his return visits did not
compensate Schaitberger for the loss of his daughters. Three times he
returned for them, but they had been raised as Catholics and could only
regard their father as a stranger. By his third visit one of his daughters was
married. Both refused to leave, though it is said that his eldest daughter,
at the age of twenty-five, came to visit him with a view to converting him

to Catholicism, was herself converted to Protestantism and stayed. At the end of his life Schaitberger saw the fruits of his work and experienced the change of context in which those fruits were reaped. Of the great trains of Protestant exiles from Salzburg whose faith no man had done more than he to revive and strengthen, one came through Nuremberg a year before he died; and he himself was taken up by the pietist party – which had not existed when he left the mines – which exploited the Salzburg crisis. His most useful biography was published in the journal edited by Johann Adam Steinmetz, the great hero of the revival at the Jesus Church in Teschen in Upper Silesia;[21] and the financial straits of his last days were eased by English subscriptions for the relief of Salzburger exiles forwarded by Samuel Urlsperger, Senior of Augsburg.[22] Urlsperger it was who did more than anyone to organise an asylum for a small part of the Salzburgers in Georgia, who raised funds for them throughout his long life and kept their memory evergreen by a series of monumental tomes.[23] He also published collected editions of Schaitberger's works[24] and gave a laudatory account of him to the SPCK.[25]

Schaitberger's career exemplifies the constant interaction between the Austrian Protestants and their neighbours and exemplifies also the options that were open to each. In practice these were limited to three. They could – and there were always some Austrian Protestants who did[26] – adopt the position known in the language of the day as 'indifferentism', the view that salvation was available to the adherents of more churches than one. This position had some attractiveness against Catholic inquisitors who persistently informed autodidact Austrian and Salzburger Protestants that the faith they claimed to hold was in fact Catholicism and that they only refused obedience from contumaciousness.[27] The peril was the understanding in the Lutheran world that the most consistent of all indifferentists had been Thomas Hobbes, who had required subjects to hold the religion of their prince as a matter not just of prudence but of conscience.[28] It was this position, above all, which Schaitberger aimed to destroy, and in the eighteenth century he probably contributed more to Protestant self-definition than the Invariata, many of the characteristic Protestant sticking-points, such as the invocation of saints, being derived from him.[29] The other two options were those of apocalyptic hope and of revival, and these were mixed in varying proportions right through the world of secret Protestantism and through Hungary. When the final crisis was approaching in Salzburg in 1731, one of the Protestants extended the prophecy of the destruction of Jerusalem to the capital city of that principality, thereby dropping a broad hint (studiously ignored) to the king of Prussia as to what was expected of him.[30] Schaitberger, himself in the Lutheran Orthodox manner, had no doubt that the end-time was near, though in him this conviction was less a threat designed to extort repentance while there was yet time than an encouragement to hold on for the short time till God and his saints were vindicated. Adapting an exposition of Daniel ix. 26[31] of the celebrated Johann Arndt, he argued that 'now is God's holy and only-saving Word rooted out by a godless world, through unbelief and idolatry and the hypocrisy of lip-serving Christians. Christ will also be rooted out and denied by those who know God's Word, but for the sake of the belly do not confess it.'[32] But in Schaitberger apocalyptic led not, as in a section of the Huguenot movement, to the pursuit of ends without consideration of means ('enthusiasm' in eighteenth-century parlance), but to a reawakening of faith, strengthened and tested by the harsh discipline of public confession. At the beginning of the eighteenth century neither the English nor the German language had a technical word to describe this revival of the dying (but not dead) embers of faith and conscience. In 1702 Cotton Mather in America used the word 'revival' in this sense; the German word *Erweckung*, which in 1700 still carried additional connotations even within the spiritual sphere, came much later to be an equivalent. On neither the Catholic nor the Protestant side did the vocabulary of confessional conflict include anything adequately to describe what Schaitberger's biographer lamely referred to as 'the grace of God as revealed in persons of the lower class'. Observed phenomenologically in the light of what was later (and still is) known as revival, the secret Protestants were clearly stumbling upon revival, and Schaitberger was one of its preachers. The subjects of the Habsburgs, like the Habsburgs themselves, were looking for new means of Christianising successive generations and were making more rapid progress than their rulers.

The new developments came first among the Protestants of Silesia.[33] In the toils after Westphalia, yet with some rights denied to their fellows in Austria and Salzburg, with the relics of a church system and some leadership, both lay and clerical, Silesian Protestantism was saved by the incursion of Charles XII of Sweden in 1707 and the Convention of Altranstädt. But the religion which then went back into the churches was not the same as that which had been deprived of them two generations before. Domestic piety, informal class meetings, had replaced public worship. Pastors, dispossessed of their livings, survived precariously, keeping in touch with their flocks as itinerants, known already as *Buschpre-diger*, the local equivalent of the Methodist field preachers. Deprived of public standing, the Silesian Protestants turned to inwardness of faith, a certain tenderness of piety which became one of the hallmarks of Protestant revival. Silesian revival was more sober in tone than some of what came later in Central Europe, Britain or America and owed much to the ability of its inherited leadership to keep the reins, a leadership in effective contact with the scholarship of the early Enlightenment. But 'persons of the lower class', less abreast of scholarship, were always likely to take the lead. When Swedish troops entered the country, there being no churches for their use, they held their church parades in the open air, introducing another familiar Methodist word, 'camp meeting' (*Feldgottesdienst*). When the troops moved on, the children of Lower Silesia appropriated this device, meeting several times daily in the open air, without adult co-operation, standing round their elected leaders in prayer and singing. Despite the winter, this 'uprising of the children', as it was called, spread across the country (as news of it was assiduously disseminated across Europe) and reached Breslau in 1708. The objectives of the camp meetings – the restoration of Protestant churches and schools – were politically sensitive in the highest degree, and the meetings were followed up by a new and fanatical race of itinerant preachers backed by Halle.

Orthodox Sweden may have saved the day in Silesia, but it was the pietist agents of Prussia from Halle who seized the advantage. Pietism began with no conception of religious revival, no idea that its prescriptions for supplementing church routines could be pressed into service in place of them. But Halle now fuelled one extraordinary religious revival among thousands of Swedish prisoners of war in Siberia[34] and exploited another based on the new Jesus Church at Teschen in Upper Silesia, which had been obtained by Swedish feats of arms.[35] In retrospect we can recognise that circumstances at Teschen were right for what became one style of Protestant revivalism. A scattered population of 40,000, long deprived of regular church ministrations, but knowing what those ordinances were, suffering a great lack of fellowship and goaded by the knowledge that neighbouring Protestants in Poland, Hungary and Bohemia were in much worse trouble, poured into the Jesus Church and created a religious situation unfamiliar to the established Churches of Prussia and abhorrent to those of Saxony. The situation gave rise to another characteristic technique of Protestant revivalism, the hours of enthusiastic hymn-singing as the scattered congregation gathered and waited for their service. It was the genius of Halle to get the place going on a basis of three or four languages, to generate hope by a rapid extension of literacy and, for over twenty years, to staff it with men of unusual calibre. Of these first, Christoph Nikolaus Voigt had been a tutor to Francke's own children. The most important and attractive, Johann Adam Steinmetz, was a native of Brieg and, as pastor of Tepliwoda, had discovered a gift for eliciting by his preaching abnormal psychological phenomena in quite the manner of the early Wesley;[36] when the preachers were expelled in 1730, he devoted himself, among other things, to making the works of the Anglo-Saxon revivalists who had drawn inspiration from him – men like Jonathan

Edwards and Philip Doddridge – available for the flocks he had left behind.[37] A third, Johann Liberda, a man in whom the political agitator and the preacher were almost indistinguishable, must have been one of the most effective revivalists of all time; it was his mission (and this was the main interest of Halle and the Prussian government in Teschen) to exploit peasant resistance in Bohemia and Moravia and bind together hatred of Catholicisation and of intensified serfdom. This had already led to peasant revolts and to considerable emigration, especially into Saxony, and to the foundation of another religious community by a convert of Steinmetz and hero of John Wesley, Christian David, on the estates of Zinzendorf at Herrnhut. Here, in similar conditions, another important revival took place in 1727. And it was this playing with fire in Bohemia which led the Jesuits to get the preachers out of Teschen. This might be a setback, but it made no difference to Prussia's new status as the defender of the Protestant interest, nor to her equivocal role, religious and political, in Bohemia. In its turn this role encouraged the Habsburgs' obsession with the notion of Prussian interference with their religious affairs in Inner Austria and other parts never penetrated by the agents of Halle.[38]

The great crisis erupted in the archbishopric of Salzburg, where it was supposed there might be a secret Protestant population of 5,000 or 6,000, but some 30,000 finally emigrated, and took everyone by surprise. Yet circumstances were not greatly different from those in Silesia and Bohemia, where developments had helped to fan the embers in Salzburg; and the favourable political conjuncture provided in the one case by the incursion of Charles XII was now provided in the other by the fact that the emperor's liberty to deal harshly with Protestants was temporarily inhibited by his need to secure international recognition, including Protestant recognition, for the Pragmatic Sanction. In a principality long disposed to persecute Protestants and witches, and susceptible to the propaganda of home-produced zealots such as Schaitberger, the advent of Archbishop Firmian and the Jesuits detonated an explosion which the acuter observers both in Germany and Britain recognised was not just confessional survival, but revival.[39] Still more striking is the fact that the Catholic polemic which Corbinian Gärtner built up from contemporary sources preserved by the Salzburg government shows that styles of piety and religious activity were now put to the service of the Augsburg Confession which did not characterise the Churches of that tradition and were a coarser version of what had already been experienced in Silesia and were to reappear in America. He speaks of night meetings at Goldegg where they sang hymns and wept so that the whole countryside could hear, of women preaching (one of the standard signs of the day of the Lord, following Joel ii. 28 and Acts ii. 17–18), of one of the Moseggers at Wagrain preaching so touchingly that his hearers broke out into tears, of the evangelists of Abtenau who went round like fanatics constraining those who had never adhered to the Augsburg Confession to join them, indeed of organised efforts to convert the Catholic population house to house and at the church door. And although the archbishop's dispute with the Dürrenberger miners has much of the industrial confrontation about it, it is here that the clearest evidence of successful Protestant evangelisation emerges. His accusation that the miners sang Lutheran hymns and neglected work was in common form with the charges made against the early meetings of Wesley and Whitefield; E.P. Thompson had not yet dreamed up the theory that Protestant revival was a device for enforcing labour discipline.[40] The final spur to the archbishop's decision to act was the discovery that, at Gastein, phenomena of this kind had been the order of the day since the beginning of the century. There had been a succession of peasant preachers and house meetings nourished by illicit literature, and when, during the crisis of 1731–2, these domestic gatherings became public assemblies held at night or during service time, there was a resource of lay preachers and familiarity with Protestant hymnody on which to draw.[41]

The final outcome in which a religious upheaval, apparently contrived in innocence to extort toleration, ended with mass migrations to the unpalatable refuges on the fringes of the Protestant world from Georgia to the Baltic, created a unique sensation in Europe. Received, preached to[42] and catechised in every town as they were marched across Europe, the Salzburgers jolted the sensibilities of their contemporaries much more sharply than the earlier scandals of the selling of Protestants or their pastors to the galleys. For almost a century German Protestants had felt themselves to be a beleaguered garrison, and could not now refuse their admiration to a lower-class defiance of government in the common cause. The press had a field day and, in the usual newspaper way, was widely reprinted and quoted abroad. The pamphlet and sermon press is reckoned to have run to 500 titles.[43] Still more striking were the line drawings and coloured illustrations on the Salzburgers turning their back on their mountain homeland for the sake of the Gospel. These are a splendid source for the history of Salzburger costume because, for the first time, workers in this medium had to pay the lower orders the compliment of naturalistic, not grotesque, representation. Of course the general agreement that the Salzburger emigration was a deeply significant event did not prevent some disagreement as to what the significance was. Fifty years before Lessing, the newspaper press championed the virtues of toleration on a great scale and translated a message from the king of England to the emperor as saying that, with the defeat of the Turkish menace, Christendom now needed a new basis for its future health.[44] For peasants to have accomplished so much showed that, contrary to received opinion, they were educable and therefore fit recipients for the shoal of improving Enlightenment literature written for them in the next generation,[45] not to mention being transformed 'from parish to patriot' thereafter.[46] The Saxon Orthodox, initially stunned that so successful a propagation of Christianity by un-ecclesiastical devices was possible,[47] began to use excited language in almost the revivalist manner.[48] Like members of the Oxford Holy Club immediately afterwards, good men and women, like Johann Jakob Moser and his wife,[49] were delighted to find they had independently undergone conversion experiences. Georg Conrad Rieger, special superintendent of Stuttgart, spoke of the Salzburger trains being preceded everywhere in Protestant communities by 'moving awakenings' (*beweglichen Erweckungen*),[50] while those more radical German writers who stood at the fountainhead of religious revival in the west of the empire now held that the secret increase of the hidden kingdom of God had reached the point where public outbreaks might be expected anywhere.[51] The works of Arnold,[52] Dippel[53] and Francke[54] had fatally undermined priestcraft in Sweden. Things were little better in Denmark or Saxony; the crown in the household of God was reserved for Zinzendorf.

Even had the miners of Berchtesgaden not now emulated the example of the Salzburgers to get out of their little *Probstei*[55] and the Czech Protestants taken new heart in their struggles,[56] the diplomatic situation would have prevented the emperor from continuing his rather temporising attitude towards the upheaval in the principality. France must somehow be prevented from getting up a religious conflict in the Reichstag and the Prussian alliance be preserved if possible.[57] The political context of Protestant life in Austria over the next fifty years was shaped by a balance of opposed factors. From the standpoint both of domestic peace and the welfare of the Catholic interest in the empire, the Habsburgs and the archbishops of Salzburg had a common interest in containing the Protestant revival and stood together in doing so, with fair consistency. The archbishop was convinced that the Protestants of Carinthia, Styria and the Tyrol were in league with his contumacious subjects, while Charles VI had long harried the bishop of Seckau to put on a drive against the Styrian Protestants.[58] In 1733 he published a resolution embracing the principles which were to underlie Habsburg policy down to the time of the Toleration Patent. Besides intensified missions, religious commissions, houses of conversions and better pastoral care, which might assist in the conversion of Protestants, the emperor was to deny the *jus emigrandi* conferred on religious minorities by the Westphalia settlement; yet he sought to break up communities of the stiff-necked by forced labour, militia service on the Hungarian frontier or transportation to Hungary or Siebenbürgen. On the ecclesiastical side Salzburg could help. There was constant correspondence between the bishops of Seckau and their metropolitan; Salzburg advised on the suspect books to be put down, provided missionaries and money for the Church in Styria;[59] and, bankrupt as the archbishorpic was,[60] it suffered constant criticism in Austria for its miserliness.[61]

The confessional policy of the Habsburgs could be very harsh, particularly under Maria Theresia, the zealous Catholic daughter of a Protestant mother. It was, however, mitigated by in-built contradictions in Habsburg policies and interrupted by circumstances. The great triumph of the Counter-Reformation in Bohemia and Moravia had been sealed and made permanent by great transfers of Protestant property to Catholic religious houses and noble families. The latter, though, had paid, as well as gained, heavily in the process. They wanted their northern flank protected by agreements with the Protestant powers and found institutional as well as political means for diverting Habsburg effort away from Catholic triumph in the empire to expansion in the south-east at the expense of the Turks.[62] The brilliant success of these policies created in turn a great need for settlers in Hungary and Siebenbürgen, which could not be met if a resolutely confessional line were pursued. This dilemma was explicit in the Salzburg crisis. The troops which the emperor sent in[63] were intended, not only to keep out Protestants who might have been useful in Hungary, but to keep *in* Carinthian Catholics trying to take advantage of the flooded land market in the principality.[64] Charles VI could not square his circle by his brutal policy of transportation, not least because it inflicted a death sentence on up to a third of its victims, a rate of 'wastage' extravagantly in excess of that achieved by the Prussians in marching the Salzburgers to the Baltic. Small wonder that Joseph II was educated upon documents which insisted that Archbishop Firmian had ruined his principality by depopulating it[65] and, as a young man, set himself the questions 'how to confront the depopulation of the empire attempted by so many foreign powers, and at the same time to draw advantages from the empire for the strengthening of the army and population of these lands?'[66] The principal answer to both those questions was to be the Patent of Toleration. The Austrian Protestants, therefore, were roughly handled by a government which knew that a 'final solution' to its problem of confessional minorities was not among the options open to it, a government, moreover, which could not keep up its policies of persecution and evangelistic pressure in time of war.[67] The result was that, from a Protestant viewpoint, the War of the Austrian Succession offered a welcome relief from the hot days of Charles VI, while the Seven Years' War formed an interlude between the violent reaction of Maria Theresia in the early 1750s and her vexation with the Moravian Protestants in the last months of her life. For quite different reasons from those which Schaitberger had offered, the worst sufferings of the Austrian Protestants were not of indefinite duration. In their instance, the wave-like pattern of revival was directly related to the fierce but erratic pressure of hostile governments: spared the worst trials of the Bohemians, they better sustained the proportion of faith.[68]

The new features of the Austrian situation were the example of the Salzburger Protestants and the fact that the open co-operation between the authorities of Salzburg on the one side and those of Vienna, Graz and Klagenfurt on the other made it clear to the Protestants on both sides that they were fighting the same battle; this fanned the enthusiasm of the Salzburgers to reproduce their own miracle in the Habsburg lands. Here the Austrian authorities, spiritual and secular, suffered from the ineptness of their notion of mission. Of this two examples may suffice. The documents of the religious commissions are instinct with the view that the Roman Catholic Church was the one Church, and hence the only missionaries were those it commissioned. Anyone else emulating this line of business was an agitator or an emissary sent by some other authority, and probably a dealer in subversive literature. This view was natural in view of the irritation the Habsburgs had suffered from the agents of Prussia and Halle in Bohemia, but no Prussian agent was ever taken up in Inner Austria, and Halle imprints are notably lacking among the quantities of Protestant literature impounded at the time or surviving in the hands of Protestant families into the age of toleration. Yet what is plain from the administrative documents is that the unrest among the Protestant population was fanned, partly by homegrown propagandists (*seductores aliorum*),[69] but quite largely by Salzburgers. Relations between the two, even before the crisis, are attested by the fact that some Salzburgers were taken up in Austria, having come to Vienna for communion, and that their fellows in the Salzkammergut appealed to the Austrians for help.[70] From the beginning the new Salzburg preachers were active in Styria and Carinthia, and the Austrian government produced circumstantial evidence to the Reichstag that some were supported by the Corpus Evangelicorum (though the allegation that one varied his disguises with perruques and liveries strains credulity).[71] Special measures were taken to keep them out in 1745; they were there in force during the most vivid outbreak of all generated by the zeal of Maria Theresia in the early 1750s,[72] and they were back again in the 1770s.[73] Small wonder that the government was hostile to the appearance of 'so-called Catholic Salzburgers'.[74] The nature of Protestant survival in Austria was being transformed by Protestant revival in Salzburg.

On the Catholic side, missions suffered from following foreign styles, all of which were losing touch with the tastes of even the Catholic population,[75] from being planned by a hierarchy which could not know how it felt to be an Austrian Protestant, and from being executed by a clergy better drilled in giving safe answers than in producing results. The bishop of Passau's instructions to his missionaries required them to brush up their knowledge of agriculture and rural life and to be 'affabiles, urbani, suaves, ab ira alieni . . . sermone & moribus hilares'. To guide them straight to the market for their wares, an entertaining profile of the secret Lutheran ('Signa diognostica occultorum Lutheranorum') was included. Beginning with slack attendance at mass and ending with eating meat or pork fat on prohibited days 'sub praetentu oblivionis, voracitatis aut simulatione magnae paupertatis', this would hardly have distinguished a Protestant from the average, carnal, rural Catholic. The missionaries were also instructed to take advantage of the indiscretions of children and to hoodwink their parents. If, after preaching on the Trinity, incarnation, Advent, the Holy Spirit, the institution of baptism or the eucharist or any other articles held in common by Catholics and Lutherans, they asked a suspect whether he believed these truths and received the expected confident affirmative answer, they should instantly add 'What about purgatory and the invocation of the saints?' Any hesitation would betray the heretic.[76] Protestant ingenuity was not so easily circumvented. The advice from Ortenburg, Bavaria, was that the domestic religious instruction of children should cease while they were at school,[77] while the demands of survival had taught the Protestants of the Upper Ennstal to manage the catechism better than their Catholic neighbours.[78] The Catholic missionaries by contrast took their cue from their bishop; the best method of conversion, they informed him with depressing unanimity, was 'praescripta mansuetudo et patientia'. Prescription was the limit of their inspiration.[79]

The second failure of Catholic imagination casts a good deal of light on the inner nature of the Austrian Protestant community. The authorities in Church and State were the victims to an extraordinary degree of the myth that Protestantism was the religion of a book. Hence the endless discussions in the documents and the secondary works how far the troubles in Styria and Carinthia were the work of Prussian agents; hence the fact that, overwhelmingly, the largest item in the indexes to the *Religionsakten* at Graz is the entry *Bücher*; hence also the mountains of repetitive information about the literature accumulated by peasants in holes and corners. Of course, if books had not mattered to the Austrian Protestants, they would not have been part of their ordinary commerce with the outside world, the stock-in-trade of the Ramsauer cattle dealers at Regensburg, of artisans on their travels and the host of travelling pedlars catering for the housewife's needs and bringing with them Protestant books with images of the Virgin on the title page and bogus Catholic approbations and places of origin.[80] The principal sources of supply were Württemberg and Nuremberg, a town later the base of an interesting merchant who forms a link between the first and the second phases of the Protestant revival, Johann Tobias Kiessling (1742–1824).[81] Converted by revival preaching and contact with Salzburger exiles, he devoted himself to getting books into Upper and Inner Austria in the course of his normal business in herbs and spices and drugs, and through other channels, and contributed notably to the founding of the Deutsche Christentumsgesellschaft and to the reconstruction of Protestant church life in Austria after the Patent of Toleration. Austrian Protestants required books of a limited range and used them in a special way. The bitter resistance of the *Toleranzgemeinden* to the introduction of new hymn books on the grounds that they were beyond their level of reading-readiness, and their resistance to the education of their children beyond the point where they could continue the family tradition of reading the prayers of Habermann and other devotional works,[82] cast a vivid light upon the role of books during the years of persecution. Reading, to the old Protestant peasantry, was a process of deciphering a text heard from childhood up, a matter of the ear as much as the eye.[83] And those texts were the predominantly devotional texts. Catechising, which had been a ministerial function, dropped out. What counted were hymn books from a variety of sources – though even here the Protestants' partial independence of the printed word is attested by the survival of manuscript hymn books, the overwhelming bulk of whose contents are to be found in no published collection[84] – books of prayers and devotions on which family piety could be sustained (Habermann was the most popular, and there were also indigenous manuscript collections), Schaitberger, sermons of Luther and Spangenberg and theological writers like Johann Arndt, who had most given themselves to sustaining practical piety. It is said that every Protestant family with three or more books had a volume of Arndt. The parallel is very close with the Reformed congregations in Bohemia, which also cherished Arndt and supplemented him with the affective English Puritan writers, Lewis Bayley, Bunyan and Richard Baxter, who seemed to Isaac Watts central to the English reformed tradition – and were certainly indispensable to the reformed practitioners of revival in New England and in Old. The Bible came fairly well down the list, and, of the parts of the Bible which were read, Revelation came first, followed, in order of importance, by the Psalms, the Gospels and Genesis;[85] strikingly absent are the epistles of Paul, and especially Romans, on which the founders of Protestant theology had leaned so heavily. The secret Protestants used those Scriptures which spoke most directly to their condition and were not too hard to read.

Doblhof, Maria Theresia's commissioner in Carinthia, reported to her in some vexation in 1752: 'Many of these people . . . *in Dogmate* are not of the same opinion, each believes what he learned from his parents or heard when he was in service or read piecemeal in books'.[86] The truth was that the bearer of Austrian Protestantism was not now the Church, nor the book, but the family or at any rate the clan*(Sippe)*.[87] This was why the pastors often had a difficult time of it when they returned after 1781 and also why the problem which perplexes Austrian Protestant historians, why one valley should stay Protestant and the next not, is not really a problem; it is like those other corporate decisions, buried in the depths of clan rancour which, at the English Reformation, led alternate side valleys in the Pennines to stay Catholic or go Protestant. This is why the manuscript hymn collections show (as Doblhof observed) doctrinal untidiness and evidence even of Protestant-Catholic syncretism at the edges but show, also, a sustained capacity to translate the original Reformation emphasis on justification into a personal devotion to the Saviour, and it is why a tenderness of piety like that of the Silesians developed here. It is why Austrian Protestantism kept free of the class distinctions of Protestantism in Germany and Hungary[88] and why what happened when Maria Theresia's government became abnormally oppressive in the early 1750s was not conspiracy, but revival accompanied by a degree of violence and obscenity against the religious statues which were among the obstrusive new features of the Austrian Baroque.[89] The lessons taught in Silesia, Upper Lusatia, Bohemia and Salzburg, that Protestant communities, fearful for their future, could pull themselves up by their bootstraps and generate a kind of enthusiastic piety not characteristic of the Churches of the Augsburg or Helvetic Confessions, lessons which had been taken to heart as far away as Wales, Scotland, England and the northern and middle colonies of America, were now embraced in Styria and Carinthia. There was, for example, a sudden expansion of the movement in Stadel.[90] The first effect of the Catholic mission in the Ennstal in 1751 was that 200 parishioners declared themselves Lutherans, saying that 'they had formerly had a dead faith, but now a living one, and went home singing and rejoicing';[91] and they had their peasant preachers, too. Revival is also the reason why secret Protestantism issued, not in the Lutheran Orthodoxy of even Schaitberger, and certainly not in the pietism of Halle or Württemberg, but in 'an awakened Christianity' of a very unconfessional character, a religion strong enough after all its trials to be capable, with foreign help, of creating a church system.

The delineation of Austrian Protestantism may be completed by comparison with Hungary where, in the second quarter of the eighteenth century, Protestants still encountered the full violence of Habsburg intolerance. Most of the factors at work in Austria also operated under the Crown of St Stephen, but, differently balanced and working in a different context, they produced different results. Revival was not a characteristic of the history of Hungarian Protestantism in this period, even though Philip Doddridge appeared in Magyar dress and even though the growth point was the so-called 'widowed' congregations without a pastor. They appeared to the tune of over 1,000 under the Toleration Patent and had kept going by the sort of informal means which were all that were open to the Austrians. Again, Hungarian Protestantism, Lutheran and Reformed, made one remarkable missionary effort, despite all the language difficulties, in getting Bohemian and Moravian Protestantism organised once more after the Toleration Patent, by supplying sixty ministers. But the balance between these efforts and apocalyptic was quite different. Austrian Protestants were addicted to the Book of Revelation, and when, after the Toleration Patent they built their churches, the highest figure above the altar was commonly the lamb with the flag of victory and the book of the seven seals.[92] That Austrian Protestantism survived to build its altars, however, was due to the fact that, in desperation, its energies went into revival on this side of the apocalypse; in Hungary, for a long time, apocalyptic fantasies had free rein.[93] Moreover, the Hungarians retained their church system, kept a foothold in those social strata with access to power and had no need for radical departures from the past to hold on to in a whirlpool in which Catholicism was never as unequivocally equated with Habsburg loyalty as it was outside the Kingdom of St Stephen. The result was that the hirsute and rebarbative bishops of the Siebenbürger Saxons could keep up a doctrinal war on three fronts against popery, pietism and Calvinism long after the Orthodox dinosaurs on whom they modelled themselves had died out in Germany.[94] And the Reformed, like the Reformed elsewhere, got over their eschatological fantasies only to begin a long slide into rationalism. In any case, the only instance in which a religious establishment took up with revival with any enthusiasm was in New England, and even there the association lasted hardly a decade. Hungary represents the rule rather than the exception. It was the Austrian and Salzburger Protestants who made a new and distinctive contribution to the old problem of Christianising successive generations. And that contribution was not lost on their fellows elsewhere.

Notes

1 For this and an indication of the literature see W.R. Ward, 'Power and piety: the origins of religious revivals in the early eighteenth century', *Bulletins of the John Rylands University Library of Manchester* lxiii (1980), 231–52. Above, Ch. 5.

2 Diözesanarchiv Graz, MS xv b. 23, Religionsberichte Protestantismus 1598–1730, 10 Oct. 1730.

3 Ibid. Religionsberichte Protestantismus 1731–35, letter to bishop of Seckau, 16 Jan. 1733.

4 H. von Zwiedineck-Südenhorst, 'Geschichte der religiösen Bewegung in Inner-Österreich im 18. Jahrhundert', *Archiv für österreichische Geschichte* liii (1875), 457–546 at p. 482.

5 Paul Dedic, 'Die Massnahmen Maria Theresias gegen die Oberennstaler Protestanten bis zur Errichtung der steirischen Konversionshaüser', *Jahrbuch der Gesellschaft für die Geschichte des Protestantismus in Österreich* (hereinafter cited as *JGGPÖ*) lxi (1940), 73–149 at p. 76.

6 Steirmärkisches Landesarchiv, Graz, MS H.S. xiii. I, Religionsakten 1749–73, passim, e.g. no. 483.

7 *Acta Historico-Ecclesiastica* (hereinafter cited as *AHE*), i. 769–808; ii. 734–47. Reporting in the *Unschuldige Nachrichten* was admittedly rather thin, probably owing to the Saxon censorship.

8 E.g. Bernhard Raupach, *Evangelisches Österreich*, Hamburg 1732. Cf. the works on neighbouring areas: J.G. Hillinger, *Beytrag zur Kirchen-Historie des Erzbischoftums Saltzburg*, Saalfield 1732; G.C. Rieger, *Der Salz-Bund Gottes mit der Evangelisch-Salzburgischen Gemeinde*, n.p. 1732–3; G.C. Rieger, *Die alte und neue Böhmische Brüder*, Züllichau 1734–9.

9 Burnet's view was that the Salzburger Protestants were descended from the Waldensians, G. Burnet, *Some letters concerning an account of what seemed most remarkable in Switzerland, Italy &c.*, London 1687 (trans. *Beschreibung seiner Reise durch die Schweiz, Italien und einiger Orter Deutschlands und Frankreichs*). This was widely discussed – e.g. by J.G. Schelhorn, *Historische Nachricht von Ursprunge, Fortgang und Schicksale der evangelischen Religion in den Salzburgischen Landen*, Leipzig 1732, 7–10 – and was rejected both by Joseph Schaitberger, the exiled Hallein miner and evangelist, *Wahrhaftiger Bericht von der Salzburgischen Reformation welche im Jahr . . . 1686 vorgegangen ist* (repr. in Hillinger, *op. cit.* 130), and by G.G.G. Göcking, *Vollkommene Emigrations . . . Geschichte . . .* Frankfurt-Leipzig 1734–7, i. 43–4. The parallel between the fate of the Waldenses, who suffered renewed persecution in the 1720s and (despite British and Prussian diplomatic support, and much Swiss assistance) emigrated on a modest scale, was too close to escape notice, *Die seuffende Salzburger oder besondere Unterredung . . . zwischen einem . . . Waldenser*, Magdeburg 1732; *Die getröstete Salzburger, oder Gespräch . . . zwischen einem Salzburger und einem . . . Waldenser*, Magdeburg 1733; *Die zweyte Unterredung . . . zwischen einem . . . Salzburger und einem . . . Waldenser*, Magdeburg 1732. Protestant scholars were too preoccupied with assessing the place of the Waldensians in the pedigree of the Reformation to explore their contemporary history, Rieger, *Salz-Bund Gottes*, 738–9; idem, *Böhmische Brüder*, i. 4–6; *Unschuldige Nachrichten* 1734, 518. The Waldensians seem not, however, to have shown the same capacity to generate revival as the Salzburgers and Austrians (or indeed as the older

Waldensian exiles absorbed into the Bohemian Brethren), perhaps because
some were settled and then resettled; some were settled in very small groups;
and some of the larger groups remained dependent on Swiss established
churches.

10 *The Present State of Germany*, i, London 1738, 344; Hillinger, *Kirchen-
    Historie Salzburg*, 13; Rieger, *Salz-Bund Gottes*, 5. In *Böhmische Brüder*, i. 3,
    Rieger aimed 'to represent . . . a continuous and unbroken succession and
    series of visible Protestant congregations from the first apostolic churches up
    to our own time'.

11 Cf. Peter F. Barton, 'Gegenreformation und Protestantismus in der habsburgis-
    chen Macht- und Einflußsphäre, vor allem im 17. Jahrhundert', in *Rebellion
    oder Religion?*, ed. Peter F. Barton and Láslo Makkai, Budapest 1977, 23–36
    at p. 25.

12 Sakrausky, 'Der österreichische Protestantismus', 12, 22–3.

13 Clergy also resisted the creation of a less inefficient parochial system for
    financial reasons, Dedic, 'Die Massnahmen Maria Theresias', 81.

14 The work of Winfried Schulze and Günter Vogler, suggesting that this peasant
    aptitude for litigation was one reason why the Reich escaped a recurrence of
    the massive revolt of 1525, is summarised with references in Günter Vogler,
    'Religion, confession and peasant resistance in the German territories in the
    sixteenth to the eighteenth centuries', in János M. Bak and Gerhard Beneke
    (eds), *Religion and Rural Revolt*, Manchester 1984, 173–87 at p. 183.

15 Adam Wandruszka, 'Geheimprotestantismus, Josephinismus und Volksliturgie
    in Österreich', *Zeitschrift für Kirchengeschichte* (hereinafter cited as *ZKg*)
    lxxviii (1967), 94–101 at p. 95.

16 Raupach, *Evangelisches Österreich*, 293–300. Fritz Dickmann lays the weight
    on the simple determination of the emperor and his councillors not to surrender
    this point, *Der Westfälische Frieden*, 2nd edn, Münster 1965, 366, 462–3.

17 Hans Widmann, *Geschichte Salzburgs*, Gotha 1907–14, iii. 326. It was
    characteristic of the confusions of jurisdiction in this area that while, for secular
    government, most of the Defereggental was subject to the Principality of
    Salzburg, part belonged to the Tirol. In matters spiritual the valley was entirely
    subject to the archdiocese of Salzburg and belonged to the archdeaconrry of
    Gmünd in Carinthia.

18 Martin Gruhlichen, *Annales Theologico-ecclesiastici. Oder historische Nachri-
    chten von allen Merckwürdigkeiten die sich in Kirchen- und Theologischen-
    Sachen seit der Reformation Lutheri bis anitzo zugetragen*, Dresden-Leipzig
    1734, 760.

19 Samuel Urlsperger, *Der noch lebende Joseph Schaitberger*, Augsburg 1732,
    21; *Evangelisch in Steiermark*, Graz 1981, 85.

20 Joseph Desput, 'Toleranz im Zeichen der Aufklärung. Zur Durchführung
    des Toleranzpatentes in der Steiermark', *Mitteilungen des Steiermärkischen
    Landesarchivs* xxxi (1981), 105–21 at p. 120.

21 The biography appeared in a series 'of reports of the grace of God as revealed
    in persons of the lower class' in the Leipzig journal *Sammlung auserlesener*

Materien zum Bau des Reiches Gottes v (1736), 589–621. The journal was founded by Traugott Immanuel Jerichovius, an ally of Zinzendorf and master of the school attached to the Jesus Church at Teschen in its heroic years, and was taken over on his death in 1734 by Steinmetz, the most important and attractive preacher of the Teschen revival before his expulsion in 1730 (on whom see below). H. Patzelt, *De Pietismus im Teschener Schlesien, 1709–1730,* Göttingen 1969, 174 n. 11; Albrecht Ritschl, *Geschichte des Pietismus,* Bonn, 1880–6, repr. Berlin 1966, ii. 471 n. 1.

22 Urlsperger, *Der noch lebende Schaitberger,* 10–11.

23 Samuel Urlsperger, *Die ausführliche Nachrichten von der Salzburger Emigranten in Amerika,* Halle 1736–50, a work partly available in English as *Detailed Reports on the Salzburger Emigrants who settled in America,* ed. George Fenwick Jones and others, 6 vols, Athens, Ga. 1968–. The *Nachrichten* were succeeded by a briefer series by the same author, *Americanisches Ackerwerk Gottes,* Augsburg, 1760–7.

24 Philoletha Evangelico (i.e. Samuel Urlsperger), *Saltzburgisches Denkmal der Evangelischen Wahrheit, das ist Joseph Schaitbergers . . . Evangelische Sendschreiben,* Frankfurt-Leipzig 1732. This text was produced to meet the demands of literate Salzburger exiles, 'almost all' of whom 'asked, "Have you any Schaitbergers" and were delighted when given a copy', Urlsperger, *Der noch lebende Schaitberger,* 8. The posthumous collection of Schaitberger's works with the writing of which he disclaimed receiving any assistance, ibid. 11–12 and app. 2, exceeded 700 pages, Joseph Schaitberger, *Neuvermehrter evangelischer Sendbrief,* Nuremberg 1736.

25 Samuel Urlsperger (1685–1772) had been pastor of the German Lutheran congregation in the Savoy 1710–12 and, when he left this country, became a corresponding member of the SPCK. The SPCK was influential with the Georgia Trustees in securing a settlement for the Salzburgers.

26 Dedic, 'Die Massnahmen Maria Theresias', 113.

27 J.T. Zauner and Corbinian Gärtner, *Neu Chronik von Salzburg,* Salzburg 1803–26, iv. 70–2.

28 Siegmund Jacob Baumgarten, *Geschichte der Religionspartheyen,* ed. J.S. Semler, Halle 1766, repr. Hildesheim 1966, 107.

29 Dedic, *op. cit.* 80, 83–4. Schaitberger was adept at producing six evidences that the Lutheran Church was the one true Church (and scorned the radical Pietists who held 'the Lutheranism of today to be more an old Bible than a new Jerusalem and [went] no more to church or communion') or a biblical confession in ten points, Urlsperger, *Salzburgisches Denkmal,* 97; Schaitberger, *Neuvermehrter Sendbrief,* 129–31, 568. Cf. Oskar Sakrausky, 'Evangelisches Glaubensleben im Gailtal zur Zeit der Reformation und Gegenreformation', *Carinthia I* clxxi (1981), 171–92 at p. 191.

30 Zauner and Gärtner, *op. cit.* iv. 89.

31 'After the sixty-two weeks the one who is anointed shall be removed [*ausgerottet* in the Luther version] with no one to take his part, and the horde of the invading prince shall work havoc on city and sanctuary.'

32 Schaitberger's first circular letter commenced with this passage; it was reprinted in Urlsperger, *Salzburgisches Denkmal*, 1.

33 For a treatment of this subject with references, see Ward, 'Power and piety'.

34 On this see Curt Friedrich Wreech, *Wahrhaffte und umständliche Historie von deren schwedischen Gefangenen in Russland und Siberien . . .*, Sorau 1725.

35 For the Jesus Church see Oskar Wagner, *Mutterkirche vieler Länder. Geschichte der evangelischen Kirche im Herzogtum Teschen. 1545–1918/20*, Vienna-Cologne-Graz 1978; and Patzelt, *Pietismus im Teschener Schlesien*.

36 Christian Friedrich Jona, *Nachricht von dem Lebens-Umständen und dem selige Abschiede des weiland hochwürdigen Herrn, Herrn Johann Adam Steinmetz*, Magdeburg 1762, contains a valuable account of Steinmetz's preaching methods.

37 Cf. Peter Kawerau, 'Johann Adam Steinmetz. Vermittler zwischen dem deutschen und amerikanischen Pietismus im 18. Jahrhundert', *ZKg* lxx (1959), 75–88.

38 Zwiedineck-Südenhorst, 'Religiöse Bewegung in Inner-Österreich', 467–8; August Leidl, 'Die religiöse und seelsorgliche Situation zur Zeit Maria Theresias (1740–1780) im Gebiet des heutigen Österreich', *Ostbairische Grenzmarken* xvi (1974), 162–78 at pp. 165, 167. Frederick the Great was too preoccupied with holding and populating Silesia (for which he looked to Bohemia and Moravia) to bother about the Protestants of Inner Austria.

39 [Johann Jakob Moser], *Acten-Mässiger Bericht von der jetzmaligen schweren Verfolgung derer Evangelischen in dem Ertz-Bisthum Salzburg*, Frankurt-Leipzig 1732, Vorrede. *The Present State of Germany*, i. 344–5.

40 Zaunerr and Gärtner, *Salzburg*, iv. 127–36, 381–93. On Mosegger's preaching, see Georg Loesche, 'Neues über die Ausrottung des Protestantismus in Salzburg, 1731/2', *JGGPÖ* 1 (1929), 1–201 at p. 30; cf. p. 66.

41 Widmann, *Geschichte Salzburgs*, iii. 389–91.

42 The British Library preserves a small collection of these sermons at MSS 1012 d. 30, 3905 ee. 63/3, 4650 df. 3, and 4660 aa 12/2.

43 This subject is elaborately treated, with reprints of many of the graphics, in Angelika Marsch, *Die Salzburger Emigration in Bildern*, 2nd edn, Weissenhorn 1979, 158ff.

44 *Reformation-Emigration. Protestanten in Salzburg*, ed. F. Zaisberger, Salzburg 1981, 110–11.

45 Heinz Otto Lichtenberg, *Unterhaltsame Bauernaufklärung. Ein Kapitel Volksbildungsgeschichte*, Tübingen 1970.

46 J.G. Gagliardo, *From Pariah to Patriot. The changing image of the German peasant, 1770–1840*, Lexington, Ky. 1969. Cf. Gerhard Kaiser, *Pietismus und Patriotismus im literarischen Deutschland*, Wiesbaden 1961, ch. vii, esp. at pp. 107–8.

47 Valentin Ernst Löscher, *Drey Predigten von der Erkenntnis und Ehre des Sohnes Gottes . . .*, Dresden-Neustadt 1733, 26.

48 'The Lord is doing a new thing in the land . . . It exults and sings; it gives thanks and praise . . . The land is becoming like the Lord. It makes all things new. It

builds new altars. It renews its old, its first love. It creates new hope. It traces new growth', Gottfried Müller, *Zulänglich Erkantnüss des jetzigen Salzburgischen Emigration-Wesens*, Dresden-Leipzig 1732, pref., 2.

49 *Lebensgeschichte J.J. Mosers, von ihm selbst beschrieben*, n. p. 1768, 55. Moser (1701–85) was a Württemberger, a celebrated lawyer who made the public law of the empire a subject of academic study. For him see references in Ward, 'Orthodoxy, Enlightenment and religious revival', *Studies in Church History* xvii (1982), 275–96 at pp. 279–80 (above, Ch. 2); and Mack Walker, *Johann Jakob Moser and the Holy Roman Empire of the German Nation*, Chapel Hill, NC 1981.

50 Rieger, *Der Salz-Bund Gottes*, 3. Rieger (1687–1743), of whom there is a useful obituary in *AHE* viii. 736–62, was pressed to extend his work on the Salzburgers to the ancient and modern history of the Brethren on the grounds that 'this kind of history had something awakening and edifying [*erweckliches und erbauliches*] in it', *Böhmishe Brüder*, i. 2.

51 *Geistliche Fama*, vii. 18–34; x. 28, 81–2; xxiii. 6–7. This journal, which ran from 1730 to 1743, was edited at first by Johann Samuel Carl and later by Konrad Dippel. Cf. Winfried Zeller, *Theologie und Frömmigkeit*, Marburg 1971–8, ii. 153–9.

52 Gottfried Arnold, (1666–1714), professor of history at Giessen 1697–8, whose *Unpartheyische Kirchen- und Ketzer-Historie* (1699–1700) saw the history of heresy as part of the history of the Church, and who believed that if there was a 'proof' of the truth of Christianity it must be established not dogmatically, but on a basis of experience and history.

53 Johann Konrad Dippel (1673–1734), the son of a Hessian pastor, moved from Orthodoxy to a radically anti-institutional kind of pietism. A scientist who always had international aristocratic support for his alchemist researches into the production of gold, he was physician to the king of Sweden; his struggles to pit observation against a mechanistic world-picture have been compared to his pietistic and experiential theology of salvation.

54 August Hermann Francke (1663–1727), the great organiser of the second generation of the pietist movement, spiritually, politically and in terms of the charitable institutions of Halle. He began close to the mystic spiritualists in Saxony and ended by putting a universal vision to the service of the Prussian government.

55 Johann Rudolf Schlegel, *Kirchengeschichte des achtzehnten Jahrhunderts*, Heilbronn 1784–6, ii. 207–8; J. Regula, 'Die Berchtesgadener . . . Emigranten in Göttingen, 1733–42', *Zeitschrift der Gesellschaft für niedersächsische Kirchengeschichte* xix (1914), 209–29; E.C.W. von Schauroth, *Vollständige Sammlung aller . . . Schreiben und anderer übrigen Verhandlungen des hochpreisslichen Corporis Evangelicorum . . .* , Regensburg 1751–2, i. 113–27. The Protestant ambassadors got over the difficulty that many of the Berchtesgadeners were serfs by paying their redemption money.

56 Eduard Winter, *Die tschechische und slovakische Emigration in Deutschland im 17. und 18. Jahrhundert*, [East] Berlin 1955, 103.

57 On these issues see Martin Naumann, *Österreich, England und das Reich, 1719–32*, Berlin 1936, 181; Hugo Hantsch, *Reichsvizekanzler Friedrich Graf von Schönborn (1674–1746). Einige Kapitel zur politischen Geschichte Kaiser Josefs I und Karls VI*, Augsburg 1929, 325–35; Josef Karl Mayr, 'Zur Geschichte der Emigration der Salzburger Protestanten von 1731/2', *JGGPÖ* lii (1931), 136–47; F. Reissenberger, 'Das Corpus Evangelicorum und die österreichischen Protestanten (1685–1764)', *JGGPÖ* xvii (1896), 212–18.

58 Zauner and Gärtner, *Salzburg*, iv. 112; Diözesanarchiv Graz, MS xv b. 23, correspondence of Charles VI with the bishop of Seckau, 13, 28 Sept. 1714, 3 Aug. 1718, 30 Mar. 1724.

59 Ibid. MS xv b. 23, archbishop of Salzburg to the bishop of Seckau, 3 Mar. 1730; Steiermärkisches Landesarchiv, Graz, MS H.S. xiii. 1, nos. 131, 146, 180, 202; H.S. xiii. 2, nos. 22, 104, 118, 137, 466, 505. Despite the rift between primate and emperor over the Protestant question at this moment, the archbishopic (as distinct from the principality) had already opened the way to smoother co-operation by clearing up many of the disputes over jurisdiction and church organisation which had existed between them.

60 K. Amon (ed.), *Die Bischöfe von Graz-Seckau*, Graz-Vienna-Cologne 1969, 338.

61 Steiermärkisches Landesarchiv, Graz, MS H.S. xiii. 1, nos. 247, 425, 615, 673.

62 This theme is pursued by Grete Klingenstein, *Der Aufstieg des Hauses Kaunitz*, Göttingen 1975.

63 Prince Eugene's dragoons were a disappointment; a considerable proportion of both officers and men were Protestants who joined in the devotions of the Protestant families on whom they were billeted. They had to be replaced by cuirassiers, Gerhard Florey, *Geschichte der Salzburger Protestanten und ihrer Emigration 1731/32*, Vienna-Cologne-Graz 1977, 110.

64 Zwiedineck-Südenhorst, 'Religiöse Bewegung', 466, 472. The secular authorities were naturally anxious to suppress news of events in Salzburg, Diözesanarchiv Graz, Religionsberichte Protestantismus 1731–5, governor of Styria and others to the bishop of Seckau, 16 Jan. 1733. As it was Protestants from the Gosautal joined the Salzburger trains, Peter F. Barton (ed.), *Im Zeichen der Toleranz*, Vienna 1981, 423.

65 Staatsarchiv, Vienna, MS W514 fos 288–9; Österreichische National Bibliothek, Vienna, Handschriftsammlung, MS S. no. 12. 109, fo. 110.

66 *Aus der Zeit Maria Theresias. Tagebuch des Fürsten Johann Josef Khevenhüller-Metsch 1742–46*, ed. Rudolf Graf Khevenhüller, Vienna 1907–25, vi. 480.

67 At the end of the seventeenth century persecution had sometimes been limited in wartime by the non co-operation of provincial authorities, Paul Dedic, 'Duldung und Aufenthalt evangelischer Ausländer in Graz am Ende des 17. Jahrhunderts', *JGGPÖ* vii. (1936), 70–8.

68 In Bohemia, apart from apocalyptic sects, there were even Judaising bodies of Christian Israelites, Rudolf Ričan, *Das Reich Gottes in dem Böhmischen Ländern. Geschichte des tschechischen Protestantismus*, Stuttgart 1957, 148.

69 Steiermärkisches Landesarchiv, Graz, MS H.S. xiii. 1, nos. 544, 656–7, 670, 687–8, 709, 712, 718, 728.

70 *AHE*, i. 634–40; Loesche, 'Die Ausrottung', 121–7.

71 Zwiedineck-Südenhorst, 'Religiöse Bewegung', 468–9, 511–15. Cf. Diözesanarchiv Graz, MS xv b. 23, Religionsberichte Protestantismus 1731–5, bishop of Seckau to the emperor, 3 Aug., 2 Oct. 1731.

72 Dedic, 'Die Massnahmen Maria Theresias', 79, 89, 96, 97, 100, 102, 112–13: Steiermärkische Landesarchiv, Graz, MS H.S. xiii. 1, no. 534. There were others from Ortenburg, Bavaria, ibid. nos. 459, 561.

73 Ibid. MS H.S. xiii. 2, nos. 1295, 1313.

74 Ibid. MS H.S. xiii. 1, no. 23.

75 The styles of mission, changes in which were resisted by the bishops, are described in Leidl, 'Die religiöse und seelsorgliche Situation', 171–4; cf. Wandruszka, 'Geheimprotestantismus', 97.

76 The instructions, dated 1752, are preserved in Steiermärkisches Landesarchiv, Graz, Box 349, Religions Acta, 1752–3. Cf. Diözesanarchiv Graz, MS Religionsberichte Protestantismus 1731–5, bundle labelled 'Gegenreformation' (1733–4). In 1749 the vicar of Schladming and Ramsau (Upper Ennstal) reported, credibly enough, that meat was cooked and eaten on fast days there.

77 Ortenburg was a Protestant county to which Protestants from Upper Austria had resorted for communion, Barton, *Im Zeichen der Toleranz*, 408.

78 Dedic, 'Massnahmen Maria Theresias', 76.

79 Huge quantities of missionaries' reports are to be found in Steiermärkisches Landesarchiv, Graz, Box 350, Religions Akten.

80 Paul Dedic, 'Die Einschmuggelung lutherischer Bücher nach Kärnten in den ersten Dezennien des 18. Jahrhunderts', *JGGPÖ* lx (1939), 126–77 at p. 126, 174; idem, 'Die Massnahmen Maria Theresias', 110, 113.

81 For him see Ernst Staehlin, *Die Christentumsgesellschaft in der Zeit der Aufklärung und der beginnenden Erweckung*, Basle 1970, 44; Barton, *Im Zeichen der Toleranz*, 407–8.

82 Franz Reischer, *Die Toleranzgemeinden Kärntens nach einem Visitationsbericht vom Jahre 1786*, Klagenfurt 1965, 57.

83 On this see Reinhard Wittmann, 'Der lesende Landmann. Zur Rezeption aufklärerischer Bemühungen durch die bäuerliche Bevölkerung im 18. Jahrhundert', in Heinz Ishreyt (ed.), *Der Bauer Mittel- und Osteuropas im sozioökonomischen Wandel des 18. und 19. Jahrhunderts*, Cologne-Vienna 1973, 142–96.

84 Oskar Sakrausky, 'Das evangelische geistliche Lied in Kärnten', *Carinthia I* clxxi (1981), 271–87.

85 Idem, 'Evangelisches Glaubenleben im Gailtal zur Zeit der Reformation und Gegenreformation', *Carinthia I* clxxi (1981), 171–92 at p. 191.

86 Dedic, 'Einschmuggelung', 173. The report is printed in Zwiedineck-Südenhorst, 'Religiöse Bewegung', 521–6.

87 Sakrausky, 'Evangelisches Glaubensleben', 189.

88 Johann Christian Edelmann, who made the pilgrimage to Ödenburg to

communion as part of the household of Count Kornfiel, liked Hungarian wine and tobacco but did not care for the spectacle in church of the gentry nodding in sumptuous pews while peasants, wearied from their own long journeys, were kept waiting in the heat, J.C. Edelmann, *Selbstbiographie*, Berlin 1849 (repr. in W. Grossman (ed.), *Sämtliche Schriften*, xii, Bad Canstatt 1976), 82–5.

89 Steiermärkisches Landesarchiv, Graz, MS H.S. xiii. 1, nos. 125, 127 (and many subsequent papers about Gewiessler), 135.

90 Zwiedineck-Südenhorst, 'Religiöse Bewegung', 526.

91 Dedic, 'Die Massnahmen Maria Theresias', 94. The persistence of this tradition into the age of toleration is hinted at in Barton, *Im Zeichen der Toleranz*, 14–15, 425.

92 Sakrausky, 'Evangelisches Glaubenleben', 191.

93 On how this came about, see Béla Obál, *Die Religionspolitik in Ungarn nach den Westfälischer Frieden Während der Regierung Leopold I*, Halle 1910, 14–18. For the Hungarian Protestants generally, see Mihály Bucsay, *Der Protestantismus in Ungarn 1521–1978*, Vienna-Cologne-Graz 1977–9; and for the context of their struggle, Béla Köpeczi, *Staatsräson und christliche Solidarität*, Vienna-Cologne-Graz 1983. For Lutherans, Johannes Borbis, *Die evangelisch-lutherische Kirche Ungarns in ihrer geschichtlichen Entwicklung*, Nördlingen 1861.

94 *Die Bischöfe der evangelischen Kirche A.B. in Siebenbürgen*, i, ed. Hermann Jekeli, Hermannstadt 1933, repr. Vienna 1978.

10

Pastoral Office and the General
Priesthood in the Great Awakening

Whatever Luther may have said about the priesthood of all believers, it took more than a century and a half for the idea to receive full-scale treatment, and Spener, who achieved this during his time as Senior of Frankfurt (1660–86), approached the goal indirectly through editing Arndt's sermons (1675). To catch the public eye he republished the introduction separately later in the year under the title *Pia Desideria, or heartfelt desires for an improvement of the true evangelical church pleasing to God, with some Christian proposals to that end.*[1] With a dedication to all the overseers and pastors of the evangelical church it was now a deliberately programmatic writing. In this tract Spener castigated every class of society for their responsibility for the lamentable state of the Church, making suggestions for improved clerical training and preaching, which might have been made at any period of Church history. The real sting came in an explicit appeal to Luther on how best to realize the priesthood of all believers. To spread the word of God more richly among the people there should be private gatherings under clerical leadership for the exchange of views and Bible study; more radically, there should be private gatherings for the exercise of the obligations of the general spiritual priesthood. The faithful should teach, warn, convert, edify each other. These gatherings should be cells for the renewal of the Church. They would also enable Spener, the expert catechist, to drive home his conviction that Christianity was a way of life, learnt by doing.

The general, or as Spener preferred to call it, the spiritual priesthood, was part of a programme of church renewal. There was nothing anti-clerical about it; the faithful of whatever order were to take a more exalted view of their vocation than hitherto, and live accordingly. But in Spener's later works, *Das geistliche Priestertum* (1677) and *Die allgemeine Gottes-gelehrtheit* (1680) the tone began to change. The basic definitions of the

First published in *Studies in Church History* 26 (1989), pp. 303–327.

spiritual priesthood conferred by Christ upon his followers still stood,[2] but the language was already one of rights; men had the right to test the doctrine of their preachers, and women most emphatically had the right to participate in these priestly offices [reference to Joel 2 vv. 28–9].[3] The upper classes had appropriated all the rights in the Church at the expense of the third estate.[4] Spener's *collegium pietatis* or class-meetings in Frankfurt had begun as an élite society, much like the groups already gathered by Jean de Labadie, but speedily it was joined by artisans and servants of both sexes; like Wesley later, Spener was surprised at the knowledge possessed by simple men, and had now no doubt that the work of the Holy Spirit was not circumscribed by boundaries of class or education.[5]

All this Spener sought to argue from the Fathers; from the young Luther who in the preface to the *Deutsche Messe* of 1526 had called for the formation of a gathering of earnest Christians much like Spener's *collegium pietatis* or Wesley's select bands;[6] from other pillars of the Lutheran tradition, especially from his own old stamping-ground in Strasbourg;[7] and not least from the very title-deed of Lutheran Orthodoxy, the Formula of Concord.[8] Yet the dominant view in Lutheran Orthodoxy had staked everything on the Pastoral Office (*Amt* in German). 'Without the Pastoral Office is there no salvation'. 'Pastors stand in a single succession to the prophets and apostles; they are to reveal the will and counsel of God to men'. To deny that the ministry so-to-speak turned on the tap was to deny the *sola fide, sola gratia*. Even Valentin Ernst Löscher who sought in the hostile climate of the next generation to maintain the notion that theology derived its intellectual and scientific character as an essential function of church office, would concede no more than that 'Theologia ideo intendit pietatem, sed non includit'.[9] Moreover, Spener's precedents in the Lutheran tradition included nothing on the scale on which he came to treat the priesthood of all believers. He put a minority theme in a major key.

Spener's programme evoked a vivid response, soon followed by a violent reaction; both owed much to the special situation of Frankfurt in the ecclesiastical geography of the Empire. A few years ago the Evangelical Church of the Rhineland published a learned analysis of the religious psychology of their own congregations, the leading feature of which was independence, an independence exemplified especially in lay emancipation and immediacy of religious experience.[10] The first of these characteristics was greatly strengthened by the experiences of the seventeenth century; the second by the revivals which followed. The Lutheran Church in Jülich, Cleves, and Berg had never had the sympathetic backing of the state which Lutheran Churches still thought they needed, and the intrusion into the area of both the Reformed House of Brandenburg and the Lutheran house of Pfalz-Neuburg added to its troubles. The latter house brought in the church order of Pfalz-Zweibrücken which was a kind of Melancthonian middle way between the Saxon order and the Reformed order in the Palatinate; Lutheran in doctrine, this order never introduced the Formula of Concord. On the morrow of these changes, the house of Pfalz-Neuburg turned Catholic, with the result that the Lower Rhine Lutheran Churches lost their old synodical constitution without ever gaining an effective monarchical consistorial constitution. Self-help must be the order of the day, and it comes as no surprise that Johannes Scheibler (1627–89), superintendent of the Church in Berg, turned to Spener for assistance, nor that a Church with no convenient access to a place of ministerial training turned first to Giessen, the earliest university in which Pietists set the tone, and then on a big scale to Halle, for their clergy. Meanwhile the self-help had made these Churches more like their Reformed neighbours.

Frankfurt belonged to the Upper Rhine area where the Reformation had been introduced from above. French intervention and dynastic conversions to Rome had brought the Counter-Reformation up to the left bank of the Rhine, but they had created problems for princes and clergy more than ordinary congregations. Despite sharp opposition in doctrine, the Churches of the upper Rhine, evangelical and Reformed, were alike in owing their origin to princely initiative, and in undergoing a powerful Melancthonian influence; they had begun gradually to approximate to each other in constitution, and in the nineteenth century were to accept union schemes relatively willingly. The Lutheran Churches of this area embodied many features which in Saxony were regarded as Reformed. In Strasbourg, for example, the Church exercised church discipline through elders, and maintained public catechizings, public confirmation, communion without confession, and baptism without exorcism. What irked Spener was that established status undermined the exercise of discipline; his remedy was to revive internal sanctions by using semi-reformed methods not unfamiliar in the Upper Rhine.

Through his godmother and original sponsor, the widowed Countess Agathe von Rappoltstein, née Countess of Solms-Laubach, Spener also enjoyed entrée to a quite different milieu, that network of counts stretching away to Lusatia and Silesia who were to form the backbone of the Pietist party. And this group were among those who put Spener in the way of appointment in 1686 as court chaplain to the Elector of Saxony, in effect Primate of Lutheran Germany.[11] In the race for this dignity Spener pipped Johann Benedict Carpzov, a Leipzig theologian of formidable polemical violence. But the storm which now descended upon him, led by Carpzov with the predictable argument that Spener's friends substituted piety for faith, owed less to personalities than to the fact that the Saxon Church embodied a Lutheranism very different from that of the Rhine Churches, and saw its metier in protecting the gospel from what it regarded as Reformed contamination. What became the Pietist party was the wretched remnant left at the end of a fearful battering, gathered under the liberal protection of the Reformed Elector of Brandenburg.[12] That shrewd old warrior Hobbes would have been delighted by this contract between the leaders of an individualist piety and a despotism on the make, concluded to mutual advantage.

Everything seemed to go wrong with the revived priesthood of all believers. Spener was a churchman to the core; but his right-hand man, Johann Jakob Schütz, took up with Labadism and led a separation, part of which confirmed the worst fears of the Orthodox by ending up in Penn's Quaker colony in America. Spener, again, had spoken up for women, but the distaff side did not respond with tact. Spener did not expect unusual or extravagant phenomena in his class meeting at Frankfurt, and did not get them. Ecstatic phenomena, mostly among women and nothing to do with Pietism, had been fairly common in seventeenth-century Germany. But when the Orthodox mounted their horrendous assault on the Pietists, a number of spectacular cases, mostly of ecstatic pietist servant-girls, cropped up in central and northern Germany. Revelations to order were, of coure, grist to the Orthodox mill, and of Magdalena of Quedlinburg it was unkindly reported that 'she is so much on heat [*brunstig*] that she can scarcely bear the name of Jesus or the memory of his love and grace; as soon as she speaks or thinks of them she goes into convulsions'.

Unlike Luther, Spener was very interested in dreams and visions – and it is notable that pietists who dropped out of the ministry often took up medicine with what might now be called a psychiatric bent – and his main contribution to theological discussion consisted of thousands of pages of expert opinions on particular cases and issues such as these. Spener was not prepared to deny that God might possibly have fresh revelation in store through these unlikely channels; though the scriptural warnings against false prophets in the last days were still to be heeded. He would not accept a simple alternative that unusual religious phenomena must be of God or of the devil, and put forward other possibilities including disturbances in the unconscious, some of which might be evidence of sickness, some beyond understanding. In many of the personal cases Spener had to judge, he declared clearly against the divine origin of the visions; but in others he abstained from judgment on the grounds that he simply did not know. This modesty, which has lately earned him the title of 'the father of theological pluralism', disappointed friends as well as enemies. In the current view, it was the job of a theologian to know. Spener might be thought not so much to be coordinating the general priesthood with the Pastoral Office, as downgrading the Pastoral Office.[13]

The Orthodox might, finally, think that Spener had given the game away in the vocabulary he used. In his programmatic writings Spener talked indeed of regeneration, but the key-word was 'spirit'. What the evangelical church lacked was not pure doctrine in preaching and liturgy, but spirit. Spiritual poverty characterized the offical Church and clergy, the habitual Christianity of the pew, the dead technicalities of the polemical theologians. Almost immediately after his call to Saxony, Spener preached in Leipzig on 'The Office of the Holy Spirit in the work of our salvation'. Spener was not merely inviting the charge that he was a Quaker, but, consciously or unconciously, was putting himself in that line of writers known in the German tradition as spiritualistic. With this there were two immediate snags. Proclaiming in 1520 that 'all Christians are truly of the spiritual order, and there is no distinction among them simply on account of office', Luther had set himself and his fellow pastors a problem of conscience. Could they exercise their office representatively? Luther sought to solve his own problem by appeal to his academic office and for the candidate for the parish by a call from the congregation in due form. Still, the nagging question remained, not whether the individual was worthy of his office, but whether the office was justified at all. This dilemma had plagued the spiritualistic tradition.[14] Not all the anxious resigned, but in 1698, in Spener's own lifetime, Gottfried Arnold, less than a year after his call to a chair at Giessen, resoundingly did so, forsaking the academic Babel on the grounds that it was ruinous to the 'tender life of Christ within'.[15] Still worse, at the very moment when Spener replied to a polemic which equated Pietism with Quakerism by a piece of contemporary church history which sought to establish the churchmanship of Pietists, Arnold produced a series of historical works culminating in his enormous *Impartial History of Churches and Heretics*, a work damned by the Orthodox as the worst book ever written and lauded by Thomasius as the best book since the Gospels. Arnold would have no truck with a conventional church history intent on elucidating God's providential care of the true church of the author's choice. He did not think that Christianity had ever quite maintained its apostolic level, but the fall had come in the time of Constantine. Christianity had then made its choice between the only two options ever open to it, accepting decline or accepting persecution. The result was that the 'true active believer had no longer any place in it and religion was established in fixed concepts and terms grasped by the intellect, and in outward confessions and other *opera operata*'. These concepts established who was orthodox, whether the orthodox were genuine Christians or not. The history of the true church was now hidden and invisible, sustained by witnesses who accepted persecution; and very often they were those who had figured in church histories hitherto as heretics.[16]

Antichrist, indeed, was to be found as often among the Protestants as among the papists. In the long run Arnold contributed enormously to transferring church history from the history of Providence to that of ordinary sinful humanity where we now expect to find it; and quite immediately he showed that Spener's attempt to revive lay vocations raised the modern question whether it is possible to have Christianity without the Church.

The opening of this question, the last thing that Spener desired, did not, however, constitute a knock-out blow for the Orthodox. For in all the areas requiring urgent attention by the Lutheran Churches, Christianity would have to survive without the Church or not at all. There were 20,000 Swedes exiled to Siberia after Charles XII's disastrous Pultava campaign; there were many times that number of Germans in America, by 1776 about 200,000; there were many times this number again of Protestants abandoned by the Westphalia settlement in the great triangle bounded by Salzburg. Transylvania, and Poland, most of them without a Church, and all of them subject to the most savage pressure of the Counter-Reformation. And then there were the endless mission-fields of the world, many still untouched even by the Catholics. Orthodoxy did a little. New Sweden on the Delaware had ended a brief and inglorious existence in 1655, but the Swedish Lutheran church continued to supply clergy and other assistance right down to the time of American independence; and the Church in the Netherlands did a good deal for New Amsterdam and other parts. By contrast, the informal devotions intended by Spener to supplement the parish round proved extraordinarily successful among church-less Protestants outside the Westphalia ring-fence in keeping the flame of Christian piety alight and in generating a new phenomenon which required a new word, viz. revival. Even in Hungary where Protestant church-systems did exist, the real progress was made by the so-called 'widowed congregations' which had no pastor. The great missionary to the Protestants of Salzburg and Austria was the ex-miner of Hallein, Joseph Schaitberger;[17] Lutheran Orthodox in views, he did a noble work in the most reduced circumstances, despite clerical discouragement, and with no ecclesiastical recognition.

Everywhere else the back-up to what was accomplished by the priesthood of all believers was supplied by the charitable institutions at Halle which were organs of neither Church nor state. In America Halle and the Moravians, who reckoned, at any rate, to be an interconfessional religious society, competed to provide assistance, and the fact that the Pastoral Office was eventually established among Lutherans in America was due to the labours of Henry Melchior Mühlenberg, who started life in the service of Zinzendorf's family, but was despatched by Halle to save the German Americans from the ravages of the Count. He succeeded in getting Swedes and Germans to form a Lutheran Church in America, an achievement which owed nothing to authority in Church or state. *Amt*, the Pastoral Office, had been saved in spite of itself.[18] It was the same story with foreign missions where there was no question either of a call by a congregation to a pastor, or of any 'sending' by the Church; Halle, the Moravians, and, much later, the *Deutsche Christentumsgesellschaft*[19] made a start on the basis of private enterprise with whatever assistance could be found. The pressure exerted on the German Pietists was such that the radicals were always tempted to withdraw altogether from ordinary social relations to a hermit-like existence, and very many did not marry; but others rediscovered a dynamic aspect to the life of the Christian community altogether neglected in Orthodoxy. This dynamic aspect was to spring further surprises in the Lower Rhine area to which Spener had spoken directly in his Frankfurt days.

On the problems of the Lower Rhine we have touched already; they were compounded by the gathering momentum of emigration, the rapid growth of certain industrial towns, especially Essen, and the indigenous mysticism of some of the artisans. In this milieu where mysticism and the desire for dynamism went hand in hand the curious idea took root among Pietists most at risk to French and Catholic aggression that monasticism had been a kind of revival movement, that had the monasteries remained true to their ideals, the Reformers would not have turned against them. Gerhard Tersteegen (1697–1769) who combined a Reformed heritage with Quietism and with an authentic power of exegetical imagination that is still hard to resist, formed a 'Brotherhood of the common life' in his youth, his followers formed *Pilgerhütten* up and down the Lower Rhine, and it was out of this German milieu in exile that the Protestant monastery at Ephrata in Pennsylvania was formed. Tersteegen in the Pietist manner spent twenty years writing a collection of *Select lives of holy souls* (1733–53); but the holy souls were all Catholic, and mostly hermits and members of religious orders of Counter-Reformation provenance.[20] It was a paradox when a radical Protestant insistence on the priesthood of all believers and an Arnoldian distaste for ecclesiastical pretension issued in veneration of a Catholic élite; but the logic of the process was as clear as the spiritual gifts which set it in motion.

Tersteegen's confessional neutrality was of course only possible to a Protestant of a special kind, and he made it clear that he had no desire to be anything but a Protestant, and a Reformed Protestant at that. Much of his work in realizing the general priesthood was done through the conventicles which the Reformed communities in the Lower Rhine had to hand as Spener did not. Tersteegen respected the officers of the Church, especially its pastors, though like Wesley he preferred those who did the job they were appointed for. He never wanted to found a separate sect, yet in practice he did not attend church or partake of the sacraments. He did not despise external props to the inner life, but hankered after the early congregation at Jerusalem which held all things in common, and had not yet turned the lovefeast into a sacramental occasion for compulsion and polemic. And through force of personality, through his preaching, pastoral care, and genuine interest in healing, Tersteegen worked revival in Reformed communities which were moving in that direction under an impetus of their own. Nor was it long before ecclesiastical barriers, particularly against his hymns, began to crumble, so that posthumously he began to reach a larger public.[21] What then was it that had begun to happen in the Reformed world?

The Reformed tradition began promisingly with the assertion that Christ had instituted not one but four kinds of office for the government of the Church, pastors, teachers, elders, and deacons,[22] with a great hostility to the idea of ordination and inherited talk of clergy and laity. The Scots reformers would not use the word 'clergy' except when referring to the Roman Catholic priesthood,[23] and late in the seventeenth century Voetius in the Netherlands could still speak of 'populus seu plebs ecclesiastica, quos in Papatu vocant laicos'. insisting that there was no distinction in Scripture between clergy and laity, only between elders and people.[24] But punditry had long since set in in the Reformed world. The later Helvetic Confession (1566) held that ministerial power in the Church was like empire (*imperio similior*) and included the power of the keys.[25] The Westminster Confession (1647) proclaimed that Christ had given the Church 'the ministry, oracles and ordinances of God . . . to the end of the world', and that the latter were in the hands of the former, 'lawfully ordained'. *The Form of Church Government* (1645) despatched other New Testament gifts and offices in short order: 'apostles, evangelists and prophets . . . are ceased'. The *Larger Catechism* (1648) was even firmer: 'Q. 156. *is the word of God to be read by all?* A. Although all are not permitted to read the word publicly to the congregation, yet all sorts of people are bound to read it apart by themselves, and with their families: to which end the Holy Scriptures are to be translated out of the original into vulgar languages', provided, in the view of the Kirk, that vulgar language was not Gaelic.[26] The Dutch adorned the cake with the thinnest of icing. In 1643 Appolonius explained that the Church was 'mixtae naturae, partim quasi aristocratica, partim quasi democratica', and there was no mistaking the balance between the two; the aristocratic part consisted of the offices through which the lordship of Christ was exercised in the Church, the democratic part consisted of the fraternal fellowship of believers. Voetius wrote with Hobbesian directness. There were two material parts to the institutional Church, rulers and ruled; the former were minsters and elders, the latter the people.[27] It is no wonder that the leaders of the Dutch Pietist movement were all clergy.

Elsewhere office could not fail to be magnified by the fact that, in Bern for example, the pastor was and is an official of the state, paid by the state, who cannot enter a pastoral appointment until he has taken an oath before a state official. As recently as 1959 the *Konsekrator* received the ordinands' vows, laid his hands on them, but omitted to go through the necesary legal requirements for the holding of church office, with the result that every candidate had to be put through the entire ordination ceremony again. The official commentary says that whether the *Konsekrator*'s omission was due to his having Catholic ordination in mind, or congregationalist indifference to the wider Church, or to simple forgetfulness, is not known. This, after the explanation that *Konsekration* is not ordination, simply an acceptance of the duties of office, and that the laying on of hands, though problematical from a Reformed standpoint, is acceptable as a long-standing custom, is very striking; small wonder that the commentary having discussed lay service in terms of organists, sacristans, and grave-diggers, is constrained to admit that the Swiss reformers expelled hierarchy with one boot and the priesthood of all believers with the other.[28]

But though new presbyter might be old priest writ large, his rule might be modified or even challenged by reference to other things in the Reformed tradition. Worship must be tested by Scripture, not least by the injunction of 1 Cor. 14 v. 1 to 'follow after charity, and desire spiritual gifts, but rather that ye may prophesy'. In Dutch circles this was understood to mean the exposition and practical application of Scripture by pastors and members of congregations jointly; comparing the various Scripture texts used in public sermons during the week gave these meetings the name of *collatio scripturaria*. This was the order of the Dutch congregation in London in 1550; the Walloon congregation of the same period had the custom of a portion of Scripture expounded by the pastor and discussed and questioned by the congregation. The idea was taken up by Dutch national synods later in the sixteenth century, but it had always been in part an instrument of control and could not survive the rigours of establishment. Voetius, exponent as he was of the *praxis pietatis* and *theologia affectiva*, explained that these prophesyings were not an indis-pensable function of the Church, and should take place not as a public exercise of the whole congregation, but in private gatherings consisting entirely of speaking participants or of a select group of non-speaking hearers. Even then the presidency or leading exposition of Scripture should be reserved for a theologically trained man.[29] Conventicles, indeed, came to be associated with rigorists who could not bear the lax discipline of a national establishment, and were constantly tempted to move off into separation.

These devices for the development of spiritual gifts were nevertheless important in the Reformed communities scattered along and outside the borders of the Netherlands, communities which came to have a powerful effect upon the Netherlands themselves. Voetianism and Coccejanism, the two great schools of Dutch Reformed Orthodoxy, each contributed something to the later growth of Pietism and revival, the former being a main channel of the affective side of English Puritanism, and encouraging preaching like that of the young Daniel Rowland in Wales,[30] while Coccejanism with its covenant theology encouraged the kind of historical reconsideration that we have observed in Arnold. What made the issue between the two schools so intractable was that the Voetians were strong in the lower middle class and in politics were devotees of the Orange family and central government; while the Coccejans moved in the world of wealth and scholarship and stood for the Patriot opposition to Orange power. That political issue could never be resolved in the Netherlands to the complete advantage of either party, but was not a problem in Bremen, East Friesland, and the Lower Rhine. Bremen, a town of strict Voetian ethos, was not merely the birthplace of Coccejus, it was a great stronghold of Coccejan theology. Of Theodor Untereyck (1635–93), a Coccejan who in his early days in Bremen ran into great trouble with the clergy of the town both on doctrinal grounds and because he held class-meetings during the time other men held church services, it was said in his funeral oration that 'what Spener is in the Lutheran church, Untereyck is in the Reformed'; and with equal justice it could have been said that Untereyck was the source of many of Spener's ideas.[31] He had a powerful influence on the publicists of the New Birth like Reitz, maintained active contact with the Quakers, and was father-in-God to various second-generation pietists, the most important of whom was Friedrich Adolf Lampe (1683–1729). Lampe united in his own education the traditions of Bremen, Franeker (the principal Coccejan faculty in the Netherlands), Utrecht, and the Lower Rhine, and was developing Pietism in the direction of what was to become revival. He himself became a Netherlands figure in 1720 when he was called back to a chair at Utrecht; his catechisms left their mark on the whole Rhine valley, even on Switzerland.[32] Thus in the early eighteenth cenutry in the Reformed Rhineland, as in Reformed New England, the necessities of the Churches were driving some of the ministry towards revivalism; Theodorus Jacobus Frelinghuysen (1692–1747), pastor of a village near Emden, became indeed the earliest of the revivalists in the American Middle Colonies, a decade before the revival in New England[33] and among the chief weapons of the proto-revivalists were those conventicles which had appealed to Spener as means of realizing the general priesthood. The experience of the torchbearers inside the Reformed Churches was here much the same as that of Tersteegen outside.

The punditry which the Reformed tradition embodied in its fully developed shape might also be challenged from within. 'We know not what you mean by your popish term of laymen' declared Elizabethan separatists; 'May any person preach who hath no office to do so?' asked John Penry, hot for the conversion of Wales, and the answer was a foregone conclusion: 'Yes, that he may'.[34] These assumptions did not necessarily imply a low view of the Pastoral Office and harmonized with the idea that both the call to the office and its exercise must take place within the covenanted circle of visible saints. As John Cotton put it to the church at Salem, Mass., in 1636: 'if you should come to crave baptism for your children, or the Lord's Supper for yourselves, of a minister whom you have not called over you, he hath no power, and therefore he cannot dispense an act of power.'[35] It was the covenanted congregation which made the ministry, not the reverse. A question from the church at Salem evoked the resolution that 'such as had been ministers in England were lawful ministers by the call of the people there, notwithstanding their acceptance of the call of the bishops &c. (for which they humbled themselves, acknowledging it their sin &c.) but being come hither, they accounted themselves no ministers, until they were called to another church, and that, upon election, they were ministers before they were solemnly ordained'.[36] And as congregational theory came to be worked out in England the whole issue of ministry was bound up with the cultivation of spiritual gifts in the congregation, the issue which so exercised Spener. If a congregation was to find ministerial gifts in its circle it must encourage them without applying opprobrious names such as 'lay-preaching';[37] and when it had sought out a pastor for itself the essence of the act of ordination (whether or not accompanied by the laying on of hands) was prayer, and this also was a collective act of the church: 'By this it appeareth that the people may perform the substantial act of Ordination, viz. Prayer'.[38] John Winthrop noted that under Cotton's approach 'more were converted and added to that church, than to all the other churches in the bay'.[39] Thus while the Quakers sought to escape priesthood by abolishing the Pastoral Office, the Congregationalists, having reshaped the Office in the context of the spiritual life of the congregation, felt able to include in their covenants far-reaching professions of 'obedience to our Pastors & governors over us in ye Lord'.

America was ruthlessly to expose the hazards of this synthesis.[40] Congregationalism became for a time the state Church in Massachusetts; a polity in which only freemen could vote and hold office, only church members could become freemen, and only those able to satisfy the clergy of a work of grace in their soul could become church members. This rule of saints proved extraordinarily difficult to perpetuate in practice. Within the first generation ministers discovered that if they admitted children of church members who could not testify to the work of grace within, they would destroy the pure church; but if they did not admit them, a political system already very oligarchic would become impossible to sustain. Temporary relief was sought in the adoption of the Half-way Covenant in 1662. Under this arrangement ministers might admit to the Church the children of members who professed a belief in Christian principles and wished to affiliate. Without proof of conversion they could not take communion and enjoy the full privileges of membership; but at least they could vote. The Congregationalists now reaped the full embarrassment of trying to make a religious establishment from a polity designed to withdraw the saints from the parish. The second problem, there from the first generation, was exacerbated by the record growth of a population which doubled every twenty-five years up to the Revolution. Immigrants poured in from Germany, Switzerland, France, Sweden, and elsewhere. Some brought a pastor with them; most brought nothing, not even the language of the country; none could be fitted into the American establishments. And the dire poverty of many of the immigrants differed in two ways from its European counterpart. The new populations were far more mobile than was usual in Europe, and their mobility was taking them into areas where not merely the kingdom of God but the kingdom of this world had to be built from the bottom upwards. None of the European Churches was used to this situation; and the Congregationalists had two particular problems. The need for basic social construction contained an implicit challenge to their attitude towards the righteousness of works; and a church polity conceived in terms of pastoral relationships was ill at ease in circumstances the overwheming requirement of which was evangelism.

Thomas Hooker, minister of Hartford, Conn., who had served in the Netherlands, spoke for many of the early settlers in finding those provinces 'wonderfully ticklish and miserable',[41] and the ministry viewed their predicament as one characterized by disorder, social and ecclesiastical, of the lamentable Dutch kind, of which they had hoped Congregational discipline would afford a cure. But discipline there must be. Hooker was adept at lobbying his elders as a church within a church;[42] Samuel Stone gave a Yankee version of Appollonius, describing the Congregational polity as 'a speaking *Aristocracy* in the face of a silent *Democracy*'.[43] Others pleaded for Presbyterianism, and thanked God they had escaped 'that *sink* of all errors, QUAKERISM'.[44] They managed to shed their ruling elders, exalted ministerial status, pushed an associational life with a view to setting bounds to local licence, and altogether changed the character of ordination ceremonies. Ministers now came to be ordained by other ministers rather than by the congregation, to claim that their office was conveyed in ordination rather than congregational election; and the quantities of mutton, beef, rum and wine ordered to celebrate these occasions are much more reminiscent of the beanfeasts required on entrance to an Old World guild than the congregational prayer of New World theory.[45] This programme of aggrandizing the Pastoral Office and shaking loose its roots in the gifts and graces of the congregation was not necessarily bloodless; in Cotton Mather whom the *Oxford English Dictionary* credits with the first use of the word 'revival' in the modern sense, an intensely renewed chiliasm, a ravishing vision of the heavenly joy awaiting the pure in heart, provided its own emotional dynamite.[46] But clerical bullying, remarkably ineffective in the Old World could not possibly work in the New.[47]

An alternative strategy was to abandon the pure church, a policy associated with that powerful character, Solomon Stoddard.[48] Called to Northampton, Mass., in 1670, he married Esther Mather, his predecessor's widow, added twelve children to her three, and created an unrivalled network of family influences right through the Connecticut valley. Morever, in a record which puts the protracted meetings of the nineteenth-century revivalists in the shade, he did not miss a Sunday sermon or weeknight lecture for illness for the next 59 years. He extended the Halfway Covenant by admitting all respectable baptized persons to church membership. Having got his flock in, Stoddard relied on a combination of powerful preaching for conversion and the converting effect of the communion ordinance itself. This system Stoddard built up throughout the Connecticut valley in opposition to the Boston policies of the Mathers, and it brought him a series of harvests of souls; the largest fell to his former assistant and successor at Northampton, his grandson Jonathan Edwards.

The experience of the Connecticut valley shows clearly enough why, when revival finally broke out on a large scale, it was more warmly received by the ministers of the Standing Order than by official clergy anywhere else, and why in 1740 Whitefield was given a hero's welcome, notwithstanding his episcopal ordination and his notoriously lax views on church order. The upshot of the Great Awakening from the standpoint of our theme was curiously contradictory. The Standing Order paid a high price for past punditry in a great outburst of attacks on unconverted ministers and in demands for the exercise of the general priesthood in itinerant and unordained preaching. The New England establishment was irrevocably broken, and a hundred separatist congregations formed in the forties. Yet on another view things changed extraordinarily little. The leadership even of the radical movements was predominantly in ministerial hands, and Gilbert Tennent who had begun with a sharp blast against unconverted ministers became apprehensive of spiritual gifts when they turned up in the shape of Zinzendorf. Still more striking was the case of the Revd James Davenport of Long Island, himself a Yale graduate, who came close to claiming the immediate direction of the Holy Spirit. This claim appeared to the authorities of Connecticut and Massachusetts evidence of mental illness. The high point of Davenport's demonstrations came in the famous bonfire at New London on which were cast 'a Quanity of Books . . . all suppos'd by them to be tinctured with Arminianism & opposed to the work of God's Spirit in ye Land'. This theatrical assault on one of the bases of professional clerical punditry is a striking index of the real state of affairs. William Tennent's famous Log College for the training of revival preachers had offered a recognizably Presbyterian education on an economical basis;[49] 'the Shepherds' Tent' founded by Davenport and Allen, who had been suspended from the ministry for declaring that in the work of conversion the reading of the Bible, unless it was accompanied by the immediate operation of the Holy Spirit, was of no more use than reading an old almanac, was a much more down-market institution, and one dedicated to attaining the immediate gifts of inspiration rather than to any educational process.[50] Founded at a favourable moment when Harvard and Yale were drained of students, The Shepherd's Tent was put down by legal proceedings against its leaders. Princeton was begun on a conservative basis by the New Side Presbyterians in 1747; but it was a long time before the heirs of the revivalists ventured to create their own foundations at Brown, Dartmouth, and Rutgers (to use their modern names), and then on much the same basis as the old New England colleges. Punditry had reasserted itself.[51]

It was the same story with church order. The Separates continued to insist that their members improve the gifts with which the Spirit had endowed them, but they imposed the controls of Scripture, a ministry, and the advice of neighbouring congregations. Many of the Separates had parted company with their parish churches because of the lax discipline prevailing. As that discipline was tightened, many returned to their original home. Most of the rest were picked up by the Baptists who now became a force in New England for the first time,[52] and whose polity came off the same Reformed stem as that of the Standing Order. They too played their part in pruning back the more inconvenient claims to spiritual gifts. There were Separates who claimed the ultimate spiritual gifts of sinlessness and immortality, but the church of Isaac Backus, the great New England Baptist leader, separated from the Easton Baptists because they condoned perfectionism, spiritual wifery, and baptism by 'unordained itinerants'.

Punditry, however, chastened, was back, and Calvinist New England was Calvinist New England still. It was not for another generation, after the excitements of the American Revolution, and after the back lands of Maine, Vermont, New Hampshire, and Massachusetts had filled up with settlers that high pressure revival could produce new religions with an almost Californian fertility.[53] In old New England, as Wesley was to note with some acerbity, revival had been killed stone dead for fifty years.

Dissenters in Old England and New pursued similar fashions[54] in dissimilar contexts, and reacted to revival in similar ways. The spiritual heart of English dissent never ceased to beat in spite of Restoration persecution and many political disappointments thereafter; and there were dissenters who adapted themselves to a colder climate by hotter preaching, and deliberate evangelism.[55] In the eighteenth century a generous man like Doddridge could sympathize with much in the revival and in Enlightenment too. But there were always others who were conscious that they had an order and a discipline to maintain, even if the church established did not. These stiffer Brethren[56] had torpedoed the Happy Union attempted in 1691, and doubtless their successors contributed to that long series of cases down the century where Methodists were refused communion or other friendly relations,[57] a series much longer than that of the obnoxious parish priests of legend. Of course, if the sacraments were an ordinance of a covenanted fellowship, many Methodists were not eligible, and Wesley's creation of an interdenominational religious society did not constitute a moral claim on their behalf. And even those who were sympathetic, like Isaac Watts and Philip Doddridge, had quite clear reservations.[58] Of course the leading Methodists were Anglicans, the Wesleys were Arminians and sometimes incautious advocates of Christian perfection, and, in his early years of field-preaching, John Wesley, with a fine sense of impartiality, balanced the irritation he gave the bishops by interfering in other men's parishes by the irritation he gave nonconformists by rebaptizing dissenters.[59] And the constitutional structure in Whitefield's Tabernacles in England or the building he created in Philadelphia were hardly churches according to the Engish Reformed understanding.[60]

What finally of the relations between the Pastoral Office and the general priesthood among religious communities created during the revival, taking as examples the Methodists and the Moravians? The Methodists, it must be said, muddied the waters very considerably.[61] Methodism in Wesley's lifetime might be thought to be an improved model of what Spener had sought, with class-meeting and love-feasts providing for the improvement of the spiritual gits of the society members, with band-meetings for the élite, and with what Wesley called the prophetic office, the right of laymen to preach, being usefully directed to evangelistic purposes for which Spener had not clearly provided. And underlying the whole were the regular ordinances of church or chapel of which Methodists were required to partake. But when, by a chapter of accidents in the generation after Wesley's death, Methodism became, not one but several, churches, Wesley's sons developed nearly the worst possible ecclesiology. At a time when other communities were seeking to realize the New Testament office of evangelist, Wesleyan Methodism turned its evangelists into pastors, and claimed for pastors an authority which ensured that, however the priesthood of all believers might be realized in Methodist practice, it would not be recognized in church government. Christ had filled the whole Pastoral Office and transmitted his authority to his ministers, in this case embodied in the Conference. The pastor wholly given up to the work, must feed and also rule the flock; his authority, which included ordination, legislation, the power of admission into the church, and of reproof, exhortation, and excision from it, was *sui generis*, and could not be shared with those who were not pastors, even if, like local preachers or class-leaders, they performed valuable spiritual functions. The passage of time, the diplomacy necessary to achieve Methodist Union in 1933, and the long-term pressure of Protestant examples which now seem to be fading from the Methodist official mind, eventually softened this to a statement in the Deed of Union that the ministry exercised no priesthood different in kind from that of other members of the Church. Moreover, as if there were a legalistic device for realizing the priesthood of all believers, the Deed of Union wrote the obituary of the class-meeting by extolling its merits in an amazing hortatory passage which was entirely out of place in a constitutional document and could be guaranteed never to be read by anyone likely to be influenced by it.[62]

The position with the Moravians was perhaps a little happier but even more confused. At the root of the difficulty was the disparity between Zinzendorf's original intention of creating a philadelphian *Schlossecclesiola* on his estate and the tenacious desire of the Moravians refugees who began to settle it to maintain dimly recollected traditions of the old Bohemian Brethren.[63] Zinzendorf believed he could provide for both by creating a movement within the evangelical church of the sort he thought Luther had provided for in the Preface to the *Deutsche Messe*.[64] Like Wesley, he was hamstrung by the inability of the Protesant establishments to cope with missionary situations beyond their borders, and for many years threatened with the loss of his base in Saxony and vociferiously denounced by the watchmen on the Lutheran ramparts. Zinzendorf's response was to secure episcopal consecration for David Nitschmann from Jablonski, the last remaining bishop in the old Moravian line, the authority to be exercised solely in the New World where there was then no Lutheran jurisdiction and where it was important (in Cranz's words) to have a status 'which the most rigid Episcopalian in the English colonies must acknowledge'.[65] Three years later Zinzendorf himself received consecration by the same route, also as a missionary bishop, the pair numbering themselves 63 and 64 in the old Moravian succession. Before this, however, Zinzendorf had braved family opposition to acquire Lutheran ordination in bizarre (and as Ritschl insisted, illicit)[66] circumstances, in what must have been one of the more hilarious ordination examinations of modern time.[67]

Aiming to obtain his orders from the Swedish Lutheran Church still entrenched on the south side of the Baltic at Stralsund, Zinzendorf obtained himself employment as a tutor in a merchant's household there under an assumed name. He also preached incognito on the ground that though the Superintendent knew who he was, it was 'not necessary for the people to know, and the effect of the sermons on their hearts was thus much more innocent and reliable'.[68] The first crisis of the examination would have sunk many candidates; required to preach a sermon, the Count was about to step into the pulpit when the examiner, white as death, came after him to say that he had given him the wrong gospel text. Zinzendorf coped with aplomb, but the examination continued severe. One of the examiners took occasion to deliver an attack on Zinzendorf which clearly embarrassed the candidate who was still incognito. When the examiners began to twig the situation 'the Superintendent asked him with these words "I ask you before God, are you not the Count himself?" He replied: "Yes, I am" and, undoing his coat, showed them upon his waistcoat the star and order of the cross, but begged them to keep quiet about his person, and to pay him no compliments. This they promised and faithfully performed'. At the next examination the Count began with name-dropping about his influence with the Cardinal de Noailles, Primate of France, and ended with his drawing his sword and promising 'never more, life-long, to wear it again. The Superintendent still [had] it in his keeping'. The Count's examiners who were men of repute ended by giving him a good testimonial, which predictably proved entirely unconvincing to his Orthodox and Hallesian enemies.[69] By this strange route Lutheran ordination and Moravian episcopacy were grafted on to what all insisted was the Renewed Unity of the Brethren, and already by the time Moravian doctrine was received in England it was a high one: 'Why does the Holy Ghost consecrate the Bishops? Because he has consecrated Jesus. Who outwardly [appoints to church office?] The Elders and Bishops. What is holy Ordination? A gift [of the Holy Spirit] through the laying on of hands'.[70]

This story is a confused one, but it may serve a purpose by showing how much more confused is the contemporary situation. The majority parties among the Churches insist on maintaining a corporative attitude towards their professional ministries, apparently oblivious of the fact that the rest of the world manages its affairs much better by contracts of service, and making up its mind what it wants from its employees. The ecumenical movement now seems clearly dedicated to making catholics of us all. And what of non-stipendiary ministries? Anglican bishops and Baptist congregations alike combine to use this device to close their mind to the general priesthood, and to create the impression, much as the pre-Reformation Church created the impression that the Christian life *par excellence* was the regular life, that the Christian vocation *par excellence* is that of ordained ministry. Churches which stoop to this kind of thing deserve all they get. It is characteristic of the present day that the spiritual gift currently in greatest demand, viz. healing, is the one about the eliciting and development of which least is known. Yet so far has the history of the Church parted company from the pursuit of spiritual gifts that there are even those who would confine healing services to the eucharist. For clergy of this ilk the Pastoral Office has clearly swallowed up the General Priesthood. They are the true Levites, not the eternally nonconformist priesthood after the order of Melchizedek.

Notes

1 This tract was reprinted in the Olms edition of *Philipp Jakob Spener. Schriften*, 1, Hildesheim, 1979, and was translated into English by Theodore G. Tappert, Philadelphia, 1964.

2 'What is the spiritual priesthood? It is the right which our Saviour Jesus Christ earned for all men, to which he anointed all his faithful through the Holy Spirit, by virtue of which they may and they ought to bring suitable sacrifices to God, to pray for themselves and others, and edify each other and their neighbours . . . From whom comes this spiritual priesthood? From Jesus Christ, the true high-priesthood according to the order of Melchizedek 1) which as he has no successor in his priesthood, but remains eternally the sole high-priest; also has 2) made his Christians to be priests 3) before his father to whom sacrifices have their sanctity solely from his son and are made acceptable to God'. *Das Geistliche Priestertum* is included in *Spener Schriften* 1. The copy here used is in P.J. Spener, *Drey erbauliche Schriften*, ed.J.G. Pritius, Frankfurt, 1717, pp. 14–15.

3 *Ibid.*, pp. 42, 74, 76. For Spener's change of tone, see Paul Grunberg, *Philipp Jakob Spener*, Göttingen, 1893–1906, 2, p. 171.

4 *Ibid.*, 2, p. 119.

5 Johannes Wallmann, 'Geistliche Erneuerung der Kirche nach Philipp Jakob Spener', *Pietismus und Neuzeit*, 12 (1986), p. 29.

6 Spener held more clearly than Wesley that membership of these groups implied not withdrawal from the world but acceptance of responsibility for it. J.O. Rüttgardt, *Heiliges Leben in der Welt. Grundzüge Christlicher Sittlichkeit nach P.J. Spener*, Bielefeld, 1978, pp. 146–7.

7 Spener, *Drey erbauliche Schriften: Das Geistliche Priestertum*, Appendix; Martin Brecht, *Martin Luther*, Stuttgart, 1981–7, 1, pp. 276, 354 *seq.*; 2, pp. 20, 36–8, 249–53; *Luther's Works*, American ed. by J. Pelikan and H.T. Lehmann, 55, Philadelphia, 1965, pp. 63–4.

8 P.J. Spener, *Die allgemeine Gottesgelehrtheit aller glaubigen Christen und rechtschaffenen Theologen*, Frankfurt, 1680, pp. 335–6. This work is to be reprinted in *Spener Schriften*, 3.

9 Cf. The Swabian Confession Art. VII: 'To attain such faith and give it to us men, God has established the Pastoral Office or spoken word; . . . nor is there any other means, nor method, neither way nor bridge to receive faith' (T. Harnack, *Die Grundbekenntnisse der Evangelich-Lutherischen Kirche*, Dorpat, 1845). For a liberal commentary on the development of Lutheran clericalism see Paul Drews, *Der evanglische Geistliche in der deutchen Vergangenheit*, Jena, 1905, pp. 24, 40–4, 51. On Lösher see Martin Greschat, *Zwischen Tradition und neuem Anfang. Valentin Ernst Löscher und der Ausgang der lutherischen Orthodoxie*, Witten, 1971, pp. 137–42: Emanuel Hirsch, *Geschichte der neurn evangelischen Theologie*, 5 edn., Gütersloh, 1975, 2, pp. 202–5: Moritz von Engelhardt, *Valentin Ernst Löscher, nach seinem Leben und Wirken*, Stuttgart, 1856, pp. 74, 107. On the Lutheran ministry in general, see Wilhelm Pauck, 'The ministry in the time of the continental Reformation' in *The Ministry in Historical Perspectives*, eds H. Richard Niebuhr and Daniel D. Williams, New York, 1956, pp. 110–48.

10 Ottfried Kietzig, *Die kirchliche Frömmigkeit in den evangelischen Gemeinden des Niederrheins*, Düsseldorf, 1971, pp. 5, 22, 64.

11 On the churches of the Upper and Lower Rhine areas, see Max Goebel, *Geschichte der christlichen Lebens in der rheinisch-westphalischen evangelischen Kirche*, Coblenz, 1849–52, 2, pp. 438–9, 459–60, 511–25.

12 There is a narrative of the conflict in Grünberg, *Spener*, 1, pp. 214–56.

13 Albrecht Ritschl, *Geschichte des Pietismus*, Bonn, 1880–86; repr. Berlin, 1966, 2, pp. 183–90: Wallmann, 'Geistliche Erneuerung', *Pietismus und Neuzeit*, 12, pp. 32–7.

14 Rudolf Mohr, 'Die Krise des Amtverstandnisses im Spiritualismus und Pietismus', in *Traditio-Krisis-Renovatio aus theologischer Sicht. Festschrift Winfried Zeller*, eds B. Jaspert and R. Mohr, Marburg, 1976, pp. 143–71.

15 Rüdiger Mack, *Pietismus und Frühaufklärung an der Universität Giessen und in Hessen-Darmstadt*, Giessen, 1984, p. 86.

16 The vast and often contentious literature about Arnold is summarized in Klaus Wetzel, *Theologische Kirchengeschichtsschreibung im deutschen Protestantismus, 1660–1760*, Giessen/Basel, 1983, pp. 175–209. See also Jürgen Büchsel, *Gottfried Arnold – sein Verständnis von Kirche und Wiedergeburt*, Witten,

1970: J.F.G. Goeters, 'Gottfried Arnolds Anschauung von der Kirchengeschichte in ihrem Werdegang' in *Traditio-Krisis-Renovatio*, pp. 241–57.

17 On Schaitberger see my paper, '"An Awakened Christianity". The Austrian Protestants and their neighbours', *JEH* 40 (1989), pp. 53–73. Above, Ch. 9.

18 For Mühlenberg see *The Journals of Henry Melchior Mühlenberg*, trans. by T.G. Tappert and John W. Doberstein, Philadelphia, 1942–58: *Die Korrespondenz Heinrich Melchior Mühlenbergs aus der Anfangszeit des deutschen Luthertums in Nordamerika*, ed. Kurt Aland, in progress, Berlin/New York, 1986–.

19 On which see Ernst Staehlin, *Die Christentumsgesellschaft in der Zeit der Aufklärung und der beginnenden Erweckung*, Basel, 1970.

20 Winfried Zeller, 'Die kirchengeschichtliche Sicht des Mönchtums im Protestantismus, insbesondere bei Gerhard Tersteegen' in his *Theologie und Frömmigkeit. Gesammelte Aufsätze*, ed. B. Jaspert, Marburg, 1971–8, 2, pp. 185–200. For the view of Tersteegen as a Protestant Carmelite see Giovanna della Croce, *Gerhard Tersteegen: Neubelebung der Mystik als Ansatz einer kommenden spiritualität*, Bern, 1979.

21 Cornelis Pieter van Andel, *Gerhard Tersteegen. Leben und Werk-sein Platz in der Kirchengeschichte* (Düsseldorf, 1973, original Dutch ed., Wageningen, 1961), esp. pp. 75, 160–6, 169.

22 *Ordonnances Ecclésiastiques* (Geneva, 1561), no. 2. The Reformed confessions from the West are conveniently collected by W. Niesel in *Bekenntnisschriften und Kirchenordnungen der nach Gottes Wort reformierte Kirche* (Munich, 5 vols, n.d., 1937 &c.). Here 1, p. 43 [for the circumstances in which this collection was produced, see Klaus Scholder, *The Churches and the Third Reich* (London, 1987), 1, pp. 296–7]. See also C. Fabricius, *Corpus Confessionum. Die Bekenntnisse der Christenheit* (18 parts Berlin/Leipzig, 1928–44).

23 Duncan Shaw, 'The Inauguration of Ministers in Scotland, 1560–1620', *Records of the Scottish Church History Society*, 16 (1966), pp. 35–8.

24 Gisbertius Voetius, *Politicae Ecclesiasticae* (Amsterdam, 1663–9), 1, pp. 12, 27; 2, pp. 8–12.

25 Niesel, *Bekenntnisschriften*, 4, p. 256.

26 These texts are conveniently gathered in *The Confession of Faith; the Larger and Shorter Catechisms with the Scripture proofs at large . . .* republished by the Free Presbyterian Church of Scotland (n. pl., 1976), pp. 108, 113, 248–9, 398. An official Gaelic Bible was not available in the Highlands till the early nineteenth century (J. MacInnes, *The Evangelical Movement in the Highlands of Scotland, 1688–1800*, Aberdeen, 1951, pp. 4, 62). Marilyn J. Westerkamp demonstrates that the Westminster Confession could be made by the Scots-Irish into an instrument of revival, and of self-assertion against English assimilation in Ulster, Scotland and America, but not that it led to 'the triumph of the laity'. *Triumph of the Laity*, New York, 1988.

27 Enno Conring, *Kirche und Staat nach der Lehre der niederlandischen Calvin-*

isten in der ersten Hälfte des 17. Jahrhunderts, Neukirchen-Vluyn, 1965, p. 103; Voetius, *Politicae Ecclesiasticae*, 1, p. 12.

28 On this paragraph see Kurt Guggisberg, *Bernische Kirchenkunde*, Bern, 1968, p. 24, 89–90, 109, 244. Wernle justly comments that old customs died very hard in the Swiss churches, even in the case of the sacraments which they did not take over from Catholicism (which of course included ordination). P. Wernle, *Der schweizerische Protestantismus im XVIII. Jahrhundert* (Tübingen, 1923–5), 1, p. 65.

29 The institution is described in *Joannis a Lasco Opera tam edita quam inedita*, ed. A. Kuyper (Amsterdam, 1866), 2, pp. 101–5 [French version in *Toute la Forme et Manière du Ministère ecclésiastique, en l'Église des estrangers, dressée a Londres en Angleterre*, tr. by Giles Clematius (n. pl., 1556)]: *Original Letters relative to the English Reformation*, ed. by Hastings Robinson (Cambridge, 1846–7), 2, pp. 575: W.D. Robson Scott, 'Josua Maler's Visit to England in 1551', *Modern Language Review*, 45 (1950), p. 351. For modern comment: Ritschl, *Geschichte des Pietismus*, 1, pp. 120–1: J. Lindeboom, *Austin Friars. A History of the Dutch Reformed Church in London, 1550–1950* (The Hague, 1950), pp. 24–7: Andrew Pettegree, *Foreign Protestant Communities in sixteenth-century London* (Oxford, 1986), pp. 63–4.

30 A Dutch pastor at Middleburg told his English colleague in 1681, 'Before the Belgick Churches were pester'd with the Dogmes of Cocceius, the ministry of the Word was exceedingly succesfull, many Hearers would weep at Sermons, proud sinners would quake and tremble at the word preached, multitudes were converted and reformed . . .' (G.F. Nuttall, 'English Dissenters in the Netherlands, 1640–1689', *Nederlands Archief voor Kerkegeschiednis*, 59 (1979), pp. 37–8). Cf Eifion Evans, *Daniel Rowland and the Great Evangelical Awakening in Wales*, Edinburgh, 1985, pp. 39, 43; Martin H. Prozesky, 'The Emergence of Dutch Pietism', *JEH* 28 (1977), pp. 29–37: F. Ernest Stoeffler, *The Rise of Evangelical Pietism*, Leiden, 1971, *passim*.

31 Gottfried Mai, *Die niederdeutsche Reformbewegung*, Hospitium Ecclesiae Bd. 12, Bremen, 1979, pp. 110–11: Heiner Faulenbach, 'Die Anfänge des Pietismus bei den Reformierten in Deutschland', *Pietismus und Neuzeit*, 4 (1977–78), pp. 205–9.

32 On Lampe see Heinrich Heppe, *Geschichte des Pietismus und der Mystik in der Reformierten Kirche, namentlich der Niederlande*, Leiden, 1879, pp. 236–40: Ritschl, *Geschichte des Pietismus*, 1, pp. 427–54: Mai, *Niederdeutsche Reformbewegung, pp. 252–301*: Gerrit Snijders, *Friedrich Adolf Lampe, ein deutsche reformierte Theologe in Holland*, Bremen, 1961: W. Hollweg, *Geschichte des älteren Pietismus in den Reformieten Gemeinden Ostfrieslands*, Aurich, 1978, pp. 151–3.

33 James Tanis, *Dutch Calvinistic Pietism in the Middle Colonies. A Study in the Life and Theology of Theodorus Jacobus Frelinghuysen*, The Hague, 1967. The attempt by Herman Hermelink III to argue that, despite the contemporary estimates of Gilbert Tennent and Jonathan Edwards, Frelinghuysen was not a revivalist at all, actually shows that Frelinghuysen was a revivalist who

approximated more nearly to the Voetian stamp than those who came later. 'Another Look at Frelinghuysen and his "Awakening"', *Church History*, 37 (1968), pp. 423–88.

34 Cf. 'The Apostle inseparablie coupleth the gathering together of the saints with the work of the ministerie', John Penry, *Three Treatises concerning Wales*, ed. D. Williams, Cardiff, 1960, p. 81.

35 *John Cotton on the Churches of New England*, ed. Larzer Ziff, Cambridge, Mass., 1968, pp. 43–4. Cf. 82–3, 98–9. Cotton would not baptize his child Seaborn, born on the Atlantic pasage, 'at sea (not for want of fresh water, for, he held, sea water would have served:) 1. because he had no settled congregation there; 2. because a minister hath no power to give the seals but in his own congregation'. E.S. Morgan, *Visible Saints. The History of a Puritan Idea*, New York, 1963, p. 97. See also the New England 'Platform of Church Discipline,' 1649. Cotton Mather, *Magnalia Christi Americana*, 3 ed., Hartford, Conn., 1852: repr. Edinburgh, 1979, 2, pp. 220–1.

36 John Winthrop, *The History of New England*, ed. J. Savage, Boston, 1825–6, 1, pp. 217.

37 John Owen preserved a nice balance: 'Spiritual gifts of themselves make no man actually a minister, yet no man can be made a minister according to the mind of Christ who is not a partaker of them . . . if the Lord Christ at any time or in any place cease to give out spiritual gifts unto men . . . then and in that place the ministry itself must cease'. *Two Discourses concerning the Holy Spirit and his work*, London, 1693, p. 232.

38 This theme is worked out in inimitable style under the heading 'The principle of fellowship' by Dr G.F. Nuttall in *Visible Saints. The Congregational Way*, Oxford, 1957, pp. 85–95. I am indebted to Dr Nuttall for much advice on the congregational doctrine of the ministry.

39 John Winthrop, *Journal, 1630–1649*, ed. James K. Hosmer, New York, 1908, 1. p. 116.

40 An admirable account of the evolution of the ministry in New England is given in David D. Hall, *The Faithful Shepherd*, Chapel Hill, N.C., 1972. The constitutional documents are collected in Williston Walker, *The Creeds and Platforms of Congregationalism*, New York, 1893. Much information about the constitution and English background of the American churches is given in John Butler, 'Power, Authority and the Origins of the American Denominational Order. The English Churches in the Delaware Valley', *Transactions of the American Philosophical Society*, 68, 1978, 2, pp. 1–81.

41 Mather, *Magnalia Christi Americana*, 1, p. 340.

42 *Ibid.*, p. 349.

43 *Ibid.*, p. 437.

44 *Ibid.*, pp. 453, 492.

45 These developments are a main theme of J.W.T. Youngs, Jnr., *God's Messengers. Religious Leadership in Colonial New England*, Baltimore, 1976, esp. pp. 30–9, 64–78. See also G. Selement, *Keepers of the Vineyard, The Puritan Ministry and Collective Culture in Colonial New England*, Lanham, 1984.

46 This is one of the themes of Robert Middlekauf, *The Mathers. Three Generations of Puritan Intellectuals, 1596–1728*, New York, 1971.

47 David Harlan argues that the whole mechanism of ministerial authority was much more frail than recent scholars have tended to suggest. (*The Clergy and the Great Awakening in New England*, Ann Arbor, 1980, pp. 13–30). When Mather came to recommend religious societies, they were not Spener's *ecclesiolae* designed to optimize the general priesthood, but socities for the reformation of manners on the English pattern, designed to add lay pressure to that of the clergy in social regulation. James W. Jones, *The Shattered Synthesis. New England Puritanism before the Great Awakening*, New Haven, 1973, pp. 85–6.

48 Stoddard is justly prominent in the literature. See e.g. Jones, *Shattered Synthesis*, pp. 104–28: Perry Miller, 'Solomon Stoddard', *Harvard Theological Review*, 34, 1941, pp. 277–320.

49 See the old classic, Archibald Alexander, *The Log College*, Philadelphia, 1851: repr. London, 1968.

50 Richard Warch, 'The Shepherd's Tent. Education and Enthusiasm in the Great Awakening', *American Quarterly*, 30, 1978, pp. 177–98.

51 The most recent and spirited account of Davenport is given in Clarke Garret, *Spirit Possession and Popular Religion. From the Camisards to the Shakers*, Baltimore, 1987, pp. 119–126.

52 W.G. McLoughlin, *New England Dissent, 1630–1833*, Cambridge, Mass., 1971, I, pp. 329–488: *The Diary of Isaac Backus*, ed. W.G. McLoughlin, Providence, 1979, 1, p. 570; 2, p. 703. Backus (*ibid.*, 1, pp. 74, 101) would not allow the power of ordination to be separated from the power of election. Cf. his *Discourse Showing the Nature and Necessity of an Internal Call to Preach the Everlasting Gospel*, 1754, in *Isaac Backus on Church, State and Calvinism. Pamphlets, 1754–1789*, ed. W.G. McLoughlin, Cambridge, Mass., 1968; D.S. Lovejoy, *Religious Enthusiasm in the New World*, Cambridge, Mass., 1985, pp. 183–4.

53 This subject is vividly recreated by Stephen A. Marini, *Radical Sects of Revolutionary New England*, Cambridge, Mass., 1982.

54 Pretty constantly keeping an eye on each other. Cf. Thomas Harmer, *Remarks on the antient and present state of the Congregational churches of Norfolk and Suffolk* (1777) in his *Miscellaneous Works*, London, 1823, pp. 137–220: Hall, *Faithful Shepherd*, pp. 221, 223–6.

55 W.R. Ward, 'The relations of Enlightenment and religious revival in Central Europe and the English-speaking world' in *Reform and Reformation. England and the Continent c.1500–c.1750*, ed. Derek Baker, Oxford, 1979, pp. 294–7.

56 How the various nuances were to be recognized in the eighteenth century is attractively described by Isaac Watts in *Posthumous Works*, London, 1779, 2, pp. 158–62.

57 'Mr Harmer . . . thinks . . . that the spirit of the Methodists is hurtful to the peace and order of our settled churches. Dr Wood, who had large experience of Methodists was very clear . . . that very few of that people could walk

comfortably and usefully with our churches'. John Browne, *History of Congregationalism and Memorials of the churches of Norfolk and Suffolk*, London, 1877, p. 199.

58 G.F. Nuttall, 'Methodism and the older Dissent. Some perspectives', *United Reformed Church Historical Journal*, 2, 1981, 272–74.

59 *The Journal of John Wesley*, ed. N. Curnock, 2 edn., London, 1938, 2, p. 135. The circumlocution Wesley uses in two later cases (*ibid.*, 5, p. 195; 7, p. 132) suggests that these ex-Baptist candidates may never have received believers' Baptism. 'Mr. Wesley . . . maintained with jealousy his high-church professions, and kept at a suspicious distance from Dissenters'. D. Bogue and J. Bennett, *The History of the Dissenters from the Revolution to the year 1808*, 2 edn., London, 1833, 2, p. 25.

60 *Ibid.*, pp. 48–9.

61 For a fuller treatment of the following see my two papers: 'The Legacy of John Wesley: The Pastoral Office in Britain and America' in *Statesmen, Scholars and Merchants. Essays in Eighteenth-Century History presented to Dame Lucy Sutherland*, eds A. Whiteman, J.S. Bromley and P.G.M. Dickson, Oxford, 1973, 323–50 (below, Ch. 12); and 'Die Methodistische Kirchen' *Theologische Realenzyclopaedie* 22. 666–80.

62 H. Spencer and E. Finch, *The Constitutional Practice and Discipline of the Methodist Church*, 5 edn., London, 1969, pp. 289, 291.

63 On this see my paper on 'The Renewed Unity of the Brethren. Ancient church, new sect, or interconfessional movement?' in *Bulletin of the John Rylands Library of the University of Manchester*, 70, 1988, pp. 77–92 (above, Ch. 7). Part of the difficulty was that the old Bohemian Brethren had more than once been forced to improvise in life-and-death emergencies. See David Cranz, *The Ancient and Modern History of the Brethren*, tr. B. Latrobe, London, 1780, pp. 26–8. Cf. *Primitive Church government . . . or the Unity of the Brethren in Bohemia*, n. pl., 1703. The old Brethren held that the ministry was not one of the essentials of Christianity, but was necessary because it mediated the Word of God, held the keys, and dispensed the sacraments, all of which were essentials. *Church constitutions of the Bohemian and Moravian Brethren*, ed. and trans. B. Seifferth, London, 1866, pp. 102–3.

64 *Luther's Works*, American edn. 53, p. 62. In the forties Zinzendorf affirmed his Lutheran orthodoxy by getting the Brethren to receive the Confessio Augustana Invariata (*Twentyone Discourses or Dissertations upon the Augsburg Confession*, trans. F. Okeley, London, 1753, pp. ii, xxix, 250–1) while admitting that 'a hierarchical state in the church was perhaps never absolutely necessary'. *An account of the Doctrine, Manners, Liturgy and Ideas of the Unitas Fratrum*. Presented to the House of Commons in 1749, London, 1749, p. 66.

65 *The Ancient and Modern History of the Brethren*, p. 196.

66 'The examination [which] followed [was conducted] not by the whole Ministerium in Stralsund, nor by the college of three pastors, but, since Zinzendorf

must expect opposition in either case, by two pastors one of whom was the Superintendent'. *Geschichte des Pietismus*, 3, p. 276.

67 A good (and respectful) modern account of this episode is given by E. Beyreuther, *Zinzendorf und die Christenheit*, Marburg-an-der-Lahn, 1961, pp. 75–81. See also A.G. Spangenberg, *Leben des Herrn. Nicolaus Ludwig Grafen . . . von Zinzendorf*, Barby, 1773–5, pp. 826–46: Cranz, *Ancient and Modern History of the Brethren*, pp. 177–9: *Büdingische Sammlung*, Büdingen, 1742–5, 3, pp. 670–7: J.G. Carpzov, *Religions-untersuchung der Böhmisch- und Mährischen Brüder . . .* Leipzig, 1742, pp. 454–9: J.P.S. Wickler, *Des Herrn Grafen Ludwig von Zinzendorfs Unternehmungen in Religions-sachen*, Leipzig, 1740, pp. 73–83, 95.

68 *Büdingische Sammlung.* Biographical footnote to vol. 1 Preface (no pagination).

69 Winckler, a Hallesian, found the Count's professions of loyalty to the Lutheran Church hypocritical (*Des Herrn Grafen . . . von Zinzendorf's Unternehmungen*, pp. 71–81). Certainly he made the curious promise to avoid the sham church in public. N.L. von Zinzendorf, *Die Gegenwärtige Gestalt des Kreuz-Reichs Jesu in seiner Unschuld . . .* Frankfurt/Leipzig, 1745, pp. 133–4.

70 *A Manual of Doctrine* [translated and published by James Hutton] London, 1742, nos 113, 1140, 1179. Cf. Fabricius, *Corpus Confessionum*, 10, pp. 4, 32–3. Spangenberg came as close as he could to treating ordination as a sacrament (A.G. Spangenberg, *Apologetiche Schluss-Schrift* Leipzig/Gorlitz, 1752, pp. 427–8), but stressed that Moravian bishops, priests and deacons were all 'under the conference of elders appointed by the synod, to whom the superintendency and counselling of the whole Unity is committed' (*A Concise Historical Account of the Present Constitution of the Unitas Fratrum . . .*, trans. B. Latrobe London, 1775, pp. 43, 46). In the next century Edmund de Schweinitz maintained that 'episcopacy is essential to [the] existence' of the Unity. *The Moravian Episcopate* (n. pl. or d.), p. 4.

11

The Baptists and the Transformation
of the Church, 1780–1830

Between the age of Gill and Brine, on the one hand, and that of Fuller and Robert Hall the younger, on the other, the period about the turn of the eighteenth and nineteenth centuries which saw the triumph of the moderate Calvinists over the hyper-Calvinists, there was a shift in the Baptist frame of mind as striking as the shift in literary style in which that mind was expressed; and friends of the Baptist Union have generally been in no doubt on which side they stand. Yet the nature of the shift and the reasons for it are still very difficult to grasp, and it must be confessed that European studies of the central development have been much less sophisticated than the treatment by American scholars of what went on at the fringe.[1] This evening, in the hope of goading someone to do better, I would like to chance my arm with the assertion that the shift arose from a transformation of the church partly effected, and partly evoked, by the transformation of the context in which it operated, and that the new frame of mind owed much to the effort to understand that transformed context. Certainly the change was not only, indeed not mainly, a theological one, for by the early nineteenth century the objection of the hypers was not just to Fullerism and offers of grace, but to a whole syndrome of activities, a renewed associational life, itinerant preaching and Sunday schools, ministerial training and foreign missions. That much of this programme had been actively canvassed by seventeenth century Baptists constitutes only part of the historian's difficulty in putting his finger upon what was new; so many of the usual explanations hardly seem to help. Like Anglican evangelicals but unlike Methodists, Baptists tend to look upon their history as a succession of personal networks, and have delighted to show how such networks took the prehistory of Fullerism right back thrugh the age of the hypers. Certainly the relatively liberal Calvinism of Beddome[2] and the

Historical lecture to the Baptist Union. First published in *Baptist Quarterly* 25 (1973), pp. 167–184.

West of England had its influence on London and the South Midlands where the future founding fathers of the Baptist Missionary Society used Jonathan Edwards to help each other over their difficulties with hyperism, and linked up through John Sutcliff of Olney, with Fawcett, Alvery Jackson and other Baptists of the North who had never owned the sway of Gill and Brine, and early made a deep impression on the Rossendale area of Lancashire. It is less often said that the age of the hypers seems to continue right into the age of the Fullerites. There were miisters like John Hirst of Bacup[3] and William Crabtree of Bradford[4] who were never very clear how they stood in relation to the great crux about offers of grace. It seemed a revolution when John Rippon succeeded Gill at Carter Lane, Tooley Street, yet he lived to write a *Memoir* of Gill defending him from the conventional evangelical charges of bigotry.[5] Still more remarkable it was in the works of Dr Gill that Fuller is said to have first found the famous distinction between man's natural and moral ability which other evangelicals drew from Jonathan Edwards to discredit the hypers.[6] English Baptists and Scots evangelicals seem to have read Gill, Edwards and the Fullerites concurrently with no sense of incongruity.[7]

Moreover there was some awkwardness of stance among the Fullerites themselves. They were committed to the claim that their movement constituted a 'new era' in the history of the denomination,[8] that they were ending a usurped power to impose a ruinous doctrinal orthodoxy.[9] Yet Fuller bent over backwards to minimise the disturbance in the reformed tradition which the hypers had been able to effect; Gill and Brine, he held, were great upright and independent-minded men who did not sustain a common orthodoxy.[10] 'The new system', it was alleged, 'is little more than a revival of the old Calvinism which subsisted before the time of Hussey and the other founders of pseudo-Calvinism'.[11] That middle path btween Arminianism and Antinomianism which Baxter had taken,[12] which Watts had perceived in the preaching of Edwards and described as 'the common plain *protestant* doctrine of the reformation',[13] was the way also of the Fullerites.[14] If the 'new era' could be represented theologically as a return to the old mainstream doctrine and could find seventeenth century precedents for many of its institutional departures, the modern combined efforts of Baptists and paedo-baptists had been variously foreshadowed on both sides of the Atlantic in the early eighteenth century; indeed the upper-crust Baptists of Massachusetts, tainted with urbanity, had been hankering for 'Fraternal Union' with the congregational establishment for a generation before the Great Awakening.[15]

I doubt whether the difference between the hypers and the Fullerites will yield to a structural theological analysis, any more than the difference between the Scottish moderates and the evangelicals of Chalmers's day.

For Fullerism, evangelical Calvinism, was avowedly a rhetorical theology,[16] aiming to persuade sizeable bodies of people to particular courses of action, and encountering in hyperism and 'rational' religion two very different kinds of resistance in very different proportions in different parts of the reformed world.[17] The English Fullerites were mainly concerned to dislodge the hypers, and their inveterate hostility to rational religion sprang from their self-consciously rhetorical standpoint; the trouble with English rationalism was that it opened the way to an aggressive popular anti-theology only too closely resembling the gospel of the Fullerites,[18] and built, as Robert Hall perceived, on metaphysical propositions derived from Jonathan Edwards himself.[19] Beyond England rational religion was not an affair of outsiders. Moderatism was strongly entrenched in the Kirk, and the Old Lights of the Standing Order in Massachusetts and Connecticut, though eventually defeated, were never routed. Thus the problems of persuasion varied greatly from place to place, and time to time, and the best the historian can hope for is to pick up changes in the tone of voice, fugitive impressions of changes not merely amongst Baptists, but right through the reformed world. The transformation to which these led constituted a new era indeed.

Gill's eschatology makes it plain that he conceived his situation quite differently from the Fullerites. To Gill the history of the church was a continuous cycle of prosperity and adversity as the people of God worked their way through the various church-states symbolically represented in the book of Revelation, until the ultimate consummation;[20] and the minister's chief job was to keep his flock apprized where they were in the great pilgrimage; indeed the best way to illustrate his functions was to expound symbolically the doctrine of the cherubim, those knowledgable messengers of God.[21] 'If it should be asked, What time is it with us now? Where about we are?', Gill was ready with his sign-post:

> We are in the Sardian church-state, in the latter part of it, which . . . brought on the Reformation, and represents that; we are in the decline of that state; . . . we have a *name*, that we *live*, and are dead; the name of reformed churches, but without the life and power of true religion . . . yet it is not totally dark . . . it is a sort of twilight with us, . . . As to what of the night is to come . . . they are the slaying of the witnesses, and the universal spread of Popery all over Christendom.

The slaying of the witnesses, their bodies lying unburied, those signs of the end so anxiously canvassed in the reformed world of the eighteenth century,[22] Gill also read symbolically, as referring to the day when the ministry, deserted by their flocks, would 'cease prophesying, their testimony being finished'. This state of affairs had already begun. 'A sleepy frame of mind has seized us . . . Coldness and indifference to spiritual things, a want of affection to God, Christ and his people, truths and ordinances, may easily be observed.'[23] There was no denying that one set of facts in Gill's day was very much as he described it, nor can one mistake the eloquence with which he encouraged the flock to hold on until the Philadelphian church-state ushered in the spiritual reign of Christ; the Lord loved Zion's gates, and had taken up residence within them.[24] Of course Gill looked at life as a closed system. The basic factors in the predicament of men and the church were known. The fundamental enemy of evangelical truth was the Church of Rome, which, though in principle defeated, would enjoy a brief supremacy again at the slaying of the witnesses. How deeply the mentality of the closed system penetrated the hypers may be gauged by its tenacity in the patron saint of their critics, Jonathan Edwards. Edwards actually believed that the Red Indians had been led into North America by the devil at the time of Constantine, in order that he might keep a people for himself safe from the spread of the Gospel.[25] The millennial significance of the Indian missions of Eliot and Brainerd was that the Indians had once again been drawn into the history of redemption as it was mostly worked out in Europe. The closed system had reasserted itself. Yet the closed system was beginning to crumble, and one of the signs of the crumbling was the emergence among the evangelical Calvinists of a view of history quite unlike that of Gill.

The famous pamphlet in which William Carey called for the formation of a Baptist Missionary Society in 1792[26] differed from Gill in both manner and substance. Carey outflanked the objection that the heathen could not be brought in till the witnesses had been slain, by showing that at various times since the New Testament it had been possible to carry out the dominical command to teach all nations, and that the heathen were now being brought in many scattered parts. The obstacles overcome by popish missionaries or English traders could certainly be surmounted by Baptists, and Carey sought to proportion the means to the end in view by a business-like survey of the length, breadth, population and beliefs of the countries of the world.[27] The important thing about Carey's historical scheme was that it was already a cliché, and would have been instantly recognized as such not merely by his immediate circle,[28] but by like-minded men right through the reformed world. Continually repeated with very little variation, the new view of history stemmed from that curious compilation, the *Historical collections relating to remarkable periods of the success of the gospel* (originally published in 1754 and kept up to date with additional volumes in 1761 and 1796) by John Gillies,[29] an eminent minister of the kirk in Glasgow, and son-in-law of another pillar of Scots evangelicalism, and patron of Jonathan Edwards, John Maclaurin. In two large volumes of reports, letters and diaries, Gillies related the acts of the latter-day apostles, leaving the sources to suggest to those with eyes to see that God was leading his church not into the dark tunnel which must precede his mighty saving acts, but into full revival. Since the Reformation, and especially since the emergence of Puritanism, the Scots revivals, the early missions to the American Indians, and the rise of Pietism in Germany in the seventeenth century, a great tide had built up. In the present century the Danish overseas missions had been followed by unprecedented revivals in America, Wales, Scotland and Ireland, by the growth of Methodism in England, by evidence of renewal in the Dutch Church. Gillies's *Historical collections* originated in the exchange of correspondence and literature between Jonathan Edwards, Thomas Prince and other American friends of Whitefield, and the spokesman for the Scots revivals of the 'forties, Maclaurin, MacCulloch, Robe, Erskine and others;[30] it bore out much of Edwards' conviction that the millenium would come on this side of the apocalypse, and that history was worth the trouble of investigating since it displayed 'the established means of success' in religion.[31] The hypers might repudiate offers of grace if they wished, but offers of grace were being made, accepted and blessed on an unheard-of scale all round the globe.

The effects of the new historical outlook among the Baptists were very striking. Rippon's *Baptist Annual Register* which ran from 1790 to 1802 aimed, like Gillies, to provide a compendious account of God's activity in the world,[32] to canalize the energies of the denomination, and to get Baptists out of the way of regarding their history as a simple chronicle of Baptist sufferings. Such a view still deeply marked the outlook of Isaac Backus, the chief figure of the remarkable efflorescence of Baptist historiography in America. But underlying his massive *History of New England*[33] and the vast archive on which it was built,[34] was the conviction that the facts of the case indicated something important about God's way with the Baptists which Dr Gill could never have inferred from Scripture symbolism. John Leland, Morgan Edwards, John Williams and others had already left their mark on American Baptist historiography and there was David Benedict to come. In England Baptists were pressed to improve their acquaintance with the Moravians by reading Thomas Haweis's *Church History*,[35] to get up their Pietism by reading Francke and others in translation,[36] and finally, a Fullerite, Joseph Ivimey, produced the first serious history of Baptist development in England, in instalments beginning in 1811, which gave evidence of a sense of having arrived which Dr Gill had not possessed.

Yet the new attitudes could not fail to direct Baptist interest beyond the denominational boundaries. The tide of revival seemed to have turned decisively in the ministry of that oddity George Whitefield; indispensable theological ammunition came from Jonathan Edwards; ministers of the Kirk had played a key role in establishing the Concert of Prayer and the literary freemasonry of the revival, and assumed a central station not merely in the Reformed world, but in the Protestant world generally. When in the 1790's, the barriers to evangelism at home and abroad began to collapse, the new panoramic view of history produced spectacular fruit in the movement known as Catholic christianity,[37] and induced in the evangelical Calvinists of England a mood of euphoria at the 'funeral of bigotry'[38] and the prospect of creating completely new Independent and Baptist denominations. The great evangelical battery of Bible, tract, missionary and Sunday school societies was in due course exported to America, where events had already moved more quickly in the same direction, and were much more powerfully injected with enlightenment. In a sermon reprinted for English Baptist readers by John Sutcliff, that faithful disciple of Edwards, Joseph Bellamy, had circumvented the hypers with Yankee verve and calculated that even on the pessimistic assumption that the population doubled every fifty years, and that all before the millenium were reprobate, those who were lost would be proportioned to those who were saved after the millenium only as $1:17456\frac{1}{3}$.[39] After American Independence even this modest restraint on optimism was intolerable to the social and spiritual technocrats who were piecing together a state, a society and even the kingdom of God. Elhanan Winchester was by no means the only Baptist to be carried over into Universalism,[40] and even Isaac Backus, much more typical of the ordinary Baptist, was driven to political combination with Methodists and Jeffersonian deists in his compulsive desire to disestablish the Standing Order in Connecticut and Massachusetts. And not long after Backus's death in 1806, Lyman Beecher himself was assuring English Baptists not only of his own Fullerite convictions, but of the rapprochement between the Baptists and the Standing Order in New England brought about by the triumph of Edwardsean views there.[41] As soon as the vestiges of establishment were destroyed, Baptists would feel free to take the middle way they coveted between establishment and rationalism, and to attempt the conversion of America and the world by evangelical association in the Benevolent System. On both sides of the Atlantic, Manifest Destiny and the work of God seemed in perfect harness. By the end of the eighteenth century American Baptists claimed about 10 per cent of the population for their community,[42] and the Philadelphia Association was almost intoxicated by 'the display of the sovereignty of God' produced by the federal constitution and the separation of church and state.[43] In England evangelical Calvinists took over the coarse Anglican chauvinism of a previous generation, asking 'why it hath been ordained that we, the most considerable among the professors of truly reformed Christianity, have of all others the most extensive commerce, and seem likely to possess the most extensive dominions in [the] new world';[44] and their hawk-like vigilance over the religious confusion in France under the Consulate provoked the creation of a series of Channel-coast bishoprics as a means of defence.[45]

Moreover, even in England, forces of movement were at work so rapid that Christendom must clearly be contrived rather than reformed. The Sunday school open to all rather than the covenanted meeting of baptized saints was the sign of the times. Evangelism rather than sanctification was the church's business, and the more the slogan of 'the missionary church' caught on, the more the kingdom of God seemed delivered over to associational principles. On both sides of the Atlantic associations had a bad name,[46] but whether for evangelism, Sunday schools or politics, they were indispensable. The Philadelphia Association was prepared to define the church simply as an association for the pursuit of ends beyond the power of individuals,[47] and in 1812 the Northamptonshire Association took it for granted that 'associations and the spirit of religion . . . kept pace with each other'.[48] With Baptists in this frame of mind the empirical and pragmatic spirit embodied in the associations could not fail to influence the spirit of religion. A veritable passion broke out against systematic divinity, as the illicit offspring of metaphysics, Platonic or scholastic.[49] Fuller's celebrated attack upon Socinianism was crudely pragmatic;[50] what he claimed as a brand-new method for assessing doctrine was to test its capacity for producing practical godliness. Later Fuller cautiously noted that although the book of nature was as unsystematically arranged as the Bible, it was equally patient of systematic exposition; but it is significant that he made the observation in a *Body of Divinity* which he did not live to complete or publish.[51]

Whatever the suspicions of metaphysics, the new attitudes in religion encouraged receptiveness to the epistemology and psychology entailed on the eighteenth century by John Locke. Brine had been quite clear that the Lockean plan simply illustrated the total otherness of revelation. Sensation, reflection and abstraction could teach much, 'but it was not possible that by these measures we should have ever discovered any evangelical truths.'[52] In similar vein, in America before the Great Awakening, John Walton had used Lockean sensationalism to explain why his contemporaries were still generally deluded by the doctrine of infant baptism; they absorbed error by ear and eye rather than the truth by revelation.[53] Edwards and the evangelicals could not solve their problems so simply, precisely because of their preoccupation with the personal response of faith. In his *Treatise Concerning religious affections* (1746) Edwards grafted the old Puritan interest in the work of the Spirit on to the Lockean scheme, arguing that the saints were distinguished from natural men by 'the sensations of a new spiritual sense, which the souls of natural men have not', and devising an elaborate series of tests by which their response to the divine beauty might be assessed.[54] Unlike Edwards, the English Fullerites were trying to get rid of the introspection encouraged by the hypers' insistence that a man could not have true faith in Christ until he had the inner evidence of an interest in Him,[55] but they could find no alternative to taking Edwards's experimentalism further. The cliché of the literature was that doctrinal religion should be founded on experimental religion,[56] and that Christian people needed more intimate opportunities for the mutual analysis of their religious experience than were provided by the traditional covenant relations of church members.[57] Moreover Lockean psychology had institutional implications; it might chart a middle course between the hypers who would have no adaptation in the machinery of the church, and restless Sandemanians or Haldaneites who regarded every scripture precedent as prescriptive. Early in the nineteenth century, Alexander Macleod sought to proceed from the variety of inspiration to be found in scripture, to the gifts, faculties or organs by which it was imparted, with a view to laying out a new map of spiritual knowledge like the 'survey of the natural and moral condition of the globe' demanded by the scientists.[58]

The institutional implications of the new turn indicated what was happening to the church, its transformation from symbol to instrument, a transformation accompanied by a great turning to empirical modes of thought. Baptists, like everyone else, tended to find the nub of the question in the ministry. Their denomination was being altered out of all recognition by itinerant evangelism which found no clear doctrinal or institutional expression in their inherited view of the church. Right down to 1800 nearly all English Baptists accepted Gill's definition of the Church as simply 'a society of saints and faithful men in Christ Jesus that . . . by agreement meet together in one place to carry on worship of God, to glorify him, and, edify one another'.[59] The office of evangelist was one of the extraordinary offices of the New Testament which had early lapsed, and the chief permanent officer of the church was the pastor.[60] When itinerant evangelism became the central concern of 'the missionary church' some adaptation was unavoidable. Should the new duty simply be laid upon the pastor with such lay assistance as he could gather? If the office of evangelist was revived, how was it to be related to the pastoral office?[61] The paradox was that after 1800 as the Methodist itinerants began to transform their status into pastors, the rest of the Protestant world, earnestly read and applauded by evangelical Baptists, was demanding either that the pastoral office be given over to evangelism or that the New Testament office of evangelist be revived. Thomas Haweis's *Church History* ascribed the real authority in the New Testament church to the itinerants;[62] biblical critics like Macknight of the Scots church and Bloomfield and Scott amongst Anglicans called for the revival of the office of evangelist.[63] Amongst Baptists, Alexander Macleod, followed by David Douglas[64] in the North-east, sought to relate the old institutions held to be outwardly symbolical of the inner life of the Church, to the new instrumental devices for evangelism, by means of the Lockean map of spiritual knowledge. If the New Testament gifts of the spirit were teamed up with the varieties of ministry through which they were normally bestowed, it was clear that the office of evangelist had a permanent work in the Church, and the missionary force a scriptural authority. Moreover, in Macleod's view, the great church conflict, which was brewing as he wrote in 1828, hinged on the office of evangelist. Episcopalians and Presbyterians preserved the office but built unwarrantable powers upon it; Congregationalists in self-defence had rejected it. John Wesley admirably organised his evangelists but failed to provide stated pastors. It was hazardous to amalgamate the office with organs of another kind, hazardous to reject it, hazardous to be a freelance innovator. Baptists ultimately proved no more successful than other parties to the church conflict in integrating evangelism effectively into a church-order at once empirically and biblically based; and already, difficulties of a religious character had been encountered in the new turn.

For new attitudes to the inner and outer life of the Christian had become apparent in new approaches to prayer and prophecy. There is no need to recapitulate the story of the Concert of Prayer,[65] that extraordinary combined effort of importunity, first called for by Edwards, instituted by the Scots revivalists in 1744, and implemented over much of the Protestant world for generations. One has the feeling that for the old Puritans, despite their willingness to plead the terms of the covenant in God's face, intercession was the work of the Holy Spirit rather than the congregation, but Edwards put the boot on quite the other foot. 'God is', he proclaimed, ' . . . at the command of the prayer of faith; and in this respect is, as it were, under the power of his people.'[66] A more explosive motto for the instrumental church could hardly have been conceived. The revival of the work of God, the great objective of the new prayer, was put squarely into the hands of the praying faithful. When deference began to crumble in England in the 1790's the amazing spread of cottage prayer meetings told its own tale, and, inevitably, the same methods were used to beat up enthusiasm for missions, and especially Baptist missions, overseas. But in the short run the exploitation of prayer as a means of impressing the importance of the missionary cause on children and servants[67] left a residue of guilt among the faithful;[68] and in the long run the barriers between the faithful and the rest became too tough to shift by the form of normal pressure exerted by the evangelistic prayer meeting. When this happened, a prayer meeting which was a means to an end became an intolerable bore.[69]

Prophecy raised difficulties of a different kind. Despite the excitement raised by the troubles of the papacy in the nineties, the status of prophecy as a sign-post to the Christian pilgrim had by that date been destroyed beyond the possibility of recovery or replacement. From Edwards onward, empiricism and induction had been used to lay bare the divine decrees. As Samuel Davies, later President of Princeton, put it in 1755, 'our readiest way to know what he [God] intended to do from Everlasting, is to enquire what he actually does in time'.[70] By this device Joseph Bellamy could expound a view of the Millenium in which the European trappings of the defeat of Anti-christ, to which the Papacy had been central, had disappeared;[71] and Baptists like Isaac Backus could brace themselves for the final defeat of the Beast in their own midst; the Beast which for Backus was Congregational establishment.[72] On both sides of the Atlantic the protagonists of the 'missionary church' became so powerfully possessed of the sense that the millenium was within the grasp of human will,[73] as to leave very little room in practice for a divine strategy full of quirks, paradoxes and tragedy. In 1792 Charles Whitfield, with unconscious irony, hit off the new status of prophecy in his advice on reading to the village lads of Hamsterly, Co. Durham. When well-grounded in the faith they might properly read for entertainment, and 'a careful comparison of prophecies with the New Testament will afford much pleasure.'[74] The slaying of the witnesses no longer really mattered, and the interpretation of prophecy had become the agreeable cross-word puzzle game familiar to readers of Edmund Gosse. Yet oddly enough, in this sphere the supplanting of symbol and allegory by empiricism was a very mixed blessing. For the facts to which the evangelicals drew attention, were the facts of religious experience, rather than the public events, political and ecclesiastical, which had constituted the apocalyptic drama. Some portion of the political ineptness of the English evangelical Baptists was due to the devious tactics which they found necessary to defend the Toleration Act;[75] but some was due to the Fullerite belief that political involvement represented the biggest menace to spiritual health.[76] And the moral of McLoughlin's immense enquiry into the American Baptists is that once they had shaken off their second-class citizenship,[77] they could neither deploy their political strength nor recognize that they had now entered an informal religious establishment which bore hardly on minorities.[78] Yet on both wings of the English Baptist movement political realism flourished on the interpretation of prophecy. James Bicheno, a protégé of Robert Robinson,[79] who became pastor at Newbury in 1793, supported an intelligent appraisal of the French Revolution and its aftermath upon a framework of prophecy, and drew from it concrete and rational conclusions for social justice and foreign policy.[80] And the opposite extreme threw up the most effective postwar Baptist politician, the comic of Manchester radicalism, William Gadsby,[81] the pioneer of Gillism in an industrial context and the greatest of the hypers.

Moreover, if the question of prophecy illustrates the hazards evangelical Baptists encountered in making empiricism work, the great controversy over open communion in the early nineteenth century suggests that they had special difficulties in reducing the role of religious symbolism. Baptists had of course a propensity to dispute the terms of communion,[82] but, even if they had not, they would have been unable to avoid the spectactular debate on baptism which engulfed the English churches in 1812 and continued for years. The pace of social change at home and the new problems of the mission field abroad compelled all the churches to reconsider their relations with the public generally, as they were worked out in their inherited baptismal doctrine and discipline. Here circumstances differed immensely on opposite sides of the Atlantic. In America the strict communion position had almost taken possession of the Particular Baptists;[83] in England, release from the grip of the hypers, development of the 'missionary church', and resistance to the Anglican establishment, all pointed to combined action, especially with the Independents, and combined evangelism, prayer and worship, were bound to lead to demands for open communion. The two striking things about this controversy, as it concerned evangelical Calvinists, are the amount of personal embarrassment it caused,[84] and the amount of common ground which all parties shared. Baptists saw plainly that the issues involved concerned not merely the history of the denomination, but the question of how far recent trends of thought and action could be taken. If Hall believed that interdenominational action and open communion were the conditions of progress,[85] the strict communionists could fairly reply that open communion simply provoked secession and the formation of strict communion churches.[86] Moreover, open communion would leave the Baptist denomination with nothing to stand for. Joseph Kinghorn saw with perfect clarity the situation (which later came to pass) in which congregations claiming to stand for a sound doctrine of baptism would consist largely of unbaptized persons, and would have none of it.[87] Moreover, the Fullerite advocates of strict communion all saw their opponents as returning to the establishmentarian policies of Solomon Stoddard, Jonathan Edwards's grandfather and predecessor in the living of Northampton, Mass.; Stoddard had welcomed all the respectability of the parish to the Lord's Table, asking no questions about conversion, with a liberality bitterly repudiated by Edwards himself.[88] The Great Awakening as well as the Baptist denomination was at stake.

The open communionists did not miss the point that even Edwards would have been refused communion by their opponents,[89] and were aware that baptism acutely raised the question how far the church could substitute empiricism for symbolism. Just as some evangelical paedobaptists felt cornered into saying that baptism was not a sacrament at all,[90] William Steadman played baptism down on the ground that there could be no baptism without conversion, and all might join in the work of evangelism,[91] and other Baptists began to say that the essential condition of communion was not water baptism, but the baptism of the Spirit.[92] Where Hall and Kinghorn differed was not in their estimate of the operation of open communion among Baptists, but in how much they were prepared to accept. Hall held that 'were that practice universally to prevail, the mixture of baptists and paedobaptists in Christian societies would probably, ere long, be such that the appellation of baptist might be found not so properly applicable to churches as to individuals, while some more comprehensive term might possibly be employed to discriminate the views of collective bodies';[93] Kinghorn declared that 'the plan of *open communion* makes the church *a society of persons who esteem each other to be Christians*'.[94] Either way the church was not a symbol of God's truth constituted by those who responded to the symbolic language and practices of the faith, even to a symbol as powerful in the recent past as believer's baptism; it was an association of people with a common intention to pursue a particular work. This Hall could swallow but Kinghorn could not.

It is not for the historian to resolve this dilemma, but it is noteworthy that the approaches of historians and theologians to it seem in late years to have gone in entirely opposite directions. The theologians have put up a great clamour for evocative symbols. One has heard it said that we must drum up a belief in demon-possession in order to see baptism as exorcism, and one has seen it written that 'there can be no new song until the angelic voices have first been heard to sing it in heaven . . . When the angels are silenced there are no communications even of partial divine knowledge'.[95] Historians, on the other hand, have been trying to assess on their own level what the symbolic and sacramental acts may be said to have accomplished. Dr Bossy, for example, regarding the parish in late medieval and early modern times as the theatre of perpetual conflict between kinship groups, sees the parish priest as a peacemaker, and the baptismal arrangements with godparents (who might on occasion be children) as devices for strengthening the kinship-group and providing future support for the candidate in baptism.[96] This might not be very sacramental, but it was very useful, and gives one an inkling why the leading Reformers were so immoderately hostile to believer's baptism becoming the norm; they did not want individual option to intensify the warfare in the parish, and their fears were faintly echoed by evangelical paedobaptists early in the nineteenth century declaring that believer's baptism was a defiance of natural affections.[97] At the same time one may infer that the determination of churchmen, protestant and catholic, to drive the parish as a unit of christianisation instead of building on the natural and associational groups which existed within it, was one of the reasons for the long-term decline of the old religious establishments; the symbols at their disposal were not strong enough to absorb the smaller units into a larger parish cohesion. My colleague, Mervyn James, finds the first appearance of Baptist practice in the North-east rooted in forms of radical Puritanism which had appeared before 1640 on the confines of Durham and Northumberland, where it expressed the sense of independence of the extended family in hill areas, over against the systems of control applied by the gentry to the nuclear families of the plain.[98] It was doubtless theologically bizarre to assert the independence of a kinship group on the basis of believer's baptism, but it is not difficult to understand how it happened; nor can one fail to note that when the north-country Baptists began to expand in the middle of the eighteenth century, they did so mostly in hill communities of a similar kind. What Hall and Kinghorn each understood Hall to be saying was that a religious appeal must take account of the forms of social cohesion with life in them; by Hall's time what counted was not the extended family, but the association,[99] and his view was that inherited symbolism and churchmanship should not be permitted to obstruct the use of this device for awakening and sustaining a Christian faith. In the century and a half since Hall died, religion has continued to escape from churches in Europe, America and Africa, into all manner of other groupings. Yet the most succesful religious society of all, the Methodist connexion, has repeatedly crucified itself upon the claim to churchly status; in an ecumenical age ministers are obsessed with churchmanship and call even for the angels. In the middle of the nineteenth century the churches refurbished and multiplied their symbols for purposes of denominational warfare; in our re-mythologising days they use them as rallying cries against decay. Perhaps Robert Hall's contribution to the transformation of the church is overdue for a fresh look.

Notes

1 Perry Miller, Alan Heimert, Richard Bushman, William McLoughlin and Sydney Ahlstrom, have no real counterparts in English scholarship.

2 Beddome, 'a true disciple of the old school . . . [who] was not afraid to press on his hearers with becoming earnestness, all those experimental and practical parts of the inspired volume' (*Evangelical Magazine* xiii. 562–3) based his sermon on 'The nature and authority of the Christian Ministry' on Matt. iv. 19 ('I will make you fishers of men') and counselled ministers to 'beseech men, in Christ's stead, to be reconciled to God'. *Sermons of the late Benjamin Beddome A.M., with a brief memoir of the author*, London, 1835, pp. 302–3.

3 James Hargreaves, *The life and memoirs of the late Rev. John Hirst*, Rochdale, 1816, pp. 272–7.

4 Isaac Mann, *Memoirs of the late Rev. Wm. Crabtree, first pastor of the Baptist Church at Bradford, Yorks.* (London, 1815, pp. 49–50.

5 John Rippon *A brief memoir of the life and writings of Rev. John Gill*, London, 1838, p. 139.

6 *Evangelical Magazine*, xxvi. 3.

7 George Pritchard, *Memoir of the Rev. Wm. Newman*, London, 1837, pp. 139, 159: John Brown, *The evangelical preacher*, 3 vols., Edinburgh, 1802–6. Long before Edwards became the vogue with progressive Baptists, he had appeared on the reading lists of the Bristol Academy cheek by jowl with Gill and Brine, and with the Scots evangelicals Maclaurin and Witherspoon. J. Rippon, *Baptist Annual Register*, London, 1790–1802, i. 253–6.

8 Joseph Ivimey, *History of the English Baptists*, London, 1811–30, iv. 41.

9 *The works of Andrew Fuller*, London, 1824, i. 273, iii. 468. John Ryland, *Pastoral Memorials*, London, 1828, ii. 325. *The works of Robert Hall* ed. O. Gregory, 2nd ed. London, 1833, ii. 401. [Jn. Fawcett jnr.], *An Account of the life, ministry and writings of Rev. John Fawcett*, London, 1818, pp. 237–8. Ivimey, *History of the Baptists*, iii. pp. ix., xi. The longer these criticisms went on, the harder they became to state moderately, cf. J.H. Hinton, *On completeness of ministerial qualification*, London, 1829,, pp. vi–x. The moderate Calvinists' public image was of men who selfconsciously refused to 'indulge a wanton curiosity to pry into what is not revealed' (Joseph Bellamy, *Sermons*, ed. J. Sutcliff, Northampton, 1783, p. iii. *Evangelical Magazine*, xxiii. 353. Cf. the important MS. letter of Joseph Hughes to John Pike, Battersea, December 14, 1807, prefixed to the Angus Library copy of J. Leifchild, *Memoir of the late Joseph Hughes, one of the secretaries of the British and Foreign Bible Society*, London, 1835), who maintained a proper proportion of faith (Rippon, *Baptist Annual Register*, i. 432), balanced a propensity to activism and committee sitting by a devotion to private prayer (J.H. Hinton, *The means of a religious revival*, London, 1829, pp. xiv–xv), and as Fuller himself put it, sustained 'a lively interest in evangelical, faithful, practical and pungent preaching; an attention to things more than to words; a taste for the affectionate more than for the curious; a disposition to read and

think rather than to dispute; a spirit to promote the kingdom of Christ.' *Baptist Magazine*, v. 232.

10 Fuller, *Works*, i. 273, 276n. Cf. Ivimey, *History of the Baptists*, iii. 260.

11 *Baptist Magazine*, vii. 267.

12 Cf. John Evans, *A brief sketch of the several denominations into which the Christian world is divided; accompanied with a persuasive to religious moderation*, London, 1795, pp. 15–16. This characteristic production of the age of 'catholic christianity' (*Evangelical Magazine*, iii. 299) by a General Baptist rapidly went through some twenty editions, and more than trebled in size.

13 Jonathan Edwards, *Faithful narrative of the surprising work of God . . . in Northampton*, ed. I. Watts and J. Guyse. Republished by J. Fawcett and W. Steadman, Halifax, 1808, p. ix. A paper on the English publishing history of Jonathan Edwards, to which the first (1737) edition of the *Faithful Narrative*, would provide an introduction, would be a useful exercise (The *explicanda* are provided by Thomas H. Johnson, *The printed writings of Jonathan Edwards, 1703–1758. A bibliography*, Princeton, 1940). Evangelical Baptists and Congregationalists seem to have reprinted his shorter pieces whenever they thought the English revival needed an impulse, and John Wesley (sometimes to the fury of Baptists) [*Circular letter of the Northamptonshire Association*, 1781] would bowdlerize them for his followers.

14 The literary devices by which Baxter, Watts and Edwards were taken up into evangelical Calvinism are illustrated in John Gillies, *Historical collections relating to remarkable periods of the success of the gospel and eminent instruments employed in promoting it*, Glasgow, 1754, i. 258. Cf. John Erskine, *The signs of the times considered: or the high probabililty that the present appearances in New England and the West of Scotland are the prelude to the glorious things promised to the church in the latter ages*, Edinburgh, 1752, p. i.

15 W.G. McLoughlin, *New England Dissent, 1630–1833. The Baptists and the separation of Church and State*, Cambridge, Mass., 1971, i. 278 seq.

16 *Evangelical Magazine*, viii. 243.

17 The two fronts on which the evangelical Calvinists contended in England may be illustrated by William Gadsby for the hypers and Walter Wilson for the old-style Congregationalists. The former proposed a text to be hung over William Roby's chapel in Manchester: 'Mangling done here' (*The works of the late Wiliam Gadsby, Manchester*, ed. J. Gadsby, London, 1851, p. 49). Wilson lamented that 'the true spirit of nonconformity has been dead by at least one generation; and its present representatives . . . consider it a happy omen for their age of liberality. The Calamys, the Bradburys, and the Robinsons, are now remembered no more, unless it be to malign their zeal, or to pity their bigotry. Dissenters of former days have been greatly blamed for not possessing what is called a 'missionary spirit' . . . It is true they did not beat up a crusade in the religious world for the wild purpose of proselyting the savage hottentot, or the untutored islander, but they conducted plans of instruction for the rising

generation of their countrymen which turned to infinitely better account.'
(Walter Wilson, *The history and antiquities of dissenting churches and meeting
houses in London, Westminster and Southwark*, London, 1808–14, i. p. xii.,
iv. 435, 541, 551). Cf. A. Peel, *These hundred years*, London, 1931, pp. 36–7.

18 *Circular letter of Kent and Sussex Particular Baptist Association*, 1793, p. 7.
Rippon, *Baptist Annual Register*, ii. 467. Charles Whitfield, *The obligations
to mental improvement stated and the use of books recommended to youth*,
Newcastle, 1792, p. 20.

19 Robert Hall, *Works*, i. 58–64.

20 John Gill, *The watchman's answer to the question, 'What of the night?'*, 6th
ed., London, 1812. The first edition was in 1751.

21 John Gill, *The doctrine of the cherubim opened and explained*, London,
1764, p. 29. (This sermon was preached again in Victorian dress without
acknowledgement by Jabez Burns in *Sketches of sermons designed for special
occasions*, London, 1860, pp. 113–6). Cf. John Gill, *The work of the gospel
minister recommended to consideration*, London, 1763. John Gill, *The duty
of a pastor*, n. pl. or d., pp. 10–11. John Brine, *Diligence in study recommended
to ministers*, London, 1757. The church was itself a symbol of God's way with
men which would do its work in due course. John Gill, *Sermon on Jeremiah*,
vi. 16, London, 1750, p. 20.

22 See, e.g., Alan Heimert, *Religion and the American mind from the Great
Awakening to the Revolution*, 2nd ed. Cambridge, Mass., 1968, pp. 85–90.

23 Gill, *The watchman's answer*, pp. 25–7.

24 *Ibid.*, p. 37. John Gill, *The practical improvement of the watchman's answer*,
5th ed., London, 1793. John Gill, *The glory of the church in the latter day*, 2nd
ed., London, 1753, p. 4. Cf. John Brine, *Christ the object of God's eternal
delight, and the church, the object of Christ's everlasting delight*, London,
1761.

25 *The works of Jonathan Edwards*, ed. H. Rogers, S.E. Dwight, and E. Hickman,
London, 1837, i. 600.

26 William Carey, *An enquiry into the obligations of Christians to use means for
the conversion of the heathens*, Leicester, 1793.

27 *Ibid.*, pp. 36–7, 11.

28 E.g., J. Fawcett, *Considerations relative to the sending of missionaries to
propagate the gospel among heathens*, Leeds, 1793. A. Fuller, *The Calvinistic
and socinian systems examined and compared as to their moral tendency*, ed.
London, 1802, pp. 28–30.

29 For a contemporary memoir of Gillies, see *Evangelical Magazine*, xvii. 89–93.

30 Edwards, *Works*, i. pp. cxiv. *seq.*, cxlv–clxiii. Sir Henry Moncreiff Wellwood,
Account of the life and writings of John Erskine, Edinburgh, 1818, pp.
160–162. Cf. *The Christian history, containing accounts of the revival and
propagation of religion in Great Britain and America*, Boston, Mass., 1743–5.

31 Edwards, *Works*, i. 569, 586.

32 After the *Register* had ceased publication the *Evangelical Magazine* maintained
similar surveys. *Evangelical Magazine*, xviii. 384, 431, 503.

33 Isaac Backus, *A history of New England with particular reference to the denomination of Christians called Baptists*, Boston, Mass., 1777–1796. Cf. Angus Library, Isaac Backus, MS. History of the Baptist Warren Association in New England, 1767–92.

34 McLoughlin, *New England Dissent*, ii. 774–6, 1286.

35 Rippon, *Baptist Annual Register*, iv. 798–805. Rippon had already published extracts from their mission reports. *Ibid.*, i. 378–84.

36 *Baptist Magazine*, v. 381–2. August Herman Frank, *A guide to the reading and study of the Holy Scriptures*. Translated with a life of the author by Wm. Jaques, London, 1813. *Evangelical Magazine*, xx. 81–7, 120–6.

37 E.g., 'A great variety of denominations dwell together, and worship before the throne of God and the Lamb, without one jarring note . . . there Whitefield and Erskine, Toplady and Wesley, Romaine and Gill, Jonathan Edwards and Latrobe, can all unite in one song of praise to that true God to whose sovereign grace and almighty influence they cheerfully own themselves indebted for their complete salvation.' *Evangelical Magazine*, xi. 207.

38 The phrase is David Bogue's; the sentiment applauded by liberal Baptists.

39 'The Millenium' in *Sermons*, p. 51.

40 Cf. John Leland (McLoughlin, *New England Dissent*, ii. 930) and Samuel Baker, *A solemn address to all Christians but specially to the Methodist and Baptist orders on the subject of christian fellowship and the union of doctrines*, Hallowell, 1814, p. 17.

41 *Baptist Magazine*, vi. 212–5. American Baptists had gone over wholesale to Fullerite views, David Benedict, *A general history of the Baptist denomination in America and other parts of the world*, Boston, Mass., 1813, ii. 456.

42 Rippon, *Baptist Annual Register*, iv. 813, 936.

43 *Ibid.*, iv. 813–4.

44 *Evangelical Magazine*, xii. 170–1. The speaker is Dr John Rotheram, fellow of University College, Oxford, and later Rector of Houghton-le-Spring.

45 Rippon, *Baptist Annual Register*, iii. 465–7; iv. 912–6, 936–9, 1064–9. S. Delacroix, *La réorganisation de l'Eglise de France après les Révolution (1801–9)*, vol. i, Paris, 1962, p. 125.

46 In America they had been used to force Old Light ministers on predominantly New Light congregations, McLoughlin, *New England Dissent*, i. 343, 364, 403.

47 'As particular members are called together and united in one body, which we call a particular church, to answer those ends and purposes that could not be accomplished by any single member, so a collection and union of churches into one associational body, may be easily conceived capable of answering those still greater purposes, that any particular church would not be equal to.' (Angus Library. Isaac Backus, MS. History of the Baptist Warren Association in New England 1767–92, fo. 11. Cf. Benedict, *Baptist Denomination in America*, ii. 464. Backus, *History of New England*, iii. 114–9). Gill would have groaned at this doctrine, but it was repeated almost to the word by the English Baptist New Connexion in 1793. Rippon, *Baptist Annual Register*, i. 549.

48 *Circular letter of Northamptonshire Association*, 1812, p. 8.

49 MS. Letter of Joseph Hughes to John Pike, Battersea, December 14, 1807, prefixed to Angus Library copy of J. Leifchild, *Memoir of Joseph Hughes*. [John Fawcett Jnr.], *Life of John Fawcett*, p. 95. Cf. David Eaton, *A familiar conversation on religious bigotry, candor and liberality; humbly intended as a persuasive to greater moderation, union and peace amongst the followers of Christ*, London, 1803, p. 8.

50 *The Calvinistic and socinian systems compared as to their moral tendency.*

51 Fuller, *Works*, iv. 319. Cf. *Evangelical Magazine*, x. 88–90.

52 John Brine, *The proper eternity of the divine decrees, and of the mediatorial office of Jesus Christ, asserted and proved*, London, 1754, pp. 33–4.

53 McLoughlin, *New England dissent*, i. 316.

54 *The works of Jonathan Edwards, Vol. II, Religious Affections*, ed. John E. Smith, New Haven, Conn., 1959, pp. 271, 449.

55 Robert Hall, *Help to Zion's travellers*, Bristol, n.d. [1781], p. 116.

56 *Evangelical Magazine*, i. 150–3: Benjamin Beddome, *Twenty short discourses adapted to village worship or the devotions of the family*, 7 series, London, 1805–19, vi. 39–40.

57 John Fawcett, *The constitution and order of a gospel church considered*, Halifax, 1797, pp. 54–5.

58 Alexander Macleod, *A view of inspiration comprehending the nature and distinctions of the spiritual gifts and offices of the apostolic age*, Glasgow, 1827, pp. 7, 9–10.

59 John Gill, *Sermon on Jer. vi. 16*, p. 20.

60 *Circular letter of Kent and Sussex Particular Baptist Association* 1788: Daniel Turner, *A compendium of social religion*, London, 1758, p. 39. Charles Whitfield, *The form and order of a Church of Christ*, Newcastle-upon-Tyne, 1775, pp. 34–6. J. Fawcett, *The constitution and order of a gospel church considered*, Halifax, 1797, pp. 29–30. Wm. Newman, *A manual for church members drawn from the New Testament*, London, 1825, p. 58. In the America of the Great Awakening, Old Lights considered itinerancy as an intrusion upon the covenant relations of minister and people, and damned the 'priest' Whitefield for introducing the 'anarchy' of episcopalianism (Heimert, *Religion and the American mind*, p. 119); it was a sign of the times in England that Gill's long church covenants went out of fashion, and that in 1793 Fuller was wishing 'we had a Whitefield' and commending Isaac Backus's itinerant missions in Virginia. Fawcett, *Life of Fawcett*, pp. 99–100, 297.

61 Fawcett, *Constitution of a gospel church*, pp. 41–2. Fawcett, *Thoughts on revival*, p. 16. *Circular letter of the Northamptonshire Association*, 1821, pp. 9–10. W. Steadman, *The Christian minister's duty and reward*, Gateshead, 1807.

62 Thomas Haweis, *An impartial and succinct history of the rise, declension and revival of the Churches of Christ*, London, 1800, i. 83–5. David Benedict, *Baptist denomination in America*, i. 43.

63 James Macknight, *A new literal translation from the original Greek of all the*

apostolical epistles with a commentary and notes, 4th ed. London, 1809, ii. 393 n. 3; i. 580 n.l. S.T. Bloomfield, *The Greek Testament with English notes*, 2nd ed. London, 1836, ii. 293. Thomas Scott, *The Holy Bible . . . with explanatory notes*, new ed., 6 vols., London, 1812–14, *sub*. Eph. iv. 11; 2 Tim. iv. 1–5; Acts xxi. 7–14.

64 Macleod, *View of Inspiration*, p. 496. David Douglas, *Essay on the nature and perpetuity of the office of primitive evangelist*, London, 1838.

65 For a characteristc contemporary account: *Evangelical Magazine*, iii. 198–201.

66 Edwards, *Works*, i. 426.

67 *Evangelical Magazine*, xxv. 9.

68 *Ibid.*, iii. 73.

69 Its epitaph amongst Baptists was written by Jabez Burns, *A retrospect of forty-five years' Christian ministry*, London, 1875, pp. 368–9.

70 Heimert, *Religion and the American mind*, p. 84.

71 *Ibid.*, p. 87: Bellamy, *Sermons* No. 2.

72 Angus Library. Isaac Backus, MS. History of the Baptist Warren Association, fo. 27. Backus, *History of New England*, ii. 406. Rippon, *Baptist Annual Register*, ii. 132.

73 The evangelical reviewers could find no higher praise for David Bogue's *Discourses on the Millenium* for example, than that no man had done more than the author to bring on the millenium, 'nor are the thoughts and emotions [the book] excites any other than such as are calculated to produce a Millenium.' *Evangelical Magazine*, xxvi. 381, 432.

74 Charles Whitfield, *The obligations to mental improvement stated*, p. 22.

75 W.R. Ward, *Religion and society in England, 1790–1850*, London, 1972, pp. 50–62.

76 Andrew Fuller, *The backslider*, 3rd ed., London, 1804, pp. 24–5. (The Kent and Sussex Association actually began a circular letter on the *Signs of the Times* (1793) with the declaration 'we do not mean to enter on a discussion of the political state of the world at large, or of these kingdoms in particular. We apprehend that subject to be foreign to our business'). Not surprisingly in a eulogy on *Christian Patriotism*, Dunstable, 1803, Fuller could find little wrong with the England of his day, negro slavery apart.

77 Cf. on the English side, Samuel Pearce, *The oppressive, unjust and prophane nature and tendency of the Corporation and Test Acts exposed*, Birmingham, 1790.

78 McLoughlin, *New England Dissent*,i. p. xviii; ii. 1269–70.

79 I am indebted to Mr David Bebblington for information about Bicheno's background. There is no suggestion that Bicheno followed Robinson into unitarianism; his tone resembles that of a Congregational 'Old Light' like Walter Wilson: 'Many religious people have a most unaccountable notion that the affairs of government should be left to the wicked.' *Dissenting Meeting Houses*, iv. 549.

80 J. Bicheno, *The signs of the times: or the overthrow of the papal tyranny in France, the prelude of destruction to the papacy and despotism; but of peace*

to mankind, 2nd ed., London, 1794; J. Bicheno, *The probable progress and issue of the commotions which have agitated Europe since the French Revolution*, London, 1797. J. Bicheno, *The fulfilment of prophecy farther illustrated by the signs of the times*, London, 1817.

81 Gadsby's political career may be best traced in the Manchester press.

82 E.P. Winter, 'The Lord's Supper: admission and exclusion among the Baptists of the seventeenth century,' *Baptist Quarterly*, xvii. 267–81.

83 The Great Awakening had given rise to numerous Separate congregations mostly conducted on mixed communion principles. But the success of the Separates in jolting the Standing Churches into greater strictness, giving up the half-way covenant, and so forth, opened the way for paedobaptists to return to the establishment, leaving the Separate movement in the hands of the advocates of believers' baptism. Until the last generation of the eighteenth century, most of the Baptist expansion in America resulted from the transformation of Separate into closed-communion Baptist churches, and after the mid-sixties their distinctive position gave them a basis for a great drive against a Congregational establishment which had no counterpart in England.

84 On the paedobaptist front it was held that the trouble was all created by a handful of ill-disposed Independent ministers in the South of England (*Baptist Magazine*, vi. 209–10); on the Baptist front Robert Hall maintained that 'the practice of strict communion rests almost entirely on *authority . . . that were the influence of a few great names withdrawn, it would sink under its own weight*,' and Fuller's death in 1815 was followed by a wrangle between the open- and strict-communionists to claim him for themselves (Halls, *Works*, ii. 5; iii. 409–10. Wm. Newman, *The admission of unbaptised persons to the Lord's Supper inconsistent with the New Testament* London, 1815, pp. 1–2, 4–6. Joseph Kinghorn, *Arguments against the practice of mixed communion*, London, 1827, pp. 23–5). The *Baptist Magazine* prohibited discussion of the question in its columns, and irritated readers of the 'Catholic Christianity' school for not prohibiting it strictly enough. *Baptist Magazine*, iv. 326; vi. 189. Cf. *Evangelical Magazine*, xxiii. 370.

85 At the crucial moment Hall received unexpected support from America. J.M. Mason, *A plea for Catholic communion in the church of God*, 2nd ed., London, 1816. (For the voluminous comment this tract received see *Evangelical Magazine*, xxv. 144–6, 177–9, 215–7, 270–2.) Robert Hall, *A reply to Rev. Joseph Kinghorn*, 2nd ed., London, 1818, pp. viii–ix.

86 G.A. Weston, 'The Baptists of North western England, 1750–1850', unpublished, Sheffield, Ph.D. thesis, 1969, pp. 208–13.

87 Kinghorn, *Arguments against mixed communion*, pp. 19–20.

88 Joseph Kinghorn, *Baptism a term of communion at the Lord's supper*, 2nd ed., Norwich, 1816, pp. 109–12. *Evangelical Magazine*, xxi. 460. Cf. W. Jones, *Memoirs of the life, ministry and writings of Rev. Rowland Hill*, London, 1834, p. 84.

89 *Evangelical Magazine*, xxii. 90.

90 *Ibid.*, xxvii. 370–1.

91 Weston, *Northwestern Baptists*, pp. 89–90, 207.

92 *The duty and importance of free communion among real Christians of every denomination, especially in the present period, with some notices of the writings of Messrs. Booth, Fuller, and R. Hall*, London, n.d., pp. 14–15. Cf. similar views among paedobaptists, Joseph Francis Burrell, *Water baptism, circumcision and the Lord's supper dissected and analized* . . . London, 1816, pp. 79, 81, 84.

93 Hall, *Works*, iii. 452.

94 Kinghorn, *Arguments against mixed communion*, p. 37.

95 T. Fawcett, *The symbolic language of religion*, London, 1970, pp. 282, 273.

96 John Bossy, 'Blood and baptism; kinship, community and Christianity in Western Europe from the fourteenth to the seventeenth centuries,' *Studies in Church History*, vol. x. 129–43. I am indebted to Dr Bossy for the kind loan of a copy of this paper before publication.

97 *Evangelical Magazine*, xxiv. 138.

98 Cf. the Independent 'Dales Men' of Swalesdale discussed by Dr G.F. Nuttall in his presidential address to the Ecclesiastical History Society, *Studies in Church History*, vol. x. 160.

99 Though in 1809 a Methodist report from the Durham coal-field described how 'whole families of several individuals unite themselves at once to our societies. This is truly conversion *per stirpes* and not merely *per capita*.' Methodist Church Archives MSS., John Ward to Jabez Bunting, 27 March, 1809.

Part Three

Methodism

12

The Legacy of John Wesley:
The Pastoral Office in Britain and America

The Wesleyan doctrine of the Pastoral Office, a closely articulated exposition of Wesley's legacy, had a hectic heyday in England in the second quarter of the nineteenth century. Theologically it has fallen upon hard times,[1] but it remains an interesting problem in the transmission of ideas, more particularly in the respective roles of ideas and events in shaping institutions. The doctrine appealed to history as well as to scripture, and assumed *a priori* that every body politic possessed sovereign legislative power.[2] The Methodist legislature was Conference, in which Wesley had chosen to exercise his plenitude of power with the preachers, and to which he had ultimately bequeathed his power to station them in their respective 'circuits' or preaching rounds by the Deed of Declaration. His general superintendence over the whole Society had been vested in each circuit in what had been known as his Assistant (that is the general overseer of the circuit) and Helpers (the other itinerants), and were now known as the Superintendent and ordinary preachers; and his daily oversight had passed to District Committees acting on behalf of Conference. This concentration of spiritual authority, it was claimed, was rooted in the New Testament. Christ had filled the whole Pastoral Office, and transmitted his authority to his ministers. The pastor, wholly given up to the work, must feed and also rule the flock; his authority, which included ordination, legislation, the power of admission into the Church, and of reproof, exhortation, and excision from it, was *sui generis*, and could not be shared with those who were not pastors, even if, like local preachers or class leaders, they performed valuable spiritual functions; and the fullness of his power was held to afford the best safeguard 'that our doctrines shall be preserved in their purity'.

First published in *Statesmen, Scholars and Merchants. Essays in Eighteenth-Century History presented to Dame Lucy Stuart Sutherland, edited by Anne Whiteman, J.S. Bromley and P.G.M. Dickson*, Oxford, 1973.

In the heyday of Jabez Bunting, from about 1825 until the 1850s, the polemical intent of this skilful double appeal to what must *a priori* be, and to the practical upshot of Methodist history and scripture, was betrayed by a certain smoothness, even slickness. For the striking feature of Methodist theological literature in the generation following Wesley's death in 1791 was its total silence on the whole matter.[3] The biblical commentators of the immediate post-Wesleyan period, too, who had to make something of the whole range of texts to which the later expositors of the Pastoral Office appealed, made very modest claims. Indeed, they altogether undermined that pillar of ministerial authority, Heb. 13: 17 – 'Obey them that have the rule over you . . . for they watch over your souls as they that shall give account'[4] – and put their polemical energy into expounding texts which rebuke the abuse of pastoral power.[5] In this they maintained the tradition of Wesley himself, whose *Notes on the New Testament* were among the authoritative standards of the Connexion. Wesley asserted for the minister 'a power of inflicting and remitting ecclesiastical censures', but his desire to justify the ministrations of his helpers led him to talk as if pastoral authority might be divided, and he was often brusque with the official shepherds of parishes, his fellow Anglican clergy.[6] Nor could the high Wesleyans of the Bunting era ever agree in their appeal to history, though they understood that if the itinerant were truly a full pastor of the Church of Christ, he must be shown to have exercised his authority independently of the Church of England at the earliest possible date. Richard Watson insisted that the preachers, while lacking the imposition of hands, had been 'virtually' ordained from the time of and by virtue of their summons to Wesley's first Conference in 1744.[7] This ran into historical difficulties: Wesley had always distinguished between the prophetic office (the right to preach and exhort), which he believed his itinerants possessed, and the priestly office (the power to administer the sacraments, etc.), which they did not; this was powerfully argued in his famous Korah sermon. Furthermore, the theory of 'virtual ordination', from 1744 onwards, failed to explain why Wesley had ordained several men in and after 1784, quite independently of their reception into full connexion. The Methodist historian Smith went so far as to date the origin of the Methodist Pastoral Office back to 1739, when Wesley began field-preaching, and thought that denominational status was complete when Wesley separated his United Society in London from the Moravians on Sunday, 20 July 1740. Methodism, he believed, had undergone no further change 'except from small to great'. But this too encountered logical obstacles. By 1740 Wesley's Society could hardly be distinguished from earlier religious societies, like those associated with Horneck and Woodward, which had never become a denomination.

Moreover, this argument undercut Smith's second line of defence that, after Wesley's death, Conference regarded reception into full connexion 'as equivalent to real or formal ordination'.[8] Uncertain as Smith was, however, he never rivalled the confusion of the American historian Nathan Bangs, who claimed that when Methodism first entered the American colonies in 1766, it 'had received a regular shape [and] was known as a distinct denomination, though still adhering to the Church of England'.[9] On neither side of the Atlantic would the untidy ways of the eighteenth-century Church of England dovetail with the stricter categories of nineteenth-century churchmanship.

Wesley himself persistently refused to admit that he had separated, and in most respects was more comfortable in the Church of England at the end of his life than at the beginning. His field-preaching and other early arrangements led to clashes with Church authority at various levels, and had to be justified by necessity. Necessity had to be reinforced by casuistry. A tacit dispensation from the rubrics and canons, Wesley concluded in 1755, had the same force as an explicit dispensation – and the connivance of the Church authorities at what they could not but know amounted to a tacit dispensation.[10] The enthusiasm with which he embraced the arguments of Lord King and Stillingfleet, that bishops and presbyters were of the same order and that Christ and the Apostles prescribed no particular form of church government, betrayed Wesley's apprehensiveness about a new move. The Conference minutes of 1744 promised obedience to bishops 'in all things indifferent'. As Wesley became embroiled with the hierarchy on matters doctrinal and practical, however, a certain desperation began to colour his pledges of loyalty. In the summer of 1755 the game seemed almost up: 'My conclusion (which I cannot give up) that it is lawful to continue in the Church stands, I know not how, almost without any premises that are able to bear its weight.'[11] Moreover, the Wesley whom the nineteenth-century orthodox remembered as the hammer of Arians and Calvinists gave vent to much eighteenth-century weariness with the entrenched theological positions of the past. The Rules of Society required of members only a desire 'to flee from the wrath to come, to be saved from their sins'. Like the pioneers of revival in America, Wesley stressed the New Birth, the conditions of vigour and energy in the faith, and yet shrank from allowing even this primitive Christianity (as he believed it to be) to become a test, a means of sifting the sheep from the goats, a process ruinous ever since the Reformation. At the end of his life, Wesley was still claiming that Methodists

do not impose, in order to their admission, any opinions whatever. Let them hold particular or general redemption, absolute or conditional decrees; let them be Churchmen or Dissenters, Presbyterians or Independents, it is no obstacle. Let them choose one mode of baptism or another, it is no bar to their admission. The Presbyterian may be Presbyterian still; the Independent or Anabaptist use his own mode of worship. . . . They think and let think. One condition and one only is required, – a real desire to save their soul.[12]

Looseness to old orthodoxy as well as to old discipline might have compounded Wesley's discomfort in the Church. In fact, the Church's very inability to generate policy enhanced in it a capacity for absorption which enabled it to cope with later movements much more prickly than Methodism. After twenty years Wesley began, indeed, to enjoy a real 'tacit dispensation'. As early as 1758 he found that 'controversy is now asleep, and we in great measure live peaceably with all men, so that we are strangely at leisure to spend our whole time in enforcing plain, practical, vital religion'.[13] If from Richard Green's bibliography of *Anti-Methodist Publications* (1902) are removed the titles produced by the Arminian controversy (a bout of evangelical in-fighting) and those evoked by the expulsions from St Edmund Hall in 1768 (which did not concern Wesley's Methodism), it appears that the number of anti-Methodist publications diminished with every decade, and by the end of Wesley's life was very small indeed. At a popular level too, 'where the movement pushed into new terrain it still encountered violence, but not on the scale of the 1740s and 1750s. In many once troubled places Methodism was soon tolerated and even welcomed'.[14] 'Prejudice seems now dying away', noted Wesley contentedly.[15] He himself became a popular public institution. At one time he had justified field-preaching by the fact that pulpits were closed to him; from 1774 onwards he peppered his *Journal* with invitations to preach, and sometimes celebrate, in the parish church, especially in Yorkshire, and occasionally with the explicit approval of the bishop. Even in the Isle of Man, where in 1776 Bishop Richmond 'for the prevention of schism' had banned Methodist preachers from communion, Wesley in 1781 (after George Mason succeeded to the see) found 'no opposition . . . from the Bishop (a good man) or from the bulk of the clergy . . . we have now rather too little than too much reproach'.[16]

While Wesley's faith in the Church seemed gradually vindicated, formal Dissent, moving deeper into rationalism, became steadily less palatable to him. Moreover, Wesley's mission was to the nation, and especially to the lower classes, whereas on both sides of the Atlantic the old Dissent became increasingly élitist, aware not merely that the populace did not take to its new liberal rationalist views, but that it might become highly dangerous if it did. It was Dissenting ministers, rather than the parish priests of legend, who excommunicated Methodists in England, and still more in America.[17] America, indeed, was calculated to confirm Wesley's antipathy to Dissent. He mishandled the ideological conflict created by colonial revolt, advising the Government of the justice of the American cause, and yet pamphleteering so strongly against it as to leave a tradition in the connexional management that he 'had like to have ruined Methodism there'.[18] American Methodism was indeed painfully rent. In 1770 the Virginia Methodists joined with the Baptists to overthrow the Anglican establishment in the colony.[19] Deprived of their legal provision, the Virginia clergy stopped work, and a hectic Methodist expansion created a case for Methodist ordination, so that the people might receive the sacraments no longer available from the clergy. The Fluvanna Conference of 1779 introduced presbyteral ordination, and administration began. The one English preacher remaining in America, Francis Asbury (1745–1816), then confined in Delaware, called a small group of northern preachers to what can only be called a schismatic Conference, established his sole authority over them, and extracted a promise that they would allow the sacraments to be received only from Anglican clergy. Asbury wrote coolly 'to our dissenting brethren in Virginia hoping to reclaim them'.[20] The Conference at Manakintown, Virginia in 1780 was critical; to the end it seemed that Asbury, representing a link with a fallen establishment and an English connexion now out of reach, must fail to convince the majority party. Yet somehow – Asbury suppressed the minutes – he got an agreement to suspend administration till Wesley could be consulted; and so the breach between a northern Methodism, over which Asbury had informally made himself bishop, and a southern Methodism which seemed to have taken the decisive step into presbyterianism was bridged over. Wesley could hardly have had a sharper warning against the perils of a dissenting Methodism.

Could Wesley cope with the American disputes and still provide for the continuance of the English movement after his death within the now congenial limits of the Church, and within his own not very singular views of church and ministry? The most recent scholarly opinion holds that 'if ever there was a year when Wesley could be said to have irrevocably severed himself and Methodism from the Church of England it was in 1784 when, by his ordinations and by the Deed of Declaration to take effect upon his death, he sought a settlement for the societies on both sides of the Atlantic'.[21] Yet more than one view of even that well-documented year is possible.

Wesley was resolved that 'no Methodist Trustees, if I can help it, shall after my death, any more than while I live, have the power of placing and displacing the preachers';[22] and by the Deed of Declaration (1784) he bequeathed his stationing power to Conference. The dispute in Virginia

showed the inadequacy of a simple reference to Conference, and so the
Deed named 100 preachers to constitute the Conference, and maintain
their numbers by co-optation. They became known as the Legal Hundred.
As John Pawson, one of the preachers keenest to administer the sacraments,
put it:

> . . . the principle of this Deed was to identify the meaning of the word
> Conference, so that it might be ascertained & acknowledged by the law
> of the nation, & by that means to secure all the chapels. But there
> certainly was no more design of paving the way for ordination, or
> separating from the church by anything that was then done than of flying
> up into the clouds.[23]

For the chapels 'situate in Ireland, or other parts out of the kingdom of
Great Britain', Conference might appoint delegates armed with its full
powers, whose acts, signed and entered into the Conference Journal,
should be deemed to be Conference acts. Of late years Wesley had held
Irish Conferences every other year, presiding alternately with Thomas
Coke, and after his death Coke became virtually perpetual President of an
annual Irish Conference. Irish preachers were also named among the Legal
Hundred. How this provision might be extended to 'other parts out of the
kingdom of Great Britain' speedily transpired.

In September 1784 a presbytery of three Anglican priests – John Wesley,
Thomas Coke, and James Creighton – ordained two itinerants, Whatcoat
and Vasey, as deacons and elders, and Wesley made Coke General
Superintendent of the American work. They took supplies of the *Sunday
Service in North America*, Wesley's reformed and abbreviated version of
the Book of Common Prayer, which contained forms of ordination, closely
modelled on those of the Church, for a threefold ministry of deacons,
elders, and superintendents. They were to make Asbury joint general
superintendent, and to ordain selected American preachers to administer
the sacraments. Wesley had long believed he was 'as real a Christian bishop
as the Archbishop of Canterbury',[24] and his clandestine transaction with
Coke (also a presbyter) makes sense in the light of the provisions of the
Deed of Declaration for 'parts out of the kingdom of Great Britain'. All
Wesley could give (and this Coke knew he could not do without) was his
explicit blessing upon the remodelling of American Methodism. He seems
to have envisaged an extension of the system operating in Ireland, with the
American Methodists linked notionally with the Church of England by the
superintendency of Thomas Coke, and substantially by a modernized
prayer-book; like the Irish, the Americans were also given a toehold in the
sovereign legislature of Methodism (which also operated in an Anglican
context) by the stationing of three members of the Legal Hundred among

them. There have always been allegations that Wesley was here pushed into schism by the ambition of Thomas Coke. Certainly his outburst against the assumption of the title of bishop by Coke and Asbury is famous.[25] Yet the American arrangements were entirely consistent with Wesley's wider disposition of his affairs, and Coke's weakness was not ambition, but the thickest vein of personal silliness ever disclosed by a Methodist leader of the first rank.[26] Coke multiplied the criticism Wesley must inevitably encounter by treating the American preachers to a slashing attack upon the Anglican clergy. John Wesley's bitterest critic was his brother Charles; he had always held straiter views of church order and for thirty years had imagined himself to 'stand in the way of [his] brother's violent counsellors, the object of both their fear and hate'; nor was he sweetened by John's willingness to act behind his back:

> Lord Mansfield told me last year [he wrote to Dr Chandler] that ordination was separation. This my brother does not and will not see; or that he has renounced the principles and practice of his whole life; that he has acted contrary to all his declarations, protestations, and writings . . . and left an indelible blot on his name . . . our partnership here is dissolved, but not our friendship.[27]

Yet this letter to an Anglican priest bound for America itself suggests that the dispute between the Wesley brothers was not so much the end-product of a long course of ecclesiastical irregularity in England, as part of a larger disagreement in the Anglican world about the unprecedented situation across the Atlantic.

'By a very uncommon train of providences', as Wesley put it in the understatement of the century, the jurisdiction exercised by the Bishop of London in America had been ended by the peace settlement of 1783. The English bishops could not ordain citizens of what was now a foreign power, men unable to take the oaths of allegiance and supremacy. The rump of episcopalian clergy in America could neither look to them for salvation, nor replace them by any ordinary procedure. William White, rector of Christ Church, Philadelphia, recommended in 1782 that the episcopalians, lay and clerical, should make a sort of social contract with each other, declaring themselves an episcopal church, and together elect 'a superior order of ministers . . . they both being interested in the choice'.[28] 'In an emergency in which a duly authorized ministry cannot be obtained', the first duty was to maintain public worship and preaching. White's programme, which entered deeply into the final constitution of the Protestant Episcopal Church of America, was far more republican than Wesley's; but its assumption that 'the duty and office of a bishop differs in nothing from that of other priests, except in the power of ordination and confirmation, and in the right of precedency in ecclesiastical meetings' was the same.

Like Wesley, White was immediately challenged. A small group of Connecticut clergy, maintaining that 'an episcopal church without an episcopacy, if it be not a contradiction in terms, would . . . be a new thing under the sun',[29] secretly chose Samuel Seabury to be their bishop, and dispatched him to England for consecration. The issue between White and Seabury could hardly be isolated from the issue between the brothers Wesley. White was kind to Coke in America, tried to promote a union with the Methodists on his own platform, and attempted to negotiate with Wesley in England in 1787.[30] Charles Wesley collected evidence of clerical alarm from New York and Seabury's correspondence with the S.P.G., and wept that the American 'poor sheep' had 'been betrayed into separation from the Church of England' by not waiting for Bishop Seabury. Two Methodist preachers were ordained by Seabury, one of whom kept Charles Wesley supplied with backstairs gossip.[31]

John Wesley's low estimate of Seabury's prospects was borne out by the result. For some years the knowledgeable had been pressing the Americans to seek 'legitimization' by ancient ecclesiastical authority from Catholic Rome to Lutheran Scandinavia, or to take direct presbyteral action: 'If the British islands were sunk in the sea (and the surface of the globe has suffered greater changes)', counselled Franklin, 'you would probably take some such method.'[32] The Primate's view that Seabury's consecration by the nonjuring Scottish bishops 'would create jealousies and schisms in the Church' was dismally fulfilled. It was held that the Scottish bishops required a *congé d'élire* from the Pretender (who must absolve Seabury from allegiance), that Seabury remained in canonical subjection to them, even that his orders were invalid. Efforts were made to exclude Seabury from the convention of his church on the grounds that he was still receiving half-pay as a former British army chaplain, a charge quaintly parried by White with the doctrine that 'an ecclesiastical body needed not to be over-righteous'.[33] Still worse, Seabury had promised to introduce the Scottish communion office with its primitive un-Anglican devotions, while White's party were as keen as Wesley to bring the Prayer Book up to date; they produced a form which omitted the Athanasian and Nicene creeds and the descent into hell. And lest anyone but Charles Wesley thought the Bishop of Connecticut more palatable to American Methodists than he was to American episcopalians, Seabury called on them to 'return to the unity of the Church which they have unreasonably, unnecessarily and wickedly broken, by their separation and schism'.[34]

The American latitudinarians were more skilful. They got their own State governments to press the ministry in England for legislation to enable sympathetic English bishops to consecrate three Americans, who might thus create an English succession independent of Seabury. This Bill 'to enable the English Bishops to consecrate [three Socinians] for foreign countries, viz. the overthrow of Bishop Seabury of Connecticut',[35] introduced by the Primate in 1786, was frustrated in its original intention by the failure of the bishop-elect of Virginia to raise the fare to come for his consecration. White and Provoost, the new Bishops of Pennsylvania and New York, had now to take Seabury seriously, and in 1789 they brought Connecticut, still making no concessions to the synodal rights of the laity acknowledged in every other diocese, into a national Protestant Episcopal Church. The discomforts of this uneasy diplomatic combination of theological opposites soon made themselves felt. In April 1791 Thomas Coke, confessing that 'I went further in the separation of our church in America than Mr Wesley . . . did intend', proposed a reunion to Bishop White, involving the reordination of the American preachers. This astonishing volte-face was probably due to the fright Coke received from the explosion of militant conservatism in England. English Methodists, it seemed, could only be safe as a religious society unequivocally within the Church, and by the same token they should make overtures to the Protestant Episcopal Church on behalf of the American Methodists; the latter, moreover, were in serious constitutional trouble, which might be salved by a fresh legitimization of the management.[36] Coke had characteristically gone behind Asbury's back; and on receiving news of Wesley's death, he scampered off to England in the hope of succeeding to Wesley's monarchical authority. White, however, responded kindly, suggesting that Coke and Asbury be consecrated bishops for the Methodists in a united Church. Seabury made no reply at all, and by 1791 the tongues of angels could hardly have united a Protestant Episcopal Church whose present energies were entirely consumed by the problem of survival and the incalculably aggressive machine being constructed by Francis Asbury. The two vehicles of the Anglican tradition in America had, therefore, already diverged decisively in style, orientation, and power.

In 1791 Coke seems to have sought an American settlement in the general interests of a Methodism in which England was the senior partner, a *coup* which had eluded him even in 1784. In that year the Christmas Conference, a specially summoned gathering of the American preachers, had undertaken to obey Wesley 'in matters belonging to church government', and after his death 'to do everything . . . to preserve and promote our union with the Methodists in Europe'. But Asbury knew that on the sacrament question he had driven Wesley's authority to the limit; his future usefulness turned on securing a vote of confidence from the American preachers which would tie their hands and might deter Wesley from stationing him out of the country, or from sending him on roving commissions as he had sent Coke and tried to send Freeborn Garretson. Asbury insisted on election by his brethren, thus creating a precedent by which future ordinands would be nominated by the Superintendent and elected by the Conference. In 1786 Wesley summoned a General Conference to meet at Baltimore the following year which was to make the Englishman, Richard Whatcoat, a Superintendent and the American, Garretson, Superintendent for missions in Nova Scotia, Newfoundland, and the West Indies. The Americans, however, had long made their own arrangements for Conferences, and were incensed. They refused to appoint the new Superintendents, extracted a written undertaking from Coke never to exercise his episcopal functions outside the United States, expunged their undertaking to accept Wesley's authority, left his name out of the minutes, and held that even he had no power to move Asbury to Europe. Moreover, they treated the proceedings, not as a General Conference, but as the Baltimore Annual Conference brought forward.

Herein lay a second problem. The Christmas Conference had been a constitutional convention: once it dispersed, the Americans lacked the sovereign conference which existed in England, the continuance of which after Wesley's death had been prescribed by the Deed of Declaration. The General Superintendent had to conduct local Annual Conferences as Wesley conducted the Irish Conference. Three were required in 1785, but as early as 1790 fourteen were needed, two beyond the Alleghenies. In 1789, in a desperate effort to secure common policy and legislation, Asbury created a Council of Bishops and presiding elders (*anglice* chairmen of districts, or assistant bishops) to safeguard the general welfare of the church. He appointed the members and retained a veto; yet this Council could not, any more than Wesley, bind any district without the support of the District Conference. The hopelessness of expecting the sovereign legislature in England to control the separatism of American district conferences was poignantly illustrated by the one modification of the American Discipline carried by the Council on its own authority, an article against dealing in slaves:[37] the most divisive moral issue they must face was outside the experience of almost all the English preachers. Assailed by James O'Kelly, a hell-raiser deeply entrenched in Virginia, and opposed by Coke, the Council was dropped in 1791.

One resort remained. Wesley was scarcely in the grave when, in July 1791, the Americans buried his scheme of government and summoned a General Conference for the following summer. This Conference led to considerable constitutional development. A great campaign by O'Kelly to allow the preachers an appeal against the stations appointed by the bishop was defeated at the cost of a substantial secession; but the whole body of preachers agreed to meet every four years, and established their power over the discipline and government of the Church; bishops were to be elected by and be responsible to them. On the other hand, the executive was strengthened by the formal recognition of the order of presiding elders, appointed by the bishops. The plenitude of power formerly exercised by Wesley was being divided among various hands; indeed, the westward march of American Methodism made some formal federalism increasingly desirable. In 1808 New York obtained the support of the 'fringe' New England, Western, and South Carolina Conferences in an effort to break the grip upon the General Conference established by the central Conferences of Baltimore, Philadelphia, and Virginia. After a deadlock which brought the church to the point of break-up, the General Conference replaced itself by a quadrennial 'Delegated Conference', composed of one-fifth of the membership of each district Annual Conference. The Delegated Conference was not to be in practice sovereign; except under stringent conditions, certain reserved matters including standards of doctrine, the system of representation and of itinerant episcopacy, and the general Rules of Society were beyond its reach. A peculiar and independent American Methodism was now in being. Coke was not present, but had to bear the odium of the revelation of his private negotiations with Bishop White in 1791. The General Conference, in effect, politely sacked him. It elected its first native-born bishop, William McKendree. But nationalism and sectionalism went hand in hand. With Asbury's support, each Annual Conference was authorized to form its own regulations relative to dealings in slaves. A pastorate untrammelled by formal lay influence, and yet constitutionally debarred from enforcing a common ethic, was a thing undreamt of in the English apologetic for the Pastoral Office.

Europe was as full of surprises for church government as America. Having ordained for America, Wesley had begun to ordain for the West Indies and elsewhere in the overseas mission field (a practice Conference continued after his death) and, in a few cases, for Scotland, where he was becoming too old to celebrate in person.[38] So far Wesley had not trespassed upon the jurisdiction of the Church of England; but at the very end of his life he ordained Rankin and Moore, who neither left the country nor themselves ordained, though Moore was to survive till ordination by imposition of hands began in Methodism in 1836. Wesley also ordained Alexander Mather, thought likely to be his successor, and was alleged to have made him a bishop. Conference became increasingly concerned with the question of separation from the Church, but Wesley himself remained adamant against it. He produced his famous Korah sermon to show that the itinerants' call to preach did not include a priestly vocation,[39] and he is said to have given Coke a fearful dressing-down when that enthusiast talked boldly of introducing the sacraments in England.[40] Not until his eighty-sixth birthday in 1789 did Wesley admit (what his preachers already knew) that he was ageing; and when he died in 1791 the constitutional future for Methodism was so obscure that the strident factions among the preachers each claimed him for themselves.

In 1787 James Creighton had tried to secure the support of the English hierarchy for Wesley's original scheme of episcopal management; he now, after Wesley's death, reported that a pale shadow of this was in favour – the Connexion to be governed by chairmen of districts appointed annually.[41] The party eager to separate from the Church and introduce the sacraments avowed that Wesley intended such a system, quite independent of regular ordination, and that he had made Mather a bishop to set it going. Their case was not helped by Mather's losing his nerve and joining the pro-Church party. John Pawson exploded:

> Wonders never cease. Would you think it after all their clamour about the church, & their quoting Mr W[esley's] authority, this self-same Mr W. ordained Mr Mather Bishop just after the London Conference [in 1788]. This was in order that he might support the Church of England. Is it possible that Mr W. could intend this? No it is not. It is rank nonsense . . . [42]

And there were those to whom the whole hierarchical principle was an un-Methodist abomination. Joseph Bradford, who claimed to know Wesley's mind, held that 'if Mr Wesley told Messrs Moore & Bradburn that he was determined that the Methodist[s] should after his decease become an Episcopal Church, he left the world with a lie in his mouth'.[43] Certainly Wesley was said to have declared: ' "As soon as I am dead, the Methodists will be a regular Presbyterian Church" . . . [and] he meant, that *his death would make us such*. While he lived, he was the head, the Bishop; but as soon as he died, all his power died with him.'[44] Whatever the form of government, no one supposed that taking a preacher into full connexion was virtual ordination. John Pawson held explicitly that

> we must have ordination among us, were it only to preserve order & to keep up a proper esteem in the minds of the people for that most sacred ordinance. Observe with regard to the far greater number of preachers now in Connexion, ordination was not so much as thought of, much less was it intended either by themselves or by those who recd. them into Connexion. Therefore these men cannot be ordained. Ordination among us was never thought of when we were admitting preachers till the last London Conference [1788]. And although at Leeds [1793] we had a most solemn and blessed time when the preachers were admitted, yet

there were some among those 24 that I would not ordain on any account . . . & we have some others in full connexion who pass along in some poor Circuits who are by no means fit to be ordained.[45]

It was soon obvious that a President changing annually and a yearly Conference session of two or three weeks could not manage the Connexion. The critical problem, however, was not administrative but political.[46] The campaign against the Test and Corporation Acts in the late eighties raised a spirit of militant resistance in the Church of England; the French Revolution raised it still further, and for a time provided the Church with sufficient mob force to nullify the guarantees of the Toleration Act. The chief victims of the mob were the old Dissenters, especially the Unitarians; but prudence conspired with the rising conservatism of the Methodist grandees, laymen and preachers, to stop the drift from the Church, and it was reinforced by resentment towards the élite among the preachers on the part of all those itinerants considered unfit to administer the sacraments. Rational and hysterical by turns[47] but always a weathercock, Coke went with the tide, and for two Conferences after the death of Wesley the conservative coalition was on top. In the autumn of 1792, however, the response of English artisan opinion to the movement of the Parisian *sans-culottes* loosed a torrent of anti-establishment opinion which in Methodism took the form of an uncontrollable clamour for separation. After pitched battles in all the Methodist urban centres, the preachers were left with no option but to follow the flock or lose it, and in 1795 they made a compact with the trustees of the Connexion. It was called the Plan of Pacification. Forbidding the general administration of the sacraments, the Plan contained escape clauses which permitted administration on condition of lay and Conference consent, and so enabled Methodists to move rapidly and overwhelmingly into practical Nonconformity. Thus an entirely unforeseeable outburst of lay anti-clericalism had thrust ministerial functions upon the preachers in conditions that made selective ordination impossible.

Moreover, administrative hierarchy also suffered defeat. In 1794 President Pawson made a serious attempt on pragmatic grounds to establish episcopacy, starting from Wesley's bishops, Coke and Mather. A small secret conclave of preachers, held at Lichfield, prepared to divide the English and Scottish work into eight districts, each with a bishop to ordain: six of these should come from the conclave. A storm was raised against this plan by William Thompson, who ascribed it to 'love of power' and bitterly assailed the coalition of Coke and his personal enemies which had promoted it. At the next Conference he defeated the scheme,[48] together with Mather's last attempts to establish himself as 'king in Israel', and thus destroyed an opportunity for a degree of institutional decentralization which Methodism later badly needed.

The Plan of Pacification, indispensable to internal order, put the Connexion in political jeopardy. The year 1795 saw the worst of a severe subsistence crisis and opened the door to an unprecedented wave of itinerant preaching – Methodist, Baptist, Congregational, and indeed undenominational – which shook the Church in its rural strongholds. With the old mobs now impossible to raise, the Church authorities called for fresh legal powers, particularly the withdrawal of legal protection from Sunday Schools and itinerant preaching under the Toleration Act. From 1795, when Coke was given to understand that some pledge of loyalty was required from the Connexion, Methodism was in danger. Coke's reply was to campaign for the exclusion of Alexander Kilham, a preacher seeking to reform Methodism by increasing lay influence, and to try once more to strengthen the Anglican connexion by obtaining episcopal ordination for a number of Methodist preachers. The rising tone of Anglican churchmanship, and its new predilection for political solutions, made this cause hopeless; but Kilham was expelled in 1796, and a great race for support between him and Conference began. In 1797 he offered extensive lay participation in the government of a New Connexion, while the old Conference made substantial concessions to the local authorities of circuit and Society, the Quarterly and Leaders' Meetings. When in 1829 and subsequent years the high Wesleyan doctrine of the Pastoral Office was formally expounded by John Beecham (1787–1856) and his successors, it was held that these concessions were purely procedural and in no way abridged the connexional principle or the authority of the Pastoral Office; at the time it was said that ministerial authority had been surrendered.[49] Moreover, in an astonishing confession, John Pawson, who had pressed so hard for the sacraments, held that 'Church hours & the sacraments have not by any means answered the expectations of either preachers or people', and should be surrendered to save the itinerancy from the government. Alas, 'the Plan of Pacification stands in the way'.[50] The idea that the rights secured by the Plan to laymen to solicit the sacrament from the preachers inhibited the latter from abandoning the Pastoral Office was not a notion entertained in the age of Jabez Bunting. Was it, however, surprising that the *Form of Discipline* of 1797 required the minister to feed and guide, but not to teach or govern the flock?[51] Or that the generation which took the torch from Wesley, and surrendered successively his scheme for an international episcopacy, ordination, and unfettered preachers' rule as they had been kept up in America, preserved a deafening silence on the question of the Pastoral Office?

Yet a change was at hand. In 1799 a young Manchester revivalist, Jabez

Bunting (1779–1858), began his probation as a Wesleyan preacher. He united force of personality with force of circumstances to effect a wholesale change in English Methodism. Faced with disorderly revivalists at Macclesfield in his second circuit, in 1803, Bunting developed a stern view of church order and discipline. From this preoccupation circumstances never permitted him to escape. Revivalism, class conflict in the flock, difficulties in the agencies of religious action, such as the Sunday Schools, related to the Methodist Societies but often imperfectly controlled by them, the dreadful financial crisis which set in after the war[52] – all, in Bunting's view, called for the determined exercise of discipline locally, reinforced by the collective action of the pastorate in Conference. Bunting inspired a vigour of central executive activity unseen since Wesley. His central administration stiffened the Methodist executive as episcopacy might have done. Zealous for the conversion of the heathen, Thomas Coke had had no conception of the elaborate logistics of modern missions: the Methodist Missionary Society, one of the great nineteenth-century charities, was Bunting's answer to that need. His Theological Institution preceded Anglican attempts to provide seminary training for the ministry. There were Conference committees to govern the raising or expenditure of funds, or to break up long-standing constitutional arrangements in the circuits. And there were continual negotiations with Government on the future of emancipated West Indian slaves, on the security of missions, on education.

Bunting published little, but his early Macclesfield letters contained the double appeal to Wesley and the New Testament, together with that exaggerated emphasis on discipline which flowered in the doctrine of the Pastoral Office as expounded by the 'high' Wesleyan party in the second quarter of the nineteenth century. He called on the preachers to return 'to the spirit & discipline of ancient Methodism, & with that resolve to stand or fall'. The church was constituted by 'that proper ministerial *pastorship & oversight* of the flock which the New Testament enjoins as universally necessary'. 'ECCLESIASTICAL DISCIPLINE . . . is to effect and maintain an open and visible separation between *the Church* and *the world*.'[53] Later the Liverpool Minutes, drafted under his presidency at the critical Conference of 1820, compellingly described the new ministry, evangelical yet resolute, and became required study for District Meetings and ordinands. Of the great Methodist authorities Bunting alone supported the lay apologists who replied to the attempts of Mark Robinson of Beverley to revive a Church Methodism in 1825, and asserted 'substantially a good and valid *presbyterian* ordination of our ministers, which every preacher receives when admitted into full connexion'.[54] In 1829, at the end of his second presidential year, Bunting gave a notable ordination charge, setting in the general context of the ministry 'that godly discipline which . . . [is], equally with the dispensation of the word and sacraments, an institution of Christ'.[55] Defeated during his first presidency, he succeeded during his third (1836) in introducing ordination by imposition of hands, instead of reception by simple vote of Conference. The Methodist preacher was now, for all to see, a minister, ordained to an undifferentiated ministry of which Wesley had known nothing. Methodism was now (according to one of Bunting's preacher friends) 'an entire system', what Wesley might have condemned as a sect.[56]

The challenge of the Methodist secessions of 1834–5 and 1850–5 consolidated in the mind of Alfred Barrett, whose works became prescribed texts for Methodist ministers, the doctrine towards which Bunting had been working. Barrett's *Essay on the Pastoral Office* explained that Christ had established different orders of ministry for different purposes. The Apostles had been commissioned to found the Church, complete its doctrine, and convince the Gentiles. Prophets had expounded the Christian sense of the Old Testament to the Jews. Pastors and teachers were to govern the settled congregations of the faithful, and had a continuing function when the work of the other two orders was done and they came to an end. Having thus inverted Wesley's order, and made his preachers almost successors of Aaron, Barrett expounded the functional Methodist view of church and ministry. Circuit superintendents were very like the 'primitive angel or bishop of the Church'; what mattered was not the succession of offices but the maintenance of pastoral oversight. English Methodism had no order of deacons, but it did not lack diaconal service.[57] The harrowing débâcle of the Wesleyan Reform secessions, which cost a third of the membership, drove Barrett still higher. In some amazing history he held that Wesley's assistants had been genuine pastors, and that this made separation from the Establishment inevitable, though it had in fact been 'compelled' 'by the exclusive acts of the clergy of that day'. But at bottom he wanted to get away from history, and even from his old functionalism, into a symbolic doctrine of the Church, 'the necessary connexion between a definite form of doctrine, and a suitable as well as definite church regimen in which to teach it to all around'. Wesleyan Methodism taught the need to attest justification by a spotless life; it stressed the hazard of losing the heavenly treasure by slothfulness and sin. This state of spiritual *angst* necessitated 'especially amongst the industrial classes . . . a subordination of one to another, with a putting away of reserve, a mutual watchfulness among the ministry'.[58] Hearty to a fault, and unashamedly regarding their religious institutions as devices for a purpose, the flock could hardly be expected to recognize this inward spiritual essence of which the outward form of the Wesleyan constitution was now held to be the symbol. Symbolism, moreover, had painful practical disadvantages, for the 1830s saw the emergence of a lunatic fringe among the preachers which wanted the legislation of 1795 and 1797 modified or repealed, in order to put the plenitude of pastoral authority beyond all doubt.[59] But conservative revolution was a pipe-dream.

As the Connexion ran into difficulties in the forties, high Wesleyans began to suspect that the vast authoritarian Methodism of America – where "there is no low Methodism and high Methodism, no *in* and *outs*, no *government* and its partisans to keep in office or to remove, [where] Methodism is one' – embodied Wesley's 'real mind'.[60] In Asbury's comments and sermon notes the familiar Wesleyan words attach themselves to ministry – 'to preach the gospel in all its essential points, to administer the ordinances; and to rule the Church of Christ'.[61] In the vast spaces of America, the itinerants much more closely resembled the prime mover described by Barrett than ever they could in England. The frontier from the extreme north to the Gulf of Mexico was mostly opened up by local preachers; but the fact that by 1820 the Methodists, starting from scratch, had overhauled the Baptists, who employed similar lay agencies, and in the next twenty years were greatly to outstrip them must owe much to the co-ordinating, organizing, and evangelistic labours of the itinerants. Asbury's journal witnesses eloquently to the way the hardships and peculiarities of the itinerant life reinforced the preachers' corporate sense, and to his understanding that they were part of a huge migration.[62] Asbury was an entrepreneur in religion, a man who perceived a market to be exploited, one of the most remarkable men of this kind there have ever been. Of limited gifts but infinite toughness, Asbury, from the moment of his arrival in America in 1771, grasped (indeed was obsessed with) the key to the situation – that the American migration could only be won by an itinerant ministry in Wesley's original sense, a ministry not church-based. Finding the preachers settling down in the eastern seaboard towns, he prized them loose and contested their every attempt to settle again. Asbury conceived himself as restoring a New Testament system of itinerant episcopacy; he found the corruption of city life, not in its sin, but in the inertia it opposed to itinerant ministry:

I wish to warn you [he wrote in his Valedictory Address] against the growing evil of locality[63] in bishops, elders, preachers or Conferences. Locality is essential to cities and towns, but traveling is essential to the country. Were I to name cities such as Jerusalem, Antioch and Rome, with all the great cities, both ancient and modern, what havoc have these made in the Churches! Alas for us! out of seven hundred traveling preachers, we have about one hundred located in towns and cities and small rich circuits. Guard particularly against two orders of preachers;

the one of the country, and the other for the cities; the latter generally
settle themselves to purchase ministers, too often men of gifts and
learning intend to set themselves to sale.[64]

The rural orientation of American Methodism was an entrepreneurial
rather than (as in England) a market fact; Asbury's machine opened up
new areas, but 'other denominations came [and] took possession of the
villages' which grew up later.[65]

Primitive itinerancy and poverty made all the difference to the American
ministry. At the Christmas Conference of 1784 the preacher's allowance
was fixed at $64 (a sum raised in 1800 to $80), with allowances in
proportion for wife and children. But the family allowances were rarely
paid, and at the end of his life Asbury reckoned that not more than one-
sixth of the preachers, in the wealthiest circuits, received their own
allowances in full. There were few preachers' houses outside the great
cities. And throughout the period of breakneck expansion from 1800, the
whole system was in the financial straits which came upon English
Methodism only after the Napoleonic wars. Asbury's power sprang from
his willingness to share not merely the labour but the deprivation of the
itinerants. Half of those who died in the ministry were under thirty; two-
thirds had travelled less than twelve years. Of course, itinerants for whom
there were in practice no houses or family allowances were single men.
The Virginia Conference of 1809 was attended by eighty-four preachers
of whom only three were married.[66] To marry meant normally to 'locate',
to find a house and settled work, and it kept terms of service short. Of the
fifteen preachers received in 1784, one-third had retired from the itinerancy
in less than two years; nearly another third in five. And so it continued for
a couple of generations. Between 1792 and 1796, 161 men entered the
itinerancy, but there was a net gain of only 27. Deaths, expulsions, and
106 locations accounted for the rest. Up to 1814, 1,616 candidates had
been received into full connexion; by 1816, 819 had located, many of them
to render yeoman service as local preachers. The Methodist Episcopal
ministry was really a militarily organized mission, largely composed of
short-service agents who could hardly be pastorally related to the flock in
the traditional European sense.[67] Of course the American flock was
different, its extreme mobility making the autocratic powers of the
itinerants more acceptable, while the rapid turnover of the itinerants in
turn created acceptance for the autocracy of the bishops and presiding
elders. Asbury understood what he was about, noting from Thomas
Haweis's *Church History* that 'the [primitive] evangelists were the chief
superintending, episcopal men; aye, so say I; and that they prescribed
forms of discipline and systematized codes of doctrine'.[68]

In England, by contrast, the commentators noted from 1800 how much less laborious the circuit rounds had become, and from 1815 how itinerancy in the old sense of sleeping, praying, and preaching with the people in their rural homes and meeting-places was coming to an end, and with it that symbolic institution, the circuit horse. Too many country circuits were neglected, and ravaged by the Ranters.[69] Before long, the comment was that home missions had ceased altogether. And it was a married ministry. In Wesley's time less than a third of the preachers were married; by 1814 it was three-quarters of a total number which had trebled since his death.[70] The cause of the increase was the great proliferation of chapels, especially urban chapels, built on debt, which provided appointments with a mini-mum of travelling and required no nights away from home. These conditions were congenial to a married ministry, but all sections of the Methodist community, including the adherents who were not members of Society, shared responsibility for the situation which produced them. 'The Meth[odist]s [it was noted in 1802] are now saying, Let us have genteel chapels that we may be like our neighbours';[71] and their version of what Asbury abused as 'locality' called, as he predicted, for a genteel ministry. Fittingly enough, Alfred Barrett, a man of 'particularly chaste and elegant mind', had a successful ministry at the Oxford Road chapel, 'attended by most of the élite of the Methodist body in Manchester'.[72]

The development of a high doctrine of the ministry to support an active central administration, in England, drove together the two causes of religious democracy and local rights. The strains to which American Methodism was subject tended to drive them apart. By 1830 the bishops of the Methodist Episcopal Church had ceased to itinerate over the whole church in Asbury's manner, and had established an informal balance of North and South. The South seemed to have effectively compromised the originally strong Methodist anti-slavery witness.[73] Unlike the supporters of local rights in England, it could appeal to a high or strict interpretation of the constitution of 1808, and especially to the restrictive rule that forbade the Delegated Conference to 'do away [with] episcopacy, or destroy the plan of our itinerant general superintendency'. Yet in the North and West strong feeling arose against appointing slave-holders to high office. In 1832 James O. Andrew owed his election to the episcopate to the need to find a southerner who did not own slaves. 'It is not my merit that has made me a Bishop', he exclaimed with tears in his eyes, 'but my poverty.' Fittingly enough, the final crisis was brought on by Andrew's acquiring slaves through inheritance and marriage, the law of Georgia forbidding manumission. The North held that it was the policy of the church not to elect slave-holders to the episcopate, for they could not itinerate in the North. Andrew had disqualified himself and should resign.

A bishop convicted of immorality might be constitutionally removed, but no proceedings were ever taken against Andrew; the North was exerting naked Conference power over the episcopate in a way the South had resisted ever since 1808. Cornered at last, the South virtually abandoned Wesley's doctrine that bishops and presbyters were equal in order and different in office:

> It is true that the Annual Conferences select the Bishops of the Church, by the suffrages of their delegates, in General Conference assembled; but the General Conference . . . does not possess the power of ordination, without which a Bishop cannot be constituted . . . Episcopacy even in the Methodist Church is not a mere appointment to labour. It is an official consecrated station, under the protection of law . . . If the doctrine against which we protest be admitted, the episcopal office is, at best, but a quadrennial term of service.[74]

In America, as in England, the hard-pressed 'high' Methodists were seeking to move from a functional to a symbolic doctrine of the church. Repudiating the Conference leverage against episcopacy, the southerners seceded in 1844; the Civil War was casting its shadow before.

On both sides of the Atlantic the attempt to save the day for the modern developments in Methodism by asserting their symbolic status had by 1850 ended in disaster. Not surprisingly, one notable writer, George Steward,[75] now returned to the view that the legacy of John Wesley consisted in the empiricism and the functional considerations which underlay the institutions he entailed upon his posterity, clearly perceiving that institutional collapse could no longer be remedied by magnifying ministerial authority. But this was a highbrow presentation of the traditions of Methodist reform, a part of the Wesleyan patrimony which falls beyond the limits of this paper.

Notes

1 For a theological treatment, see John Kent, *The Age of Disunity* (1966), pp. 44–85, and J.C. Bowmer, 'Church and Ministry in Wesleyan Methodism from the Death of Wesley to the Death of Jabuz Bunting', Ph.D. thesis, University of Leeds, 1967.

2 The following outline is based on J. Beecham, *An Essay on the Constitution of Wesleyan Methodism* (3rd edn., 1851), pp. 2–6, 42, 46–9, 81 sqq., 117, 120. This, the first major text (originally published in 1829 and republished in 1850 and 1851, when the Wesleyan Reform secessions were in full flood and Beecham

as President had to act up to his doctrine), spans the entire active history of the doctrine. Cf. Richard Watson, *Theological Institutes* (1829), iii. 361–9.

3 This negative conclusion, first reached by the most careful student of the whole matter, Dr J.C. Bowmer, 'Church and Ministry', pp. 307–9, is fully borne out by my own studies. The literature produced for, and about, the ministry even shows occasional tendencies to lapse into the very low view that the minister was simply a 'speaking brother'.

4 T. Coke, *Commentary on the New Testament* (1803), *sub loco* (cf. commentary on Acts 20: 28 and I Cor. 4: 21); J. Sutcliffe, *A Commentary on the Old and New Testament* (2 vols. 1834–5), ii. 417, 426, 620. Text quoted in Wesley's version.

5 e.g. Adam Clarke, *The New Testament . . . with a Commentary and Critical Notes* (1817), *sub* I Pet. 5: 3.

6 e.g. on I Thess. 5: 13 ('Esteem them very highly in love for their work's sake'), '*For their work's sake* . . . But how are we to esteem them that do not work at all?' Even Heb. 13: 17 required obedience not in conscience or judgement but in 'your own will in things purely indifferent'. John Wesley, *Explanatory Notes upon the New Testament* (1958 edn.), pp. 387, 761, 762, 853, 886.

7 *Life of John Wesley* (12th edn., n.d.), pp. 203–5, 372–6; A.B. Lawson, *John Wesley and the Christian Ministry* (1963), p. 111.

8 *History of Wesleyan Methodism*, i (5th edn., 1866), 162, 164, 171; ii (4th edn., 1863), 235. Taking men into full connexion every year, Conference in 1792 forbade ordination without its special consent.

9 *A History of the Methodist Episcopal Church*, 10th edn., 4 vols., New York, 1857, i. 44–5.

10 *The Journal of John Wesley*, ed. N. Curnock (8 vols., 1938), iv. 120.

11 *The Letters of John Wesley*, ed. J. Telford (8 vols., 1931), iii. 145; cf. ibid., pp. 131, 151.

12 *The Works of John Wesley*, Zondervan edn., 14 vols., Grand Rapids, Mich., n.d., xiii. 266. Cf. John Wesley, *Sermons on Several Occasions*, ed. J. Beecham (1872), iii. 182–3.

13 Wesley, *Works*, viii. 225–6.

14 J. Walsh, 'Methodism and the Mob in the Eighteenth Century', *Studies in Church History*, viii (1972), 227.

15 Wesley, *Journal*, vi. 390.

16 L. Tyerman, *Life and Times of Rev. John Wesley* (6th edn., 3 vols., 1890), iii. 229; Wesley, *Journal*, vi. 151, 321.

17 Ibid., iii. 70, 73.

18 M[ethodist] C[hurch] A[rchives], now in John Rylands University Library, Manchester], R. Pilter to Jabez Bunting, 23 Oct. 1819. Cf. *History of American Methodism*, ed. E.S. Bucke, New York, 3 vols., 1964, i. 164.

19 W.W. Sweet, *Methodism in American History*, New York, 1933, p. 101.

20 *The Journal and Letters of Francis Asbury*, ed. E.T. Clark (3 vols., 1958), i. 307; cf. ibid., iii. 22.

21 F. Baker, *John Wesley and the Church of England* (1970), p. 218.

22 Wesley, *Works*, xiii. 727.

23 M.C.A., Tyerman MSS. iii, fo. 66.

24 Wesley, *Letters*, vii. 262.

25 Asbury, *Journal and Letters*, iii. 65. As a weary old man, Asbury himself echoed Wesley: 'A Bishop, oh that it had never been named. I was elected and ordained a superintendent as my parchment will show' (ibid., iii. 378).

26 Coke never grew up; towards the end of his life his colleagues rescued him on the brink of matrimony with a woman whose record of business fraud was so bad that 'if one of our travelling preachers were to marry such a woman he would be censured, if not excluded from the Connexion. The woman's creditors were exulting in the prospect of arresting the Doctor immediately on his marriage with her.' M.C.A. Tyerman, MSS. i, fos. 349–50.

27 Tyerman, *Wesley*, ii. 247; T. Jackson, *Life of Charles Wesley*, ii (1841), 391.

28 W. White, *The Case of the Episcopal Churches in the United States considered*, Philadelphia, 1782, reprinted in *Hist[orical] Mag[azine of the] Prot[estant] Episc[opal] Ch[urch]*, xxii (1953), 435 sqq. 'Never had so strange a sight been seen before in Christendom, as this necessity of various members knitting themselves into one by such a conscious and voluntary act': Samuel Wilberforce, *History of the Protestant Episcopal Church in America* (2nd edn., 1846), pp. 195–6.

29 *Hist. Mag. Prot. Episc. Ch.* xxii. 479.

30 E.J. Drinkhouse, *History of Methodist Reform*, i, Baltimore, 1899, 267–8 n.; J. Vickers, *Thomas Coke, Apostle of Methodism* (1969), pp. 90–1.

31 MS. copies of the letters collected by Charles Wesley are in M.C.A. Cf. Jackson, *Charles Wesley*, ii. 392; Baker, p. 275.

32 Prince Hoare, *Memoirs of Granville Sharp* (1820), pp. 207 sqq.; E.J. Beardsley, *Life and Correspondence of Samuel Seabury*, Boston, 1881, pp. 97–161; Wilberforce, pp. 199–207; R.D. Middleton, *Dr Routh* (1938), pp. 48 sqq.; W. White, *Memoirs of the Protestant Episcopal Church in the United States of America*, Philadelphia, 1820, pp. 88, 91; *The Private Correspondence of Benjamin Franklin*, ed. W.T. Franklin (1817), pp. 57–8.

33 Beardsley, p. 160; Hoare, pp. 212, 231 n.; *Hist. Mag. Prot. Episc. Ch.* xxii. 484–6; White, *Memoirs*, pp. 124, 166, 172–3.

34 Wilberforce, p. 215; Beardsley, p. 230.

35 Wilberforce, p. 216.

36 M.C.A. Thomas Coke to Joseph Benson, 15 July 1791; J.J. Tigert, *A Constitutional History of American Episcopal Methodism*, 2nd edn., Nashville, Tenn., 1904, p. 317.

37 Tigert, p. 252.

38 M.C.A., Tyerman MSS. iii, fo. 150.

39 This sermon was suppressed after Wesley's death, and when in 1829 it was republished as Sermon no. cxv, it bore a footnote suggesting that it was not to be taken seriously.

40 M.C.A., Tyerman MSS. iii, fos. 142, 133 (cf. fos. 150–1); Tyerman, *Wesley*, iii. 443.

41 Lake Junaluska, N.C., United Methodist Church Archives, Creighton MSS., 4 July 1791. Cf. Smith, *Wesleyan Methodism*, ii, Appendix E.

42 M.C.A., Tyerman MSS. iii, fo. 204. Cf. S. Bradburn, *The Question, 'Are the Methodists dissenters?' fairly examined* (n. pl., 1792), p. 14. Mather had declined ordination at short notice in 1785 (Tyerman MSS. iii, fo. 54).

43 M.C.A., Tyerman MSS. i, fo. 139.

44 Bradburn, *Are Methodists dissenters?*, p. 19.

45 M.C.A., Tyerman MSS. iii, fo. 242. Cf. ibid., i, fo. 128; iii, fo. 145.

46 For a fuller discussion, see W.R. Ward, 'The French Revolution and the English Churches; a Case Study in the Impact of Revolution upon the Church', *Miscellaneous Historiae Ecclesiasticae*, iv (1972), 55–84.

47 M.C.A., Thomas Coke to Joseph Benson, 15 July 1791.

48 M.C.A., W. Thompson to R. Rodda, 9 May 1794; W. Thompson to J. Benson, 8 May 1794; Tyerman MSS. iii, fo. 249.

49 J. Crowther, *The Methodist Manual*, Halifax, 1810, p. 31.

50 M.C.A., Tyerman MSS. iii, fos. 319–20.

51 The *Form of Discipline* defined the office of a minister as 'to watch over souls as he that must give account; to feed and guide the flock'. Both these phrases came from the minutes of Wesley's first Conference (1744), where the first had applied to the ordained clergy of the Church and the second derived from his commission to his lay Assistants 'in the absence of the minister, to feed and guide, to teach and govern the flock'. On the latter powers, which the ministry most needed in the 1820s, the *Form of Discipline* was characteristically silent.

52 On these problems, see W.R. Ward, 'The Religion of the People and the Problem of Control, 1790–1830', *Studies in Church History*, viii (1972), 237–57. I have made a biographical assessment of Bunting in *The Early Correspondence of Jabez Bunting* (R. Hist. Soc., Camden 4th ser. xi, 1972).

53 M.C.A., J. Bunting to R. Reece, 15 July 1803; Bunting to G. Marsden, 13 Dec. 1803; T.P. Bunting, *Life of Jabez Bunting* (2 vols., 1859–89), i. 430.

54 M.C.A., Bunting to H. Sandwith, 10 Feb. 1825; H. Sandwith to Bunting, 12 Feb. 1825.

55 *Sermons by Jabez Bunting*, ed. W.L. Thornton (2 vols., 1861–2), ii. 375, 379.

56 M.C.A., W. Vevers to Bunting, 13 April 1830; Wesley, *Letters*, viii. 66, 71; *Works*, xiii. 272. It was still an odd system. Missionaries who had returned home after completing their probation were to be examined like the ordinands of the year; having been ordained before going overseas, they were not subject to reordination, but were at least theoretically liable to be refused reception into full connexion at this point, four or more years after ordination.

57 A. Barrett, *Essay on the Pastoral Office as a Divine Institution in the Church of Christ* (1839), pp. 10–11, 118–19, 126.

58 A. Barrett, *The Ministry and Polity of the Christian Church* (1854), pp. 15, 109–10, 31–2.

59 M.C.A., J. Bicknell to Bunting, 2 March 1835; W. Binning to [Bunting], 10 July 1851; Oliver Henwood to Thomas Clulow, 23 April 1853.

60 J. Dixon, *Methodism in America* (3rd edn., 1849), pp. 63, 241; J. Dixon,

Methodism in its Origin, Economy and Present Position (1843), p. 127. Episcopal Methodism had in fact recently become *two*, with the secession of the southern Methodists on the slavery question.

61 Asbury, *Journal and Letters*, ii. 294; cf. ibid., iii. 183.

62 Ibid., ii. 410–11, 417; iii. 453.

63 'Locality' or 'location' meant, in Methodist parlance on both sides of the Atlantic, settling in one place.

64 Asbury, *Journal and Letters*, iii. 475–6.

65 Bangs, ii. 294.

66 Drinkhouse, i. 199. For Asbury's touching account of his preference for celibacy, *Journal and Letters*, ii. 423, 591.

67 A. Stevens, *History of the Methodist Episcopal Church in the United States of America*, 4 vols., New York, 1866–7, ii. 140 and iv. 185; Bucke, *History of American Methodism* (p. 328, n. 18), i. 472. The nearest English parallel was the way the Hull Primitive Methodist Circuit, 1822–7, picked up a scattered mass of popular evangelicalism between the Humber and the Scottish Border, by means of poorly paid temporary agents, regarded by no one as ministers: *Proceedings of the Wesley Historical Society*, xxxvii (1970), 169 sqq.

68 Asbury, *Journal and Letters*, ii. 488.

69 On these problems, see W.R. Ward, *Religion and Society in England, 1790–1850* (1972), pp. 99–101.

70 M.C.A., W. Myles to Joseph Dutton, 3 June 1814.

71 M.C.A., Tyerman MSS. iii, fo. 319.

72 John Evans, *Lancashire Authors and Orators* (1850), p. 30.

73 On this whole subject, see D.G. Mathews, *Slavery and Methodism*, Princeton, N.J., 1965.

74 G.F. Moede, *The Office of Bishop in Methodism. Its History and Development* Zürich, 1964, pp. 84–102.

75 George Steward, *The Principles of Church Government and their Application to Wesleyan Methodism* (1853); also George Steward, *The Farewell to Wesleyan Controversy* (1854).

13

John Wesley, Traveller

The *DNB*, following Tyerman in an unusually cautious mood,[1] cautiously affirms that 'it is said' that Wesley travelled about a quarter of a million miles and preached about 40,000 sermons. In the eighteenth century there was as much confusion about what constituted a mile as there now is about what constitutes a sermon; but it is hardly the part of modern scholarship to try to add precision to the luminous round figures excogitated by the enthusiastic statisticians of the Victorian era. The one estimate surely qualifies him as a traveller, as the other does as a preacher; and Wesley was an itinerant preacher in a sense that my grandfather was at the beginning of his Primitive Methodist ministry in North Yorkshire, but of which modern Methodist ministers are not even pale copies.

But before we begin to follow him on his rounds it is worth noting that in the Protestant world of the late seventeenth and early eighteenth centuries there was a good deal of mobile effort on the part of both people and preachers, not all of it of the same kind. So far as the flock was concerned, the movements were a testimony to the fact that many parts of the Protestant world were less well provided with religious amenities than we are apt to imagine. Some of this was the result of persecution. Right down to the conquest of Silesia by Frederick the Great, Silesian Protestants would pour out to services in special churches built on the Saxon side of the border, and pour out especially for summer communions and especially to those churches which made the work an evangelistic speciality; there was the same weary pilgrimage of the remaining Austrian Protestant nobility and their dependents into Hungary, or to Ortenburg, Bavaria. Bohemians would go over to the County of Asch, into Upper Lusatia or the Dresden area, Protestant Poles into the Duchy of Teschen. It was also the case that when Presbyterianism was being established against much opposition in Ulster and Scotland, a tradition of mass communions with a powerful aura of revivalism about them and with people gathering from far and wide grew up, and was still of consequence in the Highlands in the

Paper presented to the Pre-Industrial Seminar, University of Durham, 1990.

eighteenth century, subject to some clerical discouragement on the grounds that in bad times the sheer impossibility of providing hospitality reduced the frequency with which the ordinance could be observed. In Wales, too, dissenters were apt to travel enormous distances for communion, and it is a serious question for historical inquiry why the revivalistic effects of these gatherings which had been common in the seventeenth century and broke out again in the nineteenth had these results less often in between.

Clergy and laymen performing pastoral functions were also on the move, following population movements; sometimes dramatically so. The first Lutheran pastor in New York had been driven out of his Hungarian parish by the Turks. Outside New England there hardly was in America a parish system as Anglican clergy would recognise it, and that was one reason why it was hard to get them to go even to a state like Virginia where there was a working Anglican establishment of sorts. Itinerancy and improvisation were the order of the day, as they had to be in other places where resources were thinly stretched, as they were, for example in Lusatia where German Lutherans attempted to something for suppressed slavonic nationalities, the Wends and Sorbs. There is still a parish church in Bautzen set aside for the use of over twenty Sorbish villages; and in our period they were served by a sort of circuit system.

There were also a series of philadelphian religious movements at the end of the seventeenth whose object was to gather the true saints out of the mass, and in the process of doing so were involved in what was not far from itinerant evangelisation. The Inspired, those hybrid offshoots of the French Prophets, did actually evangelize to the extent of creating a connexion which extended from their base behind Frankfurt to the French border and down into Switzerland. And Wesley's own labours were narrower in scope than those of Whitefield with his seven excursions to America, or those of Zinzendorf which extended from the Baltic to Pennsylvania, but they combined the evangelistic preaching of the one with the practical oversight of religious communities substantially gathered by other people of the other, and they were more systematic than either. After his conversion and visit to Herrnhut in 1738 Wesley never left the United Kingdom except for two short busman's holidays in the Netherlands in the eighties, and once his itinerant system had got going he reckoned to get right round the connexion every two years, and did indeed hold an Irish Conference every second year. Scotland he visited rather more often than Ireland, though sometimes the visits were fleeting, and towards the end of his life were generally only biennial. Nevertheless a Methodist itinerancy which began round a not very adventurous London-Bristol axis soon extended to every part of the three kingdoms with such regularity that his Journal often records his presence in quite unimportant places two years, not to the day but to the week, from the time he was there last. There has probably never been such a regular and systematic traveller in the United Kingdom, and in his own day none who tested the capacity of the means of transport for regular and punctual travel so severely.

Wesley, then, was an itinerant, but not a wandering, evangelist, and, although the evidence is almost entirely lacking, there is no doubt at all that his rounds were a highly organised affair, in their way like the circuit plans that his assistants had to organise all the time, and every superintendent must still publish quarterly. It was not an accident, for example, that when he turned up at Blanchland in March 1747, 'they were gathered out of the lead-mines from all parts; many from Allendale six miles off' or that when he paid his first visit to Allendale in July of the following year it was precisely on the lead-miners' six-monthly pay-day when every miner was down to collect his earnings, and every tradesman and stall-holder in the Tyne Valley was there to relieve him of them, and the maximum audience could be guaranteed.[2] It was the same at the other end of his life. In 1788 when Wesley was due to go north, his brother Charles was weak and known to be likely to die; John left precise instructions with the preachers where he could be found in that event, so that he might come back and minister to the family. The preachers bungled the affair and it was almost a fortnight after Charles's death that John received the news to his no small grief and chagrin. The upshot was one of the legendary memories of the aged Wesley. He was due to preach to a packed congregation of one of his favourite societies, at Bolton, where in addition to all else there was a Sunday School choir of a hundred trebles, boys and girls, not in Wesley's view to be equalled 'in any chapel, cathedral or music room in the four seas'. All went well until he attempted to give out the second hymn, Charles Wesley's hymn on wrestling Jacob 'Come, O Thou Traveller unknown'; when he came to the lines:

> My company before is gone,
> And I am left alone with Thee

he broke down in tears and had to sit in the pulpit, his face in his hands. At this point the congregation behaved far better than the preachers and left him with his grief in silence until he had recovered his composure. The rest of the service was not forgotten by either party, and what gave the occasion its peculiar poignancy was the shared knowledge that a private grief had been harrowed by the sorry failure of a normally reliable system.[3] The system was organised in two stages. Two of a number of surviving documents illustrate the first stage. One gives Wesley's travel plan in the Midlands over a period of days; the other, appeared at the very end of Wesley's life in the *Dublin Chronicle* for April 7, 1789. This commenced,

'We hear that the Rev. Mr Wesley, who arrived a few days ago in this city, intends visiting most of the principal towns in this kingdom, with his usual celerity, though in the 87th year of his age', and proceeded to list the places where he could be found for the next nine weeks, a different place each day;[4] and the Journal shows that the marathon was completed substantially according to plan. The second stage in the system we may infer from one of the most frequently reprinted documents of the revival in New England, Nathan Cole's description of Whitefield's visit to Middletown, Conn.[5] Here the organized plan is supplemented by word of mouth:

> On a sudden in the morning about 8 or 9 of the clock there came a messenger and said Mr Whitefield preached at Hartford and Wethersfield yesterday and is to preach at Middletown this morning at ten of the clock. I was in my field at work. I dropped my tool that I had in my hand and ran home to my wife . . . [When they got within sight of Middletown, the place seemed enveloped in 'a cloud of fog'] . . . , this cloud was a cloud of dust made by the horses' feet. It arose some rods into the air over the tops of hills and trees; and when I came within about 20 rods of the road, I could see men and horses slipping along in the cloud like shadows, and as I drew nearer it seemed like a steady stream of horses and their riders, scarcely a horse more than his length behind another, all of a lather and foam with sweat, their breath rolling out of their nostrils every jump . . .

The plebs of Old England were not of course as well blessed with horses as their fellows in New England, but the system of supplementing an organised itinerary by local word of mouth was the same. It did not always work: arriving at Aberdare in 1750 'we found that no notice had been given; so after resting for an hour we set out for Brecknock',[6] and it could only operate in a society suffering from chronic underemployment; but it usually worked very well, and it underlies the driving sense of urgency in the Journal. Take, for example the following reference to Hindley Hill, Christopher Hopper's farm in Allendale where a small society met.

> Having appointed before I left Hindley Hill, to preach there again on Wednesday evening, I set out about two in the afternoon, though extremely weak, having had a flux for some days [and made for Keswick. On the return journey] I took horse at half an hour past three. There was no moon or stars, but a thick mist, so that I could see neither road nor anything else; but I went as right as if it had been noonday. When I drew nigh Penruddock Moor the mist vanished, the stars appeared, and the morning dawned; so I imagined all the danger was past; but when I was on the middle of the moor, the mist fell again on every side, and I

quickly lost my way. I lifted up my heart. Immediately it cleared up, and I soon recovered the high road. On Alston Moor I missed my way again; and what, I believe, no stranger has done lately, road through all the bogs, without any stop, till I came to the vale, and thence to Hindley Hill.[7]

Hartside was often a bad crossing for Wesley; two days later he had to do it in the mist again to get over to Whitehaven. But one of the common entries in the Journal is 'the congregation was waiting', and this was the spur to get on. Considerable distances could be covered when necessary. In 1767, for example, Wesley did the journey from London to Bristol between late afternoon and noon the next day.[8]

The precisely defined purpose of Wesley's journeyings meant, of course, that his Journal could not be a travelogue; and so did his insistence on redeeming the time. Riding time would do for making up his reading in at any rate in the light-weight fields. In an aside of 1770 he remarks: '(History, poetry, and philosophy I commonly read on horseback, having other employment at other times)'.[9] By the same token, however, he subjected eighteenth-century transport to severe timetable tests, and no man showed more clearly what its possibilities were. Almost the only thing the general public knows about Wesley is that he had a horse, and the use made of this symbol by connexional artists and sculptors sufficiently illustrates the point that Wesley's mission to the lower classes was conducted from above in both senses of the word. His own incidental admissions, however, suggest that the risks to high-mileage drivers were then much what they are now. Wesley was, however, adept at 'improving' those hazards to the advantage of the Kingdom of God. In 1739 at Bristol, for example:

As I was riding to Rose Green in a smooth, plain part of the road, my horse suddenly pitched upon his head and rolled over and over. I received no other hurt than a little bruise on one side, which for the present I felt not, but preached without pain to six or seven thousand people on that important direction, 'Whether ye eat or drink, or whatever you do, do all to the glory of God'.[10]

In Bristol again in 1741 the hand of Providence was yet more immediately and doubtless more painfully felt:

Before I came to Lawrence Hill my horse fell, and attempting to rise, fell down upon me. One or two women ran out of a neighbouring house, and when I rose, helped me in. I adore the wisdom of God. In this house were three persons who began to run well, but Satan had hindered them. But they resolved to set out again. And not one of them has looked back since.[11]

Two years later it was worse again in London:

> About four I set out and rode softly to Snow Hill, where the saddle slipping quite upon my mare's neck, I fell over her head, and she ran back into Smithfield. Some boys caught her and brought her to me again, cursing and swearing all the way. I spoke plainly to them, and they promised to amend. I was setting forward when a man cried, 'Sir, you have lost your saddle-cloth'. Two or three more would needs help me to put it on; but these two swore at almost every word. I turned to one and another and spoke in love. They all took it well and thanked me much. I gave them two or three little books which they promised to read over carefully.[12]

If in England the blows of Providence were timely as well as painful, the trouble in Ireland was demon-possession. Wesley found Philipstown in 1748 'the most stupid, senseless place I have seen in all Ireland' and hence:

> I do not wonder that Satan was sorely unwilling I should go out of this place. The moment I mounted my horse, without any visible cause, he began to boggle and snort and drew backward, and from one side to the other, as if there were a stone wall just before him. Brother Williams whipped him behind and I before, but it was lost labour. He leaped from side to side, till he came to a gateway, into which he ran backwards and tumbled head over heels. My foot was under him, but I arose unhurt. He then went on as quiet as any horse in the world. Thus far only could Satan go.[13]

In May 1787 having lost four Irish horses in rapid succession, Wesley reinforced this conviction with the kind of statement he never made in England: 'The old murderer is restrained from hurting me; but, it seems he has power over my horses'.[14] Perhaps it was significant that it seems to have been the Irish Conference which adopted a minute which was incorporated into the English minutes when publication began in 1765:

> Q. Are all preachers merciful to their beasts?
> A. Perhaps not. Everyone ought 1. Never to ride hard. 2. To see with his own eyes his horse rubbed, fed and bedded.[15]

Hard riding apart, it will not surprise you that when Wesley and John Downes were riding south from Newcastle in 1743, their horses having had a good view of Ferryhill both laid down and died.[16]

Nor were the perils of horse riding all of this kind. Posses of strange horsemen were of course particularly suspect during the Forty-Five, and were one of the reasons why Methodists were suspected of Jacobitism. There was a dramatic confrontation on a hilltop near Tolcarn in Cornwall in that year. On the one side were the warden, constables and notables of the parish with a warrant from the Helston Justices, and on the other Wesley's party, besought by the congregation to go no further. Wesley, never averse to a confrontation, rode up to the notables, and was saved in the nick of time by the arrival of the parish priest of Redruth, who vouched for having known him in Oxford. One of the gentlemen from the hostile reception committee drew Wesley aside and said:

> Sir, I will tell you the ground of this. All the gentlemen of these parts say that you have been a long time in France and Spain, and are now sent hither by the Pretender; and that these societies are to join him.[17]

These tense confrontations of riders so beloved of directors of Western films did not all end so happily. In 1748 there were dreadful scenes of violence at the aptly named Roughlee in Rossendale. These were got up by George White the curate of Colne, who, having been educated at Douai, converted to the Church of England, and having been preferred by the favour of Archbishop Potter, sought to prove that he had worked his passage by deeds of violence against Methodists. Wesley replied with a threatening letter, but as his party left Roughlee between four and five in the morning,

> observing several parties of men upon the hills, and suspecting their design, we put on and passed the lane they were making for before they came. One of our brothers not riding so fast was intercepted by them. They immediately knocked him down, and how it was he got out from amongst them he knew not.

Wesley's subsequent comment on White was not complimentary:

> It was his manner first to hire, and then head the mob, when they and he were tolerably drunk. But he drank himself first into a jail, and then into his grave.[18]

These political hazards, however, illustrate another point which is apt to be obscured by the first person in which much of the Journal is written. Neither Wesley nor his preachers normally rode alone. This was more than a defence against highwaymen and other disturbers of the peace; it was an important means to the education, spiritual development and bonding together of the preachers.

If Wesley's experience was at all characteristic, however, the two great hazards to the rider, one man-made and the other natural, were ferries and the sands. Of course, then as now, some ferries were fun. In 1773 Wesley crossed to Sheerness:

over that whimsical ferry, where footmen and horses pay nothing, but every carriage four shillings![19]

In fact local sources make it clear that the King's Ferry 'for carriages, horses, cattle and passengers' was a good deal more whimsical than that. Generally ruinous, it moved its burden by hauling on a cable of 140 fathoms fixed at each end across the Swale, and carried travellers free except in the evening, on Sundays, and four public holidays a year, the principal perquisite of the ferryman being the right to dredge for oysters within the radius of the ferry loop.[20] Wesley fully shared the general conviction of his countrymen that almost everyone to do with ferries and the sands was a crook battening on the hapless traveller; and paradoxically the one case where this did not happen almost cost him his life and the Grimsby congregation their sermon. Wesley was held up at Owston Ferry, seven and a half miles south of Scunthorpe,

> the boatmen telling us we could not pass the Trent. It was as much as our lives were worth to put from the shore before the storm abated. We waited an hour. But being afraid it would do much hurt if I should disappoint the congregation at Grimsby, I asked the men if they did not think it possible to get to the other shore. They said they could not tell, but if we would venture our lives, they would venture theirs. So we put off, having six men, two women, and three horses in the boat. Many stood looking after us on the riverside; in the middle of which we were, when in an instant, the side of the boat was under water, and the horses and men rolling one over another. We expected the boat to sink every moment, but I did not doubt of being able to swim ashore. The boatmen were amazed as well as the rest, but they quickly recovered and rowed for life. And soon after our horses leaping overboard lightened the boat, and we all came unhurt to land. They wondered what was the matter, I did not rise (for I lay along in the bottom of the boat); and I wondered too till upon examination we found that a large iron crow [or grappling-hook], which the boatmen sometimes used, was (none knew how) run through the string of my boot, which pinned me down that I could not stir. So that if the boat had sunk, I should have been safe enough from swimming any further.[21]

Ferries and sands were related hazards, for up the west side of the country there were a good many crossings which could be negotiated on horse back at low tide by those who knew what they were about, but required a ferry at high tide; these included the passage from Anglesey to Holy Island for the Irish packet before Telford's road was built. At various times Wesley must have ventured upon them all, almost always with bad results, across Carmarthen Bay in South Wales,[22] the Menai Straits,[23] Morecombe Bay and the Duddon Estuary. It was this last which evoked Wesley's most choleric outburst against the sinners who screwed a living from the sands:

> I believe it is ten measured miles shorter than the other [route]; but there are four sands to pass, so far from each other that it is scarce possible to pass them all in a day – especially as you have to do with a generation of liars, who detain all strangers as long as they can, either for their own gain or their neighbours'. I can advise no stranger to go this way: he may go round by Kendal and Keswick, often in less time, always with less expense, and far less trial of his patience.[24]

This conviction left its mark on the history both of the Lake counties and of Methodism, for, only two years later, Wesley became so comprehensively lost in trying to cut through the mountains in the Lakes, that it is impossible even now to establish his route – but it may well have involved the Hard Knott pass.[25] He did not altogether forsake the route via Kendal and Keswick, but commonly kept up his link with Whitehaven from Newcastle. The result was that Methodism made little impact in southern Cumbria, until the industrial development of Barrow-in-Furness in the nineteenth century permitted a new activity based on immigration. Meanwhile, contrary to every assumption of the romantic Lakers, the Lakes continued a substantially godless region.

One crossing remained unavoidable for a few years longer – the Solway Firth. In 1766 Wesley and his companion attempted the crossing south from Dumfries:

> In ten minutes Duncan Wright was embogged. However, the horse plunged on and got through. I was inclined to turn back; but Duncan telling me I needed only go a little to the left, I did so and sunk at once to my horse's shoulders. He sprang up twice, and twice sunk again, each time deeper than before. At the third plunge he threw me on one side, and we both made shift to scramble out. I was covered with fine soft mud from my feet to the crown of my head; yet, blessed be God, not hurt at all. But we could not cross till between seven and eight o'clock. An honest man crossed with us, who went two miles out of his way to guide us over the sands to Skinburness, where we found a clean little house, and passed a comfortable night.[26]

A few months later, going in the opposite direction, they had difficulty in getting a guide, as they were all engaged in a cockfight; Wesley was made giddy by the action of the waves, and John Atlay, his companion, temporarily lost his sight, and was caught by another member of the party as he fell from his horse.[27] One more trip, successfully accomplished with a guide,[28] put paid to Wesley's adventures in the Solway Firth.

When a rider has come through as many hazards as Wesley, his advice on horse management is worthy of heed. Wesley gave his with his usual self-confidence in 1770:

> I aver that in riding above a hundred thousand miles, I scarce ever remember any horse (except two that would fall head over heels any way) to fall or make a considerable stumble, while I rode *with a slack rein* . . . I have repeated the trial more frequently than most men in the kingdom can do. A slack rein will prevent stumbling if anything will. But in some horses nothing can'.[29]

I think this may be a better account of Wesley's management of himself than of his horses. He was no longer the anxious precisian of Oxford and Georgia, and was all the better for it. But as the Journal shows, his horses had involved him in potentially fatal accidents at least every other year over a considerable period, and the horses could hardly all have been of substandard intelligence. Moreover a year or so later, another horse threw him forward on to the pommel of the saddle, and, even after the immediate pain had subsided, left a permanent injury. This, Wesley confessed in the decent obscurity of Latin, led over a few years to a badly swollen testicle, which would have totally incapacitated most men, but merely inconvenienced him. Not surprisingly the medical profession disagreed as to the prudent course – it was this operation which killed Gibbon – but finally in 1774 he underwent surgery which removed half a pint of fluid and (to the surgeon's 'no small surprise') a pearl the size of a small shot.[30] Next day Wesley professed himself a hundred per cent fit; but the writing had been on the wall for some time, and lay grandees in the connexion had been raising a subscription 'to prevent [his] riding on horseback', finally they procured him a carriage, fitted up with a desk so that he need never stop working.

Wesley's jaunts on the sands were now over, and the Journal changes subtly too. Instead of the constant phrase 'I rode to Bristol' or 'I rode to Newcastle', we find 'I went on', 'I reached'. But in other respects things changed very little. During the brief time his wife attempted to accompany him on his rounds, they had travelled by coach,[31] and it was indeed in her presence that Wesley escaped a mob at Myton Car near Hull in a coach, being rather ungallantly screened from the missiles his assailants hurled through the windows by 'a large gentlewoman who sat in my lap'. The ferries were still a menace. In 1773 he put his chaise on board for Ireland at Liverpool, and the boat immediately grounded on a sandbank.[32] At Dun Laoghaire the commissioners of customs would not permit it to be landed 'because, they said, the captain of a packet boat had no right to bring over goods'.[33] This proved to be a singular intervention of Providence, for, as Tyerman relates, the substitute which Wesley hired:

at Ballibac ferry went overboard, and, with difficulty, was recovered; and which on another occasion it took five hours to drag less than a dozen miles; which, in a third instance was disabled by the breaking of the hinder axletree; and which, more than once, was in danger of being dashed to pieces by furious mobs.[34]

Wesley had always in haste or emergencies taken the post chaise,[35] a sort of taxi service deriving its name from the fact that the vehicle or the horses were hired by post stages, and late in his life frequently took advantage of the time-tabled mailcoach services; these seem to have been relatively cheap and offered a choice of routes, but might be full up and hence exposed the prospective traveller to villainy on the part of the clerk.[36] The mailcoach had, nevertheless, its advantages, for our last hair-raiser took place in his private chaise, with Wesley inside.[37] By this time Wesley's disastrous marriage with the widow Vazeille had broken up, though without in any way weakening his affection for his stepdaughter who had married William Smith, a Methodist corn merchant in Newcastle, and for her daughters whom he always regarded as his granddaughters. In 1774 Wesley set out from Newcastle:

for Horsley, with Mr Hopper and Mr Smith. I took Mrs Smith and her two little girls in the chaise with me. About two miles from the town, just on the brow of the hill, on a sudden both the horses set out, without any visible cause, and flew down the hill like an arrow out of a bow. In a minute John fell off the coach-box. The horses then went on full speed, sometimes to the edge of the ditch on the right, sometimes on the left. A cart came up against them; they avoided it exactly as if the man had been on the box. A narrow bridge was at the foot of the hill; they went directly over the middle of it. They ran up the next hill with the same speed, many persons meeting us, but getting out of the way. Near the top of the hill was a gate, which led into a farmer's yard. It stood open. They turned short and ran through it, without touching the gate on one side or the post on the other. I thought, 'However, the gate which is on the other side of the yard, and is shut, will stop them'. But they rushed through it as if it had been a cobweb, and galloped on through the cornfield. The little girls cried out, 'Grandpapa, save us!' I told them, 'Nothing will hurt you: do not be afraid'; feeling no more fear or care (blessed be God!) than if I had been sitting in my study. The horses ran on till they came to the edge of a steep precipice. Just then Mr Smith,

who could not overtake us before, galloped in between. They stopped
in a moment. Had they gone on ever so little, he and we must have gone
down together!

I am persuaded both evil and good angels had a large share in this
transaction; how large we do not know now, but we shall know hereafter.

Wesley's Journal, like his travelling, was to serve his religious purposes
and hence his incidental comment is less than his universal interests might
have led us to expect. There is comment about the improvement wrought
by turnpikes, about the inns (or more often about the blasphemous
company to be found in them). Though the least querulous of men, Wesley
occasionally gives vent to a sense of physical weariness, rarely directly,
often indirectly in statements of the distance, 'eight (computed) miles',[38]
'four long miles',[39] 'three hours' ride (which they call eight miles)',[40] 'seven
or eight (northern) miles', 'about twenty measured miles',[41] 'our seven-
and-thirty Irish miles, so called, were little less than seventy English',[42]
'sixteen Welsh miles',[43] and so forth. The modern eye will often recognise
symptoms of fatigue in these statements, but is also wrongly tempted to
see in them statements of Wesley's undoubted prickly nationalism. For the
fact was that the English mile of modern times (eight furlongs or 1760
yards) which existed long before it was defined by statute in 1593, was for
centuries only one of several linear measures in use (quite apart from
the fact that measures of different principles were employed for the
measurement of land and of textiles). There was the 'old English mile' or
league of twelve furlongs, and the much shorter Roman mile consisting of
eight stadia or 1000 Roman paces (*mille passuum*) of five feet each, as well
as a shorter Anglo-Saxon mile. The league could be understood as a mile
and a half or as fifteen hundred paces. Moreover although the idea of a
mile as eight furlongs early took deep root, the length of the perch and
hence the furlong was variable. This ambiguity gave rise to the 'long' miles
of Lancashire and Cheshire, and to the old Irish mile of 2240 yards, based
on a perch of seven yards used by William Petty for his great 'Down Survey'
of 1654–5. When the perch was the more normal five and a half yards, the
measured mile was the same in post-Conquest times as today. Cartogra-
phers came to distinguish, as did Wesley, between 'computed' and 'statute'
miles; when milestones in Yorkshire came to be altered from the former
to the latter, mileages went up by thirty to one hundred per cent. Fynes
Moryson, a seventeenth-century commentator, foreshadowed Wesley's
experience:

> ... even in England the miles seem, and indeed are more short neere
> London, where the ways are faire and plaine, and frequently inhabited,
> as they seeme, and indeed are more long and tedious, through the desart

places of the North, over mountains, and through uninhabited and difficult passages.[44]

As a young man Wesley found that his horse tired faster than he did,[45] and even in the last year of his life he preached at Beverley before a party of forty who had come to escort him ceremonially to Hull, dined with them and raced them back to Hull before they could catch him up.[46] The old man was now too tired or perhaps his eyesight was too poor to work in his coach. He looked through the window and loved what he saw. Of two judgments made three months before his journal ends, and which he did not live to publish, one will I think seem to you very just, and the other perhaps surprising:

> We rode to Hexham through one of the pleasantest countries that I have lately seen. The road lay (from Haltwhistle) on the side of a fruitful mountain, shaded with trees, and sloping down to a clear river, which ran between ours and another fruitful mountain, well wooded and improved.
>
> We went [from Stanhope] on to Durham. Here . . . I was obliged to preach in the open air, to a multitude of people, all of whom were serious and attentive. We went through a lovely country to Sunderland.[47]

How much happier than in 1752:

> I preached in Durham to a quiet, stupid congregation, and the next day went on to Newcastle.[48]

Abbreviations:
Journal of John Wesley ed. N. Curnock (Standard ed.), 2nd edn., London, 1938: *Journal* (C).
Journals and Diaries ed. W.R. Ward & R.P. Heitzenrater (Works of John Wesley [Bicentennial ed.]), Nashville, Tenn., 1988: *Journal* (W).

Notes

1 L. Tyerman, *The life and times of Rev. John Wesley M.A. Founder of the Methodists*, 6th edn., London, 1890, 3. 658. Tyerman took his cue from one of Wesley's earliest biographers, John Whitehead.
2 *Journal* (W) 3. 164, 235–6.
3 *Journal* (C) 7. 376–7; Tyerman, *Wesley* 3. 527.
4 A letter of Wm. Severn to Saml. Bardsley, Feb. 8, 1772, inserted into JW's copy of the Journal: *Journal* (C) 5. 449 n. 2: *Proceedings of the Wesley Historical Society* 5. 78–9. In 1760 Wesley declined an offer of hospitality in Ireland on the ground that 'as my journeyings were fixed, I could not do that without

disappointing several congregations' (*Journal* (W) 4. 266). Again in 1761
Wesley writes: 'I cannot fix my route through Scotland till I hear from Mr
Gillies'. *Letters* ed. J. Telford 4. 141–2.

5 For example in *The Great Awakening* ed. A. Heimert and Perry Miller, 5th
edn., Indianapolis, 1978 184–6. Cf. *Journal* (W) 4. 484: 'Knowing they were
scattered up and down [the Gower peninsula] I had sent two persons on Sunday
that they might be there early on Monday, and so send notice of my coming
all over the country. But they came to Oxwich scarce a quarter of an hour
before me, so that the poor people had no notice at all'.

6 *Journal* (W) 3. 324.

7 *Ibid.*, 3. 301–2.

8 *Ibid.*, 3. 302. There is no reference at all in the Journal to maps; the consequence
was a frequent dependence on guides, even in civilised parts of the country.
For the London to Bristol journey, *Journal* (C) 5. 234.

9 *Ibid.*, 5. 360. Cf. *Journal* (W) 3. 322: 'In riding to Cirencester I read Dr Bates's
Elenchus Motuum nuperorum in Anglia. His Latin is not much inferior to
Caesar's, whom he seems studiously to imitate; and his thoughts are generally
just, only that he has no more mercy on the Puritans than upon Cromwell'.

10 *Ibid.*, 2. 73–74.

11 *Ibid.*, 2. 234–5.

12 *Ibid.*, 2. 330–31.

13 *Journal* (C) 3. 342. A similar spill in Canterbury in 1758 temporarily cost
Wesley the use of his right leg. *Journal* (W) 4. 169.

14 *Journal* (C) 7. 282.

15 *Minutes of the Methodist Conferences*, London, 1872 1. 49; *Wesleyan Methodist Magazine* 1865 705–9.

16 *Journal* (W) 2. 329.

17 *Ibid.*, 3. 77–8.

18 *Ibid.*, 3. 243–4. 427.

19 *Journal* (C) 6. 6.

20 E. Hasted, *History of Kent*, Canterbury, 1797–1801: repr., 6. 210–211.

21 *Journal* (W) 2. 349–50.

22 *Ibid.*, 4. 424–5.

23 *Ibid.*, 3. 267, 325.

24 *Ibid.*, 4. 190–1.

25 *Ibid.*, 4. 315.

26 *Journal* (C) 5. 172.

27 *Ibid.*, 5. 201.

28 *Ibid.*, 5. 255.

29 *Ibid.*, 5. 361.

30 *Ibid.*, 5. 447, 474: 6. 8.

31 *Journal* (W) 3. 419.

32 *Journal* (C) 5. 500.

33 *Ibid.*, 5. 501.

34 Tyerman, *Wesley* 3. 153.

35 e.g. *Journal* (C) 5. 282.
36 *Ibid.*, 7. 257, 332, 358, 417. These references are all for 1787 and 1788.
37 *Ibid.*, 7. 27.
38 *Journal* (W) 2. 305.
39 *Ibid.*, 3. 113.
40 *Ibid.*, 3. 129.
41 *Ibid.*, 2. 329.
42 *Ibid.*, 4. 266.
43 *Ibid.*, 3. 324.
44 Philip Grierson, *English linear measures. An essay in origins*, Reading, 1972; C. Close, 'The old English mile', *Geographical Journal* 76 (1930) 338–42; J.B.P. Karslake, 'Further notes on the old English mile', *Ibid.*, 77 (1931) 355–60.
45 *Journal* (W) 2. 181 & n. 19.
46 *Journal* (C) 8. 75; *Wesleyan Methodist Magazine* 1836 494.
47 *Journal* (C) 8. 68, 71.
48 *Journal* (W) 3. 422.

14

The Religion of the People and the Problem of Control, 1790–1830

The generation about which I wish to speak was, I make no doubt, the most important single generation in the modern history not merely of English religion but of the whole Christian world. For despite the holy water sprinkled by the late Dean Sykes and his pupils, there seems no doubt that the effectiveness of the Church throughout Western Europe was undermined by the same forces which were everywhere sapping the *Ancien Régime*, the whole institutional complex of which the religious establishments were part. The great crisis of the French Revolution altered for ever the terms on which religious establishments must work, and in so doing it intensified everywhere a long-felt need for private action in the world of religion. It also brought out how the balance of institutions varied from one society to another. In Germany the Protestant establishments were able to absorb evangelicalism and though they could not assimilate Roman Catholic minorities, they had rendered them by 1918 as unable to manage rationally without a Protestant establishment as the Protestants themselves. In England the legal dependence of the Church upon the state disguised a real dependence of a weak state upon networks of informal influence including those of the Church. The English state had been too weak to put down dissent, too weak to allow its clergy to play at politics in their Convocation, too weak to plant the Anglican establishment in the American colonies. In the mid-nineties a Church entirely unequipped to meet the repercussions of the revolutionary crisis in France, had to face its moment of truth with no better state backing than the episcopalians of colonial America, not because, as bewildered clergy perpetually insisted, there was a peculiar perfidy in Tory politicians, but because there was no German-style concentration of power on which they could draw. As a working establishment the Church of England collapsed even more quickly

Presidential address to the Ecclesiastical History Society. First published in *Studies in Church History* 8 (1971), pp. 237–57.

than that of France, its fate epitomised by a great non-event, whose importance has been notably unsung by historians, the failure of government to put down itinerant preaching and Sunday schools by a restriction of the Toleration Act in 1799 and 1800. Till 1870 the state owed some obligations to the Church, but already gave public notice that it could not save the day for it. In America the experience of colonial revolt had turned the sects into an informal religious establishment; the forces of public order being so much weaker and society so much more expansive even than in England, the Americans had to drive the machinery for reconstituting religious society much harder than it was ever driven by the English. But elasticity gave the American informal establishment an absorptive power greater even than the formal establishments of Germany. Methodism and the benevolent system, episcopalianism, and eventually even Roman Catholicism, were taken on board and made vehicles of American nationalism.

The problem of control in England therefore, turned upon a unique social balance; the English Church faced the new forces of the age with neither the institutional power of the German *Landeskirchen* nor the dynamism of the American churches. Concurrent endowment of different religious bodies was one of the great non-starters of the century; equally the supplanting of the formal establishment by an informal *Volkskirche* was one of its unrealised dreams. England failed to secure either a formal or informal establishment of real effectiveness. In the first decade of the century with the dismemberment of the old establishments proceeding apace, the prospect of a popular evangelical church seemed a real one. Since the mid-1790s the two growing points of the church order, the itinerancy and the Sunday Schools, had undergone a remarkable development upon an undenominational basis, and if the Anglicans had dropped out of the one and were being rapidly displaced by popular pressure from the other, there were new reinforcements in an undenominational press and that great battery of Bible, Tract and Missionary Societies which formed a pattern of Christian progress all the way from Basel to New York. The sudden weakening of traditional communal indoctrination seemed to clear the decks for associational activity of all kinds. This seemed the way to Christianise the people, and also to create new networks of informal influence which English public institutions evidently needed. The substance of this new religion of the people as proclaimed in the prospectuses of the reviews and the trust deeds of a host of Sunday schools was the XXXIX Articles of the Church itself, and it was to prove that social tension like that which in the mid-1790s had caused the Church to cut adrift from the new movements, was to break up much of the associational mechanism, and change its frame of mind. Denominational loyalties came increasingly to be pressed as a counterpoise to class antagonism within the ranks, and while anathematising the out-groups had its uses in keeping the in-groups together, it converted a social conflict into that denominational contest which formed the main substance of the politics of the thirties and forties.

In the space of one paper, I can examine this process in one community only, the Wesleyan Methodists, and for only the first twenty years of the nineteenth century. Both community and date are, however, important, for not only were the Wesleyans the fastest growing of the evangelical communities, but their connexional constitution forced up their tensions into open and central conflict more readily than among the independents. Moreover it was in the first decade of the century and not, as the books sometimes say, in the years following the Tractarian débâcle, that the Wesleyans aspired to become an informal Protestant establishment and felt assured that neither states[1] nor individuals which stood in their way would come to any good. Yet three successive and related challenges, religious, social and administrative, exposed their Achilles heel and set the problem of control within Methodism itself.

The first challenge came from revivalism, or as it is convenient to call it in an English context, from Ranterism. There is no need to repeat the oft-told tale of the Conference declaration against camp meetings in 1807, and of the formation of the Primitive Methodist Connexion in which revivalism was in a measure institutionalised. But it is important to see why Conference acted as it did. For the doings on Mow Cop had no political significance; 1807 was a year of low social tension; and it was in any case the regular itinerancy which was under political fire at that moment. The truth is that Ranterism had a considerable pre-history both in the country and more recently in the great Northern towns.

For Ranterism challenged Wesleyanism hard where it teetered between form and formalism. Wesleyans had a firmly articulated schema of the Christian life, beginning with conviction of sin and finding liberty and working up to entire sanctification, which had its own imaginative appeal. It enabled the believer to judge his progress experimentally, and guided the Class leaders through the official system of spiritual inquisition. Everyone understood its merits but there was no official recognition of its limitations, or of the signs, already discernible, that the thing was becoming a bore. There was the same formalism about Wesleyan preaching. At the bottom were the exhorters. The exhortation consisted of reproving sin, pleading with the sinner to flee from the wrath to come, describing the speaker's own experience in these matters, and testifying to his present joy. The framework of the exhortation appears to have been rigid, held together by these topics, the main scope for individuality lying in the personal testimony. The distinction between exhorters and preachers, whether itinerant or local, lay in 'taking a text'. This was a public declaration that the speaker had ceased to 'exhort', and also that he accepted a new restraint, that of dealing with the specific doctrines brought out by his 'texts'.[2] John Phillips of Osset wrote: 'The doctrines I preach are, the fall of man, repentance towards God, faith in our Lord Jesus Christ, and the holiness without which no man can see the Lord.' In 1802 Joseph Entwisle emphasised that 'the Head of the Church has put great honor upon a few *leading truths* by wch. Methodist sermons are character-ised, and a man need never lose sight of them for the sake of variety'.[3] The undertaking to preach 'our doctrines' still required regularly of Methodist itinerants, began with this technical sense, and applied to all those who had completed their apprenticeship as exhorters. One can feel the sense of relief when Hugh Bourne resolved to take his collier friends for a day's 'praying and shouting' on Mow Cop.

This system of instruction and control had little hope of containing a society as dynamic as that which was developing in the great towns, and even in the countryside the 1790s had shown that the crucial breakthrough was being made less by exhorting, preaching or class leading, than by cottage prayer meetings led by entirely unofficial persons. They exploited the new social solidarity of the lower orders in the villages, to enter private houses, and in prayer to incorporate their neighbours into the circle of the faithful.[4] It was characteristic that William Clowes, the great Primitive, was an unusually impressive man in prayer, even in silent prayer. Even in his Wesleyan days, he spared his class the official inquisition, and humanely encouraged their initiative in religious exercises of which they were capable.[5]

> The class rapidly increased until the house became so full, that there was hardly room to kneel. In leading my classes I used to get from six to ten to pray a minute or two each, and thus to get the whole up into the faith; then I found it a very easy matter to lead thirty or forty members in an hour and a quarter for I found that leading did not consist so much in talking to the members as in getting into the faith, and bringing down the cloud of God's glory, that the people might be truly blessed in their souls as well as instructed in divine things.

Of course (as he ingenuously reports) souls were converted in every room in the house, even in the larder.

Moreover, a far-reaching process not only of political but of spiritual education was going on among working men. Half the interest of the journals of Bourne and Clowes lies in the light they cast upon the progress of humble men for whom adherence to the Establishment was out of the

question and official Wesleyanism offered no way forward. One day
Bourne was struck down at one of those country corners where the saints
so often wrestled with God or with Satan.[6]

> Coming home at the praying place in Mr Heath's fields, I felt as if I was
> held by an irresistible power, and I sank down into nothing before it,
> and everything that I did was contrary to God. I felt it die away – I gave
> myself up to God. Immediately came 'the spirit of burning', and I was
> made 'a habitation of God through the Spirit.' I wondered at myself; I
> could scarcely believe what the Spirit witnessed.

But it was not all immediacy, for the men from the Potteries were in touch
not only with American revivalists but with James Crawfoot and the Magic
Methodists of Delamere Forest, who specialised in visions; with Peter
Philips, a chair maker of Warrington, who led the Quaker Methodists of
that place into contact with the spirituality of the Society of Friends; with
James Sigston, a schoolmaster notorious in the annals of Leeds Methodism.
The bizarre visions of pious women in their circle, establishing the
celestial pecking order of the prophets and seers of Cheshire and North
Staffordshire,[7] reveal a lively awareness of a range of spiritual possibilities
far beyond the Wesleyan discipline.

Then there was exorcism. Anglicans reproached Wesleyans with it, and
Wesleyans the Ranters.[8] There is no doubt that exorcism went on in
orthodox Methodism, but the Ranters did not blush to provide a service
which was evidently in lively popular demand. As a young man, Clowes
could defeat though not destroy the notorious Kidsgrove bogget,[9] and
by 1810 he and Bourne were grappling with a spirit world almost
Methodistically organised.[10]

> I visited Clowes [writes Bourne]. He has been terribly troubled by the
> woman we saw at Ramser. I believe she will prove to be a witch. These
> are the head labourers under Satan, like as the fathers are the head
> labourers under Jesus Christ. So we are fully engaged in the battle. These,
> I believe, cannot hurt Christ's little ones till the[y] have first combated
> the fathers. It appears that they have been engaged against James
> Crawfoot ever since he had a terrible time praying with and for a woman
> who was in witchcraft. For the witches throughout the world all meet
> and have connection with the power devil . . . Well the Lord is strong
> and we shall soon, I believe, have to cope with the chief powers of
> Hell . . . I am certain the Lord will give us the victory.

Revival was a rural phenomenon all the way from Pomerania and
Swabia to Lincolnshire and Kentucky, but its progress might be speeded
in areas where industrial employment replaced landlordism by forms of

economic dependence not organised on a parochial basis.[11] This was especially the case where the extractive industries, mining, quarrying and fishing, created a close cohesion of their own, whether in Siegerland, Cornwall or County Durham, but it happened also where the putting-out system in the textile industries altered the character of the whole countrysides as in Wuppertal, parts of the Black Forest, the North Midlands or the West Riding. But the brakes rarely came off more suddenly than they did now for rural immigrants to the northern industrial towns, and amongst them came a series of outbreaks of Ranterism and clashes with the Wesleyan preachers. Here especially religious antagonism was sharpened by social conflict. The uninstitutional movements of God's grace so dear to the revivalists, evoked a powerful echo in men who were at the losing end of institutions and chilled the marrow of those with a stake in institutional stability. There were always men of substance who dabbled in revivalism, but everyone knew that men's leanings one way or the other were deeply coloured by their social standing.[12] Already there was little love lost between the revivalists and the little knot of wealthy intermarried Woods, Marsdens and Burtons with whom Bunting, the future architect of early Victorian Methodism, allied himself, and who maintained a cross bench position between Methodism and the Church, with brothers in the ministry of each.

With the turn of the century the revivalists began to claim the same rights of private edification amongst Wesleyans as the latter had claimed in the Church. Separate places of worship began to go up, and secessions began in Preston, Stockport, and Macclesfield; in Leeds James Sigston and 300 of his friends were expelled and set up as the 'Kirkgate Screamers'.[13] The reactions of the Wesleyan preachers are vividly illustrated in the surviving correspondence about the Macclesfield men who published their rules as Christian Revivalists in 1803. The superintendent minister Joseph Entwisle, was a wise and kindly man whose 'simple and unaffected devotion'[14] was acknowledged far outside the connexion. He took a generally hopeful view of the circuit and ascribed its admittedly flat state partly to factory work which kept people much too late to attend weeknight meetings, and partly to the fact that the secession of the revivalists had evoked rather too much conservative backlash among 'the leading friends'.[15] But the junior preacher, Jabez Bunting, already regarded in the third year of his ministry as a preaching and organising prodigy, saw the whole matter in black-and-white terms.[16]

The people in this town are tired of parties and divisions: & in general equally of the rant & extravagancies of what is called Revivalism ... Divisions *from* the church, though awful, are perhaps after all less to be dreaded than divisions *in* the church . . . Revivalism, as of late professed & practised was [likely if] not checked, to have gradually ruined genuine Methodism. [I a]m glad, however, that they have been the first to draw the sword. But as they have drawn it, I earnestly wish that our preachers would take the opportunity of returning fully to the spirit & discipline of ancient Methodism, & with that resolve to stand or fall. The temporary loss of numbers would probably be more than recompensed by the increase of real scriptural piety, the restoration of good order & the establishment of brotherly love.

Bunting's doctrinaire conviction that he was possessed of the Wesleyan tradition in some sense in which his elders who had travelled with the great man were not, was ominous for the future of Methodism. For the next generation the older men were generally more liberal than Bunting's young hard-liners, and in 1806 the conjunction of his appointment to Manchester with a serious recession brought about a resounding rupture with the Band Room Methodists there. It was in hard times when the appeal of Methodism flagged that the revivalists were most tempted to go it alone and were most irked by the luxury as well as the formalism of the Methodist upper crust. The Manchester preachers admitted privately to have been looking for 'the annihilation of the party',[17] and Bunting was not the man to let the opportunity slip.

Revivalism then threatened not merely the peace of congregations but the forms of Wesleyan spirituality and instruction. But what moved Conference ultimately against camp meetings was not the fissiparousness of revivalism, but its capacity for union. In 1805 the first conference of Independent Methodists was held in Manchester, uniting the revivalists not merely of the Band Room, but of Oldham, Warrington, Stockport and Macclesfield as well. The Primitive Methodist connexion was another unpremeditated union of revivalists,[18] who had begun and remained in close touch with the Independents, but who obtained great expansiveness by a degree of connexionalism and a paid, though poorly paid, ministry which picked up much of that rural ranterism which had been spreading since the mid-1790s. They profited also from that more general unspiky, undenominational evangelicalism propagated at the same time. Baptist Chapels, Independent, New Connexion, even Wesleyan chapels were opened to them, and Union chapels the very cataloguing of which has not yet begun admitted them to their cycle. Though on a small scale, these coalitions created the impression, later more actively canvassed in America than in England, that revivalism rather than denominationalism was the fundamental antidote to the tensions of church and society.

That this was not quite true was one of the lessons of the last great wave of urban revival which the preachers had to face. In 1816 Methodism seemed again on the flood tide, especially in the towns of the north-west, of Derbyshire, and about Leeds.[19] But before long it was reported from York that while 400 new members 'of the lowest order' had been added, the pews were unlet as the chapel respectability were driven away to the Independents.[20] Social tension had already passed the point at which it could be sublimated in religious revival, and as events slid toward Peterloo even Bunting's much-prized unity of the church was put at hazard.

Cornwall, however, was a different story. Here the modest liberty of tinner and fisherman, the cohesiveness of village life, the indifference of the Cornish to the politics of parliament or class, made spontaneous revival possible right into the 1830s, while the unpopularity of the Cornish Church left no obvious alternative to Methodism for the more substantial classes. Revival broke out at Redruth in 1814 in a staggering meeting which would not break up for nine successive days and nights. We read that[21]

> hundreds were crying for mercy at once. Some remained in great distress of soul for one hour, some for 2, some 6, some 9, 12, and some for 15 hours before the Lord spoke peace to their souls – then they wd. rise, extend their arms, & proclaim the wonderful works of God, with such energy, that bystanders wd. be struck in a moment, & fall to the ground & roar for the disquietude of their souls.

Events of this kind continued till 1819, and broke out again in the thirties.

The Cornish revival was far too explosive for the Methodist machine. The official system of collecting weekly class monies which worked properly hardly anywhere, was here almost inoperative. Circuits made shift according to their lights, and poverty led them to keep down their ministerial staff to the lowest practicable level.[22] The Cornish local preachers never quite amassed the power of those of the Isle of Man who established themselves as an unofficial Manx Conference,[23] but they seem to have gathered huge classes during the revival and kept them under permanent oversight as class leaders. The double hold of converting power and pastoral leadership gave them an ascendancy which did not bend easily to preachers' pressure. The hazards were aggravated by poverty, for it was no sacrifice to a Cornish artisan to grasp professional status by taking a class of a hundred into separation, and living humbly as a preacher on their offerings.[24] But poverty also protected Cornwall from much in English Methodism, and in the thirties Bunting's streamlined schemes for levies per head of members in districts, seemed impossible even to ministers hottest for standard connexional practices.

Fed by reports from Cornish preachers of irregular ways, and even by demands that the President or Secretary of Conference should annually attend the Cornish District Meeting to keep things in order,[25] Bunting regarded the Cornish as 'the *mob of Methodism*, they have always been rude and refractory'.[26] Yet this judgement was to miss the main point which emerges from a splendid series of preachers' reports. George Russell who had been unbearably irked by my own forbears among the impudent Derbyshire Ranters whose religion, he declared, bore 'a near resemblance to the religion of old Nick',[27] took a cool and not unfavourable view of the Cornish revival at Helston in 1814. He perceived that the Cornish people, under native impulses, were making Methodism a popular establishment, a *Volkskirche*, without parallel in any comparable area in England.[28] Cornish society was free and disorderly, and so was Cornish Methodism. But if it could not yet be overtaken by *episkope* as officially understood, it had the strength arising from popular community observance, and hence a freedom from the quirks to which English revivalists were subject. Too much has been made of the excitements aroused by Dr Warren in 1835 and Wesleyan Reform in 1849. What finally undid Cornish Methodism was not liberty but the erosion of Cornish separateness by more powerful forces from across the Tamar. Of these, Buntingism and its Methodist rivals were only the foretaste.

The Wesleyan preachers' feud with the revivalists was soon overshadowed by the second great challenge, that of convulsive social discontent. In 1810 Daniel Isaac was risking life and limb in desperate opposition to trade unionism on the North Eastern coalfield,[29] and in the following year the Luddite movement in Yorkshire and Lancashire severely tested the cohesion of the body. In the 1790s the Methodist flock had been so much on one side of the social divide as to leave the preachers no real option but to follow them and turn against the propertied trustees who clung to the Church. Now as the preachers wept for the great Methodist Burton family who brought up the cannon to defend their print works at Rhodes, and mowed down the hands to whom they were said to be so kind,[30] it was clear not only that Methodists stood on both sides of the social conflict but that forces within the connexion were differently aligned. There were ecclesiastical as well as political inducements for the conservative stance of the Old Connexion preachers; for it brought back magnates from the New Connection, frightened, it was reported, by 'the connivance of some of their preachers and other official persons at the Luddite system and practices'. Even the Old Chapel at Huddersfield which the Kilhamites had carried off in 1797 was believed to be ripe for the picking.[31]

In 1812 Bunting was stationed at Halifax in the heart of the West Riding troubles. So firm was he with the Luddites that for months on end he could not go out at night alone. Late in January 1813, 17 Luddites were hanged at York, 6 of them sons of Methodists, and Bunting commented privately:[32]

> However solicitous to make the best of this, it is after all an *awful* fact – and it confirms me in my fixed opinion, that the progress of Methodism in the West Riding of Yorkshire has been more swift than solid; more extensive than deep, more in the increase of numbers, than in diffusion of that kind of piety which shines as brightly & operates as visibly *at home* as in the prayer meeting and the crowded love feast. I read of no people, professing serious religion, who have not as a body far outstripped us in that branch of practical godliness, which consists in the moral management & discipline of children.

The Methodist tub, in short, could no longer contain the torrent of antiestablishment sentiment: what was needed was less revival and more denominational drill, and in particular, one of Bunting's current nostrums, the control of Sunday schools.

The post-war crisis was, however, very much worse. A dramatic fall in prices made every social adjustment more painful, and in Methodism as elsewhere the hackles rose unbearably. In 1815 Bunting concluded that Manchester 'must have a firm Superintendent'.[33] At Peterloo they had John Stephens, a former Cornish tin miner, and a man of 'morbid disposition' but of stern action when roused. His junior preacher, the famous Thomas Jackson, was required to patrol the streets at night keeping order, supported as he recalled by 'a noble band of men', the flower of the Manchester Methodist plutocracy.[34] Stephens painfully enforced discipline in the Leaders' Meeting, in his first year removing 400 from the membership roll, and admonished them to go 'either to the New Connexion or the devil'.[35] He followed up the Peterloo clash by a sermon on Mark 14: 7, 'For ye have the poor with you always', explaining to the poor the advantages of this state of affairs, and proclaimed his intention to 'blow the sacred trumpet to call Jehovah's hosts to battle; and manfully unfurl the banners of his country, his Sovereign and his God'.[36] Stephens was genteelly but firmly supported by an address from the connexional Committee of Privileges.

On the other side the radical *Manchester Observer* mercilessly flayed the Wesleyans and their discipline,[37] and all over the north as desperate superintendents sought to cut the canker from the body, rumours mounted ever wilder about the confidential relations of the Methodist leadership with the government. Jacobins at Bolton claimed that Stephens had 'received a check for £10,000 for services done to Government, signed *Sidmouth*'.[38] Yorkshire radicals alleged that the connection had 'lent the Government half a million of money to buy cannon to shoot them with'.[39]

At Marple they made it a million.[40] The truth was more prosaic, but perhaps more discreditable; the upper crust were using the full Halévy doctrine that Methodism was saving society from revolution, to demand legislation making camp meetings illegal while securing the indoor gatherings of Wesleyans.[41]

Of course, in the smaller textile towns where there were few men of substance for the preachers to call on, they could be desperately isolated. J.B. Holroyd, preacher at Haslingden in Rossendale, reported that two thirds of the population in his circuit were radicals, and there being no magistrate or chief constable, they were manufacturing pikes and drilling nightly.[42] Five 'marked kingsmen' were to be assassinated on the day of revolution, including the Anglican incumbent and himself.

> One evening a few weeks since just as I came out of my own door to go into the chapel, the procession was just drawing up in front of the house. I did not judge it prudent to go through the crowd but stood inside the garden gate; they gave three of the most horrid groans I ever heard, and with each groan, a young man brandished a pike within a yard of my breast, accompanied with such dreadful oaths, enough to make one's blood run chill . . . It is with grief I say that our society is not free from the contagion. Some have left us this quarter . . . They do not think it right to give anything toward the support of those who encourage and pray for a number of tyrants . . . The above are not the sentiments of our leading friends in Haslingden, quite the reverse, but they can render the preachers no efficient support in opposing the general impetus . . . [The previous Sunday he had been attacked by a group of office-holders about Castlereagh's Six Acts] when they told me in plain terms that [the] Methodist preachers were as bad as the Church ministers in supporting Government, but it was asked, Will Lord Castlereagh support you?

So far as camp meetings went, the answer, fortunately, was that he would not.[43]

Holroyd here set out the basic pattern of the Methodist crises of the next generation, depicted in a thousand private letters; the great social division in the flock, with the poor and the radical on the one side, and the preacher in alliance with 'the leading friends' in the other, with calumny on one side opposed by church discipline on the other. The itinerant ministry which only yesterday had been a device for retrieving the lost from the highways and hedges, and compelling them to come in, was now being used as a social regulator in a way ruinous to the self-respect which had been one of Methodism's greatest gifts to many of her humble sons. The preachers did not need Bunting to tell them that Methodism hated democracy as it hated sin; recession and democracy killed their evangelistic appeal, and set the flock by the ears. Nor could the New Connexion and the sects which championed the radical cause capitalise the opportunity. A generation later the Chartists were to find that they had a hard core of leaders and organizers; a considerable and potentially stable body of the second rank who were prepared to play supporting parts and who enjoyed the fellowship of the movement; and a vast mass who were swept in and out of the movement in response to the trade cycle, and whom it was impossible to organise for long. In effect Bunting and his coadjutors were acknowledging that this was already true of Wesleyanism, and were welding the first two groups into a denomination at the cost, perhaps on a certain level of realism, the small cost, of writing off the third, that great mass which had poured into the Sunday schools and chapels since the mid-1790s.

For there was no lack of quite explicit *realpolitik* amongst the Methodist preachers.[44] One of their characteristics in the age of Bunting was an uncanny capacity to anticipate the manoeuvres of the big battalions, a shrewdness which in the forties proved intolerably irksome to men of strait principles. And already pastoral coarseness set in. By February 1821, John Stephens was monarch of all he surveyed, assured that the trade cycle would raise Manchester Methodism to more than its former glories.[45]

> The objects we have kept in view are, 1st. to give the sound part of the society a decided ascendancy. 2. So to put down the opposition, as to disable them from doing mischief. 3. to cure those of them who are worth saving. 4. To take the rest one by one, and crush them when they notoriously commit themselves . . . They are completely at our mercy . . . They are down and we intend to keep them down. That they are not annihilated is rather from want of will than power . . . Methodism stands high among the respectable people.

Even now there was a loss of 5000 members, 'such a blow', said Adam Clarke, 'as we never had since we were a people'.[46] What the preachers could not foresee was that Peterloo had for ever severed official Methodism from urban revivalism. No doubt Manchester would in time have exhibited the same metropolitan secularism as made London the graveyard of religious enthusiasm, but what actually happened was that the great flood tide of 1816 and 1817 was suddenly terminated and never returned. As happened more broadly with the Wesleyan reform secessions of the fifties, the connexional machine could repair the membership losses, but could never evoke the old expansiveness. The years 1819–20 were the moment of truth for the Wesleyans, as the years 1792–3 had been for the Church; Wesleyanism was never going to be a popular urban religion.

The alliance of the preachers with the men of substance in the denomination was clinched by the third great challenge, the direct impact of the post-war economic difficulties upon the Methodist machine. Methodism now paid cruelly for the euphoria of the previous decade, when normally sober men had believed that it was about to subdue the world, and the hundreds of young preachers were called out on whose shoulders Bunting climbed to power. In these years the connexion came to resemble a modern cut-price motor insurance company tempted or deluded by a large cash flow into prodigal disregard of its future liabilities, and falling into a number of morally venial but financially ruinous mistakes of a basically actuarial kind. The Methodist system of paying not a stipend, but allowances for travelling and the maintenance of a house and family created an open-ended liability. The problem of ministerial allowances was taking shape before the end of the war, but the collapse of prices afterwards made the burden, and especially the continual increase of preachers' families seem intolerable. Seasoned preachers could see no way between bankruptcy and exhausting the patience of the flock.[47] Anxious statisticians throughout the connexion were betting on the fertility of the manse and astonishing proposals were made to dismiss preachers with large families, or to station them according to the ability of circuits to pay.[48] In 1819, the year of Peterloo, the candle seemed consumed at both ends. The intake of new preachers had to be restricted,[49] and the Legalised Fund, a kind of group-insurance scheme by which the preachers provided for their widows, and for the retirement of aged and disabled brethren, a fund which should have been bursting at the seams with the subscriptions of recent young recruits, could not meet its obligations.[50]

Everyone knew that the principal cause for the multiplication of preachers was the multiplication of chapels, and hence of pews to be let and mortgages to be serviced, for whatever the aspirations of Conference to be the living Wesley, it was not behaving as Wesley had behaved. In his lifetime, reported William Myles,[51]

> there were never more than one third of the preachers married . . . And he would not let a chapel be built unless two thirds of the money was subscribed before a stone was laid, and it stated whether it would call for an additional preacher. Now near three fourths of the preachers are married, and chapels are built or purchased without, in some cases, one fifth of the money subscribed, and immediately a travelling preacher called out.

Every historian knows how the agricultural industry agonised to meet high wartime debts from low peacetime prices, but no industry was more heavily mortgaged than Methodism. What had been a running sore, became suddenly a disease of fatal proportions, and Conference's modest application of central control to future extensions in 1817 and 1818, could not lighten existing commitments.

I have discovered no trace that the preachers could analyse the economic roots of their difficulties; what vexed them was the loss of an impetus which they had fondly ascribed to sound doctrine and polity.

About five or six years ago [wrote Jonathan Crowther in 1817][52] our machine seemed to possess such incalculable force, that almost all things seemed to be possible to us, yea, even in temporal things ... We are now arrived at a new crisis of our affairs. The connexion is in danger of being overset by its own weight.

In 1818 Charles Atmore feared that 'the *zenith* of Methodism' was past, and could not imagine how they could get through Conference without driving 'the people mad with our collections'.[53]

It was a matter of remark, moreover, that itinerancy in the old sense was rapidly coming to an end. A market in urban religion had been discovered which could be commercially tapped. The right kind of chapel in the right site could attract a congregation of gratifying number and affluence. But as the preachers made no bones privately, the brethren were only too willing to be anchored by connubial bliss and by the financial and pastoral obligations of the new causes, to the neglect of their rural ministry. From the large Yorkshire towns ministers ventured into the country but returned home nightly.[54] They confessed their dilemma. Country congregations were being neglected, and ground lost to the Ranters; on the other hand without a resident minister the town causes in which the financial stake was so huge could not thrive. The old hands in the ministry were quite bitter.[55] 'Paul taught the people publicly and from house to house', wrote one.[56] 'We have very little of domestic teaching.'

This was a cut indeed. For if the rise of Methodism on the macroscale had been an aspect of the rise of the provinces against the centre, on the microscale it had often been an aspect of the rise of the fringes of the parish against the nuclear village, the parish church, and the central apparatus of service and control. For one remote parish in Montgomeryshire, it has been shown how the revival forwarded this process by shifting the centre of worship from the parish church to the hearths of outlying farm kitchens, and that even when domestic prayer and prophecy were institutionalised, the chapel buildings were scattered at remote intersections of routes avoiding the village, a monument to the centrifugal forces which underlay them.[57]

What was true of Llanfihangel was true of many English parishes too, and the steady decay of the old style of itinerancy which involved journeys from home sometimes of weeks on end, sleeping, praying and preaching with the people in their homes and rural meeting places, involved subtle changes thoroughly unpalatable to many who remembered what Methodism was originally like. No doubt this distaste did play into the hands of the Primitives[58] who harvested a second crop from the Wesleyan mission fields, were always more decentralised and more rural than the Wesleyans, and in some parts of the country maintained an old-style itinerancy into the present century.

There were two symbols of the new era which bore directly on the financial crisis. The first was the steady disappearance of the circuit horse.[59] For circuit stewards had it calculated that 'the expenses attending a horse support a single Preacher'[60] who might be of more service to the central chapels, but who, unlike the horse, would ere long establish a claim to additional allowances for wife, house and children, coals, candles and servant. If when the horse was exchanged for an unmarried preacher the country societies could be disposed of to a new circuit, the local financial advantage could be maximised.[61] This ruinous process, the creation of financially unsound country circuits, was the second symbol of the decline of itinerancy. It was a general abuse, particularly notorious in the old Methodist urban centres of London, Bristol and the North-East, and it aggravated the burdens created by Thomas Coke's domestic missions which gave rise to forty circuits hardly any of which were capable of spiritual or financial independence.[62]

Methodist connexionalism being what it was, these mistakes at the fringes had immediate repercussions at the centre, and the preachers in Conference found themselves struggling to pay what was due to them as individuals in the circuits. The theory of Methodist finance was that each society contributed to the support of the preachers stationed in the circuit, while the chapel supported the trust.[63] Thus pew rents serviced or reduced the chapel debts, while the society through its class monies or otherwise met the preachers' allowances. If the pew rents failed to meet the expenses of the trust, and especially the interest upon debt, then the trust also must be supported by the society. Circuits which could not meet their obligations (the chief of which were the preachers' allowances) returned a deficiency to the District Meeting; and District Meetings which could not meet their deficiency returned it to Conference. Conferences in turn must meet the accumulated deficiency from the proceeds of the Yearly Collection, a fund apparently first opened for the temporary sustenance of Coke's Home Missions, but soon used as a milch cow by all the insolvent Districts in the connexion. If Conference could not meet the deficiencies, preachers whose circuits had defaulted on their allowances did not receive them at all. Unscrupulous circuits, discovering that they were not absolutely committed to their financial undertakings, would bid for preachers by offering ample allowances they intended to return as deficiencies for someone else to pay; unscrupulous preachers connived at circuits which cooked the books and avoided returning deficiencies by contracting illicit debts for their successors to discover and pay.[65] Savage deflation had destroyed the connexion's financial control and acutely raised the question of what the proper remuneration of a preacher was. Certainly the preachers compared their lot with that of their dissenting and Anglican brethren and steadily raised their financial and pastoral pretensions. From a Conference viewpoint the interests of the work of God and the professional interests of the ministry were in this crisis inseparable; neither could survive without the money of those who had it to give, without sacrifice on their own part, or without an absolute determination to enforce discipline on themselves and their people. In 1818 the preachers could see no way of meeting a deficit of £5,000 except by bearing it themselves, relinquishing claims to unpaid allowances for half the sum, and taking up the unsold publishing stock of the Book Room for the rest;[66] in 1819 they cut back recruiting; in 1820 they elected the first President who had not travelled with John Wesley, and the youngest ever, Thomas Coke excepted. But he was Jabez Bunting, the toughest and most iron-willed of their number.

It was now too that the preachers laid claim to the full dignity of the Pastoral Office which Wesley and some of his immediate successors had been so anxious to deny them,[67] and their ideal was subtly transformed from feeding and guiding to teaching and ruling. In 1818 Conference tacitly defied the Conference rule of 1793, adding the title of Rev. to the names of all the preachers on the Missionary Committee;[68] in 1819 ex-President Jonathan Edmondson announced his intention of writing 'a Treatise on the Pastoral Office, adapted to our circumstances as itinerants';[69] in 1820 Bunting created an uproar in Conference by proposing from the Presidential chair that the young preachers be received by imposition of hands.[70] On this point Bunting could not yet carry his brethren with him, but he gathered up the Conference conversation in the Liverpool Minutes which set forth so compelling a picture of the new ideal Methodist minister that Conference required them to be read annually at District, and later, circuit meetings, and by candidates for the ministry. Thus deeply did the Peterloo crisis and Bunting leave their mark, a mark appropriately engraved at the point where the body of the preachers made their transition from a genuine itinerancy to the sham, church-based itinerancy they have maintained ever since.

In his important study of the Wesleyan doctrine of the ministry Dr Bowmer maintains that the doctrine of the Pastoral Office was not 'devised to defend an otherwise intolerable situation'.[71] I have endeavoured respectfully to suggest the contrary by examining the situation itself. One last point is in order. As the storm broke the connexion was known to be precariously dependent on four districts which paid their way, produced a surplus on their Yearly Collection and gave up the whole of their profits on the book trade to assist other Districts. The four pillars of financial salvation were Liverpool, Manchester, Leeds and Halifax.[72] It was an unfortunate accident that these were the areas where the class war was hottest; but no accident that the radicals recognised a change in preachers contending not for order but for survival, for resources that disorderly Cornwall could never produce; no accident that Bunting, John Stephens, Richard Reece and the other toughs of the connexion migrated among the town circuits which were the core of those districts; no accident that in every one of those circuits there took place between 1825 and 1835 at least one of those great constitutional conflicts in which the high Wesleyan doctrine of the ministry was hammered out.

It has often been asked whether with greater personal elasticity the age of Bunting might have been spared the damaging separations with which it ended. Upon a broad view this seems a misplaced question. The social stresses which toppled the monarchies of the continent in the forties, in Britain divided the churches. The Church of England defeated as a national church in the 1790s lost relatively little, but the Church of Scotland was disrupted, the Old and New Methodist Connexions were broken, there were great losses among the Independents and Baptists. In a community where a weak state had for so long depended on informal networks of influence, it was the informal networks rather than the state which bore the brunt. Lacking both the concentration of authority which underpinned the German establishments, and the continuing role of their American brethren, the English churches suffered terribly. Marx was right in relating their struggles to a wider contest about authority, but betrayed by continental habits of mind into supposing that religion was epiphenomenon, for here it was near the heart of the matter. The highly pitched claims, the screwed-up courage incarnate in a man like Bunting, the deductive theologies designed to bind conscience, the newly-invented ethical scruples, were the characteristic outcome of excess pressure upon the informal networks, of the apparent inseparability of Gospel, ministry and public order. Of course the private sector could not bear the weight put upon it, and because it could not, there was no escaping that apple of historians' discord, the revolution in government, the development of those formal methods of central and social adjustment, which implied that England would never be so free or so disorderly again. The *Landeskirche* and the would-be *Volkskirchen* drew their battle, lost many of their functions to the state, and surreptitiously buried the doctrinal and ethical devices for anathematising out-groups and consolidating in-groups which they had employed against each other. The religion of the people, that undenominational evangelicalism which took root when the structure of authority cracked in the 1790s, survived impervious to the Pastoral Office and the Apostolic Succession alike, and constitutes most of what religion is left in the churches and outside. The victim of the débâcle was the empirical frame of mind in which that religion was born. If there is one thing odder than the attempt to unite two bodies of Christian people by reconciling the Pastoral Office with the Apostolic Succession, it is the recent attempt to represent Methodism as a sort of *philosophia perennis* welling up opportunely in a great church metaphysically conceived.[73] But this you may think is the last rant of an old Ranter.

Notes

1 R. Reece, *A compendious martyrology, containing an account of the sufferings and constancy of Christians in the different persecutions which have raged against them under pagan and popish governments*, London 1812–15, I, pp. iii–iv.

2 Margaret Batty, Contribution of local preachers to the life of the Wesleyan Methodist Church until 1932, and to the Methodist Church after 1932 in England, Leeds MA thesis 1969, pp. 39–40.

3 M[ethodist] C[hurch] A[rchives] MSS. Joseph Entwisle to Joseph Benson, 21 June 1802.

4 Despite confusion of terminology this is evidently what is referred to in a *Report from the clergy of a district in the diocese of Lincoln*, London 1800 pp. 11–12.

5 *The Journals of William Clowes*, London 1844 p. 59.

6 J.T. Wilkinson, *Hugh Bourne 1772–1852*, London 1952 p. 42.

7 Hartley-Victoria College, Manchester, MS Journals of Hugh Bourne F fol. 131.

8 *Ibid.*, fo. 121. The charge here was that they were actually *in* witchcraft.

9 Clowes, *Journals*, pp. 43–4.

10 Hartley-Victoria College, Manchester, MS Journals of Hugh Bourne E fol. 299.

11 Cf. R.A. Ingram, *The causes of the increase of Methodism and dissension*, London 1807 pp. 85–6.

12 T.P. Bunting, *The Life of Jabez Bunting*, London 1859–87 I, p. 115.

13 Leeds Central Library, John [should be Thomas] Wray's MS. History of Methodism in Leeds, x, fols. 145–7.

14 J. Nightingale, *Portraiture of Methodism*, London 1807 p. 266.

15 MCA MSS. Joseph Entwisle to George Marsden, 30 November 1802.

16 MCA MSS. Jabez Bunting to Richard Reece, 15 July 1803 (copy). Cf. same to same, 11 June 18[03]: same to George Marsden, 10 June 1803.

17 MCA MSS. W. Jenkins to Jabez Bunting, 29 January 1806.

18 Clowes, *Journals*, pp. 94–5.

19 MCA MSS. J. Barber to George Marsden, 7 February 1816. J. Braithwaite to B. Slater, 10 September 1816; W. Leach to Jabez Bunting, 20 January 1816; James Nichols to Jabez Bunting, 8 February 1816; R. Wood to Jabez Bunting, 9 March 1816; M. Wilson to Jabez Bunting, 17 March 1816; Hartley Victoria College, Manchester, James Everett's MS, Memoranda Book I, fol. 219.

20 MCA MSS. Miles Martindale to Jabez Bunting, 9 July 1816.

21 MCA Tyerman MSS III, fol. 355. Another account of the same events by the same writer was reprinted in the *Monthly Repository*, 1814, pp. 377–8 from a flysheet published at York.

22 MCA MSS. James Blackett to Jabez Bunting, 12 September 1828; W. Dale to same, 15 July 1842; same to same, 12 July 1839.

23 MCA MSS. John Mercer to Jabez Bunting, 14 March 1820.

24 MCA MSS. John Baker to Jabez Bunting, 16 June 1834.

25 MCA MSS. W. Dale to Jabez Bunting, 15 July 1842.

26 T. Shaw, *A history of Cornish Methodism*, Truro 1967 p. 81.

27 MCA Tyerman MSS, I, fols. 358–9.

28 *Ibid.*, I, fols. 362–3.

29 MCA MS. Copy of a circular sent by Mr Isaac to the Superintendents of circuits. December 1816.

30 MCA MSS. Joseph Entwisle to T. Stanley, 27 April 1812.

31 MCA Thomas Allan MSS. J. Stamp to T. Allan, [19 June 1813].

32 MCA MSS. Jabez Bunting to George Marsden, 28 January 1813.

33 MCA MSS. Jabez Bunting to George Marsden, 24 June 1815.

34 T. Jackson, *Recollections of my own life and times*, ed. B. Frankland, London 1873 pp. 171–9.

35 *Manchester Observer*, pp. 894–5. Cf. *A letter to the Rev. John Stephens occasioned by some recent transactions and occurrences in the Methodist Society in Manchester*, Manchester 1820.

36 J. Stephens, *The mutual relations, claims and duties of the rich and poor*, Manchester 1819.

37 For a case which has the ring of truth about it see, e.g. *Manchester Observer*, p. 1000.

38 MCA MSS. J. Hanwell to J. Everett, 15 October 1821. Cf. J. Hebblewhite to J. Everett, 15 March 1820.

39 MCA MSS. J. Edmondson to J. Crowther, 16 November 1819.

40 MCA MSS. H. & S. Kellett to T. Ingham, 24 February 1820.

41 PRO, H.O. 42.198 (1819) quoted in D.A. Gowland, Methodist secessions and social conflict in South Lancashire, 1830–57, Manchester PhD thesis 1966 p. 14; MCA MSS. J. Hebblewhite to J. Everett, 15 March 1820; Robert F. Wearmouth, *Methodism and the working-class movements of England 1800–1850*, London 1947 pp. 145–6; MCA Thomas Allan MSS. Thomas Allan to John Eliot, to Rev, Mr Collison, and to Lord Liverpool, all on 3 December 1819.

42 MCA MSS. J.B. Holroyd to Jabez Bunting, 23 December 1819. Cf. same to same, 26 January 1820. A similar letter to the first reached the Home Office. Wearmouth, *Methodism and working class movements*, pp. 146–7.

43 *Ibid.*, p. 168.

44 E.g. 'The lower orders of society . . . unless led on by men of talent, wealth, and fame, can never overthrow any government possessed of even a moderate share of strength': J. Macdonald, *Memoirs of Rev. Joseph Benson*, London 1822 p. 311.

45 MCA MSS. J. Stephens to Jabez Bunting, 1 February 1821. Cf. T. Jackson to same, 26 March 1821.

46 James Everett, *Adam Clarke portrayed*, London 1843–9, III, pp. 251–2.

47 MCA MSS. Joseph Entwisle to George Marsden, 2 March 1816.

48 MCA MSS. R. Miller to R. Reece, 11 July 1816; W. Worth to Jabez Bunting, 23 January 1818; R. Miller to T. Blanchard, 13 March 1819; same to Jabez Bunting, 1 April 1819 (2 letters); Jabez Bunting to Samuel Taylor, 10 March 1814; Miles Martindale to Jabez Bunting, 9 July 1816. Eventually Conference fixed the number of children circuits should support in proportion to the membership and arranged for any surplus to be maintained by a connexional Children's Fund. MCA MSS. James Akerman to Jabez Bunting, 31 July 1821.

49 Bunting, *Life of Bunting*, II, pp. 162–3: MCA MSS. J. Edmondson to J. Crowther, 16 November 1819; J.W. Cloake to Jabez Bunting, 29 March 1820.

50 MCA MSS. J. Sharp to Jabez Bunting, 20 April 1819.

51 MCA MSS. W. Myles to Joseph Dutton, 3 June 1814.

52 J. Crowther, *Thoughts upon the finances or temporal affairs of the Methodist connexion . . .* , Leeds 1817 pp. 24–5.

53 MCA MSS. Charles Atmore to George Marsden, 3 April 1818.

54 Bunting, *Life of Bunting*, II, p. 80; MCA MSS. W. Myles to Jabez Bunting, 5 June 1819.

55 MCA MSS. M. Martindale to Jabez Bunting, 9 July 1816.

56 MCA MS. Letters of Presidents of Wesleyan Methodist Conference, I, 1744–1838, fol. 58; J. Taylor to G. Marsden, 7 February 1811.

57 Alwyn D. Rees, *Life in a Welsh countryside*, Cardiff 1968 pp. 102–6.

58 There were independent reports of great losses to the Primitives in the villages because of dissatisfaction with the Wesleyan constitution, and 'the wish for a cheaper religion'. *Monthly Repository*, 1820, p. 168.

59 MCA MSS. W. Worth to Jabez Bunting, 23 January 1818.

60 Crowther, *Thoughts upon finances*, p. 12.

61 *Ibid.*, p. 11.

62 *Ibid.*, pp. 16, 29; MCA MSS. W. Myles to R. Blunt, 1 November 1813; J. Entwisle to Jabez Bunting, n.d. [before 18 December 1812]; T. Lessey Snr. to same, 6 May 1815.

63 MCA MSS. Jabez Bunting to I. Clayton, 14 July 1815.

64 MCA MSS. Samuel Taylor to Jabez Bunting, 22 July 1819.

65 MCA MSS. E. Hare to Jabez Bunting, 12 June 1810; Z. Taft to same, [7] May

1818; John Mercer to Jabez Bunting, 14 March 1820. Cf. W. Evans to same, 2 August 1820.

66 George Smith, *History of Wesleyan Methodism*, 4 edn., London 1866, III, p. 5.

67 *Ibid.*, III, p. 34.

68 *Ibid.*, III, p. 35.

69 MCA MSS. J. Edmondson to B. Slater, 11 November 1819.

70 MCA MSS. Conference Journal, 1820–1.

71 John C. Bowmer, 'Church and ministry in Wesleyan Methodism from the death of John Wesley to the death of Jabez Bunting', Leeds PhD thesis 1967 p. 304.

72 Crowther, *Thoughts upon finances*, p. 18.

73 R.E. Davis, *Methodism*, London 1963 p. 11.

15

Revival and Class Conflict in early nineteenth-century Britain

The case I wish to argue in this paper is that under the double pressure of long term structural difficulties, and a severe social crisis in the mid-nineties the old denominational order in England which received its legal organization in the Toleration Act collapsed; that it was succeeded by a great outpouring of undenominational religion, or as it was called at the time 'Catholic' Christianity, Christian unity 1790s' style. The crisis of 1795 was followed by a series of others, everyone of which was critical in the history of popular religion, crises in which class attitudes were hammered out and in which other forms of conflict flourished. The reaction of churchmen of the day was to push denominational loyalties in a wholly new way as a counterpoise to the savage divisions in the ranks, to hold together the in-groups by anathematising the out-groups. By 1830 the undenominational enterprise had been largely overlaid by a new denominational system which could not fail to generate more hostility than the old, precisely because the nature of its operation was to ease class conflict by converting it into denominational warfare. It was this denominational warfare which was the main substance of English politics in the thirties and forties; it was this which made the Catholic Christianity of the nineties incomprehensible to the following generation.

First to the long-term problems. In the second half of the eighteenth century the effectiveness of the churches throughout Western Europe was undermined by the same forces which were everywhere sapping the *ancien régime*, the whole institutional complex of which the religious establishments were part. Underlying everything else was the rapid increase in the population which put every institution of state and society under strain. The population increase bore directly upon church order, for inevitably it evoked attempts not simply to drive the traditional mechanism

First published in *Erweckung am Beginn des 19 Jahrhunderts*, ed. U. Gabler and P. Schramm, Amsterdam, 1986, pp. 87–104.

of the church harder, but to create new means of dealing with a new problem. Sunday schools were one of the plainest examples of this; they were springing up in the 1780s even before Raikes began his propaganda, and spread like wildfire afterwards. In the school histories one reads repeatedly how the founding fathers were distressed at evils which awaited the children let loose in the streets on the Sabbath. Of course there had always been urchins up to mischief on the Day of Rest, but now there were so many more of them; a simple increase in scale had changed the whole nature of the problem, and it was apparent to laymen that the traditional institutions for the religious and secular education of the young were quite unequal to the need.

The population explosion evoked another important modification of traditional church order, the regular practice of itinerant ministry. The continuous pressure under which the parish system was now having to operate ensured that an increasing number of ordinary folk would slip through the net of pastoral oversight. This kind of spiritual destitution formed a standing invitation to the zealots to go out into the high-ways and hedges and compel the lost to come in, especially where they suspected the parish ministry to be abnormally slack. There had, of course, been itinerant preaching before; what was new in the mid-1790s was that the organised itinerancy of the Methodists was providing a working model for systematic imitation. A connexional system and an itinerant ministry were as foreign to the traditional order of the dissenters as they were to the church, but, like the Sunday schools, they were touchstones in a ferocious struggle for power and policy in which the princes of the old dissenting world, the Unitarians and Quakers, were pushed to the fringes of the enterprise, while the old Independent and Baptist denominations were broken and reconstructed both institutionally and doctrinally.

At another level, revival itself suggests that there were long-standing religious difficulties in the old order, widely diffused fears for maintenance of that cycle of conviction of sin and finding assurance of salvation on which the survival of Protestantism as a working religion depended. This was not a local thing, it went right through the Protestant world. Beginning in Central Europe, a great whirligig of personal networks, literary influences and institutional relations between Germany, Britain and America established itself quite early in the eighteenth century, flinging off at a tangent the hot coals of evangelical sentiment as it went. The fortunes of these movements depended largely upon the balance of institutions locally. In Germany the Protestant establishments were tough enough to absorb evangelicalism in the end. In America the forces of social cohesion were everywhere weaker than in Europe; the Americans had to drive the machinery for reconstituting religious society much harder than it was ever driven by the English. The American informal establishment derived from its institutional weakness a power of absorption greater even than the formal establishments of Germany. Methodism and the benevolent system, Episcopalianism and eventually Roman Catholicism were taken on board, and made vehicles of American nationalism.

Strong by American standards, the English state was weak by the standards of the Continent, and the legal dependence of the Church upon the state disguised a real dependence of a weak state upon networks of informal influence which included those of the Church. The English state had been too weak to put down dissent, too weak to allow its clergy to play at politics in their Convocation, too weak to plant the Anglican establishment in the American colonies. But in the mid-nineties institutional stability fragile as it was, suffered a sharp and sudden blow. A subsistence crisis of European proportions, so severe that the Speenhamland magistrates adopted the extraordinary expedient of subsidising the wages of labourers actually in work, was given a wholly new political edge by the response of the urban radicals to sansculottism in France. The spectacular decline of the influence of the clergy was alarmingly manifest in their sudden inability to raise the Church-and-King mobs with which they had battered the liberal dissenters into political insignificance in the early nineties. A Church establishment entirely unequipped to meet the repercussions of the revolutionary crisis in France, had to face its moment of truth with no better state backing than the Episcopalians of colonial America, not because, as bewildered clergy perpetually insisted, there was a peculiar perfidy in Tory politicians, but because there was no German-style concentration of power on which they could draw. Methodism and evangelical dissent were transformed suddenly from revivals[1] into mass movements. As a working establishment the Church of England collapsed even quicker than that of France.

Intellectual solvents had been also at work upon the old denominational order, and none more so than the Enlightenment. Everyone knows that the evangelicals had sought to go behind the fashionable modernisms to older sources of theological inspiration, but in doing so they could not shed the large infusion of empiricism they had absorbed from the Enlightenment itself. Nothing seemed more incredible to them than the metaphysical approach to theology which had characterized the reformed divines of the seventeenth century, unless it was the reprobation controversy to which that approach seemed to have led. Listen to the *Evangelical Magazine*:[2]

    ... men must pay very little attention indeed to discriminating the proper provinces of speculation and faith, when, professing to learn revealed truth, they suffered themselves to be drawn into a metaphysical labyrinth. If the Arminian controversy shall ever be decided, it will be when, with respect to the abstruse doctrines of Scripture theologians shall follow the same method which natural philosophers have learnt to do with respect to mysterious phenomena in nature; when they shall admit them as ultimate facts and be willing to confess ignorance rather than by attempting to exhibit them in a light no less ridiculous than improper.

It was system, metaphysics, which seemed to account for the unhappy embarrassments of the past, and system became the prize theological swearword of the day. The upshot of the new empiricism was to suggest that there was little practical difference in the religious appeals of evangelicals of the different schools, and by the mid-nineties they were prepared to admit the fact.

To those who looked abroad the entrenched positions of the past seemed even more irrelevant. 'In the West', it was noted, 'the Roman Anti-Christ, accursed of God and man, is sinking under the reiterated strokes of the divine vengeance,' and beyond him stretched an endless missionary field, white with the harvest, and open to the reapers for the first time. The Methodists and Baptists early put in their sickle, and in 1795 the Independents, with a good deal of support from Methodists, Anglicans and others founded the London Missionary Society on an undenominational basis. In an astonishing way denominational distinctions crumbled, and national divisions too. Most of the local missionary societies now organized in Scotland became auxiliaries of the Society, while from Rotterdam and Basle, Zurich and East Friesland, Germany and Sweden, came letters of sympathy, liberal contributions and manpower. The way was open for the astonishing career of a man like Steinkopf, stumping England and the Continent, and linking the English evangelicals with his vast circle abroad in the common causes of the Missionary Society, the Religious Tract Society and the Bible Society, that great undenominational machine which established itself as the programme of Christian progress all the way from Basel and Hamburg to New York. At home the Religious Tract Society, the British and Foreign School Society, the Hibernian Society, an undenominational press took root in the same milieu. For twenty years from the mid-nineties, there was a chorus of congratulation that bigotry was dead, that Catholic Christianity was triumphant, that 'the Christian world now see more clearly than ever the followers of Christ did since the Apostolic age, the sin and folly of contending' over matters indifferent.

More important than the effusions of the public orators of the religious world, is the evidence that the undenominational principle was assuming institutional form, and doing so at the points of growth in the church order, the itinerancy and the Sunday Schools. In the South Midlands, particularly in John Newton's old circle at Olney and Newport Pagnell there had been a long tradition of cooperation between Anglican and dissenting evangelicals, and in the mid-nineties they took advantage of the interest in missions overseas to organise village preaching on an undenominational basis. These efforts, however, were much less systematic than those of the Methodists, and it was soon clear that a gospel ministry had not made even occasional contact with more than one village in three. But why should there not be an organised and united gospel ministry? This at least is what was launched in 1797 by the circle of Newport Pagnell and Olney under the name of the Bedfordshire Union of Christians. This Union formed of Independents and Baptists, Anglicans, Methodists and Moravians, quickly supplied an itinerant ministry to 100 villages and hamlets, many of them weekly, and laid the foundations of those Union congregations in Bedfordshire which lasted until the ecumenism of our own day forced them to make their choice of denomination.

How nearly the Bedford schemes met the mood of the moment was demonstrated by the speed with which they spread, or were begun quite independently on local initiative. Cambridgeshire had established its itinerancy in 1795, but in 1797 and 1798 the dykes burst; the Bedfordshire Union moved into Huntingdonshire, and county associations for promoting itinerant evangelism, mostly on an undenominational basis were set up in Warwickshire; in Hampshire, Dorset, Wiltshire and the West of England: in Surrey, West Kent, East Kent and Greenwich; while in Berkshire similar work was undertaken by an undenominational Evangelical Society in Reading which quickly established four new congregations. Worcestershire, Herefordshire and Westmorland followed suit; and in 1798 a Northern Evangelical Society was set up to carry the gospel into the villages of Durham, Northumberland, Cumberland and Westmorland. The undenominational itinerancies, in short, seem to have been established over most of the country except where Methodist itinerancy was in process of sweeping the board on its own.

All this was very like what had happened by a quite different route in the Sunday school movement, whose connection with the revival movement was rather late and in a sense rather accidental. For in the North and some other parts the Sunday school movement was a great triumph of municipal Christianity. The Manchester Sunday Schools were launched in 1784 by an address from the borough reeve and constables, and placed under a committee on which Churchmen, Dissenters and Roman Catholics all served. The town was divided into districts in each of which collectors received subscriptions on behalf of the town's committee; most of the rest of the funds came from collections at special sermons preached by all the clergy including Roman Catholics. This pattern of organization was drawn from the undenominational schools at Leeds, and when the committee came to prepare forms of worship, they printed the Leeds prayers, together with two forms drawn up by their Anglican secretary, the Rev. James Bennett, two more from Dr Barnes, the Unitarian minister at Cross Street, the Church catechism, and a selectionn of Watt's hymns. Committees of visitors of mixed denominational character were appointed to superintend the schools in each district. The success of the scheme was staggering. 2300 children were rapidly enrolled, a score of towns and districts in the neighbourhood at once adopted their own variations on the Manchester plan, and the town's committee was swamped with inquiries from all parts of the kingdom.

The heart of the Sunday school movement, however, was in the textile towns, for the textile industries offered such brisk employment for children, that the Sabbath afforded their one opportunity for instruction. The weakness of the day school tradition and the strength of the Sunday schools were head and tail of the same penny. And in a great number of the new schools there was a strong undenominational element. The greatest of them all, that at Stockport, began in 1784 in the same way as at Manchester. At Macclesfield, where Anglican evangelicals and Methodists enjoyed unusually close relations, the Stockport pattern was followed in 1796. In neighbouring villages like Bollington and Higher Hurdsfield, the Sunday school was the first religious institution in the place, and was perforce established upon the undenominational platform. The result is particularly instructive at Bollington where the first chapel and Sunday school were both created by Methodists. But the Sunday school existed as an institution before the chapel was built in 1808; and immediately afterwards, the new chapel buildings proving inadequate for the Sunday school, buildings were erected for the scholars on an undenominational basis. The active men in Bollington were almost all Wesleyans, the Sunday school was largely kept going by Wesleyan support, but it was not a Wesleyan body, and it later acted as an umbrella to all the movements of protest against the Wesleyan establishment in the village.

North of Manchester, the Hillock School at Middleton Junction, though mostly the work of Methodists, bore on its copingstone the familiar legend, 'a School for all denominations'. At Rochdale, the first Sunday school was begun by James Hamilton, a Methodist tin-plate worker, but the children were taken in turn to the parish church, St Mary's (Anglican) Chapel, and to the chapels of the Unitarians, Wesleyans and Baptists. In brief the Manchester system prevailed throughout a wide region of SE Lancashire, NE Cheshire and West Derbyshire; in Yorkshire the undenominational system seems to have been common, perhaps the rule; it was the same in the Potteries. With Sunday schools as with itinerancy, there were similar activities further south, and in London, where there were societies for raising funds, and producing literature. Nor was there any obscurity as to the substance of the undenominational religion which underpinned all this activity. The prospectuses of the reviews and the trust deeds of a host of Sunday schools summed it up in the XXXIX Articles, that Protestantism which down to this time had united laymen and clerk, and was now revitalized by evangelical sentiment. The religion of the Church of England was the common ground on which sects and parties wished to come together, and it is a measure of the alienation between Church and people which this period was to witness that the Church did more than anyone to break up the undenominational enterprise.

For the great crisis of the mid-nineties was unprecedented and very frightening. No sooner had urban radicalism been contained by repressive legislation, than the great tide of evangelicalism began to roll across the countryside. The difficulty, once church mobs became impossible to raise was to know what to do. In Manchester in 1795 church mobs were still sacking Unitarian property; in 1796 the clergy were complaining that two-thirds of the people never came near their services; by 1802 they were exerting the united force of the civil power and police but still the people would not come; by 1804 the clergy of the collegiate church were complaining bitterly that their influence had been lost to the conventicles. Some rural areas were no better. The Bishop of Lincoln appointed a group of clergy to report on what had gone wrong in his diocese, and in 1800 their report gave a gloomy picture of the collapse of the parish ministry, with more than two thirds of the people never coming near the church.

The Lincolnshire clergy, observing the speed at which the water was pouring from the tub could only conclude that evilly-disposed persons, especially Methodists, had removed the plug, a charge to which the latter had no difficulty in pleading not guilty. R.A. Ingram, rector of Segrave, Leicestershire, had the wisdom to perceive that what was happening was a far-reaching social crisis exploited but not created by the evangelicals. The trouble was that the delicate mechanisms by which deference had been maintained had been suddenly subjected to much greater strain than they would bear. As he saw it the rapid rise of commercial wealth had weakened the hold of old families who had supported the proper influence of the clergy, and had created new forms of dependence which did not operate on a parochial basis. Thousands of outworkers depended on master tradesmen who lived miles away; many of them had no settlement, and so owed no dependence even for poor relief. And the whole question had been focused with fearful clarity by the radical development of the French

Revolution. It was to this great cataclysm that Dissenters ascribed the collapse of popular complaisance towards the establishment, the assertion of a right of private judgement in religion and a willingness to hear and follow Methodist or dissenting preachers. It was a subsistence crisis with a wholly new political edge which drew the itinerants in squadrons into the countryside, and led to what Ingram candidly admitted to be 'the dismemberment of the national church'. There never had been, and the Toleration Act had certainly never contemplated, such an organised attempt to cut through the bonds of deference as the great upsurge of itinerant preaching which began in 1797. The preachers of the Bedfordshire Union might 'particularly pray for the King, for Magistrates and the minister of the parish' in the villages they invaded, but they were plainly severing the traditional links between the upper and the lower orders at a time when everything else seemed to be conspiring in the same direction.

To all this churchmen replied theologically with a high churchmanship of a quite new stiffness and politically with a great howl against the political hazards of itinerancy, a howl which reached a climax in the famous charge of Bishop Horsley to the clergy of Rochester in 1800, and which was designed to replace the broken weapon of brute force with legal authority to act. Itinerancy by Anglican evangelicals not unnaturally ceased, and in the winter of 1799–1800 Pitt's government came to the point of action; in a portmanteau measure to suppress private meetings, political discussion and conspiracy, they proposed to put the brake on itinerant preaching, the licensing of conventicles and Sunday schools. Another bill was got up by Michael Angelo Taylor, MP for Durham. It turned out that with opposition from Wilberforce and differences within the government, neither of these bills got into the house. Moreover the crisis for the itinerants coincided to the week with that of the Union with Ireland, and Pitt could not easily ask for toleration to be extended to Catholics and restricted to Protestant dissent. Methodists and dissenters had no option but to set up formal organisations in self-defence, organisations which swung into immediate and triumphant action against Lord Sidmouth's bill to restrict itinerancy in 1811. Social conflict was forcing a new denominational organisation into being, and also giving a further twist to evangelical pietism. The itinerants were under the strongest pressure to disavow any political object, in order to retain their basic rights of prayer and preaching.

The clash which came over itinerancy can be followed in some detail in the Sunday schools. Combined action on the Manchester pattern depended, as everyone understood, on avoiding denominational imperialism. But as social schism opened in 1795, children of the lower classes poured into the non-Anglican and especially the Wesleyan schools. The fact that there was an influential and vocal dislike of the schools in Wesleyanism, did not prevent bitter Anglican charges of sheep-stealing nor a concerted agitation against the political hazards of the schools. Finally in 1799 and 1800 when Pitt was preparing legislation, two of the leading Anglican clergy in Manchester withdrew their financial support from the town's committee and then broke it up. The clergy took a proportion of the joint property and established a new committee under their sole control.

Once the Anglicans had gone, it was more difficult to appeal to the general public for funds, and for financial reasons alone the ties between the schools and particular congregations were bound to grow stronger. The Wesleyans were now so much the dominant party amongst the remnant that they virtually cornered the system, and in due course laid hands for denominational purposes on school property to which they had little claim. The same cycle of events occurred in Yorkshire, starting in Leeds in 1805 and going right through the county in the next decade; here the signal for separation was very often that the clergy insisted upon enforcing the Book of Common Prayer. Yet no county illustrated more fully than Yorkshire the flimsiness of points of church order. Decency might be saved but the price was commonly the loss of the whole school.

In Stockport the same combination of forces produced a somewhat different result. As in Manchester, the Town's Committee ran into difficulties in the mid-nineties, when the school associated with the Wesleyan Chapel in Hillgate suddenly outstripped all the others in size, but did not qualify for more than a sixth of the funds collected for the six schools in the town. Driven to seek its own financial resources the school became in fact a Methodist school. But the astonishing growth of the school ensured that this was not the end of the story. The Wesleyan trustees never did anything corporately for the Sunday School, their premises speedily became inadequate for the throngs of children, and the school committee was burdened with the immense expense of renting cottages and other unsuitable accommodation for their 2,000 children. One of the moving spirits in Stockport, however, Matthew Mayer, a Wesleyan of apostolic labours, and great business acumen, was the very embodiment of undenominational evangelicalism. He realised that it would be much easier to raise a large capital endowment for building than to keep up the annual subscriptions for rents, as well as enormously increasing the efficiency of their work. So it came about that the amazing building which till lately stood on the brow of the hill in Stockport was erected in 1805, and that in order to raise the building fund, the Sunday school appealed to the whole town upon an undenominational basis, claiming in substance to have superseded the decayed relics of the town's committee system. Within a generation the Stockport school had become the largest in the world, educating no fewer than 6000 children; its surplus of home-produced teachers was launching

one Sunday school after another, a process which vividly illuminates the
mechanics of the evangelical revival as a whole; and the school's fascinating
role as an educational publisher and pioneer became a subject in itself – it
was the Sunday school which established the first technical education in
the town, and at one stage supported its own chemistry laboratories.

In Manchester the Church challenged the undenominational principle
when it seemed to be getting out of hand; in Stockport it was the Wesleyan
Conference. No sooner had the school got into its new building, than they
began to cast around for preachers for their charity sermon. The Sunday
school committee could not understand why Bradburn, Bunting, Benson
and other Wesleyan stars who had the greatest drawing power in Stockport
all declined their invitations, and they finally discovered that Conference
was imposing economic sanctions to stop the school escaping from their
orbit. Conference's terms were that no preachers should be heard in the
school other than Anglican and Methodist, and not more than one of the
former to three of the latter. This impertinent blockade was no more
successful than the Warrenite attempt to cut off supplies to Conference a
generation later, but it excluded Methodist preachers from the school for
many years. Their next step was to organise rival schools, and the final
upshot was not that the denominations dismantled the undenominational
system as in Manchester, but that they tried to turn it into a denomination
on its own.

In the next generation this conflict was repeated, not between Methodism
and the Church, but within Methodism itself. At the crucial time in the
mid-nineties relations between the two were discussed in terms of the right
of Methodists to receive communion from their own preachers. The official
story has always been that Methodist pietism demanded surer guarantees
of godliness in the officiating minister than Anglican discipline could
provide. There was, however, more than simple pietism in the case; in their
private correspondence the preachers associated the whole business with
the torrent of opinion away from the establishment, and confessed candidly
that if they did not follow the torrent they would lose the people.
Particularly in the mind of Samuel Bradburn, the issue between the
Methodist people on the march and the trustees who were supporting the
Church connection was the local aspect of the great divide which was
opening in English life between the establishment and the rest:[3]

> I am persuaded that the contest is only like Fox and Pit(t). It is not who
> shall do the preachers most good, or who shall serve the people most,
> but who shall have the power to do their own will.

> *Unbounded liberty*, founded upon the *Rights of Man*, in all matters
> consistent with decorum and our main design to save souls (is our object).

Vox populi should be our motto. The *Leaders, not Trustees*, are the representatives of the people. I would sooner lose the whole premises belonging to the New Chapel, than submit to be governed by that tyrannical aristocratic faction.

More political language about the Eucharist is not easy to imagine. Nevertheless with radical reconstruction Wesleyanism survived the troubles of the nineties, and came through a testing time with the Ranters in the following decade.

The rise of Luddism, however, posed inescapably the question whether Methodism could any longer contain social discontent within itself or within society, and showed how the preachers had changed their social alignment since the nineties. It was Bunting's fate to be stationed at Halifax in the heart of the West Riding troubles; and so tough was his line with Methodists who took part that his life was in jeopardy, and for months on end he could not go out alone at night. His final verdict is very interesting:[4]

The progress of Methodism in the West Riding of Yorkshire has been more swift than solid; more extensive than deep; more in the increase of numbers than in the diffusion of that kind of piety which shines as brightly . . . *at home* as in the prayer meeting and the crowded love feast. I read of no people professing serious religion who have not as a body far outstripped us in that branch of practical godliness which consists in the social management and discipline of children.

How this was to be provided was revealed as Manchester moved towards the disaster of Peterloo. John Stephens, the superintendent minister, with his little knot of prosperous supporters, enforced stern discipline in the leaders' meeting, hunted down the radicals, preached against disaffection and removed 400 members from the roll. In reply the radical *Manchester Observer* flayed Wesleyan discipline weekly for two years after Peterloo with a bitterness that has to be read to be believed. On Tyneside there were even wilder episodes. The itinerant ministry which only yesterday had been a device for retrieving the lost and compelling them to come in was now a principle of exclusion; it was being used to enforce a denominational line, and to drive the dissidents, in the current phrase, to the devil or the New Connexion. Of course there was a case to be put for the connexional leadership. Neither the New Connexion nor the sects which championed the radical cause were able to capitalise their opportunity. A generation later the Chartists were to find that they had a hard core of leaders and organisers; a considerable and potentially stable body of the second rank who were prepared to play supporting parts and who enjoyed the fellowship of the movement; and a vast mass who were swept in and out of the movement in response to the trade cycle and whom it was impossible to organise for long. In effect Bunting and his coadjutors were acknowledging that this was already true of Wesleyanism, and were welding the first two groups into a denomination at the cost, perhaps on a certain level of realism, the small cost, of writing off the third, that great mass which had poured into the chapels and Sunday schools since the mid-nineties.

It was the Sunday schools which revealed most clearly what was going on, the problem being precisely that they embodied the religion of the nation rather than the denomination. At Peterloo the Anglican schools to satisfy their wealthy subscribers, came out fiercely against the radicals and resolved to exclude all children wearing drab hats and other political emblems. The Wesleyan quarterly meeting in Manchester followed suit at once and resolved to expel any teacher wearing a political emblem, and to refuse admission to children expelled from other schools. What is significant here is that the Quarterly Meeting was trying to exert a control over undenominational schools to which it had no right at all, and that under this pressure the radicals made an effort to capture the undenominational tradition for themselves. Under the wing of a schismatic group of Swedenborgians called Bible Christians they launched a successful Union (or undenominational) Sunday School.

This episode, following that at Stockport, was a sharp warning to the Methodist Conference to look to their guns. Conference responded by legislation confining Wesleyan schools to religious instruction, subjecting them to ministerial control, and finally in 1826, inviting the ministers to use the power of the purse to get control of the undenominational schools. In Manchester under Bunting's leadership they did this with considerable adroitness, establishing their own control and the exclusive use of the Wesleyan catechism. But the real problem was in the schools at Leeds, the lively spirit of democracy in the teachers' meetings where policy was settled in the absence of the minister; if leaders or local preachers who were also teachers carried this spirit into the Societies there would be an end to the preachers' claim to ministerial status:

> 'Several of them' the Conference historian records,[5] 'were known among their companions by the names of the principal members of the opposition in the House of Commons. One was called Lord John Russell; another was known as Mr Hume; a third, as Mr Grey Bennett. As these and other persons were active in fomenting discord, and promoting unmethodistic proceedings, it supposed that it would take place in the Sunday schools; where most of the mischief had been engendered;

and although trouble in 1827 broke out over the celebrated organ in Leeds Brunswick chapel, it did in fact involve a desperate struggle for the physical control of the Sunday school. In this contest, Bunting, acting with doubtful legality, secured a victory for the high Wesleyan doctrine of the ministry at the cost of 1000 members and the organisation of a secession connection, the Leeds Protestant Methodists. Socially and institutionally the Leeds clash set the pattern of the future. When serious trouble was raised in the connection in 1835 by Dr Warren and his friends, the real damage was done below the level of church membership, and has never been recorded. Huge Sunday schools decamped lock stock and barrel, four in Manchester, others in Rochdale, Moston, Bury, Bolton, Burslem, Blackburn, Chester and Newcastle upon Tyne. As vividly as in the nineties Sunday school secessions showed the separation of a broad public from the church – but this time it was Wesleyan Methodism. Nor was this the end. When the Wesleyan reform secessions began in 1849 it was the turn of the country causes. The MS Minutes of the Norwich & Lynn district Meeting of 1850 bewail the loss of 4000 out of 10,000 members and no fewer than twenty-eight Sunday schools.

Thus when religious revival was crossed with class conflict in a social context of weak public authority and moderately strong social rigidities, the result was intense assertion of ministerial power and the deplorable denominational warfare of the thirties and forties which has coloured the whole church history of Great Britain since. The social stresses which toppled the monarchies of the Continent in the forties, in Britain fell upon the informal networks and divided the Churches, dividing most violently the connexionally organized churches. The Church of England, defeated as a national church in the 1790s lost relatively little, but the Church of Scotland was disrupted, the Old and New Methodist Connexions were broken, and never regained their expansiveness, there were great losses among the Independents and Baptists. Lacking both the concentration of authority which underpinned the German establishments, and the civilising role of the American brethren, the English churches suffered terribly. Marx was right in relating their struggles to a wider context about authority, but betrayed by Continental habits of mind into supposing that religion was epiphenomenon, for here it was near the heart of the matter. Of course the private sector could not bear the weight upon it and because it could not, there was no escaping that favourite chestnut of the historians, the revolution in government, which implied that England would never be so free or so disorderly again.

Notes

1 For more evidence and full documentation see my book, *Religion and Society in England, 1790–1850*, London, 1972.
2 *Evangelical Magazine* 2. 458.
3 Methodist Church Archives (John Rylands University Library, Manchester) S. Bradburn to R. Rodda, 7 Dec. 1791; 19 April, 23 June, 1792: Tyerman MSS 1. fos. 130–1, 134–5.
4 Methodist Church Archives. Jabez Bunting to George Marsden, 28 January 1813.
5 George Smith, *History of Wesleyan Methodism* vol. 3, 4th edn., London, 1866 p. 113.

Part Four

Christianity and Society

16

The Way of the World. The Rise and Decline of Protestant Social Christianity in Britain

The social problems created by industrialisation were no respecters of national or denominational boundaries. Despite the different rhythm of the industrialising process from one country to another; despite differences in political organisation which affected the ways men dealt with their problems; despite extraordinary variations in theological fashion and the structure of church life, there is a curious parallelism in the ways churchmen looked at social problems in Western Europe and America. By the generation before the First World War, Catholic and Protestant, liberal, orthodox and pietistic evangelical, German, French, British and American, were attempting to construct a social Christianity, to preach a gospel which was corporate as well as individual, secular as well as religious; they were already bringing about important changes in the machinery of their churches, and the relations of church and state; they displayed a self-confidence which now seems astonishing, and an ignorance of the process they were dealing with has perhaps never been dispelled but is now more palpable; they had already created what was to be one of the most important bases for co-operation among the churches between the two World Wars, but had still little sense of the distance which now separated them from the levers of economic power; and, despite much study and a huge volume of publication, they had not made clear what sort of intellectual or spiritual processes underlay Christian social teaching. In 1918 Protestants, especially in Germany, were bitterly divided whether the social reference of Christianity implied revolution, reform or conservatism; two generations later when there is an oppressive sense of the universality of the social problem, these differences have become universalized. Ecumenism has not reconciled the differences, but only provided additional institutions and wider horizons within which they can be contested.

Within a single paper no more than the salient features of this process

First published in *Kirchliche Zeitgeschichte* 1 (1988), pp. 293–305.

can be sketched out; what have often been believed to be associated questions, the churches' loss of pastoral influence, the rise of religious or atheistic dissent, and so forth must be set aside. There is, however, some advantage in seeking a bird's-eye view from an English standpoint, for if English society was overrun by religious dissent to an unusual degree between about 1780 and 1900, the effort to create a social Christianity was not distorted by the political challenge of an organized Marxism. Equally the separation of the church establishment from the world of labour had mostly taken place before the Industrial Revolution began, and hence social Christianity was less likely to be confused with evangelism. The prestige of British economic development also gave peculiar resonance to the churches' role in it. Theodor Fliedner came to England to visit Elizabeth Fry, the Quaker prison reformer, and Thomas Chalmers' schemes for model parish organisation in Scotland were well known in Germany; Victor-Aimée Huber and Theodor Lohmann were impressed by British co-operatives and friendly societies; Max Weber in his *Protestant Ethic and the Spirit of Capitalism* had the curious illusion that he was laying bare the springs of British power. In the nineteenth century British and American religion diverged; but the running in America was still made mostly by churches of British derivation and the result of their close remaining links was that many of the voluntary institutions of the British religious world attained their fullest development in America, and received in turn the impress of American know-how, energy and emotional extremism.

The distinction made by nineteenth-century German commentators between natural and artificial poverty, indicates at least that poverty could take more than one form, and the response of the English churches to industrial development is not to be understood without some reference to the problem of poverty in the pre-industrial world. The social pyramid in eighteenth-century England, though very steep in terms of incomes, was very flat in terms of numbers above the base. At the end of the century it was reckoned, indeed, that about one-eighth of the population, paupers, criminals and the rest, were really below the base, and 'presumed to live chiefly or wholly upon the labours of others'. Of the remainder, almost two-thirds were members of the next rank above, lesser freeholders, shopkeepers, publicans and so forth. In all the societies of the *ancien régime* the problem of poverty was twofold, how to cope with the submerged population who were never economically viable (in England this was a matter for the Poor Law operated on a parish basis and in various ways using the machinery of the Church), and how to mount a rescue operation in times of real dearth. For the shorter-term movements of the trade cycle were still dependent on the harvest; a shortfall in the harvest directly reduced all that industrial employment which consisted in processing the harvest – threshing, milling, baking, brewing, tanning and all the rest, and by driving food prices to famine levels mopped up the purchasing power normally attracted by popular textiles, and produced unemployment in this industrial sector too. In these dark times great numbers of the two huge classes at the base of the social pyramid might be thrust into the morass beneath, magnifying the problem of public order and of destitution out of all recognition. To solve this problem the societies of the old order had no adequate resources. Francis Place, a self-confident English radical of the early nineteenth century, describes how he was perennially plagued by dreams of 'hanging from a second-floor window by my hands, scarcely able to hold on, and always with iron spikes beneath me'; his nightmare was the nightmare of all. English society differed from that of the rest of Western Europe in the eighteenth century not in kind but in degree; it had a larger landless rural population with little defence against high food prices than the rest; a larger proportion of its labour force had become unwilling or unable to accept anything but wheaten bread; the central machinery of state was much weaker than in France or Germany; and the tradition of *laisser-faire* had gone much further. Moreover, although the commercialisation of British agriculture had enabled the long-term increase in the population to be fed down to 1750, it could not, despite a remarkable effort, cope with the vast increase that then began; in a relatively short time Britain was transformed from a normal exporter to a normal importer of foodstuffs, and the problem of survival in hard times was transformed from one of food distribution to one of wages. In Britain as in most other places the food market had hitherto been inevitably for the most part limited and local, the law had capitalized upon popular hostility to middlemen, and magistrates had powers to prevent the hoarding of food and to compel its sale at fair prices. It now seems that even in England this authority was more often exercised in the bad years of the eighteenth century than was formerly thought, and it was this which constituted the 'moral economy' to which the working class appealed. In the years of high prices it was normal for the mob to come out and pit its numbers against the movement of prices on the free market, forcibly auctioning food at 'fair' prices, and particularly common in the second half of the eighteenth century when the whole national food supply was in a state of precarious balance, and in the north and west of the country outside the main wheat-growing areas. The mob was a respectable institution which sometimes enjoyed the sympathy of clergy and magistrates.

This 'moral economy' has been an object of recurrent admiration ever since its demise to those who have opposed economic individualism on Christian or other grounds, but it was a notoriously harsh system, and even before the great population explosion of the second half of the eighteenth century, it was a system which could solve neither its problem of endemic poverty, nor its problem of recurrent dearth, by any exercise of policy. It was a conventional Christian obligation to assist with the former, and a matter of self-interest to keep the ill consequences of the latter within bounds. It was improvements in agricultural technology and organisation which preserved England from Malthusian population crises, and a willingness to turn to exceptional and half-forgotten measures which got her through critical years like 1709 and 1795, the troubles of which she shared with the rest of the Continent, and which were of a gravity only less serious than famine itself.

Moreover, particularly from the standpoint of conservative churchmen, the 'moral economy' had an important legacy right into the period of full industrial development. With the introduction of the Speenhamland system in 1795 there came an extraordinary development in the Poor Law. By this system the wages of labourers actually in work were made up to a subsistence level, calculated in relation to the price of food and to the number of children in the family, and, after the Napoleonic wars, when the emergence of what might now be called a 'corn mountain' over much of Europe produced threats of food dumping, a protective Corn Law was obtained by which the agricultural interest hoped to shield itself from the worst effects of collapsing prices. On two fronts therefore a gesture was made towards the traditional manipulation of family incomes and prices to enable the countryside to maintain its population. Already, however, the 'moral' force of the system was less in evidence, for the wild agitations of the agricultural industry to reduce its overheads in a time of falling prices were assisted by a general change of attitude towards poor relief; swollen poor rates had been accepted during the war as a device for protecting the poor against the traditional calamity of food prices at famine level, but were resisted when transformed into unemployment relief or ease to the agricultural wages fund. To the advocates of a classical political economy the clamours of farmers and landlords for both protection and a reduction in the poor rate seemed a denial of justice as well as sound policy; and the combined effect of the new Poor Law of 1834 and the repeal of the Corn Laws in 1845 was to expose the agricultural sector of the economy to the full play of market forces, and to use both the carrot and the stick to get the surplus population off the land. The emotional furore generated by these triumphs of the market is, however, a measure of the revulsion felt by many ordinary people and not a few of their clergy at the triumph of the cash nexus over inherited conceptions of justice.

By this time, too, a conservative and Christian social philosophy was in being which carried important practical implications. In the England of the 1820s, as in Restoration Prussia, conservative social analysis was offered as an explicit alternative to political reform. On the conservative view of the matter, the upper and lower orders of society were related to each other as members of an organism and should accept their mutual obligations. In this process of acceptance the church had a crucial role. Apart from the sanctions of religion there seemed no reason why the lower orders should accept the hardships of their lot, and it was quite certain that apart from Christianity the upper orders would not display that altruistic concern for the welfare of the lower without which the old order clearly could not survive. The rapid growth of the towns was a particular menace; their economic dynamism, materialism and dissent were equal affronts to the conservative philosophy, and their very existence seemed destructive to that network of personal relationships which alone could prevent the degeneration of the old English mob into the probably ungovernable new English masses. This view which closely resembled the conservative Christian social philosophy, as it came to be developed in many parts of Europe, did not explain why the most frightening aspect of the reform crisis which engulfed Church and state between 1830 and 1832, came not in the towns, but in the farm labourers' revolt in the south-eastern counties, a revolt which was often directed against the clergy and the lay impropriators, and which sealed the fate of the immemorial system of supporting the clergy by tithe. Nevertheless it underlay a number of attempts to patch up the social body from the top downwards, and to reopen the possibility of a popular role for the church establishment. Of these the only one which needs mention here is Tory Radicalism, which from one point of view represented an attempt to adapt the moral economy to new circumstances.

In 1833 Lord Ashley, the future earl of Shaftesbury, took over the leadership of the Factory Movement. Not yet an evangelical, and much under the influence of the conservative theorising of Robert Southey, he seems to have been motivated by intense hatred of mill owners, those conspicuous successes of the Industrial Revolution, of whom he knew little, but whom he understood to be the principal menace to social order. A campaign with the millhands of Yorkshire and Lancashire against capitalist employers might restore the political influence of the gentry in new circumstances, and as there was considerable support for the Ten Hours agitation among Anglican clergy especially in Yorkshire, the Factory Movement might lead to the political isolation of religious dissent. The failure of the Tory radical movement is instructive. For Ashley found already, as did Adolf Stöcker in Germany in the 1890s, that none of the parties would fulfil the role allotted to it in the conservative ideology. Ashley was always complaining that the clergy, from the bishops in the House of Lords to parish priests, did not pull their weight; indeed their support did not reach its peak until the bill was on the threshold of success in 1847, by which time industrial recession had brought short-time working in so many mills that the mill owners themselves were accepting the bill. In Lancashire especially, dissenters and even Catholic priests provided the local leadership of the movement to a quite provoking degree. The southern gentry would not follow Ashley, and many of the northern workers who did, did so from class-conscious motives. Moreover if the bishops were lukewarm, the Tory government of 1841, headed by Peel and Graham, two devotees of political economy, was hostile. It had no room for Ashley, set him down as a dangerous demagogue and effected the ruin of the Tory radical programme. These failures stemmed from various sources. The Church itself had profited too greatly from the commercialisation of agriculture to be an enthusiastic or even credible supporter of the moral economy in any form; the attempt to uphold public order against radical ideas and a subsistence crisis during the period of the French Revolution had pushed English society in the direction of class stratification; and even a conservative government was now possessed of another style of economic management, also of eighteenth-century origin, created by the political economists.

Even for the eighteenth-century corn market, Adam Smith and his predecessors had offered an alternative model to that of the regulated economy. The theory was that in a free market the common good would be established. Small farmers with harvest wages and Michaelmas rents to pay would sell at relatively low prices after the harvest; the middling farmers would hold out till early spring, and the big men would hope to get the best price in the summer before the next harvest ripened. In Adam Smith's time there were in fact many areas of the country where there was no market mechanism of this kind, and during the Revolutionary and Napoleonic Wars it was not always possible for soaring prices to act as a signal for imports from abroad as he had assumed; nevertheless the growth of a national market in foodstuffs in the second half of the eighteenth century is unmistakable, and one of the compelling reasons for Peel's decision to repeal the Corn Laws in 1845 was the belief that the secure feeding of the urban areas of Western Europe now depended on enlarging the granaries of Eastern Europe and the Ukraine, and that this could only be achieved by extending the mechanism of the international grain market. The very motive which had once told in favour of paternal regulation now told against it. By the same token the social conflict which had formerly taken place over the supply of food now took place over wage levels and other matters on which the old moral economy gave less precise guidance. And of course the hope now was that the market mechanism, by breaking the fetters which bound the output of the old economy, would end the endemic poverty that economy had been unable to cure, and circumvent the dearths which must occur in every local market from time to time. This might also cut at the roots of the cyclical crises of the old kind. Pleonexia itself might have a moral appearance.

The effect of the gradual triumph of the free market economy over that of the conservative vision was to increase the confusion of the Christian social response to the new developments. It intensified an intellectual difficulty. Innumerable evangelicals were equally possessed of a personal Christian ethic of love and a highly impersonal classical market economics; individuals and those executing church discipline in congregations can be shown trying to hold the two together, but there was never any satisfactory theory explaining how it was to be done. There had always been objections to cumbering a weak state with functions it could not perform – and in no sphere more conspicuously than the criminal law – but now there seemed often to be objections in principle to using the state at all, objections which rubbed off upon the state church, which seemed to be as expensive, as unadaptable to changes in social need, and as full of jobbery as the state itself. After the Reform Bill Bishop Blomfield set out to prove the usefulness of the Church by a great programme of church and school building, but he never won parliamentary approval for the resumption of grants of money for specifically church purposes; and unhappily the church building let loose some of the worst conflicts of the century over church rates, while education became a running sore at both parliamentary and parish level. The way to bring religion to bear on many social problems seemed to be by private association, and associations became the rage. Circumstances old and new conspired also to obscure what was involved in the transition from charity to policy. France Place's nightmare of falling through the base of the social pyramid on to the iron spikes beneath, might suggest that religion itself was the best contribution to social welfare, fortifying those at risk against the hazards of intemperance, incontinence and extravagance, and perhaps enabling them to sleep sounder at nights. In a market economy economic failure was more likely to seem the result of moral or spiritual failure than in the old economy where in the best of times one-eighth of the population was not economically viable. Hence the feature of the Victorian debate which is most alien to modern prejudice – the intimate connection of moral and social reform; hence also the vast plethora of interlocking societies for the pursuit of humanitarian aims, temperance and sexual purity; and hence also their ambivalent attitude towards state intervention. Not merely was social reform on this view a largely moral thing, it was intimately connected with the fight against poverty and in favour of civilising and dignifying influences. The Charity Organisation Society which attempted to apply business principles to the relief of poverty was linked by innumerable personal connections with most of the moral reform organisations, which in their turn included the attack on poverty in their programme. For many, the prevention of cruelty to animals, sabbath observance and Sunday closing of public houses went together; for others, women's suffrage, women's temperance and opposition to the Contagious Diseases Acts were inseparable. The dignity of women, drunkards, prostitutes and animals, to none of whom had the old order extended much formal protection, was now perceived as a major concern; without these the campaign against poverty would fail, or at least turn to ashes at the moment of success. Marx condemned the whole attitude as 'false consciousness' and might himself have been condemned by it in similar terms; the dialogue with Marxism is not the sole function of political theology. One of the advantages of the battery of good-works societies was that it enabled bridges to be built across some of the chasms in English society – here evangelical and utilitarian could work together or men and women, there Anglican and dissenter or Liberal and Tory. One of the disadvantages was that no general discussion was likely of the role of the state in social reform. Sabbatarians were as interventionist as factory reformers, the protectors of children or the old anti-slavery men had been; and the upshot was that violent mass anti-sabbatarianism became the English counterpart to organized revolutionary atheism on the Continent. Josephine Butler, on the other hand, would not have prostitution licensed and disinfected. She wrote that the Contagious Diseases Acts which sought to limit the transmission of venereal disease, necessitated 'the greatest crime of which earth can be witness', the 'depriving God's creatures of freewill, of choice and of responsibility'.

The curious fragmentation of social reform in mid-Victorian England affords one clue to one of the missing factors in the concern of the English churches with the problems of an industrial society. Like its counterparts in France and in Wichern's Protestant Germany, Christian social concern in England was evoked by the emergence of very unpalatable new social relations; but whereas French conservatism developed into *intégrisme*, the demand for an 'integral Christianity' in the double sense of a closely interlocked doctrinal system in which every part supported every other, and which attempted to interpret not merely the church but the world, the Protestant *intégrisme* which developed in Germany in men like Adolf Stöcker did not appear here. The doctrinal systems which might most readily have served this purpose – those based on the Westminster Confession – had no credit in the establishment, and in the world of dissent had been driven into holes and corners by the new pietistic evangelicals. Coleridge who had talked endlessly of a grand framework of interpretation had failed to produce one. The Tractarian champions of a full Catholic programme had little appreciation of the social problems of their day, and were in any case forced into opposition within the national church. It was indeed a post-Tractarian, H.P. Liddon, who, on the theological side, best fulfilled the requirements of an English *intégrisme*, but he not only held no church office which might have led him to link his theology with some pressing practical problem, but was brought by the curious infighting within the High Church party to attach himself personally to Gladstone and the politics of liberalism. When his own pupils and junior colleagues began to seek an inductive basis for their theology, and in the eighties to take up with Christian Socialism, Liddon protested bitterly against betrayal. A situation in which a deductive systematic theology could not achieve a social doctrine, when a revived empiricism could, was one in which there would be no *intégrisme*. No one was trying to make a 'system' work, whether intellectually in the perception of social issues, or institutionally in church and state.

In the 1840s the social strains which on the continent produced revolution, in England produced religious schism, but the result on both sides of the Channel was the first real flowering of social Christianity. It was characteristic of the English situation that the Christian Socialism of Maurice and Ludlow envisaged not so much a welfare state as a welfare church; characteristic that it was peculiarly difficult to harness the French revolutionary tradition to a social programme, for while Ludlow in the French manner was organising his band of brothers to await the outbreak of revolution in London, the social revolution was being wrought out in the North; it was characteristic too that the Christian Socialists' producer-co-operatives were speedily outstripped by consumer co-operatives created by working men for themselves and realistically centred upon Manchester. Maurice's outlook, which was important for the next generation of Christian Socialists, was closely related to that of Coleridge. He craved for wholeness of vision, was so concerned to hold together the insights of opposed views as to be almost pathologically unwilling to throw in his lot with any of the theological or political factions of the day. Socialism, or the co-operative principle, like the Church, was for him a way of reasserting the apparently lost fellowship of mankind, of realising the fact of the headship of Christ. But he was no more successful in checking the independent organisation of the working class than the Tory radicals, and as social tension ebbed in the fifties, interest in social Christianity declined, as it did in France and Prussia too. Maurice himself came to put most of his interest into the Working Men's College, and came to be an admirer of Prussian militarism and Bismarck's attempt to harness the German national movement.

The continuous history of social Christianity in England, as in France,

Germany and the United States, begins in the later seventies and eighties, and in each case embodied the response of the privileged or established churches to harder times, much as the prehistory of social Christianity had marked their response to the threat of revolution. The starting point in England is conveniently marked by the formation of the Guild of St Matthew by Stewart Headlam in 1877, and the Christian Social Union, a body not unlike the Evangelisch-soziale Kongress, in 1889. Both these organisations sprang from a narrowly high-church Anglican stock, and from a conjunction of economic and social circumstances. The Great Depression which set in in 1873 and lasted through 1896 was not perhaps a very great depression, but it did involve a period of low profitability in a number of traditional British staple industries, and a fundamental reappraisal of the role of British agriculture. In the seventies the full impact of American wheat exports was felt for the first time. British farmers were faced with the unfamiliar combination of a succession of poor harvests together with very low prices for the grain they produced; in 1879 the realisation dawned that things would never be the same again for English corn growers, farm rents tumbled, and even so, tenants became hard to find. This was a double disaster for the Church. Over twenty years a great capital had been sunk in the reorganisation of church leases, the fruits of which were expected in the later seventies and eighties as the old 21-year leases were run out; those fruits would never be reaped. The English Church, like the universities and a section of the aristocracy, dug its own financial grave by accepting the best economic advice available in the middle of the century. Moreover the parish priests felt the draught almost at once; in 1836 tithe was commuted for a corn rent calculated upon seven-year averages of grain prices, an arrangement which meant gradual, but inexorable impoverishment for the clergy when prices entered upon their long decline. From one privileged sector of the economy after another came demands for a reconsideration of the gold standard or the adoption of protection, and in the Church too the dominant economic ethic was partially repudiated. In the sixties and seventies the Church had suffered considerable losses of support among those members of the upper classes who had valued the Church in the past principally as a social regulator and knew that it could serve no longer; all the more reason therefore for the Church to reconsider those social arrangements which might be held especially to estrange the sympathies of working men. Yet the reconsideration most obviously took place in liberal Catholic circles, among men who had been drawn into liberal causes by attachment to Gladstone, and completed their breach with the conservatively oriented main body of the Anglo-Catholic party by attempting from a Catholic point of view that reconciliation with progressive intellect which had been the hallmark of the liberal enterprise. In this cause inductive logic acquired from Mill, or the idea of the world as the theatre of God's self-revelation picked up from Hegel, or any version of the idea of progress, could be employed towards the construction of a theology in which the key-concept was the Incarnation. No one had found F.D. Maurice harder to swallow than the post-Tractarians, but now his theology seemed exactly calculated to support a view of the Church as the Body of Christ, committed to 'the promotion of righteousness and freedom and truth among nations'. The social reference of the new theology was encouraged by the degeneration of political liberalism into intractable sectional causes in the last twenty years of the nineteenth century; in a world in which official politics consisted of all those things which divided liberals from conservatives and in which liberalism consisted so largely of disestablishment, teetotalism and opposition to Church schools, those issues of social reform which were still regarded not as party concerns but as technical crossbench matters were increasingly attractive. At all events the propaganda of these groups evoked a wide response in the Church of England, and though it suggested explicitly that those who produced it were persecuted pioneers, it proved a fashionable route to preferment. Bishops galore were taken from the Christian Social Union.

Among those who came to the top by this route was William Temple, who became Bishop of Manchester in 1921, and Archbishop, first of York (1929) and then Canterbury (1942). Temple did more than anyone to make social Christianity a kind of orthodoxy between the wars, insisting that it was not possible to be fully a Christian in a non-Christian society; and exemplified vividly the strengths and weakness of the movement. Before he became a bishop he got going the movement which in 1924 became the Conference on Christian Politics Economics and Citizenship (COPEC). This was based on a number of years' quite serious study, and on the issue of 200,000 questionnaires whose findings were collated at seventy-five centres. Moreover, at a moment when the Church of England was losing interest in questions of church union, and when Temple himself was entering upon a senior career which made him more establishmentarian and cautious in his view, the interdenominational basis of COPEC created a confidence in his leadership on the part of the nonconformists considerably greater than the facts warranted. Moreover he brought into the movement the best thinker it ever had – R.H. Tawney, who became a professor in the London School of Economics, produced in his *Religion and the Rise of Capitalism* (1926) an argument which never quite convinced historians, but explained to the satisfaction of churchmen that social policy had once been the property of Christianity, that its demise was the consequence of doctrines which no one now held, and that the social Christians were not heretics but men laying claim to lost goods. Temple continued in the same path to the end, publishing just before his elevation to Canterbury a popular Penguin book on *Christianity and the Social Order* which sold in huge numbers. But Temple was in many ways fortunate in the moment of his death (1944). The emergence of bitter ideological divisions in the thirties gave a marginal look to English social Christianity, and especially to its view of politics. In the nineteenth century much of the substance of reform had been constituted by the idea that the way to progress was to take institutions out of politics; in modern English jargon, to 'privatize' them. Crown, civil service and universities had all been subjected to this process, and no institution had taken it upon itself more fully than the Church. Temple stood in this tradition as completely as any of his predecessors on the bench of bishops. Upon his consecration he resigned his short-lived membership of the Labour party, and behaved on the practical assumption that Christian social policies would be implemented by the sheer power of conviction of ideas. The deteriorating international situation demonstrated to all with eyes to see that real politics was about power, and exposed a range of questions to which the social Christians, acting from motives of *noblesse oblige*, had not given their mind. After the war a situation of under-used resources was replaced for many years by one of over-stretched resources of which the grand symptoms were over-full employment and inflation. But in truth Christian Socialism had always been a failure in what might have been considered two of its major concerns; it had viewed social problems too much from the top of the social pyramid ever to create a foothold for the Church in the world of labour, and it had never exercised practical influence on the policies of government. Christian Socialism was indeed the politics of a church losing contact with the practical exercise of authority. There are parallels here with German religious socialism.

Inflation in the third quarter of the twentieth century had as powerful an effect upon the ethos of the Church as the savage deflation which followed the Napoleonic Wars. At the beginning of the nineteenth century it had been maintained that a hierarchical church was necessary to sustain a hierarchical society, and that to equalize clerical stipends would drive the Church towards a subversive presbyterianism. Inflation has led to the augmentation of small livings to meet minimum standards on so broad a scale as to produce a substantially egalitarian clergy for the first time. As the nineteenth-century prophets had foreseen, this, reinforced by a sense of a great loss of political and social status, moved clergy and bishops to a political position left of centre as nothing had ever done before, and in the time of the Thatcher government baffled both Tory leadership and Church leadership with a sense of mutual incomprehension. At the same time other factors combined to revive in the Church political attitudes with a world horizon. The Church of England responded in its measure to the politicization of Third World elites brought to bear through the World Council of Churches; and the warmth of its response was kindled by the difficulties encountered by branches of the Anglican communion in various parts of Africa, especially Uganda and South Africa. This adverse experience, moreover, seemed to qualify a very uncompetitive Church to rival the liberationists of the Roman Catholic communion as advocates of the downtrodden. And in the early seventies when these influences were making themselves felt, the Church of England adopted a new constitution. Under the new arrangements the weight of the *ex officio* element in the assemblies of the Church was reduced and that of the parties strongly represented among the ordinary clergy, and especially the evangelical and Anglo-Catholic parties, increased. The effect of the changes has hitherto been to make it impossible for the Church to make any decisive changes of policy at all, each of the parties being strong enough to defeat proposals, none able to collect sufficient allies to succeed, even in conjunction with the official element in the Church, to carry them. This stalemate has generated a great deal of frustration, and a recrudescence among Anglo-Catholics of a sense of being persecuted in the Church by men who have abandoned its distinctive traditions for political ends or political management. These sentiments brought to their side men of quite different church origins, such as the late Dr Gareth Bennett, and paradoxically evoked the most distinguished Anglican contribution to political theology in this century in the work of Dr Edward Norman, Dean of Peterhouse.

A historian of note (and of strong Tory convictions) Dr Norman castigates political priests with never a reference to the Irish among whom his historical studies began. His argument is that the social Christians, by adopting the liberationist views of unrepresentative Third World elites, deceive the Third World as to what is ever likely to be accomplished by political action, and betray their own constituents by discerning the hand of God so fully in the political movements of their choice as virtually to deny the transcendental aspects of the faith. He sees the Christian radicals as politically menacing; with their naive faith that the state can be persuaded to do the church's work for it they constantly favour collectivist solutions to social problems; and in modern circumstances this simply contributes to the growth of monolithic political organizations which are likely to deny the Church the liberty to do the work peculiar to it. Strongly animated as he is against the liberal politics of ideas, Dr Norman is an equally strong advocate of the ordinary politics of management, of diplomacy, and even of nuclear deterrence; and by implication he is an advocate of ordinary politics as a christian vocation. It is here that his special contribution lies.

It is not possible to acquit him entirely of factiousness. He began by (quite properly) attacking the Maurician Christian Socialists for being basically unpolitical, and has ended in an involuted way by praising them for perceiving the limits of politics and contributing to the mind of the Church. He insists that Christ's teaching calls upon a unique authority outside historical circumstances altogether, but also that somehow a spiritual interpretation of the religious tradition can exploit the historical relativism which is a characteristic achievement of the secular world he deplores, and expound the presence of the Infinite in time without describing the faith in the secular terms of the radicals. He knows that early Catholic social Christianity could develop into Fascism and that even the Marxist language of the liberationists shows traces of the corporatist language of their social-catholic predecessors; but he does not admit that English social Christianity began as a Tory substitute for the extension of political rights. It is unlikely that even Mrs Thatcher herself knows whether Dr Norman's Tory arguments for a privatized liberal Church in a limited liberal state constitute him a Thatcherite; but he has unmistakably showed that more kinds of Christian politics are possible than those at present dominant in the marginalized churches of contemporary England.

Was the transition from charity to policy possible in the world of English dissent? Social Christianity, as we have seen, was mostly the politics of religious establishments. Lutheran rather than Reformed in Germany, Reformed rather than free church in Switzerland, prosperous Unitarian, Congregational or Episcopalian in America rather than lower-class Methodist or Baptist. It has, however, been claimed in America that the most pietistic form of revivalism, the perfectionism of Finney, precisely because of its concern with perfection, was to blossom into the social gospel itself, while the more conservative wing of the English labour movement is apt to trace its pedigree to Methodism rather than to Marx whenever the left wing threatens to get on top. The question is an important one because upon the answer to it turns one's view whether the prevalence of a social gospel in the evangelical nonconformity of the later nineteenth and early twentieth centuries developed from or displaced the old evangelicalism, and it is a question which has not been systematically investigated in an English context. My own view is that neither in England nor America is the case made out that evangelicalism was capable of rising from the conception of charity to that of policy. Indeed the one case where the transition was made by a movement within the evangelical ambience is an odd one. The teetotal movement, as distinct from the temperance crusade, originated in the 1830s as a piece of working-class self-help. They worked in the same milieu as the revivalists, and used much the same methods, seeking out the drunkard in his haunts, and, with the pledge, bringing on a crisis like conversion or believer's baptism. They understood the need for a set of alternative institutions in which the reclaimed might be protected from the pressure of ordinary social mores. By 1850 the converts of the movement numbered scores of thousands, and they were beginning to bring the church managements to terms, but the liquor problem seemed hardly to have changed. The English teetotallers then began to follow the Americans in a fundamental change of strategy. They undertook a programme of mass education in the Sunday Schools with a view to creating anti-liquor sentiment before the drinking habit began. They also attempted to reinforce the individual appeal by manipulating social arrangements by statute, securing prohibition or local option in banning liquor sales. This was a crucial moment in the history not only of the teetotal movement but of the whole milieu in which it sprang up. In most respects its prejudices were against state action, but it now began to seek theoretical justification for the solution of individual moral problems by corporate regulation. By this road teetotalism could lead to Hegelianism, even to socialism, exactly as it did with many of the Swiss religious socialists. Of course what many of the teetotallers wanted was a draconian act of prohibition, altogether beyond the capabilities of the weak English state of the mid-nineteenth century, in order to achieve a rapid social reformation which would make it possible to preserve old English traditions of weak government and personal liberty; but the step towards corporate regulation, once taken, could not be reversed.

Moreover the teetotal milieu was one in which, despite the class stratification of English life, a form of co-operation between middle- and working-class radicals was created which later gained the name of Lib-Labism [Liberal-Labour politics] and established itself as a durable political option. The social association on which this political alliance depended had roots in ordinary English life, and especially that which revolved around the chapels and Sunday Schools. Hostility to the privileges and indoctrination of an 'aristocratic' Church was here deeply rooted, and was convenient for keeping middle- and working-class forces in line. The liberal ideal of this form of labour politics had three positive advantages which the Socialist historians of labour and the catholic historians of Social Christianity have obscured. With the exception of a hankering after prohibition in a section of the teetotal movement, it did not make demands on the state which the political machinery of that day could not answer; it inclined towards self-help and a belief in the existence of a long-term beneficial economic spiral. In the second place many of its demands were concerned with justice, or at least with rectifying a sense of status deprivation; in the last generation of the nineteenth century when uncontrollable alterations in the terms of trade did more for the material welfare of British labour than all acts of policy put together, the politics of economic contrivance could hardly have the realism of the politics of justice. Finally, though the rebellious sons of the middle class and angry clerical agitators might call for Socialism, English working men had a deep-seated distrust of a state they did not run, and did not care to extend its functions. The chapel rather than the established church; trade unions rather than wage regulation; friendly societies rather than Bismarckian national insurance; the co-operative store rather than state ownership, were their characteristic enthusiasms. Particularly in the coal fields this kind of politics went on for a very long time, precisely because, unlike Christian Socialism, it stood for things which at least some working men actually wanted. In the Durham coalfield as late as the middle years of the first World War the discipline of the Primitive Methodist chapels was used as a weapon by the Lib-Lab men against those who contended for independent labour, Trotskyite or pacifist politics, with sad effect upon the chapels, when after the war, the tide of politics ran the other way.

The early origins of this sort of politics, the way it was harnessed to Gladstone's political chariot by John Bright, and its long duration are now well recognized; so too are the contributions of the Primitive Methodists and other dissenters to trade unionism and politics in the coal, textile, boot and shoe, agricultural and other industries. What is hardly known at all is the relation between the religion and the politics of the men concerned. To many, like John Wilson, the Durham miners' leader, there was a simple equation between religion and utility, justification by faith and social justice, the community of faith and political tactics. 'Whatever points of difference in opinion men may have on what we Methodists call conversion,' he wrote, 'to me and in my case it was needful if I were to be of any use to myself, my family or my kind'. Despatched to the Midlands on a trade union missionary journey in 1878, his first two meetings were at Harriseahead and Mow Cop where the Primitive Methodist revival had begun; in a single act he paid homage to the fountainhead of the religious tradition in which he was bred and laid claim to the organized recruiting power of the religious community which bore the tradition. It is an extraordinary example of the inhibiting power of dogma, political and religious, that historians have provided so little of the intellectual analysis which men like John Wilson did not provide for themselves.

Of course they were under relatively slight pressure to distinguish their religious and political attitudes. English liberals with a social attitude, unlike Naumann, Göhre and Harnack, were not confronted with a confessional Lutheranism more systematic than anything in Luther, a Marxist socialism with a doctrine more highly systematized than that of Marx, still less a systematic approach to foreign affairs like that of Max

Weber, towards which they must have an explicit stance. This meant that when things went wrong they were less likely to give up church activity than Harnack, or Christianity like Göhre, or the ministry like Naumann and all the pastors who were excluded from that profession for social-protestant views, nor were they tempted like Karl Barth and Eduard Thurneysen to reach a Christian understanding of revelation by reading Bengel and Thomas Carlyle. Unfortunately empiricism can become mindless. In politics Lib-Labism, now under the Labour banner, went on with very little social doctrine, especially among the Methodist and Christian Socialist members of Parliament, and with no doctrine at all respecting international affairs, until it was dealt a mortal blow by the inflation of the sixties and seventies. This experience encouraged trade unions to throw in their lot with the extreme left of the party in the belief that organized labour could profit best from the unearned redistribution of wealth which inflation brought with it. In its turn this realignment made the Labour party impossible to lead by traditional methods, and deprived Methodist socialists, for example, of both their constituency in the country and of their prop in the party leadership. How unpolitical the Methodist members of Parliament now were, was illustrated by the fact that they did not follow Dr Owen, a former Labour Foreign Secretary, exasperated at the isolationism of the Labour Left, into the Social Democratic Party; they became candidates for the Speakership of the House of Commons. The three Speakers before the present one were all Methodists, two of them members of the Labour Party. Nor were they helped by the formal organization of their religious communion. Taking their views from the World Council of Churches and their own Mission House, the Methodist connexional leadership wished to argue that the Marxist regime of Mr Mugabe was more Christian than Afrikaner domination in South Africa, but was at a loss to explain why. It was also taken by surprise at the violent reaction of Ulster Methodists to the proposal that the National Anthem be omitted from the new Methodist hymnbook. Culpable political innocence could hardly proceed further.

17

Max Weber and the Ritschlians

Max Weber, the unbelieving scion of a family descended on the one side form those Protestant refugees from the Habsburg lands who had so often generated religious revival, and in another branch from that ancient Huguenot community in Frankfurt whose congregation outside the walls was a permanent memorial to the pugnacious determination of the Frankfurt town council to maintain the Lutheran character of a place full of Calvinists and Jews, derived from his pedigree a degree of detachment, even alienation, from his milieu which is doubtless one of the qualifications of a sociologist. Family circumstances, political events and intellectual interests were, however, to bring him into close contact with a group of Lutheran theologians all of whom had strong reasons for wishing to remain within their *Landeskirchen*, and so made the intellectual running in these establishments, that they are now almost the only theologians of the period of intellectual interest. To this group, the neo-Ritschlians, Weber came to be important partly because of his analysis of German society, and partly because he was powerfully engaged with intellectual issues cognate with those which they had inherited from Ritschl. The intellectual significance of this group in no way disguises the fact that they were a minority, even a persecuted minority, in the great *Landeskirchen* of their day, and heavily dependent on state protection in academic appointments, protection which did not extend to providing a career for one distinguished Old Testament scholar among them, Hermann Gunkel.[1] One of the unspoken reasons for Troeltsch's transfer from theology to philosophy when he moved from Heidelberg to Berlin in 1915 may very well have been that no one wanted another row with the Evangelisch Oberkirchenrat like that which had been staged when Harnack had been brought in from Marburg in 1890.[2] Confessional Lutheranism remained as strong as ever in the Saxon church; to the fury of Ritschl, it came to provide a shelter for all the tendencies of anti-Prussian separatism in Hanover and the middle states;[3] and the power

First published in *Max Weber and his Contemporaries*, ed. Wolfgang J. Mommsen and Jurgen Osterhammed, London 1987, pp. 203–214.

of the Positive Union meticulously entrenched at the court of William I, remained unbroken in the Old Prussian Union at the time of his grandson's abdication.[4]

Political antipathy was not the only barrier between Weber and the conservatives who were in possession in the German churches. All of them still resisted in the name of dogma the historical outlook for which he stood and, even on the level of social understanding, moved in another world. Rudolf Todt had tried to read off social policy from the Bible; Stöcker was not merely an anti-Semite, but thought that agitation provided a way to sublimate the divisions in the national life in enthusiasm for God, Church and Emperor; while the whole Protestant-social enterprise was an affront to the demand for a value-free social science for which Weber came to stand. Indeed the third edition of Martin von Nathusius's book, *Die Mitarbeit der Kirche an der Lösung der sozialen Frage* (1st ed. Leipzig, 1893–4, 3rd ed. 1904) which gave Troeltsch a push towards the studies which led to his *Social Teaching of the Christian Churches*, sought to derive from Christianity the principals of a natural social order, of a Christian sociology with the virtual status of revelation. And if Weber made no contact with the various styles of conservatism dominant in the *Landeskirchen*, the interest he aroused among theologians was equally clearly terminated by the demise of the Ritschlian party. It was Karl Barth, a pupil of Wilhelm Herrmann, and one of the successors of that friend of Weber's Youth, Paul Göhre, as assistant to Martin Rade on the *Christliche Welt*, who most notably turned from his neo-Ritschlian origins to new ways; and though Barth vituperated wildly against Naumann, Troeltsch and Harnack, he left hardly a reference to Weber in the whole of his gigantic corpus. The deaths of Naumann, Weber and Troeltsch in rapid succession concluded a chapter; and that conclusion was underlined by the rise of the dialectical theology.

Weber would probably have been drawn to the Ritschlians in any case. His mother was devoted to the protestant-social cause on religious grounds,[5] and his Baumgarten cousins were also involved in it. Otto Baumgarten was a friend of the pastor and professor, Baron von Soden, who was active in the Evangelisch-soziale Kongress, and was commissioned to produce a semi-offical sheet, the *Evangelisch-soziale Zeitfragen*. In this enterprise he made use of Weber, and the national economists who gathered at the Weber household.[6] More importantly from our present point of view, among Otto Baumgarten's childhood friends had been two leading members of the Ritschlian group, Friedrich Loofs and Albert Eichhorn, and Otto Ritschl, the son and later the distinguished biographer of the great Albrecht himself.[7] Thus, although Weber was confirmed in the profession of sociologist in 1893 by an invitation from Paul Göhre, the

secretary of the ESK, to continue on behalf of that body the inquiry into
the conditions of rural labour into the provinces east of the Elbe which he
had begun for the Verein für Sozialpolitik, he already stood not far from
the Ritschlian group into whose hands the ESK fell after the secession of
Stöcker and the conservatives in the great political crisis of 1895.[8] And
although the Baumgartens were Carlylean[9] and not very rigorous in their
social views, the main intellectual preoccupations of the Ritschlian group
had a significance for Weber, as his secularized mind had for them.

Albrecht Ritschl had begun his intellectual life as a disciple of Baur and
the Tübingen school, and as a young man viewed the intellectual and
political problems of his day much in young Hegelian terms. Some bridge
must be found between the factual truth arising from the positive sciences,
and the subjectivism which seemed the last refuge of a faith in God which
had lost its grip on history and the world; some alternative to the bleak
choice between the scientific destruction of revelation in the manner of
Strauss, and the doctrinaire confessionalism of Hengstenberg; some version
of what Schleiermacher had called 'the contract' between Christian faith
and scientific research.[10] At first Ritschl thought that Hegelianism might
provide the organising concept, but, like Marx and Feuerbach, Ritschl
accepted the Left Hegelian pursuit of the concrete, of the real world and
of practical ends, and by the fifties he had got rid of Hegelianism altogether,
and reintroduced Kant as the Protestant philosopher *par excellence*.
According to Kant there was no theoretical way of transcending the limits
of finiteness; the only possibility of a breakthrough to the divine lay in the
sphere of practical reason, in the experience of the moral imperative. From
this point of view Ritschl contributed to the heavy emphasis on personality
and the cultivation of ethics in German protestant theology in the late
nineteenth century, and exemplified one of the ways in which theology like
so many other branches of scholarship was feeling the impact of historical
studies. He also provided a systematic backing for his view that the survival
of Protestantism in the Rhineland depended on the Prussian Union Church,
and that the recovery of national unity in Germany depended not on
confessionalism, but on the Prussian state.

The organising concept of the system which Ritschl had constructed by
the time of the founding of the Second Empire, which held together his
philosophy of religion and history, his exegesis, dogmatics and ethics was
that of the Kingdom of God. The kingdom of God was God's purpose for
the world; there was thus a sense in which the social and cultural
development of mankind was rooted in the nature of God himself. The
hierarchy of natural communities – family, profession, national state –
was, both statistically and morally, a pre-condition of the kingdom of God.
In one system Ritschl had despatched the world-denying attitudes of

monasticism and Pietism, the particularism of Hanover and also of the Centre party, the narrowness of the sects, and the grandiose presumption of the Hegelian idealism in which he had been raised. His recourse to history rather than metaphysics, his ethical impulse, his return to Luther, were particularly attractive to young men raised upon confessional or mediation theology.[11]

If Ritschl sought to assign a religious value to history and culture, he was also a practitioner of historical inquiry on a greater scale than is commonly allowed. In December 1885 Harnack sent Ritschl the first copy of the first volume of his *Dogmengeschichte* with the inscription: 'It is necessary for me, in putting this volume in your hands, to thank you again heartily for all I have received from you. Seventeen years ago my own theological labours began with the study of your *Rise of the old Catholic church*,[12] and since then scarcely a quarter has passed without my learning something new from you. The present book is a sort of conclusion of long years of study; without the foundations you laid, it would never have been written, imperfect as it is.'[13] It appears, indeed, that Harnack derived the framework of his famous book from Ritschl, though he built upon it in his own way.[14] Ritschl also produced a massive three volume *Geschichte des Pietismus* (Bonn, 1880–1886; reprint Berlin, 1966). This work has suffered in esteem because of its polemical object. Ritschl believed intensely that the failure of the Protestant establishments to hold the masses was the fault of the alliance between the Pietists and the confessional party in his own lifetime. They had severed the links with culture which every healthy religious appeal needed, and had sought to convert individuals out of the world instead of strengthening them ethically in it. The *History of Pietism* was designed to make this implausible charge stick. It was nevertheless a very considerable work in its own right. The Pietist literature was in Ritschl's time much more difficult to trace than it is now, and almost the only reputable work on which he could build were the studies of the religious life of the Rhineland by that remarkable historian, Max Goebel. And, at the end, with whatever defects of scholarship and partisanship, Ritschl had produced a massive general survey of the field on an international and interdenominational basis which no subsequent scholar has had the courage to rival or even revise.

More importantly from the standpoint of our present theme, Ritschl adumbrated at intervals in his treatise a typology of the Christian life, of the sort which had already concerned Max Goebel in his discussion of Rhineland sects and was later to concern Weber and Troeltsch. Ritschl held that mysticism was a Hellenistic phenomenon alien to Christianity; Christianity was world affirming and active in the world. It followed that since Pietism, and its precursors among the Anabaptists embodied mysticism and asceticism, they could not have been derived from primitive Christianity but only from Catholicism. The age of Bernard of Clairvaux and the monastic reform movement had shown that medieval Catholicism was a collection of incompatible things. The Church as a legally organized institution sought world domination, while prescribing to individuals world renunciation and mystic union with Jesus beyond the world. Power was the object of the institution; monasticism, mysticism and asceticism the aims entailed on individuals. The incompatibility was bearable at least for a time because the distance between the world and mankind, on the one hand, and God on the other, was understood in very abstract terms, but it was an inherently unstable arrangement. Ascetic mysticism was a force always ready to appeal to its ideals of other-worldly perfection against the institutions of the church and also against the content of its faith. It was prepared to burst the bonds of universal social unity for which the church stood in monasticism, sectarianism, mysticism and individualism.

Luther's achievement was to rediscover the Christian faith as a spiritual power in the world. The church now gave up the legal and political functions which inhibited its religious development, and the state, taking responsibility for legal protection and the discipline of the Christian life, cleared the way for the church to purify social life by universal love. The individual, free to appropriate God's promise of love, could realise his own value in quiet trust in God in the pursuit of his civil calling. The church, which alone had the gospel of justification and the certainty of salvation, had the job of keeping individuals up to scratch in a world necessarily imperfect. If there were difficulties in this, there was no solution at all in defending the idea of a holy congregation. It is not perfection which indicates the presence of the church but the pure preaching of the gospel. What imperilled the Lutheran church was the misapplication of the idea of 'Freedom in the Law'. Political circumstances and the struggle with Catholicism had brought into Lutheranism many of the features of the old church system to which it was opposed, separated it from the ethical and religious aspirations of the people and gave much too great a weight to doctrine. Nor was the balance preserved on the Reformed side. Here doctrine effaced the Lutheran distinction between law and religion, discipline and grace, state and church, and attempted to create a new theocracy. A hard biblicism attempted to give universal sanction to the transitory institutions of the New Testament church. Ascetic strictness approximated to monastic flight from the world. The Reformed church was well equipped to contend with the universalist as well as the separatist tendencies in Catholicism, but the logic of its own position was to dissolve into Independency. Illogicality, refusal to accept the consequences of its assumptions, was a strength in the Reformed tradition, as it was a weakness in the Lutheran.

These tendencies which had contributed to the breakup of the Catholic church system continued to ferment in the Reformed world. Having established apostolic doctrine, the Lutheran churches did not attempt to recover an apostolic church form; having recovered an apostolic church form, the Reformed churches tended to subject all moral choices to canons of apostolic sanctity, and to abolish the category of things indifferent. This moral ideal was bound to be ruinous to the idea of a *Volkskirche*, and encourage the formation of separate religious societies. Pietism was the offspring not only of Anabaptism, but also of Calvinism. There was a further typology of Anabaptism to be established, in which Franciscan features were to be observed again, the Spiritualist and the Biblicist. Again men became indifferent to natural human conditions, became 'world-deniers', and took up the cudgels not against sin, but against men's creaturely condition. This might issue in Quietism (a phenomenon which, as Ritschl had learned from Heinrich Heppe, had come in from France) or in eschatological enthusiasm which aimed a revolutionary blow at the course of history and the development of society. But either road led to separatism and to a rejection of the church's mission to reshape society. In Reformed territories this frame of mind led to the formation of free churches which sustained the utmost hostility towards the confessional churches from which they had sprung; in Lutheran territories it tended to turn against the whole congregational idea, and aspire to a sort of philadelphia without word or sacrament in the Lutheran sense, or local roots and constitution. Some barrier against this has been created by Spener who revived the domestic order in the Lutheran system and strengthened professional life. In addition to his basic typology, Ritschl offered various explanations drawn from national character and social history, as to the variety of ways in which the story had worked out in the various confessional territories; but all ended in separation, all were strong among the lower social orders (sometimes they needed the patronage of wealthy women, but only the nobility and the civil service remained true to the Landeskirchen), and all were unwilling to admit the relative nature of church conditions.[15]

Thus, very remarkably, Anabaptism, Calvinism, Pietism and enlightenment turned out to be derived from the bad features of medieval Catholicism, and it was Lutheranism which offered a model for an age of Liberalism and science. It was now a question whether Ritschl's successors could continue to derive the same organising advantage from the concept of the Kingdom of God, whether his typology and historical periodisation would be found satisfactory (Troeltsch, for example, started from Ritschl's

point and ended with something very different), and whether, when the
encouragement of the Kaiser in 1890 induced in academics of all kinds an
obsession with the 'social question', Ritschl's hints towards social policy
would be thought enough. For although his concept of the Kingdom of
God ascribed a positive significance to the world process, and hence implied
the possibility of a social dogmatic and a social ethic, Ritschl himself drew
almost no social inferences. His view of the long slow way by which
protestantism drew its adherents to the law of Christ was limited to
religious education in which the congregation, the family, and the state
took part.

Two interconnected groups of younger Ritschlians began to form, each
finding problems with the master, and it was with these younger men, and
especially with one group of them that Weber was to be connected. In
1876 Martin Rade, a theological student in his fourth semester at Leipzig,
made the acquaintance of the young Harnack, then a *Privatdozent*, and
formed a durable circle of friends who made a considerable mark on
theological studies in Germany and Switzerland, men like Wilhelm Borne-
mann, Friedrick Loofs, Paul Drews, and William Wrede. In 1886 Rade's
circle launched the journal which the following year became *Die Christliche
Welt*, and developed into one of the most famous of all liberal–Protestant
journals.[16] At first it took up the anticatholic element in Ritschl's heritage
and backed the Evangelische Bund, but in championing Harnack's claims
to appointment in Berlin, and supporting him in the doctrinal battles in
which he became engaged, the journal took a decisive turn to the left, its
editor, the only one of the younger Ritschlians to enjoy any longevity,
continuing to move leftwards till his death in 1940 at the age of 83. Like
Friedrich Naumann, whose sister Dora he met in 1887 and married in
1889, Rade was attracted to social questions by interest in the career of
Stöcker. Moreover the journal could not but be deeply affected by
the history of the Evangelisch-soziale Kongress, for with Naumann its
correspondent on Inner Mission affairs, Paul Drews on social questions,
and Paul Göhre coming in as Rade's parish assistant and the paper's expert
on Socialist affairs, the *Christliche Welt* was almost an organ of the 'young'
group at the Congress. By this time Rade was well aware of intellectual
difficulties in the heritage of Ritschl. Like Harnack, Rade was overwhelmed
by the importance of an historical approach to Christian doctrine, and was
indeed optimistic enough to think that historical studies offered a way to
peace and an end to dogmatic feuding.[17] Not surprisingly therefore, while
sharing Ritschl's hostility to natural theology, Rade was not in the
least interested in the teleological devices by which Ritschl had ascribed
theological significance to society and culture in his doctrine of the kingdom
of God. Ritschl indeed began to look like another theologian who had

sacrificed truth to system. For if theology had its basis in an historical revelation, then that basis could be established by the same methods of historical enquiry as obtained in profane history. This in turn implied that the problem of the relation of religious knowledge and knowledge of the world which Ritschl thought he had solved by his system, returned in an acute form. Moreover, history figured large in the Rade group's sense of mission, their calling to redeem the church as well as the world. This very fact, however, raised acutely the question of the relation of present and past in historical inquiry. Could historical inquiry be determined by present concerns, and what relation might there be between a present sense of mission and the Christian past? More generally if theology was an historical science, what was its relation to Christian practice, not merely to ethics but to preaching. Rade and his friends managed to convince themselves that Ritschl's unsuccessful textbook, *Unterricht in der Christlichen Religion* (Bonn, 1875) could all be preached. It became apparent however, that one's view of the relation of theory and practice would be influenced by one's understanding of the relation of theology to historical scholarship, of Christianity to culture. Abstract as these questions were, they underlay the individual's judgment of what social groups the congregation could co-operate with and what special task it could set itself. To Martin Rade, whose first choice was for a pastoral rather than an academic career, these questions were, and remained, paramount.[18]

The academic young Ritschlians, nevertheless, came by their own route to much the same point at the same time. A group jovially known as the *kleine Facultät* had begun to form under Ritschl's wing at Göttingen in the eighties; it included Eichhorn, Gunkel, Wrede (from Rade's original circle) Bousset, Weiss, and Troeltsch, all of them, except Troeltsch, North Germans, and all, except Eichhorn and Troeltsch, Bible scholars. They began to claim that the historical-critical school gave too much heed to philology and too little to the general historical background of the religious origins of the past; they disregarded the 'historical constitution' of all literary documents; still worse they sacrificed the variety of the New Testament to the necessities of system.[19] Even Harnack, the farthest left of the older group, now became uncooperative; having made himself odious in his youth by emphasising Hellenistic influences upon the history of Christian dogma, he was now assailed for not going nearly far enough. The young were impressed by the great works of secular history of Ranke and Mommsen,[20] and were concerned to insist that the religious development of Israel and the church could not be separated from general history, conceived very broadly indeed. The pressure of current social questions opened their eyes to the influence of such issues in the religious history of the past. More than this, historical research was held to have obliterated the frontiers between Christianity and non-Christian religions, between natural and supernatural areas of study. To the younger party, the Ritschlians appeared to be pushing aside the questions thrown up by history, while they themselves were seeking to subject the whole religious life of men to the same methods of research. Rade called for the foundation of new chairs in *Religionsgeschichte*, the history of religion in this general sense, while older Ritschlians stood firm against any further reduction of the absoluteness of Christianity. The issue here raised was not unlike the issue raised at the ESK whether a specifically Christian politics was possible; and the breakup of the Ritschlian party which began with an attack by Troeltsch on Julius Kaftan in 1893, coincided fairly closely with the breakup of the Congress.

By the early nineties the circle was complete. Weber was the centre of a professorial discussion group at Heidelberg which included Troeltsch among its members; he was lecturing for the ESK and assessing its work in Rade's journal, *Die Christliche Welt*;[21] and if the ESK confirmed Weber in his vocation as a sociologist, he contributed to the breakup of that body by his reports. Weber's exposure of the hollow basis of the public pretensions of the eastern aristocracy was absolutely intolerable to the Right in their great counterattack of the mid-nineties, and helped to make Stöcker's position in the ESK impossible; by contrast his analysis gave some standing ground in policy to Naumann and the left wing of that body. Weber could not have failed to draw some stimulus from the discussions in the Ritschlian circle, as well as from the investigations into which they pushed him. In return he exercised a disturbing intellectual influence on them. This has always been recognized in the case of that other outsider whom the Ritschlians drew to them, Friedrich Naumann.[22] Naumann used Ritschl's language and concepts, but seems never to have bothered with Ritschl himself, and his views were shaped by his own pastoral experience and by a reading in socialist literature uncommon amongst the clergy of the establishment. Like Ritschl, Naumann came to employ the kingdom of God as an intellectually unifying concept, but the content of the concept was derived from his own social experience. The Kingdom of God was the process of establishing social justice, a process which might find room for both the charitable activity of the Inner Mission, and the social engineering contemplated by the Socialists. The methodological clash between the younger and the older Ritschlians signalled by the onslaught of Troeltsch on Julius Kaftan in 1893, had its counterpart in a clash between Kaftan and Naumann at the ESK in the same year. Kaftan, in the Ritschlian way, addressed himself to the question of 'Christianity and the economic order', in principle two quite different things, from the standpoint of the concept of personality. He concluded that since there was no eternal life in God without moral education and activity, it was a Christian obligation so to shape the economic order that it offered scope for the Christian ideal.[23] In opening the discussion, Naumann showed how his encounter with Marx had moved him in the direction of vocabulary which became characteristic of Weber. The question was whether Christianity had an inner-worldly ideal (a term earlier employed by Max Goebel). Social democracy was the first great protestant heresy, because it had exaggerated the inner-worldly ideal of the church to the point of chiliasm, making the impossible demand that perfect conditions be introduced on earth; it was in fact an inner-worldly chiliasm. In resisting the heresy, the church had in fact forgotten the principle which the heresy perverted, had forgotten that Jesus was one who brought help to the suffering, and that some means must be found for doing this in a machine age. The two great guides were Jesus and Marx. Marx showed how the world worked and what its needs were; Jesus, 'the man of the people', offered inner dynamics, hope, faith, and liberation from the tyranny of concepts imposed by Marx's professed disciples.[24]

Though the language might be Weberian, Weber set himself to destroy the substance of Naumann's doctrine. In 1894 Rade invited Weber to review a collection of Naumann's essays in the *Christliche Welt*. In this review Weber paid tribute to Naumann personally, but derided both his claim to have created a theological politics, and his optimism about the future. This jolt to Naumann,[25] however, was as nothing to that occasioned by Weber's Freiburg inaugural. This ferocious blast, with its implicit demand for a value-free political sociology was in every way a challenge to the political theology which Naumann had been struggling to develop, and some of its thrusts – the refusal to substitute 'state help' for 'self-help', even while establishing the power interests of the nation; the attack on those who substituted 'social policy in place of politics . . . cultural and economic history in place of political history' seemed aimed directly at him. The pitiless perspective of the Freiburg Inaugural upon international politics, thoroughly upset Naumann's balance. Reporting the lecture for his own journal *Hilfe*, he asked in a famous phrase 'is he not right? Of what use to us is the best social policy, if the Cossacks come? The man who wishes to pursue domestic policy must first secure the nation, fatherland and frontiers, he must look after the national power. This is the weakest point of social democracy. We need a socialism which is fit to govern . . . Such a socialism must be German-national'. Convinced by Weber that the world was not what he and Marx had supposed it was, pressed by Rudolf Sohm to separate religion and politics in the interests of confessional purity, driven by the recognition that in the conditions of the mid-nineties the church was not a useful vehicle of social policy, Naumann

founded his Nationalsoziale Verein[26] and entered on a process of minimiz-
ing the scope of religion. This left him little to talk about beyond the
concept of personality which had so preoccupied the elder Ritschlians, and
finally silenced him as a religious writer for almost the whole of the last
decade and a half of his life.[27] On the other hand, in *Demokratie und
Kaisertum*, in 1900 Naumann skilfully used Weber's methods of social
inquiry to answer his criticisms of the Nationalsoziale Verein. Weber had
held that it was hopeless to attempt to combine working-class and middle-
class elements in a single party when modern political parties were based
on the concrete and distinct separate interests round which the classes
themselves had formed. Naumann now argued that if political realism
were induced all round, it ought to be possible to produce a grand left-
bloc 'from Bassermann to Bebel' which could force the imperial government
to negotiate; the price of cooperation would be electoral reform and
the consequence of electoral reform would be the destruction of the
parliamentary strength of the conservatives and their privileged relation
to the Kaiser. There was room in the modern Germany for capitalism,
socialism and *Weltpolitik*; no room for the alliance of Emperor and a
basically particularist coalitition of the right. If the ESK had made a
sociologist of Weber, he had in turn made a sociologist of Naumann, and
in so doing had acquired a lifelong friend and ally.

Weber's influence was equally marked upon the more theoretically
minded members of the Ritschlian group. If their preoccupation with
questions of religious typology, and the concern with problems of large-
scale historical periodization which flowed from their belief that Protestantism had taken its opportunities at the beginning of the modern era, but
seemed to be losing them now, must have propelled Weber in the direction
of the studies on the Protestant ethic and the spirit of capitalism, his
agrarian studies gave a sharp actuality to the economic influence upon
religious outlook to men who were very inclined to see religious groupings
and institutions as the expression of religious ideas, and reinforced the
assumptions of the *religionsgeschichtliche* school. Troeltsch repeatedly
looked back to Weber's dominant influence upon him[28] as he turned to
sociology at this point: 'All the previous solutions gave rise to new
problems. At the same time I came under the spell of the powerful
personality of Max Weber, for whom the marvels dawning upon me had
long been foregone conclusions. And from that point I was powerfully
gripped by the Marxist theory of infrastructure and super-structure: not
that I swallowed it without more ado.'[29] It is, however, also true that
Troeltsch gave Weber the benefit of his vast reading, when the latter gave
his mind to the social consequences of religious belief.

There were moreover further complexities in the interchange between the two. Of the older group of Ritschlians, the only one to keep in any kind of touch with the younger men was Harnack, and although Harnack publicly resisted Rade's pressure for the foundation of chairs in the field of *Religionsgeschichte*, Rade felt that he must use Harnack's *Essence of Christianity*, the most famous of all expositions of Christianity for the plain man, given as inter-faculty lectures at Berlin in the winter semester of 1899–1900, as a banner to rally the party.[30] Two difficulties lay in the way. Harnack summed Christianity up in a very individualist way – 'God and the soul – the soul and its God';[31] and although he accepted that the preaching of the Kingdom of God had social implications, and, under a political hat, was prepared to talk about the priority of the state over the individual,[32] it was now unlikely that this would satisfy either Lutheran High Churchmen beating the drum about the church, or the younger Ritschlians' preoccupation with the community-forming power of Christian groups of various kinds. More fundamental was the very notion of an 'essence' of Christianity. It is true that this notion had had a long history,[33] and that Troeltsch himself had used language of this kind in the mid-nineties. The difference now was that the younger Ritschlians had been exposed to Max Weber, who had been refining the ideas they had all played with on the subject of religious typology, into his concept of 'ideal types'. On the surface the 'essence of Christianity' appeared to be an 'ideal type' of that complex phenomenon, and Troeltsch said as much in his essay on 'Modern Philosophy of History' (1904).[34] Immediately, however, Max Weber made it clear that this was not the case.[35] He distinguished between value-related judgments which historians must make in their choice of source materials, and value judgments proper. The historian must not turn his technical operations into value judgments. Harnack's 'essence' might convey the notion of a force operating in history, and it might be a normative concept designed to recall Christianity to its true self; in neither case was it a Weberian ideal type. An ideal type for him was simply a generalisation, whose adequacy, greater or less, made it more or less useful for comparing or measuring reality.

This confusion was to be important for Troeltsch's future work. Troeltsch's reception of Harnack's book in a serial review he wrote for the *Christliche Welt* was decidedly cautious; and he silently made over seventy alterations of substance in the review when it was included in his *Gesammelte Schriften*.[36] What Troeltsch wanted in the *religionsgeschichtliche* manner was to proceed 'from general history and its methods to Christianity in its whole breadth, and to the question of the validity of Christianity,'[37] but he found that this programme did not get him out of the toils. Apart from the difficulty of explaining a religion which claimed to be a final revelation in terms of its context, there was the problem of the contradictions within the Christian tradition. Troeltsch believed (and said) that Catholicism was 'a deviation from the essence of Christianity';[38] he knew that this was a value judgment, and obscured its effect when the essay came to be included in his collected works. In his subsequent rumination upon this problem Troeltsch could not find a way of insisting on the pursuit of modern historical inquiry wherever it led, and yet stopping short of scepticism and relativism; or, to put the matter in another way, of combining an historical treatment of Christianity with actual dogmatic construction. From this dilemma Weber's emphasis on the value-free nature of his ideal types seemed to offer some way out. And when Troeltsch had got to the end of his *Social Teaching of the Christian Churches* he maintained that 'perceptions of eternal ethical values are not scientific preceptions and cannot be proved along scientific lines'.[39] He went on nevertheless to suggest four social and ethical 'ideas and energies' which had certain status as revelation. In short the logical acumen of Weber enabled Troeltsch to clarify his scholarship, but in the end did not save him from dogmatizing from a personal standpoint. Troeltsch was in the same position as the conservative Orthodox he had represented as primeval ignoramuses.

There were rumours that Troeltsch who was better at getting to press than Weber, irked him by anticipating some of his ideas in the *Social Teachings of the Christian Churches*. Whatever the truth of this, the two of them with Harnack and other Ritschlians continued to cooperate in trying to seek constitutional reform during the war, an early peace, the erection of constitutional government with generous provision for the churches, and the launching of the DDP. It was death which left them with unfinished work in both politics and scholarship.

Notes

1 Werner Klatt, *Hermann Gunkel*, Göttingen, 1969, pp. 17, 41–3.
2 Otto Baumgarten, *Meine Lebensgeschichte*, Tübingen, 1929, p. 187.
3 Otto Ritschl, *Albrecht Ritschls Leben*, Freiburg, 1892–6, 2.162–3.
4 Gottfried Kögel, *Rudolf Kögel. Sein Werden und Wirken*, Berlin, 1894–99.
5 Wolfgang J. Mommsen, *Max Weber und die deutsche Politik, 1890–1920*, 2nd ed. Tübingen, 1974, p. 20.
6 Baumgarten, pp. 215–6.
7 *Ibid.* pp. 82–4, 89.
8 All these topics are briefly treated in W.R. Ward, *Theology, Sociology and Politics. The German Protestant Social Conscience, 1890–1933*, Bern, 1979, pp. 63–73.
9 Carlyle could be taken seriously as late in Germany as in England. A three-

volume collection of his *Sozial-politische Schriften* was published at Göttingen in 1899.

10 In the second letter to Friedrich Lücke. Kurt Nowak (ed.) *F.D.E. Schleiermacher, Theologische Schriften*, Berlin East, 1983, p. 442.

11 On Ritschl, see Otto Ritschl, *Albrecht Ritschls Leben*; Gustav Ecke, *Die theologische Schule Albrecht Ritschls und die evangelische Kirche der Gegenwart*, Berlin, 1904, 2.4–25: Hermann Timm, *Theorie und Praxis in der Theologie Albrecht Ritschls und Wilhelm Hermanns*, Gütersloh, 1967, esp. pp. 29–36, 62–73, 81–5: Adolf Harnack, *Reden und Aufsätze*, Giessen, 1904–30, 4.341–4: Klatt, p. 19.

12 2nd ed. Bonn, 1857.

13 Agnes von Zahn-Harnack, *Adolf von Harnack*, Berlin, 1936, p. 135.

14 Eginhard Peter Meijering, *Theologisch Urteile über die Dogmengeschichte. Ritschls Einfuss auf von Harnack*, Leiden, 1978, p. 11.

15 Manfred Wichelhaus, *Kirchengeschichtschreibung und Soziologie im neunzehnten Jahrhundert und bei Ernst Troeltsch*, Heidelberg, 1965, pp. 44–50.

16 The history of this journal forms much of the substance of Johannes Rathje, *Die Welt des freien Protestantismus*, Stuttgart, 1952.

17 Christoph Schwöbel, *Martin Rade. Das Verhältnis von Geschichte, Religion und Moral als Grundproblem seiner Theologie*, Gütersloh, 1980, p. 39.

18 *Ibid.* pp. 31–3.

19 Klatt, pp. 18–21, 26–7. The history of the 'kleine Facultät' has recently been taken much further by Friedrich Wilhelm Graf, 'Der "Systematiker" der "Kleinen Göttinger Fakultät". Ernst Troeltsch's Promotionsthesen und ihr Göttinger Kontext' in *Troeltsch Studien* 1, Gütersloh, 1982, 235–290.

20 When Harnack found himself in the company of historians of Ranckean derivation in 1906, he was odious again, preaching toleration against the government's politically inspired anti-catholicism. Rüdiger von Bruch, *Wissenschaft, Politik und offentliche Meinung. Gelehrtenpolitik in Wilhelminischer Deutschland, 1890–1914*, Husum, 1980, p. 390.

21 *Ibid.* 254, 265 n. 208.

22 On Naumann see Theodor Heuss, *Friedrich Naumann, Der Mann, das Werk, die Zeit*, Stuttgart, 1937: 3rd ed. München/Hamburg, 1968: Hermann Timm, *Friedrich Naumann. Theologischer Widerruf Theologische Existenz Heute* no. 141, München, 1967: Ingrid Engel, *Gottesverstandnis und sozialpolitischer Handeln. Eine Untersuchung zu Friedrich Naumann*, Göttingen, 1972: Andreas Lindt, *Friedrich Naumann und Max Weber. Theologische Existenz Heute* no. *174*, München, 1973: Ward, pp. 89–118: Friedrich Naumann, *Werke*, Köln/Opladen, 1964–7.

23 Berichte des Evangelisch-sozialen Kongresses 4, 1893, 12.

24 It is another sign of the toils into which the Ritschlian school was getting, that Naumann's contribution was attacked by Harnack on historical grounds. *Ibid.* 4. 41–3.

25 Naumann, *Werke* 1. 402–24: Timm, pp. 38–40.

26 On the fate of this political association see Dieter Düding, *Der Nationalsoziale*

Verein, 1896–1903. Der gescheiterte Versuch einer parteipolitischen Synthese von Nationalismus, Sozialismus und Liberalismus, München, 1972.

27 Naumann, *Werke* 1. 632.

28 'Max Weber, one of the mightiest of Germans and one of the most comprehensive, and also methodologically one of the strictest scholars of the age.' Historismus und seine Probleme, 1922, in Ernst Troeltsch, *Gesammelte Schriften* 4. 565.

29 *Ibid.* 2. 11.

30 Schwöbel, p. 122.

31 Adolf Harnack, *What is Christianity?*, London, 1901, p. 34.

32 Adolf Harnack, *Reden und Aufsätze* 4. 280–81.

33 Hans Wagenhammer, *Das Wesen des Christentums. Eine begriffsgeschichtliche Untersuchung*, Mainz, 1973.

34 Troeltsch, *Gesammelte Schriften* 2. 723.

35 Max Brodbeck, *Readings in philosophy of Social Science*, New York, 1968, pp. 503–4.

36 On this see Stephen W. Sykes, 'Troeltsch and Christianity's essence' in John P. Clayton (ed.) *Ernst Troeltsch and the future of theology*, Cambridge, 1976, p. 143. The paper as a whole is a valuable discussion of the relations of Weber and Troeltsch at this point.

37 Troeltsch, *Gesammelte Schriften* 2. 400.

38 *Ibid.* 2. 404.

39 Ernst Troetlsch, *The social teaching of the Christian churches*, London, 1931, p. 1004.

18

Faith and Fate. *Eine Vogelperspektive* of German Social Catholicism

Of the three parts to my title the *Vogelperspektive* is the light-hearted one. It is a favourite word of Hans-Urich Wehler who uses it frequently in his *German Social History*, a work of mind-boggling proportions. To Wehler a bird's-eye view is akin to a satellite picture; and all I can offer you today is a small album of satellite shots which will not tell you whether the rain will fall in your garden but may add realism to the barometric readings. Faith and fate in the sense of unsolicited historical circumstances have rarely been as dramatically combined as in the case of the German social Catholics. For if in one sense the social doctrine of the church grows out of its age-old mission to lead men to salvation, it does not attain a very sophisticated form nor liberate itself from moral theology till the nineteenth century. Concerned with the formation of earthly ordinances which may further the evangelical mission of the church, Catholic social doctrine must struggle to raise its sights not just from alms to charity, but from charity to policy. The special mark of German social Catholicism has been not the faith which it inherited and sustained, but its early and persistent efforts to generate policy under pressure.

Nineteenth-century industrialisation paid no heed to nation or denomination; Christian social doctrines were also developed everywhere in the West, and their common characteristics were that they were in the first instance the work of religious establishments, Catholic and Protestant, often indeed of establishments trying to find an acceptable substitute for political reform, and that their common cliche, a concern for the 'social question', 'question sociale', 'soziale Frage' embodied a delusion. That delusion was that the paramount affront to conscience was that of industrial labour relations, and no country was to demonstrate more painfully than Germany that agricultural labour relations, from which the

Paper presented to the International Symposium on the Centenary of the Papal Encyclical *Rerum Novarum*, Hull, 1991.

social Christian gaze was generally averted, could be a great deal more savage. The peculiarity of German catholicism in the nineteenth century was that it was composed of a series of social establishments which had lost their political standing; that it was confronted by Protestant governments, or in the case of Bavaria by a government in which Josephinist traditions were strong, and that the most important of the former, that of Prussia, which had a record of generosity in the treatment of religious minorities unequalled by any of the German churches, was now in a peculiarly illiberal phase. All governments, Catholic and Protestant, allowed a good deal of influence in church affairs to the king or emperor as the senior lay member of the congregation. When the Elector of Brandenburg, the ruler of an overwhelmingly Lutheran people, had turned Calvinist in the seventeenth century, he had forfeited that influence, and his theorists had sought ways in which ecclesiastical authority might be derived from the idea of the state. Prussia had in fact provided a home for many non-Lutherans, and for Lutheran protests against the narrowness of the Lutheran confessionalism sustained in Saxony, and dealt more generously with the Catholics they acquired in Silesia in the eighteenth century than the latter expected. But the partition of Poland set the Prussian state problems of assimilation on a new scale, and when the peace settlement of 1815 provided Prussia with large new Catholic populations in the Rhineland, she resumed the process of assimilation under the legislation thought appropriate for 18th-century Poland. The unacceptable face of deriving ecclesiastical authority from the idea of the state was now only too apparent. And in the Rhineland this face was the more unacceptable because on the left bank Catholics benefited from the Concordat of 1801 and liberal traditions shared with France and Belgium; on the right bank Prussian law began to operate under new and unfavourable circumstances.

Protestant states, moreover, had an immediate interest in aligning Catholic diocesan administration with their new boundaries, and in replacing piecemeal the old ecclesiastical constitution of the Empire. These new arrangements required the agreement of the Papacy and the paradoxical upshot of the long series of Concordats negotiated by Cardinal Consalvi, Pius VII's peripatetic Secretary of State, was that Protestant powers brought home to their Catholic populations the reality of Papal authority more forcibly than anyone had done in the recent past. It was a question whether curial policy would be any better adapted to the needs of the German Catholics than were the policies of their political masters. The final ambiguity was that the perceived needs of a German Catholic population divided by distance, language, social standing, and in the case of Bavaria a sense of separateness still held to justify an independent political machine, were very different. Later on the Centre Party was regularly plagued by clashes between the wealthy aristocracy of Silesia, their counterparts in Westphalia, the liberal bourgeoisie of the Rhine and the peasant democracy of the south-west. But the sprawling extension of Prussia was a unifying factor, and the permanent clash between that power and Cologne ensured that the conservative social forces in German Catholicism could not, like their counterparts elsewhere, use social Christianity as a substitute for liberal politics, since liberal constitutionalism seemed to be their only defence against a most unpalatable despotism. And in turn the long-running theme in the history of German Catholicism was whether conservative social instincts and liberal politics could be held in harness.

The essence of the story came right at the beginning in the famous 'Cologne affair'. Under a Prussian royal ordinance of 1803 designed to assist the Protestantisation of Poland, the children of mixed marriages were required to follow the religion of their father; this might enable the Protestant mayor of a Catholic town to form the nucleus of a Protestant congregation. The Prussian government obtained from the Papacy an agreement to allow priests to assist passively at the celebration of mixed marriages, and got the Archbishop of Cologne to agree that priests might actually celebrate mixed marriages contrary to canon law. Resistance, however, began amongst both priests and lay people, and when the Archbishop died in 1835, it was led by the new Archbishop Droste-Vischering, and backed by the Westphalian aristocracy from whom he sprang. Before long Droste-Vischering was imprisoned, and a year later, the Archbishop of Poznan. The Pope supported his bishops; the Prussian government tried to keep his missives from their people; other German governments were delighted to break their blockade, and a new Catholic journalism in which Görres was prominent, created a whole new public opinion. What the Catholics needed, and knew they needed, was some means to translate this strength into a defensive political force. To this end the desire of the German priesthood for a new self-image offered a new means. Their loss of status since the French Revolution, and the threat to the independence of the Papacy implied in the threat to the Papal States, killed off their old establishmentarianism, and made them long to stand at the head of their people, gathered beneath a Papacy which had not yet learned how to use forces of this kind. To this new turn the lofty romantics who figure in the textbooks as the grand old men of social Catholicism like Adam Heinrich Müller and Franz von Baader had almost nothing to say.

When state authority collapsed in the revolution of 1848, however, the transformation in German Catholicism became instantly apparent. At once the Archbishop of Cologne assembled his suffragans, and, in the autumn of 1848, the bishops of all Germany gathered in almost unheard-of style at Würzburg. Sixty-two years before there had indeed been a famous Congress at Ems which championed the rights of the German hierarchy against Rome; the Würzburg gathering, by contrast, pleaded the liberties of the church against oppressive states, and began with a declaration of absolute fidelity to the Papacy, the only ally in sight. And what the bishops here gained was never again challenged even in the most reactionary years after the revolution. They were moving faster than the state towards a sort of national unity, an option never open to them in the privileged days of the Catholic *ancien régime*. Laymen who needed defence against other popular forces which had been let loose, associated equally actively. *Piusvereine* sprouted like mushrooms, not of course at first embodying much in the way of policy. But from the beginning there were two styles of action which characterised and divided Catholics right down to the time of reconstruction, post-Second World War. There was the so-called Mainz type, under strong ecclesiastical influence, aiming primarily to defend religious liberties, and submitting their statutes to Rome for approval; and there was the Cologne type, which sought its own solutions to political and social problems, and was commonly led by laymen who insisted on the necessary connection between political and religious liberty. Another long-term source of disagreement turned up in Danzig, where the Piusvereine included Lutherans and Mennonites, all, we are told, 'avid for religious liberty'. These movements also seized a national platform, holding a Katholikentag practically every year thereafter.

The mention of Mainz brings us to its remarkable bishop, Ketteler. He was among the most forward to seize the opportunities created by the revolution, and his image, like that of other great historical figures, was subsequently remodelled to meet later needs; those *fin-de-siècle* Catholics who saw safety in depoliticising their movement represented him as more of a social reformer than he was. Ketteler sprang from Westphalian aristocracy; he was authoritarian but businesslike; his social assumptions were conservative, but his formative political experience was as assistant to Droste-Vischering at the time of the Cologne crisis, and all his life he believed that the platform of human rights claimed in 1848 was the basis for a national state. This political programme had indeed a social supplement. Ketteler shared that hostility to large-scale entrepreneurs and to Manchesterism which characterised the aristocracy everywhere, Catholic and Protestant; but no one in the Rhineland could be unaware that the very idea of private property was under noisy challenge from the far Left. Ketteler therefore regarded himself as pursuing a middle path, defending private property against the communists, protesting against that capitalist abuse of property rights which he saw as the cause of the disorders of industrial society. He dabbled in Lassalle, and thought the Church should aim to secure that everyone had a maintenance. One of the difficulties with Ketteler's social outlook was that it aggravated the central problem of his political platform. In 1848 it was not unreasonable to hope to promote co-operation between Catholics and liberals on a basis of opposition to absolutism. But Ketteler could never reconcile himself to the consequences of the fact that the Prussian state had dealt more generously with deviant views than any of the churches, and held that liberalism involved a militant theological subjectivism which made it the mortal enemy of the Catholic church, and as such the heir and ally of absolutism. Not even Catholic states escaped the contagion. Ketteler strongly favoured the *grossdeutsch* solution to the problem of German nationality; but in a private memorandum which Pfülf rescued from his papers he spoke bitterly of the bad young boys sent from Austria to the National Assembly in 1848. And well he might, for with a few years of the Revolution of 1848 the first tremors of what became the Kulturkampf began to be felt in South Germany and the Habsburg Empire. Ketteler had somehow to plead for toleration in circumstances in which liberals were incensed by the Syllabus of Errors and the efforts of church authority to treat toleration as an attack on its evangelical mission. Ketteler himself wanted free trade in religion without accepting the consequences of this particular *Manchestertum*. And from his viewpoint this question had an urgency which social questions lacked.

German parties, including Catholic parties, trace their origin to the revolution of 1848, but, during the years of reaction which followed, they mostly lost their constituency organisation. The upswing did not return till the sixties. The Catholics, however, retained and developed their network of societies, and these, once the dream of a great Germany under Austrian leadership had been laid to rest, were able to develop their own national organisations, and generated both social activity and social theory. They formed a very compact, regionally structured, and hierarchically framed Catholic social milieu, which in homogeneous Catholic areas could be extremely intransigent. It was a half-political organisation, devoted to a Catholic defence which was badly needed, and it isolated the Catholic population from their neighbours in a ghetto of great durability. Moreover, under the threat of the Kulturkampf, this half-political organisation instantly adopted an effective political front, in the shape of the Centre Party, and rooted it deeply in the Catholic constituency. There was a price for this success. In Rainer Lepsius's words, the Centre was not a membership party, simply the political committee of the Catholic organisations, linked to the voters by the organisations and the clergy.

Should that co-operation be withdrawn, the Centre would collapse like a pack of cards. A long time ahead, in 1933, this happened, and the collapse of the Centre brought after it the collapse of most of what was valuable in German life.

The Kulturkampf, hectic as it was by the standards of the old absolutism, was a very 19th-century prefiguring of the crisis of 1933. Beginning with the abolition of the Catholic section of the Kultusministerium, and proceeding to establish state control over all schools and to prescribe the education of all clergy, the clash ended with the cutting off of state financial support, with a papal encyclical declaring all government measures invalid, and punishing compliance with excommunication. Bishops and clergy were jailed, and soon one third of the parishes in Prussia alone were vacant. Why did Bismarck do it, particularly a Bismarck who as recently as 1870 had seriously considered offering asylum to the Pope should he be compelled by the Italian occupation of Rome to flee abroad, and who as a somewhat quirky evangelical was not disposed to the conventional Protestant Caesaro-papism which Catholics had been contesting since 1815? No final answer to this question has ever been produced, and the best guide lies in Bismarck's general bearing. Politics, in his view, was a field of battle in which the prudent chose the ground of conflict and struck first. Long views were discouraged both by his experience of the game and his genuine trust in Providence. He had no special grievance against the Centre Party, though he did not care for the anti-Prussianism of its components in Hanover and the south-west. Still less did he care for the fact that in the south-west the Catholic network had created a popular movement on a conservative basis, for Bismarck, however revolutionary his action, was intent on presenting himself as the one conservative dam against the flood. But the attack was probably triggered off opportunistically by Ketteler's presenting a petition calling for the expulsion of Italian troops from the Papal states, and eliciting a letter from the papal secretary Antonelli declaring the solidarity of the Curia with the Centre party. When the Centre party proposed constitutional changes to secure the free development of the Church and its associations, the way was open to brand the whole movement as hostile to the Reich. This campaign guaranteed the reactionary Chancellor the enthusiastic support of most of the liberals, and killed any possibility of future co-operation between them and the Catholics.

It was of course a battle which Bismarck could not possibly win, though this did not prevent him, a few years later, pursuing a similar campaign against the Socialists, a rather different party which also underpinned their political front with a great network of social institutions. It was also an entirely unnecessary battle. In the short run it destroyed the unanimity of patriotic fervour which had greeted the victorious war against France, and in the long run it strengthened the defences which the Catholic community raised against the forces which were inexorably assimilating them to German life. In 1873 80 per cent of Catholic males voted for the Centre; by 1912 that proportion was down to 60 per cent, and by 1933 to about 40 per cent. But the impact made by the clash on the leadership élite, prolonged its effects almost to our own time. The birth dates of Matthias Erzberger (1875), the Centre leader murdered in 1920, Brüning (1885), Chancellor 1930–32, and Adenauer (1876) all fell in this crucial period. And the Centre's relatively stable base in the electorate, secured it a very steady 25 per cent of the seats in the Reichstag; indeed one of the examples of the hollowness of the public life of the later Second Empire was the degree to which the rise of Socialism caused the Protestant monarchy to depend on the parliamentary support of a Catholic Centre Party which was itself losing voters to the Socialists and peasant parties.

Bismarck was too canny a hand to launch the Kulturkampf without giving himself ample opportunity to distance himself from it when the time was convenient. It proved that a good deal more was needed than this, or even the election of a Pope in Leo XIII who was ready for a compromise. Christoph Weber, in an engaging piece of Namierisation, has shown that if the Chancellor had trouble with the instincts of his bureaucracy and some of his political allies, Leo XIII had to fight for his independence in the Vatican, and try to restrain the hardliners in the Centre Party, while Bishop Kopp, the principal negotiator in Germany, wanted a compromise with the state in order to get his ordinands into universities and break the hold of seminary scholasticism on their training. The two principal parties, the Chancellor and Pope must fight each other's battles, and did so with sufficient effect to achieve an untidy settlement in 1887. Three years later the new Emperor William II had ditched Bismarck, publicly advertised himself as a social-welfare Kaiser, called a conference at Berlin on labour protection and even invited the Pope. This contact stimulated Leo XIII to turn the long-standing work of the International Union of Social Studies which had been meeting for some years at Freiburg into the Encyclical, *Rerum Novarum*, which you are here celebrating.

This Encyclical appeared to the German Social Catholics to give authoritative blessing to the main lines of their own domestic discussions. These had given more sophisticated substance to the simple principles with which Ketteler had begun. The view that social need could be adequately met by a combination of moral renewal and church charity, had been out-gunned by the conviction that social policy was indispensable. The question whether that policy should aim at total social reconstruction based on past corporative social models or some new ones, had been answered by the less radical acceptance of the present social order, and determination to remedy some of its defects. Socialism remained anathema, but, after ferocious argument, the dominant view among the German social Catholics came to be that much greater state intervention in social issues was needed, a perhaps surprising conclusion from a community whose grievances against the state in question were so many and so recent. The call for what amounted to a moderate welfare state was a rather modest basis on which to advertise a 'Catholic solution to the social problem', but even so it concealed a new series of domestic religious problems. Ketteler had held explicitly that, by the order of creation, the state was as independent of the Church in its own sphere, as in its sphere the Church was of the state; and so too was its authority. By the same token political parties and trade unions had a claim on Christian allegiance irrespective of confessional character. The Centre party had given up the name of Catholic *Fraktion*, and if Catholics baulked at the way Socialist trade unions were built into the Marxist machinery of agitation, there were no doubt objectives for which Catholics and Protestants might legitimately combine in the same or separate unions. This at any rate was the view in the Mönchen-Gladbach section of the movement, and, in the later nineties, in the Katholikentag. But in some sections of Catholic labour, and increasingly from Rome under the influence of Benigni, then papal under-secretary of state, it was stoutly challenged, and the challenge maintained by what amounted to a party organisation in Berlin.

For a Catholic movement could not insulate itself from wider currents in the Church; and although under inspiration of *Rerum Novarum* the Volksverein got up to a membership of 800,000 before the 1914 war and did a job of organisation and social education said to have been equalled by no other Catholic organisation in the world, the wider currents in the Church were on the whole unhelpful to the movement after the turn of the century. For integralism was as hostile to social openness as to modernism. The integralists called for a systematic theology which should interpret the world as well as the Church, and in which every part should be a key support to every other. They had no doubt that 'an enduring fellow-travelling and co-operation with people of the most various outlooks and ideals could not possibly be for good, even if it were in the long run feasible', and they were prepared to match practical action to theoretical word, by almost outlawing strike action. This fracas was wound up by the Papal Encyclical *Singulari quadam* (1912) which permitted the continu-ation of the existing Christian trade unions, but showed so strong a preference for organisations closely united to the church, as to enable the Berlin party to expound the Pope as permitting interconfessional unions only a temporary toleration. In the same way when Julius Bachem exhorted the Centre party in 1906 to 'come out of the tower', he evoked a violent counterblast. And even where the Centre did not get sucked into this maelstrom, it found it hard to retain the loyalty of a younger generation of priests in whose professional judgment other things were more urgent to counteract the steady disintegration of the Catholic community, devotion to the Sacred Heart, Marian piety or the liturgical movement, for example. And at the end of 1918 the Bavarian opposition to the leadership of Erzberger did cause a schism from the Centre and the establishment of the Bavarian Volkspartei, the successors of which are still in independent existence. The case of German social Catholicism in the early twentieth century is in short rather like that and rather worse than that of English Methodism a century earlier; rather like, in that so far from providing 'a Catholic solution to the social question' or a focus of national unity, it could barely counter the forces of division in its own ranks, and rather worse in that the transformation of the Centre in the crucial years before the first World War into a usually pro-government party guaranteed that the Second Empire would not reform itself as the interests of both the Empire and the Catholic community demanded. English Methodism could not stop the unreformed British system reforming itself. But it took the last agonies of the First World War and the threat of revolution to drive the Centre to what Wilfried Loth has called a 'half-turn' to parliamentary democracy.

This ambiguous performance continued throughout the period of the Weimar Republic. Calling in the state to the cause of labour protection had in no way equipped the mind of the Centre to deal with the gigantic state-led rip-off of hyperinflation. Once again the Centre found itself an indispensable state-supporting party, and particularly in Prussia had a permanent and very profitable agreement with the Socialists. In the Reich the story was less happy. It was to the credit of the Centre that for a decade or more it helped to maintain a democratic system; but in its guidelines of 1922 it avoided the words democracy and democratic, affirming support only for a *Volksstaat*, and some of its number were already looking to a collapse of the system. Its way of preserving its own precarious cohesion was by reacting to the proposals of others rather than generating policy of its own, and by relying, at a time when the clergy were playing a diminishing role in the public life of the Catholic community, on priests to mediate in its internal affairs. It was this process which in 1928 gave the party its first clerical leader in Monsignor Kaas, who insisted that Brüning be made head of the Reichstag delegation. The unfortunate feature of this new clericalism was that it coincided with a shift in policy in Rome which left less room for political Catholicism as practised in Germany.

Notwithstanding all these ambiguities the record of the German Catholics during the period of Hitler's meteoric rise to the threshold of power was an honourable one. The bishops repeatedly condemned Nazi doctrine as anti-Christian; the Centre party kept up its share of the poll, and this indicated not only a will to fight, but the fact that the cohesion of the Catholic community, though much weakened, was holding. Early in 1933 a wave of terror directed against the Centre and the civil servants who adhered to it made it clear that something worse than a new Kulturkampf might be in prospect. The result of the clean sweep made by Hitler of the parties of the right in the elections of March 1933 was that the Centre was no longer the key to the formation of a government, but was still the key to the special majority Hitler needed to assume dictatorial powers constitutionally by means of an Enabling Act. New policies in Rome were now decisive. Pius XI's Catholic Action required the penetration of public life with the spirit of a Church now more sharply defined by canon law revision. He was moreover obsessed with the danger of Bolshevik religious persecution which was undoubtedly a bigger menace to the interests of the Church as a whole than it was to those of the German Church in particular. He and his secretary of state Pacelli sought to provide for both concerns by a series of Concordats with Bavaria (1924), Prussia (1929) and Baden (1932) based on the principles of the Italian Lateran treaties, which should provide a more certain protection to the Church than confessionally based political parties. The disastrous things about 1933 were that it was quite clear that a Reich concordat would never be obtained from a constitutional government, that the Pope became convinced that, apart from himself, Hitler was the only reliable spokesman against Bolshevism, and that Monsignor Kaas, in terms of the principles of the Concordats, was in effect the pupil of Pacelli. With Kaas as a go-between Hitler offered the Pope his concordat which was accepted over an Easter weekend behind the backs of the bishops and the Centre Party, at the price of ditching the whole machine of political Catholicism. After a dreadful scene in which Brüning insisted on the rejection of the Enabling Bill and Kaas pounded the table, saying 'Am I the leader of the Centre Party? If not who is?', the Centre Party wrote its own death sentence by providing the necessary majority for the bill, Kaas left the country while his party foundered, and the bishops, now with no protection except the Concordat, had to eat their words. Other governments, of course, made the same mistake as the Pope; the calamitous thing about this mistake was that it visited an appalling penalty on the long-term failure of the German Catholic community to harmonize its liberal political interests with its conservative social inclinations, and the failure of the Centre Party to become an ordinary political party organising its own political constituency.

Political catastrophes on this scale rarely permit their perpetrators a second chance; but by virtue of ecclesiastical cohesion German Catholicism had always been an exception to the usual rules. Twice it had inherited political power by default, once with the collapse of the *Obrigkeitsstaat* by revolution in 1848 and once with its overthrow by allied action in 1918. Amazingly it did so twice again, illustrating what is becoming familiar in Eastern Europe, that when dictatorships destroy ordinary political life, people's loyalties focus upon whatever is left to them, especially the nation and the confession, and where, as in Poland or Lithuania, these substantially coincide, one intolerance may be replaced by another. At the end of the Second World War the Church was in existence, however bruised by persecution and compromise, and its bishops were among the few function-ing native authorities. The doctrine they uttered went back to the earliest days of social Catholicism before there was any social Catholic doctrine; their view that Nazism was a consequence of men's turning away from God, was not very sophisticated, but it served to underpin successful demands for public assistance to safeguard moral objectives to which they were strongly committed, and furthered a process which has left the German churches the largest employer in the country after the state. Moreover the bishops and their agents, especially Domkapitular Wilhelm Böhler, who, in the palmy days of Weimar, had been General Secretary of the Catholic school organisation, had an important influence on the development of the West German constitutions. German life was now more confessionally mixed than it ever had been, and this made it easier for the CDU to attract conservative Protestant voters than it had ever been for the Centre, a proceeding which the bishops did not oppose, while the Socialists eventually jettisoned their Marxist baggage partly in the hope of recruiting on the Catholic Left. Add to this that the Cold War produced a Federal Republic in which Catholics were actually in a majority, and that a CDU which had begun by being heavily weighted with Catholic-social, labour-protection baggage became the exponents of the most successful capitalism in the West, and the scene was set for a surprise beyond the wildest dreams of the Centre: when Gorbachev pulled the plug on the Warsaw pact regimes, the CDU swept the board in the old Protestant and Socialist heartlands of the former East Germany. The heirs of the *reichfeindlich* party had reunited most of the old Empire and its Chancellor was making tactless noises before the German minority in Poland. Was political Catholicism finally making its way at the expense of social Catholicism? At election times the bishops trotted out pastoral letters with the regularity of liturgical amens, but gunning against liberalism saved neither Socialist nor CDU governments from dependence on FDP votes. On a theoretical level one learned Jesuit, Nell-Breuning, complained that a long series of Papal economic pronouncements had disastrously overstepped the limits of their authors' technical competence, and that the integralists, those great pioneers of social doctrine, refused to distinguish between the degrees of authority attaching to church pronouncements. Other Jesuits laboured to demythologise the peasant problem and must now be groaning at the way the world's interests in the GATT negotiations have been sacrificed on the altar of the peasant lobby. And to cap all, it is hard not to believe that a persistence of social-Catholic, labour-protection baggage was not one of the influences in the disastrous decision of Chancellor Kohl to condemn his new provinces, starved both of capital and entrepreneurial skill to mass unemployment, by granting them both currency parity and wage parity with the West. The real world is resolving the ambiguities of the German social-Catholic tradition for it.

19

The Socialist Commitment
in Karl Barth

The young Karl Barth is not an easy man to assess. It is not just that he covered a major theological revulsion by violent polemics, nor even that in the second world war he became a cult figure with hard-pressed Protestants everywhere, overwhelmed by the need to save their churches from the destructive compromises of the church leaders, and subsequently, more briefly, a cult figure with a new theological establishment. More recently the young Karl Barth has been the victim of disputes over the uses to which Barthianism can be put. In the German student revolt the need to unify thought and action in politics and theology exposed a generation gap; a burning concern to many theological students, it embarrassed many of their teachers. At the Kirchliche Hochschule in Berlin, a bastion of Barthianism, Friedrich-Wilhelm Marquardt, a pupil of Hellmut Gollwitzer, sought to bridge the gap by showing that from the beginning to end the core of Barth's theology was a socialist commitment. (The first paragraph of this book reads starkly, 'Karl Barth was Socialist'.)[1] The perspective first opened by the student movement was confirmed by Marquardt's editorial work on Barth's Safenwil remains, and especially on forty three socialist speeches. Marquardt worked out his view systematically in a *Habilitationschrift* which was rejected at the Kirchliche Hochschule as *unwissenschaftlich*. Gollwitzer made a public scene, got the book published, and took the whole argument further in a long essay of his own.[2] The clinching evidence (if that is what it really is) of the speeches is not available under the terms on which Karl Barth's unpublished remains are being edited until the volume in which they are to be incorporated is published. Yet most of the voluminous material ever likely to be available for the young Barth is now in print, and it is worth examining in its own right, as distinct from being expounded in the light of the *Church Dogmatics* with Marquardt.

Printed in *Studies in Church History* 15 (1978), pp. 453–65.

Marquardt's argument is that the socialist practice of Barth's years as a parish minister at Safenwil (1911–21) shaped not merely his social theory but his understanding of God. If Barth's socialism was in a sense pre-Marxist, apocalyptic, his conception of the unity of theory and practice was very Marxist indeed, notwithstanding current allegations from the DDR that Barth represented 'a genuine bourgeois position'.[3] For the only practice corresponding to the kingdom of God must be a practice aiming to overthrow social conditions which radically contradicted the kingdom. The living God who fetched up in the last volume of the *Church Dogmatics* as 'the partisan of the poor and finally . . . revolutionary'[4] had been the great overthrower from the beginning. As Marquardt puts it, Barth's development had been 'from "God" as a hallmark of revolution interpreted in the religious-socialist way, to "revolution" as the hallmark of God understood in revelation.'[5] If revolution implies radical discontinuity, so also do justification and the new birth as understood in the reformed tradition. The bourgeoisie had the material and moral resources to benefit by reform. The only hope for the proletariat was in a total upheaval in their inward and outward circumstances; but in its desperate helplessness the proletariat was close to the kingdom of God. The socialist understanding of the proletarian lot was a parable of the human predicament; the will to revolution was a parable of God's response. To admit, as eventually Brunner came to do, even a point of contact between natural man and the living God, was not merely an erroneous concession to humanism, it was bourgeois reformism. Indeed natural theology, an attempt by human resources to lay some hold on the riddle of existence, and to domesticate revelation by laying a foundation for it, was simply the *Verburgerlichung des Evangeliums*, the process of making the gospel respectable.[6] No discontinuity could be more discontinuous or revolutionary than the resurrection, understood not so much Christologically as apocalyptically, the secret force of God in the history of the world, the beginning of a messianic history on earth, of a new people of God who grasp the act of God and are grasped by it.[7] How do all these claims look in the light of Barth's voluminous early correspondence, the scores of sermons and addresses, and the first two editions of his *Romans* (1919 and 1921)?

Even as a student Barth had written a paper for the Zofingia society embodying conventional religious-social views, and like so many others, in Switzerland as well as England, found a way into the social question through the Blue Cross teetotal movement. He made no secret of his socialist views from the moment of his arrival in Safenwil, and was certainly considering joining the party as early as midsummer 1913.[8] The jolt Barth received from the patriotic stance of his German teachers at the outbreak of war, he steadily embroidered into one of the most famous legends of recent church history, even claiming that it justified turning against the whole theological tradition stemming from Schleiermacher,[9] a blanket condemnation from which only Schleiermacher's rough handling by the Prussian government earned him exoneration in Barth's extreme old age.[10] It ought to have been as important to Barth as it was to Ragaz that the leaders of the second international had behaved as badly as the theologians, but instead he joined the party early in 1915, explaining that 'just because I set such emphasis Sunday by Sunday on the last things, it was no longer possible for me personally to remain suspended in the clouds above the present evil world'. This eschatological gesture was, however, one of qualified solidarity, Barth limiting his party activity to paying subscriptions and giving lectures,[11] in which, among other things, he explained what was wrong with the party. 'I do it without enthusiasm', he reported in 1916, 'because it is necessary and because I cannot as yet get on to the one thing necessary with them in the way it must be done'.[12] There was also some trade union activity, and in the autumn of 1917, he became involved in a clash between fifty-five women knitters in his parish who organised and were threatened with dismissal by their employer. Barth interceded with the employer who gave him a polite reception and then declared war, adding that Barth 'was the worst enemy he has had in his whole life'. Barth claimed to have shown that the gospel was behind the knitters, and the village also backed them up; but he reported, 'I have contributed *nothing* directly other than a statement of facts to the factory workers, on which I . . . reported in the meeting, in order to make clear to them the seriousness of their position'.[13] No more indeed is heard of the united knitting workers. In all this there is something less than the practitioner of revolution being led to the God of revolution and back again. So far from the hostile mill-owner opposing Barth's re-election to the parish in 1917, he got him an increase in pay, and the relief measures Barth organised during the influenza epidemic of November 1918 were generously supported by the employers of the village. The truth is that the vast correspondence with Thurneysen is strikingly unpolitical, overwhelmingly dominated by ecclesiastical concerns, exchanges of sermons, the preparation of the commentary on Romans, professional reading and so forth. For a man preaching an eschatological hope, perceiving the breaking through of the kingdom of God, Barth's silence about the events of the time is deafening. He seems to have had a perverse sympathy with the German offensive in March 1918,[14] and his sneers against the League of Nations were even more offensive than the barbs he usually directed against Ragaz whose pro-league sympathies were doubtless what really provoked him. 'The good-boy AntiChrist in Wilson is now coming to light and the League of Nations will surely become the great whore of Babylon.'[15] Thurneysen enthused over Barth's reports of the strength of old-fashioned pietism in Württemberg, rejoiced that Germany 'did not have to be transformed into a red army camp like Hungary! And [held that] despite everything I would rather stand by Germany than by Wilson who wants to attend the peace settlement with his wife and children, apparently in high moral spirits.'[16]

The argument from silence to the conclusion that Barth was basically unpolitical is clinched by what he does not say on the theme he claimed to take seriously, that of socialism. There is not the least suggestion that he knew or cared that the party he had joined was at the centre of important developments in the world of international labour; still less that he appreciated that the labour troubles in his own parish were part of the wider resentments that led to the Zürich riots in November 1917. The year between the riots and the general strike was still more tense; Barth, the man who proclaimed from the pulpit that 'God is! signifies a revolution', had absolutely nothing to say.[17] While Ragaz was puzzling out the drift of the times from Burckhardt and Alexander Herzen, and even Thurneysen was seeking illumination from Carlyle's *French Revolution*,[18] Barth, who throughout the year had been applying himself intensively to the Württemberger pietists, was pinning his faith to the apocalyptic Bengel.[19] Thurneysen indeed reminded him that there were reactionary pietists who had interfered in politics too much, but then, as Switzerland teetered on the edge of revolution, Thurneysen was not willing to make a public proclamation, for he was not sure whether events portended Bolshevism, the last things, or a revival of the age of Metternich.[20] None of this can be reckoned a moral failing in Barth. He had his *Romans* to finish, and the pietist literature seemed one road to that goal. Nor did his literary labour exclude assisting his parishioners, as distinct from his core-congregation in their temporal necessities. Nevertheless the record seems threadbare as evidence for a Marxist union of theory and praxis, and it suggests that when Barth talked about socialism, he sometimes did so in a rather special sense.

That this is the case is the tenor of the utterances from Thurneysen's side of the partnership (whence most of the references to the affairs of the day come) and of the sermons of the two friends so far published. In 1914 Thurneysen had to prime Barth about Naumann,[21] on whom he had published a substantial paper in 1910.[22] Naumann is here perceived as significant in the sharpness of the antithesis which he discovered between Christianity and the autonomous power-state, and the way he exemplified the more general problem posed to Christianity by modern openness to autonomous culture. It was this which led to the everlasting discussions of the day on Christianity and culture, ethics and business, religion and socialism, all those things which Barth was to put under the blanket condemnation of 'hyphenated Christianity'. In 1910 Thurneysen could find no ethical basis for the state, though he was prepared to argue with Troeltsch that the state must provide for a good life according to the current level of cultural achievement, once the physical basis of existence had been met. Thus the separation of political and religious values was not as complete as was affirmed by Naumann from the side of the state, or by Tolstoy from the side of the kingdom of God. There was a positive Christian ethic distinct from all *Kulturseligkeit*, from which the achievements, crises and catastrophes of public life could not be withdrawn, but a manifold reality was not to be conceived in simple formulae; it must be laid hold of and mastered in personal act and decision. At this point Thurneysen was already fitted to absorb Barth's later doctrine that language about God and man could not proceed on the same level, and their common addiction to Russian spirituality, and especially Dostoievsky.[23] It was also significant that Thurneysen responded with genuine enthusiasm to Naumann's early period, quoting a long passage from *Was heisst christlich-sozial?* (1894): 'We feel the Christian-social cause as a force and power. It hovers over us as a new power of thought, it moves us, raises up, bears us ... The gospel is to us as a melting glow, the power of a new epoch.' Here in the young Naumann at his most unpolitical was the rhetoric needed by Kutter and the young Barth to express the action of the living God. It was perhaps too close for comfort to the stark irrationalism of the life-philosophy and was not politics at all in the ordinary sense of the word.

Echoes of the Naumann discussion recur in Barth's sermons for 1914. Jesus had fought for social justice, but now men supposed the fight could go on without him. Barth replies 'it is to stand the matter on its head if one says: indeed ... we want Socialism, but not the source from which it flowed and must flow, if it wishes to be something genuine or deep.' And the conclusion is doubly unpolitical. 'Yes, Jesus has proclaimed a new, righteous world, the Kingdom of God, but only those will enter it, only those will see it, who are of a pure heart and a good will ... whoever wants a better world must become a better man'. The conclusion of November 1914 was predictable: 'Others expect salvation from a general *revolution*, from a rising of peoples against their governments ... [But] in reality every nation has the government it deserves.'[24] To right wrong by revolution was to cast out devils by Beelzebub. The socialists had failed to stop the war, and the moral was, 'put not your trust in men (compare Ps. 146:3) whatever their names may be'.[25] In six hundred and fifty pages of sermons the momentous politics of 1914 receive a handful of banalities of this kind, banalities on the whole derogatory to socialism. The later sermons published as *Suchet Gott, so werdet ihr leben* (1917) show equally little evidence of the concurrent reading of the Bible and newspaper with which Barth is credited, though the anti-establishment tone is sharper,[26] and there is the acute feeling of social breakup which had been with the religious-socialist movement from the beginning. Yet the social movements in Russia and elsewhere were 'not the full powerful, certain wind of the spirit as it happened at Pentecost',[27] and the earth tremors 'powerfully rattling at our churches' did not alter the fact that efforts to reorder the world of work or education, politics and social relations must take second place to 'the great turn from death to life, waiting to break forth from heaven upon earth'.[28] The role of the socialist party was that of an eschatological 'sign'; it was a pointer to the Christian hope. That was why Blumhardt and Barth had joined it, and that was why Barth concluded of himself what he had elsewhere concluded of Blumhardt, that 'to hope upon God is something unpolitical and supra-political, and coincides with no party, be it socialist, conservative or liberal.'[29] Barth like Kutter was pressing the *analogia fidei*, the view that social unrest, socialism, was the earthly analogy of the action of the living God in judgement and redemption. There were two problems here. The first was that the closer socialism resembled an idea in the mind of God, the less connection it could have with any working system of politics. The second was that the closer Barth came to Kutter in insisting on the indispensability of the *analogia fidei*, the less they could agree on what it amounted to. For in 1914 Kutter had become a violent pro-German, was reported to be singing the 'Watch on the Rhine' all day and publicly maintaining that God demonstrated his purposes for mankind in the history of a particular people or state, specifically at present the German people and state, whose very authoritarianism was intended to nurture a culture of humanity for the human race at large.[30] Not for the last time, the *analogia fidei* seemed capable of producing results to order. But Kutter, counselling his young friends against destroying 'the inner processes of growth' by too much clarity,[31] encouraged work on the *Romans*, to the early editions of which we must now turn.

Barth's exposition of Romans 13.1–7 ('Let every soul be subject to the higher powers. For . . . the powers that be are ordained of God') turned into a political tirade, but was not more singular than Marquardt's exposition of Barth. On Marquardt's view ' "Revolution" becomes . . . the basic concept of his understanding of God, his eschatology, his ethics',[32] and Barth's doctrine of the state is structured like Lenin's *State and Revolution* which had recently appeared. The state embodies no values, it is simply a power organisation existing for purposes of exploitation. The difference is that while Lenin was prepared to proceed to the dictatorship of the proletariat without waiting for better men to sustain it, Barth criticized the presumption of revolutionary individuals, and called for the 'absolute revolution of God'. No Christian revolutionary cadre has the fate of the kingdom of God in its hands, but the Christian revolutionary, unlike Lenin's comrades, is in some sense already 'a new creation'. Hence Barth's throw-away phrase which matters so much to Marquardt, that his revolution (or God's) is 'more than Leninism'.[33]

The unpolitical Barth of the war years did not of course suddenly metamorphose into a Protestant Lenin. The keynote to his discussion is given at the very beginning – it is 'intended in the *Spirit* and must be understood in the *Spirit*. Only to the pure in heart will the path to be trod be and remain a *straight* path.'[34] It is a homily to the saints. History after the fall, declared Barth, is under the wrath of God, and the normal management of earthly relations through the righteousness of God can only be restored in Christ. So far from the powers that be being ordained of God in the common place sense of the words, 'the power state of the present day is diametrically opposed to the intentions of God; it is intrinsically evil'.[35] The state indeed achieved a certain interlocking balance in the affairs of fallen men, and as such is one of God's devices for keeping men in hand; but the overwhelming weight of Barth's rhetoric is directed to the point that the Christian as such has 'nothing to do with the power state,' any kind of power state or political party, with 'Gustavus Adolphus or Napoleon, Cromwell or Frederick the Great, Windthorst or Bebel . . . with monarchy, militarism, patriotism [or] liberalism.' 'All politics, as the struggle for power, as the diabolical art of legitimation, is *basically* dirty' and any Christian who goes into it, particularly bearing 'the banners of God' deserves all he gets, for he abandons the analogy of the sufferings of Christ.[36] The Christian has no fatherland, he still seeks one. 'The decisive struggle between the old and the new world will never be fought out in the political arena', and the absolute revolution of God is not to be hastened by individual initiative. 'Only through the quiet other-worldly construction of a new man according to the order of God' and through alienating the affections of the flock from this world to another, is the Christian 'to starve out the state religiously'. Right at the end of his treatment Barth returns with his left hand a little of what he has so violently taken away with his right, allowing that running away from politics has as little merit as deifying them. But the limit is 'illusionless fulfilment of duty without song-and-dance . . . *no* combinations of throne and altar, *no* Christian patriotism, no beating up of democratic crowds. Strike and general strike and street fighting if it must be, but *no* religious justification and glorification of it. Military service as soldier or officer, if it must be, but under *no* circumstances as chaplain'.[37] It was in this context that Barth uttered his now famous slogan, 'social-democratic but not religious-socialist.'[38] Barth had defended himself against the commonplace political idolatry of Germany, both Protestant and Catholic, but if pushed hard he might have had to concede at least a provisional autonomy to politics of the kind he so bitterly resented in Naumann. And the main tenor of his message, like so much of Barth in those years was pietism accompanied by an unpietist gnashing of teeth. It was not just that he gave no guidance to the Christian caught up in street-fighting to decide on which side to fight, and approved only a minimum stake in a temporal order hastening to dissolution; it is that a man who can use the word 'penultimate' as a term of abuse[39] with an abandon perhaps only possible to one committed to the ethos of an endowed establishment, feels no need for discrimination among penultimate things and does not appreciate the ingenuity required to maintain a supply of them. There may be some virtue in this position; there is none in regarding it as the theological counterpart to Lenin, the exemplar of the terrifying potentialities of political decision.

A few months after the appearance of the *Romans*, Barth resumed his struggle for a transcendent viewpoint in his address on the 'Christian in Society' at the religious-socialist conference at Tambach.[40] Disenchantment with the state, now extended to other social institutions which claimed to grasp the riddle of existence – 'authority in itself', especially academic authority, 'the family in itself . . . the voracious idol of the bourgeoisie', and, worst of all, 'religion as such . . . this power of death in its Catholic and Protestant form'.[41] Barth came within an ace of denying the possibility of policy,[42] but fetched up by saying that in Christ lay 'the overcoming of the false denial of the world and the unconditioned assurance against all *false* affirmation of the world'. The resurrection included God's 'Yes' and his 'No' to the world, just as socialism showed how it was impossible to say 'No' to the world without entering it.[43] The conclusion was that of Thurneysen in 1910: 'We will neither burn up and go mad about affirmation with Naumann until it becomes nonsense, nor go with Tolstoy into rejection until it becomes absurd'.[44] Once again Barth had, in the hottest possible language, advised the radical to play it cool.

The Tambach address opened the German market to Barth for the first time, literally as well as metaphorically, for it enabled him to find a German publisher; this in its turn led to the decision completely to rewrite the *Romans* and to twelve months of furious literary effort to which even his parish preaching took second place. Marquardt who grossly exaggerates the significance of radical political decision in Barth's earliest theology, exaggerates again in seeing in the second *Romans* 'a sensational anti-revolutionary turn',[45] but has certainly got the direction right, and may well be correct in his supposition that the new stance contributed to the book's success in Germany on its appearance in 1922. It is not quite clear why the new turn took place. At the crucial time Thurneysen was writing his paper on 'Socialism and Christianity'[46] which showed little advance on the line of Kutter and Blumhardt; the doctrine was still the unpolitical one that socialism mattered because it taught the church about justification by faith.[47] But Barth now affirmed 'too broken a position towards Socialism' to be put on the list of party speakers, and found his curate, Frau Thurneysen's cousin, Fritz Lieb, reporting him as holding that 'the social question would be the next to come *off* the order of the day.'[48] It is hard to believe that Barth was not tempted by the very success of the Russian revolution to take it down a peg; and he suspected he had misled the German religious-socialists by the blunt certainties of the first edition.[49] Above all he had to cope in the most domestic sense with Fritz Lieb, who had gone over from Syriac to Karl Marx without acquiring discretion in transit. When the Swiss socialist party split in December 1920 on the issue of affiliation to the third international, and the minority withdrew to form a communist party, Lieb was one of the hardest hardliners among them; Barth was on the other side, and subsequently had to take time off from the second *Romans* to sort out Lieb's behaviour in both pulpit and parish.[50]

The new treatment bore the marks of the Tambach address, for it was directed not narrowly to the state and revolution, but to the whole range of great social institutions which limited the rights of individuals by virtue of their claim to solve the riddle of life. To admit their authority was to concede legitimation, to reject it was to accept the principle of revolution. Barth proposed to deny both in the name of the honour of God. But on the somewhat implausible ground that no one was likely to be won for reaction reading Romans, he was specially concerned 'to wrest from . . . [the Radical's] hands the principle of revolution . . . a sacrifice of quite peculiar dignity.'[51] The revolutionary sees clearly that all human authority is fraudulently acquired, but so far from overcoming evil with good 'he too usurps a position which is not due to him, . . . an authority which, as we have grimly experienced in Bolshevism, but also in the behaviour of far more delicately-minded innovators! soon displays its essential tyranny.' The rebel stands near to God for 'he really means that Revolution which is the impossible possibility. He means forgiveness of sins and the resurrection of the dead. He means Jesus Christ – He that hath *overcome*!' He substitutes doing for 'not doing', and establishes the old order in more powerful form by contriving revolution in the Leninist fashion with men as they are.[52] The basically unpolitical conclusion of the first *Romans* was necessarily reaffirmed more starkly. 'A political career . . . becomes possibly only when it is seen to be essentially a game'. Tax paying, the most passive of political actions, now appeared as the type of that 'not doing' by which the man saved by grace and that not of himself signified his allegiance to the righteousness of God.[53]

There was perhaps more truth than Thurneysen knew in his conclusion
of February 1923 that socialism and Christianity had passed each other to
a distance which made dialogue almost impossible.[54] Barth became a
professor at Göttingen and in his own phrase 'had better things to do than
follow German politics' until the time came when paying taxes to a Nazi
government seemed a not very striking testimony to the revolution of
God,[55] not least because that government refused to accept them any
longer. Marquardt emphasises that Barth was now a guest on foreign soil,
and had to acquire the formidable technical equipment of his teaching
office.[56] But the truth was that he aspired to a viewpoint too Olympian for
politics, and this must make him attractive to conservatives. To say with
Gollwitzer that 'Barth, as the Christian theologian he was, always kept
clear of everything built on a closed ideological system; his options
always remained pragmatic, practical-political,'[57] is to put too flattering a
construction on the mid-twenties. Bultmann was nearer the truth in 1924
when he reported that at a lecture by Siegmund-Schultze, 'K. Barth's
followers get up with the Brethren [*Gemeinschaftleute*] as men who
emancipate themselves from social obligations.'[58] Real politics began with
the expulsion of Barth from the country in 1935,[59] But that is another
story.[60]

Notes

1 F.-W. Marquardt, *Theologie und Sozialismus, Das Beispiel Karl Barths*,
    Munich 1972, p. 39.
2 Helmut Gollwitzer, *Reich Gottes und Sozialismus bei Karl Barth*, Theologische
    Existenz heute no. 169, Munich 1972.
3 Robert Steigerwald, *Marxismus-Religion-Gegenwart*, [East] Berlin 1973, p.
    157.
4 Karl Barth, *Church Dogmatics*, Edinburgh 1936–69, 4/2 p. 180.
5 Marquardt, p. 27.
6 *Ibid.* pp. 117–18, 293–4: Gollwitzer p. 30: E. Brunner and K. Barth, *Natural
    theology*, London 1946: Barth, *Dogmatics* 2/1 p. 141.
7 Marquardt, p. 192.
8 K. Barth, *Gesamtausgabe 5, Barth-Thurneysen Briefwechsel*, Zurich 1973–4,
    I, pp. 4–5.
9 Eberhard Busch, *Karl Barths Lebenslauf: nach seinen Briefen und autobiogra-
    phischen Texten*, Munich 1975, pp. 93–4.
10 *Schleiermacher-Auswahl. Mit einem Nachwort von Karl Barth*, ed. H. Bolli,
    Munich/Hamburg 1968, pp. 293–4.
11 *Barth-Thurneysen Briefwechsel* 1, p. 30, partly translated into English in J.D.
    Smart, *Revolutionary theology in the making*, London 1964, p. 28.

12 *Ibid.* 1 p. 122, Smart, p. 36.

13 *Ibid.* 1 pp. 98, 208, 223, 227, 229, Smart p. 42, 230, Smart pp. 42–3 – included in wrong letter, 233.

14 *Ibid.* 1 p. 271, Smart p. 44 (This paragraph is misleading as it does not indicate the omission of two sentences).

15 *Ibid.* 1 p. 327.

16 *Ibid.* 1 p. 335, compare, K. Barth and E. Thurneysen, *Suchet Gott, so werdet ihr leben*, 2 ed. Zollikon 1928, p. 64: 'We [that is, sinful men] are President Wilson and would like to proclaim peace to half the world – and have ourselves to set the other half alight.'

17 K. Barth, *Gesamtausgabe* 1, *Predigten* 1914 p. 168: *Suchet Gott*, p. 102. Barth was prepared to explain the strike when it was all over: *Barth – Thurneysen Briefwechsel* 1 p. 321.

18 *Ibid.* 1 p. 302.

19 *Ibid.* 1 pp. 196, 201–2, 205, 214–16, 300, 307, 320, 327.

20 *Ibid.* 1 pp. 221, 303, 323.

21 *Ibid.* 1 pp. 5–7.

22 E. Thurneysen, 'Ethik und Politik in ihrem gegenseitigen Verhältnis bei Friedrich Naumann', *Centralblatt des Schweizerischen Zofingervereins* 21, Basel? 1910–11, pp. 138–60.

23 *Barth-Thurneysen Briefwechsel* 1 pp. 25, 72, 167, 324, 404. In the secular Russian tradition revolution was transformed from being the means to an end into a way of life – Theodor Schieder, *Staat und Gesellschaft im Wandel unserer Zeit*, 3 ed. Munich 1974, pp. 42–6; it was fitting that theologians given to equating resurrection and revolution should turn back to the Russian religious tradition. On the theological and political debate on revolution in Russia, see Bastiaan Wielenga, *Lenins Weg zur Revolution. Eine Konfrontation mit Sergei Bulgakov und Petr Struve im Interesse einer theologischen Besinnung*, Munich 1971.

24 *Predigten* 1914 pp. 38, 42, 591.

25 *Ibid.* pp. 435–6. Compare pp. 526, 531.

26 For example *Suchet Gott* p. 65.

27 *Ibid.* p. 93.

28 *Ibid.* pp. 133–4, 150.

29 *Ibid.* pp. 170–2.

30 Hermann Kutter jun, *Herman Kutters Lebenswerk*, Zürich 1965 p. 63. Compare *Barth-Thurneysen Briefwechsel* 1 p. 339.

31 *Ibid.* 1. p. 41.

32 Marquardt pp. 126–7.

33 *Ibid.* pp. 126–41.

34 K. Barth, *Der Römerbrief*, 1 ed. Bern 1919, p. 375.

35 *Ibid.* p. 376.

36 *Ibid.* pp. 377–8, 381–2, 384, 386.

37 *Ibid.* pp. 379, 380–1, 382, 388, 391.

38 *Ibid.* pp. 387–90.

39 *Ibid.* pp. 381, 391.

40 Given, September 1919; published, 1920. Conveniently reprinted in *Anfänge der dialectischen Theologie*, ed. J. Moltmann, Munich 1962–3. The fact that the English translation of Moltmann – James M. Robinson, *The beginnings of dialectical theology*, Richmond Va., 1968 – omits the piece gives some colour to Marquardt's charge that a theological Barth has been invented *ex eventu.*

41 Moltmann 1 pp. 15–16.

42 *Ibid.* 1 pp. 6, 8.

43 *Ibid.* 1 pp. 21, 28.

44 *Ibid.* 1 pp. 32–4, 36.

45 Marquardt p. 142.

46 *Barth-Thurneysen Briefwechsel* 1 pp. 364–5. The paper was first published in *Zwischen den Zeiten*, 2, Munich 1923, and republished in Moltmann 2, pp. 221 *seq*, and E. Thurneysen *Das Wort Gottes und die Kirche. Aufsätze und Vorträge*, Munich 1971 pp. 159 *seq.*

47 Moltmann 2, pp. 233–4. This may be what Thurneysen meant when late in life he said that Barth's socialism was to be understood theologically. E. Thurneysen, *Karl Barth, 'Theologie und Sozialismus' in den Briefen seiner Frühzeit*, Zurich 1973, p. 31.

48 *Barth-Thurneysen Briefwechsel* 1 pp. 402, 404, 430, 449 (compare p. 453).

49 *Ibid.* 1, p. 436.

50 Busch pp. 117–18, 120, 131: *Barth-Thurneysen Briefwechsel* 1 pp. 454, 486, 493, 465–6. Lieb (1892–1970) became a professor of systematic theology at Bonn 1931 (dismissed 1933) and Basel 1937. During the Second World War he was connected with the French resistance movement to which he dedicated the French translation of his book, *Russland Unterwegs* (Bern 1945: translations into French, Dutch and Czech) advocating a positive approach to the Soviet Union. In 1947 he received a chair in East European church history at Berlin.

51 K. Barth, *Der Römerbrief. Zweite Auflage in neuer Bearbeitung*, Munich 1922, p. 462. As the text did not change in subsequent editions it is convenient to use the English translation made by Sir Edwyn Hoskyns from the 6 ed., Karl Barth, *The Epistle to the Romans*, London 1972, pp. 476–8.

52 *Ibid.* pp. 480–4.

53 *Ibid.* pp. 487–8, 491–2.

54 *Barth-Thurneysen Briefwechsel* 2, pp. 146–7, Eng. tr. Smart, p. 136.

55 Karl Barth, *Letzte Zeugnisse*, Zürich 1969, p. 43. Thurneysen (p. 8) says Barth achieved a real understanding of politics only after he went to Germany.

56 Marquardt p. 45; Gollwitzer pp. 8–10. Compare Busch p. 162.

57 H. Gollwitzer in Marquardt, p. 8.

58 K. Barth, *Gesamtausgabe 5, Karl Barth – Rudolph Bultmann Briefwechsel*, ed. B. Jaspert, Zürich 1971, pp. 24–5.

59 A useful commentary is Daniel Cornu, *Karl Barth et la Politique*, Geneva 1967.

60 Since this paper was delivered Ulrich Dannemann has published his *Theologie und Politik im Denken Karl Barths*, Munich 1977, in which he confirms the

view here taken of the young Barth's inadequacies as a political thinker, but attempts to sustain Marquardt's main line of argument by ascribing them to Barth's theological immaturity.

20

Will Herberg: an American Hypothesis seen from Europe[1]

In a recent television interview André Previn remarked that what appealed to him about Aaron Copland was his 'wow' approach to music. To anyone familiar with the rather tedious annals of English religion, one of the engaging things about Americans, be they revivalists like Billy Sunday, atheists like Bob Ingersoll, or funny men like H.L. Mencken, is their 'wow' approach to religion. A strong dose of this vivacity, even downright funniness, should always make Will Herberg's *Protestant-Catholic-Jew* refreshing reading, and the book also gave an example, which other American Jews have followed, of a religious discussion showing real intellectual distinction. First published in 1955 at the peak of the post-war religious boom, Herberg's essay attempted to provide a simple and neat explanation of the double peculiarity of the American situation, on the one hand an extraordinarily high level of church membership and attendance, with a general complacency towards organized religion, and on the other the extraordinary vapidness of the religion professed. It was on this last point that much of the humour of the book turned. Between 1949 and 1953 the distribution of the Scriptures in the US increased by 140 per cent to an all-time high of 9,726,391 volumes a year; and in a commercially organized survey, four fifths of Americans declared they believed the Bible to be the revealed Word of God rather than merely great literature. Yet when these same enthusiasts for revelation were asked 'to give the names of the first four books of the New Testament of the Bible, that is the first four Gospels', 53 per cent could not name even one. Likewise with Church membership. It is said that 43 per cent of the population was in Church membership in 1926, a figure which by 1962 had reached 63 per cent, with about 45 per cent attending church each week. Impressive as these figures are, they are much lower than the 70–75 per cent who told

Paper presented to the British Association for American Studies. First published in *Durham University Journal* 65 (1973).

the pollsters that they were church members, and beyond them there were another 20–25 per cent who regarded themselves as comprised in various religious communities, though not members. And since one of the forms of the market research to which Americans continuously subject themselves is constituted by religious sociology, we are in no doubt as to what these millions believe. 96 or 97 per cent believe in God, 90 per cent pray on various occasions, 73 per cent believe in an afterlife with God as Judge, but 'only 5 per cent [had] any fear, not to say expectation of going [to hell]'. According to another source, 80 per cent admitted that what they were 'most serious about' was not the life after death in which they said they believed, but in trying to live as comfortably in this life as possible. Moreover the Last Judgment could have no terrors for a people 91 per cent of whom felt they could honestly say that they were trying to lead a good life, and 78 per cent of whom felt no hesitation in saying that they more than half measured up to their own standards of goodness; or for the over 50 per cent who asserted that they were following the rule of loving one's neighbour as oneself 'all the way'. Yet when pressed further about this great fund of grace with the question, 'Would you say your religious beliefs have any effect on your ideas of politics and business?' 54 per cent said no, 39 per cent said yes, and only 7 per cent had the wisdom to say they did not know.[2]

Herberg accounted for both the religiosity and what might be called the secularization by a theory about immigration. The first generation of immigrants, so the argument went, huddled together in the eastern seaboard towns and main railway centres, and essayed the impossible of recreating the life they had left behind. The basic cultural link was language, and ethnic groups quickly acquired a national character which many of their members had not had before they arrived. National churches were imported as part of the complex, a particular problem for Roman Catholics, among whose ethnic groups were several with competing interests and a general distaste for a church life created in the image of the Irish and dominated by them. In the second generation the national language took second place and was an embarrassment. Sons of immigrants might support the ethnic block as a profitable counter in domestic politics, or to assist the national cause in Europe. If they did, the church was part of the machinery to be kept going. Or they might simply flounder, feeling neither American nor foreign, and lose their fathers' religion in much the same way as they lost their fathers' language. The third generation was to reproduce neither of the patterns of the second; it neither remained a congeries of unassimilated nationalities, nor underwent total assimilation. The English language had triumphed; they were now American. But they could obtain a sense of individuality by an appeal to the one element in their past which they had not been asked to change – their religion. By the same token, having by now moved out of the ghetto and into the suburbs, they could acquire some social roots by affiliation with the suburban church or synagogue. Religious association, concluded Herberg, became 'the primary context of self-identification and social location' for the third generation of America's immigrants;[3] and since a hectic period of immigration had come to an end only in 1924, this was a large proportion of the people. Hence the religious boom.

Moreover the churches themselves reflected the situation of partial assimilation. Here Herberg leaned heavily on the study of intermarriage trends in New Haven, published in 1944 by Ruby Jo Kennedy. She showed that in-marriage amongst Irish and Germans, almost total in 1870, had by 1940 declined to modest proportions, but that in-marriage among Protestants, Catholics and Jews remained almost as exclusive as ever.[4] In these three religious grouping what was left of ethnic peculiarities was preserved and refined, and the dominant mores refracted in its turn. It was this in Herberg's view which accounted for the vapidness of American religion. Protestantism, Catholicism and Judaism were simply three divisions of the great American religion, inculcating the secular values of the American way of life. To be an American one did not need to believe much of the Jewish or Christian heritage, but one must fit into one division or another. To declare oneself a Buddhist would be to simply get a name as a cranky Protestant, and with 'adjustment' becoming the fashionable word in psychology, one probably wouldn't make the experiment. In this process Protestantism had some advantage, possessing an aura of social privilege, and better facilities for maintaining ethnic peculiarities than Catholicism; Judaism was at a special disadvantage in depending heavily upon a ritual which was not compatible with assimilation; yet, for whatever reason, Jews hung on to their community and stiffened it with a vast fund-raising network.

How far American religious bodies might become vehicles for secular values was amusingly illustrated by a poll conducted in 1948 by the *Ladies' Home Journal*. Respondents were asked 'to look within [themselves] and state honestly whether [they] thought [they] really obeyed the law of love under certain special conditions'; 90 per cent said yes and 5 per cent no when the one to be loved was a person belonging to a different religion; 80 per cent said yes and 12 per cent no when it was a case of a member of a different race; 78 per cent said yes and 10 per cent no when it concerned a business competitor; but only 27 per cent said yes and 57 per cent no 'in the case of a political party you think is dangerous'; while 25 per cent said yes and 63 per cent said no when it concerned an enemy of the nation.[5] Ecclesiastical transmission of political values came out in other ways. The traditional defence of episcopal church government has been that the outward form of the church should symbolize its inner essence – indeed in the eighteenth century independency was as symbolic as episcopalianism. Both these traditions exist in the United States together with a Roman Catholic episcopacy imported at a time when it was uniquely clericalized and bureaucratic. But all American church governments have become in a greater or less degree federal and democratic. There was a large lay element in the management of American Anglicanism even in the days of its establishment in Virginia, and early in the nineteenth century the belligerent Irish of Norfolk, Virginia, did not hesitate to sign a declaration to Rome announcing that 'in consequence of our inalienable right of patronage our first bishop will be elected by us'. They lost their case but in the long run made their point. It was not for nothing that Tocqueville found the Catholics 'the most republican and the most democratic class of citizens which exists in the United States'.[6] Nothing could have been more autocratic or centralized than early American Methodism, but it too moved steadily in the direction of federalism and democracy.

The neatness and coherence of Herberg's thesis constituted an irresistible temptation to the empirical sociologists, and over the next decade the computers were kept busy checking his theses and various counter-hypotheses, with mixed results. In the long-term survey of the Detroit area maintained by the University of Michigan, Gerhard Lenski bore out much of what Herberg had reckoned.[7] He found that it was only among second generation Jews that religious affiliation tended to lapse, and that otherwise there was a pattern of increasing religious activity linked with increasing Americanization and unaffected by age differences between the generations. Moreover, Herberg's theory appeared applicable to the internal migration into Detroit from the South. Southern-born white Protestants coming to Detroit found Detroit Protestantism so alien, and the congregations which attempted to keep up the flavour of southern Protestantism so unsuccessful, that their church attendance lapsed, notwithstanding the numerous generations of American pedigree behind them; but the third generation in Detroit was attending church with great frequency. If this pattern were to establish itself, urbanization might be as profitable to churches in America as it was harmful to churches elsewhere. Others thought that the third generation was more rebellious than Herberg had allowed, and Seymour Lipset was prepared to deny the whole premise that there had been a long-term increase in church attendance.[8] Again, a rehashing of the Michigan survey statistics suggested that there were quite different patterns for men and for women; that the fall-off in church attendance among second-generation Protestant men was due simply to the behaviour of second generation immigrants only one of whose parents was an immigrant, while the practice of Catholic women showed no meaningful generation difference. Lazerwitz and Rowitz triumphantly concluded that Herberg's thesis applied only to Catholic males, though it might possibly have operated for Protestants in more distant times when Protestant immigrants were rural peasants.[9] Considering that these meticulous conclusions were derived from a secondary analysis of data from a tiny sample in Detroit, one could scarcely fail to conclude empirical sociology had now crossed the line separating the tedious from the ridiculous.

The location of the Detroit sample was also suspect to a more significant group of scholars who wished to resume the discussion at the other end. Herberg had put the stress upon the function of religion as a means of social identification, and, as befitted a theologian, he was interested primarily in what happened to religion when it was used for this purpose. He had shown that, as everyone knew, assimilation was not a simple business and had called attention to the function of religion in the process. But assimilation was plainly a question in its own right. Sampling techniques overstated the degree of Catholic assimilation by missing altogether the French Canadian enclaves in Upper New England, the Polish enclaves in Detroit and Buffalo, and the various kinds of Spanish speaking Catholicism in the south-west. Moreover at the pressure point of immigration in New York, much like Liverpool in this respect, the ethnic communities showed an extraordinary durability, though the political power of the Irish machine had been successfully challenged, and though the Irish Americans of today included a great many not of unmixed Irish descent. It was this persistence which gave a cue to students like Glazer, Moynihan and Gordon, who were interested in the problem of assimilation in its own right, and in the effect of religion upon it.[10] Taking the persistence of ethnic groupings as a datum, they saw the problem not as one of cultural assimilation, but of the political reconciliation of diverging interests. Gordon argues that the structure of a society consists in a set of crystallized social relations in which men are grouped and related to the major institutional activities of the nation, crystallized relations being repetitive social links based on shared expectations. The ethnic group enables most of its members to find their primary relationships and many of their secondary relationships among themselves, and in America the ethnic subsocieties are numerous and large enough to be themselves stratified on the basis of class. The subsocieties have their own subculture, but a society, being a structured thing, can exist without its culture, though the culture cannot exist without the society. The one major impact of immigrant group culture, as distinct from the achievements of individuals, has been the transmutation of the national Protantism into the tripartite Herberg religion of Protestant-Catholic-Jew; but otherwise acculturation has been rapid and fairly complete, leaving behind a denominational jostling of a not very elegant kind. From the standpoint of religious articulateness it is particularly unfortunate that the enormous expansion of higher education and professional training seems to be creating an intellectual subsociety, which has diverted the loyalties of its members from the ethnic subsocieties, especially the non-Protestant ones (much as it has creamed off the intelligentsia of dissent in England), without in any way weakening the political power of the ethnic groups.

This seemed to be a recipe both for ecclesiastical mediocrity and for the ineffectiveness of intellect in politics, but in the sixties it was not the most urgent problem. For the massive Negro immigration into New York and other northern cities brought home the fact that there was a huge domestic population whose assimilation within a common Protestantism or a common Catholicism had barely begun, and who began to seek cohesion on a basis of race. There were some who described themselves as Black Jews; others called themselves Black Muslims; but there was no way to assimilation through these devices. Here Herberg, admitting that 'the existence of the Negro church as a segregated division of Protestantism [constituted] . . . an anomaly of considerable importance' in his scheme,[11] and saying nothing about race, was found wanting.

The most recent treatments of American religion, the first of them a work of major importance, Sydney E. Ahlstrom's *Religions history of the American people* and Robert T. Handy's *Religion in the American experience: the pluralistic style*, both published late in 1972, overwhelmed by the demoralizing clashes of the sixties, and especially by racial tension, have been driven not merely to reject Herberg's standpoint, but to demand the complete rewriting of American religious history on new principles. Conflict history is to replace consensus history, and a covert plea for mutual toleration is to be incorporated by describing the result as a history of pluralism. There is no mistaking the emotion in Ahlstrom's plea for 'justice to the pluralistic situation which has been struggling to be born ever since this country was formally dedicated to the proposition that all men are created equal'.[12] Beginning with the pluriform religion of the Indians, and making far more of the Orthodox groups than there is any evidence that, in terms of American historical significance, they are worth, Robert Handy comes close to denying that America has had a religious history, as distinct from an encyclopaedia of religious histories. How far the reaction has gone is made clear by the assertion that 'followers of a certain style of piety, or members of a given theological camp often feel more at home with like-minded persons of another denomination than they do with their own fellow denominationalists who belong to an opposition group. Hence the pluralistic style of American religion is not only a matter of religious multiplicity, but has penetrated to the inner citadels of religious institutions ... [one of the consequences] of the pluralistic style for American religious life is what can be called the internalization of pluralism'.[13] At a time when the experience of churches everywhere is that the dividing lines of religious opinion cross rather than follow the lines of denominational division, this is a sorry piece of isolationism, and suggests that the new model of American religion can already inhibit historical understanding. Is it possible to qualify Herberg's thesis in a more useful way?

I would suggest that Herberg's main argument can be strengthened by taking a longer historical perspective, but that on a comparative view his statistics do not always mean quite what they say.

Without a more substantial historical support than he chose to construct, Herberg's argument is very vulnerable to the attacks of the conflict historians. It will not do to say that religion was the one element in the immigrant's past which he was not asked to give up, for there were repeated nativist agitations to make acceptance impossible. It is the more odd that Herberg said nothing about what amounts to the politics of backlash, since his subject took its shape from the triumphant Protestant reaction of the years which followed the First World War. It was not just that the immigration law of 1924 put a ceiling on total immigration, and imposed a domestic national origins quota excluding all but a trickle of immigrants from other than the Protestant countries of northern Europe; it was that the pace was being made by men who did not want America to be even a single melting pot, but wanted the direct assimilation of the immigrants and their culture. The Prohibition Amendment was passed by Congress and ratified by forty-six states. Legislation to outlaw the teaching of evolution in the public schools was introduced into the legislatures of half the country, and was actually enacted in a few. At federal, state and local levels there was action to limit the rights of political dissenters, and still worse, organized mass action in the private sector, as the second Ku Klux Klan came to embrace between a quarter and a third of the adult native-born Protestant males. Anything further from the cosy consensus situation described by Herberg is not easy to imagine; yet the circumstances of the early twenties had been parallelled innumerable times since the 1790s, with agitations against Illuminati and Masons, against Catholics and Jews, mostly employing paranoid theories of conspiracy which again did yeoman service in the agitations against Communism after the Second World War. Lipset and Raab explain this feature of American history as the outcome of a sense of status deprivation, in a society which is exceedingly mobile, and hence creates very rapid displacements; but is also achievement-oriented to a quite uncommon degree, making displacement uncommonly painful. However, as befits men subsidized by the Anti-Defamation League, their copious account of the genesis of the Radical Right is accompanied by very little commentary on the fact that the Right has never for long succeeded in its objects;[14] that the national religion has three divisions, not one; and that some at least of what Herberg holds to be the impact of recent assimilation upon American religion, has a long history and is among the conditions of assimilation itself.

I would suggest that there are reasons of three different orders for this state of affairs, political, ecclesiastical, and social. Although American conservatives have generally been hostile to the extension of the functions of the state in the fields of business, welfare and religion, they have necessarily sought political action in the end. The American political system, however, dedicated primarily to a choice between two candidates for the management of the executive, does not lend itself to the creation of third parties; moreover the two great parties are almost necessarily coalitions of interests. The hardline campaigns of both the right and the left have therefore had the character of movements in the country much more than overtly political acts. On the right they seem to have reached their greatest vigour when the conservative party of the day has been in some confusion, and their ultimate fate has been that of absorption and compromise as a special interest in the next great conservative coalition to assert itself. In much the same way as the English whig coalitions of the nineteenth century both offered the local and sectional agitators of the left their one route to office, and on the other made it nearly impossible for them to use political authority when they had it, so American parties have acted as a brake on extremism, and the fair degree of stability that the major parties have achieved seems to have a directly dampening effect upon militant agitation in the country.

It is also the case that religious establishment in America has acted in many respects like party. In the early colonial period such a development had seemed out of the question, with a multitude of English sects with different constitutional standing in every colony, and with other religious bodies, mostly Protestant, from Germany, Austria, Switzerland, France, Sweden, Scotland and Ulster as well. But the threat from without that the British government would impose episcopacy in America, together with the threat from within that the upper crust of colonial society might find its way out of the reformed bodies and into Episcopalianism, much as it has always done in Edinburgh, was sufficient to break down the barriers of sect and colony, to create a common religious cause, compatible at once with the legend of their fathers' errand into America, with enlightenment, with the Manifest Destiny of the American people. The churches which had thus become a vehicle of colonial nationalism, were ready to be turned by Independence into an informal religious establishment, distinguished from that of England in various ways, not least by its active links with English dissent, Scottish Establishment and the Protestant Churches of Europe. American Christianity of the 1950s would no doubt have looked very odd to Ezra Stiles, but certain passages of his famous sermon on Christian Union in 1761 read very like Will Herberg: 'Providence has planted British America with a variety of sects which will unavoidably become a mutual balance upon one another. Their temporary collisions, like the action of acids and alkalis after a short ebullition, will subside in harmony and union, not by the destruction of either, but in the friendly cohabitation of all . . . The notion of erecting the policy of either sect into universal dominion to the destruction of the rest is but an airy vision . . . all the present sects will subsist and increase into distinct respectable bodies.'[15] The idea that America was blessed with a self-balancing ecclesiastical ecology, made respectable by its public functions, was to prove capable of surprising extension.

But the social pull of Episcopalianism was not the only domestic problem undermining the barriers of sect and colony. Religious revival, often treated as an Anglo-American affair, was a much broader phenomenon than this.[16] Beginning in Germany a great whirligig of personal connections, literary influences, and direct institutional links, built up between Germany, America, and Britain, going round and round, each acting on the other and flinging off hot coals of revival as they went, one into Finland and Scandinavia, others into Switzerland and the Protestant Midi, others to Ireland and in the Moravian diaspora to the four corners of the earth. The impact of these movements very sharply emphasized the differences in the balance of institutions among the various societies. In Germany the concentration of institutional strength behind the Protestant establishment was sufficient to contain the evangelical movement and finally to absorb it. In England all the social rigidities were much less, and the influence of the French Revolution was to weaken them still further; the result was that evangelicalism made a much greater splash, and from the mid-1790s began to expand like wildfire; while the very weakness of the state compelled the political establishment to drive the informal methods of control, and especially the Church, to the limit, and hence to prepare the way for a ferocious church conflict. The upshot of the peculiar balance in England was therefore that the establishment could neither contain nor absorb the great mass of evangelicalism. In America the forces of social cohesion were everywhere weaker than in Europe, and almost non-existent on the frontier. Moreover, little as the new informal establishment cared for the new ways (and early Methodists seem to have been refused communion by American dissenters much more often than by the English establishment), it was not clear that they could either put them down or do without them. The bad time which the English establishment had in the 1790s was paralleled in America; on both sides of the Atlantic the same texts were used to explain the troubles of privileged orthodoxy by the conspiracies of Bavarian Illuminati. At least the Methodists were free from suspicion on this score. Moreover while in England it was conceivable that given a sufficient degree of spiritual devotion and political resolution the establishment might be made to do its work, in America it was really impossible to regard a population doubling every twenty-five years and swarming into the wilderness as in any sense a covenant people. The machinery for reconstituting religious society had to be driven much harder in America than it was in England, because the need, not to say the opportunity, was so much greater. This difference constituted the essential Americanism of the Second Great Awakening. American Methodism took wing shortly after English Methodism had begun its most rapid phase of expansion, and rapidly outstripped it by virtue of a much more ruthless organization. Asbury exercised an autocracy unparalleled by any of Wesley's successors in England, and his preachers constituted not so much a ministry in the European sense as a military-style mission, enduring great deprivation for short periods of service, before dropping out of the ministry for marriage and a settled job.[17]

Again the great battery of societies for every good work in which the church seemed delivered over to instrumental and associational principles, which was conceived in England and exported to Germany, Switzerland and America, reached its apogee across the Atlantic under the name of the Benevolent System.[18] In the same kind of way, American need and American technological skills transformed revival into revivalism. All these developments and the instrumental attitudes towards the church which went with them were as abhorrent to styles of ministry derived from the old Puritan tradition as they might have been to English High-Churchmen or to the Lutheran orthodox in Germany. But there was in the end no means either of stopping them or of doing without them. Elasticity gave the informal establishment of America an absorptive power greater even than the formal establishments of Germany. Methodism and the benevolent system, Episcopalianism and revivalism, were taken on board, and made vehicles of American nationalism. Small wonder that Tocqueville could write, very much in the Herberg manner, that 'religion in America takes no direct part in the government of society, but nevertheless it must be regarded as the foremost of the political institutions of that country . . . I do not know whether all Americans have a sincere faith in their religion, but I am certain they hold it to be indispensable to the maintenance of

republican institutions . . . Although the Christians of America are divided
into a multitude of sects, they all look upon their religion in the same light.
This applies to Roman Catholicism as well as to other forms of belief.'
Tocqueville is not very different from the Eisenhower rather heavily
worked by Herberg, declaring that 'our government makes no sense unless
it is founded in a deeply felt religious faith – and I don't care what it is'.[19]

Thus by the time that nativism and anti-masonry became really important the American establishment had acquired a character for yielding
rather than resisting, and its domestic disagreements on the slavery issue
were making a common front impossible to achieve. It is my impression
that in the European churches the impact of liberalism, like that of revival,
was in inverse proportion to ecclesiastical institutionalization. It followed
that liberalism enjoyed much greater triumphs in the American than in
most of the European churches, and, in washing away the old orthodoxies,
further increased the capacity for absorption. A Protestantism which had
long claimed a special relationship with God's plan for America, was
perhaps specially susceptible to the usual liberal doctrine that God was at
work in the world as well as in the church, that there could not be a radical
separation of the church and the world, the elect and the damned. The
worst Horace Bushnell could say of sin was that it was deprivation, and
the 'moral inability' of which Jonathan Edwards had talked was replaced
by 'moral responsibility'. There were special American attractions too in
the progressive view of history, that things, including the church, were in
a state of improvement; that there could be no radical taint of sin to be
overcome in crisis. The whole matter was taken a stage further by the
emergence of the social gospel, ambiguously related as it was to the old
evangelicalism. Walter Rauschenbusch indeed combined an intense belief
in the sinfulness of man and institutions, with an equally intense optimism
as to their remediability. American Arminianism had found it necessary
and possible to contrive and organize the Kingdom of God in an ecclesiastical sense; Rauschenbusch went a step further and held not merely that 'the
kingdom of God is humanity organized according to the will of God', but
that it was just round the corner. On this view the proper preoccupation
of the church was with what might elsewhere be called secular values; how
deeply this frame of mind penetrated could be illustrated in various ways,
but perhaps never more strikingly than in those who in the 1930s came to
revolt against it. Richard and Reinhold Niebuhr were amongst those who
sought to do for American Protestantism what Barth, Brunner and the neo-
orthodox were doing in Europe; each of them deplored the enslavement of
the church to the national and ethnic ideologies, and sought to recover an
orthodoxy which was beyond both the old fundamentalism and the old
liberalism. Yet neither of them produced a *Dogmatik* in the German

manner; they were preoccupied by the questions to which the liberals and social gospellers had given their mind, producing lectures on the *Nature and Destiny of Man*, an *Interpretation of Christian Ethics*, and studies of the proper relation of the church to society.[20] The tendencies against which the Niebuhr brothers and people like Walter Lowrie were protesting might not have much appeal in an introverted South covering its status deprivation by the old-time religion, but they made it relatively easy in the America that was a going concern for establishment to absorb forms of Judaism and Catholicism which would not insist too hard upon divisive peculiarities.

The identification of the churches with American nationalism was of course a great risk when that nationalism, so secure when Will Herberg wrote, got into the toils in Vietnam and the race to the moon, or found its black minority organizing on a basis of race, and its middle-class children repudiating official ethics in movements of the hippy kind. If what Herberg had described was religion, then it was perhaps right to proclaim the Death of God. But in the mid-sixties as well as the mid-thirties, the rebels themselves exemplified the power of the past. The huge vogue of such a very bad book as Harvey Cox's *Secular City* (1965) illustrates how deeply rooted is the American tendency to fall back on its liberal and secularized traditions. Christianity is here presented as the greatest secularizing force of all, a religion whose job is to get rid of the magic in the world; indeed the positive remaining function of Christianity is to establish the policies and the theology for social change, some pretty modest instalments of which are suggested in the book. By this device an attempt is made to build a bridge between the older generation and the younger, by suggesting that the function of a secular Christianity is not so much to confer upon new arrivals membership of America as she is, as to create America as she might easily be for established residents. A shift of emphasis as small as this could not contain a revolt against the official values of any serious substance; the fact that it excited such immense interest is a vivid illustration of the remaining hold of American traditions of secularized Christianity.

Yet the form of the critique of Harvey Cox and that of the 'death of God' men, like that of the neo-orthodox of the 1930s, owes a great deal to European example; indeed many of the bizarre effects of recent years result from the exposure of so many ordinands trained in America to the hothouse atmosphere of German theological faculties. It is worth asking whether at a popular level the Christianity of Europe and America has again in any measure a common history, as in the main it has not had since the beginning of the nineteenth century. (Africa, I think, is still a separate story.) The question is indeed unavoidable, for much of the humour of Herberg's essay turns on his statistics. If what the statistics report is not as he assumes a peculiarly American situation, then fresh consideration is called for. There is no space in a paper to compare Herberg's statistics with those produced by various inquiries in Britain, and by the Institut Français d'Opinion Publique across the channel.[21] One inquiry conducted amongst a large sample of members of church youth clubs in Hamburg in 1959 by Hans Otto Wölber, however, deserves attention.[22] Wölber had formerly been in charge of Protestant Church youth work, and becoming Bishop of Hamburg became at once a great authoritarian and reactionary. By putting his respondents through a marathon questionnaire of 100 questions, and adding information from the Emnid Institute at Bielefeld, he sought to marry the methods of social history, sociology and social psychology in the hope of ascertaining what the religious mentality of the people was, conscious and unconscious. Many of the questions unwittingly exemplified the intellectual superiority of the German Protestant tradition and would certainly have produced 100 per cent don't knows in England or America. The surprise produced by the replies, however, was that they fell into three distinct groups. A number of questions of a general kind received affirmative answers in 85 per cent of the cases or more, corresponding to the universality of baptism and to the fact that the great gap between baptismal and confirmation figures, brought about by political action in the German Democratic Republic and by natural causes in England, still did not exist in West Germany. It was the same with general statements of belief. 'If I believe in God as a Christian, must I then believe, according to your conviction, that Jesus Christ is God's Son?' – 84 per cent came out in favour of Jesus. To the proposition that 'Jesus Christ died for us and redeemed us', 90 per cent agreed, though some of them weakly. 'Do you believe that God speaks to us in the Bible?' – 85 per cent made the orthodox answer.[23] The readiness and universality with which these answers are produced, show that they are among the foregone conclusions of Christian social existence, accepted as an inheritance without reflection and in no way distinguishing the core-congregation (*Kernkirche*) from the general constituency of the church, though this is what some of the dogmatic propositions have often been supposed to do. In the second group were questions to which consent had been cheerfully given in Group I but which now produced an assent only in the range of 51–76 per cent. To the question, for example, 'Do several religions lead to God, or only Christianity?' only 54 per cent of those who had so confidently spoken of Jesus as God's son, now spoke up for Christianity, 13 per cent hesitantly. The difference between these questions and those in Group I was that standard religious concepts requried translating into a life-situation and this produced a much greater degree of hesitancy. In the third group, the personal factor was increased nearer to the point which the Germans call *Entscheidung* (decision) and the percentages fell away again, till by the time questions were slipped in where these Protestants had received or would expect to receive help in some trying experiencd, only 23 per cent conjured up any kind of religious factor (prayer, Bible, ministry, church). From all this Wölber concluded that much of what was supposed to be central to the faith had moved out to the fringes in the minds of its adherents. Wölber's inquiry casts a curious light on the extraordinarily crude methods used by well-established American scholars like Glock and Stark in constructing indices of what they comically call orthodoxy and ethical-ism;[24] and his results make interesting reading in connection with Herberg, for Herberg's great affirmations of piety were all in response to simple general questions like those in Wölber's group one, and there is not much doubt that a properly constructed enquiry would have revealed a low level of *Entscheidung*. And of course the rising level of church affiliation on the one side, and the declining level of religious participation on the other, had brought about some resemblance between the America of the fifties and a West Germany in which almost everyone was a church member even though it cost him extra income tax, and in which there are problems of assimilation perhaps more like those of America than any other European country.

It is plain, however, that the most recent historians of American religion do not wish to be comforted by European parallels though they pursue ecumenical policies. The race issue may indeed be more than the elasticity of the American religious establishment can cope with, and has certainly plunged the black churches into even greater difficulties than the white. But it is perhaps premature to conclude that America has become a racial Belfast, its lines of conflict immovably drawn. Nor would it be wise to assume that the American economy has lost its expansiveness. In the twenties the Protestant backlash first revealed what would now be called a generation gap, and was then made to look thoroughly passé by hectic economic growth. Renewed economic progress may make possible the development of a quadripartite Herberg religion of Protestant-Catholic-Jew-Black. Certainly Ahlstrom himself shows black churchmen able to steer a course between an exclusive concern for other-worldly salvation, and an exclusive regard for the church as a device for community action.[25] And a search for springs of religious inspiration deeper than the mores of the middle class goes on amongst white as well as black. Consensus history is after all a correlate of conflict history and it may be that in another decade a fresh wave of religious historians may find the Herberg thesis worth re-examining.

Notes

1 An earlier version of this paper was read at the conference of the British Association for American Studies held in Durham in April 1972.

2 Will Herberg, *Protestant-Catholic-Jew*, revised ed., New York, 1960, pp. 2, 72–3.

3 *Ibid.*, p. 39.

4 *Ibid.*, p. 32–4.

5 *Ibid.*, p. 76.

6 Alexis de Tocqueville, *Democracy in America*, World's Classics ed. by H.S. Commager, London, 1946, p. 230.

7 Gerhard Lenski, *The religious factor: a sociologist's inquiry*, revised ed., New York, 1963.

8 Seymour M. Lipset, 'Religion in America: what religious revival?', *Columbia University Forum*, Winter 1959. Cf. C.Y. Glock 'Y a-t-il un réveil réligieux aux États-Unis?', *Archives de sociologie des religions* no. 12 (1961), pp. 35–52. In attempting to discredit the statistical evidence for long-term growth in church membership Lipset made some shrewd thrusts (S.M. Lipset, *The first new nation* (New York, 1967) ch. 4) but does not help his case by quoting literary evidence only from mid-nineteenth century commentators who had reason to compare American voluntaryism favourably with the formal establishments of Europe. Conservative spokesmen for European establishments were less impressed with the success of American voluntaryism in taking religion to the people.

9 Bernard Lazerwitz and Louis Rowitz, 'The three generations hypothesis', *American Journal of Sociology*, lxix (1964), pp. 529–38.

10 N. Glazer and D.P. Moynihan, *Beyond the Melting Pot*, 2nd ed., Cambridge, Mass., 1964: Milton M Gordon, *Assimilation in American Life*, New York, 1964. Cf. J. Fitzpatrick, 'Cultural pluralism and religious identification: a review', *Sociological Analysis*, xxv (1965), pp. 129, 134.

11 Herberg, *op. cit.*, p. 114.

12 Sydney E. Ahlstrom, *A religious history of the American people*, New Haven, 1972, p. 12.

13 *Religion in the American experience: the pluralistic style* ed. Robert T. Handy, Columbia, S.C., 1972, pp. xvii, xvi.

14 S.M. Lipset and E. Raab, *The politics of unreason. Right-wing extremism in America, 1790–1970*, London, 1971.

15 Quoted in C. Bridenbaugh, *Mitre and sceptre: Transatlantic faiths, ideas, personalities and politics, 1689–1775*, New York, 1967, pp. 10–11.

16 For a further discussion of this point see W.R. Ward, 'The French Revolution and the English churches', *Miscellanea Historiae Ecclesiasticae* iv (1972), pp. 55–84.

17 On this subject see W.R. Ward, 'The legacy of John Wesley: the Pastoral Office in Britain and America', in *Essays presented to Lucy Stuart Sutherland*, ed. J.

Bromley, P.G.M. Dickson and A.O. Whiteman, Oxford, 1973, pp. 323–50. Above, Ch. 12.

18 C.I. Foster, *An errand of mercy. The evangelical united front, 1790–1837*, Chapel Hill, N.C., 1960.

19 De Tocqueville, *op. cit.*, pp. 235–6, 308. Eisenhower in turn may be compared with Paul Tillich who reached the peak of his popularity during the religious boom, providing arguments why sympathetic intellectuals who did not hold Christian beliefs should nevertheless conform. 'Everybody who accepts the Church with its foundation [Jesus Christ], as the community to which he spiritually belongs, can be a member of the Church even if he is temporarily or permanently unable to share in its faith'. For an ingenious discussion of this point see Stuart Mews, 'Paul Tillich and the religious situation of American intellectuals', *Religion*, ii (1972), pp. 122–39.

20 Reinhold Niebuhr, *The nature and destiny of man. A Christian interpretation*, 2 vols. London, 1941–3: Reinhold Niebuhr, *An interpretation of Christian ethics*, London, 1936. This book, fittingly enough, originated in lectures given on the Rauschenbusch Foundation: H. Richard Niebuhr, *Christ and Culture*, London, 1952: H. Richard Niebuhr, *The social sources of denominationalism*, New York, 1929.

21 See, e.g., Jacques Duquesne, *Dieu, pour l'homme d'aujourdhui*, Paris, 1970.

22 H.O. Wölber, *Religion ohne Entscheidung* (3rd ed., Göttingen, 1965). A popular version of this enquiry has been translated into English: Eberhard Stammler, *Churchless Protestants*, Philadelphia, Pa., 1964.

23 The results of this part of the enquiry were confirmed by a later survey initiated by *Der Spiegel: Was glauben die Deutschen?* ed. W. Harenberg, Munich and Mainz, 1968, e.g. pp. 62–3.

24 Rodney Stark and Charles Y. Glock, *American Piety: the nature of religious commitment*, Berkeley, Cal., 1968.

25 Ahlstrom, *op. cit.*, pp. 1075 seq. With characteristic energy, American historians have in the last decade set on foot an impressive amount of work on the nature of black religion and on the growth of racism in white religion.

Part Five

Mysticism

21

Is Martyrdom Mandatory? The case of Gottfried Arnold

Nineteenth-century critics were entirely mistaken in supposing that political economy was the dismal science; it is in fact ecclesiastical history. Members of this society understand this better than any, exchanging, as they do, views and information mainly in print, and devoting their twice yearly gatherings principally to encouraging the cheerfulness both of nature and of grace. Goethe had a word for it:[1]

> Es ist die ganze Kirchengeschichte
> Mischmasch von Irrtum und Gewalt.

But then Goethe had drunk deep at an impressionable age of Gottfried Arnold's celebrated *Unparteiische Kirchen- und Ketzerhistorie* (1699) which he discovered in his father's bookcase, and to no man was ecclesiastical history more dismal than the Arnold of the *Ketzerhistorie*. On this occasion when we are celebrating the ingrained lovelessness of organized Christianity, it is worth inquiring briefly what Arnold's views in this great work, probably the last large work of church history to have substantial impact on the educated general public, were, and how it came about that he quickly moved beyond them, married and took church office. Had martyrdom ceased to be mandatory? Had cheerfulness broken in? Was it, as some vocal admirers assumed, the triumph of the world's slow stain? Or was some other factor at work?

Gottfried Arnold (1666–1714) was bred in the strictest school of Lutheran Orthodoxy at Wittenberg, but by the age of thirty, while not breaking with the church, had set himself in opposition to most of what Orthodoxy stood for, and especially its use of church history to reinforce the claims of confessional dogmatics.[2] His development, like that of so

Paper presented to a conference of the Ecclesiastical History Society on the theme of 'Martyrs and Martyrologies'. Published in *Studies in Church History* 30 (1993), pp. 311–18.

many theologians of his day, was influenced on one side by politics, and on the other by intellectual forces of a very international kind. Arnold's first two appointments were obtained for him by Spener; they were domestic tutorships, and the second of them was in Quedlinburg, a town and abbey not far from Halberstadt.[3] After much conflict not only between the town and abbey, but between Saxony and Brandenburg, the territory was finally taken by the latter from the former in 1698. Almost predictably this struggle had also been fought by the churchmen in the town, the Orthodox preachers supporting Saxony, while the Hofdiakon Sprögel, a Pietist sympathetic to the awakened and the separatists locally, was inclined to Brandenburg. He was also a friend of Arnold, who without disloyalty to the church held house meetings open to separatists, and became a sharp critic of the Orthodox (or Saxon) party.[4] He corresponded with Jane Leade and the English Philadelphians, but more importantly was impressed by the English patristic scholar, William Cave, whose *Primitive Christianity* (1673) appeared in German dress at Leipzig in 1694.[5] Arnold was not much impressed by Cave's belief that the English church was in principle the model of the church of primitive antiquity, but, like Wesley later, he was impressed by his picture of the 'divine and holy Precepts of the Christian Religion drawn down into action . . . breathing in the hearts and lives of these good old Christians', at any rate for the first three or four centuries.[6] The early Enlightenment left its mark in Thomasius. Arnold wrote for his journal, the *Historie der Weisheit und Torheit*, and took over in return his willingness to use German in scholarly discourse, his demand for toleration, his sharp separation between philosophy and theology, his venomous opposition to Aristotelianism in the latter, his notion that true church history was wisdom, while *historia philosophica* was foolishness. In these years Arnold lived the life of a scholarly recluse, intensively studying and translating the Fathers (one of his translations being the homilies of Macarius the Egyptian which had an astonishing impact in the Pietist world and helped launch Wesley on his ill-fated expedition to Georgia).[7] But the organising principle of all this learning was derived from the Netherlands. Witsius, the Utrecht Coccejan, added to the Dutch translation of Cave the disclaimer that the authority of Scripture and that of the Fathers must be strictly distinguished; this went into the German translation and was taken over by Arnold. Friederich Spanheim the younger, who secured the triumph of the Voetian party in Leiden, taught him that the fall of the church took place at the beginning of the fourth century. And this for Arnold was the mirror of his own day, when the church relied on alliance with the state rather than its inner spiritual resources.[8]

Thus in his works of the mid-nineties which secured his call to a chair at Giessen in 1697, Arnold had reached many of the positions which, after his resignation to escape the world in 1698, he took up in the *Ketzerhistorie*. As with Cave the early church was an example to all, but that church was not Cave's. It was a community of the regenerate, and among the fruits of regeneration were *Unparteilichkeit* and inwardness. 'Impartiality' in Arnold's sense was a correlate of inwardness; not only did church history issue in no normative constitution, to boast of one, such as the apostolic succession, was already to surrender inwardness of faith to outward forms. The fall of the church indeed occurred in the fourth century when it accepted outward favour and props, and persecution ceased; but the rot had begun to set in at the end of the apostolic age, and the task of history was to unravel the interweaving of true and false. Of course persecution never did cease for heretics, and got worse after the church had made its bargain with the state; there was no question but that suffering was one of the marks of the true church, and that the true church must expect to suffer from the non-Christian church as it had from the non-Christian state. Arnold was perfectly aware that dissent was not an *opus operatum*, and that there were generally some dissenters about anxious to go to the stake for a nostrum; what was at fault on both sides in such cases was the disastrous desire to formulate the faith in non-scriptural terms. A heretic in the early church had been simply a man who denied God from heathen blindness, or denied Christ by unholy living. But in general church history was the intrusion of compulsion upon a voluntary society, a process intimately associated with institutionalisation and the growth of hierarchy.[9].

All these ideas are recognizable in the *Ketzerhistorie*, by which Arnold is chiefly remembered, but more was to come. His early works had done well among Dutch separatists, and especially in the circle of Friedrich Breckling, a Schleswiger who had separated from the Lutheran churches, and now spread his ideas by a constant stream of letters and publications from Amsterdam. He now put down his own plans to write a church history, and pressed Arnold to set forth the issue between true and corrupt Christianity on a big scale. At the same time Arnold became subject to Behmenist influences which led him to produce a study of the *Signs of the Times*,[10] and took up with that Cinderella of objects of Christian devotion, the heavenly Sophia, the divine wisdom.[11] The signs of the times were partly the incessant warfare of the sixteen-nineties, but more especially the false security of Christians, and in particular of the Lutheran Church of Saxony, blind to the fate of the Huguenots, and branding as heretics the prophets and witnesses sent to warn it. This also left its mark on the *Ketzerhistorie* three-quarters of the vast bulk of which were devoted to the last two centuries.

The central concept of the *Ketzerhistorie* as of the earlier works is *Unparteilichkeit*, and Arnold makes it clear at the very beginning[12] that this did not mean mere weighing in the scale of historical scholarship, but 'true obedience to God and his eternal truths'; it meant illumination by the Holy Spirit. But there is no division of truth into secular and theological, and no division of history into profane and church history. Those enlightened by the Holy Spirit stand on God's side, but not on the side of any particular church, since God is not bound to any human institution. Arnold was here moving towards a difficulty. From the standpoint of the plain historian the history of the institutional church may be dismal, but it can at least be written out of the sources in the usual way; the history of the invisible church can hardly be written from invisible sources. Arnold was feeling this difficulty before the end of the *Ketzerhistorie*, and proceeded to supply some of the illumination he had derived from the spirit in three more works, a *Vitae Patrum* (1700), *Das Leben der Glaubigen* (1701) covering the true saints of the last two centuries, and his *Historia et Descriptio Theologiae Mysticae* (1702, German ed. 1703).

In the *Ketzerhistorie* the exemplary picture of the early church is tightened up. The early Christians went in not for empty opinions but for 'active Christianity',[13] and the way to distinguish teachers from heretics was in practice by their works, by their pressure for freedom of conscience and suffering. There was no infallible measure for distinguishing the two, but the pairs of opposites freedom – compulsion, works – empty doctrine, suffering – power, gave a good practical guide to who was who. As soon as the teachers in the church gained the power to throw their weight about with impunity Arnold christened them opprobriously *Clerisey*, a term which in English has strangely come back into favour. At any rate church history is a history of decay, especially after Constantine, when external persecution was succeeded by internal rancour. After the fifth century Arnold scarcely speaks of *Gemeinde*, congregation or community.

It is notable that Arnold speaks of Lutheran churches, but not Lutheran *Gemeinden*, indeed the Reformation was not much to his taste. Luther indubitably began well, 'seeking to awaken in all the true fruit of the gospel, namely repentance and renewal'[14] and gave a great impulse to preaching, preaching from a full heart; but the end product was speedily clerical control and moral impotence.[15] The best that could be said was that there were some witnesses of the truth left, who pilloried the decline in Lutheranism.[16] Nor were the Protestant sects any better; there was no essential difference between the churches and sects[17] – both pushed their own authority instead of establishing Christ in the heart.[18] Arnold was now much more radical than he had been. It had once been the historian's task to separate the true from the false in the church's record; now it was impossible to associate the two. 'Because the kingdom of God is always inward . . . the true church of Christ among all parties, peoples and tongues is for good and all invisible and hidden'.[19] There was indeed no church or sect to which the true seeker after God could commit himself without anxiety. What had begun as the primitive Christian community had been so eaten out by its faithlessness as to leave no option to the faithful but total separation, at whatever the cost. The one hope was the eschatological hope that the time was drawing near when sects and names and parties would indeed fall, and God would be all in all.[20]

The *Ketzerhistorie* was first published in 1699 and 1700; yet in 1701 Arnold was married, and in 1702 he was back in church office, thus accepting two of the main institutions of society. How had yesterday's radical accommodated himself to what had then been the sinful world?

The key to this apparent revolution has already been noted. There had been considerable development in Arnold not only between his youth and the mid-nineties, and between the mid-nineties and the *Ketzerhistorie*, but also within the latter work itself. And this development continued. In one respect this was surprising, for after resigning his chair Arnold went back to Quedlinburg where religious disputes were as bitter as ever, were only inflamed by his intervention, and caused the Elector of Brandenburg to interfere by commission.[21] But Arnold's resignation of his chair owed something to the discovery that it did not offer an independent base from which to operate upon a church which had lost its way. Another period of inwardness followed; a period of influence by the English Behmenists, a remarkable personal vision of the heavenly Sophia,[22] an outpouring of lyric verse.[23] Even in the conclusion to the last part of the *Ketzerhistorie* he had begun slightly to soften his total rejection of institutional outwardness and to reveal the first signs of a possible connection between inwardness and the world.[24] Soon came the admission that even a community making its pilgrimage to Christ would contain the imperfect and the weak, and might even contain teachers, though they were in apostolic style to bring people to Christ, not exercise force over them.[25] The next admission was that separatism as well as conformity might be due to self-will rather than the will of God, and that it was no prophylactic against temptation and danger. In any case something was due to those who had no choice but to live under a fallen church. Arnold's return to church office was justified by love of his neighbour.[26] Paradoxically the very force of his inward mystical experience increased the assurance with which he could handle imperfect outward institutions.[27] Thundering against the abomination of desolation in the *Ketzerhistorie* had after all done no good, and at the end of 1700 he even referred to it in a private letter as 'an alien work'.[28] This did not mean that he was repudiating the book, but it clearly marked a major shift in personal attitude. The biographical collections to which reference was made above were bound to witness to the intermingling of good and evil in the church as in the world, and the *History of Mystical Theology* on which Tersteegen built so splendidly two generations later was avowedly 'the immemorial theology of the truly wise . . . maintained and propagated alongside the doctrine of the schools'.[29]

Marriage required more than a shift of emphasis, required indeed another treatise, to justify.[30] Arnold did not surrender the notion that Adam before the fall had been androgynous, but had then lost his immortal paradise body for a mortal frame akin to the beasts. But instead of pursuing the mystical assertion that the saint wed to the heavenly Sophia recovered the ground lost in Eden, Arnold came round to the view that marriage was created by God not as a requirement but as a possibility for post-Adamic man, and not for his temporal comfort, but for his spiritual well-being. Marriage, in short, was rooted in the love of God, and that was why in Ephesians 5 it could be used as an image of the union of Christ with his congregation. Arnold, at least, was prepared to try it.

How comfortably Arnold settled into matrimony and church office in the last dozen years of his life is sufficiently indicated by the paucity of his references to either.[31] Martyrdom was no longer mandatory, and this, not because a great breach with the Old Adam of Arnold's early middle age had taken place, but because of a steady develoment powered by a basic conviction which did not change at all, that faith and life were inseparably connected, and that an active faith was the hallmark of the true Christian. Sophia had warned him to be at peace. Another unchanging conviction was that suffering was the lot of the true Christian. But whereas the radical Arnold had sought its origin in the fall of both world and church, it now seemed to be an aspect of the relation of imperfect man to God, and not to be remedied by such otherwise desirable achievements as religious toleration. Seen in this light, even Lutheran Orthodoxy appeared to have something to be said for it. For the suffering of the Christian had given Arnold to doubt whether assurance of salvation could be had from mystical union with God. Assurance was available only through the sufferings of Christ, appropriated through the promise of God that they were for us. If therefore neither resignation nor rejection of the world were a necessary part of preparation for union with God, it was possible to live simultaneously in grace and in the flesh, and even to stomach the institutional church.[32] Martyrdom was no longer needed. But there is a sting in the tail. Let no ecclesiastical historian be made complacent by the story of the taming of Gottfried Arnold; for Arnold's principal vehicle of future influence,[33] that greater and better man, Gerhard Tersteegen,[34] was inspired by the radical of the *Ketzerhistorie*, the heavenly Sophia and the *Mystical Theology*, not by the relatively painless Arnold *simul justus und peccator*.

Notes

1 J.W. von Goethe, *Zahme Xenien, Gedenkausgabe der Werke* 2. 402; *The Autobiography of J.W. von Goethe* ed. K.J. Weintraub, Chicago, 1974 1. 379–80.

2 The most useful of the older works on Arnold are Franz Dibelius, *Gottfried Arnold. Sein Leben und seine Bedeutung fur Kirche und Theologie*, Berlin, 1873; Max Goebel, *Geschichte des christlichen Lebens in der rhenisch-westphalischen evangelischen Kirche*, Coblenz, 1849–52, 2. 698–735. The most useful modern works are Erich Seeberg, *Gottfried Arnold, die Wissensch-aft und die Mystik seiner Zeit*, Meerane i. Sa., 1923; Hermann Dörries, *Geist und Geschichte bei Gottfried Arnold*, Göttingen, 1963; Ernst Benz, *Die protestantische Thebais*, Mainz/Wiesbaden, 1963; Jürgen Büchsel, *Gottfried Arnold. Sein Verständnis von Kirche und Wiedergeburt*, Witten, 1970; J.F.G. Goeters, 'Gottfried Arnolds Anschauung von der Kirchengeschichte in ihrem Werdegang', in *Traditio-Krisis-Renovatio aus theologischer Sicht. Festschrift Winfried Zeller* ed. B. Jaspert & R. Mohr, Marburg, 1976 241–57; F.W. Kantzenbach, 'Gottfried Arnold', in *Gestalten der Kirchengeschichte 7.Ortho-doxie und Pietismus* ed. M. Greschat, Stuttgart, 1982, 261–75; T. Stählin, *Gottfried Arnolds geistliche Dichtung, Glaube und Mystik*, Göttingen, 1966. See also Klaus Wetzel, *Theologische Kirchengeschichtsschreibung im deutschen Protestantismus, 1660–1760*, Giessen/Basel, 1983; J. Büchsel & D. Blaufuss, 'Gottfried Arnolds Briefwechsel', in *Pietismus-Herrnhutertum-Erweckungs-bewegung. Festschrift fur Erich Beyreuther* ed. D. Meyer, Cologne, 1982 71–107.

3 On Quedlinburg see J.B. Neveux, *Vie spirituelle et vie sociale entre Rhin et Baltique au XVIIᵐᵉ siecle*, Paris, 1967 12 *et passim*.

4 There are a few details about this in Martin Schmidt, 'Gottfried Arnold – seine Eigenart, seine Bedeutung, seine Beziehung zu Quedlinburg', in his *Wiedergeburt und neuer Mensch*, Witten, 1969 331–41. Sprögel officiated at the wedding of August Hermann Francke in 1694. See also Dibelius, *Gottfried Arnold* 55–67.

5 W. Cave, *Erstes Christentum oder Gottesdienst der alten Christen in den ersten Zeiten des Evangelii* tr. J.C. Frauendorf.

6 Eamon Duffy, 'Primitive Christianity Revived: religious renewal in Augustan England', *SCH* 14 (1977) 287–300.

7 On this see Benz, *Die protestantische Thebais*; H.D. Rack, *Reasonable Enthusi-ast. John Wesley and the Rise of Methodism*, London, 1989, 102, 347.

8 Goeters, 'Gottfried Arnolds Anschauung' 247, 249.

9 Büchsel, *Gottfried Arnold* 32–75.

10 *Die Zeichen dieser Zeit, bei dem Anfang der instehenden Trubsalen erwogen*

von einem der damit gute Absichten hat (Aschersleben, 1698). Cf. Goeters, op. cit. 252 & n. 44.

11 On this cult see Ernst Benz, *Die Vision. Erfahrungsformen und Bildwelt*, Stuttgart, 1969 575–86. An English example of Sophiolatry, with its characteristic ambivalence as to the gender of the object of the cult, is Charles Wesley's hymn, 'Happy the man that finds the grace', no. 674 in the current British Methodist hymnbook, *Hymns and Psalms*.

12 Gottfried Arnold, *Unpartheyische Kirchen- und Ketzerhistorie*, Frankfurt, 1729 [cited below as *KKH*] Vorrede (n.p.) vol. 1 § 1, 3, 5, 35.

13 *KKH* 1. 202a.

14 *KKH* 1. 509a.

15 *KKH* 1. 574–5, 578.

16 *KKH* 1. 927.

17 *KKH* 1. 20.

18 *KKH* 1. 1201 § 5.

19 *KKH* 2. 1178 § 13: 1. 1200 – 2.

20 *KKH* 2. 1202 § 9.

21 Dibelius, *Arnold* 107, 131–147.

22 On this see Seeberg, *Arnold* 22–29.

23 K.C.E. Ehmann (ed.), *Gottfried Arnolds sämmtliche Lieder mit einer reichen Auswahl aus den freieren Dichtungen . . .* Stuttgart, 1856.

24 Büchsel, *Arnold* 112; *KKH* 2. 1179 § 17.

25 Büchsel, *Arnold* 115.

26 *Ibid.* 116–7; Gottfried Arnold, *Die geistliche Gestalt eines evangelischen Lehrers*, Halle, 1704 579–80, 615.

27 J. Christoph Coler, *Historia Gothofredi Arnold . . .* , Wittenberg, 1718 237.

28 *Ibid.* 231.

29 Gottfried Arnold, *Historia et descriptio theologiae mysticae*, Frankfurt, 1702 22.

30 *Das eheliche und unverehlichte Leben der ersten Christen*, Frankfurt, 1702.

31 On the later Arnold see, besides the biographies quoted, Walter Delius, 'Gottfried Arnold in Perleburg (1707–1714)', *Jahrbuch fur Berlin-Brandenburgische Kirchengeschichte* 43 (1968) 155–160.

32 Büchsel, *Arnold* 201.

33 It is of interest to English readers to note that a proposal, perhaps occasioned by the publication of the enlarged edition of the *KKH* at Schaffhausen (1740–42), to produce an English translation in weekly instalments of three sheets, though commended by a quotation from Bayle's *Dictionary*, seems to have failed for lack of subscribers (*Certain queries with their respective answers; by way of introduction to the Rev. Mr Godfrey Arnold's Impartial History of the Church and Hereticks*, London, 1744 [B.L. T. 1794 (6)]). I have not discovered the source of the proposal.

34 See my forthcoming paper on 'Mysticism and Revival: the case of Gerhard Tersteegen' in the Festschrift for Dr J.D. Walsh.

22

Anglicanism & Assimilation; or Mysticism & Mayhem in the Eighteenth Century

The English church in the eighteenth century is not in common perception a very good candidate for inclusion in a conference devoted to the theme of church and society in northern Europe. A byword for isolation and torpor, it has not been quite restored to life by either Dean Sykes's insistence that things were not as bad as nineteenth-century zealots found it convenient to make out, or the more recent refurbishments of Jonathan Clark. Today without entering into dialogue with them or going over too much of the ground I have covered recently in delineating the European context of all the Protestant churches, including the churches in America, I would like to talk about another side of Anglican life, very international in its bearings, and not lacking in vigour though rather unpredictable in its outcome.

Social Christianity is more problematic now than it was in the early eighteenth century. The fact that statesmen could assume with ease that the business of churches was to provide an ideological platform for the great game of international politics and to assimilate restive populations, owed much to the fact that everyone assumed that the best way to care for the welfare of peasants, for example, was to Christianise them more thoroughly, and to put down at any rate those superstitious observances which they did not share with their social betters.

The two great aims of the statesmen were of course often incompatible, or at least inconvenient for each other. The Counter-Reformation provided an ideology for both Habsburg and Bourbon, but it did not illuminate their mutual hostility, nor solely determine their relations with their own churches or even the Pope. Lutheran Orthodoxy provided a platform for the aggression of Sweden and Saxony against Prussia, even after the Elector of the latter had turned Catholic, and in some respects hampered what

Paper presented to the International Conference on Religion and Society in Northern Europe, 1992.

either could do for the savagely oppressed Protestants of the Habsburg lands and Hungary. By the early eighteenth century what was left of the Reformed confessional interest was taken up with keeping anti-French propaganda at fever heat, with providing for a mass of refugees, and with salvaging something from the wreck of the Reformed interest in Rhinelands.

It was at points like this that the ideological interests of the states linked up with their domestic interests or conflicted with them in new ways. The whole of eastern Europe was very short of labour, and the simple solution of fixing what labour there was to the soil by ever more rigorous forms of serfdom created problems as well as solving them; labour resistance might take the form of peasant revolts which in the Habsburg lands were frequent, or more frequently still, of peasant flight to Poland, to the Baltic where there were thousands of vacant peasant lots, or to the Ukraine. Labour shortages, and still more shortages of skilled labour were damaging to the confessional purity of states which took most pride in it. The sudden Habsburg acquisition of an enormous empire in the south-east at the expense of the Turks created a tremendous demand for settlers and for skilled assistance. Narrowly Catholic as was the Habsburg dynasty it did not mind lining the Turkish frontier with Protestants, and using the plums of empire as a bait for selected Protestant conversions. Altogether they absorbed far more German immigrants, many of them Protestants, than even the American colonies, creating problems in Croatia and elsewhere which are still with us.

The Tsars stiffly defended the privileges of the Russian Orthodox establishment, but they could not modernize their empire without German Protestant assistance, govern the provinces they acquired along the Baltic littoral without the German Protestant gentry, nor populate the lower Volga without German settlers. The first two cases opened the door to German Pietism and the last to German-speaking Mennonites. The whole business was most skilfully managed by the kings of Prussia who advertised for settlers every year, and took them in on a basis of state-managed toleration by the thousands annually. Most of them were Reformed, but in 1731 they acquired 20,000 Salzburgers, those fascinating revivalistic Lutherans, and fished hard and treasonably in Bohemia for Czechs, and acquired some, though not the scores of thousands with whom they conspired and who were kept at home by an eighteenth-century version of the Iron Curtain.

What states could do, private enterprise could also do. If the Protestant gentry of Saxony's most recently acquired and restive province in Upper Lusatia sought to develop their own estates (and incidentally resist assimilation by Saxony) by Christianising their own suppressed populations of

Wends and Sorbs, and smuggling out Czechs and Moravians from the old kingdom of Bohemia, the von Dietrichstein estates across that border were busy smuggling settlers in the opposite direction. If Oglethorpe, the governor of Georgia in the 1730s, who had served with Prince Eugene in the great campaign in which the Habsburgs had routed the Turks and knew all about their frontier settlement policies, advertised in German Pietist journals for settlers to man the Georgia frontier against the Spanish in Florida, the Spanish sought to disrupt the process from within, just like the kings of Prussia in Bohemia, by promoting the mass flight of negro slaves.

There was, morevoer, a further complication. If settlement policies could only be carried through in defiance of the claims to confessional purity which so frequently were used to justify the international policies of states, attempts at assimilation proved much more difficult than anyone expected at first, and often generated a religious response which no one quite knew how to handle, what we call religious revival. This first became obvious in the Habsburg lands, where Protestant populations deprived of their church systems and of the inherited leadership of nobility and clergy, began forcibly to pull themselves up by their own bootstraps, but it also was prepared in the most pagan part of Europe, east of the Baltic. Here the Swedish church, given the task of assimilating those territories to Sweden, made a determined assault on the old deities of nature and of fire. Its work was not complete when those territories fell to Russia, but the old paganism seems to have been fatally undermined, and when in the thirties Pietists and Moravians whose expectations were shaped by places where religious revival was breaking out, arrived, one of the most dramatic of all religious revivals took place. And it was this change in expectations which affected the whole religious situation, not only in the West of Europe, but in America as well. For here was another division of spirits. Everywhere the Orthodox parties tried to convict Pietists and revivalists on the score of false doctrine, a charge vehemently repudiated, or of breach of discipline. On this latter point the more enthusiastic spirits on the other side convinced themselves not merely that revival was the normal condition of the church, but that since NT times the true church was the *Wanderkirche* or itinerant church. If anyone was in breach of discipline it was the Orthodox devotees of the parish pump.

So far I have hardly mentioned the British situation, but if anyone were to imagine that the picture I have painted is somehow remote from the British experience, he would simply be confessing to the way the isolation of the modern Church of England has imposed itself upon its historiography. For if Anglicanism was hardly a crusading platform for British courts, British support for the threatened Greek Orthodox interest at

Constantinople and the menaced Protestant interest in Europe was implied by their guarantees to successive peace settlements, and was expected by friends abroad, some of whom like the Swiss could give little in turn. Even the Lutheran Orthodox who had limited sympathy with the Church of England, did not, from the standpoint of their own interests, want to see the triumph of Jacobitism; and even the Lutheran Orthodox exposed themselves voluntarily to the biggest bombardment of English devotional, theological and exegetical literature ever mounted. Moreover British courts and ministers had the same work of assimilation for the Church to do as had their colleagues abroad. In England the field for assimilation was in one direction limited by the creation of a second-class establishment for dissenters under the Toleration Act. But the standard continental work of assimilation remained where the large contingent of Huguenots, and the smaller contingents of Palatines who had mostly been established upon estates in southern Ireland were concerned; and there were two major additional works in getting the Welsh on to the broader and safer paths of English Christianity, and making something of the American colonies. There was a fourth major work of assimilation of critical immediate importance, the defeat of Jacobitism in the Scottish Highlands and their conquest for Lowland religion and the English Bible, but this fell to the Church of Scotland.

Mention of America and Scotland brings out a complication in the position of the Church of England which had its parallel in various parts of Protestant Europe, but was made by that fact no easier to cope with. The churches of England and Scotland were not made partners by their sharing a common head and having some common tasks. In fact in the long and bitter struggle in which the Kirk fought its way north of the Tay and into the Highlands, Episcopalianism was one of the persecuted parties. Nor was it endeared to the Presbytrian zealots by the fact that their own pressure made Scottish Episcopalians look more to England than they ever had before, nor that in 1712 it obtained legalized dissenting status under a Toleration Act passed during a rabid Tory reaction. This concession apparently infringed of the terms of the Act of Union, and went in the teeth of that rabid minority in Scotland which still aspired to the full severity of the Solemn League and Covenant. The embarrassments of the Kirk, at once assimilating and threatened with assimilation are not my theme today; the very unusual Anglican experience of persecution is. Before turning to that subject, however, I would ask you to hold in mind the fact that although the Church approached its work in America through the same organisations as it employed in Wales, the SPCK and SPG, it had here to face the consequences of the fact that the Protestant succession had only been saved by importing a series of foreign monarchs, and that even good Queen Anne had been happily married to a Lutheran, Prince George of Denmark. He it was who appointed as his court chaplain a Halle Pietist, Anton Wilhelm Böhme; Böhme was retained in office by George I, and succeeded on his death in 1722 by a still more important chaplain, Friedrich Wilhelm Ziegenhagen. These gentlemen not only linked the SPCK with the Halle policies of universal regeneration, and steered the Hanoverian court away from the policies of narrow Orthodoxy they maintained in the electorate, but did it major service in helping to populate the American colonies with Germans and civilising those who settled, and had an impact on the Church in England which reinforced that already made by Scotland. Thus the work of the Church in America was complicated not just by a Puritan establishment in New England, a minuscule Dutch establishment in New York secured by treaty, and continuous Presbyterian immigration from Ulster and Scotland, but by the informal representation of the Lutheran establishments at the London court.

The peculiarity of the north-east of Scotland was that in spite of hard times Episcopalianism went on working normally for some twenty years after the Revolution, supported by a good deal of unanimity between clergy, gentry and people. Most of the clergy qualified themselves by taking oaths of loyalty to the government, but some like George Garden who did not, went on ministering. Where churches were claimed for the Presbyterians, heritors would refuse access to the building and keep hold of the communion vessels and the session records. There was no Presbyterian communion in Aberdeen 1690–1704. It was clear that the Episcopalians of the north-east would not be got out without a fight, for which the Presbyterians were only too ready. In this fight they had one powerful political weapon, to pin the charge of Jacobitism upon their opponents. This charge stuck only too well, for when it came to rebellion in 1715, virtually all the spiritual leaders and gentry of north-eastern Episcopalianism came out for the Pretender. George Garden returned to the pulpit from which he had been expelled to announce that a Stuart victory would lead to the reintroduction of episcopacy, he and his brother James presented an address of loyalty when the Pretender arrived, and the Earl of Mar who set up the Pretender's standard at Braemar, promised to restore episcopacy, and amongst his troops used only the English liturgy. Whatever one may think of the political judgment of the Scots Episcopalians, all this was perhaps only to be expected from men who had all along been stout defenders of episcopacy and opponents of the Covenant. What is interesting about the spiritual leaders of this movement, however, and eventually made them important for the church south of the border, was that they were not simply Scottish Sacheverells, but had developed a distinctive religious position.

Like so many in the early eighteenth-century the north-eastern Episcopalians reacted hard against the religious controversy of the previous century,
against the notion that the core of Christian belief and practice could be
encompassed in systematic statements like the Westminster confession, or
indeed, unyielding apologists for episcopacy as they might be, in forms of
church government. Their reaction against Presbyterianism was centred
on worship and took the double form of an interest in liturgy and a
propensity to mysticism. The interest in liturgy was something new.
Scottish episcopal services in the seventeenth century differed little from
Presbyterian ones in the seventeenth century, though they did make use of
the Lord's Prayer, Ten Commandments, and the Baptismal Service. After
the Toleration Act of 1712, however, the English Prayer Book, came into
very general use, much furthered by George Garden, now deprived of the
cathedral parish in Aberdeen, and his brother James, deprived of a divinity
professorship there. Once into liturgy, however, the Episcopalians could
display as much of the Old Adam as the Presbyterians, and the Gardens
together with Principal George Middleton soon became leading supporters
in the north-east of Laud's prayer book, divisive as this was and has
remained among Episcopalians of the north.

Their roots in mysticism go further back and produced in the end more
palatable fruit. The north-east made three special contributions to the
literature of mysticism, the *Spiritual Exercises* of John Forbes of Corse,
Henry Scougall's *Life of God in the Soul of Man*, and James Garden's
Comparative Theology. All these authors were professors of theology at
King's College, Aberdeen, and the spiritual leaders of the region were
intimately involved in them all. George Garden, the soul of that movement,
translated Forbes's *Spiritual Exercises* into Latin and published them in
the collected edition of Forbes's works which he brought out in Amsterdam
in 1702–3, and remains the chief authority on Forbes's life and character.
With the Scougalls Garden was intimately associated. Bishop Patrick
Scougall, Henry's father, ordained Garden, Henry preached at Garden's
first induction to a parish, when Henry became a professor in 1673 Garden
was recalled to his old college, and, in 1678 when Henry died at the early
age of 28, Garden preached his funeral sermon. James Garden, as we have
seen, was George's brother, and the full title of his work, *Comparative
Theology, or the True and Solid Grounds of a Pure and Peaceable Theology*
represented the objects of them both. They were buried side by side in the
churchyard of Old Machar, Aberdeen.

Garden's title represented a frame of mind which the group had inherited
from Forbes, a stout champion of episcopacy and opponent of the
Covenant, indeed, but a man who preserved the proportion of faith, did
not dabble in the technical language of mysticism, and insisted that what

came first was personal communion with a faithful and loving God. In Scougall's *Life of God in the Soul of Man*, the best known Scottish contribution to devotional literature, the net was cast wider. The book was first published by Bishop Burnet in 1677, and a fifth edition was eventually produced by the SPCK. Sixty years ago Professor Henderson described it as the work of a lover of Thomas à Kempis and S. Teresa, a great admirer of M. de Renty, a friend of the saintly Archbishop Leighton, and disciple of the Cambridge Platonists. With George Garden, a man esteemed equally for learning and gentleness and influential as a spiritual director to the gentry, the net was cast wider again. He was a devotee of a catholic spiritual tradition to which Protestants in various parts of Europe were turning for a new spiritual impetus and escape from polemic, Augustine and Bernard, Tauler and S. Teresa, de Renty and John of the Cross, François de Sales and Thomas à Kempis. Indeed, as the bibliographers have now made clear the old reaches of this tradition had always been common to Protestant and Catholic, and had been the mainstay for the former during a terrible century; and those now seeking new ways to Christianize their world were all of them middlemen seeking to mediate between the world of ecclesiastical precision and this common stock of spiritual nutriment. And it was at this point that Garden got into a conflict with his church which was never resolved.

Garden came to look with favour on two contemporary Catholic mystics who, partly because they got into severe trouble with their own church authorities, became the object of intense Protestant interest, Antoinette Bourignon and Mme Guyon. To the former he was introduced by her editor, that curious hypermarket of mysticism, Pierre Poiret, and himself published and introduced translations of a number of her works. It was *An Apology for M. Antonia Bourignon* (1699) attributed to him and not disavowed, which brought about his condemnation by the General Assembly, a verdict in practice upheld by the Scottish bishops after the Hanoverian accession. The connection with Poiret brought the Gardens into an entirely different religious world which had also been under the hammer. Poiret had begun as a Reformed pastor in the Rhineland, and his forsaking that vocation for mysticism had been in part a statement that the sacrifices the Reformed community had made to maintain their shibboleths against Louis XIV had been more than the cause was worth. He followed Bourignon around, published her works, collected a great library of mystical texts, and left it after his death to the most notable of his followers, Gerhard Tersteegen, by whom it was transmuted into a saintly life of the finest water, and into his peculiar contribution to the Protestant heritage, three huge volumes of *Select Lives of Holy Souls*, all of them Catholic and mostly Counter-Reformation saints. There was mutual give-and-take between Poiret and the Jacobite mystics of the north-east. He introduced them to Bourignon as the way of life; they made her works available to their countrymen. Poiret learnedly defended James Garden's *Comparative Theology*, describing its author as 'vir doctrina solida, . . . vir integer, pius, pacificus' and again as 'auctorem innocentissi-mum, admirabilemque, et amabilem'; they made arrangements for the circulation of Poiret's works at home. The key figure here was a medical doctor, John Keith, who was also part of the Gardens' circle. His father had succeeded George Garden in the ministry of Old Machar, and he had been introduced by Garden to the mystics. By the time of his death he had acquired a valuable collection of mystical literature in Dutch, German, Spanish, Polish and other languages, and used it to cultivate an attitude of complete passivity, abandonment and acquiescence in God's will. But he was not passive in daily life; he helped Garden with his English editions of Bourignon and did more than anyone to get Poiret's output into the gentry libraries of the north-east.

Above all when Poiret turned from Bourignon to Mme Guyon, he took Garden and Scottish circle with him. The great contests which had earlier raged round Mme Guyon, in which she had been accused by Bossuet, and defended by Fénelon who was finally disgraced, were now past, as was her own imprisonment in the Bastille; but their general European resonance had been felt even in Scotland. For Fénelon's secretary before he died in 1715, who then wrote an idealized *Life* of his hero and edited his works was a Scot who had gone over to Rome, Andrew Michael Ramsay. Ramsay's *Life* of Fenelon deeply impressed Alexander, 4th Lord Forbes of Pitsligo, whose house at Rosehearty became George Garden's HQ for spreading the influence of Bourignon. From all this Pitsligo concluded that 'God was All, and the whole creation in itself . . . was nothing', perhaps an appropriate inspiration for a man who came out for the Stuarts in both the '15 and the '45, and lost all the family estates. But Ramsay operated directly upon the Scottish situation. Having lost Fénelon he came to assist Mme Guyon. She dictated to him letters to her Scottish followers, while their letters for her were directed to him and translated into French for her to read.

Such was sway which Mme Guyon came to exercise over the Scottish group, that contact between them could not be confined to book and letter. Ramsay stayed three years with her at Blois, Lord Forbes of Pitsligo and the brothers William and James Forbes made very long stays; Lord Deskford confessed to her his secret penchant for Jacobitism, and was described by Ramsay as one of Mme Guyon's dearest children. George Garden was present at her deathbed. The sight of Mme Guyon holding court at home to a crowd of Protestant Scottish Jacobites is I think one of the most extraordinary images of the early eighteenth century, even more than their making off with copies of the *Lettres Spirituelles* and the *Life of Gregory Lopez*.

At this point I can imagine your saying that you have heard all this before, and that it is part of the conventional background to the young John Wesley. It is quite true that the whole body of literature we have been discussing from Scougal to Gregory Lopez, from M. de Renty to Bourignon and Mme Guyon, formed part of the furniture of Wesley's mind in his earnest pursuit of sanctity, and stayed with him and his propaganda lifelong. The connection between the Scottish story and Wesley is indeed closer than a mere literary one. One of the medical friends of Dr Keith, the distribution agent for the works of Poiret, was the celebrated George Cheyne. Cheyne is remembered for having increased in weight to 33 stones, and having to be followed by a manservant bearing a stool for him to sit on every few yards; however he got his weight down to viable proportions by a strict diet, and made a good thing out of becoming a gout specialist at Bath. He was, however also a member of the mystical circle of the north-east, and an admirer of Poiret's work for the mystics. Wesley as a young man, followed Cheyne's dietary prescriptions, and always remembered them with gratitude; he read his *Natural Method of curing diseases* (1742) with enthusiasm, and was touched by a private account of his good death. Still closer to home, the north-eastern group were intimate with John Heylyn, 'the mystic doctor', rector of St Mary-le-Strand 1724–59, the favourite preacher of the London religious societies at the time when they formed the context of the work of Whitefield and Wesley, and a man at that time admired by Wesley himself. Still closer to home Wesley records having been led in the early thirties deeper into the mystics by 'a contemplative man'; and prominent on a very short list for identification with this character is James Garden, a familiar of the Byrom circle in Manchester and a neighbour in Lincolnshire.

However, what I want to argue is not the rather implausible case that Wesley was what he was because the Scottish circle were what they were, but that the cycle of experience of the Scottish Jacobite Episcopalians was very closely recapitulated in the next generation among Anglicans of Jacobite propensities. Here Wesley affords a very striking illustration. His parents, though both former dissenters, were both very high Tories and almost equally high royalists. Samuel, however, accepted William III as king; Susanna did not. This difference of opinion had a practical bearing upon the obligation to pray for the king, and, as is now well known, led to a breach of conjugal relations which was not healed by the death of William III. The fruit of the ultimate reconciliation was the birth of John Wesley himself, and, if he may be believed, old Samuel made good any defect in his Toryism by helping to write the defence speech in the trial of Sacheverell. This tradition the young Wesleys maintained. Educated in Oxford at its most treasonable, John's elder brother was a protégé of Bishop Atterbury, and believed his preferment had been blocked by the Walpole interest, while John himself had a lifelong hostility to Walpole, and in the thirties sought preferment through the Jacobite Bolingbroke. Unlike the Scots, Episcopalians of Wesley's hue were not subject to persecution, but they had the vision that Walpole was corrupting the fabric of church and state from the top, and although by origin Little Englanders of the narrowest stripe, found consolation for their defeat in the church they loved in the Quietism which had suffered like defeat upon the continent.

The fact that, unlike the Scots, men like the Wesleys were still within the establishment rather than outside it exposed them to court influence in unexpected ways. The SPCK had been intended to put down Quakerism at home and dissent generally in America, but from a very early stage had been consumed by enthusiasm for Francke's schemes of universal regeneration, and had been kept up to the mark in this by successive German court chaplains and a strong Halle Pietist influence in the distaff side at the court of George I. The great moment for this alliance came over the winter of 1731–2 when international rescue schemes had to be mounted to save some 30,000 Protestants who resolved to leave the diocese and principality of Salzburg. A small party of them were settled in the new colony of Georgia through the efforts of the SPCK and the Georgia trustees. The SPCK had to involve many more people in the rescue operation, approaching old Samuel Wesley, his curate, John Whitelamb, John's pupil, and finally John himself to go out and provide pastoral oversight. The extraordinary feature of this nexus, inspired by 'the genuine fruit of a true saving faith' among the non-Episcopalian Salzburgers, is the strong Jacobite influence it reveals. Sir John Philipps, the Welsh baronet who was the moving spirit in the SPCK was a Jacobite; Oglethorpe, the governor of Georgia, had been christened James Edward for the Old Pretender, and his sisters devoted themselves to Jacobite conspiracy. This time, however, Wesley received an introduction to the outside world more powerful than the mysticism he had so far taken on board. He learned German and Spanish, in the case of the former, also acquiring an introduction to the main schools of current Lutheran spirituality, by translating hymns from the Moravian hymnbooks; he picked up the new Lutheran view of the religious significance of the New World, and the Pietist understanding of children's and heathen missions; he was indoctrinated with the significance of the great international feud between Halle and Herrnhut. And he returned to England so overburdened with religious claims and counter-claims as to be enabled to find escape only through conversion. In other respects things had only changed in his absence for the worse. The alliance between Walpole and Bishop Gibson had broken down humiliatingly. Clearly the church would be saved by private enterprise or not at all; the radical programme of reform envisaged by the Jacobite country party alliance needed its religious counterpart, a spreading of scriptural holiness through the land. And it is worth noting that Wesley's brand of red-blooded religion proved more succesful than that of the establishment as a whole in one of that institution's main tasks, that of assimilation first of the Huguenots and later of the Palatines settled in Ireland. And his friend Whitefield was much more successful than the SPCK in Wales, though Welshness rather than Englishness rode on the back of revival.

There was one more surprise to be sprung by Scottish Jacobitism, this time Presbyterian, on behalf of the great cause of a national revival of religion. The great hope of the English revivalists lay in the fact that not only did it prove possible to pull Walpole down, but that there was now once again an alternative centre of political influence, the Leicester House interest led by Frederick, Prince of Wales, which seemed to have the future before it. By the early forties, the prince's secretary, James Erskine, Lord Grange, was building up a broad-bottomed Methodist coalition of alternative religion around the skirts of Leicester House, including the Countess of Huntingdon, Howell Harris and the Wesleys, not to mention Whitefield, of whose prospective elevation to the bench of bishops there were constant rumours. Grange was invited to Wesley's Conference in 1745, and actually attended in 1748. He and Charles Wesley seemed able to reduce each other to happy tears at will; he helped to get John Nelson out of pressed army service by providing a substitute; Charles Wesley rescued a lost daughter of his from Deism and reconciled her with her father. The extraordinary feature of all this was that Grange was one of the most equivocal figures of that age. The younger brother of the Old Pretender's general, the Earl of Mar, Grange kept just on the side of legitimacy in the interests of the family estates, but recent scholars have no doubt of his Jacobite involvement; even in 1745 he encouraged the Young Pretender's adventure, whilst condemning his arrival without an army. Mar's wife suffered from occasional insanity, and Grange was thwarted in an attempt to carry her off to Scotland in 1731 by her sister, Lady Mary Wortley Montagu, armed with a warrant from the King's Bench. At the same time Grange's relation with his own wife reached a stormy climax. Violent, drunken and an occasional imbecile, she is said to have accused him of treason and stolen letters to prove it. At any rate in 1732, Grange celebrated her death, having in fact had her abducted by men in Lovat (Jacobite) tartan to confinement for many years in St Kilda, and later in Assynt and Skye, where she truly died in 1745. The simplest explanation of these adventures is that both wives had access to secrets ruinous to the Erskine family. Grange, however, was not only engaged in an attempt to shift the balance in the English church prior to the succession of the reversionary interest. He also endeavoured to shift the balance in Scotland by bringing in Zinzendorf and the Moravians in the wake of Whitefield's successes at Cambuslang, and sent the Count a huge twenty-three page analysis of the Scots religious situation, seeking to show that the time was now ripe. Zinzendorf was too preoccupied with other things to take the opportunity, and the original Methodist hope of political as well as religious regeneration came to an end with the untimely death of Frederick Prince of Wales in 1751, almost a decade before his father. Bishops and others in possession could breathe easy again.

There is a moral in this tangled story. Like most of the religious establishments of Europe (though unlike the Kirk) the Church of England failed in the tasks of assimilation which it was set in the eighteenth century; but those parts of the church which were, or felt themselves, painfully subject to assimilation, generated remarkable energies of both a spiritual and practical kind. In this respect what I have called the mayhem of mysticism was a parable of religious revival all over Europe, and among the European disapora in America.

Index